ANTITRUST

STATUTES, TREATIES, REGULATIONS, GUIDELINES, POLICIES

2014–2015 Edition

by

JOHN J. FLYNN
Late Hugh B. Brown Professor of Law Emeritus
S.J. Quinney College of Law, University of Utah

HARRY FIRST
Charles L. Denison Professor of Law
New York University School of Law

DARREN BUSH
Law Foundation Professor of Law
University of Houston Law Center

Mat #41657600

444 Cedar Street, Suite 700
St. Paul, MN 55101
1-877-888-1330

Printed in the United States of America

ISBN: 978-1-62810-146-1

PREFACE

The growing complex of amendments to the basic antitrust laws and adoption of special industry statutes and exemptions, enforcement agency "Guidelines" and agency "Policies" requires the publication of a convenient compilation of these materials for the practitioner, the academic and the student of antitrust law.[1] The materials selected include the full text of the Sherman, Clayton and Federal Trade Commission acts. Significant statutes defining exemptions from the antitrust laws like those applying to health care, local government regulation, insurance, baseball (The Curt Flood Act of 1998 adding § 27a to The Clayton Act) and other activities are included. The "Antitrust Civil Process Act" is included because of its significance for the unique discovery tools used in antitrust investigations.

The full text of "Guidelines" and "Policies" commonly used in law practice and referred to in law school basic and advanced antitrust classes are also included. Among the "Guidelines" included are the "2010 Horizontal Merger Guidelines." The Guidelines for Intellectual Property, International Trade and Collaborations Among Competitors are also included. The issuance of "Policy" statements by the enforcement agencies providing guidance in understanding the circumstances in which the Antitrust Division and the F.T.C. exercise enforcement discretion are of significance to both students and practitioners of antitrust law. Policy statements like those concerning health care regulation provide insights into how the Antitrust Division and the F.T.C. view a complex and emerging new area of antitrust counseling and litigation. Sentencing guidelines for antitrust violations and the Antitrust Division's Corporate Leniency Policy are also included because of the important role of criminal sanctions in antitrust enforcement.

The growing significance of international antitrust issues is reflected by the inclusion of excerpts from the Treaty Establishing the European Economic Community, the International Antitrust Enforcement Assistance Act of 1994, and the Antitrust Division's International Guidelines.

It is believed that providing these significant but otherwise widely scattered antitrust materials in a single volume will provide a convenient and useful reference tool for the student, teacher and practitioner of antitrust law.

HARRY FIRST
DARREN BUSH

April 25, 2014

[1] [Eds. We have not corrected any spelling errors that occur in original source materials.]

ACKNOWLEDGMENTS

While the responsibility for this volume of statutory and other antitrust law materials is ours, we owe a debt to the late Louis B. Schwartz, formerly Benjamin Franklin Professor of Law at the University of Pennsylvania and Professor of Law at the University of California, Hastings College of Law. He served as our common mentor and was, throughout his distinguished career, a leading teacher, scholar, and practitioner of antitrust law. Louis B. Schwartz established the standard of excellence to which we can only aspire. Louis B. Schwartz passed away in February, 2003, leaving behind a great legacy in the realms of antitrust and criminal law.

We also owe a great debt to our friend, mentor, colleague and co-author John J. Flynn, who passed away in April, 2010. John J. Flynn was the Hugh B. Brown Professor of Law at the S.J. Quinney College of Law at the University of Utah. John J. Flynn was behind the scenes in many of the antitrust laws we now take for granted, including but not limited to the drafting of the Tunney Act and the case United States v. El Paso Natural Gas Co., 276 U.S. 651 (1964). Apart from being on the front lines of antitrust, John J. Flynn was an excellent scholar and teacher. He leaves behind not only a legacy of antitrust and regulated industries articles, but also a legacy of students who with great love and admiration simply called him "Flynn."

Prior versions were accomplished thanks to the invaluable efforts of Lisa Baiocchi-Mooney, Cynthia Mabry, Suzanne Clevenger, Shelby Boseman, Jeff Burke, all graduates of the University of Houston Law Center, and Ms. Barbara McFarlane, Administrative Assistant, University of Utah College of Law.

H.F.
D.B.

April 25, 2014

TABLE OF CONTENTS

TABLE OF CONTENTS

PART 4. POLICY STATEMENTS AND AGREEMENTS

PART 5. PROCEDURAL STATUTES AND EXEMPTIONS

PART 6. TREATIES AND INTERNATIONAL AGREEMENTS

ANTITRUST

STATUTES, TREATIES, REGULATIONS, GUIDELINES, POLICIES

2014–2015 Edition

PART 1
BASIC STATUTES

1

SHERMAN ANTITRUST ACT

§ 1 [15 U.S.C. § 1]. Trusts, etc., in restraint of trade illegal; penalty

Every contract, combination in the form of trust or otherwise, or conspiracy, in restraint of trade or commerce among the several States, or with foreign nations, is declared to be illegal. Every person who shall make any contract or engage in any combination or conspiracy hereby declared to be illegal shall be deemed guilty of a felony, and, on conviction thereof, shall be punished by fine not exceeding $100,000,000 if a corporation, or, if any other person, $1,000,000, or by imprisonment not exceeding 10 years, or by both said punishments, in the discretion of the court.[1]

(July 2, 1890, c. 647, § 1, 26 Stat. 209; Aug. 17, 1937, c. 690, Title VIII, 50 Stat. 693; July 7, 1955, c. 281, 69 Stat. 282. Dec. 21, 1974, Pub.L. 93-528, § 3, 88 Stat. 1708; Dec. 12, 1975, Pub.L. 94-145, § 2, 89 Stat. 801; Nov. 16, 1990, Pub.L. 101-588, § 4(a), 104 Stat. 2880; June 22, 2004, Pub.L. 108-237, Title II, § 215(a), 118 Stat. 668.)

§ 2 [15 U.S.C. § 2]. Monopolizing trade a felony; penalty

Every person who shall monopolize, or attempt to monopolize, or combine or conspire with any other person or persons, to monopolize any part of the trade or commerce among the several States, or with foreign nations, shall be deemed guilty of a felony, and, on conviction thereof, shall be punished by fine not exceeding $100,000,000 if a corporation, or, if any other person, $1,000,000, or by imprisonment not exceeding 10 years, or by both said punishments, in the discretion of the court.[2]

(July 2, 1890, c. 647, § 2, 26 Stat. 209; July 7, 1955, c. 281, 69 Stat. 282. Dec. 21, 1974, Pub.L. 93-528, § 3, 88 Stat. 1708; Nov. 16, 1990, Pub.L. 101-588, § 4(b), 104 Stat. 2880; June 22, 2004, Pub.L. 108-237, Title II, § 215(b), 118 Stat. 668.)

§ 3 [15 U.S.C. § 3]. Trusts in Territories or District of Columbia illegal; combination a felony

(a) Every contract, combination in form of trust or otherwise, or conspiracy, in restraint of trade or commerce in any Territory of the United States or of the District of Columbia, or in restraint of trade or commerce between any such Territory and another, or between any such Territory or Territories and any State or States or the District of Columbia, or with foreign nations, or between the District of Columbia and any State or States or foreign nations, is declared illegal. Every person who shall make any such contract or engage in any such combination or conspiracy, shall be deemed guilty of a felony, and, on conviction thereof, shall be punished by fine not exceeding $100,000,000 if a corporation, or, if any other person, $1,000,000, or by imprisonment not exceeding 10 years, or by both said punishments, in the discretion of the court.

(b) Every person who shall monopolize, or attempt to monopolize, or combine or conspire with any other person or persons, to monopolize any part of the trade or commerce in any Territory of the United States or of the District of Columbia, or between any such Territory and another, or

---

[1] The Criminal Fines Improvements Act of 1987, 18 U.S.C. § 3571, provides that a court may impose a larger alternative fine for individuals and corporations equal to twice the gain or loss caused by the crime.

[2] *Id.*

between any such Territory or Territories and any State or States or the District of Columbia, or with foreign nations, or between the District of Columbia, and any State or States or foreign nations, shall be deemed guilty of a felony, and, on conviction thereof, shall be punished by fine not exceeding $100,000,000 if a corporation, or, if any other person, $1,000,000, or by imprisonment not exceeding 10 years, or by both said punishments, in the discretion of the court.[3]

(July 2, 1890, c. 647, § 3, 26 Stat. 209; July 7, 1955, c. 281, 69 Stat. 282; Dec. 21, 1974, Pub.L. 93-528, § 3, 88 Stat. 1708; Nov. 16, 1990, Pub.L. 101-588, § 4(c), 104 Stat. 2880., Nov. 2, 2002, Pub.L. 107-273, Div. C, Title IV, § 14102(b), 116 Stat. 1921; June 22, 2004, Pub.L. 108-237, Title II, § 215(c), 118 Stat. 668.)

§ 4 [15 U.S.C. § 4]. Jurisdiction of courts; duty of United States attorneys; procedure

The several district courts of the United States are invested with jurisdiction to prevent and restrain violations of sections 1 to 7 of this title; and it shall be the duty of the several United States attorneys, in their respective districts, under the direction of the Attorney General, to institute proceedings in equity to prevent and restrain such violations. Such proceedings may be by way of petition setting forth the case and praying that such violation shall be enjoined or otherwise prohibited. When the parties complained of shall have been duly notified of such petition the court shall proceed, as soon as may be, to the hearing and determination of the case; and pending such petition and before final decree, the court may at any time make such temporary restraining order or prohibition as shall be deemed just in the premises.

(July 2, 1890, c. 647, § 4, 26 Stat. 209; Mar. 3, 1911, c. 231, § 291, 36 Stat. 1167; June 25, 1948, c. 646, § 1, 62 Stat. 909.)

§ 5 [15 U.S.C. § 5]. Bringing in additional parties

Whenever it shall appear to the court before which any proceeding under section 4 of this title may be pending, that the ends of justice require that other parties should be brought before the court, the court may cause them to be summoned, whether they reside in the district in which the court is held or not; and subpoenas to that end may be served in any district by the marshal thereof.

(July 2, 1890, c. 647, § 5, 26 Stat. 210.)

§ 6 [15 U.S.C. § 6]. Forfeiture of property in transit

Any property owned under any contract or by any combination, or pursuant to any conspiracy (and being the subject thereof) mentioned in section 1 of this title, and being in the course of transportation from one State to another, or to a foreign country, shall be forfeited to the United States, and may be seized and condemned by like proceedings as those provided by law for the forfeiture, seizure, and condemnation of property imported into the United States contrary to law.

(July 2, 1890, c. 647, § 6, 26 Stat. 210.)

---

[3] *Id.*

§ 6a [15 U.S.C. § 6a]. Conduct involving trade or commerce with foreign nations

Sections 1 to 7 of this title shall not apply to conduct involving trade or commerce (other than import trade or import commerce) with foreign nations unless—

(1) such conduct has a direct, substantial, and reasonably foreseeable effect—

(A) on trade or commerce which is not trade or commerce with foreign nations, or on import trade or import commerce with foreign nations; or

(B) on export trade or export commerce with foreign nations, of a person engaged in such trade or commerce in the United States; and

(2) such effect gives rise to a claim under the provisions of sections 1 to 7 of this title, other than this section.

If sections 1 to 7 of this title apply to such conduct only because of the operation of paragraph (1) (B), then sections 1 to 7 of this title shall apply to such conduct only for injury to export business in the United States.

(July 2, 1890, c. 647, § 7, as added Oct. 8, 1982, Pub.L. 97-290, Title IV, § 402, 96 Stat. 1246.)

§ 7 [15 U.S.C. § 7]. "Person" or "persons" defined

The word "person," or "persons," wherever used in sections 1 to 7 of this title shall be deemed to include corporations and associations existing under or authorized by the laws of either the United States, the laws of any of the Territories, the laws of any State, or the laws of any foreign country.

(July 2, 1890, c. 647, § 8, 26 Stat. 210.)

2

CLAYTON ACT, AS AMENDED BY THE ROBINSON-PATMAN ACT

§ 1 [15 U.S.C. § 12]. Definitions;[1] short title

(a) "Antitrust laws," as used herein, includes the Act entitled "An Act to protect trade and commerce against unlawful restraints and monopolies," approved July second, eighteen hundred and ninety; sections seventy-three to seventy-six, inclusive, of an Act entitled "An Act to reduce taxation, to provide revenue for the Government, and for other purposes," of August twenty-seventh, eighteen hundred and ninety-four; an Act entitled "An Act to amend sections seventy-three and seventy-six of the Act of August twenty-seventh, eighteen hundred and ninety-four, entitled 'An Act to reduce taxation, to provide revenue for the Government, and for other purposes,' " approved February twelfth, nineteen hundred and thirteen; and also this Act.

"Commerce," as used herein, means trade or commerce among the several States and with foreign nations, or between the District of Columbia or any Territory of the United States and any State, Territory, or foreign nation, or between any insular possessions or other places under the jurisdiction of the United States, or between any such possession or place and any State or Territory of the United States or the District of Columbia or any foreign nation, or within the District of Columbia or any Territory or any insular possession or other place under the jurisdiction of the United States: *Provided*, That nothing in this Act contained shall apply to the Philippine Islands.

The word "person" or "persons" wherever used in this Act shall be deemed to include corporations and associations existing under or authorized by the laws of either the United States, the laws of any of the Territories, the laws of any State, or the laws of any foreign country.

(b) This Act may be cited as the "Clayton Act."

(Oct. 15, 1914, c. 323, 38 Stat. 730, Sept. 30, 1976, Pub.L. 94-435, Title III, § 305(b), 90 Stat. 1397; Nov. 2, 2002, Pub.L. 107-273, Div. C, Title IV, § 14102(c)(2)(A), 116 Stat. 1921.)

§ 2 [15 U.S.C. § 13]. Discrimination in price, services, or facilities

(As amended by The Robinson-Patman Act)

(a) Price; selection of customers

It shall be unlawful for any person engaged in commerce, in the course of such commerce, either directly or indirectly, to discriminate in price between different purchasers of commodities of like grade and quality, where either or any of the purchases involved in such discrimination are in

---

[1] **§ 1. [moved to 29 U.S.C. § 53] "Person" or "persons" defined**

The word "person" or "persons" wherever used in section 52 of this title shall be deemed to include corporations and associations existing under or authorized by the laws of either the United States, the laws of any of the Territories, the laws of any State, or the laws of any foreign country. (Oct. 15, 1914, c. 323, § 1, 38 Stat. 730.)

commerce, where such commodities are sold for use, consumption, or resale within the United States or any Territory thereof or the District of Columbia or any insular possession or other place under the jurisdiction of the United States, and where the effect of such discrimination may be substantially to lessen competition or tend to create a monopoly in any line of commerce, or to injure, destroy, or prevent competition with any person who either grants or knowingly receives the benefit of such discrimination, or with customers of either of them: *Provided*, That nothing herein contained shall prevent differentials which make only due allowance for differences in the cost of manufacture, sale, or delivery resulting from the differing methods or quantities in which such commodities are to such purchasers sold or delivered: *Provided, however*, That the Federal Trade Commission may, after due investigation and hearing to all interested parties, fix and establish quantity limits, and revise the same as it finds necessary, as to particular commodities or classes of commodities, where it finds that available purchasers in greater quantities are so few as to render differentials on account thereof unjustly discriminatory or promotive of monopoly in any line of commerce; and the foregoing shall then not be construed to permit differentials based on differences in quantities greater than those so fixed and established: *And provided further*, That nothing herein contained shall prevent persons engaged in selling goods, wares, or merchandise in commerce from selecting their own customers in bona fide transactions and not in restraint of trade: *And provided further*, That nothing herein contained shall prevent price changes from time to time where in response to changing conditions affecting the market for or the marketability of the goods concerned, such as but not limited to actual or imminent deterioration of perishable goods, obsolescence of seasonal goods, distress sales under court process, or sales in good faith in discontinuance of business in the goods concerned.

(b) Burden of rebutting prima-facie case of discrimination

Upon proof being made, at any hearing on a complaint under this section, that there has been discrimination in price or services or facilities furnished, the burden of rebutting the prima-facie case thus made by showing justification shall be upon the person charged with a violation of this section, and unless justification shall be affirmatively shown, the Commission is authorized to issue an order terminating the discrimination: *Provided, however,* That nothing herein contained shall prevent a seller rebutting the prima-facie case thus made by showing that his lower price or the furnishing of services or facilities to any purchaser or purchasers was made in good faith to meet an equally low price of a competitor, or the services or facilities furnished by a competitor.

(c) Payment or acceptance of commission, brokerage, or other compensation

It shall be unlawful for any person engaged in commerce, in the course of such commerce, to pay or grant, or to receive or accept, anything of value as a commission, brokerage, or other compensation, or any allowance or discount in lieu thereof, except for services rendered in connection with the sale or purchase of goods, wares, or merchandise, either to the other party to such transaction or to an agent, representative, or other intermediary therein where such intermediary is acting in fact for or in behalf, or is subject to the direct or indirect control, of any party to such transaction other than the person by whom such compensation is so granted or paid.

(d) Payment for services or facilities for processing or sale

It shall be unlawful for any person engaged in commerce to pay or contract for the payment of anything of value to or for the benefit of a customer of such person in the course of such commerce as compensation or in consideration for any services or facilities furnished by or through such customer in connection with the processing, handling, sale, or offering for sale of any products or commodities manufactured, sold, or offered for sale by such person, unless such payment or consideration is available on proportionally equal terms to all other customers competing in the distribution of such products or commodities.

(e) Furnishing services or facilities for processing, handling, etc.

It shall be unlawful for any person to discriminate in favor of one purchaser against another purchaser or purchasers of a commodity bought for resale, with or without processing, by contracting to furnish or furnishing, or by contributing to the furnishing of, any services or facilities connected with the processing, handling, sale, or offering for sale of such commodity so purchased upon terms not accorded to all purchasers on proportionally equal terms.

(f) Knowingly inducing or receiving discriminatory price

It shall be unlawful for any person engaged in commerce, in the course of such commerce, knowingly to induce or receive a discrimination in price which is prohibited by this section.

(Oct. 15, 1914, c. 323, § 2, 38 Stat. 730; June 19, 1936, c. 592, § 1, 49 Stat. 1526.)[2]

---

[2] Section 2 of the Robinson-Patman Act, c. 592, § 2, 49 Stat. 1527, provides that pending and prior actions and orders under § 2 of the original Clayton Act were not affected by the Robinson-Patman Act Amendment to § 2 of the Clayton Act.

Sections 3 and 4 of the Robinson-Patman Act provide as follows:

§ 3 [15 U.S.C. § 13a]. Discrimination in rebates, discounts, or advertising service charges; underselling in particular localities; penalties

(As amended by The Robinson-Patman Act)

It shall be unlawful for any person engaged in commerce, in the course of such commerce, to be a party to, or assist in, any transaction of sale, or contract to sell, which discriminates to his knowledge against competitors of the purchaser, in that, any discount, rebate, allowance, or advertising service charge is granted to the purchaser over and above any discount, rebate, allowance, or advertising service charge available at the time of such transaction to said competitors in respect of a sale of goods of like grade, quality, and quantity; to sell, or contract to sell, goods in any part of the United States at prices lower than those exacted by said person elsewhere in the United States for the purpose of destroying competition, or eliminating a competitor in such part of the United States; or, to sell, or contract to sell, goods at unreasonably low prices for the purpose of destroying competition or eliminating a competitor.

Any person violating any of the provisions of this section shall, upon conviction thereof, be fined not more than $5,000 or imprisoned not more than one year, or both.

(June 19, 1936, c. 592, § 3, 49 Stat. 1528.)

§ 4 [15 U.S.C. § 13b]. Cooperative association; return of net earnings or surplus

(As amended by The Robinson-Patman Act)

Nothing in this Act shall prevent a cooperative association from returning to its members, producers, or consumers the whole, or any part of, the net earnings or surplus resulting from its trading operations, in proportion to their purchases or sales from, to, or through the association.

(June 19, 1936, c. 592, § 4, 49 Stat. 1528.)

A further section of the Robinson-Patman Act, unnumbered, provides:

[15 U.S.C. § 13c]. Exemption of non-profit institutions from price discrimination provisions

§ 3 [15 U.S.C. § 14]. Sale, etc., on agreement not to use goods of competitor

It shall be unlawful for any person engaged in commerce, in the course of such commerce, to lease or make a sale or contract for sale of goods, wares, merchandise, machinery, supplies, or other commodities, whether patented or unpatented, for use, consumption, or resale within the United States or any Territory thereof or the District of Columbia or any insular possession or other place under the jurisdiction of the United States, or fix a price charged therefor, or discount from, or rebate upon, such price, on the condition, agreement, or understanding that the lessee or purchaser thereof shall not use or deal in the goods, wares, merchandise, machinery, supplies, or other commodities of a competitor or competitors of the lessor or seller, where the effect of such lease, sale, or contract for sale or such condition, agreement, or understanding may be to substantially lessen competition or tend to create a monopoly in any line of commerce.

(Oct. 15, 1914, c. 323, § 3, 38 Stat. 731.)

§ 4 [15 U.S.C. § 15]. Suits by persons injured

(a) Amount of recovery; prejudgment interest

Except as provided in subsection (b) of this section, any person who shall be injured in his business or property by reason of anything forbidden in the antitrust laws may sue therefor in any district court of the United States in the district in which the defendant resides or is found or has an agent, without respect to the amount in controversy, and shall recover threefold the damages by him sustained, and the cost of suit, including a reasonable attorney's fee. The court may award under this section, pursuant to a motion by such person promptly made, simple interest on actual damages for the period beginning on the date of service of such person's pleading setting forth a claim under the antitrust laws and ending on the date of judgment, or for any shorter period therein, if the court finds that the award of such interest for such period is just in the circumstances. In determining whether an award of interest under this section for any period is just in the circumstances, the court shall consider only—

(1) whether such person or the opposing party, or either party's representative, made motions or asserted claims or defenses so lacking in merit as to show that such party or representative acted intentionally for delay, or otherwise acted in bad faith;

(2) whether, in the course of the action involved, such person or the opposing party, or either party's representative, violated any applicable rule, statute, or court order providing for sanctions for dilatory behavior or otherwise providing for expeditious proceedings; and

(3) whether such person or the opposing party, or either party's representative, engaged in conduct primarily for the purpose of delaying the litigation or increasing the cost thereof.

(As amended by The Robinson-Patman Act)

Nothing in the Act approved June 19, 1936, known as the Robinson-Patman Antidiscrimination Act,, shall apply to purchases of their supplies for their own use by schools, colleges, universities, public libraries, churches, hospitals, and charitable institutions not operated for profit.

(May 26, 1938, c. 283, 52 Stat. 446.)

(b) Amount of damages payable to foreign states and instrumentalities of foreign states

(1) Except as provided in paragraph (2), any person who is a foreign state may not recover under subsection (a) of this section an amount in excess of the actual damages sustained by it and the cost of suit, including a reasonable attorney's fee.

(2) Paragraph (1) shall not apply to a foreign state if—

(A) such foreign state would be denied, under section 1605(a) (2) of Title 28, immunity in a case in which the action is based upon a commercial activity, or an act, that is the subject matter of its claim under this section;

(B) such foreign state waives all defenses based upon or arising out of its status as a foreign state, to any claims brought against it in the same action;

(C) such foreign state engages primarily in commercial activities; and

(D) such foreign state does not function, with respect to the commercial activity, or the act, that is the subject matter of its claim under this section as a procurement entity for itself or for another foreign state.

(c) Definitions

For purposes of this section—

(1) the term "commercial activity" shall have the meaning given it in section 1603(d) of Title 28, and

(2) the term "foreign state" shall have the meaning given it in section 1 603(a) of Title 28.

(Oct. 15, 1914, c. 323, § 4, 38 Stat. 731; Sept. 12, 1980, Pub.L. 96-349, § 4(a) (1), 94 Stat. 1156; Dec. 29, 1982, Pub.L. 97-393, 96 Stat. 1964.)

§ 4A [15 U.S.C. § 15a]. Suits by United States; amount of recovery; prejudgment interest

Whenever the United States is hereafter injured in its business or property by reason of anything forbidden in the antitrust laws it may sue therefor in the United States district court for the district in which the defendant resides or is found or has an agent, without respect to the amount in controversy, and shall recover threefold the damages by it sustained and the cost of suit. The court may award under this section, pursuant to a motion by the United States promptly made, simple interest on actual damages for the period beginning on the date of service of the pleading of the United States setting forth a claim under the antitrust laws and ending on the date of judgment, or for any shorter period therein, if the court finds that the award of such interest for such period is just in the circumstances. In determining whether an award of interest under this section for any period is just in the circumstances, the court shall consider only—

(1) whether the United States or the opposing party, or either party's representative, made motions or asserted claims or defenses so lacking in merit as to show that such party or representative acted intentionally for delay or otherwise acted in bad faith;

(2) whether, in the course of the action involved, the United States or the opposing party, or either party's representative, violated any applicable rule, statute, or court order providing for sanctions for dilatory behavior or otherwise providing for expeditious proceedings;

(3) whether the United States or the opposing party, or either party's representative, engaged in conduct primarily for the purpose of delaying the litigation or increasing the cost thereof; and

(4) whether the award of such interest is necessary to compensate the United States adequately for the injury sustained by the United States.

(Oct. 15, 1914, c. 323, § 4A, as added July 7, 1955, c. 283, § 1, 69 Stat. 282, and as amended Sept. 12, 1980, Pub.L. 96-349, § 4(a) (2), 94 Stat. 1156; Nov. 16, 1990, Pub.L. 101-588, § 5, 104 Stat. 2880.)

§ 4B [15 U.S.C. § 15b]. Limitation of actions

Any action to enforce any cause of action under sections 15, 15a, or 15c of this title shall be forever barred unless commenced within four years after the cause of action accrued. No cause of action barred under existing law on the effective date of this Act shall be revived by this Act.

(Oct. 15, 1914, c. 323, § 4B, as added July 7, 1955, c. 283, § 1, 69 Stat. 283, and as amended Sept. 30, 1976, Pub.L. 94-435, Title III, § 302(1), 90 Stat. 1396.)

§ 4C [15 U.S.C. 15c]. Actions by State attorneys general

(a) Parens patriae; monetary relief; damages; prejudgment interest

(1) Any attorney general of a State may bring a civil action in the name of such State, as parens patriae on behalf of natural persons residing in such State, in any district court of the United States having jurisdiction of the defendant, to secure monetary relief as provided in this section for injury sustained by such natural persons to their property by reason of any violation of sections 1 to 7 of this title. The court shall exclude from the amount of monetary relief awarded in such action any amount of monetary relief (A) which duplicates amounts which have been awarded for the same injury, or (B) which is properly allocable to (i) natural persons who have excluded their claims pursuant to subsection (b)(2) of this section, and (ii) any business entity.

(2) The court shall award the State as monetary relief threefold the total damage sustained as described in paragraph (1) of this subsection, and the cost of suit, including a reasonable attorney's fee. The court may award under this paragraph, pursuant to a motion by such State promptly made, simple interest on the total damage for the period beginning on the date of service of such State's pleading setting forth a claim under the antitrust laws and ending on the date of judgment, or for any shorter period therein, if the court finds that the award of such interest for such period is just in the circumstances. In determining whether an award of interest under this paragraph for any period is just in the circumstances, the court shall consider only—

(A) whether such State or the opposing party, or either party's representative, made motions or asserted claims or defenses so lacking in merit as to show that such party or representative acted intentionally for delay or otherwise acted in bad faith;

(B) whether, in the course of the action involved, such State or the opposing party, or either party's representative, violated any applicable rule, statute, or court order providing for sanctions for dilatory behavior or otherwise providing for expeditious proceedings; and

(C) whether such State or the opposing party, or either party's representative, engaged in conduct primarily for the purpose of delaying the litigation or increasing the cost thereof.

(b) Notice; exclusion election; final judgment

(1) In any action brought under subsection (a)(1) of this section, the State attorney general shall, at such times, in such manner, and with such content as the court may direct, cause notice thereof to be given by publication. If the court finds that notice given solely by publication would deny due process of law to any person or persons, the court may direct further notice to such person or persons according to the circumstances of the case.

(2) Any person on whose behalf an action is brought under subsection (a)(1) of this section may elect to exclude from adjudication the portion of the State claim for monetary relief attributable to him by filing notice of such election with the court within such time as specified in the notice given pursuant to paragraph (1) of this subsection.

(3) The final judgment in an action under subsection (a)(1) of this section shall be res judicata as to any claim under section 15 of this title by any person on behalf of whom such action was brought and who fails to give such notice within the period specified in the notice given pursuant to paragraph (1) of this subsection.

(c) Dismissal or compromise of action

An action under subsection (a) (1) of this section shall not be dismissed or compromised without the approval of the court, and notice of any proposed dismissal or compromise shall be given in such manner as the court directs.

(d) Attorneys' fees

In any action under subsection (a) of this section—

(1) the amount of the plaintiffs' attorney's fee, if any, shall be determined by the court; and

(2) the court may, in its discretion, award a reasonable attorney's fee to a prevailing defendant upon a finding that the State attorney general has acted in bad faith, vexatiously, wantonly, or for oppressive reasons.

(Oct. 15, 1914, c. 323, § 4C, as added Sept. 30, 1976, Pub.L. 94-435, Title III, § 301, 90 Stat. 1394, and amended Sept. 12, 1980, Pub.L. 96-349, § 4(a)(3), 94 Stat. 1157.)

§ 4D [15 U.S.C. § 15d]. Measurement of damages

In any action under section 15c(a)(1) of this title, in which there has been a determination that a defendant agreed to fix prices in violation of sections 1 to 7 of this title, damages may be proved and assessed in the aggregate by statistical or sampling methods, by the computation of illegal overcharges, or by such other reasonable system of estimating aggregate damages as the court in its discretion may permit without the necessity of separately proving the individual claim of, or amount of damage to, persons on whose behalf the suit was brought.

(Oct. 15, 1914, c. 323, § 4D, as added Sept. 30, 1976, Pub.L. 94-435, Title III, § 301, 90 Stat. 1395.)

§ 4E [15 U.S.C. § 15e]. Distribution of damages

Monetary relief recovered in an action under section 15c(a)(1) of this title shall—

(1) be distributed in such manner as the district court in its discretion may authorize; or

(2) be deemed a civil penalty by the court and deposited with the State as general revenues;

subject in either case to the requirement that any distribution procedure adopted afford each person a reasonable opportunity to secure his appropriate portion of the net monetary relief.

(Oct. 15, 1914, c. 323, § 4E, as added Sept. 30, 1976, Pub.L. 94-435, Title III, § 301, 90 Stat. 1395.)

§ 4F [15 U.S.C. § 15f]. Actions by Attorney General

(a) Notification to State attorney general

Whenever the Attorney General of the United States has brought an action under the antitrust laws, and he has reason to believe that any State attorney general would be entitled to bring an action under this Act based substantially on the same alleged violation of the antitrust laws, he shall promptly give written notification thereof to such State attorney general.

(b) Availability of files and other materials

To assist a State attorney general in evaluating the notice or in bringing any action under this Act, the Attorney General of the United States shall, upon request by such State attorney general, make available to him, to the extent permitted by law, any investigative files or other materials which are or may be relevant or material to the actual or potential cause of action under this Act.

(Oct. 15, 1914, c. 323, § 4F, as added Sept. 30, 1976, Pub.L. 94-435, Title III, § 301, 90 Stat. 1395.)

§ 4G [15 U.S.C. § 15g]. Definitions

For the purposes of sections 15c, 15d, 15e, and 15f of this title:

(1) The term "State attorney general" means the chief legal officer of a State, or any other person authorized by State law to bring actions under section 15c of this title, and includes the Corporation Counsel of the District of Columbia, except that such term does not include any person employed or retained on—

(A) a contingency fee based on a percentage of the monetary relief awarded under this section; or

(B) any other contingency fee basis, unless the amount of the award of a reasonable attorney's fee to a prevailing plaintiff is determined by the court under section 15c(d)(1) of this title.

(2) The term "State" means a State, the District of Columbia, the Commonwealth of Puerto Rico, and any other territory or possession of the United States.

(3) The term "natural persons" does not include proprietorships or partnerships.

(Oct. 15, 1914, c. 323, § 4G, as added Sept. 30, 1976, Pub.L. 94-435, Title III, § 301, 90 Stat. 1396.)

§ 4H [15 U.S.C. § 15h]. Applicability of parens patriae actions

Sections 15c, 15d, 15e, 15f, and 15g of this title shall apply in any State, unless such State provides by law for its nonapplicability in such State.

(Oct. 15, 1914, c. 323, § 4H, as added Sept. 30, 1976, Pub.L. 94-435, Title III, § 301, 90 Stat. 1396.)

§ 5 [15 U.S.C. § 16]. Judgments

(a) Prima facie evidence; collateral estoppel[3]

A final judgment or decree heretofore or hereafter rendered in any civil or criminal proceeding brought by or on behalf of the United States under the antitrust laws to the effect that a defendant has violated said laws shall be prima facie evidence against such defendant in any action or proceeding brought by any other party against such defendant under said laws as to all matters respecting which said judgment or decree would be an estoppel as between the parties thereto: *Provided*, That this section shall not apply to consent judgments or decrees entered before any testimony has been taken. Nothing contained in this section shall be construed to impose any limitation on the application of collateral estoppel, except that, in any action or proceeding brought under the antitrust laws, collateral estoppel effect shall not be given to any finding made by the Federal Trade Commission under the antitrust laws or under section 45 of this title which could give rise to a claim for relief under the antitrust laws.

(b) Consent judgments and competitive impact statements; publication in Federal Register; availability of copies to the public

---

[3] Pub.L. 108-237, Title II, § 221(a), June 22, 2004, 118 Stat. 661, provides that:

"(a) Congressional findings and declaration of purposes.—

(1) Findings.—Congress finds that—

(A) the purpose of the Tunney Act [Pub.L. 93-528, Dec. 21, 1974, 88 Stat. 1706; see Short Title note under 15 U.S.C.A. § 1 and Tables for classification] was to ensure that the entry of antitrust consent judgments is in the public interest; and

(B) it would misconstrue the meaning and Congressional intent in enacting the Tunney Act to limit the discretion of district courts to review antitrust consent judgments solely to determining whether entry of those consent judgments would make a 'mockery of the judicial function'.

(2) Purposes.—The purpose of this section is to effectuate the original Congressional intent in enacting the Tunney Act and to ensure that United States settlements of civil antitrust suits are in the public interest."

Any proposal for a consent judgment submitted by the United States for entry in any civil proceeding brought by or on behalf of the United States under the antitrust laws shall be filed with the district court before which such proceeding is pending and published by the United States in the Federal Register at least 60 days prior to the effective date of such judgment. Any written comments relating to such proposal and any responses by the United States thereto, shall also be filed with such district court and published by the United States in the Federal Register within such sixty-day period. Copies of such proposal and any other materials and documents which the United States considered determinative in formulating such proposal, shall also be made available to the public at the district court and in such other districts as the court may subsequently direct. Simultaneously with the filing of such proposal, unless otherwise instructed by the court, the United States shall file with the district court, publish in the Federal Register, and thereafter furnish to any person upon request, a competitive impact statement which shall recite—

(1) the nature and purpose of the proceeding;

(2) a description of the practices or events giving rise to the alleged violation of the antitrust laws;

(3) an explanation of the proposal for a consent judgment, including an explanation of any unusual circumstances giving rise to such proposal or any provision contained therein, relief to be obtained thereby, and the anticipated effects on competition of such relief;

(4) the remedies available to potential private plaintiffs damaged by the alleged violation in the event that such proposal for the consent judgment is entered in such proceeding;

(5) a description of the procedures available for modification of such proposal; and

(6) a description and evaluation of alternatives to such proposal actually considered by the United States.

(c) Publication of summaries in newspapers

The United States shall also cause to be published, commencing at least 60 days prior to the effective date of the judgment described in subsection (b) of this section, for 7 days over a period of 2 weeks in newspapers of general circulation of the district in which the case has been filed, in the District of Columbia, and in such other districts as the court may direct—

(i) a summary of the terms of the proposal for the consent judgment,

(ii) a summary of the competitive impact statement filed under subsection (b) of this section,

(iii) and a list of the materials and documents under subsection (b) of this section which the United States shall make available for purposes of meaningful public comment, and the place where such materials and documents are available for public inspection.

(d) Consideration of public comments by Attorney General and publication of response

During the 60-day period as specified in subsection (b) of this section, and such additional time as the United States may request and the court may grant, the United States shall receive and consider any written comments relating to the proposal for the consent judgment submitted under subsection (b) of this section. The Attorney General or his designee shall establish procedures to carry out the provisions of this subsection, but such 60-day time period shall not be shortened except by order of the district court upon a showing that (1) extraordinary circumstances require such shortening and (2) such shortening is not adverse to the public interest. At the close of the period during which such comments may be received, the United States shall file with the district court and cause to be published in the Federal Register a response to such comments. Upon application by the United States, the district court may, for good cause (based on a finding that the expense of publication in the Federal Register exceeds the public interest benefits to be gained from such publication), authorize an alternative method of public dissemination of the public comments received and the response to those comments.

(e) Public interest determination

(1) Before entering any consent judgment proposed by the United States under this section, the court shall determine that the entry of such judgment is in the public interest. For the purpose of such determination, the court shall consider—

(A) the competitive impact of such judgment, including termination of alleged violations, provisions for enforcement and modification, duration or relief sought, anticipated effects of alternative remedies actually considered, whether its terms are ambiguous, and any other competitive considerations bearing upon the adequacy of such judgment that the court deems necessary to a determination of whether the consent judgment is in the public interest; and

(B) the impact of entry of such judgment upon competition in the relevant market or markets, upon the public generally and individuals alleging specific injury from the violations set forth in the complaint including consideration of the public benefit, if any, to be derived from a determination of the issues at trial.

(2) Nothing in this section shall be construed to require the court to conduct an evidentiary hearing or to require the court to permit anyone to intervene.

(f) Procedure for public interest determination

In making its determination under subsection (e) of this section, the court may—

(1) take testimony of Government officials or experts or such other expert witnesses, upon motion of any party or participant or upon its own motion, as the court may deem appropriate;

(2) appoint a special master and such outside consultants or expert witnesses as the court may deem appropriate; and request and obtain the views, evaluations, or advice of any individual, group or agency of government with respect to any aspects of the proposed judgment or the effect of such judgment, in such manner as the court deems appropriate;

(3) authorize full or limited participation in proceedings before the court by interested persons or agencies, including appearance amicus curiae, intervention as a party pursuant to the Federal Rules of Civil Procedure, examination of witnesses or documentary materials, or participation in any other manner and extent which serves the public interest as the court may deem appropriate;

(4) review any comments including any objections filed with the United States under subsection (d) of this section concerning the proposed judgment and the responses of the United States to such comments and objections; and

(5) take such other action in the public interest as the court may deem appropriate.

(g) Filing of written or oral communications with the district court

Not later than 10 days following the date of the filing of any proposal for a consent judgment under subsection (b) of this section, each defendant shall file with the district court a description of any and all written or oral communications by or on behalf of such defendant, including any and all written or oral communications on behalf of such defendant by any officer, director, employee, or agent of such defendant, or other person, with any officer or employee of the United States concerning or relevant to such proposal, except that any such communications made by counsel of record alone with the Attorney General or the employees of the Department of Justice alone shall be excluded from the requirements of this subsection. Prior to the entry of any consent judgment pursuant to the antitrust laws, each defendant shall certify to the district court that the requirements of this subsection have been complied with and that such filing is a true and complete description of such communications known to the defendant or which the defendant reasonably should have known.

(h) Inadmissibility as evidence of proceedings before the district court and the competitive impact statement

Proceedings before the district court under subsections (e) and (f) of this section, and the competitive impact statement filed under subsection (b) of this section, shall not be admissible against any defendant in any action or proceeding brought by any other party against such defendant under the antitrust laws or by the United States under section 15a of this title nor constitute a basis for the introduction of the consent judgment as prima facie evidence against such defendant in any such action or proceeding.

(i) Suspension of limitations

Whenever any civil or criminal proceeding is instituted by the United States to prevent, restrain, or punish violations of any of the antitrust laws, but not including an action under section 15a of this title, the running of the statute of limitations in respect of every private or State right of action arising under said laws and based in whole or in part on any matter complained of in said proceeding shall be suspended during the pendency thereof and for one year thereafter: *Provided, however,* That whenever the running of the statute of limitations in respect of a cause of action arising under section 15 or 15c of this title is suspended hereunder, any action to enforce such cause of action shall be forever barred unless commenced either within the period of suspension or within four years after the cause of action accrued.

(Oct. 15, 1914, c. 323, § 5, 38 Stat. 731; July 7, 1955, c. 283, § 2, 69 Stat. 283; Dec. 21, 1974, Pub.L. 93-528, § 2, 88 Stat. 1706; Sept. 30, 1976, Pub.L. 94-435, Title III, § 302(2), 90 Stat. 1396; Sept. 12, 1980, Pub.L. 96-349, § 5(a), 94 Stat. 1157; June 22, 2004, Pub.L. 108-237, Title II, § 221(b), 118 Stat. 661.)

§ 6 [15 U.S.C. § 17]. Antitrust laws not applicable to labor organizations

The labor of a human being is not a commodity or article of commerce. Nothing contained in the antitrust laws shall be construed to forbid the existence and operation of labor, agricultural, or horticultural organizations, instituted for the purposes of mutual help, and not having capital stock or conducted for profit, or to forbid or restrain individual members of such organizations from lawfully carrying out the legitimate objects thereof; nor shall such organizations, or the members thereof, be held or construed to be illegal combinations or conspiracies in restraint of trade, under the antitrust laws.[4]

(Oct. 15, 1914, c. 323, § 6, 38 Stat. 731.)

§ 7 [15 U.S.C. § 18]. Acquisition by one corporation of stock of another

No person engaged in commerce or in any activity affecting commerce shall acquire, directly or indirectly, the whole or any part of the stock or other share capital and no person subject to the jurisdiction of the Federal Trade Commission shall acquire the whole or any part of the assets of another person engaged also in commerce or in any activity affecting commerce, where in any line of commerce or in any activity affecting commerce in any section of the country, the effect of such acquisition may be substantially to lessen competition, or to tend to create a monopoly.

No person shall acquire, directly or indirectly, the whole or any part of the stock or other share capital and no person subject to the jurisdiction of the Federal Trade Commission shall acquire the whole or any part of the

---

[4] Section 20 of the original Clayton Act, now codified in 29 U.S.C. § 52, [Statutory restriction of injunctive relief], provides:

> No restraining order or injunction shall be granted by any court of the United States, or a judge or the judges thereof, in any case between an employer and employees, or between employers and employees, or between employees, or between persons employed and persons seeking employment, involving, or growing out of, a dispute concerning terms or conditions of employment, unless necessary to prevent irreparable injury to property, or to a property right, of the party making the application, for which injury there is no adequate remedy at law, and such property or property right must be described with particularity in the application, which must be in writing and sworn to by the applicant or by his agent or attorney.
>
> And no such restraining order or injunction shall prohibit any person or persons, whether singly or in concert, from terminating any relation of employment, or from ceasing to perform any work or labor, or from recommending, advising, or persuading others by peaceful means so to do; or from attending at any place where any such person or persons may lawfully be, for the purpose of peacefully obtaining or communicating information, or from peacefully persuading any person to work or to abstain from working; or from ceasing to patronize or to employ any party to such dispute, or from recommending, advising, or persuading others by peaceful and lawful means so to do; or from paying or giving to, or withholding from, any person engaged in such dispute, any strike benefits or other moneys or things of value; or from peaceably assembling in a lawful manner, and for lawful purposes; or from doing any act or thing which might lawfully be done in the absence of such dispute by any party thereto; nor shall any of the acts specified in this paragraph be considered or held to be violations of any law of the United States.

(Oct. 15, 1914, c. 323, § 20, 38 Stat. 738.)

assets of one or more persons engaged in commerce or in any activity affecting commerce, where in any line of commerce or in any activity affecting commerce in any section of the country, the effect of such acquisition, of such stocks or assets, or of the use of such stock by the voting or granting of proxies or otherwise, may be substantially to lessen competition, or to tend to create a monopoly.

This section shall not apply to persons purchasing such stock solely for investment and not using the same by voting or otherwise to bring about, or in attempting to bring about, the substantial lessening of competition. Nor shall anything contained in this section prevent a corporation engaged in commerce or in any activity affecting commerce from causing the formation of subsidiary corporations for the actual carrying on of their immediate lawful business, or the natural and legitimate branches or extensions thereof, or from owning and holding all or a part of the stock of such subsidiary corporations, when the effect of such formation is not to substantially lessen competition.

Nor shall anything herein contained be construed to prohibit any common carrier subject to the laws to regulate commerce from aiding in the construction of branches or short lines so located as to become feeders to the main line of the company so aiding in such construction or from acquiring or owning all or any part of the stock of such branch lines, nor to prevent any such common carrier from acquiring and owning all or any part of the stock of a branch or short line constructed by an independent company where there is no substantial competition between the company owning the branch line so constructed and the company owning the main line acquiring the property or an interest therein, nor to prevent such common carrier from extending any of its lines through the medium of the acquisition of stock or otherwise of any other common carrier where there is no substantial competition between the company extending its lines and the company whose stock, property, or an interest therein is so acquired.

Nothing contained in this section shall be held to affect or impair any right heretofore legally acquired: *Provided,* That nothing in this section shall be held or construed to authorize or make lawful anything heretofore prohibited or made illegal by the antitrust laws, nor to exempt any person from the penal provisions thereof or the civil remedies therein provided.

Nothing contained in this section shall apply to transactions duly consummated pursuant to authority given by the Secretary of Transportation, Federal Power Commission, Surface Transportation Board, the Securities and Exchange Commission in the exercise of its jurisdiction under section 79j of this title, the United States Maritime Commission, or the Secretary of Agriculture under any statutory provision vesting such power in such Commission, Board, or Secretary.

(Oct. 15,1914, c. 323, § 7, 38 Stat. 731; Dec. 29, 1950, c. 1184, 64 Stat. 1125; Sept. 12, 1980, Pub.L. 96-349, § 6(a), 94 Stat. 1157; Oct. 4, 1984, Pub.L. 98-443, § 9(1), 98 Stat. 1708; Dec. 29, 1995, Pub.L. 104-88, Title III, § 318(1), 109 Stat. 949; Feb. 8, 1996, Pub.L. 104-104, Title VI, § 601(b)(3), 110 Stat. 143.)

§ 7A [15 U.S.C. § 18a] Premerger notification and waiting period

(a) Filing

Except as exempted pursuant to subsection (c) of this section, no person shall acquire, directly or indirectly, any voting securities or assets of any other person, unless both persons (or in the case of a tender offer, the acquiring person) file notification pursuant to rules under subsection (d)(1) of this section and the waiting period described in subsection (b)(1) of this section has expired, if

(1) the acquiring person, or the person whose voting securities or assets are being acquired, is engaged in commerce or in any activity affecting commerce; and

(2) as a result of such acquisition, the acquiring person would hold an aggregate total amount of the voting securities and assets of the acquired person—

(A) in excess of $200,000,000 (as adjusted and published for each fiscal year beginning after September 30, 2004, in the same manner as provided in section 19(a)(5) of this title to reflect the percentage change in the gross national product for such fiscal year compared to the gross national product for the year ending September 30, 2003); or

(B) (i) in excess of $50,000,000 (as so adjusted and published) but not in excess of $200,000,000 (as so adjusted and published); and

(ii) (I) any voting securities or assets of a person engaged in manufacturing which has annual net sales or total assets of $10,000,000 (as so adjusted and published) or more are being acquired by any person which has total assets or annual net sales of $100,000,000 (as so adjusted and published) or more;

(II) any voting securities or assets of a person not engaged in manufacturing which has total assets of $10,000,000 (as so adjusted and published) or more are being acquired by any person which has total assets or annual net sales of $100,000,000 (as so adjusted and published) or more; or

(III) any voting securities or assets of a person with annual net sales or total assets of $100,000,000 (as so adjusted and published) or more are being acquired by any person with total assets or annual net sales of $10,000,000 (as so adjusted and published) or more.

In the case of a tender offer, the person whose voting securities are sought to be acquired by a person required to file notification under this subsection shall file notification pursuant to rules under subsection (d) of this section.

(b) Waiting period; publication; voting securities

(1) The waiting period required under subsection (a) of this section shall—

(A) begin on the date of the receipt by the Federal Trade Commission and the Assistant Attorney General in charge of the Antitrust Division of the Department of Justice (hereinafter referred to in this section as the "Assistant Attorney General") of—

(i) the completed notification required under subsection (a) of this section, or

(ii) if such notification is not completed, the notification to the extent completed and a statement of the reasons for such noncompliance,

from both persons, or, in the case of a tender offer, the acquiring person; and

(B) end on the thirtieth day after the date of such receipt (or in the case of a cash tender offer, the fifteenth day), or on such later date as may be set under subsection (e)(2) or (g)(2) of this section.

(2) The Federal Trade Commission and the Assistant Attorney General may, in individual cases, terminate the waiting period specified in paragraph (1) and allow any person to proceed with any acquisition subject to this section, and promptly shall cause to be published in the Federal Register a notice that neither intends to take any action within such period with respect to such acquisition.

(3) As used in this section—

(A) The term "voting securities" means any securities which at present or upon conversion entitle the owner or holder thereof to vote for the election of directors of the issuer or, with respect to unincorporated issuers, persons exercising similar functions.

(B) The amount or percentage of voting securities or assets of a person which are acquired or held by another person shall be determined by aggregating the amount or percentage of such voting securities or assets held or acquired by such other person and each affiliate thereof.

(c) Exempt transactions

The following classes of transactions are exempt from the requirements of this section—

(1) acquisitions of goods or realty transferred in the ordinary course of business;

(2) acquisitions of bonds, mortgages, deeds of trust, or other obligations which are not voting securities;

(3) acquisitions of voting securities of an issuer at least 50 per centum of the voting securities of which are owned by the acquiring person prior to such acquisition;

(4) transfers to or from a Federal agency or a State or political subdivision thereof;

(5) transactions specifically exempted from the antitrust laws by Federal statute;

(6) transactions specifically exempted from the antitrust laws by Federal statute if approved by a Federal agency, if copies of all information and documentary material filed with such agency are contemporaneously filed with the Federal Trade Commission and the Assistant Attorney General;

(7) transactions which require agency approval under section 1467a(e) of title 12, section 1828(c) of title 12, or section 1842 of

Title 12, except that a portion of a transaction is not exempt under this paragraph if such portion of the transaction (A) is subject to section 1843(k) of Title 12; and (B) does not require agency approval under section 1842 of Title 12;

(8) transactions which require agency approval under section 1843 of Title 12 or section 1464 of Title 12, if copies of all information and documentary material filed with any such agency are contemporaneously filed with the Federal Trade Commission and the Assistant Attorney General at least 30 days prior to consummation of the proposed transaction, except that a portion of a transaction is not exempt under this paragraph if such portion of the transaction (A) is subject to section 1843(k) of Title 12; and (B) does not require agency approval under section 1843 of Title 12;

(9) acquisitions, solely for the purpose of investment, of voting securities, if, as a result of such acquisition, the securities acquired or held do not exceed 10 per centum of the outstanding voting securities of the issuer;

(10) acquisitions of voting securities, if, as a result of such acquisition, the voting securities acquired do not increase, directly or indirectly, the acquiring person's per centum share of outstanding voting securities of the issuer;

(11) acquisitions, solely for the purpose of investment, by any bank, banking association, trust company, investment company, or insurance company, of (A) voting securities pursuant to a plan of reorganization or dissolution; or (B) assets in the ordinary course of its business; and

(12) such other acquisitions, transfers, or transactions, as may be exempted under subsection (d)(2)(B) of this section.

(d) Commission rules

The Federal Trade Commission, with the concurrence of the Assistant Attorney General and by rule in accordance with section 553 of Title 5, consistent with the purposes of this section—

(1) shall require that the notification required under subsection (a) of this section be in such form and contain such documentary material and information relevant to a proposed acquisition as is necessary and appropriate to enable the Federal Trade Commission and the Assistant Attorney General to determine whether such acquisition may, if consummated, violate the antitrust laws; and

(2) may—

(A) define the terms used in this section;

(B) exempt, from the requirements of this section, classes of persons, acquisitions, transfers, or transactions which are not likely to violate the antitrust laws; and

(C) prescribe such other rules as may be necessary and appropriate to carry out the purposes of this section.

(e) Additional information; waiting period extensions

(1)(A) The Federal Trade Commission or the Assistant Attorney General may, prior to the expiration of the 30-day waiting period (or in the case of a cash tender offer, the 15-day waiting period) specified in subsection (b)(1) of this section, require the submission of additional information or documentary material relevant to the proposed acquisition, from a person required to file notification with respect to such acquisition under subsection (a) of this section prior to the expiration of the waiting period specified in subsection (b)(1) of this section, or from any officer, director, partner, agent, or employee of such person.

(B)(i) The assistant attorney general and the Federal trade Commission shall each designate a senior official who does not have direct responsibility for the review of any enforcement recommendation under this section concerning the transaction at issue, to hear any petition filed by such person to determine

(I) whether the request for additional information or documentary material is unreasonably cumulative, unduly burdensome, or duplicative; or

(II) whether the request for additional information or documentary material has been substantially complied with by the petitioning person.

(ii) Internal review procedures for petitions filed pursuant to clause (i) shall include reasonable deadlines for expedited review of such petitions, after reasonable negotiations with investigative staff, in order to avoid undue delay of the merger review process.

(iii) Not later than 90 days after December 21, 2000, the Assistant Attorney General and the Federal Trade Commission shall conduct an internal review and implement reforms of the merger review process in order to eliminate unnecessary burden, remove costly duplication, and eliminate undue delay, in order to achieve a more effective and more efficient merger review process.

(iv) Not later than 120 days after December 21, 2000, the Assistant Attorney General and the Federal Trade Commission shall issue or amend their respective industry guidance, regulations, operating manuals and relevant policy documents, to the extent appropriate, to implement each reform in this subparagraph.

(v) Not later than 180 days after December 21, 2000, the assistant attorney general and the Federal trade Commission shall each report to Congress

(I) which reforms each agency has adopted under this subparagraph;

(II) which steps each has taken to implement such internal reforms; and

(III) the effects of such reforms.

(2) The Federal Trade Commission or the Assistant Attorney General, in its or his discretion, may extend the 30-day waiting

period (or in the case of a cash tender offer, the 15-day waiting period) specified in subsection (b) (1) of this section for an additional period of not more than 30 days (or in the case of a cash tender offer, 10 days) after the date on which the Federal Trade Commission or the Assistant Attorney General, as the case may be, receives from any person to whom a request is made under paragraph (1), or in the case of tender offers, the acquiring person, (A) all the information and documentary material required to be submitted pursuant to such a request, or (B) if such request is not fully complied with, the information and documentary material submitted and a statement of the reasons for such noncompliance. Such additional period may be further extended only by the United States district court, upon an application by the Federal Trade Commission or the Assistant Attorney General pursuant to subsection (g) (2) of this section.

(f) Preliminary injunctions; hearings

If a proceeding is instituted or an action is filed by the Federal Trade Commission, alleging that a proposed acquisition violates section 18 of this title, or section 45 of this title, or an action is filed by the United States, alleging that a proposed acquisition violates such section 18 of this title, or section 1 or 2 of this title, and the Federal Trade Commission or the Assistant Attorney General (1) files a motion for a preliminary injunction against consummation of such acquisition pendente lite, and (2) certifies the United States district court for the judicial district within which the respondent resides or carries on business, or in which the action is brought, that it or he believes that the public interest requires relief pendente lite pursuant to this subsection, then upon the filing of such motion and certification, the chief judge of such district court shall immediately notify the chief judge of the United States court of appeals for the circuit in which such district court is located, who shall designate a United States district judge to whom such action shall be assigned for all purposes.

(g) Civil penalty; compliance; power of court

(1) Any person, or any officer, director, or partner thereof, who fails to comply with any provision of this section shall be liable to the United States for a civil penalty of not more than $10,000 for each day during which such person is in violation of this section. Such penalty may be recovered in a civil action brought by the United States.

(2) If any person, or any officer, director, partner, agent, or employee thereof, fails substantially to comply with the notification requirement under subsection (a) of this section or any request for the submission of additional information or documentary material under subsection (e)(1) of this section within the waiting period specified in subsection (b)(1) of this section and as may be extended under subsection (e)(2) of this section, the United States district court—

(A) may order compliance;

(B) shall extend the waiting period specified in subsection (b)(1) of this section and as may have been extended under subsection (e)(2) of this section until there has been substantial compliance, except that, in the case of a tender offer, the court may not extend such waiting period on the basis of a failure, by the person whose stock is sought to be acquired, to comply substantially with such notification requirement or any such request; and

(C) may grant such other equitable relief as the court in its discretion determines necessary or appropriate, upon application of the Federal Trade Commission or the Assistant Attorney General.

(h) Disclosure exemption

Any information or documentary material filed with the Assistant Attorney General or the Federal Trade Commission pursuant to this section shall be exempt from disclosure under section 552 of Title 5, and no such information or documentary material may be made public, except as may be relevant to any administrative or judicial action or proceeding. Nothing in this section is intended to prevent disclosure to either body of Congress or to any duly authorized committee or subcommittee of the Congress.

(i) Construction with other laws

(1) Any action taken by the Federal Trade Commission or the Assistant Attorney General or any failure of the Federal Trade Commission or the Assistant Attorney General to take any action under this section shall not bar any proceeding or any action with respect to such acquisition at any time under any other section of this Act or any other provision of law.

(2) Nothing contained in this section shall limit the authority of the Assistant Attorney General or the Federal Trade Commission to secure at any time from any person documentary material, oral testimony, or other information under the Antitrust Civil Process Act [15 U.S.C.A. § 1311 et seq.], the Federal Trade Commission Act [15 U.S.C.A. § 41 et seq.], or any other provision of law.

(j) Omitted

(k) Computation of time

If the end of any period of time provided in this section falls on a Saturday, Sunday, or legal public holiday (as defined in section 6103(a) of title 5), then such period shall be extended to the end of the next day that is not a Saturday, Sunday, or legal public holiday.

(Oct. 15, 1914, c. 323, § 7A, as added Sept. 30, 1976, Pub.L. 94-435, Title II, § 201, 90 Stat. 1390, and amended Nov. 8, 1984, Pub.L. 98-620, Title IV, § 402(10)(A), 98 Stat. 3358; Aug. 9, 1989, Pub.L. 101-73, Title XII, § 1214, 103 Stat. 529.; Nov. 12, 1999, Pub.L. 106-102, Title I, § 133(c), 113 Stat. 1383; Dec. 21, 2000, Pub.L. 106-553, § 1(a)(2) [Title VI, § 630(a), (c) to (d)], 114 Stat. 2762, 2762A-108, 2762A-110.)

§ 8 [15 U.S.C. § 19]. Interlocking directorates and officers

(a)(1) No person shall, at the same time, serve as a director or officer in any two corporations (other than banks, banking associations, and trust companies) that are—

(A) engaged in whole or in part in commerce; and

(B) by virtue of their business and location of operation, competitors, so that the elimination of competition by agreement between them would constitute a violation of any of the antitrust laws;

if each of the corporations has capital, surplus, and undivided profits aggregating more than $10,000,000 as adjusted pursuant to paragraph (5) of this subsection.

(2) Notwithstanding the provisions of paragraph (1), simultaneous service as a director or officer in any two corporations shall not be prohibited by this section if—

(A) the competitive sales of either corporation are less than $1,000,000, as adjusted pursuant to paragraph (5) of this subsection;

(B) the competitive sales of either corporation are less than 2 per centum of that corporation's total sales; or

(C) the competitive sales of each corporation are less than 4 per centum of that corporation's total sales.

For purposes of this paragraph, "competitive sales" means the gross revenues for all products and services sold by one corporation in competition with the other, determined on the basis of annual gross revenues for such products and services in that corporation's last completed fiscal year. For the purposes of this paragraph, "total sales" means the gross revenues for all products and services sold by one corporation over that corporation's last completed fiscal year.

(3) The eligibility of a director or officer under the provisions of paragraph (1) shall be determined by the capital, surplus and undivided profits, exclusive of dividends declared but not paid to stockholders, of each corporation at the end of that corporation's last completed fiscal year.

(4) For purposes of this section, the term "officer" means an officer elected or chosen by the Board of Directors.

(5) For each fiscal year commencing after September 30, 1990, the $10,000,000 and $1,000,000 thresholds in this subsection shall be increased (or decreased) as of October 1 each year by an amount equal to the percentage increase (or decrease) in the gross national product, as determined by the Department of Commerce or its successor, for the year then ended over the level so established for the year ending September 30, 1989. As soon as practicable, but not later than October 30 of each year, the Federal Trade Commission shall publish the adjusted amounts required by this paragraph.

(b) When any person elected or chosen as a director or officer of any corporation subject to the provisions hereof is eligible at the time of his election or selection to act for such corporation in such capacity, his eligibility to act in such capacity shall not be affected by any of the provisions hereof by reason of any change in the capital, surplus and undivided profits, or affairs of such corporation from whatever cause, until the expiration of one year from the date on which the event causing ineligibility occurred.

(Oct. 15, 1914, c. 323, § 8, 38 Stat. 732; May 15, 1916, c. 120, 39 Stat. 121; May 26, 1920, c. 206, 41 Stat. 626; Mar. 9, 1928, c. 165, 45 Stat. 253; Mar. 2, 1929, c. 581, 45 Stat. 1536; Aug. 23, 1935, c. 614, § 329, 49 Stat. 717; Nov. 16, 1990,

Pub.L. 101-588, § 2, 104 Stat. 2879; Dec. 17, 1993, Pub.L. 103-203, § 1, 107 Stat. 2368.)

§ 9 [18 U.S.C. § 660]. Carrier's funds derived from commerce; State prosecutions

Whoever, being a president, director, officer, or manager of any firm, association, or corporation engaged in commerce as a common carrier, or whoever, being an employee of such common carrier riding in or upon any railroad car, motortruck, steamboat, vessel, aircraft or other vehicle of such carrier moving in interstate commerce, embezzles, steals, abstracts, or willfully misapplies, or willfully permits to be misapplied, any of the moneys, funds, credits, securities, property, or assets of such firm, association, or corporation arising or accruing from, or used in, such commerce, in whole or in part, or willfully or knowingly converts the same to his own use or to the use of another, shall be fined under this title or imprisoned not more than ten years, or both.

The offense shall be deemed to have been committed not only in the district where the violation first occurred but also in any district in which the defendant may have taken or had possession of such moneys, funds, credits, securities, property or assets.

A judgment of conviction or acquittal on the merits under the laws of any State shall be a bar to any prosecution hereunder for the same act or acts.

(June 25, 1948, c. 645, 62 Stat. 730; Sept. 13, 1994, Pub.L. 103-322, Title XXXIII, § 330016(1)(K), 108 Stat. 2147.)

§ 11 [15 U.S.C. § 21]. Enforcement provisions

(a) Commissions, Board, or Secretary authorized to enforce compliance

Authority to enforce compliance with sections 13, 14, 18, and 19 of this title by the persons respectively subject thereto is vested in the Surface Transportation Board where applicable to common carriers subject to jurisdiction under subtitle IV of Title 49; in the Federal Communications Commission where applicable to common carriers engaged in wire or radio communication or radio transmission of energy; in the Secretary of Transportation where applicable to air carriers and foreign air carriers subject to part A of subtitle VII of Title 49; in the Board of Governors of the Federal Reserve System where applicable to banks, banking associations, and trust companies; and in the Federal Trade Commission where applicable to all other character of commerce to be exercised as follows:

(b) Issuance of complaints for violations; hearing; intervention; filing of testimony; report; cease and desist orders; reopening and alteration of reports or orders

Whenever the Commission, Board, or Secretary vested with jurisdiction thereof shall have reason to believe that any person is violating or has violated any of the provisions of sections 13, 14, 18, and 19 of this title, it shall issue and serve upon such person and the Attorney General a complaint stating its charges in that respect, and containing a notice of a hearing upon a day and at a place therein fixed at least thirty days after the service of said complaint. The person so complained of shall have the right to appear at the place and time so fixed and show cause why an order should not be entered by the Commission, Board, or Secretary requiring such person to cease and desist from the violation of the law so charged in said complaint. The Attorney General shall have the right to intervene and appear in said proceeding and any person may make application, and upon good cause shown may be allowed by the Commission, Board, or Secretary, to intervene and appear in said proceeding by counsel or in person. The testimony in any such proceeding shall be reduced to writing and filed in the office of the Commission, Board, or Secretary. If upon such hearing the Commission, Board, or Secretary, as the case may be, shall be of the opinion that any of the provisions of said sections have been or are being violated, it shall make a report in writing, in which it shall state its findings as to the facts, and shall issue and cause to be served on such person an order requiring such person to cease and desist from such violations, and divest itself of the stock, or other share capital, or assets, held or rid itself of the directors chosen contrary to the provisions of sections 18 and 19 of this title, if any there be, in the manner and within the time fixed by said order. Until the expiration of the time allowed for filing a petition for review, if no such petition has been duly filed within such time, or, if a petition for review has been filed within such time then until the record in the proceeding has been filed in a court of appeals of the United States, as hereinafter provided, the Commission, Board, or Secretary may at any time, upon such notice and in such manner as it shall deem proper, modify or set aside, in whole or in part, any report or any order made or issued by it under this section. After the expiration of the time allowed for filing a petition for review, if no such petition has been duly filed within such time, the Commission, Board, or Secretary may at any time, after notice and opportunity for hearing, reopen and alter, modify, or set aside, in whole or in part, any report or order made or issued by it under this section, whenever in the opinion of the Commission, Board, or Secretary conditions of fact or of law have so changed as to require such action or if the public interest shall so require: *Provided, however,* That the said person may, within sixty days after service upon him or it of said report or order entered after such a reopening, obtain a review thereof in the appropriate court of appeals of the United States, in the manner provided in subsection (c) of this section.

(c) Review of orders; jurisdiction; filing of petition and record of proceeding; conclusiveness of findings; additional evidence; modification of findings; finality of judgment and decree

Any person required by such order of the commission, board, or Secretary to cease and desist from any such violation may obtain a review of such order in the court of appeals of the United States for any circuit within which such violation occurred or within which such person resides or carries on business, by filing in the court, within sixty days after the date of the service of such order, a written petition praying that the order of the commission, board, or Secretary be set aside. A copy of such petition shall be forthwith transmitted by the clerk of the court to the commission, board, or Secretary, and thereupon the commission, board, or Secretary shall file in the court the record in the proceeding, as provided in section 2112 of Title 28. Upon such filing of the petition the court shall have jurisdiction of the proceeding and of the question determined therein concurrently with the commission, board, or Secretary until the filing of the record, and shall have power to make and enter a decree affirming, modifying, or setting aside the order of the commission, board, or Secretary, and enforcing the same to the extent that such order is affirmed, and to issue such writs as are ancillary to its jurisdiction or are necessary in its judgment to prevent injury to the public or to competitors pendente lite. The findings of the commission, board, or Secretary as to the facts, if supported by substantial evidence, shall be conclusive. To the extent that the order of the commission, board, or

Secretary is affirmed, the court shall issue its own order commanding obedience to the terms of such order of the commission, board, or Secretary. If either party shall apply to the court for leave to adduce additional evidence, and shall show to the satisfaction of the court that such additional evidence is material and that there were reasonable grounds for the failure to adduce such evidence in the proceeding before the commission, board, or Secretary, the court may order such additional evidence to be taken before the commission, board, or Secretary, and to be adduced upon the hearing in such manner and upon such terms and conditions as to the court may seem proper. The commission, board, or Secretary may modify its findings as to the facts, or make new findings, by reason of the additional evidence so taken, and shall file such modified or new findings, which if supported by substantial evidence, shall be conclusive, and its recommendation, if any, for the modification or setting aside of its original order, with the return of such additional evidence. The judgment and decree of the court shall be final, except that the same shall be subject to review by the Supreme Court upon certiorari, as provided in section 1254 of Title 28.

(d) Exclusive jurisdiction of Court of Appeals

Upon the filing of the record with its jurisdiction of the court of appeals to affirm, enforce, modify, or set aside orders of the commission, board, or Secretary shall be exclusive.

(e) Liability under antitrust laws

No order of the commission, board, or Secretary or judgment of the court to enforce the same shall in anywise relieve or absolve any person from any liability under the antitrust laws.

(f) Service of complaints, orders and other processes

Complaints, orders, and other processes of the commission, board, or Secretary under this section may be served by anyone duly authorized by the commission, board, or Secretary, either (1) by delivering a copy thereof to the person to be served, or to a member of the partnership to be served, or to the president, secretary, or other executive officer or a director of the corporation to be served; or (2) by leaving a copy thereof at the residence or the principal office or place of business of such person; or (3) by mailing by registered or certified mail a copy thereof addressed to such person at his or its residence or principal office or place of business. The verified return by the person so serving said complaint, order, or other process setting forth the manner of said service shall be proof of the same, and the return post office receipt for said complaint, order, or other process mailed by registered or certified mail as aforesaid shall be proof of the service of the same.

(g) Finality of orders generally

Any order issued under subsection (b) of this section shall become final—

(1) upon the expiration of the time allowed for filing a petition for review, if no such petition has been duly filed within such time; but the commission, board, or Secretary may thereafter modify or set aside its order to the extent provided in the last sentence of subsection (b) of this section; or

(2) upon the expiration of the time allowed for filing a petition for certiorari, if the order of the commission, board, or Secretary has been affirmed, or the petition for review has been dismissed by the court of appeals, and no petition for certiorari has been duly filed; or

(3) upon the denial of a petition for certiorari, if the order of the commission, board, or Secretary has been affirmed or the petition for review has been dismissed by the court of appeals; or

(4) upon the expiration of thirty days from the date of issuance of the mandate of the Supreme Court if such Court directs that the order of the commission, board, or Secretary be affirmed or the petition for review be dismissed.

(h) Finality of orders modified by Supreme Court

If the Supreme Court directs that the order of the commission, board, or Secretary be modified or set aside, the order of the commission, board, or Secretary rendered in accordance with the mandate of the Supreme Court shall become final upon the expiration of thirty days from the time it was rendered, unless within such thirty days either party has instituted proceedings to have such order corrected to accord with the mandate, in which event the order of the commission, board, or Secretary shall become final when so corrected.

(i) Finality of orders modified by Court of Appeals

If the order of the commission, board, or Secretary is modified or set aside by the court of appeals, and if (1) the time allowed for filing a petition for certiorari has expired and no such petition has been duly filed, or (2) the petition for certiorari has been denied, or (3) the decision of the court has been affirmed by the Supreme Court, then the order of the commission, board, or Secretary rendered in accordance with the mandate of the court of appeals shall become final on the expiration of thirty days from the time such order of the commission, board, or Secretary was rendered, unless within such thirty days either party has instituted proceedings to have such order corrected so that it will accord with the mandate, in which event the order of the commission, board, or Secretary shall become final when so corrected.

(j) Finality of orders issued on rehearing ordered by Court of Appeals or Supreme Court

If the Supreme Court orders a rehearing; or if the case is remanded by the court of appeals to the commission, board, or Secretary for a rehearing, and if (1) the time allowed for filing a petition for certiorari has expired, and no such petition has been duly filed, or (2) the petition for certiorari has been denied, or (3) the decision of the court has been affirmed by the Supreme Court, then the order of the commission, board, or Secretary rendered upon such rehearing shall become final in the same manner as though no prior order of the commission, board, or Secretary had been rendered.

(k) "Mandate" defined

As used in this section the term "mandate," in case a mandate has been recalled prior to the expiration of thirty days from the date of issuance thereof, means the final mandate.

(l) Penalties

Any person who violates any order issued by the commission, board, or Secretary under subsection (b) of this section after such order has become final, and while such order is in effect, shall forfeit and pay to the United States a civil penalty of not more than $5,000 for each violation, which shall accrue to the United States and may be recovered in a civil action brought by the United States. Each separate violation of any such order shall be a separate offense, except that in the case of a violation through continuing failure or neglect to obey a final order of the commission, board, or Secretary each day of continuance of such failure or neglect shall be deemed a separate offense.

(Oct. 15, 1914, c. 323, § 11, 38 Stat. 734; June 19, 1934, c. 652, Title VII, § 702(d), formerly Title VI, § 602(d), 48 Stat. 1102; renumbered Oct. 30, 1984, Pub.L. 98-549, § 6(a), 98 Stat. 2804; Aug. 23, 1935, c. 614, § 203(a), 49 Stat. 704; June 23, 1938, c. 601, § 1107(g), 52 Stat. 1028; June 25, 1948, c. 646, § 32(a), 62 Stat. 991; May 24, 1949, c. 139, § 127, 63 Stat. 107; Dec. 29, 1950, c. 1184, 64 Stat. 1125; Aug. 23, 1958, Pub.L. 85-726, Title XIV, § 1401(b), 72 Stat. 806; Aug. 28, 1958, Pub.L. 85-791, § 4, 72 Stat. 943; July 23, 1959, Pub.L. 86-107, § 1, 73 Stat. 243; Oct. 4, 1984, Pub.L. 98-443, § 9(m), 98 Stat. 1708; Nov. 8, 1984, Pub.L. 98-620, Title IV, § 402(10)(B), 98 Stat. 3358; Dec. 29, 1995, Pub.L. 104-88, Title III, § 318(2), 109 Stat. 949.)

§ 12 [15 U.S.C. § 22]. District in which to sue corporation

Any suit, action, or proceeding under the antitrust laws against a corporation may be brought not only in the judicial district whereof it is an inhabitant, but also in any district wherein it may be found or transacts business; and all process in such cases may be served in the district of which it is an inhabitant, or wherever it may be found.

(Oct. 15, 1914, c. 323, § 12, 38 Stat. 736.)

§ 13 [15 U.S.C. § 23]. Suits by United States; subpoenas for witnesses

In any suit, action, or proceeding brought by or on behalf of the United States subpoenas for witnesses who are required to attend a court of the United States in any judicial district in any case, civil or criminal, arising under the antitrust laws may run into any other district: *Provided,* That in civil cases no writ of subpoena shall issue for witnesses living out of the district in which the court is held at a greater distance than one hundred miles from the place of holding the same without the permission of the trial court being first had upon proper application and cause shown.

(Oct. 15, 1914, c. 323, § 13, 38 Stat. 736.)

§ 14 [15 U.S.C. § 24]. Liability of directors and agents of corporation

Whenever a corporation shall violate any of the penal provisions of the antitrust laws, such violation shall be deemed to be also that of the individual directors, officers, or agents of such corporation who shall have authorized, ordered, or done any of the acts constituting in whole or in part such violation, and such violation shall be deemed a misdemeanor, and upon conviction therefor of any such director, officer, or agent he shall be punished by a fine of not exceeding $5,000 or by imprisonment for not exceeding one year, or by both, in the discretion of the court.

(Oct. 15, 1914, c. 323, § 14, 38 Stat. 736.)

§ 15 [15 U.S.C. § 25]. Restraining violations; procedure

The several district courts of the United States are invested with jurisdiction to prevent and restrain violations of this Act, and it shall be the duty of the several United States attorneys, in their respective districts, under the direction of the Attorney General, to institute proceedings in equity to prevent and restrain such violations. Such proceedings may be by way of petition setting forth the case and praying that such violation shall be enjoined or otherwise prohibited. When the parties complained of shall have been duly notified of such petition, the court shall proceed, as soon as may be, to the hearing and determination of the case; and pending such petition, and before final decree, the court may at any time make such temporary restraining order or prohibition as shall be deemed just in the premises. Whenever it shall appear to the court before which any such proceeding may be pending that the ends of justice require that other parties should be brought before the court, the court may cause them to be summoned whether they reside in the district in which the court is held or not, and subpoenas to that end may be served in any district by the marshal thereof.

(Oct. 15, 1914, c. 323, § 15, 38 Stat. 736; June 25, 1948, c. 646, § 1, 62 Stat. 909.)

§ 16 [15 U.S.C.§ 26]. Injunctive relief for private parties; exception; costs

Any person, firm, corporation, or association shall be entitled to sue for and have injunctive relief, in any court of the United States having jurisdiction over the parties, against threatened loss or damage by a violation of the antitrust laws, including sections 13, 14, 18, and 19 of this title, when and under the same conditions and principles as injunctive relief against threatened conduct that will cause loss or damage is granted by courts of equity, under the rules governing such proceedings, and upon the execution of proper bond against damages for an injunction improvidently granted and a showing that the danger of irreparable loss or damage is immediate, a preliminary injunction may issue: *Provided,* That nothing herein contained shall be construed to entitle any person, firm, corporation, or association, except the United States, to bring suit for injunctive relief against any common carrier subject to the jurisdiction of the Surface Transportation Board under subtitle IV of Title 49. In any action under this section in which the plaintiff substantially prevails, the court shall award the cost of suit, including a reasonable attorney's fee, to such plaintiff.

(Oct. 15, 1914, c. 323, § 16, 38 Stat. 737. Sept. 30, 1976, Pub.L. 94-435, Title III, § 302(3), 90 Stat. 1396; Dec. 29, 1995, Pub.L. 104-88, Title III, § 318(3), 109 Stat. 949.)

§ 26 [15 U.S.C. § 26a]. Restrictions on the purchase of gasohol and synthetic motor fuel

(a) Limitations on the use of credit instruments; sales, resales, and transfers

Except as provided in subsection (b) of this section, it shall be unlawful for any person engaged in commerce, in the course of such commerce, directly or indirectly to impose any condition, restriction, agreement, or understanding that—

(1) limits the use of credit instruments in any transaction concerning the sale, resale, or transfer of gasohol or other synthetic motor fuel of equivalent usability in any case in which there is no similar limitation on transactions concerning such person's conventional motor fuel; or

(2) otherwise unreasonably discriminates against or unreasonably limits the sale, resale, or transfer of gasohol or other synthetic motor fuel of equivalent usability in any case in which such synthetic or conventional motor fuel is sold for use, consumption, or resale within the United States.

(b) Credit fees; equivalent conventional motor fuel sales; labeling of pumps; product liability disclaimers; advertising support; furnishing facilities

(1) Nothing in this section or in any other provision of law in effect on December 2, 1980, which is specifically applicable to the sale of petroleum products shall preclude any person referred to in subsection (a) of this section from imposing a reasonable fee for credit on the sale, resale, or transfer of the gasohol or other synthetic motor fuel referred to in subsection (a) of this section if such fee equals no more than the actual costs to such person of extending that credit.

(2) The prohibitions in this section shall not apply to any person who makes available sufficient supplies of gasohol and other synthetic motor fuels of equivalent usability to satisfy his customers' needs for such products, if the gasohol and other synthetic fuels are made available on terms and conditions which are equivalent to the terms and conditions on which such person's conventional motor fuel products are made available.

(3) Nothing in this section shall—

(A) preclude any person referred to in subsection (a) of this section from requiring reasonable labeling of pumps dispensing the gasohol or other synthetic motor fuel referred to in subsection (a) of this section to indicate, as appropriate, that such gasohol or other synthetic motor fuel is not manufactured, distributed, or sold by such person;

(B) preclude such person from issuing appropriate disclaimers of product liability for damage resulting from use of the gasohol or other synthetic motor fuel;

(C) require such person to provide advertising support for the gasohol or other synthetic motor fuel; or

(D) require such person to furnish or provide, at such person's own expense, any additional pumps, tanks, or other related facilities required for the sale of the gasohol or other synthetic motor fuel.

(c) "United States" defined

As used in this section, "United States" includes the several States, the District of Columbia, any territory of the United States, and any insular possession or other place under the jurisdiction of the United States.

(Oct. 15, 1914, c. 323, § 26, as added Dec. 2, 1980, Pub.L. 96-493, § 2, 94 Stat. 2568.)

§ 26b. [15 U.S.C. § 26b]. The Curt Flood Act of 1998[5]

(a) Major league baseball subject to antitrust laws

Subject to subsections (b) through (d) of this section, the conduct, acts, practices, or agreements of persons in the business of organized professional major league baseball directly relating to or affecting employment of major league baseball players to play baseball at the major league level are subject to the antitrust laws to the same extent such conduct, acts, practices, or agreements would be subject to the antitrust laws if engaged in by persons in any other professional sports business affecting interstate commerce.

(b) Limitation of section

No court shall rely on the enactment of this section as a basis for changing the application of the antitrust laws to any conduct, acts, practices, or agreements other than those set forth in subsection (a) of this section. This section does not create, permit or imply a cause of action by which to challenge under the antitrust laws, or otherwise apply the antitrust laws to, any conduct, acts, practices, or agreements that do not directly relate to or affect employment of major league baseball players to play baseball at the major league level, including but not limited to

(1) any conduct, acts, practices, or agreements of persons engaging in, conducting or participating in the business of organized professional baseball relating to or affecting employment to play baseball at the minor league level, any organized professional baseball amateur or first-year player draft, or any reserve clause as applied to minor league players;

(2) the agreement between organized professional major league baseball teams and the teams of the National Association of Professional Baseball Leagues, commonly known as the "Professional Baseball Agreement," the relationship between organized professional major league baseball and organized professional minor league baseball, or any other matter relating to organized professional baseball's minor leagues;

(3) any conduct, acts, practices, or agreements of persons engaging in, conducting or participating in the business of organized professional baseball relating to or affecting franchise expansion, location or relocation, franchise ownership issues, including ownership transfers, the relationship between the Office of the Commissioner and franchise owners, the marketing or sales of the entertainment product of organized professional baseball and the licensing of intellectual property rights owned or held by organized professional baseball teams individually or collectively;

---

[5] Section 1 of the amendment provides: This Act may be cited as the "Curt Flood Act of 1998."

Section 2 of the Act provides:

It is the purpose of this legislation to state that major league baseball players are covered under the antitrust laws (i.e., that major league baseball players will have the same rights under the antitrust laws as do other professional athletes, e.g., football and basketball players), along with a provision that makes it clear that the passage of this Act does not change the application of the antitrust laws in any other context or with respect to any other person or entity.

(4) any conduct, acts, practices, or agreements protected by Public Law 87-331 (15 U.S.C. 1291 et seq.) (commonly known as the "Sports Broadcasting Act of 1961");

(5) the relationship between persons in the business of organized professional baseball and umpires or other individuals who are employed in the business of organized professional baseball by such persons; or

(6) any conduct, acts, practices, or agreements of persons not in the business of organized professional major league baseball.

(c) Standing to sue

Only a major league baseball player has standing to sue under this section. For the purposes of this section, a major league baseball player is—

(1) a person who is a party to a major league player's contract, or is playing baseball at the major league level; or

(2) a person who was a party to a major league player's contract or playing baseball at the major league level at the time of the injury that is the subject of the complaint; or

(3) a person who has been a party to a major league player's contract or who has played baseball at the major league level, and who claims he has been injured in his efforts to secure a subsequent major league player's contract by an alleged violation of the antitrust laws: *Provided however,* That for the purposes of this paragraph, the alleged antitrust violation shall not include any conduct, acts, practices, or agreements of persons in the business of organized professional baseball relating to or affecting employment to play baseball at the minor league level, including any organized professional baseball amateur or first-year player draft, or any reserve clause as applied to minor league players; or

(4) a person who was a party to a major league player's contract or who was playing baseball at the major league level at the conclusion of the last full championship season immediately preceding the expiration of the last collective bargaining agreement between persons in the business of organized professional major league baseball and the exclusive collective bargaining representative of major league baseball players.

(d) Conduct, acts, practices, or agreements subject to antitrust laws

(1) As used in this section, "person" means any entity, including an individual, partnership, corporation, trust or unincorporated association or any combination or association thereof. As used in this section, the National Association of Professional Baseball Leagues, its member leagues and the clubs of those leagues, are not "in the business of organized professional major league baseball."

(2) In cases involving conduct, acts, practices, or agreements that directly relate to or affect both employment of major league baseball players to play baseball at the major league level and also relate to or affect any other aspect of organized professional baseball, including but not limited to employment to play baseball at the minor league level and the other areas set forth in subsection (b) of this section, only those components, portions or

aspects of such conduct, acts, practices, or agreements that directly relate to or affect employment of major league players to play baseball at the major league level may be challenged under subsection (a) of this section and then only to the extent that they directly relate to or affect employment of major league baseball players to play baseball at the major league level.

(3) As used in subsection (a) of this section, interpretation of the term "directly" shall not be governed by any interpretation of section 151 et seq. of Title 29 (as amended).

(4) Nothing in this section shall be construed to affect the application to organized professional baseball of the nonstatutory labor exemption from the antitrust laws.

(5) The scope of the conduct, acts, practices, or agreements covered by subsection (b) of this section shall not be strictly or narrowly construed.

(Oct. 15, 1914, c. 323, § 27, as added Oct. 27, 1998, Pub.L. 105-297, § 3, 112 Stat. 2824.)

§ 29 [15 U.S.C. § 29]. Appeals

(a) Court of appeals; review by Supreme Court

Except as otherwise expressly provided by this section, in every civil action brought in any district court of the United States under the Act entitled "An Act to protect trade and commerce against unlawful restraints and monopolies," approved July 2, 1890, or any other Acts having like purpose that have been or hereafter may be enacted, in which the United States is the complainant and equitable relief is sought, any appeal from a final judgment entered in any such action shall be taken to the court of appeals pursuant to sections 1291 and 2107 of Title 28. Any appeal from an interlocutory order entered in any such action shall be taken to the court of appeals pursuant to sections 1292(a)(1) and 2107 of Title 28 but not otherwise. Any judgment entered by the court of appeals in any such action shall be subject to review by the Supreme Court upon a writ of certiorari as provided in section 1254(1) of Title 28.

(b) Direct appeals to Supreme Court

An appeal from a final judgment pursuant to subsection (a) of this section shall lie directly to the Supreme Court if, upon application of a party filed within fifteen days of the filing of a notice of appeal, the district judge who adjudicated the case enters an order stating that immediate consideration of the appeal by the Supreme Court is of general public importance in the administration of justice. Such order shall be filed within thirty days after the filing of a notice of appeal. When such an order is filed, the appeal and any cross appeal shall be docketed in the time and manner prescribed by the rules of the Supreme Court. The Supreme Court shall thereupon either (1) dispose of the appeal and any cross appeal in the same manner as any other direct appeal authorized by law, or (2) in its discretion, deny the direct appeal and remand the case to the court of appeals, which shall then have jurisdiction to hear and determine the same as if the appeal and any cross appeal therein had been docketed in the court of appeals in the first instance pursuant to subsection (a) of this section.

(Feb. 11, 1903, c. 544, § 2, 32 Stat. 823; Mar. 3, 1911, c. 231, § 291, 36 Stat. 1167; June 9, 1944, c. 239, 58 Stat. 272; June 25, 1948, c. 646, § 17, 62 Stat. 989; Dec. 21, 1974, Pub.L. 93-528, § 5, 88 Stat. 1709.)

3

FEDERAL TRADE COMMISSION ACT

§ 1. [15 U.S.C. § 41] Federal Trade Commission established; membership; vacancies; seal

A commission is created and established, to be known as the Federal Trade Commission (hereinafter referred to as the Commission), which shall be composed of five Commissioners, who shall be appointed by the President, by and with the advice and consent of the Senate. Not more than three of the Commissioners shall be members of the same political party. The first Commissioners appointed shall continue in office for terms of three, four, five, six, and seven years, respectively, from September 26, 1914, the term of each to be designated by the President, but their successors shall be appointed for terms of seven years, except that any person chosen to fill a vacancy shall be appointed only for the unexpired term of the Commissioner whom he shall succeed: *Provided, however,* That upon the expiration of his term of office a Commissioner shall continue to serve until his successor shall have been appointed and shall have qualified. The President shall choose a chairman from the Commission's membership. No Commissioner shall engage in any other business, vocation, or employment. Any Commissioner may be removed by the President for inefficiency, neglect of duty, or malfeasance in office. A vacancy in the Commission shall not impair the right of the remaining Commissioners to exercise all the powers of the Commission.

The Commission shall have an official seal, which shall be judicially noticed.

(Sept. 26, 1914, c. 311, § 1, 38 Stat. 717; Mar. 21, 1938, c. 49, § 1, 52 Stat. 111; 1950 Reorg. Plan No. 8, § 3, eff. May 24, 1950, 15 F.R. 3175, 64 Stat. 1265.)

§ 2. [15 U.S.C. § 42] Employees; expenses

Each commissioner shall receive a salary, payable in the same manner as the salaries of the judges of the courts of the United States. The Commission shall appoint a secretary, who shall receive a salary, and it shall have authority to employ and fix the compensation of such attorneys, special experts, examiners, clerks, and other employees as it may from time to time find necessary for the proper performance of its duties and as may be from time to time appropriated for by Congress.

With the exception of the secretary, a clerk to each Commissioner, the attorneys, and such special experts and examiners as the Commission may from time to time find necessary for the conduct of its work, all employees of the Commission shall be a part of the classified civil service, and shall enter the service under such rules and regulations as may be prescribed by the Commission and by the Director of the Office of Personnel Management.

All of the expenses of the Commission, including all necessary expenses for transportation incurred by the Commissioners or by their employees under their orders, in making any investigation, or upon official business in any other places than in the city of Washington, shall be allowed and paid on the presentation of itemized vouchers therefor approved by the Commission.

Until otherwise provided by law, the Commission may rent suitable offices for its use.

The Government Accountability Office shall receive and examine all accounts of expenditures of the Commission.

(Sept. 26, 1914, c. 311, § 2, 38 Stat. 718; June 10, 1921, c. 18, Title III, § 304, 42 Stat. 24; 1978 Reorg. Plan No. 2, § 102, 43 F.R. 36037, 92 Stat. 3783; July 7, 2004, Pub.L. 108-271, § 8(b), 118 Stat. 814.)

§ 3. [15 U.S.C. § 43] Office and place of meeting

The principal office of the Commission shall be in the city of Washington, but it may meet and exercise all its powers at any other place. The Commission may, by one or more of its members, or by such examiners as it may designate, prosecute any inquiry necessary to its duties in any part of the United States.

(Sept. 26, 1914, c. 311, § 3, 38 Stat. 719.)

§ 4. [15 U.S.C. § 44] Definitions

The words defined in this section shall have the following meaning when found in this subchapter, to wit:

"Commerce" means commerce among the several States or with foreign nations, or in any Territory of the United States or in the District of Columbia, or between any such Territory and another, or between any such Territory and any State or foreign nation, or between the District of Columbia and any State or Territory or foreign nation.

"Corporation" shall be deemed to include any company, trust, so-called Massachusetts trust, or association, incorporated or unincorporated, which is organized to carry on business for its own profit or that of its members, and has shares of capital or capital stock or certificates of interest, and any company, trust, so-called Massachusetts trust, or association, incorporated or unincorporated, without shares of capital or capital stock or certificates of interest, except partnerships, which is organized to carry on business for its own profit or that of its members.

"Documentary evidence" includes all documents, papers, correspondence, books of account, and financial and corporate records.

"Acts to regulate commerce" means subtitle IV of Title 49 and the Communications Act of 1934 [47 U.S.C.A. § 151 et seq.] and all Acts amendatory thereof and supplementary thereto.

"Antitrust Acts" means the Act entitled "An Act to protect trade and commerce against unlawful restraints and monopolies," approved July 2, 1890; also sections 73 to 76, inclusive, of an Act entitled "An Act to reduce taxation, to provide revenue for the Government, and for other purposes," approved August 27, 1894; also the Act entitled "An Act to amend sections 73 and 76 of the Act of August 27, 1894, entitled 'An Act to reduce taxation, to provide revenue for the Government, and for other purposes' ," approved February 12, 1913; and also the Act entitled "An Act of supplement existing laws against unlawful restraints and monopolies, and for other purposes," approved October 15, 1914.

"Banks" means the types of banks and other financial institutions referred to in section 57a(f)(2) of this title.

"Foreign law enforcement agency" means—

(1) any agency or judicial authority of a foreign government, including a foreign state, a political subdivision of a foreign state, or a multinational organization constituted by and comprised of foreign states, that is vested with law enforcement or investigative authority in civil, criminal, or administrative matters; and

(2) any multinational organization, to the extent that it is acting on behalf of an entity described in paragraph (1).

(Sept. 26, 1914, c. 311, § 4, 38 Stat. 719; Mar. 21, 1938, c. 49, § 2, 52 Stat. 111; Dec. 19, 1991, Pub.L. 102-242, Title II, § 212(g)(1), 105 Stat. 2302; Nov. 2, 2002, Pub.L. 107-273, Div. C, Title IV, § 14102(c)(2)(B), 116 Stat. 1921; Dec. 22, 2006, Pub.L. 109-455, § 2, 120 Stat. 3372.)

§ 5. [15 U.S.C. § 45] Unfair methods of competition unlawful; prevention by Commission

(a) Declaration of unlawfulness; power to prohibit unfair practices; inapplicability to foreign trade

(1) Unfair methods of competition in or affecting commerce, and unfair or deceptive acts or practices in or affecting commerce, are hereby declared unlawful.

(2) The Commission is hereby empowered and directed to prevent persons, partnerships, or corporations, except banks, savings and loan institutions described in section 57a(f)(3) of this title, Federal credit unions described in section 57a(f)(4) of this title, common carriers subject to the Acts to regulate commerce, air carriers and foreign air carriers subject to part A of subtitle VII of Title 49, and persons, partnerships, or corporations insofar as they are subject to the Packers and Stockyards Act, 1921, as amended [7 U.S.C.A. § 181 et seq.], except as provided in section 406(b) of said Act [7 U.S.C.A. § 227(b)], from using unfair methods of competition in or affecting commerce and unfair or deceptive acts or practices in or affecting commerce.

(3) This subsection shall not apply to unfair methods of competition involving commerce with foreign nations (other than import commerce) unless—

(A) such methods of competition have a direct, substantial, and reasonably foreseeable effect—

(i) on commerce which is not commerce with foreign nations, or on import commerce with foreign nations; or

(ii) on export commerce with foreign nations, of a person engaged in such commerce in the United States; and

(B) such effect gives rise to a claim under the provisions of this subsection, other than this paragraph.

If this subsection applies to such methods of competition only because of the operation of subparagraph (A)(ii), this subsection shall apply to such conduct only for injury to export business in the United States.

(4) (A) For purposes of subsection (a) of this section, the term "unfair or deceptive acts or practices" includes such acts or practices involving foreign commerce that—

(i) cause or are likely to cause reasonably foreseeable injury within the United States; or

(ii) involve material conduct occurring within the United States.

(B) All remedies available to the Commission with respect to unfair and deceptive acts or practices shall be available for acts and practices described in this paragraph, including restitution to domestic or foreign victims.

(b) Proceeding by Commission; modifying and setting aside orders

Whenever the Commission shall have reason to believe that any such person, partnership, or corporation has been or is using any unfair method of competition or unfair or deceptive act or practice in or affecting commerce, and if it shall appear to the Commission that a proceeding by it in respect thereof would be to the interest of the public, it shall issue and serve upon such person, partnership, or corporation a complaint stating its charges in that respect and containing a notice of a hearing upon a day and at a place therein fixed at least thirty days after the service of said complaint. The person, partnership, or corporation so complained of shall have the right to appear at the place and time so fixed and show cause why an order should not be entered by the Commission requiring such person, partnership, or corporation to cease and desist from the violation of the law so charged in said complaint. Any person, partnership, or corporation may make application, and upon good cause shown may be allowed by the Commission to intervene and appear in said proceeding by counsel or in person. The testimony in any such proceeding shall be reduced to writing and filed in the office of the Commission. If upon such hearing the Commission shall be of the opinion that the method of competition or the act or practice in question is prohibited by this subchapter, it shall make a report in writing in which it shall state its findings as to the facts and shall issue and cause to be served on such person, partnership, or corporation an order requiring such person, partnership, or corporation to cease and desist from using such method of competition or such act or practice. Until the expiration of the time allowed for filing a petition for review, if no such petition has been duly filed within such time, or, if a petition for review has been filed within such time then until the record in the proceeding has been filed in a court of appeals of the United States, as hereinafter provided, the Commission may at any time, upon such notice and in such manner as it shall deem proper, modify or set aside, in whole or in part, any report or any order made or issued by it under this section. After the expiration of the time allowed for filing a petition for review, if no such petition has been duly filed within such time, the Commission may at any time, after notice and opportunity for hearing, reopen and alter, modify, or set aside, in whole or in part, any report or order made or issued by it under this section, whenever in the opinion of the Commission conditions of fact or of law have so changed as to require such action or if the public interest shall so require, except that (1) the said person, partnership, or corporation may, within sixty days after service upon him or it of said report or order entered after such a reopening, obtain a review thereof in the appropriate court of appeals of the United States, in the manner provided in subsection (c) of this section; and (2) in the case of an order, the Commission shall reopen any such order to consider whether such order (including any affirmative relief provision contained in such order) should be altered, modified, or set aside, in whole or in part, if the person, partnership, or corporation involved files a request with the Commission which makes a satisfactory showing that changed conditions of law or fact require such order to be altered, modified, or set aside, in whole or in part. The Commission shall determine whether to alter, modify, or set aside any order of the Commission in response to a request made by a person, partnership, or corporation under paragraph[1] (2) not later than 120 days after the date of the filing of such request.

(c) Review of order; rehearing

Any person, partnership, or corporation required by an order of the Commission to cease and desist from using any method of competition or act or practice may obtain a review of such order in the court of appeals of the United States, within any circuit where the method of competition or the act or practice in question was used or where such person, partnership, or corporation resides or carries on business, by filing in the court, within sixty days from the date of the service of such order, a written petition praying that the order of the Commission be set aside. A copy of such petition shall be forthwith transmitted by the clerk of the court to the Commission, and thereupon the Commission shall file in the court the record in the proceeding, as provided in section 2112 of Title 28. Upon such filing of the petition the court shall have jurisdiction of the proceeding and of the question determined therein concurrently with the Commission until the filing of the record and shall have power to make and enter a decree affirming, modifying, or setting aside the order of the Commission, and enforcing the same to the extent that such order is affirmed and to issue such writs as are ancillary to its jurisdiction or are necessary in its judgment to prevent injury to the public or to competitors pendente lite. The findings of the Commission as to the facts, if supported by evidence, shall be conclusive. To the extent that the order of the Commission is affirmed, the court shall thereupon issue its own order commanding obedience to the terms of such order of the Commission. If either party shall apply to the court for leave to adduce additional evidence, and shall show to the satisfaction of the court that such additional evidence is material and that there were reasonable grounds for the failure to adduce such evidence in the proceeding before the Commission, the court may order such additional evidence to be taken before the Commission and to be adduced upon the hearing in such manner and upon such terms and conditions as to the court may seem proper. The Commission may modify its findings as to the facts, or make new findings, by reason of the additional evidence so taken, and it shall file such modified or new findings, which, if supported by evidence, shall be conclusive, and its recommendation, if any, for the modification or setting aside of its original order, with the return of such additional evidence. The judgment and decree of the court shall be final, except that the same shall be subject to review by the Supreme Court upon certiorari, as provided in section 1254 of Title 28.

(d) Jurisdiction of court

Upon the filing of the record with it the jurisdiction of the court of appeals of the United States to affirm, enforce, modify, or set aside orders of the Commission shall be exclusive.

(e) Exemption from liability

No order of the Commission or judgment of court to enforce the same shall in anywise relieve or absolve any person, partnership, or corporation from any liability under the Antitrust Acts.

---

[1] So in original. Probably should be "clause."

(f) Service of complaints, orders and other processes; return

Complaints, orders, and other processes of the Commission under this section may be served by anyone duly authorized by the Commission, either (a) by delivering a copy thereof to the person to be served, or to a member of the partnership to be served, or the president, secretary, or other executive officer or a director of the corporation to be served; or (b) by leaving a copy thereof at the residence or the principal office or place of business of such person, partnership, or corporation; or (c) by mailing a copy thereof by registered mail or by certified mail addressed to such person, partnership, or corporation at his or its residence or principal office or place of business. The verified return by the person so serving said complaint, order, or other process setting forth the manner of said service shall be proof of the same, and the return post office receipt for said complaint, order, or other process mailed by registered mail or by certified mail as aforesaid shall be proof of the service of the same.

(g) Finality of order

An order of the Commission to cease and desist shall become final—

(1) Upon the expiration of the time allowed for filing a petition for review, if no such petition has been duly filed within such time; but the Commission may thereafter modify or set aside its order to the extent provided in the last sentence of subsection (b).

(2) Except as to any order provision subject to paragraph (4), upon the sixtieth day after such order is served, if a petition for review has been duly filed; except that any such order may be stayed, in whole or in part and subject to such conditions as may be appropriate, by—

(A) the Commission;

(B) an appropriate court of appeals of the United States, if (i) a petition for review of such order is pending in such court, and (ii) an application for such a stay was previously submitted to the Commission and the Commission, within the 30-day period beginning on the date the application was received by the Commission, either denied the application or did not grant or deny the application; or

(C) the Supreme Court, if an applicable petition for certiorari is pending.

(3) For purposes of subsection (m)(1)(B) of this section and of section 57b(a)(2) of this title, if a petition for review of the order of the Commission has been filed—

(A) upon the expiration of the time allowed for filing a petition for certiorari, if the order of the Commission has been affirmed or the petition for review has been dismissed by the court of appeals and no petition for certiorari has been duly filed;

(B) upon the denial of a petition for certiorari, if the order of the Commission has been affirmed or the petition for review has been dismissed by the court of appeals; or

(C) upon the expiration of 30 days from the date of issuance of a mandate of the Supreme Court directing that the order of the Commission be affirmed or the petition for review be dismissed.

(4) In the case of an order provision requiring a person, partnership, or corporation to divest itself of stock, other share capital, or assets, if a petition for review of such order of the Commission has been filed—

(A) upon the expiration of the time allowed for filing a petition for certiorari, if the order of the Commission has been affirmed or the petition for review has been dismissed by the court of appeals and no petition for certiorari has been duly filed;

(B) upon the denial of a petition for certiorari, if the order of the Commission has been affirmed or the petition for review has been dismissed by the court of appeals; or

(C) upon the expiration of 30 days from the date of issuance of a mandate of the Supreme Court directing that the order of the Commission be affirmed or the petition for review be dismissed.

(h) Modification or setting aside of order by Supreme Court

If the Supreme Court directs that the order of the Commission be modified or set aside, the order of the Commission rendered in accordance with the mandate of the Supreme Court shall become final upon the expiration of thirty days from the time it was rendered, unless within such thirty days either party has instituted proceedings to have such order corrected to accord with the mandate, in which event the order of the Commission shall become final when so corrected.

(i) Modification or setting aside of order by Court of Appeals

If the order of the Commission is modified or set aside by the court of appeals, and if (1) the time allowed for filing a petition for certiorari has expired and no such petition has been duly filed, or (2) the petition for certiorari has been denied, or (3) the decision of the court has been affirmed by the Supreme Court, then the order of the Commission rendered in accordance with the mandate of the court of appeals shall become final on the expiration of thirty days from the time such order of the Commission was rendered, unless within such thirty days either party has instituted proceedings to have such order corrected so that it will accord with the mandate, in which event the order of the Commission shall become final when so corrected.

(j) Rehearing upon order or remand

If the Supreme Court orders a rehearing; or if the case is remanded by the court of appeals to the Commission for a rehearing, and if (1) the time allowed for filing a petition for certiorari has expired, and no such petition has been duly filed, or (2) the petition for certiorari has been denied, or (3) the decision of the court has been affirmed by the Supreme Court, then the order of the Commission rendered upon such rehearing shall become final in the same manner as though no prior order of the Commission had been rendered.

(k) "Mandate" defined

As used in this section the term "mandate," in case a mandate has been recalled prior to the expiration of thirty days from the date of issuance thereof, means the final mandate.

(l) Penalty for violation of order; injunctions and other appropriate equitable relief

Any person, partnership, or corporation who violates an order of the Commission after it has become final, and while such order is in effect, shall forfeit and pay to the United States a civil penalty of not more than $10,000 for each violation, which shall accrue to the United States and may be recovered in a civil action brought by the Attorney General of the United States. Each separate violation of such an order shall be a separate offense, except that in the case of a violation through continuing failure to obey or neglect to obey a final order of the Commission, each day of continuance of such failure or neglect shall be deemed a separate offense. In such actions, the United States district courts are empowered to grant mandatory injunctions and such other and further equitable relief as they deem appropriate in the enforcement of such final orders of the Commission.

(m) Civil actions for recovery of penalties for knowing violations of rules and cease and desist orders respecting unfair or deceptive acts or practices; jurisdiction; maximum amount of penalties; continuing violations; de novo determinations; compromise or settlement procedure

(1) (A) The Commission may commence a civil action to recover a civil penalty in a district court of the United States against any person, partnership, or corporation which violates any rule under this chapter respecting unfair or deceptive acts or practices (other than an interpretive rule or a rule violation of which the Commission has provided is not an unfair or deceptive act or practice in violation of subsection (a)(1) of this section) with actual knowledge or knowledge fairly implied on the basis of objective circumstances that such act is unfair or deceptive and is prohibited by such rule. In such action, such person, partnership, or corporation shall be liable for a civil penalty of not more than $10,000 for each violation.

(B) If the Commission determines in a proceeding under subsection (b) of this section that any act or practice is unfair or deceptive, and issues a final cease and desist order, other than a consent order, with respect to such act or practice, then the Commission may commence a civil action to obtain a civil penalty in a district court of the United States against any person, partnership, or corporation which engages in such act or practice—

(1) after such cease and desist order becomes final (whether or not such person, partnership, or corporation was subject to such cease and desist order), and

(2) with actual knowledge that such act or practice is unfair or deceptive and is unlawful under subsection (a)(1) of this section.

In such action, such person, partnership, or corporation shall be liable for a civil penalty of not more than $10,000 for each violation.

(C) In the case of a violation through continuing failure to comply with a rule or with subsection (a) (1) of this section, each day of continuance of such failure shall be treated as a separate violation, for purposes of subparagraphs (A) and (B). In determining the amount of such a civil penalty, the court shall take into account the degree of culpability, any history of prior such conduct, ability to pay, effect on ability to continue to do business, and such other matters as justice may require.

(2) If the cease and desist order establishing that the act or practice is unfair or deceptive was not issued against the defendant in a civil penalty action under paragraph (1)(B) the issues of fact in such action against such defendant shall be tried de novo. Upon request of any party to such an action against such defendant, the court shall also review the determination of law made by the Commission in the proceeding under subsection (b) of this section that the act or practice which was the subject of such proceeding constituted an unfair or deceptive act or practice in violation of subsection (a) of this section.

(3) The Commission may compromise or settle any action for a civil penalty if such compromise or settlement is accompanied by a public statement of its reasons and is approved by the court.

(n) Standard of proof; public policy consideration

The Commission shall have no authority under this section or section 57a of this title to declare unlawful an act or practice on the grounds that such act or practice is unfair unless the act or practice causes or is likely to cause substantial injury to consumers which is not reasonably avoidable by consumers themselves and not outweighed by countervailing benefits to consumers or to competition. In determining whether an act or practice is unfair, the Commission may consider established public policies as evidence to be considered with all other evidence. Such public policy considerations may not serve as a primary basis for such determination.

(Sept. 26, 1914, c. 311, § 5, 38 Stat. 719; Mar. 21, 1938, c. 49, § 3, 52 Stat. 111; June 23, 1938, c. 601, Title XI, § 1107(f), 52 Stat. 1028; June 25, 1948, c. 646, § 32(a), 62 Stat. 991; May 24, 1949, c. 139, § 127, 63 Stat. 107; Mar. 16, 1950, c. 61, § 4(c), 64 Stat. 21; July 14, 1952, c. 745, § 2, 66 Stat. 632; Aug. 23, 1958, Pub.L. 85-726, Title XIV, §§ 1401(b), 1411, 72 Stat. 806, 809; Aug. 28, 1958, Pub.L. 85-791, § 3, 72 Stat. 942; Sept. 2, 1958, Pub.L. 85-909, § 3, 72 Stat. 1750; June 11, 1960, Pub.L. 86-507, § 1(13), 74 Stat. 200; Nov. 16, 1973, Pub.L. 93-153, Title IV, § 408(c), (d), 87 Stat. 591, 592; Jan. 4, 1975, Pub.L. 93-637, Title II, §§ 201(a), 204(b), 205(a), 88 Stat. 2193, 2200; Dec. 12, 1975, Pub.L. 94-145, § 3, 89 Stat. 801; July 23, 1979, Pub.L. 96-37, § 1(a), 93 Stat. 95; May 28, 1980, Pub.L. 96-252, § 2, 94 Stat. 374; Oct. 8, 1982, Pub.L. 97-290, Title IV, § 403, 96 Stat. 1246; Nov. 8, 1984, Pub.L. 98-620, Title IV, § 402(12), 98 Stat. 3358; Aug. 10, 1987, Pub.L. 100-86, Title VII, § 715(a)(1), 101 Stat. 655; Aug. 26, 1994, Pub.L. 103-312, §§ 4, 6, 9, 108 Stat. 1691, 1692, 1695; Dec. 22, 2006, Pub.L. 109-455, § 3, 120 Stat. 3372.)

§ 6. [15 U.S.C. § 46] Additional powers of Commission

The Commission shall also have power—

(a) Investigation of persons, partnerships, or corporations

To gather and compile information concerning, and to investigate from time to time the organization, business, conduct, practices, and management of any person, partnership, or corporation engaged in or whose business affects commerce, excepting banks, savings and loan institutions described in section 57a(f)(3) of this title, Federal credit unions described in section 57a(f)(4) of this title, and common carriers subject to the Act to regulate commerce, and its relation to other persons, partnerships, and corporations.

(b) Reports of persons, partnerships, and corporations

To require, by general or special orders, persons, partnerships, and corporations, engaged in or whose business affects commerce, excepting banks, savings and loan institutions described in section 57a(f)(3) of this title, Federal credit unions described in section 57a(f)(4) of this title, and common carriers subject to the Act to regulate commerce, or any class of them, or any of them, respectively, to file with the Commission in such form as the Commission may prescribe annual or special, or both annual and special, reports or answers in writing to specific questions, furnishing to the Commission such information as it may require as to the organization, business, conduct, practices, management, and relation to other corporations, partnerships, and individuals of the respective persons, partnerships, and corporations filing such reports or answers in writing. Such reports and answers shall be made under oath, or otherwise, as the Commission may prescribe, and shall be filed with the Commission within such reasonable period as the Commission may prescribe, unless additional time be granted in any case by the Commission.

(c) Investigation of compliance with antitrust decrees

Whenever a final decree has been entered against any defendant corporation in any suit brought by the United States to prevent and restrain any violation of the antitrust Acts, to make investigation, upon its own initiative, of the manner in which the decree has been or is being carried out, and upon the application of the Attorney General it shall be its duty to make such investigation. It shall transmit to the Attorney General a report embodying its findings and recommendations as a result of any such investigation, and the report shall be made public in the discretion of the Commission.

(d) Investigations of violations of antitrust statutes

Upon the direction of the President or either House of Congress to investigate and report the facts relating to any alleged violations of the antitrust Acts by any corporation.

(e) Readjustment of business of corporations violating antitrust statutes

Upon the application of the Attorney General to investigate and make recommendations for the readjustment of the business of any corporation alleged to be violating the antitrust Acts in order that the corporation may thereafter maintain its organization, management, and conduct of business in accordance with law.

(f) Publication of information; reports

To make public from time to time such portions of the information obtained by it hereunder as are in the public interest; and to make annual and special reports to the Congress and to submit therewith recommendations for additional legislation; and to provide for the publication of its reports and decisions in such form and manner as may be best adapted for public information and use: *Provided,* That the Commission shall not have any authority to make public any trade secret or any commercial or financial information which is obtained from any person and which is privileged or confidential, except that the Commission may disclose such information (1) to officers and employees of appropriate Federal law enforcement agencies or to any officer or employee of any State law enforcement agency upon the prior certification of an officer of any such Federal or State law enforcement agency that such information will be maintained in confidence and will be used only for official law enforcement purposes, and (2) to any officer or employee of any foreign law enforcement agency under the same circumstances that making material available to foreign law enforcement agencies is permitted under section 57b-2(b) of this title.

(g) Classification of corporations; regulations

From time to time to classify corporations and (except as provided in section 57a(a)(2) of this title) to make rules and regulations for the purpose of carrying out the provisions of this subchapter.

(h) Investigations of foreign trade conditions; reports

To investigate, from time to time, trade conditions in and with foreign countries where associations, combinations, or practices of manufacturers, merchants, or traders, or other conditions, may affect the foreign trade of the United States, and to report to Congress thereon, with such recommendations as it deems advisable.

(i) Investigations of foreign antitrust law violations

With respect to the International Antitrust Enforcement Assistance Act of 1994 [15 U.S.C.A. § 6201 et seq.], to conduct investigations of possible violations of foreign antitrust laws (as defined in section 12 of such Act [15 U.S.C.A. § 6211]).

(j) Investigative assistance for foreign law enforcement agencies

(1) In general

Upon a written request from a foreign law enforcement agency to provide assistance in accordance with this subsection, if the requesting agency states that it is investigating, or engaging in enforcement proceedings against, possible violations of laws prohibiting fraudulent or deceptive commercial practices, or other practices substantially similar to practices prohibited by any provision of the laws administered by the Commission, other than Federal antitrust laws (as defined in section 6211(5) of this title, to provide the assistance described in paragraph (2) without requiring that the conduct identified in the request constitute a violation of the laws of the United States.

(2) Type of assistance

In providing assistance to a foreign law enforcement agency under this subsection, the Commission may—

(A) conduct such investigation as the Commission deems necessary to collect information and evidence pertinent to the request for assistance, using all investigative powers authorized by this subchapter; and

(B) when the request is from an agency acting to investigate or pursue the enforcement of civil laws, or when the Attorney General refers a request to the Commission from an agency acting to investigate or pursue the enforcement of criminal laws, seek and accept appointment by a United States district court of Commission attorneys to provide assistance to foreign and international tribunals and to litigants before such tribunals on behalf of a foreign law enforcement agency pursuant to section 1782 of Title 28.

(3) Criteria for determination

In deciding whether to provide such assistance, the Commission shall consider all relevant factors, including—

(A) whether the requesting agency has agreed to provide or will provide reciprocal assistance to the Commission;

(B) whether compliance with the request would prejudice the public interest of the United States; and

(C) whether the requesting agency's investigation or enforcement proceeding concerns acts or practices that cause or are likely to cause injury to a significant number of persons.

(4) International agreements

If a foreign law enforcement agency has set forth a legal basis for requiring execution of an international agreement as a condition for reciprocal assistance, or as a condition for provision of materials or information to the Commission, the Commission, with prior approval and ongoing oversight of the Secretary of State, and with final approval of the agreement by the Secretary of State, may negotiate and conclude an international agreement, in the name of either the United States or the Commission, for the purpose of obtaining such assistance, materials, or information. The Commission may undertake in such an international agreement to—

(A) provide assistance using the powers set forth in this subsection;

(B) disclose materials and information in accordance with subsection (f) of this section and section 57b-2(b) of this title; and

(C) engage in further cooperation, and protect materials and information received from disclosure, as authorized by this subchapter.

(5) Additional authority

The authority provided by this subsection is in addition to, and not in lieu of, any other authority vested in the Commission or any other officer of the United States.

(6) Limitation

The authority granted by this subsection shall not authorize the Commission to take any action or exercise any power with respect to a bank, a savings and loan institution described in section 57a(f)(3) of this title, a Federal credit union described in section 57a(f)(4) of this title, or a common carrier subject to the Act to regulate commerce, except in accordance with the undesignated proviso following the last designated subsection of this section.

(7) Assistance to certain countries

The Commission may not provide investigative assistance under this subsection to a foreign law enforcement agency from a foreign state that the Secretary of State has determined, in accordance with section 2405(j) of the Appendix to Title 50, has repeatedly provided support for acts of international terrorism, unless and until such determination is rescinded pursuant to section 2405(j)(4) of the Appendix to Title 50

(k) Referral of evidence for criminal proceedings

(1) In general

Whenever the Commission obtains evidence that any person, partnership, or corporation, either domestic or foreign, has engaged in conduct that may constitute a violation of Federal criminal law, to transmit such evidence to the Attorney General, who may institute criminal proceedings under appropriate statutes. Nothing in this paragraph affects any other authority of the Commission to disclose information.

(2) International information

The Commission shall endeavor to ensure, with respect to memoranda of understanding and international agreements it may conclude, that material it has obtained from foreign law enforcement agencies acting to investigate or pursue the enforcement of foreign criminal laws may be used for the purpose of investigation, prosecution, or prevention of violations of United States criminal laws.

(l) Expenditures for cooperative arrangements

To expend appropriated funds for—

(1) operating expenses and other costs of bilateral and multilateral cooperative law enforcement groups conducting activities of interest to the Commission and in which the Commission participates; and

(2) expenses for consultations and meetings hosted by the Commission with foreign government agency officials, members of their delegations, appropriate representatives and staff to exchange views concerning developments relating to the Commission's mission, development and implementation of cooperation agreements, and provision of technical assistance for the development of foreign consumer protection or competition regimes, such expenses to include necessary administrative and logistic expenses and the expenses of Commission staff and foreign invitees in attendance at such consultations and meetings including—

(A) such incidental expenses as meals taken in the course of such attendance;

(B) any travel and transportation to or from such meetings; and

(C) any other related lodging or subsistence

Provided, That the exception of "banks, savings and loan institutions described in section 57a(f)(3) of this title, Federal credit unions described in section 57a(f)(3) of this title, and common carriers subject to the Act to regulate commerce" from the Commission's powers defined in subsections (a), (b), and (j) of this section, of this section, shall not be construed to limit the Commission's authority to gather and compile information, to investigate, or to require reports or answers from, any person, partnership, or corporation to the extent that such action is necessary to the investigation of any person, partnership, or corporation, group of persons, partnerships, or corporations, or industry which is not engaged or is engaged only incidentally in banking, in business as a savings and loan institution, in business as a Federal credit union, or in business as a common carrier subject to the Act to regulate commerce.

The Commission shall establish a plan designed to substantially reduce burdens imposed upon small businesses as a result of requirements established by the Commission under clause (b) relating to the filing of quarterly financial reports. Such plan shall (1) be established after consultation with small businesses and persons who use the information contained in such quarterly financial reports; (2) provide for a reduction of the number of small businesses required to file such quarterly financial reports; and (3) make revisions in the forms used for such quarterly financial reports for the purpose of reducing the complexity of such forms. The Commission, not later than December 31, 1980, shall submit such plan to the Committee on Commerce, Science, and Transportation of the Senate and to the Committee on Energy and Commerce of the House of Representatives. Such plan shall take effect not later than October 31, 1981.

No officer or employee of the Commission or any Commissioner may publish or disclose information to the public, or to any Federal agency, whereby any line-of-business data furnished by a particular establishment or individual can be identified. No one other than designated sworn officers and employees of the Commission may examine the line-of-business reports from individual firms, and information provided in the line-of-business program administered by the Commission shall be used only for statistical purposes. Information for carrying out specific law enforcement responsibilities of the Commission shall be obtained under practices and procedures in effect on May 28, 1980, or as changed by law.

Nothing in this section (other than the provisions of clause (c) and clause (d)) shall apply to the business of insurance, except that the Commission shall have authority to conduct studies and prepare reports relating to the business of insurance. The Commission may exercise such authority only upon receiving a request which is agreed to by a majority of the members of the Committee on Commerce, Science, and Transportation of the Senate or the Committee on Energy and Commerce of the House of Representatives. The authority to conduct any such study shall expire at the end of the Congress during which the request for such study was made.

(Sept. 26, 1914, c. 311, § 6, 38 Stat. 721; Nov. 16, 1973, Pub.L. 93-153, Title IV, § 408(e), 87 Stat. 592; Jan. 4, 1975, Pub.L. 93-637, Title II, §§ 201(b), 202(b), 203(a), 88 Stat. 2193, 2198; July 23, 1979, Pub.L. 96-37, § 1(b), 93 Stat. 95; May 28, 1980, Pub.L. 96-252, §§ 3–5(a), 94 Stat. 374, 375; Aug. 10, 1987, Pub.L. 100-86, Title VII, § 715(a), (b), 101 Stat. 655; Nov. 2, 1994, Pub.L. 103-437, § 5(a), 108 Stat. 4582; Nov. 2, 1994, Pub.L. 103-438, § 3(e)(2)(A), 108 Stat. 4598; Dec. 22, 2006, Pub.L. 109-455, § 4(a), (b), (d), 120 Stat. 3372, 3373, 3375.)

§ 7. [15 U.S.C. § 47] Reference of suits under antitrust statutes to Commission

In any suit in equity brought by or under the direction of the Attorney General as provided in the antitrust Acts, the court may, upon the conclusion of the testimony therein, if it shall be then of opinion that the complainant is entitled to relief, refer said suit to the Commission, as a master in chancery, to ascertain and report an appropriate form of decree therein. The Commission shall proceed upon such notice to the parties and under such rules of procedure as the court may prescribe, and upon the coming in of such report such exceptions may be filed and such proceedings had in relation thereto as upon the report of a master in other equity causes, but the court may adopt or reject such report, in whole or in part, and enter such decree as the nature of the case may in its judgment require.

(Sept. 26, 1914, c. 311, § 7, 38 Stat. 722.)

§ 8. [15 U.S.C. § 48] Information and assistance from departments

The several departments and bureaus of the Government when directed by the President shall furnish the Commission, upon its request, all records, papers, and information in their possession relating to any corporation subject to any of the provisions of this subchapter, and shall detail from time to time such officials and employees to the Commission as he may direct.

(Sept. 26, 1914, c. 311, § 8, 38 Stat. 722.)

§ 9. [15 U.S.C. § 49] Documentary evidence; depositions; witnesses

For the purposes of this subchapter the Commission, or its duly authorized agent or agents, shall at all reasonable times have access to, for the purpose of examination, and the right to copy any documentary evidence of any person, partnership, or corporation being investigated or proceeded against; and the Commission shall have power to require by subpoena the attendance and testimony of witnesses and the production of all such documentary evidence relating to any matter under investigation. Any member of the Commission may sign subpoenas, and members and examiners of the Commission may administer oaths and affirmations, examine witnesses, and receive evidence.

Such attendance of witnesses, and the production of such documentary evidence, may be required from any place in the United States, at any designated place of hearing. And in case of disobedience to a subpoena the Commission may invoke the aid of any court of the United States in requiring the attendance and testimony of witnesses and the production of documentary evidence.

Any of the district courts of the United States within the jurisdiction of which such inquiry is carried on may, in case of contumacy or refusal to obey a subpoena issued to any person, partnership, or corporation issue an order requiring such person, partnership, or corporation to appear before the Commission, or to produce documentary evidence if so ordered, or to give evidence touching the matter in question; and any failure to obey such order of the court may be punished by such court as a contempt thereof.

Upon the application of the Attorney General of the United States, at the request of the Commission, the district courts of the United States shall have jurisdiction to issue writs of mandamus commanding any person, partnership, or corporation to comply with the provisions of this subchapter or any order of the Commission made in pursuance thereof.

The Commission may order testimony to be taken by deposition in any proceeding or investigation pending under this subchapter at any stage of such proceeding or investigation. Such depositions may be taken before any person designated by the Commission and having power to administer oaths. Such testimony shall be reduced to writing by the person taking the deposition, or under his direction, and shall then be subscribed by the deponent. Any person may be compelled to appear and depose and to produce documentary evidence in the same manner as witnesses may be compelled to appear and testify and produce documentary evidence before the Commission as hereinbefore provided.

Witnesses summoned before the Commission shall be paid the same fees and mileage that are paid witnesses in the courts of the United States and witnesses whose depositions are taken and the persons taking the same shall severally be entitled to the same fees as are paid for like services in the courts of the United States.

(Sept. 26, 1914, c. 311, § 9, 38 Stat. 722; Oct. 15, 1970, Pub.L. 91-452, Title II, § 211, 84 Stat. 929; Jan. 4, 1975, Pub.L. 93-637, Title II, § 203(b), 88 Stat. 2198.)

§ 10. [15 U.S.C. § 50] Offenses and penalties

Any person who shall neglect or refuse to attend and testify, or to answer any lawful inquiry or to produce any documentary evidence, if in his power to do so, in obedience to an order of a district court of the United States directing compliance with the subpoena or lawful requirement of the Commission, shall be guilty of an offense and upon conviction thereof by a court of competent jurisdiction shall be punished by a fine of not less than $1,000 nor more than $5,000, or by imprisonment for not more than one year, or by both such fine and imprisonment.

Any person who shall willfully make, or cause to be made, any false entry or statement of fact in any report required to be made under this subchapter, or who shall willfully make, or cause to be made, any false entry in any account, record, or memorandum kept by any person, partnership, or corporation subject to this subchapter, or who shall willfully neglect or fail to make, or to cause to be made, full, true, and correct entries in such accounts, records, or memoranda of all facts and transactions appertaining to the business of such person, partnership, or corporation, or who shall willfully remove out of the jurisdiction of the United States, or willfully mutilate, alter, or by any other means falsify any documentary evidence of such person, partnership, or corporation or who shall willfully refuse to submit to the Commission or to any of its authorized agents, for the purpose of inspection and taking copies, any documentary evidence of such person, partnership, or corporation in his possession or within his control, shall be deemed guilty of an offense against the United States, and shall be subject, upon conviction in any court of the United States of competent jurisdiction, to a fine of not less than $1,000 nor more than $5,000, or to imprisonment for a term of not more than three years, or to both such fine and imprisonment.

If any persons, partnership, or corporation required by this subchapter to file any annual or special report shall fail so to do within the time fixed by the Commission for filing the same, and such failure shall continue for thirty days after notice of such default, the corporation shall forfeit to the United States the sum of $100 for each and every day of the continuance of such failure, which forfeiture shall be payable into the Treasury of the United States, and shall be recoverable in a civil suit in the name of the United States brought in the case of a corporation or partnership in the district where the corporation or partnership has its principal office or in any district in which it shall do business, and in the case of any person in the district where such person resides or has his principal place of business. It shall be the duty of the various United States attorneys, under the direction of the Attorney General of the United States, to prosecute for the recovery of the forfeitures. The costs and expenses of such prosecution shall be paid out of the appropriation for the expenses of the courts of the United States.

Any officer or employee of the Commission who shall make public any information obtained by the Commission without its authority, unless directed by a court, shall be deemed guilty of a misdemeanor, and, upon conviction thereof, shall be punished by a fine not exceeding $5,000, or by imprisonment not exceeding one year, or by fine and imprisonment, in the discretion of the court.

(Sept. 26, 1914, c. 311, § 10, 38 Stat. 723; June 25, 1948, c. 646, § 1, 62 Stat. 909; Jan. 4, 1975, Pub.L. 93-637, Title II, § 203(c), 88 Stat. 2199; May 28, 1980, Pub.L. 96-252, § 6, 94 Stat. 376.)

§ 11. [15 U.S.C. § 51] Effect on other statutory provisions

Nothing contained in this subchapter shall be construed to prevent or interfere with the enforcement of the provisions of the antitrust Acts or the Acts to regulate commerce, nor shall anything contained in this subchapter be construed to alter, modify, or repeal the said antitrust Acts or the Acts to regulate commerce or any part or parts thereof.

(Sept. 26, 1914, c. 311, § 11, 38 Stat. 724.)

§ 12. [15 U.S.C. § 52] Dissemination of false advertisements

(a) Unlawfulness

It shall be unlawful for any person, partnership, or corporation to disseminate, or cause to be disseminated, any false advertisement—

(1) By United States mails, or in or having an effect upon commerce, by any means, for the purpose of inducing, or which is likely to induce, directly or indirectly the purchase of food, drugs, devices, services, or cosmetics; or

(2) By any means, for the purpose of inducing, or which is likely to induce, directly or indirectly, the purchase in or having an effect upon commerce, of food, drugs, devices, services, or cosmetics.

(b) Unfair or deceptive act or practice

The dissemination or the causing to be disseminated of any false advertisement within the provisions of subsection (a) of this section shall be an unfair or deceptive act or practice in or affecting commerce within the meaning of section 45 of this title.

(Sept. 26, 1914, c. 311, § 12, as added Mar. 21, 1938, c. 49, § 4, 52 Stat. 114, and amended Jan. 4, 1975, Pub.L. 93-637, Title II, § 201(c), 88 Stat. 2193; Aug. 16, 1994, Pub.L. 103-297, § 8, 108 Stat. 1550.)

§ 13. [15 U.S.C. § 53] False advertisements; injunctions and restraining orders

(a) Power of Commission; jurisdiction of courts

Whenever the Commission has reason to believe—

(1) that any person, partnership, or corporation is engaged in, or is about to engage in, the dissemination or the causing of the dissemination of any advertisement in violation of section 52 of this title, and

(2) that the enjoining thereof pending the issuance of a complaint by the Commission under section 45 of this title, and until such complaint is dismissed by the Commission or set aside by the court on review, or the order of the Commission to cease and desist made thereon has become final within the meaning of section 45 of this title, would be to the interest of the public,

the Commission by any of its attorneys designated by it for such purpose may bring suit in a district court of the United States or in the United States court of any Territory, to enjoin the dissemination or the causing of the dissemination of such advertisement. Upon proper showing a temporary injunction or restraining order shall be granted without bond. Any suit may be brought where such person, partnership, or corporation resides or transacts business, or wherever venue is proper under section 1391 of Title 28. In addition, the court may, if the court determines that the interests of justice require that any other person, partnership, or corporation should be a party in such suit, cause such other person, partnership, or corporation to be added as a party without regard to whether venue is otherwise proper in the district in which the suit is brought. In any suit under this section, process may be served on any person, partnership, or corporation wherever it may be found.

(b) Temporary restraining orders; preliminary injunctions

Whenever the Commission has reason to believe—

(1) that any person, partnership, or corporation is violating, or is about to violate, any provision of law enforced by the Federal Trade Commission, and

(2) that the enjoining thereof pending the issuance of a complaint by the Commission and until such complaint is dismissed by the Commission or set aside by the court on review, or until the order of the Commission made thereon has become final, would be in the interest of the public—

the Commission by any of its attorneys designated by it for such purpose may bring suit in a district court of the United States to enjoin any such act or practice. Upon a proper showing that, weighing the equities and considering the Commission's likelihood of ultimate success, such action would be in the public interest, and after notice to the defendant, a temporary restraining order or a preliminary injunction may be granted without bond: *Provided, however,* That if a complaint is not filed within such period (not exceeding 20 days) as may be specified by the court after issuance of the temporary restraining order or preliminary injunction, the order or injunction shall be dissolved by the court and be of no further force and effect: *Provided further*, That in proper cases the Commission may seek, and after proper proof, the court may issue, a permanent injunction. Any suit may be brought where such person, partnership, or corporation resides or transacts business, or wherever venue is proper under section 1391 of Title 28. In addition, the court may, if the court determines that the interests of justice require that any other person, partnership, or corporation should be a party in such suit, cause such other person, partnership, or corporation to be added as a party without regard to whether venue is otherwise proper in the district in which the suit is brought. In any suit under this section, process may be served on any person, partnership, or corporation wherever it may be found.

(c) Service of process; proof of service

Any process of the Commission under this section may be served by any person duly authorized by the Commission—

> (1) by delivering a copy of such process to the person to be served, to a member of the partnership to be served, or to the president, secretary, or other executive officer or a director of the corporation to be served;
>
> (2) by leaving a copy of such process at the residence or the principal office or place of business of such person, partnership, or corporation; or
>
> (3) by mailing a copy of such process by registered mail or certified mail addressed to such person, partnership, or corporation at his, or her, or its residence, principal office, or principal place or business.

The verified return by the person serving such process setting forth the manner of such service shall be proof of the same.

(d) Exception of periodical publications

Whenever it appears to the satisfaction of the court in the case of a newspaper, magazine, periodical, or other publication, published at regular intervals—

> (1) that restraining the dissemination of a false advertisement in any particular issue of such publication would delay the delivery of such issue after the regular time therefor, and
>
> (2) that such delay would be due to the method by which the manufacture and distribution of such publication is customarily conducted by the publisher in accordance with sound business practice, and not to any method or device adopted for the evasion of this section or to prevent or delay the issuance of an injunction or restraining order with respect to such false advertisement or any other advertisement,

the court shall exclude such issue from the operation of the restraining order or injunction.

(Sept. 26, 1914, c. 311, § 13, as added Mar. 21, 1938, c. 49, § 4, 52 Stat. 114, and amended Nov. 16, 1973, Pub.L. 93-153, Title IV, § 408(f), 87 Stat. 592; Aug. 26, 1994, Pub.L. 103-312, § 10, 108 Stat. 1695.)

§ 14. [15 U.S.C. § 54] False advertisements; penalties

(a) Imposition of penalties

Any person, partnership, or corporation who violates any provision of section 52(a) of this title shall, if the use of the commodity advertised may be injurious to health because of results from such use under the conditions prescribed in the advertisement thereof, or under such conditions as are customary or usual, or if such violation is with intent to defraud or mislead, be guilty of a misdemeanor, and upon conviction shall be punished by a fine of not more than $5,000 or by imprisonment for not more than six months, or by both such fine and imprisonment; except that if the conviction is for a violation committed after a first conviction of such person, partnership, or corporation, for any violation of such section, punishment shall be by a fine of not more than $10,000 or by imprisonment for not more than one year, or by both such fine and imprisonment: *Provided,* That for the purposes of this section meats and meat food products duly inspected, marked, and labeled in accordance with rules and regulations issued under the Meat Inspection Act [21 U.S.C.A. § 601 et seq.] shall be conclusively presumed not injurious to health at the time the same leave official "establishments."

(b) Exception of advertising medium or agency

No publisher, radio-broadcast licensee, or agency or medium for the dissemination of advertising, except the manufacturer, packer, distributor, or seller of the commodity to which the false advertisement relates, shall be liable under this section by reason of the dissemination by him of any false advertisement, unless he has refused, on the request of the Commission, to furnish the Commission the name and post-office address of the manufacturer, packer, distributor, seller, or advertising agency, residing in the United States, who caused him to disseminate such advertisement. No advertising agency shall be liable under this section by reason of the causing by it of the dissemination of any false advertisement, unless it has refused, on the request of the Commission, to furnish the Commission the name and post-office address of the manufacturer, packer, distributor, or seller, residing in the United States, who caused it to cause the dissemination of such advertisement.

(Sept. 26, 1914, c. 311, § 14, as added Mar. 21, 1938, c. 49, § 4, 52 Stat. 114.)

§ 15. [15 U.S.C. § 55] Additional definitions

For the purposes of sections 52 to 54 of this title—

(a) False advertisement

(1) The term "false advertisement" means an advertisement, other than labeling, which is misleading in a material respect; and in determining whether any advertisement is misleading, there shall be taken into account (among other things) not only representations made or suggested by statement, word, design, device, sound, or any combination thereof, but also the extent to which the advertisement fails to reveal facts material in the light of such representations or material with respect to consequences which may result from the use of the commodity to which the advertisement relates under the conditions prescribed in said advertisement, or under such conditions as are customary or usual. No advertisement of a drug shall be deemed to be false if it is disseminated only to members of the medical profession, contains no false representation of a material fact, and includes, or is accompanied in each instance by truthful disclosure of, the formula showing quantitatively each ingredient of such drug.

(2) In the case of oleomargarine or margarine an advertisement shall be deemed misleading in a material respect if in such advertisement representations are made or suggested by statement, word, grade designation, design, device, symbol, sound, or any combination thereof, that such oleomargarine or margarine is a dairy product, except that nothing contained herein shall prevent a truthful, accurate, and full statement in any such advertisement of all the ingredients contained in such oleomargarine or margarine.

(b) Food

The term "food" means (1) articles used for food or drink for man or other animals, (2) chewing gum, and (3) articles used for components of any such article.

(c) Drug

The term "drug" means (1) articles recognized in the official United States Pharmacopoeia, official Homeopathic[2] Pharmacopoeia of the United States, or official National Formulary, or any supplement to any of them; and (2) articles intended for use in the diagnosis, cure, mitigation, treatment, or prevention of disease in man or other animals; and (3) articles (other than food) intended to affect the structure or any function of the body of man or other animals; and (4) articles intended for use as a component of any article specified in clauses (1), (2), or (3); but does not include devices or their components, parts, or accessories.

(d) Device

The term "device" (except when used in subsection (a) of this section) means an instrument, apparatus, implement, machine, contrivance, implant, in vitro reagent, or other similar or related article, including any component, part, or accessory, which is—

(1) recognized in the official National Formulary, or the United States Pharmacopeia, or any supplement to them,

(2) intended for use in the diagnosis of disease or other conditions, or in the cure, mitigation, treatment, or prevention of disease, in man or other animals, or

(3) intended to affect the structure or any function of the body of man or other animals, and

which does not achieve any of its principal intended purposes through chemical action within or on the body of man or other animals and which is not dependent upon being metabolized for the achievement of any of its principal intended purposes.

(e) Cosmetic

The term "cosmetic" means (1) articles to be rubbed, poured, sprinkled, or sprayed on, introduced into, or otherwise applied to the human body or any part thereof intended for cleansing, beautifying, promoting attractiveness, or altering the appearance, and (2) articles intended for use as a component of any such article; except that such term shall not include soap.

(f) Oleomargarine or margarine

For the purposes of this section and section 347 of Title 21, the term "oleomargarine" or "margarine" includes—

(1) all substances, mixtures, and compounds known as oleomargarine or margarine;

(2) all substances, mixtures, and compounds which have a consistence similar to that of butter and which contain any edible oils or fats other than milk fat if made in imitation or semblance of butter.

(Sept. 26, 1914, c. 311, § 15, as added Mar. 21, 1938, c. 49, § 4, 52 Stat. 114, and amended Mar. 16, 1950, c. 61, § 4(a), (b), 64 Stat. 21; May 28, 1976, Pub.L. 94-295, § 3(a)(1)(B), 90 Stat. 575.)

---

[2] So in original. Probably should be "Homeopathic."

§ 16. [15 U.S.C. § 56] Commencement, defense, intervention and supervision of litigation and appeal by Commission or Attorney General

(a) Procedure for exercise of authority to litigate or appeal

(1) Except as otherwise provided in paragraph (2) or (3), if—

(A) before commencing, defending, or intervening in, any civil action involving this subchapter (including an action to collect a civil penalty) which the Commission, or the Attorney General on behalf of the Commission, is authorized to commence, defend, or intervene in, the Commission gives written notification and undertakes to consult with the Attorney General with respect to such action; and

(B) the Attorney General fails within 45 days after receipt of such notification to commence, defend, or intervene in, such action;

the Commission may commence, defend, or intervene in, and supervise the litigation of, such action and any appeal of such action in its own name by any of its attorneys designated by it for such purpose.

(2) Except as otherwise provided in paragraph (3), in any civil action—

(A) under section 53 of this title (relating to injunctive relief);

(B) under section 57b of this title (relating to consumer redress);

(C) to obtain judicial review of a rule prescribed by the Commission, or a cease and desist order issued under section 45 of this title;

(D) under the second paragraph of section 49 of this title (relating to enforcement of a subpena) and under the fourth paragraph of such section (relating to compliance with section 46 of this title); or

(E) under section 57b-2a of this title;

the Commission shall have exclusive authority to commence or defend, and supervise the litigation of, such action and any appeal of such action in its own name by any of its attorneys designated by it for such purpose, unless the Commission authorizes the Attorney General to do so. The Commission shall inform the Attorney General of the exercise of such authority and such exercise shall not preclude the Attorney General from intervening on behalf of the United States in such action and any appeal of such action as may be otherwise provided by law.

(3) (A) If the Commission makes a written request to the Attorney General, within the 10-day period which begins on the date of the entry of the judgment in any civil action in which the Commission represented itself pursuant to paragraph (1) or (2), to represent itself through any of its attorneys designated by it for such purpose before the Supreme Court in such action, it may do so, if—

(i) the Attorney General concurs with such request; or

(ii) the Attorney General, within the 60-day period which begins on the date of the entry of such judgment—

(a) refuses to appeal or file a petition for writ of certiorari with respect to such civil action, in which case he shall give written notification to the Commission of the reasons for such refusal within such 60-day period; or

(b) the Attorney General fails to take any action with respect to the Commission's request.

(B) In any case where the Attorney General represents the Commission before the Supreme Court in any civil action in which the Commission represented itself pursuant to paragraph (1) or (2), the Attorney General may not agree to any settlement, compromise, or dismissal of such action, or confess error in the Supreme Court with respect to such action, unless the Commission concurs.

(C) For purposes of this paragraph (with respect to representation before the Supreme Court), the term "Attorney General" includes the Solicitor General.

(4) If, prior to the expiration of the 45-day period specified in paragraph (1) of this section or a 60-day period specified in paragraph (3), any right of the Commission to commence, defend, or intervene in, any such action or appeal may be extinguished due to any procedural requirement of any court with respect to the time in which any pleadings, notice of appeal, or other acts pertaining to such action or appeal may be taken, the Attorney General shall have one-half of the time required to comply with any such procedural requirement of the court (including any extension of such time granted by the court) for the purpose of commencing, defending, or intervening in the civil action pursuant to paragraph (1) or for the purpose of refusing to appeal or file a petition for writ of certiorari and the written notification or failing to take any action pursuant to paragraph 3(A)(ii).

(5) The provisions of this subsection shall apply notwithstanding chapter 31 of Title 28, or any other provision of law.

(b) Certification by Commission to Attorney General for criminal proceedings

Whenever the Commission has reason to believe that any person, partnership, or corporation is liable for a criminal penalty under this subchapter, the Commission shall certify the facts to the Attorney General, whose duty it shall be to cause appropriate criminal proceedings to be brought.

(c) Foreign litigation

(1) Commission attorneys

With the concurrence of the Attorney General, the Commission may designate Commission attorneys to assist the Attorney General in connection with litigation in foreign courts on particular matters in which the Commission has an interest.

(2) Reimbursement for foreign counsel

The Commission is authorized to expend appropriated funds, upon agreement with the Attorney General, to reimburse the Attorney General for the retention of foreign counsel for litigation in foreign courts and for expenses related to litigation in foreign courts in which the Commission has an interest.

(3) Limitation on use of funds

Nothing in this subsection authorizes the payment of claims or judgments from any source other than the permanent and indefinite appropriation authorized by section 1304 of Title 31

(4) Other authority

The authority provided by this subsection is in addition to any other authority of the Commission or the Attorney General.

(Sept. 26, 1914, c. 311, § 16, as added Mar. 21, 1938, c. 49, § 4, 52 Stat. 114, and amended Nov. 16, 1973, Pub.L. 93-153, Title IV, § 408(g), 87 Stat. 592; Jan. 4, 1975, Pub.L. 93-637, Title II, § 204(a), 88 Stat. 2199; Dec. 22, 2006, Pub.L. 109-455, §§ 5, 7(b), 120 Stat. 3375, 3380.)

§ 17. [15 U.S.C. § 57] Separability clause

If any provision of this subchapter, or the application thereof to any person, partnership, or corporation, or circumstance, is held invalid, the remainder of this subchapter, and the application of such provision to any other person, partnership, corporation, or circumstance, shall not be affected thereby.

(Sept. 26, 1914, c. 311, § 17, as added Mar. 21, 1938, c. 49, § 4, 52 Stat. 114.)

§ 18. [15 U.S.C. § 57a] Unfair or deceptive acts or practices rulemaking proceedings

(a) Authority of Commission to prescribe rules and general statements of policy

(1) Except as provided in subsection (h) of this section, the Commission may prescribe—

(A) interpretive rules and general statements of policy with respect to unfair or deceptive acts or practices in or affecting commerce (within the meaning of section 45(a)(1) of this title), and

(B) rules which define with specificity acts or practices which are unfair or deceptive acts or practices in or affecting commerce (within the meaning of section 45(a)(1) of this title), except that the Commission shall not develop or promulgate any trade rule or regulation with regard to the regulation of the development and utilization of the standards and certification activities pursuant to this section. Rules under this subparagraph may include requirements prescribed for the purpose of preventing such acts or practices.

(2) The Commission shall have no authority under this subchapter, other than its authority under this section, to prescribe any rule with respect to unfair or deceptive acts or practices in or affecting commerce (within the meaning of section 45(a)(1) of this title). The preceding sentence shall not affect any authority of the Commission to prescribe rules (including

interpretive rules), and general statements of policy, with respect to unfair methods of competition in or affecting commerce.

(b) Procedures applicable

(1) When prescribing a rule under subsection (a)(1)(B) of this section, the Commission shall proceed in accordance with section 553 of Title 5 (without regard to any reference in such section to sections 556 and 557 of such title), and shall also (A) publish a notice of proposed rulemaking stating with particularity the text of the rule, including any alternatives, which the Commission proposes to promulgate, and the reason for the proposed rule; (B) allow interested persons to submit written data, views, and arguments, and make all such submissions publicly available; (C) provide an opportunity for an informal hearing in accordance with subsection (c) of this section; and (D) promulgate, if appropriate, a final rule based on the matter in the rulemaking record (as defined in subsection (e)(1)(B) of this section), together with a statement of basis and purpose.

(2) (A) Prior to the publication of any notice of proposed rulemaking pursuant to paragraph (1)(A), the Commission shall publish an advance notice of proposed rulemaking in the Federal Register. Such advance notice shall—

(i) contain a brief description of the area of inquiry under consideration, the objectives which the Commission seeks to achieve, and possible regulatory alternatives under consideration by the Commission; and

(ii) invite the response of interested parties with respect to such proposed rulemaking, including any suggestions or alternative methods for achieving such objectives.

(B) The Commission shall submit such advance notice of proposed rulemaking to the Committee on Commerce, Science, and Transportation of the Senate and to the Committee on Energy and Commerce of the House of Representatives. The Commission may use such additional mechanisms as the Commission considers useful to obtain suggestions regarding the content of the area of inquiry before the publication of a general notice of proposed rulemaking under paragraph (1)(A).

(C) The Commission shall, 30 days before the publication of a notice of proposed rulemaking pursuant to paragraph (1)(A), submit such notice to the Committee on Commerce, Science, and Transportation of the Senate and to the Committee on Energy and Commerce of the House of Representatives.

(3) The Commission shall issue a notice of proposed rulemaking pursuant to paragraph (1)(A) only where it has reason to believe that the unfair or deceptive acts or practices which are the subject of the proposed rulemaking are prevalent. The Commission shall make a determination that unfair or deceptive acts or practices are prevalent under this paragraph only if—

(A) it has issued cease and desist orders regarding such acts or practices, or

(B) any other information available to the Commission indicates a widespread pattern of unfair or deceptive acts or practices.

(c) Informal hearing procedure

The Commission shall conduct any informal hearings required by subsection (b)(1)(C) of this section in accordance with the following procedure:

(1) (A) The Commission shall provide for the conduct of proceedings under this subsection by hearing officers who shall perform their functions in accordance with the requirements of this subsection.

(B) The officer who presides over the rulemaking proceedings shall be responsible to a chief presiding officer who shall not be responsible to any other officer or employee of the Commission. The officer who presides over the rulemaking proceeding shall make a recommended decision based upon the findings and conclusions of such officer as to all relevant and material evidence, except that such recommended decision may be made by another officer if the officer who presided over the proceeding is no longer available to the Commission.

(C) Except as required for the disposition of ex parte matters as authorized by law, no presiding officer shall consult any person or party with respect to any fact in issue unless such officer gives notice and opportunity for all parties to participate.

(2) Subject to paragraph (3) of this subsection, an interested person is entitled—

(A) to present his position orally or by documentary submissions (or both), and

(B) if the Commission determines that there are disputed issues of material fact it is necessary to resolve, to present such rebuttal submissions and to conduct (or have conducted under paragraph (3)(B)) such cross-examination of persons as the Commission determines (i) to be appropriate, and (ii) to be required for a full and true disclosure with respect to such issues.

(3) The Commission may prescribe such rules and make such rulings concerning proceedings in such hearings as may tend to avoid unnecessary costs or delay. Such rules or rulings may include (A) imposition of reasonable time limits on each interested person's oral presentations, and (B) requirements that any cross-examination to which a person may be entitled under paragraph (2) be conducted by the Commission on behalf of that person in such manner as the Commission determines (i) to be appropriate, and (ii) to be required for a full and true disclosure with respect to disputed issues of material fact.

(4) (A) Except as provided in subparagraph (B), if a group of persons each of whom under paragraphs (2) and (3) would be entitled to conduct (or have conducted) cross-examination and who are determined by the Commission to have the same or similar interests in the proceeding cannot agree upon a single representative of such interests for purposes of cross-examination, the Commission may make rules and rulings (i) limiting the representation of such interest, for such purposes, and (ii) governing the manner in which such cross-examination shall be limited.

(B) When any person who is a member of a group with respect to which the Commission has made a determination under subparagraph (A) is unable to agree upon group representation with the other members of the group, then such person shall not be denied under the authority of subparagraph (A) the opportunity to conduct (or have conducted) cross-examination as to issues affecting his particular interests if (i) he satisfies the Commission that he has made a reasonable and good faith effort to reach agreement upon group representation with the other members of the group and (ii) the Commission determines that there are substantial and relevant issues which are not adequately presented by the group representative.

(5) A verbatim transcript shall be taken of any oral presentation, and cross-examination, in an informal hearing to which this subsection applies. Such transcript shall be available to the public.

(d) Statement of basis and purpose accompanying rule; "Commission" defined; judicial review of amendment or repeal of rule; violation of rules

(1) The Commission's statement of basis and purpose to accompany a rule promulgated under subsection (a)(1)(B) of this section shall include (A) a statement as to the prevalence of the acts or practices treated by the rule; (B) a statement as to the manner and context in which such acts or practices are unfair or deceptive; and (C) a statement as to the economic effect of the rule, taking into account the effect on small business and consumers.

(2) (A) The term "Commission" as used in this subsection and subsections (b) and (c) of this section includes any person authorized to act in behalf of the Commission in any part of the rulemaking proceeding.

(B) A substantive amendment to, or repeal of, a rule promulgated under subsection (a)(1)(B) of this section shall be prescribed, and subject to judicial review, in the same manner as a rule prescribed under such subsection. An exemption under subsection (g) of this section shall not be treated as an amendment or repeal of a rule.

(3) When any rule under subsection (a)(1)(B) of this section takes effect a subsequent violation thereof shall constitute an unfair or deceptive act or practice in violation of section 45(a)(1) of

this title, unless the Commission otherwise expressly provides in such rule.

(e) Judicial review; petition; jurisdiction and venue; rulemaking record; additional submissions and presentations; scope of review and relief; review by Supreme Court; additional remedies

(1) (A) Not later than 60 days after a rule is promulgated under subsection (a)(1)(B) of this section by the Commission, any interested person (including a consumer or consumer organization) may file a petition, in the United States Court of Appeals for the District of Columbia circuit or for the circuit in which such person resides or has his principal place of business, for judicial review of such rule. Copies of the petition shall be forthwith transmitted by the clerk of the court to the Commission or other officer designated by it for that purpose. The provisions of section 2112 of Title 28 shall apply to the filing of the rulemaking record of proceedings on which the Commission based its rule and to the transfer of proceedings in the courts of appeals.

(B) For purpose of this section, the term "rulemaking record" means the rule, its statement of basis and purpose, the transcript required by subsection (c)(5) of this section, any written submissions, and any other information which the Commission considers relevant to such rule.

(2) If the petitioner or the Commission applies to the court for leave to make additional oral submissions or written presentations and shows to the satisfaction of the court that such submissions and presentations would be material and that there were reasonable grounds for the submissions and failure to make such submissions and presentations in the proceeding before the Commission, the court may order the Commission to provide additional opportunity to make such submissions and presentations. The Commission may modify or set aside its rule or make a new rule by reason of the additional submissions and presentations and shall file such modified or new rule, and the rule's statement of basis of purpose, with the return of such submissions and presentations. The court shall thereafter review such new or modified rule.

(3) Upon the filing of the petition under paragraph (1) of this subsection, the court shall have jurisdiction to review the rule in accordance with chapter 7 of Title 5 and to grant appropriate relief, including interim relief, as provided in such chapter. The court shall hold unlawful and set aside the rule on any ground specified in subparagraphs (A), (B), (C), or (D) of section 706(2) of Title 5 (taking due account of the rule of prejudicial error), or if—

(A) the court finds that the Commission's action is not supported by substantial evidence in the rulemaking record (as defined in paragraph (1)(B) of this subsection) taken as a whole, or

(B) the court finds that—

(i) a Commission determination under subsection (c) of this section that the petitioner is not entitled to conduct cross-examination or make rebuttal submissions, or

(ii) a Commission rule or ruling under subsection (c) of this section limiting the petitioner's cross-examination or rebuttal submissions, has precluded disclosure of disputed material facts which was necessary for fair determination by the Commission of the rulemaking proceeding taken as a whole.

The term "evidence," as used in this paragraph, means any matter in the rulemaking record.

(4) The judgment of the court affirming or setting aside, in whole or in part, any such rule shall be final, subject to review by the Supreme Court of the United States upon certiorari or certification, as provided in section 1254 of Title 28.

(5) (A) Remedies under the preceding paragraphs of this subsection are in addition to and not in lieu of any other remedies provided by law.

(B) The United States Courts of Appeal shall have exclusive jurisdiction of any action to obtain judicial review (other than in an enforcement proceeding) of a rule prescribed under subsection (a)(1)(B) of this section, if any district court of the United States would have had jurisdiction of such action but for this subparagraph. Any such action shall be brought in the United States Court of Appeals for the District of Columbia circuit, or for any circuit which includes a judicial district in which the action could have been brought but for this subparagraph.

(C) A determination, rule, or ruling of the Commission described in paragraph (3)(B)(i) or (ii) may be reviewed only in a proceeding under this subsection and only in accordance with paragraph (3)(B). Section 706(2)(E) of Title 5 shall not apply to any rule promulgated under subsection (a)(1)(B) of this section. The contents and adequacy of any statement required by subsection (b)(1)(D) of this section shall not be subject to judicial review in any respect.

(f) Unfair or deceptive acts or practices by banks, savings and loan institutions, or Federal credit unions; promulgation of regulations by Board of Governors of Federal Reserve System, Federal Home Loan Bank Board, and National Credit Union Administration Board; agency enforcement and compliance proceedings; violations; power of other Federal agencies unaffected; reporting requirements

(1) In order to prevent unfair or deceptive acts or practices in or affecting commerce (including acts or practices which are unfair or deceptive to consumers) by banks or savings and loan institutions described in paragraph (3), each agency specified in paragraph (2) or (3) of this subsection shall establish a separate division of consumer affairs which shall receive and take appropriate action upon complaints with respect to such acts or practices by banks or savings and loan institutions described in paragraph (3) subject to its jurisdiction. The Board of Governors of the Federal Reserve System (with respect to banks) and the Federal Home Loan Bank Board (with respect to savings and loan

institutions described in paragraph (3)) and the National Credit Union Administration Board (with respect to Federal credit unions described in paragraph (4)) shall prescribe regulations to carry out the purposes of this section, including regulations defining with specificity such unfair or deceptive acts or practices, and containing requirements prescribed for the purpose of preventing such acts or practices. Whenever the Commission prescribes a rule under subsection (a)(1)(B) of this section, then within 60 days after such rule takes effect each such Board shall promulgate substantially similar regulations prohibiting acts or practices of banks or savings and loan institutions described in paragraph (3), or Federal credit unions described in paragraph (4), as the case may be, which are substantially similar to those prohibited by rules of the Commission and which impose substantially similar requirements, unless (A) any such Board finds that such acts or practices of banks or savings and loan institutions described in paragraph (3), or Federal credit unions described in paragraph (4), as the case may be, are not unfair or deceptive, or (B) the Board of Governors of the Federal Reserve System finds that implementation of similar regulations with respect to banks, savings and loan institutions or Federal credit unions would seriously conflict with essential monetary and payments systems policies of such Board, and publishes any such finding, and the reasons therefor, in the Federal Register.

(2) Enforcement. Compliance with regulations prescribed under this subsection shall be enforced under section 1818 of Title 12, in the case of—

(A) national banks and Federal branches and Federal agencies of foreign banks, by the division of consumer affairs established by the Office of the Comptroller of the Currency;

(B) member banks of the Federal Reserve System (other than national banks), branches and agencies of foreign banks (other than Federal branches, Federal agencies, and insured State branches of foreign banks), commercial lending companies owned or controlled by foreign banks, and organizations operating under section 25 or 25(a) of the Federal Reserve Act [12 U.S.C.A. §§ 601 et seq., 611 et seq.], by the division of consumer affairs established by the Board of Governors of the Federal Reserve System; and

(C) banks insured by the Federal Deposit Insurance Corporation (other banks[3] referred to in subparagraph (A) or (B)) and insured State branches of foreign banks, by the division of consumer affairs established by the Board of Directors of the Federal Deposit Insurance Corporation.

(3) Compliance with regulations prescribed under this subsection shall be enforced under section 1818 of Title 12 with respect to savings associations as defined in section 1813 of Title 12.

(4) Compliance with regulations prescribed under this subsection shall be enforced with respect to Federal credit unions under sections 1766 and 1786 of title 12.

---

[3] So in original. Probably should be "(other than."

(5) For the purpose of the exercise by any agency referred to in paragraph (2) of its powers under any Act referred to in that paragraph, a violation of any regulation prescribed under this subsection shall be deemed to be a violation of a requirement imposed under that Act. In addition to its powers under any provision of law specifically referred to in paragraph (2), each of the agencies referred to in that paragraph may exercise, for the purpose of enforcing compliance with any regulation prescribed under this subsection, any other authority conferred on it by law.

(6) The authority of the Board of Governors of the Federal Reserve System to issue regulations under this subsection does not impair the authority of any other agency designated in this subsection to make rules respecting its own procedures in enforcing compliance with regulations prescribed under this subsection.

(7) Each agency exercising authority under this subsection shall transmit to the Congress each year a detailed report on its activities under this paragraph during the preceding calendar year.

The terms used in this paragraph that are not defined in this subchapter or otherwise defined in section 1813(s) of Title 12 shall have the meaning given to them in section 3101 of Title 12.

(g) Exemptions and stays from application of rules; procedures

(1) Any person to whom a rule under subsection (a)(1)(B) of this section applies may petition the Commission for an exemption from such rule.

(2) If, on its own motion or on the basis of a petition under paragraph (1), the Commission finds that the application of a rule prescribed under subsection (a)(1)(B) of this section to any person or class or[4] persons is not necessary to prevent the unfair or deceptive act or practice to which the rule relates, the Commission may exempt such person or class from all or part of such rule. Section 553 of Title 5 shall apply to action under this paragraph.

(3) Neither the pendency of a proceeding under this subsection respecting an exemption from a rule, nor the pendency of judicial proceedings to review the Commission's action or failure to act under this subsection, shall stay the applicability of such rule under subsection (a)(1)(B) of this section.

(h) Restriction on rulemaking authority of Commission respecting children's advertising proceedings pending on May 28, 1980

The Commission shall not have any authority to promulgate any rule in the children's advertising proceeding pending on May 28, 1980, or in any substantially similar proceeding on the basis of a determination by the Commission that such advertising constitutes an unfair act or practice in or affecting commerce.

(i) Meetings with outside parties

(1) For purposes of this subsection, the term "outside party" means any person other than (A) a Commissioner; (B) an officer or

---

[4] So in original. Probably should be "of."

employee of the Commission; or (C) any person who has entered into a contract or any other agreement or arrangement with the Commission to provide any goods or services (including consulting services) to the Commission.

(2) Not later than 60 days after May 28, 1980, the Commission shall publish a proposed rule, and not later than 180 days after May 28, 1980, the Commission shall promulgate a final rule, which shall authorize the Commission or any Commissioner to meet with any outside party concerning any rulemaking proceeding of the Commission. Such rule shall provide that—

(A) notice of any such meeting shall be included in any weekly calendar prepared by the Commission; and

(B) a verbatim record or a summary of any such meeting, or of any communication relating to any such meeting, shall be kept, made available to the public, and included in the rulemaking record.

(j) Communications by investigative personnel with staff of Commission concerning matters outside rulemaking record prohibited

Not later than 60 days after May 28, 1980, the Commission shall publish a proposed rule, and not later than 180 days after May 28, 1980, the Commission shall promulgate a final rule, which shall prohibit any officer, employee, or agent of the Commission with any investigative responsibility or other responsibility relating to any rulemaking proceeding within any operating bureau of the Commission, from communicating or causing to be communicated to any Commissioner or to the personal staff of any Commissioner any fact which is relevant to the merits of such proceeding and which is not on the rulemaking record of such proceeding, unless such communication is made available to the public and is included in the rulemaking record. The provisions of this subsection shall not apply to any communication to the extent such communication is required for the disposition of ex parte matters as authorized by law.

(Sept. 26, 1914, c. 311, § 18, as added Jan. 4, 1975, Pub.L. 93-637, Title II, § 202(a), 88 Stat. 2193, and amended July 23, 1979, Pub.L. 96-37, § 1(c), 93 Stat. 95; Mar. 31, 1980, Pub.L. 96-221, Title VI, § 610(b), 94 Stat. 174; May 28, 1980, Pub.L. 96-252, §§ 7 to 11(a), 12, 94 Stat. 376 to 379; Aug. 10, 1987, Pub.L. 100-86, Title VII, § 715(c), 101 Stat. 655; Aug. 9, 1989, Pub.L. 101-73, Title VII, § 744(t), 103 Stat. 441; Dec. 19, 1991, Pub.L. 102-242, Title II, § 212(g)(2), 105 Stat. 2302; Oct. 28, 1992, Pub.L. 102-550, Title XVI, § 1604(a)(9), 106 Stat. 4082; Aug. 26, 1994, Pub.L. 103-312, §§ 3, 5, 108 Stat. 1691, 1692; Nov. 2, 1994, Pub.L. 103-437, § 5(a), 108 Stat. 4582; Oct. 13, 2006, Pub.L. 109-351, Title VII, § 725(g), 120 Stat. 2002; Oct. 16, 2006, Pub.L. 109-356, § 123(g), 120 Stat. 2029.)

§ 19. [15 U.S.C. § 57b]. Civil actions for violations of rules and cease and desist orders respecting unfair or deceptive acts or practices

(a) Suits by Commission against persons, partnerships, or corporations; jurisdiction; relief for dishonest or fraudulent acts

(1) If any person, partnership, or corporation violates any rule under this subchapter respecting unfair or deceptive acts or practices (other than an interpretive rule, or a rule violation of which the Commission has provided is not an unfair or deceptive act or practice in violation of section 45(a) of this title), then the

Commission may commence a civil action against such person, partnership, or corporation for relief under subsection (b) of this section in a United States district court or in any court of competent jurisdiction of a State.

(2) If any person, partnership, or corporation engages in any unfair or deceptive act or practice (within the meaning of section 45(a)(1) of this title) with respect to which the Commission has issued a final cease and desist order which is applicable to such person, partnership, or corporation, then the Commission may commence a civil action against such person, partnership, or corporation in a United States district court or in any court of competent jurisdiction of a State. If the Commission satisfies the court that the act or practice to which the cease and desist order relates is one which a reasonable man would have known under the circumstances was dishonest or fraudulent, the court may grant relief under subsection (b) of this section.

(b) Nature of relief available

The court in an action under subsection (a) of this section shall have jurisdiction to grant such relief as the court finds necessary to redress injury to consumers or other persons, partnerships, and corporations resulting from the rule violation or the unfair or deceptive act or practice, as the case may be. Such relief may include, but shall not be limited to, rescission or reformation of contracts, the refund of money or return of property, the payment of damages, and public notification respecting the rule violation or the unfair or deceptive act or practice, as the case may be; except that nothing in this subsection is intended to authorize the imposition of any exemplary or punitive damages.

(c) Conclusiveness of findings of Commission in cease and desist proceedings; notice of judicial proceedings to injured persons, etc.

(1) If (A) a cease and desist order issued under section 45(b) of this title has become final under section 45(g) of this title with respect to any person's, partnership's, or corporation's rule violation or unfair or deceptive act or practice, and (B) an action under this section is brought with respect to such person's[5] partnership's, or corporation's rule violation or act or practice, then the findings of the Commission as to the material facts in the proceeding under section 45(b) of this title with respect to such person's, partnership's, or corporation's rule violation or act or practice, shall be conclusive unless (i) the terms of such cease and desist order expressly provide that the Commission's findings shall not be conclusive, or (ii) the order became final by reason of section 45(g)(1) of this title, in which case such finding shall be conclusive if supported by evidence.

(2) The court shall cause notice of an action under this section to be given in a manner which is reasonably calculated, under all of the circumstances, to apprise the persons, partnerships, and corporations allegedly injured by the defendant's rule violation or act or practice of the pendency of such action. Such notice may, in the discretion of the court, be given by publication.

(d) Time for bringing of actions

---

[5] So in original. A comma was probably intended.

No action may be brought by the Commission under this section more than 3 years after the rule violation to which an action under subsection (a)(1) of this section relates, or the unfair or deceptive act or practice to which an action under subsection (a)(2) of this section relates; except that if a cease and desist order with respect to any person's, partnership's, or corporation's rule violation or unfair or deceptive act or practice has become final and such order was issued in a proceeding under section 45(b) of this title which was commenced not later than 3 years after the rule violation or act or practice occurred, a civil action may be commenced under this section against such person, partnership, or corporation at any time before the expiration of one year after such order becomes final.

(e) Availability of additional Federal or State remedies; other authority of Commission unaffected

Remedies provided in this section are in addition to, and not in lieu of, any other remedy or right of action provided by State or Federal law. Nothing in this section shall be construed to affect any authority of the Commission under any other provision of law.

(Sept. 26, 1914, c. 311, § 19, as added Jan. 4, 1975, Pub.L. 93-637, Title II, § 206(a), 88 Stat. 2201.)

§ 20. [15 U.S.C. § 57b-1]. Civil investigative demands

(a) Definitions

For purposes of this section:

(1) The terms "civil investigative demand" and "demand" mean any demand issued by the Commission under subsection (c)(1) of this section.

(2) The term "Commission investigation" means any inquiry conducted by a Commission investigator for the purpose of ascertaining whether any person is or has been engaged in any unfair or deceptive acts or practices in or affecting commerce (within the meaning of section 45(a)(1) of this title) or in any antitrust violations.

(3) The term "Commission investigator" means any attorney or investigator employed by the Commission who is charged with the duty of enforcing or carrying into effect any provisions relating to unfair or deceptive acts or practices in or affecting commerce (within the meaning of section 45(a)(1) of this title) or any provisions relating to antitrust violations.

(4) The term "custodian" means the custodian or any deputy custodian designated under section 57b-2(b)(2)(A) of this title.

(5) The term "documentary material" includes the original or any copy of any book, record, report, memorandum, paper, communication, tabulation, chart, or other document.

(6) The term "person" means any natural person, partnership, corporation, association, or other legal entity, including any person acting under color or authority of State law.

(7) The term "violation" means any act or omission constituting an unfair or deceptive act or practice in or affecting commerce (within the meaning of section 45(a)(1) of this title) or any antitrust violation.

(8) The term "antitrust violation" means—

(A) any unfair method of competition (within the meaning of section 45(a)(1) of this title);

(B) any violation of the Clayton Act [15 U.S.C.A. § 12 et seq.] or of any other Federal statute that prohibits, or makes available to the Commission a civil remedy with respect to, any restraint upon or monopolization of interstate or foreign trade or commerce;

(C) with respect to the International Antitrust Enforcement Assistance Act of 1994 [15 U.S.C.A. § 6201 et seq.], any violation of any of the foreign antitrust laws (as defined in section 12 of such Act [15 U.S.C.A. § 6211]) with respect to which a request is made under section 3 of such Act [15 U.S.C.A. § 6202]; or

(D) any activity in preparation for a merger, acquisition, joint venture, or similar transaction, which if consummated, may result in any such unfair method of competition or in any such violation.

(b) Actions conducted by Commission respecting unfair or deceptive acts or practices in or affecting commerce

For the purpose of investigations performed pursuant to this section with respect to unfair or deceptive acts or practices in or affecting commerce (within the meaning of section 45(a)(1) of this title), all actions of the Commission taken under section 46 and section 49 of this title shall be conducted pursuant to subsection (c) of this section.

(c) Issuance of demand; contents; service; verified return; sworn certificate; answers; taking of oral testimony

(1) Whenever the Commission has reason to believe that any person may be in possession, custody, or control of any documentary material or tangible things, or may have any information, relevant to unfair or deceptive acts or practices in or affecting commerce (within the meaning of section 45(a)(1) of this title), or to antitrust violations, the Commission may, before the institution of any proceedings under this subchapter, issue in writing, and cause to be served upon such person, a civil investigative demand requiring such person to produce such documentary material for inspection and copying or reproduction, to submit such tangible things, to file written reports or answers to questions, to give oral testimony concerning documentary material or other information, or to furnish any combination of such material, answers, or testimony.

(2) Each civil investigative demand shall state the nature of the conduct constituting the alleged violation which is under investigation and the provision of law applicable to such violation.

(3) Each civil investigative demand for the production of documentary material shall—

(A) describe each class of documentary material to be produced under the demand with such definiteness and certainty as to permit such material to be fairly identified;

(B) prescribe a return date or dates which will provide a reasonable period of time within which the material so demanded may be assembled and made available for inspection and copying or reproduction; and

(C) identify the custodian to whom such material shall be made available.

(4) Each civil investigative demand for the submission of tangible things shall—

(A) describe each class of tangible things to be submitted under the demand with such definiteness and certainty as to permit such things to be fairly identified;

(B) prescribe a return date or dates which will provide a reasonable period of time within which the things so demanded may be assembled and submitted; and

(C) identify the custodian to whom such things shall be submitted.

(5) Each civil investigative demand for written reports or answers to questions shall—

(A) propound with definiteness and certainty the reports to be produced or the questions to be answered;

(B) prescribe a date or dates at which time written reports or answers to questions shall be submitted; and

(C) identify the custodian to whom such reports or answers shall be submitted.

(6) Each civil investigative demand for the giving of oral testimony shall—

(A) prescribe a date, time, and place at which oral testimony shall be commenced; and

(B) identify a Commission investigator who shall conduct the investigation and the custodian to whom the transcript of such investigation shall be submitted.

(7) (A) Any civil investigative demand may be served by any Commission investigator at any place within the territorial jurisdiction of any court of the United States.

(B) Any such demand or any enforcement petition filed under this section may be served upon any person who is not found within the territorial jurisdiction of any court of the United States, in such manner as the Federal Rules of Civil Procedure prescribe for service in a foreign nation.

(C) To the extent that the courts of the United States have authority to assert jurisdiction over such person consistent with due process, the United States District Court for the District of Columbia shall have the same jurisdiction to take any action respecting compliance with this section by such person that such district court would have if such person were personally within the jurisdiction of such district court.

(8) Service of any civil investigative demand or any enforcement petition filed under this section may be made upon a partnership, corporation, association, or other legal entity by—

(A) delivering a duly executed copy of such demand or petition to any partner, executive officer, managing agent, or general agent of such partnership, corporation, association, or other legal entity, or to any agent of such partnership, corporation, association, or other legal entity authorized by appointment or by law to receive service of process on behalf of such partnership, corporation, association, or other legal entity;

(B) delivering a duly executed copy of such demand or petition to the principal office or place of business of the partnership, corporation, association, or other legal entity to be served; or

(C) depositing a duly executed copy in the United States mails, by registered or certified mail, return receipt requested, duly addressed to such partnership, corporation, association, or other legal entity at its principal office or place of business.

(9) Service of any civil investigative demand or of any enforcement petition filed under this section may be made upon any natural person by—

(A) delivering a duly executed copy of such demand or petition to the person to be served; or

(B) depositing a duly executed copy in the United States mails by registered or certified mail, return receipt requested, duly addressed to such person at his residence or principal office or place of business.

(10) A verified return by the individual serving any civil investigative demand or any enforcement petition filed under this section setting forth the manner of such service shall be proof of such service. In the case of service by registered or certified mail, such return shall be accompanied by the return post office receipt of delivery of such demand or enforcement petition.

(11) The production of documentary material in response to a civil investigative demand shall be made under a sworn certificate, in such form as the demand designates, by the person, if a natural person, to whom the demand is directed or, if not a natural person, by any person having knowledge of the facts and circumstances relating to such production, to the effect that all of the documentary material required by the demand and in the possession, custody, or control of the person to whom the demand is directed has been produced and made available to the custodian.

(12) The submission of tangible things in response to a civil investigative demand shall be made under a sworn certificate, in such form as the demand designates, by the person to whom the demand is directed or, if not a natural person, by any person having knowledge of the facts and circumstances relating to such production, to the effect that all of the tangible things required by

the demand and in the possession, custody, or control of the person to whom the demand is directed have been submitted to the custodian.

(13) Each reporting requirement or question in a civil investigative demand shall be answered separately and fully in writing under oath, unless it is objected to, in which event the reasons for the objection shall be stated in lieu of an answer, and it shall be submitted under a sworn certificate, in such form as the demand designates, by the person, if a natural person, to whom the demand is directed or, if not a natural person, by any person responsible for answering each reporting requirement or question, to the effect that all information required by the demand and in the possession, custody, control, or knowledge of the person to whom the demand is directed has been submitted.

(14) (A) Any Commission investigator before whom oral testimony is to be taken shall put the witness on oath or affirmation and shall personally, or by any individual acting under his direction and in his presence, record the testimony of the witness. The testimony shall be taken stenographically and transcribed. After the testimony is fully transcribed, the Commission investigator before whom the testimony is taken shall promptly transmit a copy of the transcript of the testimony to the custodian.

(B) Any Commission investigator before whom oral testimony is to be taken shall exclude from the place where the testimony is to be taken all other persons except the person giving the testimony, his attorney, the officer before whom the testimony is to be taken, and any stenographer taking such testimony.

(C) The oral testimony of any person taken pursuant to a civil investigative demand shall be taken in the judicial district of the United States in which such person resides, is found, or transacts business, or in such other place as may be agreed upon by the Commission investigator before whom the oral testimony of such person is to be taken and such person.

(D) (i) Any person compelled to appear under a civil investigative demand for oral testimony pursuant to this section may be accompanied, represented, and advised by an attorney. The attorney may advise such person, in confidence, either upon the request of such person or upon the initiative of the attorney, with respect to any question asked of such person.

(ii) Such person or attorney may object on the record to any question, in whole or in part, and shall briefly state for the record the reason for the objection. An objection may properly be made, received, and entered upon the record when it is claimed that such person is entitled to refuse to answer the question on grounds of any constitutional or other legal right or privilege, including the privilege against self-incrimination. Such person shall not otherwise object to or refuse to answer any question, and shall not himself or through his attorney otherwise interrupt the oral examination. If such person refuses to answer any question, the Commission may petition the district court of the United States pursuant to this section for an order compelling such person to answer such question.

(iii) If such person refuses to answer any question on grounds of the privilege against self-incrimination, the testimony of such person may be compelled in accordance with the provisions of section 6004 of Title 18.

(E) (i) After the testimony of any witness is fully transcribed, the Commission investigator shall afford the witness (who may be accompanied by an attorney) a reasonable opportunity to examine the transcript. The transcript shall be read to or by the witness, unless such examination and reading are waived by the witness. Any changes in form or substance which the witness desires to make shall be entered and identified upon the transcript by the Commission investigator with a statement of the reasons given by the witness for making such changes. The transcript shall then be signed by the witness, unless the witness in writing waives the signing, is ill, cannot be found, or refuses to sign.

(ii) If the transcript is not signed by the witness during the 30-day period following the date upon which the witness is first afforded a reasonable opportunity to examine it, the Commission investigator shall sign the transcript and state on the record the fact of the waiver, illness, absence of the witness, or the refusal to sign, together with any reasons given for the failure to sign.

(F) The Commission investigator shall certify on the transcript that the witness was duly sworn by him and that the transcript is a true record of the testimony given by the witness, and the Commission investigator shall promptly deliver the transcript or send it by registered or certified mail to the custodian.

(G) The Commission investigator shall furnish a copy of the transcript (upon payment of reasonable charges for the transcript) to the witness only, except that the Commission may for good cause limit such witness to inspection of the official transcript of his testimony.

(H) Any witness appearing for the taking of oral testimony pursuant to a civil investigative demand shall be entitled to the same fees and mileage which are paid to witnesses in the district courts of the United States.

(d) Procedures for demand material

Materials received as a result of a civil investigative demand shall be subject to the procedures established in section 57b-2 of this title.

(e) Petition for enforcement

Whenever any person fails to comply with any civil investigative demand duly served upon him under this section, or whenever satisfactory copying or reproduction of material requested pursuant to the demand cannot be accomplished and such person refuses to surrender such material, the Commission, through such officers or attorneys as it may designate, may file, in the district court of the United States for any judicial district in which such person resides, is found, or transacts business, and serve upon such person, a petition for an order of such court for the enforcement of this section. All process of any court to which application may be made as provided in this subsection may be served in any judicial district.

(f) Petition for order modifying or setting aside demand

(1) Not later than 20 days after the service of any civil investigative demand upon any person under subsection (c) of this section, or at any time before the return date specified in the demand, whichever period is shorter, or within such period exceeding 20 days after service or in excess of such return date as may be prescribed in writing, subsequent to service, by any Commission investigator named in the demand, such person may file with the Commission a petition for an order by the Commission modifying or setting aside the demand.

(2) The time permitted for compliance with the demand in whole or in part, as deemed proper and ordered by the Commission, shall not run during the pendency of such petition at the Commission, except that such person shall comply with any portions of the demand not sought to be modified or set aside. Such petition shall specify each ground upon which the petitioner relies in seeking such relief, and may be based upon any failure of the demand to comply with the provisions of this section, or upon any constitutional or other legal right or privilege of such person.

(g) Custodial control of documentary material, tangible things, reports, etc.

At any time during which any custodian is in custody or control of any documentary material, tangible things, reports, answers to questions, or transcripts of oral testimony given by any person in compliance with any civil investigative demand, such person may file, in the district court of the United States for the judicial district within which the office of such custodian is situated, and serve upon such custodian, a petition for an order of such court requiring the performance by such custodian of any duty imposed upon him by this section or section 57b-2 of this title.

(h) Jurisdiction of court

Whenever any petition is filed in any district court of the United States under this section, such court shall have jurisdiction to hear and determine the matter so presented, and to enter such order or orders as may be required to carry into effect the provisions of this section. Any final order so entered shall be subject to appeal pursuant to section 1291 of Title 28. Any disobedience of any final order entered under this section by any court shall be punished as a contempt of such court.

(i) Commission authority to issue subpoenas or make demand for information

Notwithstanding any other provision of law, the Commission shall have no authority to issue a subpoena or make a demand for information, under authority of this subchapter or any other provision of law, unless such subpoena or demand for information is signed by a Commissioner acting pursuant to a Commission resolution. The Commission shall not delegate the power conferred by this section to sign subpoenas or demands for information to any other person.

(j) Applicability of this section

The provisions of this section shall not—

(1) apply to any proceeding under section 45(b) of this title, any proceeding under section 11(b) of the Clayton Act (15 U.S.C. 21(b)), or any adjudicative proceeding under any other provision of law; or

(2) apply to or affect the jurisdiction, duties, or powers of any agency of the Federal Government, other than the Commission, regardless of whether such jurisdiction, duties, or powers are derived in whole or in part, by reference to this subchapter.

(Sept. 26, 1914, c. 311, § 20, as added May 28, 1980, Pub.L. 96-252, § 13, 94 Stat. 380, and amended Aug. 26, 1994, Pub.L. 103-312, § 7, 108 Stat. 1693; Nov. 2, 1994, Pub.L. 103-438, § 3(e)(2)(B), 108 Stat. 4598.)

§ 21 [15 U.S.C. § 57b-2]. Confidentiality

(a) Definitions

For purposes of this section:

(1) The term "material" means documentary material, tangible things, written reports or answers to questions, and transcripts of oral testimony.

(2) The term "Federal agency" has the meaning given it in section 552(e) of Title 5.

(b) Procedures respecting documents, tangible things, or transcripts of oral testimony received pursuant to compulsory process or investigation

(1) With respect to any document, tangible thing, or transcript of oral testimony received by the Commission pursuant to compulsory process in an investigation, a purpose of which is to determine whether any person may have violated any provision of the laws administered by the Commission, the procedures established in paragraph (2) through paragraph (7) shall apply.

(2) (A) The Commission shall designate a duly authorized agent to serve as custodian of documentary material, tangible things, or written reports or answers to questions, and transcripts of oral testimony, and such additional duly authorized agents as the Commission shall determine from time to time to be necessary to serve as deputies to the custodian.

(B) Any person upon whom any demand for the production of documentary material has been duly served shall make such material available for inspection and copying or reproduction to the custodian designated in such demand at the principal place of business of such person (or at such other place as such custodian and such person thereafter may agree and prescribe in writing or as the court may direct pursuant to section 57b-1(h) of this title) on the return date specified in such demand (or on such later date as such custodian may prescribe in writing). Such person may upon written agreement between such person and the custodian substitute copies for originals of all or any part of such material.

(3) (A) The custodian to whom any documentary material, tangible things, written reports or answers to questions, and transcripts of oral testimony are delivered shall take physical possession of such material, reports or answers, and transcripts, and shall be responsible for the use made of such material, reports or answers, and transcripts, and for the return of material, pursuant to the requirements of this section.

(B) The custodian may prepare such copies of the documentary material, written reports or answers to questions, and transcripts of oral testimony, and may make tangible things available, as may be required for official use by any duly authorized officer or employee of the Commission under regulations which shall be promulgated by the Commission. Notwithstanding subparagraph (C), such material, things, and transcripts may be used by any such officer or employee in connection with the taking of oral testimony under this section.

(C) Except as otherwise provided in this section, while in the possession of the custodian, no documentary material, tangible things, reports or answers to questions, and transcripts of oral testimony shall be available for examination by any individual other than a duly authorized officer or employee of the Commission without the consent of the person who produced the material, things, or transcripts. Nothing in this section is intended to prevent disclosure to either House of the Congress or to any committee or subcommittee of the Congress, except that the Commission immediately shall notify the owner or provider of any such information of a request for information designated as confidential by the owner or provider.

(D) While in the possession of the custodian and under such reasonable terms and conditions as the Commission shall prescribe—

(i) documentary material, tangible things, or written reports shall be available for examination by the person who produced the material, or by any duly authorized representative of such person; and

(ii) answers to questions in writing and transcripts of oral testimony shall be available for examination by the person who produced the testimony or by his attorney.

(4) Whenever the Commission has instituted a proceeding against a person, partnership, or corporation, the custodian may deliver to any officer or employee of the Commission documentary material, tangible things, written reports or answers to questions, and transcripts of oral testimony for official use in connection with such proceeding. Upon the completion of the proceeding, the

officer or employee shall return to the custodian any such material so delivered which has not been received into the record of the proceeding.

(5) if any documentary material, tangible things, written reports or answers to questions, and transcripts of oral testimony have been produced in the course of any investigation by any person pursuant to compulsory process and—

(A) any proceeding arising out of the investigation has been completed; or

(B) no proceeding in which the material may be used has been commenced within a reasonable time after completion of the examination and analysis of all such material and other information assembled in the course of the investigation;

then the custodian shall, upon written request of the person who produced the material, return to the person any such material which has not been received into the record of any such proceeding (other than copies of such material made by the custodian pursuant to paragraph (3)(B)).

(6) The custodian of any documentary material, written reports or answers to questions, and transcripts of oral testimony may deliver to any officers or employees of appropriate Federal law enforcement agencies, in response to a written request, copies of such material for use in connection with an investigation or proceeding under the jurisdiction of any such agency. The custodian of any tangible things may make such things available for inspection to such persons on the same basis. Such materials shall not be made available to any such agency until the custodian receives certification of any officer of such agency that such information will be maintained in confidence and will be used only for official law enforcement purposes. Such documentary material, results of inspections of tangible things, written reports or answers to questions, and transcripts of oral testimony may be used by any officer or employee of such agency only in such manner and subject to such conditions as apply to the Commission under this section. The custodian may make such materials available to any State law enforcement agency upon the prior certification of any officer of such agency that such information will be maintained in confidence and will be used only for official law enforcement purposes. The custodian may make such material available to any foreign law enforcement agency upon the prior certification of an appropriate official of any such foreign law enforcement agency, either by a prior agreement or memorandum of understanding with the Commission or by other written certification, that such material will be maintained in confidence and will be used only for official law enforcement purposes, if—

(A) the foreign law enforcement agency has set forth a bona fide legal basis for its authority to maintain the material in confidence;

(B) the materials are to be used for purposes of investigating, or engaging in enforcement proceedings related to, possible violations of—

(i) foreign laws prohibiting fraudulent or deceptive commercial practices, or other practices substantially similar to practices prohibited by any law administered by the Commission;

(ii) a law administered by the Commission, if disclosure of the material would further a Commission investigation or enforcement proceeding; or

(iii) with the approval of the Attorney General, other foreign criminal laws, if such foreign criminal laws are offenses defined in or covered by a criminal mutual legal assistance treaty in force between the government of the United States and the foreign law enforcement agency's government

(C) the appropriate Federal banking agency (as defined in section 1813(q) of Title 12) or, in the case of a Federal credit union, the National Credit Union Administration, has given its prior approval if the materials to be provided under subparagraph (B) are requested by the foreign law enforcement agency for the purpose of investigating, or engaging in enforcement proceedings based on, possible violations of law by a bank, a savings and loan institution described in section 57a(f)(3) of this title, or a Federal credit union described in section 57a(f)(4) of this title; and

(D) the foreign law enforcement agency is not from a foreign state that the Secretary of State has determined, in accordance with section 2405(j) of the Appendix to Title 50, has repeatedly provided support for acts of international terrorism, unless and until such determination is rescinded pursuant to section 2405(j)(4) of the Appendix to Title 50.

Nothing in the preceding sentence authorizes the disclosure of material obtained in connection with the administration of the Federal antitrust laws or foreign antitrust laws (as defined in paragraphs (5) and (7), respectively, of section 6211 of this title to any officer or employee of a foreign law enforcement agency.

(7) In the event of the death, disability, or separation from service in the Commission of the custodian of any documentary material, tangible things, written reports or answers to questions, and transcripts of oral testimony produced under any demand issued under this subchapter, or the official relief of the custodian from responsibility for the custody and control of such material, the Commission promptly shall—

(A) designate under paragraph (2)(A) another duly authorized agent to serve as custodian of such material; and

(B) transmit in writing to the person who produced the material or testimony notice as to the identity and address of the successor so designated.

Any successor designated under paragraph (2)(A) as a result of the requirements of this paragraph shall have (with regard to the material involved) all duties and responsibilities imposed by this section upon his predecessor in office with regard to such material, except that he shall not be held responsible for any default or dereliction which occurred before his designation.

(c) Information considered confidential

(1) All information reported to or otherwise obtained by the Commission which is not subject to the requirements of subsection (b) of this section shall be considered confidential when so marked by the person supplying the information and shall not be disclosed, except in accordance with the procedures established in paragraph (2) and paragraph (3).

(2) If the Commission determines that a document marked confidential by the person supplying it may be disclosed because it is not a trade secret or commercial or financial information which is obtained from any person and which is privileged or confidential, within the meaning of section 46(f) of this title, then the Commission shall notify such person in writing that the Commission intends to disclose the document at a date not less than 10 days after the date of receipt of notification.

(3) Any person receiving such notification may, if he believes disclosure of the document would cause disclosure of a trade secret, or commercial or financial information which is obtained from any person and which is privileged or confidential, within the meaning of section 46(f) of this title, before the date set for release of the document, bring an action in the district court of the United States for the district within which the documents are located or in the United States District Court for the District of Columbia to restrain disclosure of the document. Any person receiving such notification may file with the appropriate district court or court of appeals of the United States, as appropriate, an application for a stay of disclosure. The documents shall not be disclosed until the court has ruled on the application for a stay.

(d) Particular disclosures allowed

(1) The provisions of subsection (c) of this section shall not be construed to prohibit—

(A) the disclosure of information to either House of the Congress or to any committee or subcommittee of the Congress, except that the Commission immediately shall notify the owner or provider of any such information of a request for information designated as confidential by the owner or provider;

(B) the disclosure of the results of any investigation or study carried out or prepared by the Commission, except that no information shall be identified nor shall information be disclosed in such a manner as to disclose a trade secret of any person supplying the trade secret, or to disclose any commercial or financial information which is obtained from any person and which is privileged or confidential;

(C) the disclosure of relevant and material information in Commission adjudicative proceedings or in judicial proceedings to which the Commission is a party; or

(D) the disclosure to a Federal agency of disaggregated information obtained in accordance with section 3512 of Title

44, except that the recipient agency shall use such disaggregated information for economic, statistical, or policymaking purposes only, and shall not disclose such information in an individually identifiable form.

(2) Any disclosure of relevant and material information in Commission adjudicative proceedings or in judicial proceedings to which the Commission is a party shall be governed by the rules of the Commission for adjudicative proceedings or by court rules or orders, except that the rules of the Commission shall not be amended in a manner inconsistent with the purposes of this section

(e) Effect on other statutory provisions limiting disclosure

Nothing in this section shall supersede any statutory provision which expressly prohibits or limits particular disclosures by the Commission, or which authorizes disclosures to any other Federal agency.

(f) Exemption from public disclosure

(1) In general.

Any material which is received by the Commission in any investigation, a purpose of which is to determine whether any person may have violated any provision of the laws administered by the Commission, and which is provided pursuant to any compulsory process under this subchapter or which is provided voluntarily in place of such compulsory process shall not be required to be disclosed under section 552 of Title 5, or any other provision of law, except as provided in paragraph (2)(B) of this section

(2) Material obtained from a foreign source

(A) In general

Any material which is received by the Commission in any investigation, a purpose of which is to determine whether any person may have violated any provision of the laws administered by the Commission, and which is provided pursuant to any compulsory process under this subchapter or which is provided voluntarily in place of such compulsory process shall not be required to be disclosed under section 552 of Title 5, or any other provision of law, except as provided in paragraph (2)(B) of this section

(i) any material obtained from a foreign law enforcement agency or other foreign government agency, if the foreign law enforcement agency or other foreign government agency has requested confidential treatment, or has precluded such disclosure under other use limitations, as a condition of providing the material;

(ii) any material reflecting a consumer complaint obtained from any other foreign source, if that foreign source supplying the material has requested confidential treatment as a condition of providing the material; or

(iii) any material reflecting a consumer complaint submitted to a Commission reporting mechanism sponsored in part by foreign law enforcement agencies or other foreign government agencies.

(B) Savings provision

Nothing in this subsection shall authorize the Commission to withhold information from the Congress or prevent the Commission from complying with an order of a court of the United States in an action commenced by the United States or the Commission.

(Sept. 26, 1914, c. 311, § 21, as added May 28, 1980, Pub.L. 96-252, § 14, 94 Stat. 385, and amended Aug. 26, 1994, Pub.L. 103-312, § 8, 108 Stat. 1694; Dec. 22, 2006, Pub.L. 109-455, § 6, 120 Stat. 3376.)

§ 22. [15 U.S.C. § 57b-3]. Rulemaking process

(a) Definitions

For purposes of this section:

(1) The term "rule" means any rule promulgated by the Commission under section 46 or section 57a of this title, except that such term does not include interpretive rules, rules involving Commission management or personnel, general statements of policy, or rules relating to Commission organization, procedure, or practice. Such term does not include any amendment to a rule unless the Commission—

(A) estimates that such amendment will have an annual effect on the national economy of $100,000,000 or more;

(B) estimates that such amendment will cause a substantial change in the cost or price of goods or services which are used extensively by particular industries, which are supplied extensively in particular geographic regions, or which are acquired in significant quantities by the Federal Government, or by State or local governments; or

(C) otherwise determines that such amendment will have a significant impact upon persons subject to regulation under such amendment and upon consumers.

(2) The term "rulemaking" means any Commission process for formulating or amending a rule.

(b) Notice of proposed rulemaking; regulatory analysis; contents; issuance

(1) In any case in which the Commission publishes notice of a proposed rulemaking, the Commission shall issue a preliminary regulatory analysis relating to the proposed rule involved. Each preliminary regulatory analysis shall contain—

(A) a concise statement of the need for, and the objectives of, the proposed rule;

(B) a description of any reasonable alternatives to the proposed rule which may accomplish the stated objective of the rule in a manner consistent with applicable law; and

(C) for the proposed rule, and for each of the alternatives described in the analysis, a preliminary analysis of the projected benefits and any adverse economic effects and any other effects, and of the effectiveness of the proposed rule and each alternative in meeting the stated objectives of the proposed rule.

(2) In any case in which the Commission promulgates a final rule, the Commission shall issue a final regulatory analysis relating to the final rule. Each final regulatory analysis shall contain—

(A) a concise statement of the need for, and the objectives of, the final rule;

(B) a description of any alternatives to the final rule which were considered by the Commission;

(C) an analysis of the projected benefits and any adverse economic effects and any other effects of the final rule;

(D) an explanation of the reasons for the determination of the Commission that the final rule will attain its objectives in a manner consistent with applicable law and the reasons the particular alternative was chosen; and

(E) a summary of any significant issues raised by the comments submitted during the public comment period in response to the preliminary regulatory analysis, and a summary of the assessment by the Commission of such issues.

(3) (A) In order to avoid duplication or waste, the Commission is authorized to—

(i) consider a series of closely related rules as one rule for purposes of this subsection; and

(ii) whenever appropriate, incorporate any data or analysis contained in a regulatory analysis issued under this subsection in the statement of basis and purpose to accompany any rule promulgated under section 57a(a)(1)(B) of this title, and incorporate by reference in any preliminary or final regulatory analysis information contained in a notice of proposed rulemaking or a statement of basis and purpose.

(B) The Commission shall include, in each notice of proposed rulemaking and in each publication of a final rule, a statement of the manner in which the public may obtain copies of the preliminary and final regulatory analyses. The Commission may charge a reasonable fee for the copying and mailing of regulatory analyses. The regulatory analyses shall be furnished without charge or at a reduced charge if the Commission determines that waiver or reduction of the fee is in the public interest because furnishing the information primarily benefits the general public.

(4) The Commission is authorized to delay the completion of any of the requirements established in this subsection by publishing in the Federal Register, not later than the date of publication of the final rule involved, a finding that the final rule is being promulgated in response to an emergency which makes timely compliance with the provisions of this subsection impracticable.

Such publication shall include a statement of the reasons for such finding.

(5) The requirements of this subsection shall not be construed to alter in any manner the substantive standards applicable to any action by the Commission, or the procedural standards otherwise applicable to such action.

(c) Judicial review

(1) The contents and adequacy of any regulatory analysis prepared or issued by the Commission under this section, including the adequacy of any procedure involved in such preparation or issuance, shall not be subject to any judicial review in any court, except that a court, upon review of a rule pursuant to section 57a(e) of this title, may set aside such rule if the Commission has failed entirely to prepare a regulatory analysis.

(2) Except as specified in paragraph (1), no Commission action may be invalidated, remanded, or otherwise affected by any court on account of any failure to comply with the requirements of this section.

(3) The provisions of this subsection do not alter the substantive or procedural standards otherwise applicable to judicial review of any action by the Commission.

(d) Regulatory agenda; contents; publication dates in Federal Register

(1) The Commission shall publish at least semiannually a regulatory agenda. Each regulatory agenda shall contain a list of rules which the Commission intends to propose or promulgate during the 12-month period following the publication of the agenda. On the first Monday in October of each year, the Commission shall publish in the Federal Register a schedule showing the dates during the current fiscal year on which the semiannual regulatory agenda of the Commission will be published.

(2) For each rule listed in a regulatory agenda, the Commission shall—

(A) describe the rule;

(B) state the objectives of and the legal basis for the rule; and

(C) specify any dates established or anticipated by the Commission for taking action, including dates for advance notice of proposed rulemaking, notices of proposed rulemaking, and final action by the Commission.

(3) Each regulatory agenda shall state the name, office address, and office telephone number of the Commission officer or employee responsible for responding to any inquiry relating to each rule listed.

(4) The Commission shall not propose or promulgate a rule which was not listed on a regulatory agenda unless the Commission publishes with the rule an explanation of the reasons the rule was omitted from such agenda.

(Sept. 26, 1914, c. 311, § 22, as added May 28, 1980, Pub.L. 96-252, § 15, 94 Stat. 388.)

§ 23. [15 U.S.C. § 57b-4]. Good faith reliance on actions of Board of Governors

(a) "Board of Governors" defined

For purposes of this section, the term "Board of Governors" means the Board of Governors of the Federal Reserve System.

(b) Use as defense

Notwithstanding any other provision of law, if—

(1) any person, partnership, or corporation engages in any conduct or practice which allegedly constitutes a violation of any Federal law with respect to which the Board of Governors of the Federal Reserve System has rulemaking authority; and

(2) such person, partnership, or corporation engaged in such conduct or practice in good faith reliance upon, and in conformity with, any rule, regulation, statement of interpretation, or statement of approval prescribed or issued by the Board of Governors under such Federal law;

then such good faith reliance shall constitute a defense in any administrative or judicial proceeding commenced against such person, partnership, or corporation by the Commission under this subchapter or in any administrative or judicial proceeding commenced against such person, partnership, or corporation by the Attorney General of the United States, upon request made by the Commission, under any provision of law.

(c) Applicability of subsection (b)

The provisions of subsection (b) of this section shall apply regardless of whether any rule, regulation, statement of interpretation, or statement of approval prescribed or issued by the Board of Governors is amended, rescinded, or held to be invalid by judicial authority or any other authority after a person, partnership, or corporation has engaged in any conduct or practice in good faith reliance upon, and in conformity with, such rule, regulation, statement of interpretation, or statement of approval.

(d) Request for issuance of statement or interpretation concerning conduct or practice

If, in any case in which—

(1) the Board of Governors has rulemaking authority with respect to any Federal law; and

(2) the Commission is authorized to enforce the requirements of such Federal law;

any person, partnership, or corporation submits a request to the Board of Governors for the issuance of any statement of interpretation or statement of approval relating to any conduct or practice of such person, partnership, or corporation which may be subject to the requirements of such Federal law, then the Board of Governors shall dispose of such request as soon as practicable after the receipt of such request.

(Sept. 26, 1914, c. 311, § 23, as added May 28, 1980, Pub.L. 96-252, § 16, 94 Stat. 390.)

§ 24. [15 U.S.C. 57b-5]. Agricultural cooperatives.

(a) The Commission shall not have any authority to conduct any study, investigation, or prosecution of any agricultural cooperative for any conduct which, because of the provisions of sections 291 and 292 of Title 7, is not a violation of any of the antitrust Acts or this subchapter.

(b) The Commission shall not have any authority to conduct any study or investigation of any agricultural marketing orders.

(Sept. 26, 1914, c. 311, § 24, as added Aug. 26, 1994, Pub.L. 103-312, § 2, 108 Stat. 1691.)

§ 25. [15 U.S.C. § 57c]. Authorization of appropriations

There are authorized to be appropriated to carry out the functions, powers, and duties of the Commission not to exceed $92,700,000 for fiscal year 1994; not to exceed $99,000,000 for fiscal year 1995; not to exceed $102,000,000 for fiscal year 1996; not to exceed $107,000,000 for fiscal year 1997; and not to exceed $111,000,000 for fiscal year 1998.

(Sept. 26, 1914, c. 311, § 25, formerly § 20, as added Jan. 4, 1975, Pub.L. 93-637, Title II, § 207, 88 Stat. 2203, and amended May 29, 1976, Pub.L. 94-299, § 1, 90 Stat. 588; renumbered § 24 and amended May 28, 1980, Pub.L. 96-252, §§ 13, 17, 94 Stat. 380, 391; renumbered § 25 and amended Aug. 26, 1994, Pub.L. 103-312, §§ 2, 14, 108 Stat. 1691, 1697; Oct. 1, 1996, Pub.L. 104-216, § 2, 110 Stat. 3019.)

§ 26. [15 U.S.C. § 58] Short title

This subchapter may be cited as the "Federal Trade Commission Act."

(Sept. 26, 1914, c. 311, § 26, formerly § 18, as added Mar. 21, 1938, c. 49, § 4, 52 Stat. 114; renumbered § 21, Jan. 4, 1975, Pub.L. 93-637, Title II, § 202(a), 88 Stat. 2193; renumbered § 25, May 28, 1980, Pub.L. 96-252, § 13, 94 Stat. 380; renumbered § 26, Aug. 26, 1994, Pub.L. 103-312, § 2, 108 Stat. 1691; renumbered § 28, Dec. 22, 2006, Pub.L. 109-455, § 11(1), 120 Stat. 3381.)

PART 2
REGULATIONS

4

BUSINESS ADVISORY OPINIONS

FEDERAL TRADE COMMISSION

16 C.F.R. § 1.1–1.4

§ 1.1 Policy.

(a) Any person, partnership, or corporation may request advice from the Commission with respect to a course of action which the requesting party proposes to pursue. The Commission will consider such requests for advice and inform the requesting party of the Commission's views, where practicable, under the following circumstances.

(1) The matter involves a substantial or novel question of fact or law and there is no clear Commission or court precedent; or

(2) The subject matter of the request and consequent publication of Commission advice is of significant public interest.

(b) The Commission has authorized its staff to consider all requests for advice and to render advice, where practicable, in those circumstances in which a Commission opinion would not be warranted. Hypothetical questions will not be answered, and a request for advice will ordinarily be considered inappropriate where:

(1) The same or substantially the same course of action is under investigation or is or has been the subject of a current proceeding involving the Commission or another governmental agency, or

(2) an informed opinion cannot be made or could be made only after extensive investigation, clinical study, testing, or collateral inquiry.

[44 FR 21624, Apr. 11, 1979; 44 FR 23515, Apr. 20, 1979; 54 FR 14072, April 7, 1989]

SOURCE: 32 FR 8444, June 13, 1967, unless otherwise noted.

AUTHORITY: Sec. 6, 38 Stat. 721; 15 U.S.C. 46, unless otherwise noted.

§ 1.2 Procedure.

(a) Application. The request for advice or interpretation should be submitted in writing (one original and two copies) to the Secretary of the Commission and should: (1) State clearly the question(s) that the applicant wishes resolved; (2) cite the provision of law under which the question arises; and (3) state all facts which the applicant believes to be material. In addition, the identity of the companies and other persons involved should be disclosed. Letters relating to unnamed companies or persons may not be answered. Submittal of additional facts may be requested prior to the rendering of any advice.

(b) Compliance matters. If the request is for advice as to whether the proposed course of action may violate an outstanding order to cease and desist issued by the Commission, such request will be considered as provided for in § 2.41 of this chapter.

[44 FR 21624, Apr. 11, 1979, as amended at 44 FR 40638, July 12, 1979]

SOURCE: 32 FR 8444, June 13, 1967, unless otherwise noted.

AUTHORITY: Sec. 6, 38 Stat. 721; 15 U.S.C. 46, unless otherwise noted.

§ 1.3 Advice.

(a) On the basis of the materials submitted, as well as any other information available, and if practicable, the Commission or its staff will inform the requesting party of its views.

(b) Any advice given by the Commission is without prejudice to the right of the Commission to reconsider the questions involved and, where the public interest requires, to rescind or revoke the action. Notice of such rescission or revocation will be given to the requesting party so that he may discontinue the course of action taken pursuant to the Commission's advice. The Commission will not proceed against the requesting party with respect to any action taken in good faith reliance upon the Commission's advice under this section, where all the relevant facts were fully, completely, and accurately presented to the Commission and where such action was promptly discontinued upon notification of rescission or revocation of the Commission's approval.

(c) Advice rendered by the staff is without prejudice to the right of the Commission later to rescind the advice and, where appropriate, to commence an enforcement proceeding.

[44 FR 21624, Apr. 11, 1979]

SOURCE: 32 FR 8444, June 13, 1967, unless otherwise noted.

AUTHORITY: Sec. 6, 38 Stat. 721; 15 U.S.C. 46, unless otherwise noted.

§ 1.4 Public disclosure.

Written advice rendered pursuant to this Section and requests therefor, including names and details, will be placed in the Commission's public record immediately after the requesting party has received the advice, subject to any limitations on public disclosure arising from statutory restrictions, the Commission's rules, and the public interest. A request for confidential treatment of information submitted in connection with the questions should be made separately.

[44 FR 21624, Apr. 11, 1979]

SOURCE: 32 FR 8444, June 13, 1967, unless otherwise noted.

AUTHORITY: Sec. 6, 38 Stat. 721; 15 U.S.C. 46, unless otherwise noted.

5

BUSINESS REVIEW PROCEDURE

ANTITRUST DIVISION, U.S. DEPARTMENT OF JUSTICE

28 C.F.R. § 50.6

§ 50.6 Antitrust Division business review procedure.

Although the Department of Justice is not authorized to give advisory opinions to private parties, for several decades the Antitrust Division has been willing in certain circumstances to review proposed business conduct and state its enforcement intentions. This originated with a "railroad release" procedure under which the Division would forego the initiation of criminal antitrust proceedings. The procedure was subsequently expanded to encompass a "merger clearance" procedure under which the Division would state its present enforcement intention with respect to a merger or acquisition; and the Department issued a written statement entitled "Business Review Procedure." That statement has been revised several times.

1. A request for a business review letter must be submitted in writing to the Assistant Attorney General, Antitrust Division, Department of Justice, Washington, D.C. 20530.

2. The Division will consider only requests with respect to proposed business conduct, which may involve either domestic or foreign commerce.

3. The Division may, in its discretion, refuse to consider a request.

4. A business review letter shall have no application to any party which does not join in the request therefor.

5. The requesting parties are under an affirmative obligation to make full and true disclosure with respect to the business conduct for which review is requested. Each request must be accompanied by all relevant data including background information, complete copies of all operative documents and detailed statements of all collateral oral understandings, if any. All parties requesting the review letter must provide the Division with whatever additional information or documents the Division may thereafter request in order to review the matter. Such additional information, if furnished orally, shall be promptly confirmed in writing. In connection with any request for review the Division will also conduct whatever independent investigation it believes is appropriate.

6. No oral clearance, release or other statement purporting to bind the enforcement discretion of the Division may be given. The requesting party may rely upon only a written business review letter signed by the Assistant Attorney General in charge of the Antitrust Division or his delegate.

7. (a) If the business conduct for which review is requested is subject to approval by a regulatory agency, a review request may be considered before agency approval has been obtained only where it appears that exceptional and unnecessary burdens might otherwise be imposed on the party or

parties requesting review, or where the agency specifically requests that a party or parties request review. However, any business review letter issued in these as in any other circumstances will state only the Department's present enforcement intentions under the antitrust laws. It shall in no way be taken to indicate the Department's views on the legal or factual issues that may be raised before the regulatory agency, or in an appeal from the regulatory agency's decision. In particular, the issuance of such a letter is not to be represented to mean that the Division believes that there are no anticompetitive consequences warranting agency consideration.

(b) The submission of a request for a business review, or its pendency, shall in no way alter any responsibility of any party to comply with the Premerger Notification provisions of the Antitrust Improvements Act of 1976, 15 U.S.C. 18A, and the regulations promulgated thereunder, 16 CFR, Part 801.

8. After review of a request submitted hereunder the Division may: state its present enforcement intention with respect to the proposed business conduct; decline to pass on the request; or take such other position or action as it considers appropriate.

9. A business review letter states only the enforcement intention of the Division as of the date of the letter, and the Division remains completely free to bring whatever action or proceeding it subsequently comes to believe is required by the public interest. As to a stated present intention not to bring an action, however, the Division has never exercised its right to bring a criminal action where there has been full and true disclosure at the time of presenting the request.

10. (a) Simultaneously upon notifying the requesting party of and Division action described in paragraph 8, the business review request, and the Division's letter in response shall be indexed and placed in a file available to the public upon request.

(b) On that date or within thirty days after the date upon which the Division takes any action as described in paragraph 8, the information supplied to support the business review request and any other information supplied by the requesting party in connection with the transaction that is the subject of the business review request, shall be indexed and placed in a file with the request and the Division's letter, available to the public upon request. This file shall remain open for one year, after which time it shall be closed and the documents either returned to the requesting party or otherwise disposed of, at the discretion of the Antitrust Division.

(c) Prior to the time the information described in subparagraphs (a) and (b) is indexed and made publicly available in accordance with the terms of that subparagraph, the requesting party may ask the Division to delay making public some or all of such information. However the requesting party must: (1) Specify precisely the documents or parts thereof that he asks not be made public; (2) state the minimum period of time during which nondisclosure is considered necessary; and (3) justify the request for non-disclosure, both as to content and time, by showing good cause therefor, including a showing that disclosure would have a detrimental effect upon the requesting party's operations or relationships with actual or potential customers, employees, suppliers (including suppliers of credit), stockholders, or competitors. The Department of Justice, in its discretion, shall make the final determination as to whether good cause for non-disclosure has been shown.

(d) Nothing contained in subparagraphs (a), (b) and (c) shall limit the Division's right, in its discretion, to issue a press release describing generally the identity of the requesting party or parties and the nature of action taken by the Division upon the request.

(e) This paragraph reflects a policy determination by the Justice Department and is subject to any limitations on public disclosure arising from statutory restrictions, Executive Order, or the national interest

11. Any requesting party may withdraw a request for review at any time. The Division remains free, however, to submit such comments to such requesting party as it deems appropriate. Failure to take action after receipt of documents or information whether submitted pursuant to this procedure or otherwise, does not in any way limit or stop the Division from taking such action at such time thereafter as it deems appropriate. The Division reserves the right to retain documents submitted to it under this procedure or otherwise and to use them for all governmental purposes.

[42 FR 11831, Mar. 1, 1977]

SOURCE: 50 FR 51677, Dec. 19, 1985; 51 FR 27022, July 29, 1986; 53 FR 8452, March 15, 1988; 56 FR 32327, July 16, 1991; Order No. 2013–96, 61 FR 13764, March 28, 1996; 61 FR 49260, Sept. 19, 1996; Order No. 2667–2003, 68 FR 18120, April 15, 2003; Order No. 2807–2006, 71 FR 11160, March 6, 2006; Order No. 3314–2011, 76 FR 76042, Dec. 6, 2011; Order No. 3420–2014, 79 FR 10990, Feb. 27, 2014.

AUTHORITY: 5 U.S.C. 301; 18 U.S.C. 1162; 28 U.S.C. 509, 510, 516, and 519; 42 U.S.C. 1921 et seq.,1973c; and Pub.L. 107–273, 116 Stat. 1758, 1824.

6

PILOT EXPEDITED BUSINESS REVIEW PROGRAM

ANTITRUST DIVISION, U.S. DEPARTMENT OF JUSTICE

58 FEDERAL REGISTER 6132 (JANUARY 26, 1993)

Business Reviews

Persons concerned about the legality under the antitrust laws of proposed business conduct may ask the Department of Justice for a statement of its current enforcement intentions with respect to that conduct pursuant to the Department's Business Review Procedure. See 28 CFR § 50.6.

The Department believes that the business review process provides the business community an important opportunity to receive guidance from the Department with respect to the scope, interpretation, and application of the antitrust laws to particular proposed conduct. The Department realizes, however, that if the business review process is not timely, the value of the process, and therefore its utilization, may be diminished.

Two of the most frequent types of business review requests the Department has received have involved proposals to form joint ventures or to collect and disseminate business information. Because of the nature of these requests, the Department often finds it difficult to opine on such matters based solely on the information typically provided with the initial requests. Consequently, the Department must subsequently seek additional information. This inevitably adds time and expense to the business review procedure.

In an effort to expedite the business review process with respect to these two types of requests, the Department will offer parties seeking a business review determination the option of providing certain specified information and documents contemporaneously with their initial business review submissions. Where the specified information and documents are provided, and where such submissions provide an adequate basis upon which to determine the Department's enforcement intentions, the Department will make its best effort to resolve the business review request within sixty to ninety days.

This program is subject to the following conditions:

1. The request must comply with the procedures for business reviews specified in 28 CFR 50.6.

2. Parties invoking this expedited procedure must represent in writing that they have undertaken a good faith search for the documents and information specified herein and, where applicable, have provided all responsive material.

3. The expedited procedure should not be interpreted as a representation by the Department that it will not request additional documents and information where necessary to assess the conduct under review.

4. The Department is unable to commit to a rigid deadline for processing business review requests. The time frames specified herein are targets, not deadlines.

5. This program is being implemented on a pilot basis. The Department reserves the right to alter the expedited review procedure at any time.

Parties seeking review determinations are welcome to submit such additional information as they deem appropriate to assist the Department in understanding the proposed conduct.

Information and Documents to Be Submitted

A. Joint Ventures

Information sufficient to show:

1. The name of the venture, the address of its principal place of business, and its legal form and ownership structure;

2. The persons or firms expected to participate in the venture and the nature of their contribution;

3. The purposes and objectives of the venture, together with any limitations on the nature or scope of its activities or operations;

4. The products or services the venture will develop, produce, market or distribute;

5. The extent to which participants in the venture currently develop, produce, market or distribute products or services that will be developed, produced, marketed or distributed by the venture;

6. The identity and competitive significance (described in terms of market shares, capacities, etc.) of all persons or firms that participate in the relevant product and geographic markets in which the venture will operate;

7. Any restrictions on the ability of participants in the venture to compete with the venture, individually or through other entities;

8. Any restrictions on the flow of information from the venture to its owners;

9. The ten largest customers (actual or projected) for any products or services that will be offered by the venture in the relevant geographic market and an estimate of their annual purchases;

10. The requirements for entry into any relevant product or geographic market in which the venture will operate, together with the identity of other persons or firms believed to be positioned to enter within one or two years; and

11. Any business synergies, efficiencies or other benefits likely to flow from the venture.

All documents:

1. Reflecting or effectuating formation of the venture, including charters, by-laws, articles of incorporation, and partnership, joint venture or asset purchase agreements, or the most recent drafts of such documents;

2. Discussing, reflecting or representing the business plans or strategies for the venture;

3. Prepared within two years prior to formation of the venture, discussing, reflecting or representing the business plans or strategies of any venture participant with respect to any product or service that will be offered by the venture; and

4. Discussing or relating to the legality or illegality under the antitrust laws of the venture, or the impact of the venture on competition or the price of any product or service.

B. Information Exchanges

Information sufficient to show:

1. The persons or firms expected to participate in the information exchange;

2. The purposes and objectives of the information exchange;

3. The nature, type, timeliness, and specificity of the information to be exchanged (a sample of all information to be exchanged should be provided);

4. The method by which the information will be exchanged;

5. The characteristics of the market(s) in which the information will be exchanged, including the product(s) or services(s) related to the information to be exchanged, the homogeneity of the product(s) or service(s), the pricing and marketing practices typically employed by firms in the market(s), and the availability of information concerning market conditions, individual transactions and individual competitors;

6. The identity and competitive significance (described in terms of market shares, capacities, etc.) of persons or firms that participate in the relevant product and geographic markets, but will not participate in the information exchange;

7. The ten largest customers in the relevant geographic market for any product(s) or service(s) involved in the information exchange and an estimate of their annual purchases;

8. Any safeguards that are planned to prevent disclosure of firm-specific information to competitors; and

9. Any business synergies, efficiencies or other benefits likely to flow from the venture.

All documents:

1. Reflecting or representing the agreement(s) among the parties to exchange information or the most recent drafts of such documents; and

2. Discussing or relating to the legality or illegality under the antitrust laws of the information exchange or the impact of the information exchange on competition or the price of any product or service.

7

SENTENCING GUIDELINES FOR THE UNITED STATES COURTS

U.S. SENTENCING COMMISSION[1]

TITLE 18. CRIMES AND CRIMINAL PROCEDURE

CHAPTER TWO. OFFENSE CONDUCT

PART R. ANTITRUST OFFENSES

18 U.S.C. Appx § 2R1.1

§ 2R1.1. Bid-Rigging, Price-Fixing or Market-Allocation Agreements Among Competitors

(a) Base Offense Level: 12.

(b) Specific Offense Characteristics

(1) If the conduct involved participation in an agreement to submit non-competitive bids, increase by 1 level.

(2) If the volume of commerce attributable to the defendant was more than $ 1,000,000, adjust the offense level as follows:

Volume of Commerce (Apply the Greatest)	Adjustment to Offense Level
(A) More than $1,000,000	add 2
(B) More than $10,000,000	add 4
(C) More than $40,000,000	add 6
(D) More than $100,000,000	add 8
(E) More than $250,000,000	add 10
(F) More than $500,000,000	add 12
(G) More than $1,000,000,000	add 14
(H) More than $1,500,000,000	add 16

For purposes of this guideline, the volume of commerce attributable to an individual participant in a conspiracy is the volume of commerce done by him or his principal in goods or services that were affected by the violation. When multiple counts or conspiracies are involved, the volume of commerce should be treated cumulatively to determine a single, combined offense level.

(c) Special Instructions for Fines

(1) For an individual, the guideline fine range shall be from one to five percent of the volume of commerce, but not less than $ 20,000.

(d) Special Instructions for Fines—Organizations

[1] Following United States v. Booker, 125 S. Ct. 738 (2005), the Sentencing Guidelines are no longer mandatory in the federal courts, although they continue to guide sentencing discretion.

(1) In lieu of the pecuniary loss under subsection (a)(3) of § 8C2.4 (Base Fine), use 20 percent of the volume of affected commerce.

(2) When applying § 8C2.6 (Minimum and Maximum Multipliers), neither the minimum nor maximum multiplier shall be less than 0.75.

(3) In a bid-rigging case in which the organization submitted one or more complementary bids, use as the organization's volume of commerce the greater of (A) the volume of commerce done by the organization in the goods or services that were affected by the violation, or (B) the largest contract on which the organization submitted a complementary bid in connection with the bid-rigging conspiracy.

Commentary

Statutory Provisions: 15 U.S.C. §§ 1, 3(b). For additional statutory provision(s), see Appendix A (Statutory Index).

Application Notes:

1. Application of Chapter Three (Adjustments). Sections 3B1.1 (Aggravating Role), 3B1.2 (Mitigating Role), 3B1.3 (Abuse of Position of Trust or Use of Special Skill), and 3C1.1 (Obstructing or Impeding the Administration of Justice) may be relevant in determining the seriousness of the defendant's offense. For example, if a sales manager organizes or leads the price-fixing activity of five or more participants, the 4-level increase at § 3B1.1 (a) should be applied to reflect the defendant's aggravated role in the offense. For purposes of applying § 3B1.2, an individual defendant should be considered for a mitigating role adjustment only if he were responsible in some minor way for his firm's participation in the conspiracy.

2. Considerations in Setting Fine for Individuals. In setting the fine for individuals, the court should consider the extent of the defendant's participation in the offense, the defendant's role, and the degree to which the defendant personally profited from the offense (including salary, bonuses, and career enhancement). If the court concludes that the defendant lacks the ability to pay the guideline fine, it should impose community service in lieu of a portion of the fine. The community service should be equally as burdensome as a fine.

3. The fine for an organization is determined by applying Chapter Eight (Sentencing of Organizations). In selecting a fine for an organization within the guideline fine range, the court should consider both the gain to the organization from the offense and the loss caused by the organization. It is estimated that the average gain from price-fixing is 10 percent of the selling price. The loss from price-fixing exceeds the gain because, among other things, injury is inflicted upon consumers who are unable or for other reasons do not buy the product at the higher prices. Because the loss from price-fixing exceeds the gain, subsection (d)(1) provides that 20 percent of the volume of affected commerce is to be used in lieu of the pecuniary loss under § 8C2.4(a)(3). The purpose for specifying a percent of the volume of commerce is to avoid the time and expense that would be required for the court to determine the actual gain or loss. In cases in which the actual monopoly overcharge appears to be either substantially more or substantially less than 10 percent, this factor should be considered in setting the fine within the guideline fine range.

4. Another consideration in setting the fine is that the average level of mark-up due to price-fixing may tend to decline with the volume of commerce involved.

5. It is the intent of the Commission that alternatives such as community confinement not be used to avoid imprisonment of antitrust offenders.

6. Understatement of seriousness is especially likely in cases involving complementary bids. If, for example, the defendant participated in an agreement not to submit a bid, or to submit an unreasonably high bid, on one occasion, in exchange for his being allowed to win a subsequent bid that he did not in fact win, his volume of commerce would be zero, although he would have contributed to harm that possibly was quite substantial. The court should consider sentences near the top of the guideline range in such cases.

7. In the case of a defendant with previous antitrust convictions, a sentence at the maximum of the applicable guideline range, or an upward departure, may be warranted. See § 4A1.3 (Adequacy of Criminal History Category).

Background: These guidelines apply to violations of the antitrust laws. Although they are not unlawful in all countries, there is near universal agreement that restrictive agreements among competitors, such as horizontal price-fixing (including bid-rigging) and horizontal market-allocation, can cause serious economic harm. There is no consensus, however, about the harmfulness of other types of antitrust offenses, which furthermore are rarely prosecuted and may involve unsettled issues of law. Consequently, only one guideline, which deals with horizontal agreements in restraint of trade, has been promulgated.

The agreements among competitors covered by this section are almost invariably covert conspiracies that are intended to, and serve no purpose other than to, restrict output and raise prices, and that are so plainly anticompetitive that they have been recognized as illegal per se, i.e., without any inquiry in individual cases as to their actual competitive effect.

Under the guidelines, prison terms for these offenders should be much more common, and usually somewhat longer, than typical under pre-guidelines practice. Absent adjustments, the guidelines require some period of confinement in the great majority of cases that are prosecuted, including all bid-rigging cases. The court will have the discretion to impose considerably longer sentences within the guideline ranges. Adjustments from Chapter Three, Part E (Acceptance of Responsibility) and, in rare instances, Chapter Three, Part B (Role in the Offense), may decrease these minimum sentences; nonetheless, in very few cases will the guidelines not require that some confinement be imposed. Adjustments will not affect the level of fines.

Tying the offense level to the scale or scope of the offense is important in order to ensure that the sanction is in fact punitive and that there is an incentive to desist from a violation once it has begun. The offense levels are not based directly on the damage caused or profit made by the defendant because damages are difficult and time consuming to establish. The volume of commerce is an acceptable and more readily measurable substitute. The limited empirical data available as to pre-guidelines practice showed that fines increased with the volume of commerce and the term of imprisonment probably did as well.

The Commission believes that the volume of commerce is liable to be an understated measure of seriousness in some bid-rigging cases. For this reason, and consistent with pre-guidelines practice, the Commission has specified a 1-level increase for bid-rigging.

Substantial fines are an essential part of the sentence. For an individual, the guideline fine range is from one to five percent of the volume of commerce, but not less than $ 20,000. For an organization, the guideline fine range is determined under Chapter Eight (Sentencing of Organizations), but pursuant to subsection (d)(2), the minimum multiplier is at least 0.75. This multiplier, which requires a minimum fine of 15 percent of the volume of commerce for the least serious case, was selected to provide an effective deterrent to antitrust offenses. At the same time, this minimum multiplier maintains incentives for desired organizational behavior. Because the Department of Justice has a well-established amnesty program for organizations that self-report antitrust offenses, no lower minimum multiplier is needed as an incentive for self-reporting. A minimum multiplier of at least 0.75 ensures that fines imposed in antitrust cases will exceed the average monopoly overcharge.

The Commission believes that most antitrust defendants have the resources and earning capacity to pay the fines called for by this guideline, at least over time on an installment basis.

* * *

CHAPTER EIGHT. SENTENCING OF ORGANIZATIONS

PART A. GENERAL APPLICATION PRINCIPLES

18 U.S.C. Appx § 8A1.2

§ 8A1.2. Application Instructions—Organizations

* * *

Commentary

Application Notes:

* * *

3. The following are definitions of terms used frequently in this chapter:

* * *

(b) "High-level personnel of the organization" means individuals who have substantial control over the organization or who have a substantial role in the making of policy within the organization. The term includes: a director, an executive officer; an individual in charge of a major business or functional unit of the organization, such as sales, administration, or finance; and an individual with a substantial ownership interest. "High-level personnel of a unit of the organization" is defined in the Commentary to § 8C2.5 (Culpability Score).

(c) "Substantial authority personnel" means individuals who within the scope of their authority exercise a substantial measure of discretion in acting on behalf of an organization. The term includes high-level personnel, individuals who exercise substantial supervisory authority (e.g., a plant manager, a sales manager), and any other individuals who, although not a part of an organization's management, nevertheless exercise substantial discretion when acting within the scope of their authority (e.g., an individual with authority in an organization to negotiate or set price levels or an individual authorized to negotiate or approve significant contracts). Whether an individual falls within this category must be determined on a case-by-case basis.

* * *

(j) An individual was "willfully ignorant of the offense" if the individual did not investigate the possible occurrence of unlawful conduct despite knowledge of circumstances that would lead a reasonable person to investigate whether unlawful conduct had occurred.

* * *

PART C. FINES

2. DETERMINING THE FINE—OTHER ORGANIZATIONS

18 U.S.C. Appx §§ 8C2.5, 8C2.6, 8C2.7

§ 8C2.5. Culpability Score

(a) Start with 5 points and apply subsections (b) through (g) below.

(b) Involvement in or Tolerance of Criminal Activity

If more than one applies, use the greatest:

(1) If—

(A) the organization had 5,000 or more employees and

(i) an individual within high-level personnel of the organization participated in, condoned, or was willfully ignorant of the offense; or

(ii) tolerance of the offense by substantial authority personnel was pervasive throughout the organization; or

(B) the unit of the organization within which the offense was committed had 5,000 or more employees and

(i) an individual within high-level personnel of the unit participated in, condoned, or was willfully ignorant of the offense; or

(ii) tolerance of the offense by substantial authority personnel was pervasive throughout such unit,

add 5 points; or

(2) If—

(A) the organization had 1,000 or more employees and

(i) an individual within high-level personnel of the organization participated in, condoned, or was willfully ignorant of the offense; or

(ii) tolerance of the offense by substantial authority personnel was pervasive throughout the organization; or

(B) the unit of the organization within which the offense was committed had 1,000 or more employees and

(i) an individual within high-level personnel of the unit participated in, condoned, or was willfully ignorant of the offense; or

(ii) tolerance of the offense by substantial authority personnel was pervasive throughout such unit,

add 4 points; or

(3) If—

(A) the organization had 200 or more employees and

(i) an individual within high-level personnel of the organization participated in, condoned, or was willfully ignorant of the offense; or

(ii) tolerance of the offense by substantial authority personnel was pervasive throughout the organization; or

(B) the unit of the organization within which the offense was committed had 200 or more employees and

(i) an individual within high-level personnel of the unit participated in, condoned, or was willfully ignorant of the offense; or

(ii) tolerance of the offense by substantial authority personnel was pervasive throughout such unit,

add 3 points; or

(4) If the organization had 50 or more employees and an individual within substantial authority personnel participated in, condoned, or was willfully ignorant of the offense, add 2 points; or

(5) If the organization had 10 or more employees and an individual within substantial authority personnel participated in, condoned, or was willfully ignorant of the offense, add 1 point.

(c) Prior History

If more than one applies, use the greater:

(1) If the organization (or separately-managed line of business) committed any part of the instant offense less than 10 years after (A) a criminal adjudication based on similar misconduct; or (B) civil or administrative adjudication(s) based on two or more separate instances of similar misconduct, add 1 point; or

(2) If the organization (or separately-managed line of business) committed any part of the instant offense less than 5 years after (A) a criminal adjudication based on similar misconduct; or (B) civil or administrative adjudication(s) based on two or more separate instances of similar misconduct, add 2 points.

(d) Violation of an Order

If more than one applies, use the greater:

(1) (A) If the commission of the instant offense violated a judicial order or injunction, other than a violation of a condition of probation; or (B) if the organization (or separately-managed line of business) violated a condition of probation by engaging in similar misconduct, i.e., misconduct similar to that for which it was placed on probation, add 2 points; or

(2) If the commission of the instant offense violated a condition of probation, add 1 point.

(e) Obstruction of Justice

If the organization willfully obstructed or impeded, attempted to obstruct or impede, or aided, abetted, or encouraged obstruction of justice during the investigation, prosecution, or sentencing of the instant offense, or, with knowledge thereof, failed to take reasonable steps to prevent such obstruction or impedance or attempted obstruction or impedance, add 3 points.

(f) Effective Compliance and Ethics Program

(1) If the offense occurred even though the organization had in place at the time of the offense an effective compliance and ethics program, as provided in § 8B2.1 (Effective Compliance and Ethics Program), subtract 3 points.

(2) Subsection (f)(1) shall not apply if, after becoming aware of an offense, the organization unreasonably delayed reporting the offense to appropriate governmental authorities.

(3) (A) Except as provided in subdivision (B), subsection (f)(1) shall not apply if an individual within high-level personnel of the organization, a person within high-level personnel of the unit of the organization within which the offense was committed where the unit had 200 or more employees, or an individual described in § 8B2.1(b)(2)(B) or (C), participated in, condoned, or was willfully ignorant of the offense.

(B) There is a rebuttable presumption, for purposes of subsection (f)(1), that the organization did not have an effective compliance and ethics program if an individual—

(i) within high-level personnel of a small organization; or

(ii) within substantial authority personnel, but not within high-level personnel, of any organization,

participated in, condoned, or was willfully ignorant of, the offense.

(g) Self-Reporting, Cooperation, and Acceptance of Responsibility

If more than one applies, use the greatest:

(1) If the organization (A) prior to an imminent threat of disclosure or government investigation; and (B) within a reasonably prompt time after becoming aware of the offense, reported the offense to appropriate governmental authorities, fully cooperated in the investigation, and clearly demonstrated recognition and affirmative acceptance of responsibility for its criminal conduct, subtract 5 points; or

(2) If the organization fully cooperated in the investigation and clearly demonstrated recognition and affirmative acceptance of responsibility for its criminal conduct, subtract 2 points; or

(3) If the organization clearly demonstrated recognition and affirmative acceptance of responsibility for its criminal conduct, subtract 1 point.

Commentary

Application Notes:

1. Definitions. For purposes of this guideline, "condoned," "prior criminal adjudication," "similar misconduct," "substantial authority personnel," and "willfully ignorant of the offense" have the meaning given those terms in Application Note 3 of the Commentary to § 8A1.2 (Application Instructions—Organizations).

"Small Organization," for purposes of subsection (f)(3), means an organization that, at the time of the instant offense, had fewer than 200 employees.

2. For purposes of subsection (b), "unit of the organization" means any reasonably distinct operational component of the organization. For example, a large organization may have several large units such as divisions or subsidiaries, as well as many smaller units such as specialized manufacturing, marketing, or accounting operations within these larger units. For purposes of this definition, all of these types of units are encompassed within the term "unit of the organization."

3. "High-level personnel of the organization" is defined in the Commentary to § 8A1.2 (Application Instructions—Organizations). With respect to a unit with 200 or more employees, "high-level personnel of a unit of the organization" means agents within the unit who set the policy for or control that unit. For example, if the managing agent of a unit with 200 employees participated in an offense, three points would be added under subsection (b)(3); if that organization had 1,000 employees and the managing agent of the unit with 200 employees were also within high-level personnel of the organization in its entirety, four points (rather than three) would be added under subsection (b)(2).

4. Pervasiveness under subsection (b) will be case specific and depend on the number, and degree of responsibility, of individuals within substantial authority personnel who participated in, condoned, or were willfully ignorant of the offense. Fewer individuals need to be involved for a finding of pervasiveness if those individuals exercised a relatively high degree of authority. Pervasiveness can occur either within an organization as a whole or within a unit of an organization. For example, if an offense were committed in an organization with 1,000 employees but the tolerance of the offense was pervasive only within a unit of the organization with 200 employees (and no high-level personnel of the organization participated in, condoned, or was willfully ignorant of the offense), three points would be added under subsection (b)(3). If, in the same organization, tolerance of the offense was pervasive throughout the organization as a whole, or an individual within high-level personnel of the organization participated in the offense, four points (rather than three) would be added under subsection (b)(2).

5. A "separately managed line of business," as used in subsections (c) and (d), is a subpart of a for-profit organization that has its own management, has a high degree of autonomy from higher managerial authority, and maintains its own separate books of account. Corporate subsidiaries and divisions frequently are separately managed lines of business. Under subsection (c), in determining the prior history of an organization with separately managed lines of business, only the prior conduct or criminal record of the separately managed line of business involved in the instant offense is to be used. Under subsection (d), in the context of an organization

with separately managed lines of business, in making the determination whether a violation of a condition of probation involved engaging in similar misconduct, only the prior misconduct of the separately managed line of business involved in the instant offense is to be considered.

6. Under subsection (c), in determining the prior history of an organization or separately managed line of business, the conduct of the underlying economic entity shall be considered without regard to its legal structure or ownership. For example, if two companies merged and became separate divisions and separately managed lines of business within the merged company, each division would retain the prior history of its predecessor company. If a company reorganized and became a new legal entity, the new company would retain the prior history of the predecessor company. In contrast, if one company purchased the physical assets but not the ongoing business of another company, the prior history of the company selling the physical assets would not be transferred to the company purchasing the assets. However, if an organization is acquired by another organization in response to solicitations by appropriate federal government officials, the prior history of the acquired organization shall not be attributed to the acquiring organization.

7. Under subsections (c)(1)(B) and (c)(2)(B), the civil or administrative adjudication(s) must have occurred within the specified period (ten or five years) of the instant offense.

8. Adjust the culpability score for the factors listed in subsection (e) whether or not the offense guideline incorporates that factor, or that factor is inherent in the offense.

9. Subsection (e) applies where the obstruction is committed on behalf of the organization; it does not apply where an individual or individuals have attempted to conceal their misconduct from the organization. The Commentary to § 3C1.1 (Obstructing or Impeding the Administration of Justice) provides guidance regarding the types of conduct that constitute obstruction.

10. Subsection (f)(2) contemplates that the organization will be allowed a reasonable period of time to conduct an internal investigation. In addition, no reporting is required by subsection (f)(2) if the organization reasonably concluded, based on the information then available, that no offense had been committed.

11. "Appropriate governmental authorities," as used in subsections (f) and (g)(1), means the federal or state law enforcement, regulatory, or program officials having jurisdiction over such matter. To qualify for a reduction under subsection (g)(1), the report to appropriate governmental authorities must be made under the direction of the organization.

12. To qualify for a reduction under subsection (g)(1) or (g)(2), cooperation must be both timely and thorough. To be timely, the cooperation must begin essentially at the same time as the organization is officially notified of a criminal investigation. To be thorough, the cooperation should include the disclosure of all pertinent information known by the organization. A prime test of whether the organization has disclosed all pertinent information is whether the information is sufficient for law enforcement personnel to identify the nature and extent of the offense and the individual(s) responsible for the criminal conduct. However, the cooperation to be measured is the cooperation of the organization itself, not the cooperation of individuals within the organization. If, because of the lack of cooperation of

particular individual(s), neither the organization nor law enforcement personnel are able to identify the culpable individual(s) within the organization despite the organization's efforts to cooperate fully, the organization may still be given credit for full cooperation.

13. Entry of a plea of guilty prior to the commencement of trial combined with truthful admission of involvement in the offense and related conduct ordinarily will constitute significant evidence of affirmative acceptance of responsibility under subsection (g), unless outweighed by conduct of the organization that is inconsistent with such acceptance of responsibility. This adjustment is not intended to apply to an organization that puts the government to its burden of proof at trial by denying the essential factual elements of guilt, is convicted, and only then admits guilt and expresses remorse. Conviction by trial, however, does not automatically preclude an organization from consideration for such a reduction. In rare situations, an organization may clearly demonstrate an acceptance of responsibility for its criminal conduct even though it exercises its constitutional right to a trial. This may occur, for example, where an organization goes to trial to assert and preserve issues that do not relate to factual guilt (e.g., to make a constitutional challenge to a statute or a challenge to the applicability of a statute to its conduct). In each such instance, however, a determination that an organization has accepted responsibility will be based primarily upon pretrial statements and conduct.

14. In making a determination with respect to subsection (g), the court may determine that the chief executive officer or highest ranking employee of an organization should appear at sentencing in order to signify that the organization has clearly demonstrated recognition and affirmative acceptance of responsibility.

Background: The increased culpability scores under subsection (b) are based on three interrelated principles. First, an organization is more culpable when individuals who manage the organization or who have substantial discretion in acting for the organization participate in, condone, or are willfully ignorant of criminal conduct. Second, as organizations become larger and their managements become more professional, participation in, condonation of, or willful ignorance of criminal conduct by such management is increasingly a breach of trust or abuse of position. Third, as organizations increase in size, the risk of criminal conduct beyond that reflected in the instant offense also increases whenever management's tolerance of that offense is pervasive. Because of the continuum of sizes of organizations and professionalization of management, subsection (b) gradually increases the culpability score based upon the size of the organization and the level and extent of the substantial authority personnel involvement.

§ 8C2.6 Minimum and Maximum Multipliers

Using the culpability score from § 8C2.5 (Culpability Score) and applying any applicable special instruction for fines in chapter Two, determine the applicable minimum and maximum fine multipliers from the table below.

Culpability Score	Minimum Multiplier	Maximum Multiplier
10 or more	2.00	4.00
9	1.80	3.60
8	1.60	3.20
7	1.40	2.80
6	1.20	2.40
5	1.00	2.00
4	0.80	1.60
3	0.60	1.20
2	0.40	0.80
1	0.20	0.40
0 or less	0.05	0.20

Commentary

Application Note:

1. A special instruction for fines in § 2R1.1 (Bid-Rigging, Price-Fixing or Market-Allocation Agreements Among Competitors) sets a floor for minimum and maximum multipliers in cases covered by that guideline.

§ 8C2.7 Guideline Fine Range—Organizations

(a) The minimum of the guideline fine range is determined by multiplying the base fine determined under § 8C2.4 (Base Fine) by the applicable minimum multiplier determined under § 8C2.6 (Minimum and Maximum Multipliers).

(b) The maximum of the guideline fine range is determined by multiplying the base fine determined under § 8C2.4 (Base fine) by the applicable maximum multiplier determined under § 8C2.6 (Minimum and Maximum Multipliers).

PART 3
GUIDELINES

8

HORIZONTAL MERGER GUIDELINES

U.S. DEPARTMENT OF JUSTICE AND THE FEDERAL TRADE COMMISSION

AUGUST 19, 2010

TABLE OF CONTENTS

SECTION 1: OVERVIEW

These Guidelines outline the principal analytical techniques, practices, and the enforcement policy of the Department of Justice and the Federal Trade Commission (the "Agencies") with respect to mergers and acquisitions involving actual or potential competitors ("horizontal mergers") under the federal antitrust laws.[1] The relevant statutory provisions include Section 7 of the Clayton Act, 15 U.S.C. § 18, Sections 1 and 2 of the Sherman Act, 15 U.S.C. § 1, 2, and Section 5 of the Federal Trade Commission Act, 15 U.S.C. § 45. Most particularly, Section 7 of the Clayton Act prohibits mergers if "in any line of commerce or in any activity affecting commerce in any section of the country, the effect of such acquisition may be substantially to lessen competition, or to tend to create a monopoly."

The Agencies seek to identify and challenge competitively harmful mergers while avoiding unnecessary interference with mergers that are either competitively beneficial or neutral. Most merger analysis is necessarily predictive, requiring an assessment of what will likely happen if a merger proceeds as compared to what will likely happen if it does not. Given this inherent need for prediction, these Guidelines reflect the congressional intent that merger enforcement should interdict competitive problems in their incipiency and that certainty about anticompetitive effect is seldom possible and not required for a merger to be illegal.

These Guidelines describe the principal analytical techniques and the main types of evidence on which the Agencies usually rely to predict whether a horizontal merger may substantially lessen competition. They are not intended to describe how the Agencies analyze cases other than horizontal mergers. These Guidelines are intended to assist the business community and antitrust practitioners by increasing the transparency of the analytical

---

[1] These Guidelines replace the Horizontal Merger Guidelines issued in 1992, revised in 1997. They reflect the ongoing accumulation of experience at the Agencies. The Commentary on the Horizontal Merger Guidelines issued by the Agencies in 2006 remains a valuable supplement to these Guidelines. These Guidelines may be revised from time to time as necessary to reflect significant changes in enforcement policy, to clarify existing policy, or to reflect new learning. These Guidelines do not cover vertical or other types of non-horizontal acquisitions.

process underlying the Agencies' enforcement decisions. They may also assist the courts in developing an appropriate framework for interpreting and applying the antitrust laws in the horizontal merger context.

These Guidelines should be read with the awareness that merger analysis does not consist of uniform application of a single methodology. Rather, it is a fact-specific process through which the Agencies, guided by their extensive experience, apply a range of analytical tools to the reasonably available and reliable evidence to evaluate competitive concerns in a limited period of time. Where these Guidelines provide examples, they are illustrative and do not exhaust the applications of the relevant principle.[2]

The unifying theme of these Guidelines is that mergers should not be permitted to create, enhance, or entrench market power or to facilitate its exercise. For simplicity of exposition, these Guidelines generally refer to all of these effects as enhancing market power. A merger enhances market power if it is likely to encourage one or more firms to raise price, reduce output, diminish innovation, or otherwise harm customers as a result of diminished competitive constraints or incentives. In evaluating how a merger will likely change a firm's behavior, the Agencies focus primarily on how the merger affects conduct that would be most profitable for the firm.

A merger can enhance market power simply by eliminating competition between the merging parties. This effect can arise even if the merger causes no changes in the way other firms behave. Adverse competitive effects arising in this manner are referred to as "unilateral effects." A merger also can enhance market power by increasing the risk of coordinated, accommodating, or interdependent behavior among rivals. Adverse competitive effects arising in this manner are referred to as "coordinated effects." In any given case, either or both types of effects may be present, and the distinction between them may be blurred.

These Guidelines principally describe how the Agencies analyze mergers between rival suppliers that may enhance their market power as sellers. Enhancement of market power by sellers often elevates the prices charged to customers. For simplicity of exposition, these Guidelines generally discuss the analysis in terms of such price effects. Enhanced market power can also be manifested in non-price terms and conditions that adversely affect customers, including reduced product quality, reduced product variety, reduced service, or diminished innovation. Such non-price effects may coexist with price effects, or can arise in their absence. When the Agencies investigate whether a merger may lead to a substantial lessening of non-price competition, they employ an approach analogous to that used to evaluate price competition. Enhanced market power may also make it more likely that the merged entity can profitably and effectively engage in exclusionary conduct. Regardless of how enhanced market power likely would be manifested, the Agencies normally evaluate mergers based on their impact on customers. The Agencies examine effects on either or both of the direct customers and the final consumers. The Agencies presume, absent convincing evidence to the contrary, that adverse effects on direct customers also cause adverse effects on final consumers.

Enhancement of market power by buyers, sometimes called "monopsony power," has adverse effects comparable to enhancement of market power by

---

[2] These Guidelines are not intended to describe how the Agencies will conduct the litigation of cases they decide to bring. Although relevant in that context, these Guidelines neither dictate nor exhaust the range of evidence the Agencies may introduce in litigation.

sellers. The Agencies employ an analogous framework to analyze mergers between rival purchasers that may enhance their market power as buyers. See Section 12.

SECTION 2: EVIDENCE OF ADVERSE COMPETITIVE EFFECTS

The Agencies consider any reasonably available and reliable evidence to address the central question of whether a merger may substantially lessen competition. This section discusses several categories and sources of evidence that the Agencies, in their experience, have found most informative in predicting the likely competitive effects of mergers. The list provided here is not exhaustive. In any given case, reliable evidence may be available in only some categories or from some sources. For each category of evidence, the Agencies consider evidence indicating that the merger may enhance competition as well as evidence indicating that it may lessen competition.

2.1 Types of Evidence

2.1.1 Actual Effects Observed in Consummated Mergers

When evaluating a consummated merger, the ultimate issue is not only whether adverse competitive effects have already resulted from the merger, but also whether such effects are likely to arise in the future. Evidence of observed post-merger price increases or other changes adverse to customers is given substantial weight. The Agencies evaluate whether such changes are anticompetitive effects resulting from the merger, in which case they can be dispositive. However, a consummated merger may be anticompetitive even if such effects have not yet been observed, perhaps because the merged firm may be aware of the possibility of post-merger antitrust review and moderating its conduct. Consequently, the Agencies also consider the same types of evidence they consider when evaluating unconsummated mergers.

2.1.2 Direct Comparisons Based on Experience

The Agencies look for historical events, or "natural experiments," that are informative regarding the competitive effects of the merger. For example, the Agencies may examine the impact of recent mergers, entry, expansion, or exit in the relevant market. Effects of analogous events in similar markets may also be informative.

The Agencies also look for reliable evidence based on variations among similar markets. For example, if the merging firms compete in some locales but not others, comparisons of prices charged in regions where they do and do not compete may be informative regarding post-merger prices. In some cases, however, prices are set on such a broad geographic basis that such comparisons are not informative. The Agencies also may examine how prices in similar markets vary with the number of significant competitors in those markets.

2.1.3 Market Shares and Concentration in a Relevant Market

The Agencies give weight to the merging parties' market shares in a relevant market, the level of concentration, and the change in concentration caused by the merger. See Sections 4 and 5. Mergers that cause a significant increase in concentration and result in highly concentrated markets are presumed to be likely to enhance market power, but this presumption can be rebutted by persuasive evidence showing that the merger is unlikely to enhance market power.

2.1.4 Substantial Head-to-Head Competition

The Agencies consider whether the merging firms have been, or likely will become absent the merger, substantial head-to-head competitors. Such evidence can be especially relevant for evaluating adverse unilateral effects, which result directly from the loss of that competition. See Section 6. This evidence can also inform market definition. See Section 4.

2.1.5 Disruptive Role of a Merging Party

The Agencies consider whether a merger may lessen competition by eliminating a "maverick" firm, i.e., a firm that plays a disruptive role in the market to the benefit of customers. For example, if one of the merging firms has a strong incumbency position and the other merging firm threatens to disrupt market conditions with a new technology or business model, their merger can involve the loss of actual or potential competition. Likewise, one of the merging firms may have the incentive to take the lead in price cutting or other competitive conduct or to resist increases in industry prices. A firm that may discipline prices based on its ability and incentive to expand production rapidly using available capacity also can be a maverick, as can a firm that has often resisted otherwise prevailing industry norms to cooperate on price setting or other terms of competition.

2.2 Sources of Evidence

The Agencies consider many sources of evidence in their merger analysis. The most common sources of reasonably available and reliable evidence are the merging parties, customers, other industry participants, and industry observers.

2.2.1 Merging Parties

The Agencies typically obtain substantial information from the merging parties. This information can take the form of documents, testimony, or data, and can consist of descriptions of competitively relevant conditions or reflect actual business conduct and decisions. Documents created in the normal course are more probative than documents created as advocacy materials in merger review. Documents describing industry conditions can be informative regarding the operation of the market and how a firm identifies and assesses its rivals, particularly when business decisions are made in reliance on the accuracy of those descriptions. The business decisions taken by the merging firms also can be informative about industry conditions. For example, if a firm sets price well above incremental cost, that normally indicates either that the firm believes its customers are not highly sensitive to price (not in itself of antitrust concern, see Section 4.1.3[3]) or that the firm and its rivals are engaged in coordinated interaction (see Section 7). Incremental cost depends on the relevant increment in output as well as on the time period involved, and in the case of large increments and sustained changes in output it may include some costs that would be fixed for smaller increments of output or shorter time periods.

---

[3] High margins commonly arise for products that are significantly differentiated. Products involving substantial fixed costs typically will be developed only if suppliers expect there to be enough differentiation to support margins sufficient to cover those fixed costs. High margins can be consistent with incumbent firms earning competitive returns.

Explicit or implicit evidence that the merging parties intend to raise prices, reduce output or capacity, reduce product quality or variety, withdraw products or delay their introduction, or curtail research and development efforts after the merger, or explicit or implicit evidence that the ability to engage in such conduct motivated the merger, can be highly informative in evaluating the likely effects of a merger. Likewise, the Agencies look for reliable evidence that the merger is likely to result in efficiencies. The Agencies give careful consideration to the views of individuals whose responsibilities, expertise, and experience relating to the issues in question provide particular indicia of reliability. The financial terms of the transaction may also be informative regarding competitive effects. For example, a purchase price in excess of the acquired firm's stand-alone market value may indicate that the acquiring firm is paying a premium because it expects to be able to reduce competition or to achieve efficiencies.

2.2.2 Customers

Customers can provide a variety of information to the Agencies, ranging from information about their own purchasing behavior and choices to their views about the effects of the merger itself.

Information from customers about how they would likely respond to a price increase, and the relative attractiveness of different products or suppliers, may be highly relevant, especially when corroborated by other evidence such as historical purchasing patterns and practices. Customers also can provide valuable information about the impact of historical events such as entry by a new supplier.

The conclusions of well-informed and sophisticated customers on the likely impact of the merger itself can also help the Agencies investigate competitive effects, because customers typically feel the consequences of both competitively beneficial and competitively harmful mergers. In evaluating such evidence, the Agencies are mindful that customers may oppose, or favor, a merger for reasons unrelated to the antitrust issues raised by that merger.

When some customers express concerns about the competitive effects of a merger while others view the merger as beneficial or neutral, the Agencies take account of this divergence in using the information provided by customers and consider the likely reasons for such divergence of views. For example, if for regulatory reasons some customers cannot buy imported products, while others can, a merger between domestic suppliers may harm the former customers even if it leaves the more flexible customers unharmed. See Section 3.

When direct customers of the merging firms compete against one another in a downstream market, their interests may not be aligned with the interests of final consumers, especially if the direct customers expect to pass on any anticompetitive price increase. A customer that is protected from adverse competitive effects by a long-term contract, or otherwise relatively immune from the merger's harmful effects, may even welcome an anticompetitive merger that provides that customer with a competitive advantage over its downstream rivals.

> *Example 1:* As a result of the merger, Customer C will experience a price increase for an input used in producing its final product, raising its costs. Customer C's rivals use this input more intensively than Customer C, and the same price increase applied to them will raise their costs more than it raises Customer C's costs. On balance,

Customer C may benefit from the merger even though the merger involves a substantial lessening of competition.

2.2.3 Other Industry Participants and Observers

Suppliers, indirect customers, distributors, other industry participants, and industry analysts can also provide information helpful to a merger inquiry. The interests of firms selling products complementary to those offered by the merging firms often are well aligned with those of customers, making their informed views valuable.

Information from firms that are rivals to the merging parties can help illuminate how the market operates. The interests of rival firms often diverge from the interests of customers, since customers normally lose, but rival firms gain, if the merged entity raises its prices. For that reason, the Agencies do not routinely rely on the overall views of rival firms regarding the competitive effects of the merger. However, rival firms may provide relevant facts, and even their overall views may be instructive, especially in cases where the Agencies are concerned that the merged entity may engage in exclusionary conduct.

Example 2: Merging Firms A and B operate in a market in which network effects are significant, implying that any firm's product is significantly more valuable if it commands a large market share or if it is interconnected with others that in aggregate command such a share. Prior to the merger, they and their rivals voluntarily interconnect with one another. The merger would create an entity with a large enough share that a strategy of ending voluntary interconnection would have a dangerous probability of creating monopoly power in this market. The interests of rivals and of consumers would be broadly aligned in preventing such a merger.

SECTION 3: TARGETED CUSTOMERS AND PRICE DISCRIMINATION

When examining possible adverse competitive effects from a merger, the Agencies consider whether those effects vary significantly for different customers purchasing the same or similar products. Such differential impacts are possible when sellers can discriminate, e.g., by profitably raising price to certain targeted customers but not to others. The possibility of price discrimination influences market definition (see Section 4), the measurement of market shares (see Section 5), and the evaluation of competitive effects (see Sections 6 and 7).

When price discrimination is feasible, adverse competitive effects on targeted customers can arise, even if such effects will not arise for other customers. A price increase for targeted customers may be profitable even if a price increase for all customers would not be profitable because too many other customers would substitute away. When discrimination is reasonably likely, the Agencies may evaluate competitive effects separately by type of customer. The Agencies may have access to information unavailable to customers that is relevant to evaluating whether discrimination is reasonably likely.

For price discrimination to be feasible, two conditions typically must be met: differential pricing and limited arbitrage.

First, the suppliers engaging in price discrimination must be able to price differently to targeted customers than to other customers. This may involve identification of individual customers to which different prices are offered or offering different prices to different types of customers based on observable characteristics.

> *Example 3:* Suppliers can distinguish large buyers from small buyers. Large buyers are more likely than small buyers to self-supply in response to a significant price increase. The merger may lead to price discrimination against small buyers, harming them, even if large buyers are not harmed. Such discrimination can occur even if there is no discrete gap in size between the classes of large and small buyers.

In other cases, suppliers may be unable to distinguish among different types of customers but can offer multiple products that sort customers based on their purchase decisions.

Second, the targeted customers must not be able to defeat the price increase of concern by arbitrage, e.g., by purchasing indirectly from or through other customers. Arbitrage may be difficult if it would void warranties or make service more difficult or costly for customers. Arbitrage is inherently impossible for many services. Arbitrage between customers at different geographic locations may be impractical due to transportation costs. Arbitrage on a modest scale may be possible but sufficiently costly or limited that it would not deter or defeat a discriminatory pricing strategy.

SECTION 4: MARKET DEFINITION

When the Agencies identify a potential competitive concern with a horizontal merger, market definition plays two roles. First, market definition helps specify the line of commerce and section of the country in which the competitive concern arises. In any merger enforcement action, the Agencies will normally identify one or more relevant markets in which the merger may substantially lessen competition. Second, market definition allows the Agencies to identify market participants and measure market shares and market concentration. See Section 5. The measurement of market shares and market concentration is not an end in itself, but is useful to the extent it illuminates the merger's likely competitive effects.

The Agencies' analysis need not start with market definition. Some of the analytical tools used by the Agencies to assess competitive effects do not rely on market definition, although evaluation of competitive alternatives available to customers is always necessary at some point in the analysis.

Evidence of competitive effects can inform market definition, just as market definition can be informative regarding competitive effects. For example, evidence that a reduction in the number of significant rivals offering a group of products causes prices for those products to rise significantly can itself establish that those products form a relevant market. Such evidence also may more directly predict the competitive effects of a merger, reducing the role of inferences from market definition and market shares. Where analysis suggests alternative and reasonably plausible candidate markets, and where the resulting market shares lead to very different inferences regarding competitive effects, it is particularly valuable to examine more direct forms of evidence concerning those effects.

Market definition focuses solely on demand substitution factors, i.e., on customers' ability and willingness to substitute away from one product to another in response to a price increase or a corresponding non-price change such as a reduction in product quality or service. The responsive actions of suppliers are also important in competitive analysis. They are considered in these Guidelines in the sections addressing the identification of market participants, the measurement of market shares, the analysis of competitive effects, and entry.

Customers often confront a range of possible substitutes for the products of the merging firms. Some substitutes may be closer, and others more distant, either geographically or in terms of product attributes and perceptions. Additionally, customers may assess the proximity of different products differently. When products or suppliers in different geographic areas are substitutes for one another to varying degrees, defining a market to include some substitutes and exclude others is inevitably a simplification that cannot capture the full variation in the extent to which different products compete against each other. The principles of market definition outlined below seek to make this inevitable simplification as useful and informative as is practically possible. Relevant markets need not have precise metes and bounds.

Defining a market broadly to include relatively distant product or geographic substitutes can lead to misleading market shares. This is because the competitive significance of distant substitutes is unlikely to be commensurate with their shares in a broad market. Although excluding more distant substitutes from the market inevitably understates their competitive significance to some degree, doing so often provides a more accurate indicator of the competitive effects of the merger than would the alternative of including them and overstating their competitive significance as proportional to their shares in an expanded market.

> *Example 4:* Firms A and B, sellers of two leading brands of motorcycles, propose to merge. If Brand A motorcycle prices were to rise, some buyers would substitute to Brand B, and some others would substitute to cars. However, motorcycle buyers see Brand B motorcycles as much more similar to Brand A motorcycles than are cars. Far more cars are sold than motorcycles. Evaluating shares in a market that includes cars would greatly underestimate the competitive significance of Brand B motorcycles in constraining Brand A's prices and greatly overestimate the significance of cars.

Market shares of different products in narrowly defined markets are more likely to capture the relative competitive significance of these products, and often more accurately reflect competition between close substitutes. As a result, properly defined antitrust markets often exclude some substitutes to which some customers might turn in the face of a price increase even if such substitutes provide alternatives for those customers. However, a group of products is too narrow to constitute a relevant market if competition from products outside that group is so ample that even the complete elimination of competition within the group would not significantly harm either direct customers or downstream consumers. The hypothetical monopolist test (see Section 4.1.1) is designed to ensure that candidate markets are not overly narrow in this respect.

The Agencies implement these principles of market definition flexibly when evaluating different possible candidate markets. Relevant antitrust markets defined according to the hypothetical monopolist test are not always intuitive and may not align with how industry members use the term "market."

Section 4.1 describes the principles that apply to product market definition, and gives guidance on how the Agencies most often apply those principles. Section 4.2 describes how the same principles apply to geographic market definition. Although discussed separately for simplicity of exposition, the principles described in Sections 4.1 and 4.2 are combined to define a relevant market, which has both a product and a geographic dimension. In particular, the hypothetical monopolist test is applied to a group of products together with a geographic region to determine a relevant market.

4.1 Product Market Definition

When a product sold by one merging firm (Product A) competes against one or more products sold by the other merging firm, the Agencies define a relevant product market around Product A to evaluate the importance of that competition. Such a relevant product market consists of a group of substitute products including Product A. Multiple relevant product markets may thus be identified.

4.1.1 The Hypothetical Monopolist Test

The Agencies employ the hypothetical monopolist test to evaluate whether groups of products in candidate markets are sufficiently broad to constitute relevant antitrust markets. The Agencies use the hypothetical monopolist test to identify a set of products that are reasonably interchangeable with a product sold by one of the merging firms.

The hypothetical monopolist test requires that a product market contain enough substitute products so that it could be subject to post-merger exercise of market power significantly exceeding that existing absent the merger. Specifically, the test requires that a hypothetical profit-maximizing firm, not subject to price regulation, that was the only present and future seller of those products ("hypothetical monopolist") likely would impose at least a small but significant and non-transitory increase in price ("SSNIP") on at least one product in the market, including at least one product sold by one of the merging firms.[4] For the purpose of analyzing this issue, the terms of sale of products outside the candidate market are held constant. The SSNIP is employed solely as a methodological tool for performing the hypothetical monopolist test; it is not a tolerance level for price increases resulting from a merger.

Groups of products may satisfy the hypothetical monopolist test without including the full range of substitutes from which customers choose. The hypothetical monopolist test may identify a group of products as a relevant market even if customers would substitute significantly to products outside that group in response to a price increase.

> *Example 5:* Products A and B are being tested as a candidate market. Each sells for $100, has an incremental cost of $60, and sells 1200 units. For every dollar increase in the price of Product A, for any given price of Product B, Product A loses twenty units of sales to products outside the candidate market and ten units of sales to Product B, and likewise for Product B. Under these conditions, economic analysis shows that a hypothetical profit-maximizing monopolist controlling

[4] If the pricing incentives of the firms supplying the products in the candidate market differ substantially from those of the hypothetical monopolist, for reasons other than the latter's control over a larger group of substitutes, the Agencies may instead employ the concept of a hypothetical profit-maximizing cartel comprised of the firms (with all their products) that sell the products in the candidate market. This approach is most likely to be appropriate if the merging firms sell products outside the candidate market that significantly affect their pricing incentives for products in the candidate market. This could occur, for example, if the candidate market is one for durable equipment and the firms selling that equipment derive substantial net revenues from selling spare parts and service for that equipment.

Products A and B would raise both of their prices by ten percent, to $110. Therefore, Products A and B satisfy the hypothetical monopolist test using a five percent SSNIP, and indeed for any SSNIP size up to ten percent. This is true even though two-thirds of the sales lost by one product when it raises its price are diverted to products outside the relevant market.

When applying the hypothetical monopolist test to define a market around a product offered by one of the merging firms, if the market includes a second product, the Agencies will normally also include a third product if that third product is a closer substitute for the first product than is the second product. The third product is a closer substitute if, in response to a SSNIP on the first product, greater revenues are diverted to the third product than to the second product.

Example 6: In Example 5, suppose that half of the unit sales lost by Product A when it raises its price are diverted to Product C, which also has a price of $100, while one-third are diverted to Product B. Product C is a closer substitute for Product A than is Product B. Thus Product C will normally be included in the relevant market, even though Products A and B together satisfy the hypothetical monopolist test.

The hypothetical monopolist test ensures that markets are not defined too narrowly, but it does not lead to a single relevant market. The Agencies may evaluate a merger in any relevant market satisfying the test, guided by the overarching principle that the purpose of defining the market and measuring market shares is to illuminate the evaluation of competitive effects. Because the relative competitive significance of more distant substitutes is apt to be overstated by their share of sales, when the Agencies rely on market shares and concentration, they usually do so in the smallest relevant market satisfying the hypothetical monopolist test.

Example 7: In Example 4, including cars in the market will lead to misleadingly small market shares for motorcycle producers. Unless motorcycles fail the hypothetical monopolist test, the Agencies would not include cars in the market in analyzing this motorcycle merger.

4.1.2 Benchmark Prices and SSNIP Size

The Agencies apply the SSNIP starting from prices that would likely prevail absent the merger. If prices are not likely to change absent the merger, these benchmark prices can reasonably be taken to be the prices prevailing prior to the merger.[5] If prices are likely to change absent the merger, e.g., because of innovation or entry, the Agencies may use anticipated future prices as the benchmark for the test. If prices might fall absent the merger due to the breakdown of pre-merger coordination, the Agencies may use those lower prices as the benchmark for the test. In some cases, the techniques employed by the Agencies to implement the hypothetical monopolist test focus on the difference in incentives between pre-merger firms and the hypothetical monopolist and do not require specifying the benchmark prices.

The SSNIP is intended to represent a "small but significant" increase in the prices charged by firms in the candidate market for the value they contribute to the products or services used by customers. This properly

5 Market definition for the evaluation of non-merger antitrust concerns such as monopolization or facilitating practices will differ in this respect if the effects resulting from the conduct of concern are already occurring at the time of evaluation.

directs attention to the effects of price changes commensurate with those that might result from a significant lessening of competition caused by the merger. This methodology is used because normally it is possible to quantify "small but significant" adverse price effects on customers and analyze their likely reactions, not because price effects are more important than non-price effects.

The Agencies most often use a SSNIP of five percent of the price paid by customers for the products or services to which the merging firms contribute value. However, what constitutes a "small but significant" increase in price, commensurate with a significant loss of competition caused by the merger, depends upon the nature of the industry and the merging firms' positions in it, and the Agencies may accordingly use a price increase that is larger or smaller than five percent. Where explicit or implicit prices for the firms' specific contribution to value can be identified with reasonable clarity, the Agencies may base the SSNIP on those prices.

> *Example 8:* In a merger between two oil pipelines, the SSNIP would be based on the price charged for transporting the oil, not on the price of the oil itself. If pipelines buy the oil at one end and sell it at the other, the price charged for transporting the oil is implicit, equal to the difference between the price paid for oil at the input end and the price charged for oil at the output end. The relevant product sold by the pipelines is better described as "pipeline transportation of oil from point A to point B" than as "oil at point B."

> *Example 9:* In a merger between two firms that install computers purchased from third parties, the SSNIP would be based on their fees, not on the price of installed computers. If these firms purchase the computers and charge their customers one package price, the implicit installation fee is equal to the package charge to customers less the price of the computers.

> *Example 10:* In Example 9, suppose that the prices paid by the merging firms to purchase computers are opaque, but account for at least ninety-five percent of the prices they charge for installed computers, with profits or implicit fees making up five percent of those prices at most. A five percent SSNIP on the total price paid by customers would at least double those fees or profits. Even if that would be unprofitable for a hypothetical monopolist, a significant increase in fees might well be profitable. If the SSNIP is based on the total price paid by customers, a lower percentage will be used.

4.1.3 Implementing the Hypothetical Monopolist Test

The hypothetical monopolist's incentive to raise prices depends both on the extent to which customers would likely substitute away from the products in the candidate market in response to such a price increase and on the profit margins earned on those products. The profit margin on incremental units is the difference between price and incremental cost on those units. The Agencies often estimate incremental costs, for example using merging parties' documents or data the merging parties use to make business decisions. Incremental cost is measured over the change in output that would be caused by the price increase under consideration.

In considering customers' likely responses to higher prices, the Agencies take into account any reasonably available and reliable evidence, including, but not limited to:

- how customers have shifted purchases in the past in response to relative changes in price or other terms and conditions;
- information from buyers, including surveys, concerning how they would respond to price changes;
- the conduct of industry participants, notably:
    - sellers' business decisions or business documents indicating sellers' informed beliefs concerning how customers would substitute among products in response to relative changes in price;
    - industry participants' behavior in tracking and responding to price changes by some or all rivals;
- objective information about product characteristics and the costs and delays of switching products, especially switching from products in the candidate market to products outside the candidate market;
- the percentage of sales lost by one product in the candidate market, when its price alone rises, that is recaptured by other products in the candidate market, with a higher recapture percentage making a price increase more profitable for the hypothetical monopolist;
- evidence from other industry participants, such as sellers of complementary products;
- legal or regulatory requirements; and
- the influence of downstream competition faced by customers in their output markets.

When the necessary data are available, the Agencies also may consider a "critical loss analysis" to assess the extent to which it corroborates inferences drawn from the evidence noted above. Critical loss analysis asks whether imposing at least a SSNIP on one or more products in a candidate market would raise or lower the hypothetical monopolist's profits. While this "breakeven" analysis differs from the profit-maximizing analysis called for by the hypothetical monopolist test in Section 4.1.1, merging parties sometimes present this type of analysis to the Agencies. A price increase raises profits on sales made at the higher price, but this will be offset to the extent customers substitute away from products in the candidate market. Critical loss analysis compares the magnitude of these two offsetting effects resulting from the price increase. The "critical loss" is defined as the number of lost unit sales that would leave profits unchanged. The "predicted loss" is defined as the number of unit sales that the hypothetical monopolist is predicted to lose due to the price increase. The price increase raises the hypothetical monopolist's profits if the predicted loss is less than the critical loss.

The Agencies consider all of the evidence of customer substitution noted above in assessing the predicted loss. The Agencies require that estimates of the predicted loss be consistent with that evidence, including the pre-merger margins of products in the candidate market used to calculate the critical loss. Unless the firms are engaging in coordinated interaction (see Section 7), high pre-merger margins normally indicate that each firm's product individually faces demand that is not highly sensitive to price.[6] Higher pre-merger margins thus indicate a smaller predicted loss as well as a smaller critical loss. The higher the pre-merger margin, the smaller the recapture percentage necessary for the candidate market to satisfy the hypothetical monopolist test.

Even when the evidence necessary to perform the hypothetical monopolist test quantitatively is not available, the conceptual framework of the test provides a useful methodological tool for gathering and analyzing evidence pertinent to customer substitution and to market definition. The Agencies follow the hypothetical monopolist test to the extent possible given the available evidence, bearing in mind that the ultimate goal of market definition is to help determine whether the merger may substantially lessen competition.

4.1.4 Product Market Definition with Targeted Customers

If a hypothetical monopolist could profitably target a subset of customers for price increases, the Agencies may identify relevant markets defined around those targeted customers, to whom a hypothetical monopolist would profitably and separately impose at least a SSNIP. Markets to serve targeted customers are also known as price discrimination markets. In practice, the Agencies identify price discrimination markets only where they believe there is a realistic prospect of an adverse competitive effect on a group of targeted customers.

> *Example 11:* Glass containers have many uses. In response to a price increase for glass containers, some users would substitute substantially to plastic or metal containers, but baby food manufacturers would not. If a hypothetical monopolist could price separately and limit arbitrage, baby food manufacturers would be vulnerable to a targeted increase in the price of glass containers. The Agencies could define a distinct market for glass containers used to package baby food.

The Agencies also often consider markets for targeted customers when prices are individually negotiated and suppliers have information about customers that would allow a hypothetical monopolist to identify customers that are likely to pay a higher price for the relevant product. If prices are negotiated individually with customers, the hypothetical monopolist test may suggest relevant markets that are as narrow as individual customers (see also Section 6.2 on bargaining and auctions). Nonetheless, the Agencies often define markets for groups of targeted customers, i.e., by type of customer, rather than by individual customer. By so doing, the Agencies are able to rely on aggregated market shares that can be more helpful in predicting the competitive effects of the merger.

4.2 Geographic Market Definition

The arena of competition affected by the merger may be geographically bounded if geography limits some customers' willingness or ability to substitute to some products, or some suppliers' willingness or ability to serve some customers. Both supplier and customer locations can affect this. The Agencies apply the principles of market definition described here and in Section 4.1 to define a relevant market with a geographic dimension as well as a product dimension.

---

[6] While margins are important for implementing the hypothetical monopolist test, high margins are not in themselves of antitrust concern.

The scope of geographic markets often depends on transportation costs. Other factors such as language, regulation, tariff and non-tariff trade barriers, custom and familiarity, reputation, and service availability may impede long-distance or international transactions. The competitive significance of foreign firms may be assessed at various exchange rates, especially if exchange rates have fluctuated in the recent past.

In the absence of price discrimination based on customer location, the Agencies normally define geographic markets based on the locations of suppliers, as explained in subsection 4.2.1. In other cases, notably if price discrimination based on customer location is feasible as is often the case when delivered pricing is commonly used in the industry, the Agencies may define geographic markets based on the locations of customers, as explained in subsection 4.2.2.

4.2.1 Geographic Markets Based on the Locations of Suppliers

Geographic markets based on the locations of suppliers encompass the region from which sales are made. Geographic markets of this type often apply when customers receive goods or services at suppliers' locations. Competitors in the market are firms with relevant production, sales, or service facilities in that region. Some customers who buy from these firms may be located outside the boundaries of the geographic market.

The hypothetical monopolist test requires that a hypothetical profit-maximizing firm that was the only present or future producer of the relevant product(s) located in the region would impose at least a SSNIP from at least one location, including at least one location of one of the merging firms. In this exercise the terms of sale for all products produced elsewhere are held constant. A single firm may operate in a number of different geographic markets, even for a single product.

> *Example 12:* The merging parties both have manufacturing plants in City X. The relevant product is expensive to transport and suppliers price their products for pickup at their locations. Rival plants are some distance away in City Y. A hypothetical monopolist controlling all plants in City X could profitably impose a SSNIP at these plants. Competition from more distant plants would not defeat the price increase because supplies coming from more distant plants require expensive transportation. The relevant geographic market is defined around the plants in City X.

When the geographic market is defined based on supplier locations, sales made by suppliers located in the geographic market are counted, regardless of the location of the customer making the purchase.

In considering likely reactions of customers to price increases for the relevant product(s) imposed in a candidate geographic market, the Agencies consider any reasonably available and reliable evidence, including:

- how customers have shifted purchases in the past between different geographic locations in response to relative changes in price or other terms and conditions;
- the cost and difficulty of transporting the product (or the cost and difficulty of a customer traveling to a seller's location), in relation to its price;
- whether suppliers need a presence near customers to provide service or support;

- evidence on whether sellers base business decisions on the prospect of customers switching between geographic locations in response to relative changes in price or other competitive variables;
- the costs and delays of switching from suppliers in the candidate geographic market to suppliers outside the candidate geographic market; and
- the influence of downstream competition faced by customers in their output markets.

4.2.2 Geographic Markets Based on the Locations of Customers

When the hypothetical monopolist could discriminate based on customer location, the Agencies may define geographic markets based on the locations of targeted customers.[7] Geographic markets of this type often apply when suppliers deliver their products or services to customers' locations. Geographic markets of this type encompass the region into which sales are made. Competitors in the market are firms that sell to customers in the specified region. Some suppliers that sell into the relevant market may be located outside the boundaries of the geographic market.

The hypothetical monopolist test requires that a hypothetical profit-maximizing firm that was the only present or future seller of the relevant product(s) to customers in the region would impose at least a SSNIP on some customers in that region. A region forms a relevant geographic market if this price increase would not be defeated by substitution away from the relevant product or by arbitrage, e.g., customers in the region travelling outside it to purchase the relevant product. In this exercise, the terms of sale for products sold to all customers outside the region are held constant.

> *Example 13:* Customers require local sales and support. Suppliers have sales and service operations in many geographic areas and can discriminate based on customer location. The geographic market can be defined around the locations of customers.

> *Example 14:* Each merging firm has a single manufacturing plant and delivers the relevant product to customers in City X and in City Y. The relevant product is expensive to transport. The merging firms' plants are by far the closest to City X, but no closer to City Y than are numerous rival plants. This fact pattern suggests that customers in City X may be harmed by the merger even if customers in City Y are not. For that reason, the Agencies consider a relevant geographic market defined around customers in City X. Such a market could be defined even if the region around the merging firms' plants would not be a relevant geographic market defined based on the location of sellers because a hypothetical monopolist controlling all plants in that region would find a SSNIP imposed on all of its customers unprofitable due to the loss of sales to customers in City Y.

When the geographic market is defined based on customer locations, sales made to those customers are counted, regardless of the location of the supplier making those sales.

> *Example 15:* Customers in the United States must use products approved by U.S. regulators. Foreign customers use products not

[7] For customers operating in multiple locations, only those customer locations within the targeted zone are included in the market.

approved by U.S. regulators. The relevant product market consists of products approved by U.S. regulators. The geographic market is defined around U.S. customers. Any sales made to U.S. customers by foreign suppliers are included in the market, and those foreign suppliers are participants in the U.S. market even though located outside it.

SECTION 5: MARKET PARTICIPANTS, MARKET SHARES, AND MARKET PARTICIPATION

The Agencies normally consider measures of market shares and market concentration as part of their evaluation of competitive effects. The Agencies evaluate market shares and concentration in conjunction with other reasonably available and reliable evidence for the ultimate purpose of determining whether a merger may substantially lessen competition.

Market shares can directly influence firms' competitive incentives. For example, if a price reduction to gain new customers would also apply to a firm's existing customers, a firm with a large market share may be more reluctant to implement a price reduction than one with a small share. Likewise, a firm with a large market share may not feel pressure to reduce price even if a smaller rival does. Market shares also can reflect firms' capabilities. For example, a firm with a large market share may be able to expand output rapidly by a larger absolute amount than can a small firm. Similarly, a large market share tends to indicate low costs, an attractive product, or both.

5.1 Market Participants

All firms that currently earn revenues in the relevant market are considered market participants. Vertically integrated firms are also included to the extent that their inclusion accurately reflects their competitive significance. Firms not currently earning revenues in the relevant market, but that have committed to entering the market in the near future, are also considered market participants.

Firms that are not current producers in a relevant market, but that would very likely provide rapid supply responses with direct competitive impact in the event of a SSNIP, without incurring significant sunk costs, are also considered market participants. These firms are termed "rapid entrants." Sunk costs are entry or exit costs that cannot be recovered outside the relevant market. Entry that would take place more slowly in response to adverse competitive effects, or that requires firms to incur significant sunk costs, is considered in Section 9.

Firms that produce the relevant product but do not sell it in the relevant geographic market may be rapid entrants. Other things equal, such firms are most likely to be rapid entrants if they are close to the geographic market.

> *Example 16:* Farm A grows tomatoes halfway between Cities X and Y. Currently, it ships its tomatoes to City X because prices there are two percent higher. Previously it has varied the destination of its shipments in response to small price variations. Farm A would likely be a rapid entrant participant in a market for tomatoes in City Y.

> *Example 17:* Firm B has bid multiple times to supply milk to School District S, and actually supplies milk to schools in some adjacent areas. It has never won a bid in School District S, but is well qualified to serve that district and has often nearly won. Firm B would be

counted as a rapid entrant in a market for school milk in School District S.

More generally, if the relevant market is defined around targeted customers, firms that produce relevant products but do not sell them to those customers may be rapid entrants if they can easily and rapidly begin selling to the targeted customers.

Firms that clearly possess the necessary assets to supply into the relevant market rapidly may also be rapid entrants. In markets for relatively homogeneous goods where a supplier's ability to compete depends predominantly on its costs and its capacity, and not on other factors such as experience or reputation in the relevant market, a supplier with efficient idle capacity, or readily available "swing" capacity currently used in adjacent markets that can easily and profitably be shifted to serve the relevant market, may be a rapid entrant.[8] However, idle capacity may be inefficient, and capacity used in adjacent markets may not be available, so a firm's possession of idle or swing capacity alone does not make that firm a rapid entrant.

5.2 Market Shares

The Agencies normally calculate market shares for all firms that currently produce products in the relevant market, subject to the availability of data. The Agencies also calculate market shares for other market participants if this can be done to reliably reflect their competitive significance.

Market concentration and market share data are normally based on historical evidence. However, recent or ongoing changes in market conditions may indicate that the current market share of a particular firm either understates or overstates the firm's future competitive significance. The Agencies consider reasonably predictable effects of recent or ongoing changes in market conditions when calculating and interpreting market share data. For example, if a new technology that is important to long-term competitive viability is available to other firms in the market, but is not available to a particular firm, the Agencies may conclude that that firm's historical market share overstates its future competitive significance. The Agencies may project historical market shares into the foreseeable future when this can be done reliably.

The Agencies measure market shares based on the best available indicator of firms' future competitive significance in the relevant market. This may depend upon the type of competitive effect being considered, and on the availability of data. Typically, annual data are used, but where individual transactions are large and infrequent so annual data may be unrepresentative, the Agencies may measure market shares over a longer period of time.

In most contexts, the Agencies measure each firm's market share based on its actual or projected revenues in the relevant market. Revenues in the relevant market tend to be the best measure of attractiveness to customers, since they reflect the real-world ability of firms to surmount all of the obstacles necessary to offer products on terms and conditions that are attractive to customers. In cases where one unit of a low-priced product can substitute for one unit of a higher-priced product, unit sales may measure

---

[8] If this type of supply side substitution is nearly universal among the firms selling one or more of a group of products, the Agencies may use an aggregate description of markets for those products as a matter of convenience.

competitive significance better than revenues. For example, a new, much less expensive product may have great competitive significance if it substantially erodes the revenues earned by older, higher-priced products, even if it earns relatively few revenues. In cases where customers sign long-term contracts, face switching costs, or tend to re-evaluate their suppliers only occasionally, revenues earned from recently acquired customers may better reflect the competitive significance of suppliers than do total revenues.

In markets for homogeneous products, a firm's competitive significance may derive principally from its ability and incentive to rapidly expand production in the relevant market in response to a price increase or output reduction by others in that market. As a result, a firm's competitive significance may depend upon its level of readily available capacity to serve the relevant market if that capacity is efficient enough to make such expansion profitable. In such markets, capacities or reserves may better reflect the future competitive significance of suppliers than revenues, and the Agencies may calculate market shares using those measures. Market participants that are not current producers may then be assigned positive market shares, but only if a measure of their competitive significance properly comparable to that of current producers is available. When market shares are measured based on firms' readily available capacities, the Agencies do not include capacity that is committed or so profitably employed outside the relevant market, or so high-cost, that it would not likely be used to respond to a SSNIP in the relevant market.

> *Example 18:* The geographic market is defined around customers in the United States. Firm X produces the relevant product outside the United States, and most of its sales are made to customers outside the United States. In most contexts, Firm X's market share will be based on its sales to U.S. customers, not its total sales or total capacity. However, if the relevant product is homogeneous, and if Firm X would significantly expand sales to U.S. customers rapidly and without incurring significant sunk costs in response to a SSNIP, the Agencies may base Firm X's market share on its readily available capacity to serve U.S. customers.

When the Agencies define markets serving targeted customers, these same principles are used to measure market shares, as they apply to those customers. In most contexts, each firm's market share is based on its actual or projected revenues from the targeted customers. However, the Agencies may instead measure market shares based on revenues from a broader group of customers if doing so would more accurately reflect the competitive significance of different suppliers in the relevant market. Revenues earned from a broader group of customers may also be used when better data are thereby available.

5.3 Market Concentration

Market concentration is often one useful indicator of likely competitive effects of a merger. In evaluating market concentration, the Agencies consider both the post-merger level of market concentration and the change in concentration resulting from a merger. Market shares may not fully reflect the competitive significance of firms in the market or the impact of a merger. They are used in conjunction with other evidence of competitive effects. See Sections 6 and 7.

In analyzing mergers between an incumbent and a recent or potential entrant, to the extent the Agencies use the change in concentration to evaluate competitive effects, they will do so using projected market shares. A merger between an incumbent and a potential entrant can raise significant competitive concerns. The lessening of competition resulting from such a merger is more likely to be substantial, the larger is the market share of the incumbent, the greater is the competitive significance of the potential entrant, and the greater is the competitive threat posed by this potential entrant relative to others.

The Agencies give more weight to market concentration when market shares have been stable over time, especially in the face of historical changes in relative prices or costs. If a firm has retained its market share even after its price has increased relative to those of its rivals, that firm already faces limited competitive constraints, making it less likely that its remaining rivals will replace the competition lost if one of that firm's important rivals is eliminated due to a merger. By contrast, even a highly concentrated market can be very competitive if market shares fluctuate substantially over short periods of time in response to changes in competitive offerings. However, if competition by one of the merging firms has significantly contributed to these fluctuations, perhaps because it has acted as a maverick, the Agencies will consider whether the merger will enhance market power by combining that firm with one of its significant rivals.

The Agencies may measure market concentration using the number of significant competitors in the market. This measure is most useful when there is a gap in market share between significant competitors and smaller rivals or when it is difficult to measure revenues in the relevant market. The Agencies also may consider the combined market share of the merging firms as an indicator of the extent to which others in the market may not be able readily to replace competition between the merging firms that is lost through the merger.

The Agencies often calculate the Herfindahl-Hirschman Index ("HHI") of market concentration. The HHI is calculated by summing the squares of the individual firms' market shares,[9] and thus gives proportionately greater weight to the larger market shares. When using the HHI, the Agencies consider both the post-merger level of the HHI and the increase in the HHI resulting from the merger. The increase in the HHI is equal to twice the product of the market shares of the merging firms.[10]

Based on their experience, the Agencies generally classify markets into three types:

- Unconcentrated Markets: HHI below 1500
- Moderately Concentrated Markets: HHI between 1500 and 2500
- Highly Concentrated Markets: HHI above 2500

The Agencies employ the following general standards for the relevant markets they have defined:

---

[9] For example, a market consisting of four firms with market shares of thirty percent, thirty percent, twenty percent, and twenty percent has an HHI of 2600 (302 + 302 + 202 + 202 = 2600). The HHI ranges from 10,000 (in the case of a pure monopoly) to a number approaching zero (in the case of an atomistic market). Although it is desirable to include all firms in the calculation, lack of information about firms with small shares is not critical because such firms do not affect the HHI significantly.

[10] For example, the merger of firms with shares of five percent and ten percent of the market would increase the HHI by 100 (5 × 10 × 2 = 100).

- *Small Change in Concentration:* Mergers involving an increase in the HHI of less than 100 points are unlikely to have adverse competitive effects and ordinarily require no further analysis.
- *Unconcentrated Markets:* Mergers resulting in unconcentrated markets are unlikely to have adverse competitive effects and ordinarily require no further analysis.
- *Moderately Concentrated Markets:* Mergers resulting in moderately concentrated markets that involve an increase in the HHI of more than 100 points potentially raise significant competitive concerns and often warrant scrutiny.
- *Highly Concentrated Markets:* Mergers resulting in highly concentrated markets that involve an increase in the HHI of between 100 points and 200 points potentially raise significant competitive concerns and often warrant scrutiny. Mergers resulting in highly concentrated markets that involve an increase in the HHI of more than 200 points will be presumed to be likely to enhance market power. The presumption may be rebutted by persuasive evidence showing that the merger is unlikely to enhance market power.

The purpose of these thresholds is not to provide a rigid screen to separate competitively benign mergers from anticompetitive ones, although high levels of concentration do raise concerns. Rather, they provide one way to identify some mergers unlikely to raise competitive concerns and some others for which it is particularly important to examine whether other competitive factors confirm, reinforce, or counteract the potentially harmful effects of increased concentration. The higher the post-merger HHI and the increase in the HHI, the greater are the Agencies' potential competitive concerns and the greater is the likelihood that the Agencies will request additional information to conduct their analysis.

SECTION 6: UNILATERAL EFFECTS

The elimination of competition between two firms that results from their merger may alone constitute a substantial lessening of competition. Such unilateral effects are most apparent in a merger to monopoly in a relevant market, but are by no means limited to that case. Whether cognizable efficiencies resulting from the merger are likely to reduce or reverse adverse unilateral effects is addressed in Section 10.

Several common types of unilateral effects are discussed in this section. Section 6.1 discusses unilateral price effects in markets with differentiated products. Section 6.2 discusses unilateral effects in markets where sellers negotiate with buyers or prices are determined through auctions. Section 6.3 discusses unilateral effects relating to reductions in output or capacity in markets for relatively homogeneous products. Section 6.4 discusses unilateral effects arising from diminished innovation or reduced product variety. These effects do not exhaust the types of possible unilateral effects; for example, exclusionary unilateral effects also can arise.

A merger may result in different unilateral effects along different dimensions of competition. For example, a merger may increase prices in the short term but not raise longer-term concerns about innovation, either because rivals will provide sufficient innovation competition or because the merger will generate cognizable research and development efficiencies. See Section 10.

6.1 Pricing of Differentiated Products

In differentiated product industries, some products can be very close substitutes and compete strongly with each other, while other products are more distant substitutes and compete less strongly. For example, one high-end product may compete much more directly with another high-end product than with any low-end product.

A merger between firms selling differentiated products may diminish competition by enabling the merged firm to profit by unilaterally raising the price of one or both products above the pre-merger level. Some of the sales lost due to the price rise will merely be diverted to the product of the merger partner and, depending on relative margins, capturing such sales loss through merger may make the price increase profitable even though it would not have been profitable prior to the merger.

The extent of direct competition between the products sold by the merging parties is central to the evaluation of unilateral price effects. Unilateral price effects are greater, the more the buyers of products sold by one merging firm consider products sold by the other merging firm to be their next choice. The Agencies consider any reasonably available and reliable information to evaluate the extent of direct competition between the products sold by the merging firms. This includes documentary and testimonial evidence, win/loss reports and evidence from discount approval processes, customer switching patterns, and customer surveys. The types of evidence relied on often overlap substantially with the types of evidence of customer substitution relevant to the hypothetical monopolist test. See Section 4.1.1.

Substantial unilateral price elevation post-merger for a product formerly sold by one of the merging firms normally requires that a significant fraction of the customers purchasing that product view products formerly sold by the other merging firm as their next-best choice. However, unless pre-merger margins between price and incremental cost are low, that significant fraction need not approach a majority. For this purpose, incremental cost is measured over the change in output that would be caused by the price change considered. A merger may produce significant unilateral effects for a given product even though many more sales are diverted to products sold by non-merging firms than to products previously sold by the merger partner.

> *Example 19:* In Example 5, the merged entity controlling Products A and B would raise prices ten percent, given the product offerings and prices of other firms. In that example, one-third of the sales lost by Product A when its price alone is raised are diverted to Product B. Further analysis is required to account for repositioning, entry, and efficiencies.

In some cases, the Agencies may seek to quantify the extent of direct competition between a product sold by one merging firm and a second product sold by the other merging firm by estimating the diversion ratio from the first product to the second product. The diversion ratio is the fraction of unit sales lost by the first product due to an increase in its price that would be diverted to the second product. Diversion ratios between products sold by one merging firm and products sold by the other merging firm can be very informative for assessing unilateral price effects, with higher diversion ratios indicating a greater likelihood of such effects. Diversion ratios between products sold by merging firms and those sold by non-merging firms have at most secondary predictive value.

Adverse unilateral price effects can arise when the merger gives the merged entity an incentive to raise the price of a product previously sold by one merging firm and thereby divert sales to products previously sold by the other merging firm, boosting the profits on the latter products. Taking as given other prices and product offerings, that boost to profits is equal to the value to the merged firm of the sales diverted to those products. The value of sales diverted to a product is equal to the number of units diverted to that product multiplied by the margin between price and incremental cost on that product. In some cases, where sufficient information is available, the Agencies assess the value of diverted sales, which can serve as an indicator of the upward pricing pressure on the first product resulting from the merger. Diagnosing unilateral price effects based on the value of diverted sales need not rely on market definition or the calculation of market shares and concentration. The Agencies rely much more on the value of diverted sales than on the level of the HHI for diagnosing unilateral price effects in markets with differentiated products. If the value of diverted sales is proportionately small, significant unilateral price effects are unlikely.[11]

Where sufficient data are available, the Agencies may construct economic models designed to quantify the unilateral price effects resulting from the merger. These models often include independent price responses by non-merging firms. They also can incorporate merger-specific efficiencies. These merger simulation methods need not rely on market definition. The Agencies do not treat merger simulation evidence as conclusive in itself, and they place more weight on whether their merger simulations consistently predict substantial price increases than on the precise prediction of any single simulation.

A merger is unlikely to generate substantial unilateral price increases if non-merging parties offer very close substitutes for the products offered by the merging firms. In some cases, non-merging firms may be able to reposition their products to offer close substitutes for the products offered by the merging firms. Repositioning is a supply-side response that is evaluated much like entry, with consideration given to timeliness, likelihood, and sufficiency. See Section 9. The Agencies consider whether repositioning would be sufficient to deter or counteract what otherwise would be significant anticompetitive unilateral effects from a differentiated products merger.

6.2 Bargaining and Auctions

In many industries, especially those involving intermediate goods and services, buyers and sellers negotiate to determine prices and other terms of trade. In that process, buyers commonly negotiate with more than one seller, and may play sellers off against one another. Some highly structured forms of such competition are known as auctions. Negotiations often combine aspects of an auction with aspects of one-on-one negotiation, although pure auctions are sometimes used in government procurement and elsewhere.

A merger between two competing sellers prevents buyers from playing those sellers off against each other in negotiations. This alone can significantly enhance the ability and incentive of the merged entity to obtain a result

[11] For this purpose, the value of diverted sales is measured in proportion to the lost revenues attributable to the reduction in unit sales resulting from the price increase. Those lost revenues equal the reduction in the number of units sold of that product multiplied by that product's price.

more favorable to it, and less favorable to the buyer, than the merging firms would have offered separately absent the merger. The Agencies analyze unilateral effects of this type using similar approaches to those described in Section 6.1.

Anticompetitive unilateral effects in these settings are likely in proportion to the frequency or probability with which, prior to the merger, one of the merging sellers had been the runner-up when the other won the business. These effects also are likely to be greater, the greater advantage the runner-up merging firm has over other suppliers in meeting customers' needs. These effects also tend to be greater, the more profitable were the pre-merger winning bids. All of these factors are likely to be small if there are many equally placed bidders.

The mechanisms of these anticompetitive unilateral effects, and the indicia of their likelihood, differ somewhat according to the bargaining practices used, the auction format, and the sellers' information about one another's costs and about buyers' preferences. For example, when the merging sellers are likely to know which buyers they are best and second best placed to serve, any anticompetitive unilateral effects are apt to be targeted at those buyers; when sellers are less well informed, such effects are more apt to be spread over a broader class of buyers.

6.3 Capacity and Output for Homogeneous Products

In markets involving relatively undifferentiated products, the Agencies may evaluate whether the merged firm will find it profitable unilaterally to suppress output and elevate the market price. A firm may leave capacity idle, refrain from building or obtaining capacity that would have been obtained absent the merger, or eliminate pre-existing production capabilities. A firm may also divert the use of capacity away from one relevant market and into another so as to raise the price in the former market. The competitive analyses of these alternative modes of output suppression may differ.

A unilateral output suppression strategy is more likely to be profitable when (1) the merged firm's market share is relatively high; (2) the share of the merged firm's output already committed for sale at prices unaffected by the output suppression is relatively low; (3) the margin on the suppressed output is relatively low; (4) the supply responses of rivals are relatively small; and (5) the market elasticity of demand is relatively low.

A merger may provide the merged firm a larger base of sales on which to benefit from the resulting price rise, or it may eliminate a competitor that otherwise could have expanded its output in response to the price rise.

> *Example 20:* Firms A and B both produce an industrial commodity and propose to merge. The demand for this commodity is insensitive to price. Firm A is the market leader. Firm B produces substantial output, but its operating margins are low because it operates high-cost plants. The other suppliers are operating very near capacity. The merged firm has an incentive to reduce output at the high-cost plants, perhaps shutting down some of that capacity, thus driving up the price it receives on the remainder of its output. The merger harms customers, notwithstanding that the merged firm shifts some output from high-cost plants to low-cost plants.

In some cases, a merger between a firm with a substantial share of the sales in the market and a firm with significant excess capacity to serve that market can make an output suppression strategy profitable.[12] This can occur even if the firm with the excess capacity has a relatively small share of sales, if that firm's ability to expand, and thus keep price from rising, has been making an output suppression strategy unprofitable for the firm with the larger market share.

6.4 Innovation and Product Variety

Competition often spurs firms to innovate. The Agencies may consider whether a merger is likely to diminish innovation competition by encouraging the merged firm to curtail its innovative efforts below the level that would prevail in the absence of the merger. That curtailment of innovation could take the form of reduced incentive to continue with an existing product-development effort or reduced incentive to initiate development of new products.

The first of these effects is most likely to occur if at least one of the merging firms is engaging in efforts to introduce new products that would capture substantial revenues from the other merging firm. The second, longer-run effect is most likely to occur if at least one of the merging firms has capabilities that are likely to lead it to develop new products in the future that would capture substantial revenues from the other merging firm. The Agencies therefore also consider whether a merger will diminish innovation competition by combining two of a very small number of firms with the strongest capabilities to successfully innovate in a specific direction.

The Agencies evaluate the extent to which successful innovation by one merging firm is likely to take sales from the other, and the extent to which post-merger incentives for future innovation will be lower than those that would prevail in the absence of the merger. The Agencies also consider whether the merger is likely to enable innovation that would not otherwise take place, by bringing together complementary capabilities that cannot be otherwise combined or for some other merger-specific reason. See Section 10.

The Agencies also consider whether a merger is likely to give the merged firm an incentive to cease offering one of the relevant products sold by the merging parties. Reductions in variety following a merger may or may not be anticompetitive. Mergers can lead to the efficient consolidation of products when variety offers little in value to customers. In other cases, a merger may increase variety by encouraging the merged firm to reposition its products to be more differentiated from one another.

If the merged firm would withdraw a product that a significant number of customers strongly prefer to those products that would remain available, this can constitute a harm to customers over and above any effects on the price or quality of any given product. If there is evidence of such an effect, the Agencies may inquire whether the reduction in variety is largely due to a loss of competitive incentives attributable to the merger. An anticompetitive incentive to eliminate a product as a result of the merger is greater and more likely, the larger is the share of profits from that product coming at the expense of profits from products sold by the merger partner. Where a merger substantially reduces competition by bringing two close substitute products under common ownership, and one of those products is eliminated, the merger will often also lead to a price increase on the

[12] Such a merger also can cause adverse coordinated effects, especially if the acquired firm with excess capacity was disrupting effective coordination.

remaining product, but that is not a necessary condition for anticompetitive effect.

Example 21: Firm A sells a high-end product at a premium price. Firm B sells a mid-range product at a lower price, serving customers who are more price sensitive. Several other firms have low-end products. Firms A and B together have a large share of the relevant market. Firm A proposes to acquire Firm B and discontinue Firm B's product. Firm A expects to retain most of Firm B's customers. Firm A may not find it profitable to raise the price of its high-end product after the merger, because doing so would reduce its ability to retain Firm B's more price-sensitive customers. The Agencies may conclude that the withdrawal of Firm B's product results from a loss of competition and materially harms customers.

SECTION 7: COORDINATED EFFECTS

A merger may diminish competition by enabling or encouraging post-merger coordinated interaction among firms in the relevant market that harms customers. Coordinated interaction involves conduct by multiple firms that is profitable for each of them only as a result of the accommodating reactions of the others. These reactions can blunt a firm's incentive to offer customers better deals by undercutting the extent to which such a move would win business away from rivals. They also can enhance a firm's incentive to raise prices, by assuaging the fear that such a move would lose customers to rivals.

Coordinated interaction includes a range of conduct. Coordinated interaction can involve the explicit negotiation of a common understanding of how firms will compete or refrain from competing. Such conduct typically would itself violate the antitrust laws. Coordinated interaction also can involve a similar common understanding that is not explicitly negotiated but would be enforced by the detection and punishment of deviations that would undermine the coordinated interaction. Coordinated interaction alternatively can involve parallel accommodating conduct not pursuant to a prior understanding. Parallel accommodating conduct includes situations in which each rival's response to competitive moves made by others is individually rational, and not motivated by retaliation or deterrence nor intended to sustain an agreed-upon market outcome, but nevertheless emboldens price increases and weakens competitive incentives to reduce prices or offer customers better terms. Coordinated interaction includes conduct not otherwise condemned by the antitrust laws.

The ability of rival firms to engage in coordinated conduct depends on the strength and predictability of rivals' responses to a price change or other competitive initiative. Under some circumstances, a merger can result in market concentration sufficient to strengthen such responses or enable multiple firms in the market to predict them more confidently, thereby affecting the competitive incentives of multiple firms in the market, not just the merged firm.

7.1 Impact of Merger on Coordinated Interaction

The Agencies examine whether a merger is likely to change the manner in which market participants interact, inducing substantially more coordinated interaction. The Agencies seek to identify how a merger might significantly weaken competitive incentives through an increase in the strength, extent, or likelihood of coordinated conduct. There are, however, numerous forms of coordination, and the risk that a merger will induce adverse coordinated effects may not be susceptible to quantification or detailed proof. Therefore, the Agencies evaluate the risk of coordinated effects using measures of market concentration (see Section 5) in conjunction with an assessment of whether a market is vulnerable to coordinated conduct. See Section 7.2. The analysis in Section 7.2 applies to moderately and highly concentrated markets, as unconcentrated markets are unlikely to be vulnerable to coordinated conduct.

Pursuant to the Clayton Act's incipiency standard, the Agencies may challenge mergers that in their judgment pose a real danger of harm through coordinated effects, even without specific evidence showing precisely how the coordination likely would take place. The Agencies are likely to challenge a merger if the following three conditions are all met: (1) the merger would significantly increase concentration and lead to a moderately or highly concentrated market; (2) that market shows signs of vulnerability to coordinated conduct (see Section 7.2); and (3) the Agencies have a credible basis on which to conclude that the merger may enhance that vulnerability. An acquisition eliminating a maverick firm (see Section 2.1.5) in a market vulnerable to coordinated conduct is likely to cause adverse coordinated effects.

7.2 Evidence a Market Is Vulnerable to Coordinated Conduct

The Agencies presume that market conditions are conducive to coordinated interaction if firms representing a substantial share in the relevant market appear to have previously engaged in express collusion affecting the relevant market, unless competitive conditions in the market have since changed significantly. Previous express collusion in another geographic market will have the same weight if the salient characteristics of that other market at the time of the collusion are comparable to those in the relevant market. Failed previous attempts at collusion in the relevant market suggest that successful collusion was difficult pre-merger but not so difficult as to deter attempts, and a merger may tend to make success more likely. Previous collusion or attempted collusion in another product market may also be given substantial weight if the salient characteristics of that other market at the time of the collusion are closely comparable to those in the relevant market.

A market typically is more vulnerable to coordinated conduct if each competitively important firm's significant competitive initiatives can be promptly and confidently observed by that firm's rivals. This is more likely to be the case if the terms offered to customers are relatively transparent. Price transparency can be greater for relatively homogeneous products. Even if terms of dealing are not transparent, transparency regarding the identities of the firms serving particular customers can give rise to coordination, e.g., through customer or territorial allocation. Regular monitoring by suppliers of one another's prices or customers can indicate that the terms offered to customers are relatively transparent.

A market typically is more vulnerable to coordinated conduct if a firm's prospective competitive reward from attracting customers away from its rivals will be significantly diminished by likely responses of those rivals. This is more likely to be the case, the stronger and faster are the responses the firm anticipates from its rivals. The firm is more likely to anticipate strong responses if there are few significant competitors, if products in the relevant market are relatively homogeneous, if customers find it relatively easy to switch between suppliers, or if suppliers use meeting-competition clauses.

A firm is more likely to be deterred from making competitive initiatives by whatever responses occur if sales are small and frequent rather than via occasional large and long-term contracts or if relatively few customers will switch to it before rivals are able to respond. A firm is less likely to be deterred by whatever responses occur if the firm has little stake in the status quo. For example, a firm with a small market share that can quickly and dramatically expand, constrained neither by limits on production nor by customer reluctance to switch providers or to entrust business to a historically small provider, is unlikely to be deterred. Firms are also less likely to be deterred by whatever responses occur if competition in the relevant market is marked by leapfrogging technological innovation, so that responses by competitors leave the gains from successful innovation largely intact.

A market is more apt to be vulnerable to coordinated conduct if the firm initiating a price increase will lose relatively few customers after rivals respond to the increase. Similarly, a market is more apt to be vulnerable to coordinated conduct if a firm that first offers a lower price or improved product to customers will retain relatively few customers thus attracted away from its rivals after those rivals respond.

The Agencies regard coordinated interaction as more likely, the more the participants stand to gain from successful coordination. Coordination generally is more profitable, the lower is the market elasticity of demand.

Coordinated conduct can harm customers even if not all firms in the relevant market engage in the coordination, but significant harm normally is likely only if a substantial part of the market is subject to such conduct. The prospect of harm depends on the collective market power, in the relevant market, of firms whose incentives to compete are substantially weakened by coordinated conduct. This collective market power is greater, the lower is the market elasticity of demand. This collective market power is diminished by the presence of other market participants with small market shares and little stake in the outcome resulting from the coordinated conduct, if these firms can rapidly expand their sales in the relevant market.

Buyer characteristics and the nature of the procurement process can affect coordination. For example, sellers may have the incentive to bid aggressively for a large contract even if they expect strong responses by rivals. This is especially the case for sellers with small market shares, if they can realistically win such large contracts. In some cases, a large buyer may be able to strategically undermine coordinated conduct, at least as it pertains to that buyer's needs, by choosing to put up for bid a few large contracts rather than many smaller ones, and by making its procurement decisions opaque to suppliers.

SECTION 8: POWERFUL BUYERS

Powerful buyers are often able to negotiate favorable terms with their suppliers. Such terms may reflect the lower costs of serving these buyers, but they also can reflect price discrimination in their favor.

The Agencies consider the possibility that powerful buyers may constrain the ability of the merging parties to raise prices. This can occur, for example, if powerful buyers have the ability and incentive to vertically integrate upstream or sponsor entry, or if the conduct or presence of large buyers undermines coordinated effects. However, the Agencies do not presume that the presence of powerful buyers alone forestalls adverse competitive effects flowing from the merger. Even buyers that can negotiate favorable terms may be harmed by an increase in market power. The Agencies examine the choices available to powerful buyers and how those choices likely would change due to the merger. Normally, a merger that eliminates a supplier whose presence contributed significantly to a buyer's negotiating leverage will harm that buyer.

> *Example 22:* Customer C has been able to negotiate lower pre-merger prices than other customers by threatening to shift its large volume of purchases from one merging firm to the other. No other suppliers are as well placed to meet Customer C's needs for volume and reliability. The merger is likely to harm Customer C. In this situation, the Agencies could identify a price discrimination market consisting of Customer C and similarly placed customers. The merger threatens to end previous price discrimination in their favor.

Furthermore, even if some powerful buyers could protect themselves, the Agencies also consider whether market power can be exercised against other buyers.

> *Example 23:* In Example 22, if Customer C instead obtained the lower pre-merger prices based on a credible threat to supply its own needs, or to sponsor new entry, Customer C might not be harmed. However, even in this case, other customers may still be harmed.

SECTION 9: ENTRY

The analysis of competitive effects in Sections 6 and 7 focuses on current participants in the relevant market. That analysis may also include some forms of entry. Firms that would rapidly and easily enter the market in response to a SSNIP are market participants and may be assigned market shares. See Sections 5.1 and 5.2. Firms that have, prior to the merger, committed to entering the market also will normally be treated as market participants. See Section 5.1. This section concerns entry or adjustments to pre-existing entry plans that are induced by the merger.

As part of their full assessment of competitive effects, the Agencies consider entry into the relevant market. The prospect of entry into the relevant market will alleviate concerns about adverse competitive effects only if such entry will deter or counteract any competitive effects of concern so the merger will not substantially harm customers.

The Agencies consider the actual history of entry into the relevant market and give substantial weight to this evidence. Lack of successful and effective entry in the face of non-transitory increases in the margins earned on products in the relevant market tends to suggest that successful entry is slow or difficult. Market values of incumbent firms greatly exceeding the replacement costs of their tangible assets may indicate that these firms have valuable intangible assets, which may be difficult or time consuming for an entrant to replicate.

A merger is not likely to enhance market power if entry into the market is so easy that the merged firm and its remaining rivals in the market, either unilaterally or collectively, could not profitably raise price or otherwise reduce competition compared to the level that would prevail in the absence of the merger. Entry is that easy if entry would be timely, likely, and sufficient in its magnitude, character, and scope to deter or counteract the competitive effects of concern.

The Agencies examine the timeliness, likelihood, and sufficiency of the entry efforts an entrant might practically employ. An entry effort is defined by the actions the firm must undertake to produce and sell in the market. Various elements of the entry effort will be considered. These elements can include: planning, design, and management; permitting, licensing, or other approvals; construction, debugging, and operation of production facilities; and promotion (including necessary introductory discounts), marketing, distribution, and satisfaction of customer testing and qualification requirements. Recent examples of entry, whether successful or unsuccessful, generally provide the starting point for identifying the elements of practical entry efforts. They also can be informative regarding the scale necessary for an entrant to be successful, the presence or absence of entry barriers, the factors that influence the timing of entry, the costs and risk associated with entry, and the sales opportunities realistically available to entrants.

If the assets necessary for an effective and profitable entry effort are widely available, the Agencies will not necessarily attempt to identify which firms might enter. Where an identifiable set of firms appears to have necessary assets that others lack, or to have particularly strong incentives to enter, the Agencies focus their entry analysis on those firms. Firms operating in adjacent or complementary markets, or large customers themselves, may be best placed to enter. However, the Agencies will not presume that a powerful firm in an adjacent market or a large customer will enter the relevant market unless there is reliable evidence supporting that conclusion.

In assessing whether entry will be timely, likely, and sufficient, the Agencies recognize that precise and detailed information may be difficult or impossible to obtain. The Agencies consider reasonably available and reliable evidence bearing on whether entry will satisfy the conditions of timeliness, likelihood, and sufficiency.

9.1 Timeliness

In order to deter the competitive effects of concern, entry must be rapid enough to make unprofitable overall the actions causing those effects and thus leading to entry, even though those actions would be profitable until entry takes effect.

Even if the prospect of entry does not deter the competitive effects of concern, post-merger entry may counteract them. This requires that the impact of entrants in the relevant market be rapid enough that customers are not significantly harmed by the merger, despite any anticompetitive harm that occurs prior to the entry.

The Agencies will not presume that an entrant can have a significant impact on prices before that entrant is ready to provide the relevant product to customers unless there is reliable evidence that anticipated future entry would have such an effect on prices.

9.2 Likelihood

Entry is likely if it would be profitable, accounting for the assets, capabilities, and capital needed and the risks involved, including the need for the entrant to incur costs that would not be recovered if the entrant later exits. Profitability depends upon (a) the output level the entrant is likely to obtain, accounting for the obstacles facing new entrants; (b) the price the entrant would likely obtain in the post-merger market, accounting for the impact of that entry itself on prices; and (c) the cost per unit the entrant would likely incur, which may depend upon the scale at which the entrant would operate.

9.3 Sufficiency

Even where timely and likely, entry may not be sufficient to deter or counteract the competitive effects of concern. For example, in a differentiated product industry, entry may be insufficient because the products offered by entrants are not close enough substitutes to the products offered by the merged firm to render a price increase by the merged firm unprofitable. Entry may also be insufficient due to constraints that limit entrants' competitive effectiveness, such as limitations on the capabilities of the firms best placed to enter or reputational barriers to rapid expansion by new entrants. Entry by a single firm that will replicate at least the scale and strength of one of the merging firms is sufficient. Entry by one or more firms operating at a smaller scale may be sufficient if such firms are not at a significant competitive disadvantage.

SECTION 10: EFFICIENCIES

Competition usually spurs firms to achieve efficiencies internally. Nevertheless, a primary benefit of mergers to the economy is their potential to generate significant efficiencies and thus enhance the merged firm's ability and incentive to compete, which may result in lower prices, improved quality, enhanced service, or new products. For example, merger-generated efficiencies may enhance competition by permitting two ineffective competitors to form a more effective competitor, e.g., by combining complementary assets. In a unilateral effects context, incremental cost reductions may reduce or reverse any increases in the merged firm's incentive to elevate price. Efficiencies also may lead to new or improved products, even if they do not immediately and directly affect price. In a coordinated effects context, incremental cost reductions may make coordination less likely or effective by enhancing the incentive of a maverick to lower price or by creating a new maverick firm. Even when efficiencies generated through a merger enhance a firm's ability to compete, however, a merger may have other effects that may lessen competition and make the merger anticompetitive.

The Agencies credit only those efficiencies likely to be accomplished with the proposed merger and unlikely to be accomplished in the absence of either the proposed merger or another means having comparable anticompetitive effects. These are termed merger-specific efficiencies.[13] Only alternatives that are practical in the business situation faced by the merging firms are considered in making this determination. The Agencies do not insist upon a less restrictive alternative that is merely theoretical.

Efficiencies are difficult to verify and quantify, in part because much of the information relating to efficiencies is uniquely in the possession of the merging firms. Moreover, efficiencies projected reasonably and in good faith by the merging firms may not be realized. Therefore, it is incumbent upon the merging firms to substantiate efficiency claims so that the Agencies can verify by reasonable means the likelihood and magnitude of each asserted efficiency, how and when each would be achieved (and any costs of doing so),

[13] The Agencies will not deem efficiencies to be merger-specific if they could be attained by practical alternatives that mitigate competitive concerns, such as divestiture or licensing. If a merger affects not whether but only when an efficiency would be achieved, only the timing advantage is a merger-specific efficiency.

how each would enhance the merged firm's ability and incentive to compete, and why each would be merger-specific.

Efficiency claims will not be considered if they are vague, speculative, or otherwise cannot be verified by reasonable means. Projections of efficiencies may be viewed with skepticism, particularly when generated outside of the usual business planning process. By contrast, efficiency claims substantiated by analogous past experience are those most likely to be credited.

Cognizable efficiencies are merger-specific efficiencies that have been verified and do not arise from anticompetitive reductions in output or service. Cognizable efficiencies are assessed net of costs produced by the merger or incurred in achieving those efficiencies.

The Agencies will not challenge a merger if cognizable efficiencies are of a character and magnitude such that the merger is not likely to be anticompetitive in any relevant market.[14] To make the requisite determination, the Agencies consider whether cognizable efficiencies likely would be sufficient to reverse the merger's potential to harm customers in the relevant market, e.g., by preventing price increases in that market.[15] In conducting this analysis, the Agencies will not simply compare the magnitude of the cognizable efficiencies with the magnitude of the likely harm to competition absent the efficiencies. The greater the potential adverse competitive effect of a merger, the greater must be the cognizable efficiencies, and the more they must be passed through to customers, for the Agencies to conclude that the merger will not have an anticompetitive effect in the relevant market. When the potential adverse competitive effect of a merger is likely to be particularly substantial, extraordinarily great cognizable efficiencies would be necessary to prevent the merger from being anticompetitive. In adhering to this approach, the Agencies are mindful that the antitrust laws give competition, not internal operational efficiency, primacy in protecting customers.

In the Agencies' experience, efficiencies are most likely to make a difference in merger analysis when the likely adverse competitive effects, absent the efficiencies, are not great. Efficiencies almost never justify a merger to monopoly or near-monopoly. Just as adverse competitive effects can arise along multiple dimensions of conduct, such as pricing and new product development, so too can efficiencies operate along multiple dimensions. Similarly, purported efficiency claims based on lower prices can be

---

[14] The Agencies normally assess competition in each relevant market affected by a merger independently and normally will challenge the merger if it is likely to be anticompetitive in any relevant market. In some cases, however, the Agencies in their prosecutorial discretion will consider efficiencies not strictly in the relevant market, but so inextricably linked with it that a partial divestiture or other remedy could not feasibly eliminate the anticompetitive effect in the relevant market without sacrificing the efficiencies in the other market(s). Inextricably linked efficiencies are most likely to make a difference when they are great and the likely anticompetitive effect in the relevant market(s) is small so the merger is likely to benefit customers overall.

[15] The Agencies normally give the most weight to the results of this analysis over the short term. The Agencies also may consider the effects of cognizable efficiencies with no short-term, direct effect on prices in the relevant market. Delayed benefits from efficiencies (due to delay in the achievement of, or the realization of customer benefits from, the efficiencies) will be given less weight because they are less proximate and more difficult to predict. Efficiencies relating to costs that are fixed in the short term are unlikely to benefit customers in the short term, but can benefit customers in the longer run, e.g., if they make new product introduction less expensive.

undermined if they rest on reductions in product quality or variety that customers value.

The Agencies have found that certain types of efficiencies are more likely to be cognizable and substantial than others. For example, efficiencies resulting from shifting production among facilities formerly owned separately, which enable the merging firms to reduce the incremental cost of production, are more likely to be susceptible to verification and are less likely to result from anticompetitive reductions in output. Other efficiencies, such as those relating to research and development, are potentially substantial but are generally less susceptible to verification and may be the result of anticompetitive output reductions. Yet others, such as those relating to procurement, management, or capital cost, are less likely to be merger-specific or substantial, or may not be cognizable for other reasons.

When evaluating the effects of a merger on innovation, the Agencies consider the ability of the merged firm to conduct research or development more effectively. Such efficiencies may spur innovation but not affect short-term pricing. The Agencies also consider the ability of the merged firm to appropriate a greater fraction of the benefits resulting from its innovations. Licensing and intellectual property conditions may be important to this enquiry, as they affect the ability of a firm to appropriate the benefits of its innovation. Research and development cost savings may be substantial and yet not be cognizable efficiencies because they are difficult to verify or result from anticompetitive reductions in innovative activities.

SECTION 11: FAILURE AND EXITING ASSETS

Notwithstanding the analysis above, a merger is not likely to enhance market power if imminent failure, as defined below, of one of the merging firms would cause the assets of that firm to exit the relevant market. This is an extreme instance of the more general circumstance in which the competitive significance of one of the merging firms is declining: the projected market share and significance of the exiting firm is zero. If the relevant assets would otherwise exit the market, customers are not worse off after the merger than they would have been had the merger been enjoined.

The Agencies do not normally credit claims that the assets of the failing firm would exit the relevant market unless all of the following circumstances are met: (1) the allegedly failing firm would be unable to meet its financial obligations in the near future; (2) it would not be able to reorganize successfully under Chapter 11 of the Bankruptcy Act; and (3) it has made unsuccessful good-faith efforts to elicit reasonable alternative offers that would keep its tangible and intangible assets in the relevant market and pose a less severe danger to competition than does the proposed merger.[16]

Similarly, a merger is unlikely to cause competitive harm if the risks to competition arise from the acquisition of a failing division. The Agencies do not normally credit claims that the assets of a division would exit the relevant market in the near future unless both of the following conditions are met: (1) applying cost allocation rules that reflect true economic costs, the division has a persistently negative cash flow on an operating basis, and such negative cash flow is not economically justified for the firm by benefits

[16] Any offer to purchase the assets of the failing firm for a price above the liquidation value of those assets will be regarded as a reasonable alternative offer. Liquidation value is the highest value the assets could command for use outside the relevant market.

such as added sales in complementary markets or enhanced customer goodwill;[17] and (2) the owner of the failing division has made unsuccessful good-faith efforts to elicit reasonable alternative offers that would keep its tangible and intangible assets in the relevant market and pose a less severe danger to competition than does the proposed acquisition.

SECTION 12: MERGERS OF COMPETING BUYERS

Mergers of competing buyers can enhance market power on the buying side of the market, just as mergers of competing sellers can enhance market power on the selling side of the market. Buyer market power is sometimes called "monopsony power."

To evaluate whether a merger is likely to enhance market power on the buying side of the market, the Agencies employ essentially the framework described above for evaluating whether a merger is likely to enhance market power on the selling side of the market. In defining relevant markets, the Agencies focus on the alternatives available to sellers in the face of a decrease in the price paid by a hypothetical monopsonist.

Market power on the buying side of the market is not a significant concern if suppliers have numerous attractive outlets for their goods or services. However, when that is not the case, the Agencies may conclude that the merger of competing buyers is likely to lessen competition in a manner harmful to sellers.

The Agencies distinguish between effects on sellers arising from a lessening of competition and effects arising in other ways. A merger that does not enhance market power on the buying side of the market can nevertheless lead to a reduction in prices paid by the merged firm, for example, by reducing transactions costs or allowing the merged firm to take advantage of volume-based discounts. Reduction in prices paid by the merging firms not arising from the enhancement of market power can be significant in the evaluation of efficiencies from a merger, as discussed in Section 10.

The Agencies do not view a short-run reduction in the quantity purchased as the only, or best, indicator of whether a merger enhances buyer market power. Nor do the Agencies evaluate the competitive effects of mergers between competing buyers strictly, or even primarily, on the basis of effects in the downstream markets in which the merging firms sell.

> *Example 24:* Merging Firms A and B are the only two buyers in the relevant geographic market for an agricultural product. Their merger will enhance buyer power and depress the price paid to farmers for this product, causing a transfer of wealth from farmers to the merged firm and inefficiently reducing supply. These effects can arise even if the merger will not lead to any increase in the price charged by the merged firm for its output.

SECTION 13: PARTIAL ACQUISITIONS

In most horizontal mergers, two competitors come under common ownership and control, completely and permanently eliminating competition between them. This elimination of competition is a basic element of merger analysis. However, the statutory provisions referenced in Section 1 also apply to one

---

[17] Because the parent firm can allocate costs, revenues, and intra-company transactions among itself and its subsidiaries and divisions, the Agencies require evidence on these two points that is not solely based on management plans that could have been prepared for the purpose of demonstrating negative cash flow or the prospect of exit from the relevant market.

firm's partial acquisition of a competitor. The Agencies therefore also review acquisitions of minority positions involving competing firms, even if such minority positions do not necessarily or completely eliminate competition between the parties to the transaction.

When the Agencies determine that a partial acquisition results in effective control of the target firm, or involves substantially all of the relevant assets of the target firm, they analyze the transaction much as they do a merger. Partial acquisitions that do not result in effective control may nevertheless present significant competitive concerns and may require a somewhat distinct analysis from that applied to full mergers or to acquisitions involving effective control. The details of the post-acquisition relationship between the parties, and how those details are likely to affect competition, can be important. While the Agencies will consider any way in which a partial acquisition may affect competition, they generally focus on three principal effects.

First, a partial acquisition can lessen competition by giving the acquiring firm the ability to influence the competitive conduct of the target firm. A voting interest in the target firm or specific governance rights, such as the right to appoint members to the board of directors, can permit such influence. Such influence can lessen competition because the acquiring firm can use its influence to induce the target firm to compete less aggressively or to coordinate its conduct with that of the acquiring firm.

Second, a partial acquisition can lessen competition by reducing the incentive of the acquiring firm to compete. Acquiring a minority position in a rival might significantly blunt the incentive of the acquiring firm to compete aggressively because it shares in the losses thereby inflicted on that rival. This reduction in the incentive of the acquiring firm to compete arises even if cannot influence the conduct of the target firm. As compared with the unilateral competitive effect of a full merger, this effect is likely attenuated by the fact that the ownership is only partial.

Third, a partial acquisition can lessen competition by giving the acquiring firm access to non-public, competitively sensitive information from the target firm. Even absent any ability to influence the conduct of the target firm, access to competitively sensitive information can lead to adverse unilateral or coordinated effects. For example, it can enhance the ability of the two firms to coordinate their behavior, and make other accommodating responses faster and more targeted. The risk of coordinated effects is greater if the transaction also facilitates the flow of competitively sensitive information from the acquiring firm to the target firm.

Partial acquisitions, like mergers, vary greatly in their potential for anticompetitive effects. Accordingly, the specific facts of each case must be examined to assess the likelihood of harm to competition. While partial acquisitions usually do not enable many of the types of efficiencies associated with mergers, the Agencies consider whether a partial acquisition is likely to create cognizable efficiencies.

9

ANTITRUST GUIDELINES FOR COLLABORATIONS AMONG COMPETITORS

FEDERAL TRADE COMMISSION AND U.S. DEPARTMENT OF JUSTICE ANTITRUST DIVISION

APRIL 7, 2000

TABLE OF CONTENTS

PREAMBLE

In order to compete in modern markets, competitors sometimes need to collaborate. Competitive forces are driving firms toward complex collaborations to achieve goals such as expanding into foreign markets, funding expensive innovation efforts, and lowering production and other costs.

Such collaborations often are not only benign but procompetitive. Indeed, in the last two decades, the federal antitrust agencies have brought relatively few civil cases against competitor collaborations. Nevertheless, a perception that antitrust laws are skeptical about agreements among actual or potential competitors may deter the development of procompetitive collaborations.[1]

To provide guidance to business people, the Federal Trade Commission ("FTC") and the U.S. Department of Justice ("DOJ") (collectively, "the Agencies") previously issued guidelines addressing several special circumstances in which antitrust issues related to competitor collaborations may arise.[2] But none of these Guidelines represents a general statement of

---

1 Congress has protected certain collaborations from full antitrust liability by passing the National Cooperative Research Act of 1984 ("NCRA") and the National Cooperative Research and Production Act of 1993 ("NCRPA") (codified together at 15 U.S.C. §§ 4301–06). Relatively few participants in research and production collaborations have sought to take advantage of the protections afforded by the NCRA and NCRPA, however.

2 The *Statements of Antitrust Enforcement Policy in Health Care* ("*Health Care Statements*") outline the Agencies' approach to certain health care collaborations, among other things. The *Antitrust Guidelines for the Licensing of Intellectual Property* ("*Intellectual Property Guidelines*") outline the Agencies' enforcement policy with respect to intellectual property licensing agreements among competitors, among other things. The *1992* DOJ/FTC *Horizontal Merger Guidelines*, as amended in 1997 ("*Horizontal Merger*

the Agencies' analytical approach to competitor collaborations. The increasing varieties and use of competitor collaborations have yielded requests for improved clarity regarding their treatment under the antitrust laws.

The new Antitrust Guidelines for Collaborations among Competitors ("Competitor Collaboration Guidelines") are intended to explain how the Agencies analyze certain antitrust issues raised by collaborations among competitors. Competitor collaborations and the market circumstances in which they operate vary widely. No set of guidelines can provide specific answers to every antitrust question that might arise from a competitor collaboration. These Guidelines describe an analytical framework to assist businesses in assessing the likelihood of an antitrust challenge to a collaboration with one or more competitors. They should enable businesses to evaluate proposed transactions with greater understanding of possible antitrust implications, thus encouraging procompetitive collaborations, deterring collaborations likely to harm competition and consumers, and facilitating the Agencies' investigations of collaborations.

SECTION 1: PURPOSE, DEFINITIONS, AND OVERVIEW

1.1 Purpose and Definitions

These Guidelines state the antitrust enforcement policy of the Agencies with respect to competitor collaborations. By stating their general policy, the Agencies hope to assist businesses in assessing whether the Agencies will challenge a competitor collaboration or any of the agreements of which it is comprised.[3] However, these Guidelines cannot remove judgment and discretion in antitrust law enforcement. The Agencies evaluate each case in light of its own facts and apply the analytical framework set forth in these Guidelines reasonably and flexibly.[4]

A "competitor collaboration" comprises a set of one or more agreements, other than merger agreements, between or among competitors to engage in economic activity, and the economic activity resulting therefrom.[5] "Competitors" include firms that are actual or potential competitors[6] in a relevant market.[7] Competitor collaborations involve one or more business activities, such as research and development ("R&D"), production, marketing, distribution, sales or purchasing. Information sharing and various trade association activities also may take place through competitor collaborations.

Guidelines"), outline the Agencies' approach to horizontal mergers and acquisitions, and certain competitor collaborations.

[3] These Guidelines neither describe how the Agencies litigate cases nor assign burdens of proof or production.

[4] The analytical framework set forth in these Guidelines is consistent with the analytical frameworks in the *Health Care Statements* and the *Intellectual Property Guidelines*, which remain in effect to address issues in their special contexts.

[5] These Guidelines do not address the possible exclusionary effects of agreements among competitors that may foreclose or limit competition by rivals.

[6] A firm is treated as a potential competitor if there is evidence that entry by that firm is reasonably probable in the absence of the relevant agreement, or that competitively significant decisions by actual competitors are constrained by concerns that anticompetitive conduct likely would induce the firm to enter.

[7] Firms also may be in a buyer-seller or other relationship, but that does not eliminate the need to examine the competitor relationship, if present.

These Guidelines use the terms "anticompetitive harm," "procompetitive benefit," and "overall competitive effect" in analyzing the competitive effects of agreements among competitors. All of these terms include actual and likely competitive effects. The Guidelines use the term "anticompetitive harm" to refer to an agreement's adverse competitive consequences, without taking account of offsetting procompetitive benefits. Conversely, the term "procompetitive benefit" refers to an agreement's favorable competitive consequences, without taking account of its anticompetitive harm. The terms "overall competitive effect" or "competitive effect" are used in discussing the combination of an agreement's anticompetitive harm and procompetitive benefit.

1.2 Overview of Analytical Framework

Two types of analysis are used by the Supreme Court to determine the lawfulness of an agreement among competitors: per se and rule of reason.[8] Certain types of agreements are so likely to harm competition and to have no significant procompetitive benefit that they do not warrant the time and expense required for particularized inquiry into their effects. Once identified, such agreements are challenged as per se unlawful.[9] All other agreements are evaluated under the rule of reason, which involves a factual inquiry into an agreement's overall competitive effect. As the Supreme Court has explained, rule of reason analysis entails a flexible inquiry and varies in focus and detail depending on the nature of the agreement and market circumstances.[10]

This overview briefly sets forth questions and factors that the Agencies assess in analyzing an agreement among competitors. The rest of the Guidelines should be consulted for the detailed definitions and discussion that underlie this analysis.

Agreements Challenged as Per Se Illegal. Agreements of a type that always or almost always tends to raise price or to reduce output are per se illegal. The Agencies challenge such agreements, once identified, as per se illegal. Types of agreements that have been held per se illegal include agreements among competitors to fix prices or output, rig bids, or share or divide markets by allocating customers, suppliers, territories, or lines of commerce. The Department of Justice prosecutes participants in such hard-core cartel agreements criminally. Because the courts conclusively presume such hard-core cartel agreements to be illegal, the Department of Justice treats them as such without inquiring into their claimed business purposes, anticompetitive harms, procompetitive benefits, or overall competitive effects.

Agreements Analyzed under the Rule of Reason. Agreements not challenged as per se illegal are analyzed under the rule of reason to determine their overall competitive effect. These include agreements of a type that otherwise might be considered per se illegal, provided they are reasonably related to, and reasonably necessary to achieve procompetitive benefits from, an efficiency-enhancing integration of economic activity.

Rule of reason analysis focuses on the state of competition with, as compared to without, the relevant agreement. The central question is

---

[8] *See* National Soc'y of Profl. Eng'rs v. United States, 435 U.S. 679, 692 (1978).

[9] *See* FTC v. Superior Court Trial Lawyers Ass'n, 493 U.S. 411, 432–36 (1990).

[10] *See* California Dental Ass'n v. FTC, 119 S. Ct. 1604, 1617–18 (1999); FTC v. Indiana Fed'n of Dentists, 476 U.S. 447, 459–61 (1986); National Collegiate Athletic Ass'n v. Board of Regents of the Univ. of Okla., 468 U.S. 85, 104–13 (1984).

whether the relevant agreement likely harms competition by increasing the ability or incentive profitably to raise price above or reduce output, quality, service, or innovation below what likely would prevail in the absence of the relevant agreement.

Rule of reason analysis entails a flexible inquiry and varies in focus and detail depending on the nature of the agreement and market circumstances. The Agencies focus on only those factors, and undertake only that factual inquiry, necessary to make a sound determination of the overall competitive effect of the relevant agreement. Ordinarily, however, no one factor is dispositive in the analysis.

The Agencies' analysis begins with an examination of the nature of the relevant agreement. As part of this examination, the Agencies ask about the business purpose of the agreement and examine whether the agreement, if already in operation, has caused anticompetitive harm. In some cases, the nature of the agreement and the absence of market power together may demonstrate the absence of anticompetitive harm. In such cases, the Agencies do not challenge the agreement. Alternatively, where the likelihood of anticompetitive harm is evident from the nature of the agreement, or anticompetitive harm has resulted from an agreement already in operation, then, absent overriding benefits that could offset the anticompetitive harm, the Agencies challenge such agreements without a detailed market analysis.

If the initial examination of the nature of the agreement indicates possible competitive concerns, but the agreement is not one that would be challenged without a detailed market analysis, the Agencies analyze the agreement in greater depth. The Agencies typically define relevant markets and calculate market shares and concentration as an initial step in assessing whether the agreement may create or increase market power or facilitate its exercise. The Agencies examine the extent to which the participants and the collaboration have the ability and incentive to compete independently. The Agencies also evaluate other market circumstances, e.g. entry, that may foster or prevent anticompetitive harms.

If the examination of these factors indicates no potential for anticompetitive harm, the Agencies end the investigation without considering procompetitive benefits. If investigation indicates anticompetitive harm, the Agencies examine whether the relevant agreement is reasonably necessary to achieve procompetitive benefits that likely would offset anticompetitive harms.

1.3 Competitor Collaborations Distinguished from Mergers

The competitive effects from competitor collaborations may differ from those of mergers due to a number of factors. Mergers completely end competition between the merging parties in the relevant market(s). By contrast, most competitor collaborations preserve some form of competition among the participants. This remaining competition may reduce competitive concerns, but also may raise questions about whether participants have agreed to anticompetitive restraints on the remaining competition.

Mergers are designed to be permanent, while competitor collaborations are more typically of limited duration. Thus, participants in a collaboration typically remain potential competitors, even if they are not actual competitors for certain purposes (e.g., R&D) during the collaboration. The potential for future competition between participants in a collaboration requires antitrust scrutiny different from that required for mergers.

Nonetheless, in some cases, competitor collaborations have competitive effects identical to those that would arise if the participants merged in whole or in part. The Agencies treat a competitor collaboration as a horizontal merger in a relevant market and analyze the collaboration pursuant to the *Horizontal Merger Guidelines* if: (a) the participants are competitors in that relevant market; (b) the formation of the collaboration involves an efficiency-enhancing integration of economic activity in the relevant market; (c) the integration eliminates all competition among the participants in the relevant market; and (d) the collaboration does not terminate within a sufficiently limited period[11] by its own specific and express terms.[12] Effects of the collaboration on competition in other markets are analyzed as appropriate under these Guidelines or other applicable precedent. See Example 1.[13]

SECTION 2: GENERAL PRINCIPLES FOR EVALUATING AGREEMENTS AMONG COMPETITORS

2.1 Potential Procompetitive Benefits

The Agencies recognize that consumers may benefit from competitor collaborations in a variety of ways. For example, a competitor collaboration may enable participants to offer goods or services that are cheaper, more valuable to consumers, or brought to market faster than would be possible absent the collaboration. A collaboration may allow its participants to better use existing assets, or may provide incentives for them to make output-enhancing investments that would not occur absent the collaboration. The potential efficiencies from competitor collaborations may be achieved through a variety of contractual arrangements including joint ventures, trade or professional associations, licensing arrangements, or strategic alliances.

Efficiency gains from competitor collaborations often stem from combinations of different capabilities or resources. For example, one participant may have special technical expertise that usefully complements another participant's manufacturing process, allowing the latter participant to lower its production cost or improve the quality of its product. In other instances, a collaboration may facilitate the attainment of scale or scope economies beyond the reach of any single participant. For example, two firms may be able to combine their research or marketing activities to lower their cost of bringing their products to market, or reduce the time needed to develop and begin commercial sales of new products. Consumers may benefit from these collaborations as the participants are able to lower prices, improve quality, or bring new products to market faster.

2.2 Potential Anticompetitive Harms

Competitor collaborations may harm competition and consumers by increasing the ability or incentive profitably to raise price above or reduce output, quality, service, or innovation below what likely would prevail in the absence of the relevant agreement. Such effects may arise through a

---

[11] In general, the Agencies use ten years as a term indicating sufficient permanence to justify treatment of a competitor collaboration as analogous to a merger. The length of this term may vary, however, depending on industry-specific circumstances, such as technology life cycles.

[12] This definition, however, does not determine obligations arising under the Hart-Scott-Rodino Antitrust Improvements Act of 1976, 15 U.S.C. § 18a.

[13] Examples illustrating this and other points set forth in these Guidelines are included in the Appendix.

variety of mechanisms. Among other things, agreements may limit independent decision making or combine the control of or financial interests in production, key assets, or decisions regarding price, output, or other competitively sensitive variables, or may otherwise reduce the participants' ability or incentive to compete independently.

Competitor collaborations also may facilitate explicit or tacit collusion through facilitating practices such as the exchange or disclosure of competitively sensitive information or through increased market concentration. Such collusion may involve the relevant market in which the collaboration operates or another market in which the participants in the collaboration are actual or potential competitors.

2.3 Analysis of the Overall Collaboration and the Agreements of Which It Consists

A competitor collaboration comprises a set of one or more agreements, other than merger agreements, between or among competitors to engage in economic activity, and the economic activity resulting therefrom. In general, the Agencies assess the competitive effects of the overall collaboration and any individual agreement or set of agreements within the collaboration that may harm competition. For purposes of these Guidelines, the phrase "relevant agreement" refers to whichever of these three the evaluating Agency is assessing. Two or more agreements are assessed together if their procompetitive benefits or anticompetitive harms are so intertwined that they cannot meaningfully be isolated and attributed to any individual agreement. *See* Example 2.

2.4 Competitive Effects Are Assessed as of the Time of Possible Harm to Competition

The competitive effects of a relevant agreement may change over time, depending on changes in circumstances such as internal reorganization, adoption of new agreements as part of the collaboration, addition or departure of participants, new market conditions, or changes in market share. The Agencies assess the competitive effects of a relevant agreement as of the time of possible harm to competition, whether at formation of the collaboration or at a later time, as appropriate. *See* Example 3. However, an assessment after a collaboration has been formed is sensitive to the reasonable expectations of participants whose significant sunk cost investments in reliance on the relevant agreement were made before it became anticompetitive.

SECTION 3: ANALYTICAL FRAMEWORK FOR EVALUATING AGREEMENTS AMONG COMPETITORS

3.1 Introduction

Section 3 sets forth the analytical framework that the Agencies use to evaluate the competitive effects of a competitor collaboration and the agreements of which it consists. Certain types of agreements are so likely to be harmful to competition and to have no significant benefits that they do not warrant the time and expense required for particularized inquiry into their effects.[14] Once identified, such agreements are challenged as per se illegal.[15]

[14] *See* Continental TV, Inc. v. GTE Sylvania Inc., 433 U.S. 36, 50 n.16 (1977).

[15] *See Superior Court Trial Lawyers Ass'n*, 493 U.S. at 432–36.

Agreements not challenged as per se illegal are analyzed under the rule of reason. Rule of reason analysis focuses on the state of competition with, as compared to without, the relevant agreement. Under the rule of reason, the central question is whether the relevant agreement likely harms competition by increasing the ability or incentive profitably to raise price above or reduce output, quality, service, or innovation below what likely would prevail in the absence of the relevant agreement. Given the great variety of competitor collaborations, rule of reason analysis entails a flexible inquiry and varies in focus and detail depending on the nature of the agreement and market circumstances. Rule of reason analysis focuses on only those factors, and undertakes only the degree of factual inquiry, necessary to assess accurately the overall competitive effect of the relevant agreement.[16]

The following sections describe in detail the Agencies' analytical framework.

3.2 Agreements Challenged as Per Se Illegal

Agreements of a type that always or almost always tends to raise price or reduce output are per se illegal.[17] The Agencies challenge such agreements, once identified, as per se illegal. Typically these are agreements not to compete on price or output. Types of agreements that have been held per se illegal include agreements among competitors to fix prices or output, rig bids, or share or divide markets by allocating customers, suppliers, territories or lines of commerce.[18] The Department of Justice prosecutes participants in such hard-core cartel agreements criminally. Because the courts conclusively presume such hard-core cartel agreements to be illegal, the Department of Justice treats them as such without inquiring into their claimed business purposes, anticompetitive harms, procompetitive benefits, or overall competitive effects.

If, however, participants in an efficiency-enhancing integration of economic activity enter into an agreement that is reasonably related to the integration and reasonably necessary to achieve its procompetitive benefits, the Agencies analyze the agreement under the rule of reason, even if it is of a type that might otherwise be considered per se illegal.[19] *See* Example 4. In an efficiency-enhancing integration, participants collaborate to perform or cause to be performed (by a joint venture entity created by the collaboration or by one or more participants or by a third party acting on behalf of other participants) one or more business functions, such as production, distribution, or R&D, and thereby benefit, or potentially benefit, consumers by expanding output, reducing price, or enhancing quality, service, or innovation. Participants in an efficiency-enhancing integration typically combine, by contract or otherwise, significant capital, technology, or other complementary assets to achieve procompetitive benefits that the participants could not achieve separately. The mere coordination of decisions on price, output, customers, territories, and the like is not integration, and cost savings without integration are not a basis for avoiding per se condemnation. The integration must promote procompetitive benefits that are cognizable under the efficiencies analysis

---

[16] *See California Dental Ass'n*, 119 S. Ct. at 1617–18; *Indiana Fed'n of Dentists*, 476 U.S. at 459–61; NCAA, 468 U.S. at 104–13.

[17] *See* Broadcast Music, Inc. v. Columbia Broadcasting Sys., 441 U.S. 1, 19–20 (1979).

[18] *See, e.g.,* Palmer v. BRG of Georgia, Inc., 498 U.S. 46 (1990) (market allocation); United States v. Trenton Potteries Co., 273 U.S. 392 (1927) (price fixing).

[19] *See* Arizona v. Maricopa County Medical Soc'y, 457 U.S. 332, 339 n.7, 356–57 (1982) (finding no integration).

set forth in Section 3.36 below. Such procompetitive benefits may enhance the participants' ability or incentives to compete and thus may offset an agreement's anticompetitive tendencies. *See* Examples 5 through 7.

An agreement may be "reasonably necessary" without being essential. However, if the participants could achieve an equivalent or comparable efficiency-enhancing integration through practical, significantly less restrictive means, then the Agencies conclude that the agreement is not reasonably necessary.[20] In making this assessment, except in unusual circumstances, the Agencies consider whether practical, significantly less restrictive means were reasonably available when the agreement was entered into, but do not search for a theoretically less restrictive alternative that was not practical given the business realities.

Before accepting a claim that an agreement is reasonably necessary to achieve procompetitive benefits from an integration of economic activity, the Agencies undertake a limited factual inquiry to evaluate the claim.[21] Such an inquiry may reveal that efficiencies from an agreement that are possible in theory are not plausible in the context of the particular collaboration. Some claims—such as those premised on the notion that competition itself is unreasonable—are insufficient as a matter of law,[22] and others may be implausible on their face. In any case, labeling an arrangement a "joint venture" will not protect what is merely a device to raise price or restrict output;[23] the nature of the conduct, not its designation, is determinative.

3.3 Agreements Analyzed under the Rule of Reason

Agreements not challenged as per se illegal are analyzed under the rule of reason to determine their overall competitive effect. Rule of reason analysis focuses on the state of competition with, as compared to without, the relevant agreement. The central question is whether the relevant agreement likely harms competition by increasing the ability or incentive profitably to raise price above or reduce output, quality, service, or innovation below what likely would prevail in the absence of the relevant agreement.[24]

Rule of reason analysis entails a flexible inquiry and varies in focus and detail depending on the nature of the agreement and market circumstances.[25] The Agencies focus on only those factors, and undertake only that factual inquiry, necessary to make a sound determination of the

---

[20] *See id.* at 352–53 (observing that even if a maximum fee schedule for physicians' services were desirable, it was not necessary that the schedule be established by physicians rather than by insurers); *Broadcast Music*, 441 U.S. at 20–21 (setting of price "necessary" for the blanket license).

[21] *See Maricopa*, 457 U.S. at 352–53, 356–57 (scrutinizing the defendant medical foundations for indicia of integration and evaluating the record evidence regarding less restrictive alternatives).

[22] *See Indiana Fed'n of Dentists*, 476 U.S. at 463–64; NCAA, 468 U.S. at 116–17; *Prof'l. Eng'rs*, 435 U.S. at 693–96. Other claims, such as an absence of market power, are no defense to per se illegality. *See Superior Court Trial Lawyers Ass'n*, 493 U.S. at 434–36; United States v. Socony-Vacuum Oil Co., 310 U.S. 150, 224–26 & n.59 (1940).

[23] *See* Timken Roller Bearing Co. v. United States, 341 U.S. 593, 598 (1951).

[24] In addition, concerns may arise where an agreement increases the ability or incentive of buyers to exercise monopsony power. *See infra* Section 3.31(a).

[25] *See California Dental Ass'n*, 119 S. Ct. at 1612–13, 1617 ("What is required . . . is an enquiry meet for the case, looking to the circumstances, details, and logic of a restraint."); *NCAA*, 468 U.S. 109 n.39 ("the rule of reason can sometimes be applied in the twinkling of an eye") (quoting Phillip E. Areeda, *The "Rule of Reason" in Antitrust Analysis: General Issues* 37–38 (Federal Judicial Center, June 1981)).

overall competitive effect of the relevant agreement. Ordinarily, however, no one factor is dispositive in the analysis.

Under the rule of reason, the Agencies' analysis begins with an examination of the nature of the relevant agreement, since the nature of the agreement determines the types of anticompetitive harms that may be of concern. As part of this examination, the Agencies ask about the business purpose of the agreement and examine whether the agreement, if already in operation, has caused anticompetitive harm.[26] If the nature of the agreement and the absence of market power[27] together demonstrate the absence of anticompetitive harm, the Agencies do not challenge the agreement. *See* Example 8. Alternatively, where the likelihood of anticompetitive harm is evident from the nature of the agreement,[28] or anticompetitive harm has resulted from an agreement already in operation,[29] then, absent overriding benefits that could offset the anticompetitive harm, the Agencies challenge such agreements without a detailed market analysis.[30]

If the initial examination of the nature of the agreement indicates possible competitive concerns, but the agreement is not one that would be challenged without a detailed market analysis, the Agencies analyze the agreement in greater depth. The Agencies typically define relevant markets and calculate market shares and concentration as an initial step in assessing whether the agreement may create or increase market power[31] or facilitate its exercise and thus poses risks to competition.[32] The Agencies examine factors relevant to the extent to which the participants and the collaboration have the ability and incentive to compete independently, such as whether an agreement is exclusive or non-exclusive and its duration.[33] The Agencies also evaluate whether entry would be timely, likely, and sufficient to deter or counteract any anticompetitive harms. In addition, the

---

[26] *See* Board of Trade of the City of Chicago v. United States, 246 U.S. 231, 238 (1918).

[27] That market power is absent may be determined without defining a relevant market. For example, if no market power is likely under any plausible market definition, it does not matter which one is correct.

[28] *See California Dental Ass'n*, 119 S. Ct. at 1612–13, 1617 (an "obvious anticompetitive effect" would warrant quick condemnation); *Indiana Fed'n of Dentists*, 476 U.S. at 459; *NCAA*, 468 U.S. at 104, 106–10.

[29] *See Indiana Fed'n of Dentists*, 476 U.S. at 460–61 ("Since the purpose of the inquiries into market definition and market power is to determine whether an arrangement has the potential for genuine adverse effects on competition, 'proof of actual detrimental effects, such as a reduction of output,' can obviate the need for an inquiry into market power, which is but a 'surrogate for detrimental effects.' ") (quoting 7 Phillip E. Areeda, *Antitrust Law* ¶ 1511, at 424 (1986)); *NCAA*, 468 U.S. at 104–08, 110 n.42.

[30] *See Indiana Fed'n of Dentists*, 476 U.S. at 459–60 (condemning without "detailed market analysis" an agreement to limit competition by withholding x-rays from patients' insurers after finding no competitive justification).

[31] Market power to a seller is the ability profitably to maintain prices above competitive levels for a significant period of time. Sellers also may exercise market power with respect to significant competitive dimensions other than price, such as quality, service, or innovation. Market power to a buyer is the ability profitably to depress the price paid for a product below the competitive level for a significant period of time and thereby depress output.

[32] *See* Eastman Kodak Co. v. Image Technical Services, Inc., 504 U.S. 451, 464 (1992).

[33] *Compare NCAA*, 468 U.S. at 113–15, 119–20 (noting that colleges were not permitted to televise their own games without restraint), *with Broadcast Music*, 441 U.S. at 23–24 (finding no legal or practical impediment to individual licenses).

Agencies assess any other market circumstances that may foster or impede anticompetitive harms.

If the examination of these factors indicates no potential for anticompetitive harm, the Agencies end the investigation without considering procompetitive benefits. If investigation indicates anticompetitive harm, the Agencies examine whether the relevant agreement is reasonably necessary to achieve procompetitive benefits that likely would offset anticompetitive harms.[34]

3.31 Nature of the Relevant Agreement: Business Purpose, Operation in the Marketplace and Possible Competitive Concerns

The nature of the agreement is relevant to whether it may cause anticompetitive harm. For example, by limiting independent decision making or combining control over or financial interests in production, key assets, or decisions on price, output, or other competitively sensitive variables, an agreement may create or increase market power or facilitate its exercise by the collaboration, its participants, or both. An agreement to limit independent decision making or to combine control or financial interests may reduce the ability or incentive to compete independently. An agreement also may increase the likelihood of an exercise of market power by facilitating explicit or tacit collusion,[35] either through facilitating practices such as an exchange of competitively sensitive information or through increased market concentration.

In examining the nature of the relevant agreement, the Agencies take into account inferences about business purposes for the agreement that can be drawn from objective facts. The Agencies also consider evidence of the subjective intent of the participants to the extent that it sheds light on competitive effects.[36] The Agencies do not undertake a full analysis of procompetitive benefits pursuant to Section 3.36 below, however, unless an anticompetitive harm appears likely.

The Agencies also examine whether an agreement already in operation has caused anticompetitive harm.[37] Anticompetitive harm may be observed, for example, if a competitor collaboration successfully mandates new, anticompetitive conduct or successfully eliminates procompetitive pre-collaboration conduct, such as withholding services that were desired by consumers when offered in a competitive market. If anticompetitive harm is found, examination of market power ordinarily is not required. In some cases, however, a determination of anticompetitive harm may be informed by consideration of market power.

---

[34] *See NCAA*, 468 U.S. at 113–15 (rejecting efficiency claims when production was limited, not enhanced); *Prof'l. Eng'rs*, 435 U.S. at 696 (dictum) (distinguishing restraints that promote competition from those that eliminate competition); *Chicago Bd. of Trade*, 246 U.S. at 238 (same).

[35] As used in these Guidelines, "collusion" is not limited to conduct that involves an agreement under the antitrust laws.

[36] Anticompetitive intent alone does not establish an antitrust violation, and procompetitive intent does not preclude a violation. *See, e.g., Chicago Bd. of Trade*, 246 U.S. at 238. But extrinsic evidence of intent may aid in evaluating market power, the likelihood of anticompetitive harm, and claimed procompetitive justifications where an agreement's effects are otherwise ambiguous.

[37] *See id.*

The following sections illustrate competitive concerns that may arise from the nature of particular types of competitor collaborations. This list is not exhaustive. In addition, where these sections address agreements of a type that otherwise might be considered per se illegal, such as agreements on price, the discussion assumes that the agreements already have been determined to be subject to rule of reason analysis because they are reasonably related to, and reasonably necessary to achieve procompetitive benefits from, an efficiency-enhancing integration of economic activity. See supra Section 3.2.

3.31(a) Relevant Agreements that Limit Independent Decision Making or Combine Control or Financial Interests

The following is intended to illustrate but not exhaust the types of agreements that might harm competition by eliminating independent decision making or combining control or financial interests.

Production Collaborations. Competitor collaborations may involve agreements jointly to produce a product sold to others or used by the participants as an input. Such agreements are often procompetitive.[38] Participants may combine complementary technologies, know-how, or other assets to enable the collaboration to produce a good more efficiently or to produce a good that no one participant alone could produce. However, production collaborations may involve agreements on the level of output or the use of key assets, or on the price at which the product will be marketed by the collaboration, or on other competitively significant variables, such as quality, service, or promotional strategies, that can result in anticompetitive harm. Such agreements can create or increase market power or facilitate its exercise by limiting independent decision making or by combining in the collaboration, or in certain participants, the control over some or all production or key assets or decisions about key competitive variables that otherwise would be controlled independently.[39] Such agreements could reduce individual participants' control over assets necessary to compete and thereby reduce their ability to compete independently, combine financial interests in ways that undermine incentives to compete independently, or both.

Marketing Collaborations. Competitor collaborations may involve agreements jointly to sell, distribute, or promote goods or services that are either jointly or individually produced. Such agreements may be procompetitive, for example, where a combination of complementary assets enables products more quickly and efficiently to reach the marketplace. However, marketing collaborations may involve agreements on price, output, or other competitively significant variables, or on the use of competitively significant assets, such as an extensive distribution network, that can result in anticompetitive harm. Such agreements can create or

---

[38] The *NCRPA* accords rule of reason treatment to certain production collaborations. However, the statute permits per se challenges, in appropriate circumstances, to a variety of activities, including agreements to jointly market the goods or services produced or to limit the participants' independent sale of goods or services produced outside the collaboration. *NCRPA*, 15 U.S.C. §§ 4301–02.

[39] For example, where output resulting from a collaboration is transferred to participants for independent marketing, anticompetitive harm could result if that output is restricted or if the transfer takes place at a supracompetitive price. Such conduct could raise participants' marginal costs through inflated per-unit charges on the transfer of the collaboration's output. Anticompetitive harm could occur even if there is vigorous competition among collaboration participants in the output market, since all the participants would have paid the same inflated transfer price.

increase market power or facilitate its exercise by limiting independent decision making; by combining in the collaboration, or in certain participants, control over competitively significant assets or decisions about competitively significant variables that otherwise would be controlled independently; or by combining financial interests in ways that undermine incentives to compete independently. For example, joint promotion might reduce or eliminate comparative advertising, thus harming competition by restricting information to consumers on price and other competitively significant variables.

Buying Collaborations. Competitor collaborations may involve agreements jointly to purchase necessary inputs. Many such agreements do not raise antitrust concerns and indeed may be procompetitive. Purchasing collaborations, for example, may enable participants to centralize ordering, to combine warehousing or distribution functions more efficiently, or to achieve other efficiencies. However, such agreements can create or increase market power (which, in the case of buyers, is called "monopsony power") or facilitate its exercise by increasing the ability or incentive to drive the price of the purchased product, and thereby depress output, below what likely would prevail in the absence of the relevant agreement. Buying collaborations also may facilitate collusion by standardizing participants' costs or by enhancing the ability to project or monitor a participant's output level through knowledge of its input purchases.

Research & Development Collaborations. Competitor collaborations may involve agreements to engage in joint research and development ("R&D"). Most such agreements are procompetitive, and they typically are analyzed under the rule of reason.[40] Through the combination of complementary assets, technology, or know-how, an R&D collaboration may enable participants more quickly or more efficiently to research and develop new or improved goods, services, or production processes. Joint R&D agreements, however, can create or increase market power or facilitate its exercise by limiting independent decision making or by combining in the collaboration, or in certain participants, control over competitively significant assets or all or a portion of participants' individual competitive R&D efforts. Although R&D collaborations also may facilitate tacit collusion on R&D efforts, achieving, monitoring, and punishing departures from collusion is sometimes difficult in the R&D context.

An exercise of market power may injure consumers by reducing innovation below the level that otherwise would prevail, leading to fewer or no products for consumers to choose from, lower quality products, or products that reach consumers more slowly than they otherwise would. An exercise of market power also may injure consumers by reducing the number of independent competitors in the market for the goods, services, or production processes derived from the R&D collaboration, leading to higher prices or reduced output, quality, or service. A central question is whether the agreement increases the ability or incentive anticompetitively to reduce R&D efforts pursued independently or through the collaboration, for example, by slowing the pace at which R&D efforts are pursued. Other considerations being equal, R&D agreements are more likely to raise competitive concerns when the collaboration or its participants already possess a secure source of

---

[40] *See NCRPA*, 15 U.S.C. §§ 4301–02. However, the statute permits per se challenges, in appropriate circumstances, to a variety of activities, including agreements to jointly market the fruits of collaborative R&D or to limit the participants' independent R&D or their sale or licensing of goods, services, or processes developed outside the collaboration. *Id.*

market power over an existing product and the new R&D efforts might cannibalize their supracompetitive earnings. In addition, anticompetitive harm generally is more likely when R&D competition is confined to firms with specialized characteristics or assets, such as intellectual property, or when a regulatory approval process limits the ability of late-comers to catch up with competitors already engaged in the R&D.

3.31(b) Relevant Agreements that May Facilitate Collusion

Each of the types of competitor collaborations outlined above can facilitate collusion. Competitor collaborations may provide an opportunity for participants to discuss and agree on anticompetitive terms, or otherwise to collude anticompetitively, as well as a greater ability to detect and punish deviations that would undermine the collusion. Certain marketing, production, and buying collaborations, for example, may provide opportunities for their participants to collude on price, output, customers, territories, or other competitively sensitive variables. R&D collaborations, however, may be less likely to facilitate collusion regarding R&D activities since R&D often is conducted in secret, and it thus may be difficult to monitor an agreement to coordinate R&D. In addition, collaborations can increase concentration in a relevant market and thus increase the likelihood of collusion among all firms, including the collaboration and its participants.

Agreements that facilitate collusion sometimes involve the exchange or disclosure of information. The Agencies recognize that the sharing of information among competitors may be procompetitive and is often reasonably necessary to achieve the procompetitive benefits of certain collaborations; for example, sharing certain technology, know-how, or other intellectual property may be essential to achieve the procompetitive benefits of an R&D collaboration. Nevertheless, in some cases, the sharing of information related to a market in which the collaboration operates or in which the participants are actual or potential competitors may increase the likelihood of collusion on matters such as price, output, or other competitively sensitive variables. The competitive concern depends on the nature of the information shared. Other things being equal, the sharing of information relating to price, output, costs, or strategic planning is more likely to raise competitive concern than the sharing of information relating to less competitively sensitive variables. Similarly, other things being equal, the sharing of information on current operating and future business plans is more likely to raise concerns than the sharing of historical information. Finally, other things being equal, the sharing of individual company data is more likely to raise concern than the sharing of aggregated data that does not permit recipients to identify individual firm data.

3.32 Relevant Markets Affected by the Collaboration

The Agencies typically identify and assess competitive effects in all of the relevant product and geographic markets in which competition may be affected by a competitor collaboration, although in some cases it may be possible to assess competitive effects directly without defining a particular relevant market(s). Markets affected by a competitor collaboration include all markets in which the economic integration of the participants' operations occurs or in which the collaboration operates or will operate,[41]

[41] For example, where a production joint venture buys inputs from an upstream market to incorporate in products to be sold in a downstream market, both upstream and downstream markets may be "markets affected by a competitor collaboration."

and may also include additional markets in which any participant is an actual or potential competitor.[42]

3.32(a) Goods Markets

In general, for goods[43] markets affected by a competitor collaboration, the Agencies approach relevant market definition as described in Section 1 of the *Horizontal Merger Guidelines*. To determine the relevant market, the Agencies generally consider the likely reaction of buyers to a price increase and typically ask, among other things, how buyers would respond to increases over prevailing price levels. However, when circumstances strongly suggest that the prevailing price exceeds what likely would have prevailed absent the relevant agreement, the Agencies use a price more reflective of the price that likely would have prevailed. Once a market has been defined, market shares are assigned both to firms currently in the relevant market and to firms that are able to make "uncommitted" supply responses. See Sections 1.31 and 1.32 of the *Horizontal Merger Guidelines*.

3.32(b) Technology Markets

When rights to intellectual property are marketed separately from the products in which they are used, the Agencies may define technology markets in assessing the competitive effects of a competitor collaboration that includes an agreement to license intellectual property. Technology markets consist of the intellectual property that is licensed and its close substitutes; that is, the technologies or goods that are close enough substitutes significantly to constrain the exercise of market power with respect to the intellectual property that is licensed. The Agencies approach the definition of a relevant technology market and the measurement of market share as described in Section 3.2.2 of the Intellectual Property Guidelines.

3.32(c) Research and Development: Innovation Markets

In many cases, an agreement's competitive effects on innovation are analyzed as a separate competitive effect in a relevant goods market. However, if a competitor collaboration may have competitive effects on innovation that cannot be adequately addressed through the analysis of goods or technology markets, the Agencies may define and analyze an innovation market as described in Section 3.2.3 of the Intellectual Property Guidelines. An innovation market consists of the research and development directed to particular new or improved goods or processes and the close substitutes for that research and development. The Agencies define an innovation market only when the capabilities to engage in the relevant research and development can be associated with specialized assets or characteristics of specific firms.

3.33 Market Shares and Market Concentration

Market share and market concentration affect the likelihood that the relevant agreement will create or increase market power or facilitate its exercise. The creation, increase, or facilitation of market power will likely increase the ability and incentive profitably to raise price above or reduce output, quality, service, or innovation below what likely would prevail in the absence of the relevant agreement.

---

[42] Participation in the collaboration may change the participants' behavior in this third category of markets, for example, by altering incentives and available information, or by providing an opportunity to form additional agreements among participants.

[43] The term "goods" also includes services.

Other things being equal, market share affects the extent to which participants or the collaboration must restrict their own output in order to achieve anticompetitive effects in a relevant market. The smaller the percentage of total supply that a firm controls, the more severely it must restrict its own output in order to produce a given price increase, and the less likely it is that an output restriction will be profitable. In assessing whether an agreement may cause anticompetitive harm, the Agencies typically calculate the market shares of the participants and of the collaboration.[44] The Agencies assign a range of market shares to the collaboration. The high end of that range is the sum of the market shares of the collaboration and its participants. The low end is the share of the collaboration in isolation. In general, the Agencies approach the calculation of market share as set forth in Section 1.4 of the *Horizontal Merger Guidelines.*

Other things being equal, market concentration affects the difficulties and costs of achieving and enforcing collusion in a relevant market. Accordingly, in assessing whether an agreement may increase the likelihood of collusion, the Agencies calculate market concentration. In general, the Agencies approach the calculation of market concentration as set forth in Section 1.5 of the *Horizontal Merger Guidelines*, ascribing to the competitor collaboration the same range of market shares described above.

Market share and market concentration provide only a starting point for evaluating the competitive effect of the relevant agreement. The Agencies also examine other factors outlined in the *Horizontal Merger Guidelines* as set forth below:

> The Agencies consider whether factors such as those discussed in Section 1.52 of the *Horizontal Merger Guidelines* indicate that market share and concentration data overstate or understate the likely competitive significance of participants and their collaboration.
>
> In assessing whether anticompetitive harm may arise from an agreement that combines control over or financial interests in assets or otherwise limits independent decision making, the Agencies consider whether factors such as those discussed in Section 2.2 of the *Horizontal Merger Guidelines* suggest that anticompetitive harm is more or less likely.
>
> In assessing whether anticompetitive harms may arise from an agreement that may increase the likelihood of collusion, the Agencies consider whether factors such as those discussed in Section 2.1 of the *Horizontal Merger Guidelines* suggest that anticompetitive harm is more or less likely.
>
> In evaluating the significance of market share and market concentration data and interpreting the range of market shares ascribed to the collaboration, the Agencies also examine factors beyond those set forth in the *Horizontal Merger Guidelines*. The following section describes which factors are relevant and the issues that the Agencies examine in evaluating those factors.

---

[44] When the competitive concern is that a limitation on independent decision making or a combination of control or financial interests may yield an anticompetitive reduction of research and development, the Agencies typically frame their inquiries more generally, looking to the strength, scope, and number of competing R&D efforts and their close substitutes. *See supra* Sections 3.31(a) and 3.32(c).

3.34 Factors Relevant to the Ability and Incentive of the Participants and the Collaboration to Compete

Competitor collaborations sometimes do not end competition among the participants and the collaboration. Participants may continue to compete against each other and their collaboration, either through separate, independent business operations or through membership in other collaborations. Collaborations may be managed by decision makers independent of the individual participants. Control over key competitive variables may remain outside the collaboration, such as where participants independently market and set prices for the collaboration's output.

Sometimes, however, competition among the participants and the collaboration may be restrained through explicit contractual terms or through financial or other provisions that reduce or eliminate the incentive to compete. The Agencies look to the competitive benefits and harms of the relevant agreement, not merely the formal terms of agreements among the participants.

Where the nature of the agreement and market share and market concentration data reveal a likelihood of anticompetitive harm, the Agencies more closely examine the extent to which the participants and the collaboration have the ability and incentive to compete independent of each other. The Agencies are likely to focus on six factors: (a) the extent to which the relevant agreement is non-exclusive in that participants are likely to continue to compete independently outside the collaboration in the market in which the collaboration operates; (b) the extent to which participants retain independent control of assets necessary to compete; (c) the nature and extent of participants' financial interests in the collaboration or in each other; (d) the control of the collaboration's competitively significant decision making; (e) the likelihood of anticompetitive information sharing; and (f) the duration of the collaboration.

Each of these factors is discussed in further detail below. Consideration of these factors may reduce or increase competitive concern. The analysis necessarily is flexible: the relevance and significance of each factor depends upon the facts and circumstances of each case, and any additional factors pertinent under the circumstances are considered. For example, when an agreement is examined subsequent to formation of the collaboration, the Agencies also examine factual evidence concerning participants' actual conduct.

3.34(a) Exclusivity

The Agencies consider whether, to what extent, and in what manner the relevant agreement permits participants to continue to compete against each other and their collaboration, either through separate, independent business operations or through membership in other collaborations. The Agencies inquire whether a collaboration is non-exclusive in fact as well as in name and consider any costs or other impediments to competing with the collaboration. In assessing exclusivity when an agreement already is in operation, the Agencies examine whether, to what extent, and in what manner participants actually have continued to compete against each other and the collaboration. In general, competitive concern likely is reduced to the extent that participants actually have continued to compete, either through separate, independent business operations or through membership in other collaborations, or are permitted to do so.

3.34(b) Control over Assets

The Agencies ask whether the relevant agreement requires participants to contribute to the collaboration significant assets that previously have enabled or likely would enable participants to be effective independent competitors in markets affected by the collaboration. If such resources must be contributed to the collaboration and are specialized in that they cannot readily be replaced, the participants may have lost all or some of their ability to compete against each other and their collaboration, even if they retain the contractual right to do so.[45] In general, the greater the contribution of specialized assets to the collaboration that is required, the less the participants may be relied upon to provide independent competition.

3.34(c) Financial Interests in the Collaboration or in Other Participants

The Agencies assess each participant's financial interest in the collaboration and its potential impact on the participant's incentive to compete independently with the collaboration. The potential impact may vary depending on the size and nature of the financial interest (e.g., whether the financial interest is debt or equity). In general, the greater the financial interest in the collaboration, the less likely is the participant to compete with the collaboration.[46] The Agencies also assess direct equity investments between or among the participants. Such investments may reduce the incentives of the participants to compete with each other. In either case, the analysis is sensitive to the level of financial interest in the collaboration or in another participant relative to the level of the participant's investment in its independent business operations in the markets affected by the collaboration.

3.34(d) Control of the Collaboration's Competitively Significant Decision Making

The Agencies consider the manner in which a collaboration is organized and governed in assessing the extent to which participants and their collaboration have the ability and incentive to compete independently. Thus, the Agencies consider the extent to which the collaboration's governance structure enables the collaboration to act as an independent decision maker. For example, the Agencies ask whether participants are allowed to appoint members of a board of directors for the collaboration, if incorporated, or otherwise to exercise significant control over the operations of the collaboration. In general, the collaboration is less likely to compete independently as participants gain greater control over the collaboration's price, output, and other competitively significant decisions.[47]

To the extent that the collaboration's decision making is subject to the participants' control, the Agencies consider whether that control could be

---

[45] For example, if participants in a production collaboration must contribute most of their productive capacity to the collaboration, the collaboration may impair the ability of its participants to remain effective independent competitors regardless of the terms of the agreement.

[46] Similarly, a collaboration's financial interest in a participant may diminish the collaboration's incentive to compete with that participant.

[47] Control may diverge from financial interests. For example, a small equity investment may be coupled with a right to veto large capital expenditures and, thereby, to effectively limit output. The Agencies examine a collaboration's actual governance structure in assessing issues of control.

exercised jointly. Joint control over the collaboration's price and output levels could create or increase market power and raise competitive concerns. Depending on the nature of the collaboration, competitive concern also may arise due to joint control over other competitively significant decisions, such as the level and scope of R&D efforts and investment. In contrast, to the extent that participants independently set the price and quantity[48] of their share of a collaboration's output and independently control other competitively significant decisions, an agreement's likely anticompetitive harm is reduced.[49]

3.34(e) Likelihood of Anticompetitive Information Sharing

The Agencies evaluate the extent to which competitively sensitive information concerning markets affected by the collaboration likely would be disclosed. This likelihood depends on, among other things, the nature of the collaboration, its organization and governance, and safeguards implemented to prevent or minimize such disclosure. For example, participants might refrain from assigning marketing personnel to an R&D collaboration, or, in a marketing collaboration, participants might limit access to competitively sensitive information regarding their respective operations to only certain individuals or to an independent third party. Similarly, a buying collaboration might use an independent third party to handle negotiations in which its participants' input requirements or other competitively sensitive information could be revealed. In general, it is less likely that the collaboration will facilitate collusion on competitively sensitive variables if appropriate safeguards governing information sharing are in place.

3.34(f) Duration of the Collaboration

The Agencies consider the duration of the collaboration in assessing whether participants retain the ability and incentive to compete against each other and their collaboration. In general, the shorter the duration, the more likely participants are to compete against each other and their collaboration.

3.35 Entry

Easy entry may deter or prevent profitably maintaining price above, or output, quality, service or innovation below, what likely would prevail in the absence of the relevant agreement. Where the nature of the agreement and market share and concentration data suggest a likelihood of anticompetitive harm that is not sufficiently mitigated by any continuing competition identified through the analysis in Section 3.34, the Agencies inquire whether entry would be timely, likely, and sufficient in its magnitude, character and scope to deter or counteract the anticompetitive harm of concern. If so, the relevant agreement ordinarily requires no further analysis.

---

48 Even if prices to consumers are set independently, anticompetitive harms may still occur if participants jointly set the collaboration's level of output. For example, participants may effectively coordinate price increases by reducing the collaboration's level of output and collecting their profits through high transfer prices, *i.e.*, through the amounts that participants contribute to the collaboration in exchange for each unit of the collaboration's output. Where a transfer price is determined by reference to an objective measure not under the control of the participants, (*e.g.*, average price in a different unconcentrated geographic market), competitive concern may be less likely.

49 Anticompetitive harm also is less likely if individual participants may independently increase the overall output of the collaboration.

As a general matter, the Agencies assess timeliness, likelihood, and sufficiency of committed entry under principles set forth in Section 3 of the *Horizontal Merger Guidelines*.[50] However, unlike mergers, competitor collaborations often restrict only certain business activities, while preserving competition among participants in other respects, and they may be designed to terminate after a limited duration. Consequently, the extent to which an agreement creates opportunities that would induce entry and the conditions under which ease of entry may deter or counteract anticompetitive harms may be more complex and less direct than for mergers and will vary somewhat according to the nature of the relevant agreement. For example, the likelihood of entry may be affected by what potential entrants believe about the probable duration of an anticompetitive agreement. Other things being equal, the shorter the anticipated duration of an anticompetitive agreement, the smaller the profit opportunities for potential entrants, and the lower the likelihood that it will induce committed entry. Examples of other differences are set forth below.

For certain collaborations, sufficiency of entry may be affected by the possibility that entrants will participate in the anticompetitive agreement. To the extent that such participation raises the amount of entry needed to deter or counteract anticompetitive harms, and assets required for entry are not adequately available for entrants to respond fully to their sales opportunities, or otherwise renders entry inadequate in magnitude, character or scope, sufficient entry may be more difficult to achieve.[51]

In the context of research and development collaborations, widespread availability of R&D capabilities and the large gains that may accrue to successful innovators often suggest a high likelihood that entry will deter or counteract anticompetitive reductions of R&D efforts. Nonetheless, such conditions do not always pertain, and the Agencies ask whether entry may deter or counteract anticompetitive R&D reductions, taking into account the following:

- Where market participants typically can observe the level and type of R&D efforts within a market, the principles of Section 3 of the *Horizontal Merger Guidelines* may be applied flexibly to determine whether entry is likely to deter or counteract a lessening of the quality, diversity, or pace of research and development. To be timely, entry must be sufficiently prompt to deter or counteract such harms. The Agencies evaluate the likelihood of entry based on

[50] Committed entry is defined as new competition that requires expenditure of significant sunk costs of entry and exit. *See* Section 3.0 of the *Horizontal Merger Guidelines.*

[51] Under the same principles applied to production and marketing collaborations, the exercise of monopsony power by a buying collaboration may be deterred or counteracted by the entry of new purchasers. To the extent that collaborators reduce their purchases, they may create an opportunity for new buyers to make purchases without forcing the price of the input above pre-relevant agreement levels. Committed purchasing entry, defined as new purchasing competition that requires expenditure of significant sunk costs of entry and exit—such as a new steel factory built in response to a reduction in the price of iron ore—is analyzed under principles analogous to those articulated in Section 3 of the *Horizontal Merger Guidelines*. Under that analysis, the Agencies assess whether a monopsonistic price reduction is likely to attract committed purchasing entry, profitable at pre-relevant agreement prices, that would not have occurred before the relevant agreement at those same prices. (Uncommitted new buyers are identified as participants in the relevant market if their demand responses to a price decrease are likely to occur within one year and without the expenditure of significant sunk costs of entry and exit. *See id.* at Sections 1.32 and 1.41.)

the extent to which potential entrants have (1) core competencies (and the ability to acquire any necessary specialized assets) that give them the ability to enter into competing R&D and (2) incentives to enter into competing R&D in response to a post-collaboration reduction in R&D efforts. The sufficiency of entry depends on whether the character and scope of the entrants' R&D efforts are close enough to the reduced R&D efforts to be likely to achieve similar innovations in the same time frame or otherwise to render a collaborative reduction of R&D unprofitable.

- Where market participants typically cannot observe the level and type of R&D efforts by others within a market, there may be significant questions as to whether entry would occur in response to a collaborative lessening of the quality, diversity, or pace of research and development, since such effects would not likely be observed. In such cases, the Agencies may conclude that entry would not deter or counteract anticompetitive harms.

3.36 Identifying Procompetitive Benefits of the Collaboration

Competition usually spurs firms to achieve efficiencies internally. Nevertheless, as explained above, competitor collaborations have the potential to generate significant efficiencies that benefit consumers in a variety of ways. For example, a competitor collaboration may enable firms to offer goods or services that are cheaper, more valuable to consumers, or brought to market faster than would otherwise be possible. Efficiency gains from competitor collaborations often stem from combinations of different capabilities or resources. *See supra* Section 2.1. Indeed, the primary benefit of competitor collaborations to the economy is their potential to generate such efficiencies.

Efficiencies generated through a competitor collaboration can enhance the ability and incentive of the collaboration and its participants to compete, which may result in lower prices, improved quality, enhanced service, or new products. For example, through collaboration, competitors may be able to produce an input more efficiently than any one participant could individually; such collaboration-generated efficiencies may enhance competition by permitting two or more ineffective (e.g., high cost) participants to become more effective, lower cost competitors. Even when efficiencies generated through a competitor collaboration enhance the collaboration's or the participants' ability to compete, however, a competitor collaboration may have other effects that may lessen competition and ultimately may make the relevant agreement anticompetitive.

If the Agencies conclude that the relevant agreement has caused, or is likely to cause, anticompetitive harm, they consider whether the agreement is reasonably necessary to achieve "cognizable efficiencies." "Cognizable efficiencies" are efficiencies that have been verified by the Agencies, that do not arise from anticompetitive reductions in output or service, and that cannot be achieved through practical, significantly less restrictive means. *See infra* Sections 3.36(a) and 3.36(b). Cognizable efficiencies are assessed net of costs produced by the competitor collaboration or incurred in achieving those efficiencies.

3.36(a) Cognizable Efficiencies Must Be Verifiable and Potentially Procompetitive

Efficiencies are difficult to verify and quantify, in part because much of the information relating to efficiencies is uniquely in the possession of the collaboration's participants. Moreover, efficiencies projected reasonably and in good faith by the participants may not be realized. Therefore, the participants must substantiate efficiency claims so that the Agencies can verify by reasonable means the likelihood and magnitude of each asserted efficiency; how and when each would be achieved; any costs of doing so; how each would enhance the collaboration's or its participants' ability and incentive to compete; and why the relevant agreement is reasonably necessary to achieve the claimed efficiencies (see Section 3.36 (b)). Efficiency claims are not considered if they are vague or speculative or otherwise cannot be verified by reasonable means.

Moreover, cognizable efficiencies must be potentially procompetitive. Some asserted efficiencies, such as those premised on the notion that competition itself is unreasonable, are insufficient as a matter of law. Similarly, cost savings that arise from anticompetitive output or service reductions are not treated as cognizable efficiencies. *See* Example 9.

3.36(b) Reasonable Necessity and Less Restrictive Alternatives

The Agencies consider only those efficiencies for which the relevant agreement is reasonably necessary. An agreement may be "reasonably necessary" without being essential. However, if the participants could have achieved or could achieve similar efficiencies by practical, significantly less restrictive means, then the Agencies conclude that the relevant agreement is not reasonably necessary to their achievement. In making this assessment, the Agencies consider only alternatives that are practical in the business situation faced by the participants; the Agencies do not search for a theoretically less restrictive alternative that is not realistic given business realities.

The reasonable necessity of an agreement may depend upon the market context and upon the duration of the agreement. An agreement that may be justified by the needs of a new entrant, for example, may not be reasonably necessary to achieve cognizable efficiencies in different market circumstances. The reasonable necessity of an agreement also may depend on whether it deters individual participants from undertaking free riding or other opportunistic conduct that could reduce significantly the ability of the collaboration to achieve cognizable efficiencies. Collaborations sometimes include agreements to discourage any one participant from appropriating an undue share of the fruits of the collaboration or to align participants' incentives to encourage cooperation in achieving the efficiency goals of the collaboration. The Agencies assess whether such agreements are reasonably necessary to deter opportunistic conduct that otherwise would likely prevent the achievement of cognizable efficiencies. *See* Example 10.

3.37 Overall Competitive Effect

If the relevant agreement is reasonably necessary to achieve cognizable efficiencies, the Agencies assess the likelihood and magnitude of cognizable efficiencies and anticompetitive harms to determine the agreement's overall actual or likely effect on competition in the relevant market. To make the requisite determination, the Agencies consider whether cognizable efficiencies likely would be sufficient to offset the potential of the agreement to harm consumers in the relevant market, for example, by preventing price increases.[52]

---

[52] In most cases, the Agencies' enforcement decisions depend on their analysis of the overall effect of the relevant agreement over the short term. The Agencies also will consider the effects of cognizable efficiencies with no short-term, direct effect on prices in

The Agencies' comparison of cognizable efficiencies and anticompetitive harms is necessarily an approximate judgment. In assessing the overall competitive effect of an agreement, the Agencies consider the magnitude and likelihood of both the anticompetitive harms and cognizable efficiencies from the relevant agreement. The likelihood and magnitude of anticompetitive harms in a particular case may be insignificant compared to the expected cognizable efficiencies, or vice versa. As the expected anticompetitive harm of the agreement increases, the Agencies require evidence establishing a greater level of expected cognizable efficiencies in order to avoid the conclusion that the agreement will have an anticompetitive effect overall. When the anticompetitive harm of the agreement is likely to be particularly large, extraordinarily great cognizable efficiencies would be necessary to prevent the agreement from having an anticompetitive effect overall.

SECTION 4: ANTITRUST SAFETY ZONES

4.1 Overview

Because competitor collaborations are often procompetitive, the Agencies believe that "safety zones" are useful in order to encourage such activity. The safety zones set out below are designed to provide participants in a competitor collaboration with a degree of certainty in those situations in which anticompetitive effects are so unlikely that the Agencies presume the arrangements to be lawful without inquiring into particular circumstances. They are not intended to discourage competitor collaborations that fall outside the safety zones.

The Agencies emphasize that competitor collaborations are not anticompetitive merely because they fall outside the safety zones. Indeed, many competitor collaborations falling outside the safety zones are procompetitive or competitively neutral. The Agencies analyze arrangements outside the safety zones based on the principles outlined in Section 3 above.

The following sections articulate two safety zones. Section 4.2 sets out a general safety zone applicable to any competitor collaboration.[53] Section 4.3 establishes a safety zone applicable to research and development collaborations whose competitive effects are analyzed within an innovation market. These safety zones are intended to supplement safety zone provisions in the Agencies' other guidelines and statements of enforcement policy.[54]

4.2 Safety Zone for Competitor Collaborations in General

Absent extraordinary circumstances, the Agencies do not challenge a competitor collaboration when the market shares of the collaboration and its participants collectively account for no more than twenty percent of each

---

the relevant market. Delayed benefits from the efficiencies (due to delay in the achievement of, or the realization of consumer benefits from, the efficiencies) will be given less weight because they are less proximate and more difficult to predict.

[53] *See* Sections 1.1 and 1.3 above.

[54] The Agencies have articulated antitrust safety zones in *Health Care Statements 7 & 8* and the *Intellectual Property Guidelines*, as well as in the *Horizontal Merger Guidelines*. The antitrust safety zones in these other guidelines relate to particular facts in a specific industry or to particular types of transactions.

relevant market in which competition may be affected.[55] The safety zone, however, does not apply to agreements that are per se illegal, or that would be challenged without a detailed market analysis,[56] or to competitor collaborations to which a merger analysis is applied.[57]

4.3 Safety Zone for Research and Development Competition Analyzed in Terms of Innovation Markets

Absent extraordinary circumstances, the Agencies do not challenge a competitor collaboration on the basis of effects on competition in an innovation market where three or more independently controlled research efforts in addition to those of the collaboration possess the required specialized assets or characteristics and the incentive to engage in R&D that is a close substitute for the R&D activity of the collaboration. In determining whether independently controlled R&D efforts are close substitutes, the Agencies consider, among other things, the nature, scope, and magnitude of the R&D efforts; their access to financial support; their access to intellectual property, skilled personnel, or other specialized assets; their timing; and their ability, either acting alone or through others, to successfully commercialize innovations. The antitrust safety zone does not apply to agreements that are per se illegal, or that would be challenged without a detailed market analysis,[58] or to competitor collaborations to which a merger analysis is applied.[59]

Appendix

Section 1.3

Example 1 (Competitor Collaboration/Merger)

Facts

Two oil companies agree to integrate all of their refining and refined product marketing operations. Under terms of the agreement, the collaboration will expire after twelve years; prior to that expiration date, it may be terminated by either participant on six months' prior notice. The two oil companies maintain separate crude oil production operations.

Analysis

The formation of the collaboration involves an efficiency-enhancing integration of operations in the refining and refined product markets, and the integration eliminates all competition between the participants in those markets. The evaluating Agency likely would conclude that expiration after

---

[55] For purposes of the safety zone, the Agencies consider the combined market shares of the participants and the collaboration. For example, with a collaboration among two competitors where each participant individually holds a 6 percent market share in the relevant market and the collaboration separately holds a 3 percent market share in the relevant market, the combined market share in the relevant market for purposes of the safety zone would be 15 percent. This collaboration, therefore, would fall within the safety zone. However, if the collaboration involved three competitors, each with a 6 percent market share in the relevant market, the combined market share in the relevant market for purposes of the safety zone would be 21 percent, and the collaboration would fall outside the safety zone. Including market shares of the participants takes into account possible spillover effects on competition within the relevant market among the participants and their collaboration.

[56] *See supra* notes 28–30 and accompanying text in Section 3.3.

[57] *See* Section 1.3 above.

[58] *See supra* notes 28–30 and accompanying text in Section 3.3.

[59] *See* Section 1.3 above.

twelve years does not constitute termination "within a sufficiently limited period." The participants' entitlement to terminate the collaboration at any time after giving prior notice is not termination by the collaboration's "own specific and express terms." Based on the facts presented, the evaluating Agency likely would analyze the collaboration under the *Horizontal Merger Guidelines*, rather than as a competitor collaboration under these Guidelines. Any agreements restricting competition on crude oil production would be analyzed under these Guidelines.

Section 2.3

Example 2 (Analysis of Individual Agreements/Set of Agreements)

Facts

Two firms enter a joint venture to develop and produce a new software product to be sold independently by the participants. The product will be useful in two areas, biotechnology research and pharmaceuticals research, but doing business with each of the two classes of purchasers would require a different distribution network and a separate marketing campaign. Successful penetration of one market is likely to stimulate sales in the other by enhancing the reputation of the software and by facilitating the ability of biotechnology and pharmaceutical researchers to use the fruits of each other's efforts. Although the software is to be marketed independently by the participants rather than by the joint venture, the participants agree that one will sell only to biotechnology researchers and the other will sell only to pharmaceutical researchers. The participants also agree to fix the maximum price that either firm may charge. The parties assert that the combination of these two requirements is necessary for the successful marketing of the new product. They argue that the market allocation provides each participant with adequate incentives to commercialize the product in its sector without fear that the other participant will free-ride on its efforts and that the maximum price prevents either participant from unduly exploiting its sector of the market to the detriment of sales efforts in the other sector.

Analysis

The evaluating Agency would assess overall competitive effects associated with the collaboration in its entirety and with individual agreements, such as the agreement to allocate markets, the agreement to fix maximum prices, and any of the sundry other agreements associated with joint development and production and independent marketing of the software. From the facts presented, it appears that the agreements to allocate markets and to fix maximum prices may be so intertwined that their benefits and harms "cannot meaningfully be isolated." The two agreements arguably operate together to ensure a particular blend of incentives to achieve the potential procompetitive benefits of successful commercialization of the new product. Moreover, the effects of the agreement to fix maximum prices may mitigate the price effects of the agreement to allocate markets. Based on the facts presented, the evaluating Agency likely would conclude that the agreements to allocate markets and to fix maximum prices should be analyzed as a whole.

Section 2.4

Example 3 (Time of Possible Harm to Competition)

Facts

A group of 25 small-to-mid-size banks formed a joint venture to establish an automatic teller machine network. To ensure sufficient business to justify launching the venture, the joint venture agreement specified that participants would not participate in any other ATM networks. Numerous other ATM networks were forming in roughly the same time period.

Over time, the joint venture expanded by adding more and more banks, and the number of its competitors fell. Now, ten years after formation, the joint venture has 900 member banks and controls 60% of the ATM outlets in a relevant geographic market. Following complaints from consumers that ATM fees have rapidly escalated, the evaluating Agency assesses the rule barring participation in other ATM networks, which now binds 900 banks.

Analysis

The circumstances in which the venture operates have changed over time, and the evaluating Agency would determine whether the exclusivity rule now harms competition. In assessing the exclusivity rule's competitive effect, the evaluating Agency would take account of the collaboration's substantial current market share and any procompetitive benefits of exclusivity under present circumstances, along with other factors discussed in Section 3.

Section 3.2

Example 4 (Agreement Not to Compete on Price)

Facts

Net-Business and Net-Company are two start-up companies. Each has developed and begun sales of software for the networks that link users within a particular business to each other and, in some cases, to entities outside the business. Both Net-Business and Net-Company were formed by computer specialists with no prior business expertise, and they are having trouble implementing marketing strategies, distributing their inventory, and managing their sales forces. The two companies decide to form a partnership joint venture, NET-FIRM, whose sole function will be to market and distribute the network software products of Net-Business and Net-Company. NET-FIRM will be the exclusive marketer of network software produced by Net-Business and Net-Company. Net-Business and Net-Company will each have 50% control of NET-FIRM, but each will derive profits from NET-FIRM in proportion to the revenues from sales of that partner's products. The documents setting up NET-FIRM specify that Net-Business and Net-Company will agree on the prices for the products that NET-FIRM will sell.

Analysis

Net-Business and Net-Company will agree on the prices at which NET-FIRM will sell their individually-produced software. The agreement is one "not to compete on price," and it is of a type that always or almost always tends to raise price or reduce output. The agreement to jointly set price may be challenged as per se illegal, unless it is reasonably related to, and reasonably necessary to achieve procompetitive benefits from, an efficiency-enhancing integration of economic activity.

Example 5 (Specialization without Integration)

Facts

Firm A and Firm B are two of only three producers of automobile carburetors. Minor engine variations from year to year, even within given models of a particular automobile manufacturer, require re-design of each year's carburetor and re-tooling for carburetor production. Firms A and B meet and agree that henceforth Firm A will design and produce carburetors only for automobile models of even-numbered years and Firm B will design and produce carburetors only for automobile models of odd-numbered years. Some design and re-tooling costs would be saved, but automobile manufacturers would face only two suppliers each year, rather than three.

Analysis

The agreement allocates sales by automobile model year and constitutes an agreement "not to compete on . . . output." The participants do not combine production; rather, the collaboration consists solely of an agreement not to produce certain carburetors. The mere coordination of decisions on output is not integration, and cost-savings without integration, such as the costs saved by refraining from design and production for any given model year, are not a basis for avoiding per se condemnation. The agreement is of a type so likely to harm competition and to have no significant benefits that particularized inquiry into its competitive effect is deemed by the antitrust laws not to be worth the time and expense that would be required. Consequently, the evaluating Agency likely would conclude that the agreement is per se illegal.

Example 6 (Efficiency-Enhancing Integration Present)

Facts

Compu-Max and Compu-Pro are two major producers of a variety of computer software. Each has a large, world-wide sales department. Each firm has developed and sold its own word-processing software. However, despite all efforts to develop a strong market presence in word processing, each firm has achieved only slightly more than a 10% market share, and neither is a major competitor to the two firms that dominate the word-processing software market.

Compu-Max and Compu-Pro determine that in light of their complementary areas of design expertise they could develop a markedly better word-processing program together than either can produce on its own. Compu-Max and Compu-Pro form a joint venture, WORD-FIRM, to jointly develop and market a new word-processing program, with expenses and profits to be split equally. Compu-Max and Compu-Pro both contribute to WORD-FIRM software developers experienced with word processing.

Analysis

Compu-Max and Compu-Pro have combined their word-processing design efforts, reflecting complementary areas of design expertise, in a common endeavor to develop new word-processing software that they could not have developed separately. Each participant has contributed significant assets—the time and know-how of its word-processing software developers—to the joint effort. Consequently, the evaluating Agency likely would conclude that the joint word-processing software development project is an efficiency-enhancing integration of economic activity that promotes procompetitive benefits.

Example 7 (Efficiency-Enhancing Integration Absent)

Facts

Each of the three major producers of flashlight batteries has a patent on a process for manufacturing a revolutionary new flashlight battery—the Century Battery—that would last 100 years without requiring recharging or replacement. There is little chance that another firm could produce such a battery without infringing one of the patents. Based on consumer surveys, each firm believes that aggregate profits will be less if all three sold the Century Battery than if all three sold only conventional batteries, but that any one firm could maximize profits by being the first to introduce a Century Battery. All three are capable of introducing the Century Battery within two years, although it is uncertain who would be first to market.

One component in all conventional batteries is a copper widget. An essential element in each producers' Century Battery would be a zinc, rather than a copper widget. Instead of introducing the Century Battery, the three producers agree that their batteries will use only copper widgets. Adherence to the agreement precludes any of the producers from introducing a Century Battery.

Analysis

The agreement to use only copper widgets is merely an agreement not to produce any zinc-based batteries, in particular, the Century Battery. It is "an agreement not to compete on . . . output" and is "of a type that always or almost always tends to raise price or reduce output." The participants do not collaborate to perform any business functions, and there are no procompetitive benefits from an efficiency-enhancing integration of economic activity. The evaluating Agency likely would challenge the agreement to use only copper widgets as per se illegal.

Section 3.3

Example 8 (Rule-of-Reason: Agreement Quickly Exculpated)

Facts

Under the facts of Example 4, Net-Business and Net-Company jointly market their independently-produced network software products through NET-FIRM. Those facts are changed in one respect: rather than jointly setting the prices of their products, Net-Business and Net-Company will each independently specify the prices at which its products are to be sold by NET-FIRM. The participants explicitly agree that each company will decide on the prices for its own software independently of the other company. The collaboration also includes a requirement that NET-FIRM compile and transmit to each participant quarterly reports summarizing any comments received from customers in the course of NET-FIRM's marketing efforts regarding the desirable/undesirable features of and desirable improvements to (1) that participant's product and (2) network software in general. Sufficient provisions are included to prevent the company-specific information reported to one participant from being disclosed to the other, and those provisions are followed. The information pertaining to network software in general is to be reported simultaneously to both participants.

Analysis

Under these revised facts, there is no agreement "not to compete on price or output." Absent any agreement of a type that always or almost always tends to raise price or reduce output, and absent any subsequent conduct suggesting that the firms did not follow their explicit agreement to set prices independently, no aspect of the partnership arrangement might be subjected to per se analysis. Analysis would continue under the rule of reason.

The information disclosure arrangements provide for the sharing of a very limited category of information: customer-response data pertaining to network software in general. Collection and sharing of information of this nature is unlikely to increase the ability or incentive of Net-Business or Net-Company to raise price or reduce output, quality, service, or innovation. There is no evidence that the disclosure arrangements have caused anticompetitive harm and no evidence that the prohibitions against disclosure of firm-specific information have been violated. Under any plausible relevant market definition, Net-Business and Net-Company have small market shares, and there is no other evidence to suggest that they have market power. In light of these facts, the evaluating Agency would refrain from further investigation.

Section 3.36(a)

Example 9 (Cost Savings from Anticompetitive Output or Service Reductions)

Facts

Two widget manufacturers enter a marketing collaboration. Each will continue to manufacture and set the price for its own widget, but the widgets will be promoted by a joint sales force. The two manufacturers conclude that through this collaboration they can increase their profits using only half of their aggregate pre-collaboration sales forces by (1) taking advantage of economies of scale—presenting both widgets during the same customer call—and (2) refraining from time-consuming demonstrations highlighting the relative advantages of one manufacturer's widgets over the other manufacturer's widgets. Prior to their collaboration, both manufacturers had engaged in the demonstrations.

Analysis

The savings attributable to economies of scale would be cognizable efficiencies. In contrast, eliminating demonstrations that highlight the relative advantages of one manufacturer's widgets over the other manufacturer's widgets deprives customers of information useful to their decision making. Cost savings from this source arise from an anticompetitive output or service reduction and would not be cognizable efficiencies.

Section 3.36(b)

Example 10 (Efficiencies from Restrictions on Competitive Independence)

Facts

Under the facts of Example 6, Compu-Max and Compu-Pro decide to collaborate on developing and marketing word-processing software. The firms agree that neither one will engage in R&D for designing word-processing software outside of their WORD-FIRM joint venture. Compu-Max papers drafted during the negotiations cite the concern that absent a restriction on outside word-processing R&D, Compu-Pro might withhold its best ideas, use the joint venture to learn Compu-Max's approaches to design problems, and then use that information to design an improved word-processing software product on its own. Compu-Pro's files contain similar documents regarding Compu-Max.

Compu-Max and Compu-Pro further agree that neither will sell its previously designed word-processing program once their jointly developed product is ready to be introduced. Papers in both firms' files, dating from the time of the negotiations, state that this latter restraint was designed to foster greater trust between the participants and thereby enable the collaboration to function more smoothly. As further support, the parties point to a recent failed collaboration involving other firms who sought to collaborate on developing and selling a new spread-sheet program while independently marketing their older spread-sheet software.

Analysis

The restraints on outside R&D efforts and on outside sales both restrict the competitive independence of the participants and could cause competitive harm. The evaluating Agency would inquire whether each restraint is reasonably necessary to achieve cognizable efficiencies. In the given context, that inquiry would entail an assessment of whether, by aligning the participants' incentives, the restraints in fact are reasonably necessary to deter opportunistic conduct that otherwise would likely prevent achieving cognizable efficiency goals of the collaboration.

With respect to the limitation on independent R&D efforts, possible alternatives might include agreements specifying the level and quality of each participant's R&D contributions to WORD-FIRM or requiring the sharing of all relevant R&D. The evaluating Agency would assess whether any alternatives would permit each participant to adequately monitor the scope and quality of the other's R&D contributions and whether they would effectively prevent the misappropriation of the other participant's know-how. In some circumstances, there may be no "practical, significantly less restrictive" alternative.

Although the agreement prohibiting outside sales might be challenged as per se illegal if not reasonably necessary for achieving the procompetitive benefits of the integration discussed in Example 6, the evaluating Agency likely would analyze the agreement under the rule of reason if it could not adequately assess the claim of reasonable necessity through limited factual inquiry. As a general matter, participants' contributions of marketing assets to the collaboration could more readily be monitored than their contributions of know-how, and neither participant may be capable of misappropriating the other's marketing contributions as readily as it could misappropriate know-how. Consequently, the specification and monitoring of each participant's marketing contributions could be a "practical, significantly less restrictive" alternative to prohibiting outside sales of pre-existing products. The evaluating Agency, however, would examine the experiences of the failed spread-sheet collaboration and any other facts presented by the parties to better assess whether such specification and monitoring would likely enable the achievement of cognizable efficiencies.

10

ANTITRUST ENFORCEMENT GUIDELINES FOR INTERNATIONAL OPERATIONS

U.S. DEPARTMENT OF JUSTICE AND FEDERAL TRADE COMMISSION

April 5, 1995

TABLE OF CONTENTS

1. INTRODUCTION

For more than a century, the U.S. antitrust laws have stood as the ultimate protector of the competitive process that underlies our free market economy. Through this process, which enhances consumer choice and promotes competitive prices, society as a whole benefits from the best possible allocation of resources.

Although the federal antitrust laws have always applied to foreign commerce, that application is particularly important today. Throughout the world, the importance of antitrust law as a means to ensure open and free markets, protect consumers, and prevent conduct that impedes competition is becoming more apparent. The Department of Justice ("the Department") and the Federal Trade Commission ("the Commission" or "FTC") (when referred to collectively, "the Agencies"), as the federal agencies charged with the responsibility of enforcing the antitrust laws, thus have made it a high priority to enforce the antitrust laws with respect to international operations and to cooperate wherever appropriate with foreign authorities regarding such enforcement. In furtherance of this priority, the Agencies have revised and updated the Department's 1988 Antitrust Enforcement Guidelines for International Operations, which are hereby withdrawn.[1]

The 1995 Antitrust Enforcement Guidelines for International Operations (hereinafter "Guidelines") are intended to provide antitrust guidance to businesses engaged in international operations on questions that relate specifically to the Agencies' international enforcement policy.[2] They do not, therefore, provide a complete statement of the Agencies' general enforcement policies. The topics covered include the Agencies' subject matter jurisdiction over conduct and entities outside the United States and the considerations, issues, policies, and processes that govern their decision to exercise that jurisdiction; comity; mutual assistance in international antitrust enforcement; and the effects of foreign governmental involvement on the antitrust liability of private entities. In addition, the Guidelines discuss the relationship between antitrust and international trade initiatives. Finally, to illustrate how these principles may operate in certain contexts, the Guidelines include a number of examples.

As is the case with all guidelines, users should rely on qualified counsel to assist them in evaluating the antitrust risk associated with any contemplated transaction or activity. No set of guidelines can possibly indicate how the Agencies will assess the particular facts of every case. Persons seeking more specific advance statements of enforcement intentions with respect to the matters treated in these Guidelines should use the Department's Business Review procedure,[3] the Commission's Advisory Opinion procedure,[4] or one of the more specific procedures described below for particular types of transactions.

2. ANTITRUST LAWS ENFORCED BY THE AGENCIES

Foreign commerce cases can involve almost any provision of the antitrust laws. The Agencies do not discriminate in the enforcement of the antitrust laws on the basis of the nationality of the parties. Nor do the Agencies employ their statutory authority to further non-antitrust goals. Once jurisdictional requirements, comity, and doctrines of foreign governmental involvement have been considered and satisfied, the same substantive rules apply to all cases. The following is a brief summary of the laws enforced by the Agencies that are likely to have the greatest significance for international transactions.

---

[1] The U.S. Department of Justice and Federal Trade Commission Antitrust Guidelines for the Licensing of Intellectual Property (1995), the U.S. Department of Justice and Federal Trade Commission Horizontal Merger Guidelines (1992), and the Statements of Antitrust Enforcement Policy and Analytical Principles Relating to Health Care and Antitrust, Jointly Issued by the U.S. Department of Justice and Federal Trade Commission (1994), are not qualified, modified, or otherwise amended by the issuance of these Guidelines.

[2] Readers should separately evaluate the risk of private litigation by competitors, consumers and suppliers, as well as the risk of enforcement by state prosecutors under state and federal antitrust laws.

[3] 28 C.F.R. 50.6 (1994).

[4] 16 C.F.R. 1.1–1.4 (1994).

2.1 Sherman Act

Section 1 of the Sherman Act, 15 U.S.C. 1, sets forth the basic antitrust prohibition against contracts, combinations, and conspiracies "in restraint of trade or commerce among the several States or with foreign nations." Section 2 of the Act, 15 U.S.C. 2, prohibits monopolization, attempts to monopolize, and conspiracies to monopolize "any part of trade or commerce among the several States or with foreign nations." Section 6a of the Sherman Act, 15 U.S.C. 6a, defines the jurisdictional reach of the Act with respect to non-import foreign commerce.

Violations of the Sherman Act may be prosecuted as civil or criminal offenses. Conduct that the Department prosecutes criminally is limited to traditional per se offenses of the law, which typically involve price-fixing, customer allocation, bid-rigging or other cartel activities that would also be violations of the law in many countries. Criminal violations of the Act are punishable by fines and imprisonment. The Sherman Act provides that corporate defendants may be fined up to $10 million, other defendants may be fined up to $350,000, and individuals may be sentenced to up to 3 years imprisonment.[5] The Department has sole responsibility for the criminal enforcement of the Sherman Act. In a civil proceeding, the Department may obtain injunctive relief against prohibited practices. It may also obtain treble damages if the U.S. government is the purchaser of affected goods or services.[6] Private plaintiffs may also obtain injunctive and treble damage relief for violations of the Sherman Act.[7] Before the Commission, conduct that violates the Sherman Act may be challenged pursuant to the Commission's power under Section 5 of the Federal Trade Commission Act, described below.

2.2 Clayton Act

The Clayton Act, 15 U.S.C. 12 et seq., expands on the general prohibitions of the Sherman Act and addresses anticompetitive problems in their incipiency.[8] Section 7 of the Clayton Act, 15 U.S.C. 18, prohibits any merger or acquisition of stock or assets "where in any line of commerce or in any activity affecting commerce in any section of the country, the effect of such acquisition may be substantially to lessen competition, or to tend to create a monopoly."[9] Section 15 of the Clayton Act empowers the Attorney General, and Section 13(b) of the FTC Act empowers the Commission, to seek a court order enjoining consummation of a merger that would violate Section 7. In addition, the Commission may seek a cease and desist order in an administrative proceeding against a merger under Section 11 of the Clayton Act, Section 5 of the FTC Act, or both. Private parties may also seek injunctive relief under 15 U.S.C. 26. Section 3 of the Clayton Act prohibits

---

[5] Defendants may be fined up to twice the gross pecuniary gain or loss caused by their offense in lieu of the Sherman Act fines, pursuant to 18 U.S.C. 3571(d) (1988 & Supp. 1993). In addition, the U.S. Sentencing Commission Guidelines provide further information about possible criminal sanctions for individual antitrust defendants in 2R1.1 and for organizational defendants in Chapter 8.

[6] See 15 U.S.C. 4 (1988) (injunctive relief); 15 U.S.C. 15(a) (1988 & Supp. 1993) (damages).

[7] See 15 U.S.C. 16, 26 (1988).

[8] Under the Clayton Act, "commerce" includes "trade or commerce among the several States and with foreign nations." "Persons" include corporations or associations existing under or authorized either by the laws of the United States or any of its states or territories, or by the laws of any foreign country. 15 U.S.C. 12 (1988 & Supp. 1993).

[9] 15 U.S.C. 18 (1988). The asset acquisition clause applies to "person[s] subject to the jurisdiction of the Federal Trade Commission" under the Clayton Act.

any person engaged in commerce from conditioning the lease or sale of goods or commodities upon the purchaser's agreement not to use the products of a competitor, if the effect may be "to substantially lessen competition or to tend to create a monopoly in any line of commerce."[10] In evaluating transactions, the trend of recent authority is to use the same analysis employed in the evaluation of tying under Section 1 of the Sherman Act to assess a defendant's liability under Section 3 of the Clayton Act.[11] Section 2 of the Clayton Act, known as the Robinson-Patman Act,[12] prohibits price discrimination in certain circumstances. In practice, the Commission has exercised primary enforcement responsibility for this provision.

2.3 Federal Trade Commission Act

Section 5 of the Federal Trade Commission Act ("FTC Act") declares unlawful "unfair methods of competition in or affecting commerce, and unfair or deceptive acts or practices in or affecting commerce."[13] Pursuant to its authority over unfair methods of competition, the Commission may take administrative action against conduct that violates the Sherman Act and the Clayton Act, as well as anticompetitive practices that do not fall within the scope of the Sherman or Clayton Acts. The Commission may also seek injunctive relief in federal court against any such conduct under Section 13(b) of the FTC Act. Although enforcement at the Commission relating to international deceptive practices has become increasingly important over time, these Guidelines are limited to the Commission's antitrust authority under the unfair methods of competition language of Section 5.

2.4 Hart-Scott-Rodino Antitrust Improvements Act of 1976

Title II of the Hart-Scott-Rodino Antitrust Improvements Act of 1976 ("HSR Act"), 15 U.S.C. 18a, provides the Department and the Commission with several procedural devices to facilitate enforcement of the antitrust laws with respect to anticompetitive mergers and acquisitions.[14] The HSR Act requires persons engaged in commerce or in any activity affecting commerce to notify the Agencies of proposed mergers or acquisitions that would exceed

---

[10] 15 U.S.C. 14 (1988).

[11] See, e.g., Mozart Co. v. Mercedes-Benz of N. Am., Inc., 833 F.2d 1342, 1352 (9th Cir. 1987), cert. denied, 488 U.S. 870 (1988).

[12] 15 U.S.C. 13–13b, 21a (1988). The Robinson-Patman Act applies only to purchases involving commodities "for use, consumption, or resale within the United States." Id. at 13. It has been construed not to apply to sales for export. See, e.g., General Chem., Inc. v. Exxon Chem. Co., 625 F.2d 1231, 1234 (5th Cir. 1980). Intervening domestic sales, however, would be subject to the Act. See Raul Int'l Corp. v. Sealed Power Corp., 586 F. Supp. 349, 351–55 (D.N.J. 1984).

[13] 15 U.S.C. 45 (1988 & Supp. 1993).

[14] The scope of the Agencies' jurisdiction under Clayton 7 exceeds the scope of those transactions subject to the premerger notification requirements of the HSR Act. Whether or not the HSR Act premerger notification thresholds are satisfied, either Agency may request the parties to a merger affecting U.S. commerce to provide information voluntarily concerning the transaction. In addition, the Department may issue Civil Investigative Demands ("CIDs") pursuant to the Antitrust Civil Process Act, 15 U.S.C. 1311–1314 (1988), and the Commission may issue administrative CIDs pursuant to the Act of Aug. 26, 1994, Pub. L. No. 103-312, 7; 108 Stat. 1691 (1994). The Commission may also issue administrative subpoenas and orders to file special reports under Sections 9 and 6(b) of the FTC Act, respectively. 15 U.S.C. 49, 46(b) (1988). Authority in particular cases is allocated to either the Department or the Commission pursuant to a voluntary clearance protocol. See Antitrust & Trade Reg. Daily (BNA), Dec. 6, 1993, and U.S. Department of Justice and Federal Trade Commission, Hart-Scott-Rodino Premerger Program Improvements (March 23, 1995).

statutory size-of-party and size-of-transaction thresholds,[15] to provide certain information relating to reportable transactions, and to wait for a prescribed period—15 days for cash tender offers and 30 days for most other transactions—before consummating the transaction.[16] The Agency may, before the end of the waiting period, request additional information concerning a transaction (make a "Second Request") and thereby extend the waiting period beyond the initial one prescribed, to a specified number of days after the receipt of the material required by the Second Request—10 days for cash tender offers and 20 days for most other transactions.[17]

The HSR Act and the FTC rules implementing the HSR Act[18] exempt from the premerger notification requirements certain international transactions (typically those having little nexus to U.S. commerce) that otherwise meet the statutory thresholds.[19] Failure to comply with the HSR Act is punishable by court-imposed civil penalties of up to $10,000 for each day a violation continues. The court may also order injunctive relief to remedy a failure substantially to comply with the HSR Act. Businesses may seek an interpretation of their obligations under the HSR Act from the Commission.[20]

2.5 National Cooperative Research and Production Act

The National Cooperative Research and Production Act ("NCRPA"), 15 U.S.C. 4301–06, clarifies the substantive application of the U.S. antitrust laws to joint research and development ("R&D") activities and joint

---

[15] Unless exempted pursuant to the HSR Act, the parties must provide premerger notification to the Agencies if

1. the acquiring person, or the person whose voting securities or assets are being acquired, is engaged in commerce or any activity affecting commerce; and
2.
   a. any voting securities or assets of a person engaged in manufacturing which has annual net sales or total assets of $10 million or more are being acquired by any person which has total assets or annual net sales of $100 million or more, or
   b. any voting securities or assets of a person not engaged in manufacturing which has total assets of $10 million or more are being acquired by any person which has total assets or annual sales of $100 million or more; or
   c. any voting securities or assets of a person with annual net sales or total assets of $100 million or more are being acquired by any person with total assets or annual net sales of $ 10 million or more;

   and
3. as a result of such acquisition, the acquiring person would hold 15 percent or more of the voting securities or assets of the acquired person, or
   a. an aggregate total amount of the voting securities and assets of the acquired person of $15 million. 15 U.S.C. 18a(a) (1988).

The size of the transaction test set forth in (3) must be read in conjunction with 16 C.F.R. 802.20 (1994). This Section exempts asset acquisitions valued at $15 million or less. It also exempts voting securities acquisitions of $15 million or less unless, if as a result of the acquisition, the acquiring person would hold 50 percent or more of the voting securities of an issuer that has annual net sales or total assets of $25 million or more. The HSR rules are necessarily technical, contain other exemptions, and should be consulted, rather than relying on this summary.

[16] 15 U.S.C. 18a(b) (1988 & Supp. 1993); 16 C.F.R. 803.1 (1994); see also 11 U.S.C. 363 (b)(2).

[17] 15 U.S.C. 18a(e) (1988).

[18] 16 C.F.R. 801–803 (1994).

[19] 16 C.F.R. 801.1(e), (k), 802.50–52 (1994). See infra at Section 4.22.

[20] See 16 C.F.R. 803.30 (1994).

production activities. Originally drafted to encourage research and development by providing a special antitrust regime for research and development joint ventures, the NCRPA requires U.S. courts to judge the competitive effects of a challenged joint R&D or joint production venture, or a combination of the two, in properly defined relevant markets and under a rule-of-reason standard. The statute specifies that the conduct "shall be judged on the basis of its reasonableness, taking into account all relevant factors affecting competition, including, but not limited to, effects on competition in properly defined, relevant research, development, product, process, and service markets."[21] This approach is consistent with the Agencies' general analysis of joint ventures.[22]

The NCRPA also establishes a voluntary procedure pursuant to which the Attorney General and the FTC may be notified of a joint R&D or production venture. The statute limits the monetary relief that may be obtained in private civil suits against the participants in a notified venture to actual rather than treble damages, if the challenged conduct is within the scope of the notification. With respect to joint production ventures, the National Cooperative Production Amendments of 1993[23] provide that the benefits of the limitation on recoverable damages for claims resulting from conduct within the scope of a notification are not available unless

1. the principal facilities for the production are located within the United States or its territories, and
2. "each person who controls any party to such venture (including such party itself) is a United States person, or a foreign person from a country whose law accords antitrust treatment no less favorable to United States persons than to such country's domestic persons with respect to participation in joint ventures for production."[24]

2.6 Webb-Pomerene Act

The Webb-Pomerene Act, 15 U.S.C. 61–65, provides a limited antitrust exemption for the formation and operation of associations of otherwise competing businesses to engage in collective export sales. The exemption applies only to the export of "goods, wares, or merchandise."[25] It does not apply to conduct that has an anticompetitive effect in the United States or that injures domestic competitors of the members of an export association. Nor does it provide any immunity from prosecution under foreign antitrust laws.[26] Associations seeking an exemption under the Webb-Pomerene Act must file their articles of agreement and annual reports with the Commission, but pre-formation approval from the Commission is not required.

---

[21] 15 U.S.C. 4302 (1988 & Supp. 1993).

[22] See, e.g., U.S. Department of Justice and Federal Trade Commission Antitrust Guidelines for the Licensing of Intellectual Property, 4 (1995); Statements of Antitrust Enforcement Policy and Analytical Principles Relating to Health Care and Antitrust, Jointly Issued by the U.S. Department of Justice and the Federal Trade Commission (1994), Statement 2 (outlining a four-step approach for joint venture analysis). See generally National Collegiate Athletic Ass'n v. Board of Regents of Univ. of Okla., 468 U.S. 85 (1984); Federal Trade Comm'n v. Indiana Fed'n of Dentists, 476 U.S. 447 (1986). See also Massachusetts Board of Registration in Optometry, 110 F.T.C. 549 (1988).

[23] Pub. L. No. 103-42, 107 Stat. 117, 119 (1993).

[24] 15 U.S.C. 4306 (2) (Supp. 1993).

[25] 15 U.S.C. 61 (1988).

[26] See, e.g., Cases 89/85, etc., A. Ahlstrom Osakeyhtio v. Commission ("Wood Pulp"), 1988 E.C.R. 5193, [1987–1988 Transfer Binder] Common Mkt. Rep. (CCH) 14,491 (1988).

2.7 Export Trading Company Act of 1982

The Export Trading Company Act of 1982 (the "ETC Act"), Pub. L. No. 97-290, 96 Stat. 1234, is designed to increase U.S. exports of goods and services. It addresses that goal in several ways. First, in Title II, it encourages more efficient provision of export trade services to U.S. producers and suppliers by reducing restrictions on trade financing provided by financial institutions.[27] Second, in Title III, it reduces uncertainty concerning the application of the U.S. antitrust laws to export trade through the creation of a procedure by which persons engaged in U.S. export trade may obtain an export trade certificate of review ("ETCR").[28] Third, in Title IV, it clarifies the jurisdictional rules applicable to non-import cases brought under the Sherman Act and the FTC Act.[29] The Title III certificates are discussed briefly here; the jurisdictional rules are treated below in Section 3.1.

Export trade certificates of review are issued by the Secretary of Commerce with the concurrence of the Attorney General. Persons named in the ETCR obtain limited immunity from suit under both state and federal antitrust laws for activities that are specified in the certificate and that comply with the terms of the certificate. To obtain an ETCR, an applicant must show that proposed export conduct will:

1. result in neither a substantial lessening of competition or restraint of trade within the United States nor a substantial restraint of the export trade of any competitor of the applicant;
2. not unreasonably enhance, stabilize, or depress prices in the United States of the class of goods or services covered by the application;
3. not constitute unfair methods of competition against competitors engaged in the export of the class of goods or services exported by the applicant; and
4. not include any act that may reasonably be expected to result in the sale for consumption or resale in the United States of such goods or services.[30]

Congress intended that these standards "encompass the full range of the antitrust laws," as defined in the ETC Act.[31]

Although an ETCR provides significant protection under the antitrust laws, it has certain limitations. First, conduct that falls outside the scope of a certificate remains fully subject to private and governmental enforcement actions. Second, an ETCR that is obtained by fraud is void from the outset and thus offers no protection under the antitrust laws. Third, any person that has been injured by certified conduct may recover actual (though not treble) damages if that conduct is found to violate any of the statutory criteria described above. In any such action, certified conduct enjoys a presumption of legality, and the prevailing party is entitled to recover costs and attorneys' fees.[32] Fourth, an ETCR does not constitute, explicitly or

---

[27] See 12 U.S.C. 372, 635 a-4, 1841, 1843 (1988 & Supp. 1993) (Because Title II does not implicate the antitrust laws, it is not discussed further in these Guidelines.)

[28] 15 U.S.C. 4011–21 (1988 & Supp. 1993).

[29] 15 U.S.C. 6a (1988); 15 U.S.C. 45(a)(3) (1988).

[30] 15 U.S.C. 4013(a) (1988).

[31] H.R. Rep. No. 924, 97th Cong., 2d Sess. 26 (1982). See 15 U.S.C. 4021(6).

[32] See 15 U.S.C. 4016(b)(1) (1988) (injured party) and 4016(b)(4) (1988) (party against whom claim is brought).

implicitly, an endorsement or opinion by the Secretary of Commerce or by the Attorney General concerning the legality of such business plans under the laws of any foreign country.

The Secretary of Commerce may revoke or modify an ETCR if the Secretary or the Attorney General determines that the applicant's export activities have ceased to comply with the statutory criteria for obtaining a certificate. The Attorney General may also bring suit under Section 15 of the Clayton Act to enjoin conduct that threatens "a clear and irreparable harm to the national interest,"[33] even if the conduct has been pre-approved as part of an ETCR.

The Commerce Department, in consultation with the Department, has issued guidelines setting forth the standards used in reviewing ETCR applications.[34] The ETC Guidelines contain several examples illustrating application of the certification standards to specific export trade conduct, including the use of vertical and horizontal restraints and technology licensing arrangements. In addition, the Commerce Department's Export Trading Company Guidebook[35] provides information on the functions and advantages of establishing or using an export trading company, including factors to consider in applying for an ETCR. The Commerce Department's Office of Export Trading Company Affairs provides advice and information on the formation of export trading companies and facilitates contacts between producers of exportable goods and services and firms offering export trade services.

2.8 Other Pertinent Legislation

2.81 Wilson Tariff Act

The Wilson Tariff Act, 15 U.S.C. 8–11, prohibits "every combination, conspiracy, trust, agreement, or contract" made by or between two or more persons or corporations, either of whom is engaged in importing any article from a foreign country into the United States, where the agreement is intended to restrain trade or increase the market price in any part of the United States of the imported articles, or of "any manufacture into which such imported article enters or is intended to enter." Violation of the Act is a misdemeanor, punishable by a maximum fine of $5,000 or one year in prison. The Act also provides for seizure of the imported articles.[36]

2.82 Antidumping Act of 1916

The Revenue Act of 1916, better known as the Antidumping Act, 15 U.S.C. 71–74, is not an antitrust statute, but its subject matter is closely related to the antitrust rules regarding predation. It is a trade statute that creates a private claim against importers who sell goods into the United States at prices substantially below the prices charged for the same goods in their home market. In order to state a claim, a plaintiff must show both that such lower prices were commonly and systematically charged, and that the importer had the specific intent to injure or destroy an industry in the United States, or to prevent the establishment of an industry. Dumping

---

[33] 15 U.S.C. 4016(b)(5) (1988); see 15 U.S.C. 25 (1988).

[34] See Department of Commerce, International Trade Administration, Guidelines for the Issuance of Export Trade Certificates of Review (2d ed.), 50 Fed. Reg. 1786 (1985) (hereinafter "ETC Guidelines").

[35] U.S. Department of Commerce, International Trade Administration, The Export Trading Company Guidebook (1984).

[36] 15 U.S.C. 11 (1988).

cases are more commonly brought using the administrative procedures of the Tariff Act of 1930, discussed below.

2.83 Tariff Act of 1930

A comprehensive discussion of the trade remedies available under the Tariff Act is beyond the scope of these Guidelines. However, because antitrust questions sometimes arise in the context of trade actions, it is appropriate to describe these laws briefly.

2.831 Countervailing Duties

Pursuant to Title VII.A of the Tariff Act,[37] U.S. manufacturers, producers, wholesalers, unions, and trade associations may petition for the imposition of offsetting duties on subsidized foreign imports.[38] The Department of Commerce's International Trade Administration ("ITA") must make a determination that the foreign government in question is subsidizing the imports, and in almost all cases the International Trade Commission ("ITC") must determine that a domestic industry is materially injured or threatened with material injury by reason of these imports.

2.832 Antidumping Duties

Pursuant to Title VII.B of the Tariff Act,[39] parties designated in the statute (the same parties as in the countervailing duties provision) may petition for antidumping duties, which must be imposed on foreign merchandise that is being, or is likely to be, sold in the United States at "less than fair value" ("LTFV"), if the U.S. industry is materially injured or threatened with material injury by imports of the foreign merchandise. The ITA makes the LTFV determination, and the ITC is responsible for the injury decision.

2.833 Section 337

Section 337 of the Tariff Act, 19 U.S.C. 1337, prohibits "unfair methods of competition and unfair acts in the importation of articles into the United States," if the effect is to destroy or substantially injure a U.S. industry, or where the acts relate to importation of articles infringing U.S. patents, copyrights, trademarks, or registered mask works.[40] Complaints are filed with the ITC. The principal remedies under Section 337 are an exclusion order directing that any offending goods be excluded from entry into the United States, and a cease and desist order directed toward any offending U.S. firms and individuals.[41] The ITC is required to give the Agencies an opportunity to comment before making a final determination.[42] In addition, the Department participates in the interagency group that prepares recommendations for the President to approve, disapprove, or allow to take effect the import relief proposed by the ITC.

---

[37] See 19 U.S.C. 1671 et seq. (1988 & Supp. 1993), amended by Uruguay Round Agreements Act, Pub. L. No. 103-465, 108 Stat. 4809 (1994).

[38] Some alternative procedures exist under Tariff Act 701(c) for countries that have not subscribed to the World Trade Organization ("WTO") Agreement on Subsidies and Countervailing Measures or measures equivalent to it. 19 U.S.C. 1671(c) (1988 & Supp. 1993), amended by the Uruguay Round Agreements Act, Pub. L. No. 103-465, 108 Stat. 4809 (1994).

[39] See 19 U.S.C. 1673 et seq. (1988).

[40] 19 U.S.C. 1337 (1988), amended by the Uruguay Round Agreements Act, Pub. L. No. 103-465, 108 Stat. 4809 (1994).

[41] 19 U.S.C. 1337(d), (f) (1988).

[42] 19 U.S.C. 1337(b)(2) (1988).

2.84 Trade Act of 1974

2.841 Section 201

Section 201 of the Trade Act of 1974, 19 U.S.C. 2251 et seq., provides that American businesses claiming serious injury due to significant increases in imports may petition the ITC for relief or modification under the so-called "escape clause." If the ITC makes a determination that "an article is being imported into the United States in such increased quantities as to be a substantial cause of serious injury, or the threat thereof, to the domestic industry producing an article like or directly competitive with the imported article," and formulates its recommendation for appropriate relief, the Department participates in the interagency committee that conducts the investigations and advises the President whether to adopt, modify, or reject the import relief recommended by the ITC.

2.842 Section 301

Section 301 of the Trade Act of 1974, 19 U.S.C. 2411, provides that the U.S. Trade Representative ("USTR"), subject to the specific direction, if any, of the President, may take action, including restricting imports, to enforce rights of the United States under any trade agreement, to address acts inconsistent with the international legal rights of the United States, or to respond to unjustifiable, unreasonable or discriminatory practices of foreign governments that burden or restrict U.S. commerce. Interested parties may initiate such actions through petitions to the USTR, or the USTR may itself initiate proceedings.[43] Of particular interest to antitrust enforcement is Section 301(d)(3)(B)(i)(IV), which includes among the "unreasonable" practices of foreign governments that might justify a proceeding the "toleration by a foreign government of systematic anticompetitive activities by enterprises or among enterprises in the foreign country that have the effect of restricting . . . access of United States goods or services to a foreign market."[44] The Department participates in the interagency committee that makes recommendations to the President on what actions, if any, should be taken.

2.9 Relevant International Agreements

To further the twin goals of promoting enforcement cooperation between the United States and foreign governments and of reducing any tensions that may arise in particular proceedings, the Agencies have developed close relationships with antitrust and competition policy officials of many different countries. In some instances, understandings have been reached with respect to notifications, consultations, and cooperation in antitrust matters.[45] In other instances, more general rules endorsed by multilateral organizations such as the Organization for Economic Cooperation and Development ("OECD") provide the basis for the Agencies' cooperative

---

[43] 19 U.S.C. 2412 (a), (b) (1988), amended by the Uruguay Round Agreements Act, Pub. L. No. 103-465, 108 Stat. 4809 (1994); see also Identification of Trade Expansion Priorities, Exec. Order No. 12,901, 59 Fed. Reg. 10,727 (1994).

[44] 19 U.S.C. 2411(d)(3)(B)(i)(IV) (1988), amended by the Uruguay Round Agreements Act, Pub. L. No. 103-465, 108 Stat. 4809 (1994), 314(c).

[45] Chapter 15 of the North American Free Trade Agreement ("NAFTA") addresses competition policy matters and commits the Parties to cooperate on antitrust matters. North American Free Trade Agreement Between the Government of the United States of America, the Government of Canada and the Government of the United Mexican States, 32 I.L.M. 605, 663 (1993), reprinted in H.R. Doc. No. 159, 103d Cong., 1st Sess. 712, 1170–1174 (1993).

policies. Finally, even in the absence of specific or general international understandings or recommendations, the Agencies often seek cooperation with foreign authorities.

2.91 Bilateral Cooperation Agreements

Formal written bilateral arrangements exist between the United States and the Federal Republic of Germany, Australia, and Canada.[46] International antitrust cooperation can also occur through mutual legal assistance treaties ("MLATs"), which are treaties of general application pursuant to which the United States and a foreign country agree to assist one another in criminal law enforcement matters. MLATs currently are in force with over one dozen countries, and many more are in the process of ratification or negotiation. However, only the MLAT with Canada has been used to date to obtain assistance in antitrust investigations.[47] The Agencies also hold regular consultations with the antitrust officials of Canada, the European Commission, and Japan, and have close, informal ties with the antitrust authorities of many other countries. Since 1990, the Agencies have cooperated closely with countries in the process of establishing competition agencies, assisted by funding provided by the Agency for International Development.

On November 2, 1994, President Clinton signed into law the International Antitrust Enforcement Assistance Act of 1994,[48] which authorizes the Agencies to enter into antitrust mutual assistance agreements in accordance with the legislation.

2.92 International Guidelines and Recommendations

The Agencies have agreed with respect to member countries of the OECD to consider the legitimate interests of other nations in accordance with relevant OECD recommendations.[49] Under the terms of a 1986 recommendation, the United States agency with responsibility for a particular case notifies a member country whenever an antitrust enforcement action may affect important interests of that country or its

---

[46] See Agreement Relating to Mutual Cooperation Regarding Restrictive Business Practices, June 23, 1976, U.S.-Federal Republic of Germany, 27 U.S.T. 1956, T.I.S. No. 8291, reprinted in 4 Trade Reg. Rep. (CCH) 13,501; Agreement Between the Government of the United States of America and the Government of Australia Relating to Cooperation on Antitrust Matters, June 29, 1982, U.S.-Australia, T.I.A.S. No. 10365, reprinted in 4 Trade Reg. Rep. (CCH) 13,502; and Memorandum of Understanding as to Notification, Consultation, and Cooperation with Respect to the Application of National Antitrust Laws, March 9, 1984, U.S.-Canada, reprinted in 4 Trade Reg. Rep. (CCH) 13,503. The Agencies also signed a similar agreement with the Commission of the European Communities in 1991. See Agreement Between the Government of the United States of America and the Commission of the European Communities Regarding the Application of Their Competition Laws, Sept. 23, 1991, 30 I.L.M. 1491 (Nov. 1991), reprinted in 4 Trade Reg. Rep. (CCH) 13,504. However, on August 9, 1994, the European Court of Justice ruled that the conclusion of the Agreement did not comply with institutional requirements of the law of the European Union ("EU"). Under the Court's decision, action by the EU Council of Ministers is necessary for this type of agreement. See French Republic v. Commission of European Communities (No. C-327/91) (Aug. 9, 1994).

[47] Treaty with Canada on Mutual Legal Assistance in Criminal Matters, S. Treaty Doc. No. 28, 100th Cong., 2d Sess. (1988).

[48] Pub. L. No. 103-438, 108 Stat. 4597 (1994).

[49] See Revised Recommendation of the OECD Council Concerning Cooperation Between Member Countries on Restrictive Business Practices Affecting International Trade, OECD Doc. No. C(86)44 (Final) (May 21, 1986). The Recommendation also calls for countries to consult with each other in appropriate situations, with the aim of promoting enforcement cooperation and minimizing differences that may arise.

nationals.[50] Examples of potentially notifiable actions include requests for documents located outside the United States, attempts to obtain information from potential witnesses located outside the United States, and cases or investigations with significant foreign conduct or involvement of foreign persons.

3. THRESHOLD INTERNATIONAL ENFORCEMENT ISSUES

3.1 Jurisdiction

Just as the acts of U.S. citizens in a foreign nation ordinarily are subject to the law of the country in which they occur, the acts of foreign citizens in the United States ordinarily are subject to U.S. law. The reach of the U.S. antitrust laws is not limited, however, to conduct and transactions that occur within the boundaries of the United States. Anticompetitive conduct that affects U.S. domestic or foreign commerce may violate the U.S. antitrust laws regardless of where such conduct occurs or the nationality of the parties involved.

Under the Sherman Act and the FTC Act, there are two principal tests for subject matter jurisdiction in foreign commerce cases. With respect to foreign import commerce, the Supreme Court has recently stated in Hartford Fire Insurance Co. v. California that "the Sherman Act applies to foreign conduct that was meant to produce and did in fact produce some substantial effect in the United States."[51] There has been no such authoritative ruling on the scope of the FTC Act, but both Acts apply to commerce "with foreign nations" and the Commission has held that terms used by both Acts should be construed together.[52] Second, with respect to foreign commerce other than imports, the Foreign Trade Antitrust Improvements Act of 1982 ("FTAIA") applies to foreign conduct that has a direct, substantial, and reasonably foreseeable effect on U.S. commerce. [53]

3.11 Jurisdiction over Conduct Involving Import Commerce

Imports into the United States by definition affect the U.S. domestic market directly, and will, therefore, almost invariably satisfy the intent part of the Hartford Fire test. Whether they in fact produce the requisite substantial effects will depend on the facts of each case.

---

[50] The OECD has 25 member countries and the European Commission takes part in its work. The OECD's membership includes many of the most advanced market economies in the world. The OECD also has several observer nations, which have made rapid progress toward open market economies. The Agencies follow recommended OECD practices with respect to all member countries.

[51] 113 S. Ct. 2891, 2909 (1993). In a world in which economic transactions observe no boundaries, international recognition of the "effects doctrine" of jurisdiction has become more widespread. In the context of import trade, the "implementation" test adopted in the European Court of Justice usually produces the same outcome as the "effects" test employed in the United States. See Cases 89/85, etc., Ahlstrom v. Commission, supra at note 26. The merger laws of the European Union, Canada, Germany, France, Australia, and the Czech and Slovak Republics, among others, take a similar approach.

[52] In re Massachusetts Bd. of Registration in Optometry, 110 F.T.C. 598, 609 (1988).

[53] 15 U.S.C. 6a (1988) (Sherman Act) and 45(a)(3) (1988) (FTC Act).

ILLUSTRATIVE EXAMPLE A[54]

Situation:
A, B, C, and D are foreign companies that produce a product in various foreign countries. None has any U.S. production, nor any U.S. subsidiaries. They organize a cartel for the purpose of raising the price for the product in question. Collectively, the cartel members make substantial sales into the United States, both in absolute terms and relative to total U.S. consumption.

Discussion:
These facts present the straightforward case of cartel participants selling products directly into the United States. In this situation, the transaction is unambiguously an import into the U.S. market, and the sale is not complete until the goods reach the United States. Thus, U.S. subject matter jurisdiction is clear under the general principles of antitrust law expressed most recently in Hartford Fire. The facts presented here demonstrate actual and intended participation in U.S. commerce.[55] The separate question of personal jurisdiction under the facts presented here would be analyzed using the principles discussed infra in Section 4.1.

3.12 Jurisdiction over Conduct Involving Other Foreign Commerce

With respect to foreign commerce other than imports, the jurisdictional limits of the Sherman Act and the FTC Act are delineated in the FTAIA. The FTAIA amended the Sherman Act to provide that it:

shall not apply to conduct involving trade or commerce (other than import trade or commerce) with foreign nations unless

1. such conduct has a direct, substantial, and reasonably foreseeable effect:
   A. on trade or commerce which is not trade or commerce with foreign nations, or on import trade or import commerce with foreign nations; or
   B. on export trade or export commerce with foreign nations, of a person engaged in such trade or commerce in the United States;[56]
2. such effect gives rise to a claim under the provisions of [the Sherman Act], other than this section.

The FTAIA uses slightly different statutory language for the FTC Act,[57] but produces the same jurisdictional outcomes.

---

[54] The examples incorporated into the text are intended solely to illustrate how the Agencies would apply the principles articulated in the Guidelines in differing fact situations. In each case, of course, the ultimate outcome of the analysis, i.e. whether or not a violation of the antitrust laws has occurred, would depend on the specific facts and circumstances of the case. These examples, therefore, do not address many of the factual and economic questions the Agencies would ask in analyzing particular conduct or transactions under the antitrust laws. Therefore, certain hypothetical situations presented here may, when fully analyzed, not violate any provision of the antitrust laws.

[55] See infra at Section 3.12.

[56] If the Sherman Act applies to such conduct only because of the operation of paragraph (1)(B), then that Act shall apply to such conduct only for injury to export business in the United States. 15 U.S.C. 6a (1988).

3.121 Jurisdiction in Cases Under Subsection 1(A) of the FTAIA

To the extent that conduct in foreign countries does not "involve" import commerce but does have an "effect" on either import transactions or commerce within the United States, the Agencies apply the "direct, substantial, and reasonably foreseeable" standard of the FTAIA. That standard is applied, for example, in cases in which a cartel of foreign enterprises, or a foreign monopolist, reaches the U.S. market through any mechanism that goes beyond direct sales, such as the use of an unrelated intermediary, as well as in cases in which foreign vertical restrictions or intellectual property licensing arrangements have an anticompetitive effect on U.S. commerce.

ILLUSTRATIVE EXAMPLE B

Situation:
As in Illustrative Example A, the foreign cartel produces a product in several foreign countries. None of its members has any U.S. production, nor do any of them have U.S. subsidiaries. They organize a cartel for the purpose of raising the price for the product in question. Rather than selling directly into the United States, however, the cartel sells to an intermediary outside the United States, which they know will resell the product in the United States. The intermediary is not part of the cartel.

Discussion:
The jurisdictional analysis would change slightly from the one presented in Example A, because not only is the conduct being challenged entered into by cartelists in a foreign country, but it is also initially implemented through a sale made in a foreign country. Despite the different test, however, the outcome on these facts would in all likelihood remain the same. The fact that the illegal conduct occurs prior to the import would trigger the application of the FTAIA. The Agencies would have to determine whether the challenged conduct had "direct, substantial and reasonably foreseeable effects" on U.S. domestic or import commerce. Furthermore, since "the essence of any violation of Section 1 [of the Sherman Act] is the illegal agreement itself—rather than the overt acts performed in furtherance of it,"[58] the Agencies would focus on the potential harm that would ensue if the conspiracy were successful, not on whether the actual conduct in furtherance of the conspiracy had in fact the prohibited effect upon interstate or foreign commerce.

ILLUSTRATIVE EXAMPLE C

Situation:

Variant (1):

Widgets are manufactured in both the United States and various other countries around the world. The non-U.S. manufacturers meet privately outside the United States and agree among themselves to raise prices to specified levels. Their agreement clearly indicates that sales in or into the United States are not within the scope of the agreement, and thus that each participant is free independently to set its prices for the U.S. market. Over time, the cartel members begin to sell excess production into the United States. These sales have the effect of stabilizing the cartel for the

---

[57] See 15 U.S.C. 45(a)(3) (1988).

[58] Summit Health, Ltd. v. Pinhas, 500 U.S. 322, 330–31 (1991).

foreign markets. In the U.S. market, these "excess" sales are priced at levels below those that would have prevailed in the U.S. market but for the cartel, but there is no evidence that the prices are predatory. As a result of these events, several U.S. widget manufacturers curtail their production, overall domestic output falls, and remaining manufacturers fail to invest in new or improved capacity.

Variant (2):

Assume now that the cartel agreement specifically provides that cartel members will set agreed prices for the U.S. market at levels designed to soak up excess quantities that arise as a result of price increases in foreign markets. The U.S. price level is set at periodic meetings where each participant indicates how much it must off-load in this way. Thus, the cartel members sell goods in the U.S. market at fixed prices that undercut prevailing U.S. price levels, with consequences similar to those in Variant 1.

Discussion:

Variant (1):

The jurisdictional issue is whether the predictable economic consequences of the original cartel agreement and the independent sales into the United States are sufficient to support jurisdiction. The mere fact that the existence of U.S. sales or the level of U.S. prices may ultimately be affected by the cartel agreement is not enough for either Hartford Fire jurisdiction or the FTAIA.[59] Furthermore, in the absence of an agreement with respect to the U.S. market, sales into the U.S. market at non-predatory levels do not raise antitrust concerns.[60]

Variant (2):

The critical element of a foreign price-fixing agreement with direct, intended effects in the United States is now present. The fact that the cartel believes its U.S. prices are "reasonable," or that it may be exerting downward pressure on U.S. price levels, does not exonerate it.[61] Variant 2 presents a case where the Agencies would need clear evidence of the prohibited agreement before they would consider moving forward. They would be particularly cautious if the apparent effects in the U.S. market appeared to be beneficial to consumers.

3.122 Jurisdiction in Cases Under Subsection 1(B) of the FTAIA

Two categories of "export cases" fall within the FTAIA's jurisdictional test. First, the Agencies may, in appropriate cases, take enforcement action against anticompetitive conduct, wherever occurring, that restrains U.S. exports, if

---

[59] If the Agencies lack jurisdiction under the FTAIA to challenge the cartel, the facts of this example would nonetheless lend themselves well to cooperative enforcement action among antitrust agencies. Virtually every country with an antitrust law prohibits horizontal cartels and the Agencies would willingly cooperate with foreign authorities taking direct action against the cartel in the countries where the agreement has raised the price of widgets to the extent such cooperation is allowed under U.S. law and any agreement executed pursuant to U.S. law with foreign agencies or governments.

[60] Cf. Matsushita Elec. Indus. Co. v. Zenith Radio Corp., 475 U.S. 574 (1986).

[61] Cf. Arizona v. Maricopa County Medical Soc'y, 457 U.S. 332 (1982); United States v. Socony-Vacuum Oil Co., 310 U.S. 150 (1940); United States v. Trenton Potteries Co., 273 U.S. 392 (1927).

1. the conduct has a direct, substantial, and reasonably foreseeable effect on exports of goods or services from the United States, and
2. the U.S. courts can obtain jurisdiction over persons or corporations engaged in such conduct.[62]

As Section 3.2 below explains more fully, if the conduct is unlawful under the importing country's antitrust laws as well, the Agencies are also prepared to work with that country's authorities if they are better situated to remedy the conduct, and if they are prepared to take action that will address the U.S. concerns, pursuant to their antitrust laws.

Second, the Agencies may in appropriate cases take enforcement action against conduct by U.S. exporters that has a direct, substantial, and reasonably foreseeable effect on trade or commerce within the United States, or on import trade or commerce. This can arise in two principal ways. First, if U.S. supply and demand were not particularly elastic, an agreement among U.S. firms accounting for a substantial share of the relevant market, regarding the level of their exports, could reduce supply and raise prices in the United States.[63] Second, conduct ostensibly export-related could affect the price of products sold or resold in the United States. This kind of effect could occur if, for example, U.S. firms fixed the price of an input used to manufacture a product overseas for ultimate resale in the United States.

ILLUSTRATIVE EXAMPLE D

Situation:
Companies E and F are the only producers of product Q in country Epsilon, one of the biggest markets for sales of Q in the world. E and F together account for 99 percent of the sales of product Q in Epsilon.[64] In order to prevent a competing U.S. producer from entering the market in Epsilon, E and F agree that neither one of them will purchase or distribute the U.S. product, and that they will take "all feasible" measures to keep the U.S. company out of their market. Without specifically discussing what other measures they will take to carry out this plan, E and F meet with their distributors and, through a variety of threats and inducements, obtain agreement of all of the distributors not to carry the U.S. product. There are no commercially feasible substitute distribution channels available to the U.S. producer. Because of the actions of E and F, the U.S. producer cannot find any distributors to carry its product and is unable to make any sales in Epsilon.

Discussion:
The agreement between E and F not to purchase or distribute the U.S. product would clearly have a direct and reasonably foreseeable effect on U.S. export commerce, since it is aimed at a U.S. exporter. The

---

62 See U.S. Department of Justice Press Release dated April 3, 1992 (announcing enforcement policy that would permit the Department to challenge foreign business conduct that harms U.S. exports when the conduct would have violated U.S. antitrust laws if it occurred in the United States).

63 One would need to show more than indirect price effects resulting from legitimate export efforts to support an antitrust challenge. See ETC Guidelines, supra at note 34, 50 Fed. Reg. at 1791.

64 That E and F together have an overwhelmingly dominant share in Epsilon may or may not, depending on the market conditions for Q, satisfy the requirement of "substantial effect on U.S. exports" as required by the FTAIA. Foreclosure of exports to a single country, such as Epsilon, may satisfy the statutory threshold if that country's market accounts for a significant part of the export opportunities for U.S. firms.

substantiality of the effects on U.S. exports would depend on the significance of E and F as purchasers and distributors of Q, although on these facts the virtually total foreclosure from Epsilon would almost certainly qualify as a substantial effect for jurisdictional purposes. However, if the Agencies believe that they may encounter difficulties in establishing personal jurisdiction or in obtaining effective relief, the case may be one in which the Agencies would seek to resolve their concerns by working with other authorities who are examining the transaction.

ILLUSTRATIVE EXAMPLE E

Situation:

Companies P, Q, R, and S, organized under the laws of country Alpha, all manufacture and distribute construction equipment. Much of that equipment is protected by patents in the various countries where it is sold, including Alpha. The companies all belong to a private trade association, which develops industry standards that are often (although not always) adopted by Alpha's regulatory authorities. Feeling threatened by competition from the United States, the companies agree at a trade association meeting to refuse to adopt any U.S. company technology as an industry standard, and to boycott the distribution of U.S. construction equipment. The U.S. companies have taken all necessary steps to protect their intellectual property under the law of Alpha.

Discussion:

In this example, the collective activity impedes U.S. companies in two ways: their technology is boycotted (even if U.S. companies are willing to license their intellectual property) and they are foreclosed from access to distribution channels. The jurisdictional question is whether these actions create a direct, substantial, and reasonably foreseeable effect on the exports of U.S. companies. The mere fact that only the market of Alpha appears to be foreclosed is not enough to defeat such an effect. Only if exclusion from Alpha as a quantitative measure were so de minimis in terms of actual volume of trade that there would not be a substantial effect on U.S. export commerce would jurisdiction be lacking. Given that this example involves construction equipment, a generally highly priced capital good, the exclusion from Alpha would probably satisfy the substantiality requirement for FTAIA jurisdiction. This arrangement appears to have been created with particular reference to competition from the United States, which indicates that the effects on U.S. exports are both direct and foreseeable.

3.13 Jurisdiction When U.S. Government Finances or Purchases

The Agencies may, in appropriate cases, take enforcement action when the U.S. Government is a purchaser, or substantially funds the purchase, of goods or services for consumption or use abroad. Cases in which the effect of anticompetitive conduct with respect to the sale of these goods or services falls primarily on U.S. taxpayers may qualify for redress under the federal antitrust laws.[65] As a general matter, the Agencies consider there to be a

[65] Cf. United States v. Concentrated Phosphate Export Ass'n, 393 U.S. 199, 208 (1968) ("[A]lthough the fertilizer shipments were consigned to Korea and although in most cases Korea formally let the contracts, American participation was the overwhelmingly dominant feature. The burden of noncompetitive pricing fell, not on any foreign purchaser, but on the American taxpayer. The United States was, in essence, furnishing fertilizer to Korea. . . . The foreign elements in the transaction were, by comparison, insignificant."); United States v. Standard Tallow Corp., 1988-1 Trade Cas. (CCH) 67,913 (S.D.N.Y. 1988)

sufficient effect on U.S. commerce to support the assertion of jurisdiction if, as a result of its payment or financing, the U.S. Government bears more than half the cost of the transaction. For purposes of this determination, the Agencies apply the standards used in certifying export conduct under the ETC Act of 1982, 15 U.S.C. 4011–21(1982).[66]

ILLUSTRATIVE EXAMPLE F

Situation:
A combination of U.S. firms and local firms in country Beta create a U.S.-based joint venture for the purpose of building a major pollution control facility for Beta's Environmental Control Agency ("BECA"). The venture has received preferential funding from the U.S. Government, which has the effect of making the present value of expected future repayment of the principal and interest on the loan less than half its face value. Once the venture has begun work, it appears that its members secretly have agreed to inflate the price quoted to BECA, in order to secure more funding.

Discussion:
The fact that the U.S. Government bears more than half the financial risk of the transaction is sufficient for jurisdiction. With jurisdiction established, the Agencies would proceed to investigate whether the apparent bid-rigging actually occurred.[67]

ILLUSTRATIVE EXAMPLE G

Situation:
The United States has many military bases and other facilities located in other countries. These facilities procure substantial goods and services from suppliers in the host country. In country X, it comes to the attention of the local U.S. military base commander that bids to supply certain construction services have been rigged.

Discussion:
Sales made by a foreign party to the U.S. Government, including to a U.S. facility located in a foreign country, are within U.S. antitrust jurisdiction when they fall within the rule of Section 3.13. Bid-rigging of sales to the U.S. Government represents the kind of conduct that can lead to an antitrust action. Indeed, in the United States this type of behavior is normally prosecuted by the Department as a criminal offense. In practice, the Department has whenever possible worked closely with the host

---

(consent decree) (barring suppliers from fixing prices or rigging bids for the sale of tallow financed in whole or in part through grants or loans by the U.S. Government); United States v. Anthracite Export Ass'n, 1970 Trade Cas. (CCH) 73,348 (M.D. Pa. 1970) (consent decree) (barring price-fixing, bid-rigging, and market allocation in Army foreign aid program).

[66] See ETC Guidelines, supra at note 34, 50 Fed. Reg. at 1799–1800. The requisite U.S. Government involvement could include the actual purchase of goods by the U.S. Government for shipment abroad, a U.S. Government grant to a foreign government that is specifically earmarked for the transaction, or a U.S. Government loan specifically earmarked for the transaction that is made on such generous terms that it amounts to a grant. U.S. Government interests would not be considered to be sufficiently implicated with respect to a transaction that is funded by an international agency, or a transaction in which the foreign government received non-earmarked funds from the United States as part of a general government-to-government aid program.

[67] Such conduct might also violate the False Claims Act, 31 U.S.C. 3729–3733 (1988 & Supp. 1993).

country antitrust authorities to explore remedies under local law. This has been successful in a number of instances.[68]

3.14 Jurisdiction Under Section 7 of the Clayton Act

Section 7 of the Clayton Act applies to mergers and acquisitions between firms that are engaged in commerce or in any activity affecting commerce. The Agencies would apply the same principles regarding their foreign commerce jurisdiction to Clayton Section 7 cases as they would apply in Sherman Act cases.

ILLUSTRATIVE EXAMPLE H

Situation:
Two foreign firms, one in Europe and the other in Canada, account together for a substantial percentage of U.S. sales of a particular product through direct imports. Both firms have sales offices and are subject to personal jurisdiction in the United States, although neither has productive assets in the United States. They enter into an agreement to merge.

Discussion:
The express language of Section 7 of the Clayton Act reaches the stock and asset acquisitions of persons engaged in trade and commerce "with foreign nations."[69] Thus, in assessing jurisdiction for this merger outside the United States the Agencies could establish U.S. subject matter jurisdiction based on its effect on U.S. imports. If the facts stated above were modified to show that the proposed merger would have effects on U.S. export commerce, as opposed to import trade, then in assessing jurisdiction under the Clayton Act the Agencies would analyze the question of effects on commerce in a manner consistent with the FTAIA: that is, they would look to see whether the effects on U.S. domestic or import commerce are direct, substantial, and reasonably foreseeable.[70] It is appropriate to do so because the FTAIA sheds light on the type of effects Congress considered necessary for foreign commerce cases, even though the FTAIA did not amend the Clayton Act.

In both these situations, the Agencies would conclude that Section 7 jurisdiction technically exists. However, if effective relief is difficult to obtain, the case may be one in which the Agencies would seek to coordinate their efforts with other authorities who are examining the transaction.[71]

3.2 Comity

In enforcing the antitrust laws, the Agencies consider international comity. Comity itself reflects the broad concept of respect among co-equal sovereign nations and plays a role in determining "the recognition which one nation allows within its territory to the legislative, executive or judicial acts of

---

[68] If, however, local law does not provide adequate remedies, or the local authorities are not prepared to take action, the Department will weigh the comity factors, discussed infra at Section 3.2, and take such action as is appropriate.

[69] Clayton Act 1, 15 U.S.C. 12 (1988).

[70] See supra at Section 3.121.

[71] Through concepts such as "positive comity," one country's authorities may ask another country to take measures that address possible harm to competition in the requesting country's market.

another nation."[72] Thus, in determining whether to assert jurisdiction to investigate or bring an action, or to seek particular remedies in a given case, each Agency takes into account whether significant interests of any foreign sovereign would be affected.[73]

In performing a comity analysis, the Agencies take into account all relevant factors. Among others, these may include

1. the relative significance to the alleged violation of conduct within the United States, as compared to conduct abroad;
2. the nationality of the persons involved in or affected by the conduct;
3. the presence or absence of a purpose to affect U.S. consumers, markets, or exporters;
4. the relative significance and foreseeability of the effects of the conduct on the United States as compared to the effects abroad;
5. the existence of reasonable expectations that would be furthered or defeated by the action;
6. the degree of conflict with foreign law or articulated foreign economic policies;
7. the extent to which the enforcement activities of another country with respect to the same persons, including remedies resulting from those activities, may be affected; and
8. the effectiveness of foreign enforcement as compared to U.S. enforcement action.[74]

The relative weight that each factor should be given depends on the facts and circumstances of each case. With respect to the factor concerning conflict with foreign law, the Supreme Court made clear in Hartford Fire[75] that no conflict exists for purposes of an international comity analysis in the courts if the person subject to regulation by two states can comply with the laws of both. Bearing this in mind, the Agencies first ask what laws or policies of the arguably interested foreign jurisdictions are implicated by the conduct in question. There may be no actual conflict between the antitrust enforcement interests of the United States and the laws or policies of a foreign sovereign. This is increasingly true as more countries adopt antitrust or competition laws that are compatible with those of the United States. In these cases, the anticompetitive conduct in question may also be prohibited under the pertinent foreign laws, and thus the possible conflict would relate to enforcement practices or remedy. If the laws or policies of a foreign nation are neutral, it is again possible for the parties in question to comply with the U.S. prohibition without violating foreign law.

The Agencies also take full account of comity factors beyond whether there is a conflict with foreign law. In deciding whether or not to challenge an alleged antitrust violation, the Agencies would, as part of a comity analysis,

---

[72] Hilton v. Guyot, 159 U.S. 113, 164 (1895).

[73] The Agencies have agreed to consider the legitimate interests of other nations in accordance with the recommendations of the OECD and various bilateral agreements, see supra at Section 2.9.

[74] The first six of these factors are based on previous Department Guidelines. The seventh and eighth factors are derived from considerations in the U.S.-EC Antitrust Cooperation Agreement. See supra at note 46.

[75] 113 S. Ct. 2891, 2910.

consider whether one country encourages a certain course of conduct, leaves parties free to choose among different strategies, or prohibits some of those strategies. In addition, the Agencies take into account the effect of their enforcement activities on related enforcement activities of a foreign antitrust authority. For example, the Agencies would consider whether their activities would interfere with or reinforce the objectives of the foreign proceeding, including any remedies contemplated or obtained by the foreign antitrust authority.

The Agencies also will consider whether the objectives sought to be obtained by the assertion of U.S. law would be achieved in a particular instance by foreign enforcement. In lieu of bringing an enforcement action, the Agencies may consult with interested foreign sovereigns through appropriate diplomatic channels to attempt to eliminate anticompetitive effects in the United States. In cases where the United States decides to prosecute an antitrust action, such a decision represents a determination by the Executive Branch that the importance of antitrust enforcement outweighs any relevant foreign policy concerns.[76] The Department does not believe that it is the role of the courts to "second-guess the executive branch's judgment as to the proper role of comity concerns under these circumstances."[77] To date, no Commission cases have presented the issue of the degree of deference that courts should give to the Commission's comity decisions.[78] It is important also to note that in disputes between private parties, many courts are willing to undertake a comity analysis.[79]

ILLUSTRATIVE EXAMPLE I

Situation:
A group of buyers in one foreign country decide that they will agree on the price that they will offer to U.S. suppliers of a particular product. The agreement results in substantial loss of sales and capacity reductions in the United States.

Discussion:
From a jurisdictional point of view, the FTAIA standard appears to be satisfied because the effects on U.S. exporters presented here are direct and the percentage of supply accounted for by the buyers' cartel is substantial given the fact that the U.S. suppliers are "major." The Agencies, however, would also take into consideration the comity aspects presented before deciding whether or not to proceed.

Consistent with their consideration of comity and its obligations under various international agreements, the Agencies would ordinarily notify the antitrust authority in the cartel's home country. If that authority were in a better position to address the competitive problem, and were prepared to take effective action to address the adverse effects on U.S. commerce, the Agencies would consider working cooperatively with the foreign authority or staying their own remedy pending enforcement efforts by the foreign

---

[76] Foreign policy concerns may also lead the United States not to prosecute a case. See, e.g., U.S. Department of Justice Press Release dated Nov. 19, 1984 (announcing the termination, based on foreign policy concerns, of a grand jury investigation into passenger air travel between the United States and the United Kingdom).

[77] United States v. Baker Hughes, Inc., 731 F. Supp. 3, 6 n.5 (D.D.C. 1990), aff'd, 908 F.2d 981 (D.C. Cir. 1990).

[78] Like the Department, the Commission considers comity issues and consults with foreign antitrust authorities, but the Commission is not part of the Executive Branch.

[79] See, e.g., Timberlane Lumber Co. v. Bank of America, 549 F.2d 597 (9th Cir. 1976).

country. In deciding whether to proceed, the Agencies would weigh the factors relating to comity set forth above. Factors weighing in favor of bringing such an action include the substantial and purposeful harm caused by the cartel to the United States.

ILLUSTRATIVE EXAMPLE J

Situation:
A and B manufacture a consumer product for which there are no readily available substitutes in ten different countries around the world, including the United States, Canada, Mexico, Spain, Australia, and others. When they decide to merge, it becomes necessary for them to file premerger notifications in many of these countries, and to subject themselves to the merger law of all ten.[80]

Discussion:
Under the 1986 OECD Recommendation, OECD countries notify one another when a proceeding such as a merger review is underway that might affect the interests of other countries. Within the strict limits of national confidentiality laws, agencies attempt to cooperate with one another in processing these reviews. This might extend to exchanges of publicly available information, agreements to let the other agencies know when a decision to institute a proceeding is taken, and to consult for purposes of international comity with respect to proposed remedial measures and investigatory methods. The parties can facilitate faster resolution of these cases if they are willing voluntarily to waive confidentiality protections and to cooperate with a joint investigation. At present, confidentiality provisions in U.S. and foreign laws do not usually permit effective coordination of a single international investigation in the absence of such waivers.

3.3 Effects of Foreign Government Involvement

Foreign governments may be involved in a variety of ways in conduct that may have antitrust consequences. To address the implications of such foreign governmental involvement, Congress and the courts have developed four special doctrines: the doctrine of foreign sovereign immunity; the doctrine of foreign sovereign compulsion; the act of state doctrine; and the application of the Noerr-Pennington doctrine to immunize the lobbying of foreign governments. Although these doctrines are interrelated, for purposes of discussion the Guidelines discuss each one individually.

3.31 Foreign Sovereign Immunity

The scope of immunity of a foreign government or its agencies and instrumentalities (hereinafter foreign government)[81] from the jurisdiction of the U.S. courts for all causes of action, including antitrust, is governed by

[80] Not every country has compulsory premerger notification, and the events triggering duties to notify vary from country to country.

[81] Section 1603(b) of the Foreign Sovereign Immunities Act of 1976 defines an "agency or instrumentality of a foreign state" to be any entity "(1) which is a separate legal person, corporate or otherwise; and (2) which is an organ of a foreign state or political subdivision thereof, or a majority of whose shares or other ownership interest is owned by a foreign state or political subdivision thereof; and (3) which is neither a citizen of a State of the United States as defined in Section 1332(c) and (d) of [Title 28, U.S. Code], nor created under the laws of any third country." 28 U.S.C. 1603(b) (1988). It is not uncommon in antitrust cases to see state-owned enterprises meeting this definition.

the Foreign Sovereign Immunities Act of 1976 ("FSIA").[82] Subject to the treaties in place at the time of FSIA's enactment, a foreign government is immune from suit except where designated in the FSIA. [83]

Under the FSIA, a U.S. court has jurisdiction if the foreign government has:

a) waived its immunity explicitly or by implication,

b) engaged in commercial activity as described in the statute,

c) expropriated property in violation of international law,

d) acquired rights to U.S. property,

e) committed certain torts within the United States, or agreed to arbitration of a dispute.[84]

The commercial activities exception is a frequently invoked exception to sovereign immunity under the FSIA. Under the FSIA, a foreign government is not immune in any case:

> in which the action is based upon a commercial activity carried on in the United States by the foreign state; or upon an act performed in the United States in connection with a commercial activity of the foreign state elsewhere; or upon an act outside the territory of the United States in connection with a commercial activity of the foreign state elsewhere and that act causes a direct effect in the United States.[85]

"Commercial activity of the foreign state" is not defined in the FSIA, but is to be determined by the "nature of the course of conduct or particular transaction or act, rather than by reference to its purpose."[86] In attempting to differentiate commercial from sovereign activity, courts have considered whether the conduct being challenged is customarily performed for profit[87] and whether the conduct is of a type that only a sovereign government can perform.[88] As a practical matter, most activities of foreign government-owned corporations operating in the commercial marketplace will be subject to U.S. antitrust laws to the same extent as the activities of foreign privately-owned firms.

The commercial activity also must have a substantial nexus with the United States before a foreign government is subject to suit. The FSIA sets out three different standards for meeting this requirement. First, the challenged conduct by the foreign government may occur in the United States.[89] Alternatively, the challenged commercial activity may entail an act

---

[82] 28 U.S.C. 1602, et seq. (1988).

[83] 28 U.S.C. 1604 (1988 & Supp. 1993).

[84] 28 U.S.C. 1605(a)(1–6) (1988).

[85] 28 U.S.C. 1605(a)(2) (1988).

[86] 28 U.S.C. 1603(d) (1988).

[87] See, e.g., Republic of Argentina v. Weltover, Inc., 112 S. Ct. 2160 (1992); Schoenberg v. Exportadora de Sal, S.A. de C.V., 930 F.2d 777 (9th Cir. 1991); Rush-Presbyterian-St. Luke's Medical Ctr. v. Hellenic Republic, 877 F.2d 574, 578 n.4 (7th Cir.), cert. denied, 493 U.S. 937 (1989).

[88] See, e.g., Saudi Arabia v. Nelson, 113 S. Ct. 1471 (1993); de Sanchez v. Banco Central de Nicaragua, 770 F.2d 1385 (5th Cir. 1985); Letelier v. Republic of Chile, 748 F.2d 790, 797–98 (2d Cir. 1984), cert. denied, 471 U.S. 1125 (1985); International Ass'n of Machinists & Aerospace Workers v. Organization of Petroleum Exporting Countries, 477 F. Supp. 553 (C.D. Cal. 1979), aff'd on other grounds, 649 F.2d 1354 (9th Cir. 1981), cert. denied, 454 U.S. 1163 (1982).

[89] 28 U.S.C. 1603(e) (1988).

performed in the United States in connection with a commercial activity of the foreign government elsewhere.[90] Or, finally, the challenged commercial activity of a foreign government outside of the United States may produce a direct effect within the United States, i.e., an effect which follows "as an immediate consequence of the defendant's . . . activity." [91]

3.32 Foreign Sovereign Compulsion

Although U.S. antitrust jurisdiction extends to conduct and parties in foreign countries whose actions have the required effects on U.S. commerce, as discussed above, those parties may find themselves subject to conflicting requirements from the other country (or countries) where they are located.[92] Under Hartford Fire, if it is possible for the party to comply both with the foreign law and the U.S. antitrust laws, the existence of the foreign law does not provide any legal excuse for actions that do not comply with U.S. law. However, a direct conflict may arise when the facts demonstrate that the foreign sovereign has compelled the very conduct that the U.S. antitrust law prohibits.

In these circumstances, at least one court has recognized a defense under the U.S. antitrust laws, and the Agencies will also recognize it.[93] There are two rationales underlying the defense of foreign sovereign compulsion. First, Congress enacted the U.S. antitrust laws against the background of well recognized principles of international law and comity among nations, pursuant to which U.S. authorities give due deference to the official acts of foreign governments. A defense for actions taken under the circumstances spelled out below serves to accommodate two equal sovereigns. Second, important considerations of fairness to the defendant require some

---

[90] See H.R. Rep. No. 1487, 94th Cong., 2d Sess. 18–19 (1976), reprinted in 1976 U.S.C.C.A.N. 6604, 6617–18 (providing as an example the wrongful termination in the United States of an employee of a foreign state employed in connection with commercial activity in a third country.) But see Filus v. LOT Polish Airlines, 907 F.2d 1328, 1333 (2d Cir. 1990) (holding as too attenuated the failure to warn of a defective product sold outside of the United States in connection with an accident outside the United States.)

[91] Republic of Argentina, 112 S. Ct. at 2168. This test is similar to proximate cause formulations adopted by other courts. See Martin v. Republic of South Africa, 836 F.2d 91, 95 (2d Cir. 1987) (a direct effect is one with no intervening element which flows in a straight line without deviation or interruption), quoting Upton v. Empire of Iran, 459 F. Supp. 264, 266 (D.D.C. 1978), aff'd mem., 607 F.2d 494 (D.C. Cir. 1979).

[92] Conduct by private entities not required by law is entirely outside of the protections afforded by this defense. See Continental Ore Co. v. Union Carbide & Carbon Corp., 370 U.S. 690, 706 (1962); United States v. Watchmakers of Switzerland Info. Ctr., Inc., 1963 Trade Cas. (CCH) 70,600 at 77,456–57 (S.D.N.Y. 1962) ("[T]he fact that the Swiss Government may, as a practical matter, approve the effects of this private activity cannot convert what is essentially a vulnerable private conspiracy into an unassailable system resulting from a foreign government mandate.") See supra at Section 3.2.

[93] Interamerican Refining Corp. v. Texaco Maracaibo, Inc., 307 F. Supp. 1291 (D. Del. 1970) (defendant, having been ordered by the government of Venezuela not to sell oil to a particular refiner out of favor with the current political regime, held not subject to antitrust liability under the Sherman Act for an illegal group boycott). The defense of foreign sovereign compulsion is distinguished from the federalism-based state action doctrine. The state action doctrine applies not just to the actions of states and their subdivisions, but also to private anticompetitive conduct that is both undertaken pursuant to clearly articulated state policies, and is actively supervised by the state. See Federal Trade Comm'n v. Ticor Title Insurance Co., 112 S. Ct. 2169 (1992); California Retail Liquor Dealers Ass'n v. Midcal Aluminum, Inc., 445 U.S. 97, 105 (1980); Parker v. Brown, 317 U.S. 341 (1943).

mechanism that provides a predictable rule of decision for those seeking to conform their behavior to all pertinent laws. Because of the limited scope of the defense, the Agencies will refrain from enforcement actions on the ground of foreign sovereign compulsion only when certain criteria are satisfied. First, the foreign government must have compelled the anticompetitive conduct under circumstances in which a refusal to comply with the foreign government's command would give rise to the imposition of penal or other severe sanctions. As a general matter, the Agencies regard the foreign government's formal representation that refusal to comply with its command would have such a result as being sufficient to establish that the conduct in question has been compelled, as long as that representation contains sufficient detail to enable the Agencies to see precisely how the compulsion would be accomplished under local law.[94] Foreign government measures short of compulsion do not suffice for this defense, although they can be relevant in a comity analysis.

Second, although there can be no strict territorial test for this defense, the defense normally applies only when the foreign government compels conduct which can be accomplished entirely within its own territory. If the compelled conduct occurs in the United States, the Agencies will not recognize the defense.[95] For example, no defense arises when a foreign government requires the U.S. subsidiaries of several firms to organize a cartel in the United States to fix the price at which products would be sold in the United States, or when it requires its firms to fix mandatory resale prices for their U.S. distributors to use in the United States. Third, with reference to the discussion of foreign sovereign immunity in Section 3.31 above, the order must come from the foreign government acting in its governmental capacity. The defense does not arise from conduct that would fall within the FSIA commercial activity exception.

ILLUSTRATIVE EXAMPLE K

Situation:
Greatly increased quantities of commodity X have flooded into the world market over the last two or three years, including substantial amounts indirectly coming into the United States. Because they are unsure whether they would prevail in an antidumping and countervailing duty case, U.S. industry participants have refrained from filing trade law petitions. The officials of three foreign countries meet with their respective domestic firms and urge them to "rationalize" production by cooperatively cutting back. Going one step further, one of the interested governments orders cutbacks from its firms, subject to substantial penalties for non-compliance. Producers from the other two countries agree among themselves to institute comparable cutbacks, but their governments do not require them to do so.

Discussion:
Assume for the purpose of this example that the overseas production cutbacks have the necessary effects on U.S. commerce to support

[94] For example, the Agencies may not regard as dispositive a statement that is ambiguous or that on its face appears to be internally inconsistent. The Agencies may inquire into the circumstances underlying the statement and they may also request further information if the source of the power to compel is unclear.

[95] See Linseman v. World Hockey Ass'n, 439 F. Supp. 1315, 1325 (D. Conn. 1977).

jurisdiction. As for the participants from the two countries that did not impose any penalty for a failure to reduce production, the Agencies would not find that sovereign compulsion precluded prosecution of this agreement.[96] As for participants from the country that did compel production cut-backs through the imposition of severe penalties, the Agencies would acknowledge a defense of sovereign compulsion.

3.33 Acts of State

The act of state doctrine is a judge-made rule of federal common law.[97] It is a doctrine of judicial abstention based on considerations of international comity and separation of powers, and applies only if the specific conduct complained of is a public act of the foreign sovereign within its territorial jurisdiction on matters pertaining to its governmental sovereignty. The act of state doctrine arises when the validity of the acts of a foreign government is an unavoidable issue in a case.[98]

Courts have refused to adjudicate claims or issues that would require the court to judge the legality (as a matter of U.S. law or international law) of the sovereign act of a foreign state.[99] Although in some cases the sovereign act in question may compel private behavior, such compulsion is not required by the doctrine.[100] While the act of state doctrine does not compel dismissal as a matter of course, judicial abstention is appropriate in a case where the court must "declare invalid, and thus ineffective as a rule of decision in the U.S. courts, . . . the official act of a foreign sovereign."[101]

When a restraint on competition arises directly from the act of a foreign sovereign, such as the grant of a license, award of a contract, expropriation of property, or the like, the Agencies may refrain from bringing an enforcement action based on the act of state doctrine. For example, the Agencies will not challenge foreign acts of state if the facts and circumstances indicate that: (1) the specific conduct complained of is a public act of the sovereign, (2) the act was taken within the territorial jurisdiction of the sovereign, and (3) the matter is governmental, rather than commercial.

3.34 Petitioning of Sovereigns

Under the Noerr-Pennington doctrine, a genuine effort to obtain or influence action by governmental entities in the United States is immune from application of the Sherman Act, even if the intent or effect of that effort is to restrain or monopolize trade.[102] Whatever the basis asserted for

---

[96] As in all such cases, the Agencies would consider comity factors as part of their analysis. See supra at Section 3.2.

[97] Banco Nacional de Cuba v. Sabbatino, 376 U.S. 398, 421–22 n.21 (1964) (noting that other countries do not adhere in any formulaic way to an act of state doctrine).

[98] See W.S. Kirkpatrick & Co. v. Environmental Tectonics Corp., 493 U.S. 400 (1990).

[99] International Ass'n of Machinists and Aerospace Workers v. Organization of Petroleum Exporting Countries, 649 F.2d 1354, 1358 (9th Cir. 1981), cert. denied, 454 U.S. 1163 (1982).

[100] See Timberlane, supra at note 79, 549 F.2d at 606–08.

[101] Kirkpatrick, 493 U.S. at 405, quoting Ricaud v. American Metal Co., 246 U.S. 304, 310 (1918).

[102] See Eastern R.R. Presidents Conference v. Noerr Motor Freight, Inc., 365 U.S. 127 (1961); United Mine Workers of Am. v. Pennington, 381 U.S. 657 (1965); California Motor Transp. Co. v. Trucking Unlimited, 404 U.S. 508 (1972) (extending protection to

Noerr-Pennington immunity (either as an application of the First Amendment or as a limit on the statutory reach of the Sherman Act, or both), the Agencies will apply it in the same manner to the petitioning of foreign governments and the U.S. Government.

ILLUSTRATIVE EXAMPLE L

Situation:
In the course of preparing an antidumping case, which requires the U.S. industry to demonstrate that it has been injured through the effects of the dumped imports, producers representing 75 percent of U.S. output exchange the information required for the adjudication. All the information is exchanged indirectly through third parties and in an aggregated form that makes the identity of any particular producer's information impossible to discern.

Discussion:
Information exchanged by competitors within the context of an antidumping proceeding implicates the Noerr-Pennington petitioning immunity. To the extent that these exchanges are reasonably necessary in order for them to prepare their joint petition, which is permitted under the trade laws, Noerr is available to protect against antitrust liability that would otherwise arise. On these facts the parties are likely to be immunized by Noerr if they have taken the necessary measures to ensure that the provision of sensitive information called for by the Commerce Department and the ITC cannot be used for anticompetitive purposes. In such a situation, the information exchange is incidental to genuine petitioning and is not subject to the antitrust laws. Conversely, were the parties directly to exchange extensive information relating to their costs, the prices each has charged for the product, pricing trends, and profitability, including information about specific transactions that went beyond the scope of those facts required for the adjudication, such conduct would go beyond the contemplated protection of Noerr immunity.

3.4 Antitrust Enforcement and International Trade Regulation

There has always been a close relationship between the international application of the antitrust laws and the policies and rules governing the international trade of the United States. Restrictions such as tariffs or quotas on the free flow of goods affect market definition, consumer choice, and supply options for U.S. producers. In certain instances, the U.S. trade laws set forth specific procedures for settling disputes under those laws, which can involve price and quantity agreements by the foreign firms involved. When those procedures are followed, an implied antitrust

petitioning before "all departments of Government," including the courts); Professional Real Estate Investors, Inc. v. Columbia Pictures Indus., 113 S. Ct. 1920 (1993). However, this immunity has never applied to "sham" activities, in which petitioning "ostensibly directed toward influencing governmental action, is a mere sham to cover . . . an attempt to interfere directly with the business relationships of a competitor." Professional Real Estate Investors, 113 S. Ct. at 1926, quoting Noerr, 365 U.S. at 144. See also USS-Posco Indus. v. Contra Costa Cty. Bldg. Constr. Council, AFL-CIO, 31 F.3d 800 (9th Cir. 1994).

immunity results.[103] However, agreements among competitors that do not comply with the law, or go beyond the measures authorized by the law, do not enjoy antitrust immunity. In the absence of legal authority, the fact, without more, that U.S. or foreign government officials were involved in or encouraged measures that would otherwise violate the antitrust laws does not immunize such arrangements.[104]

If a particular voluntary export restraint does not qualify for express or implied immunity from the antitrust laws, then the legality of the arrangement would depend upon the existence of the ordinary elements of an antitrust offense, such as whether or not a prohibited agreement exists or whether defenses such as foreign sovereign compulsion can be invoked.

ILLUSTRATIVE EXAMPLE M

Situation:
Six U.S. producers of product Q have initiated an antidumping action alleging that imports of Q from country Sigma at less than fair value are causing material injury to the U.S. Q industry. The ITC has made a preliminary decision that there is a reasonable indication that the U.S. industry is suffering material injury from Q imported from Sigma. The Department of Commerce has preliminarily concluded that the foreign market value of Q imported into the United States by Sigma's Q producers exceeds the price at which they are selling Q in this country by margins of 10 to 40 percent. Sigma's Q producers jointly initiate discussions with the Department of Commerce that lead to suspension of the investigation in accordance with Section 734 of the Tariff Act of 1930, 19 U.S.C. 1673c. The suspension agreement provides that each of Sigma's Q producers will sell product Q in the United States at no less than its individual foreign market value, as determined periodically by the Department of Commerce in accordance with the Tariff Act. Before determining to suspend the investigation, the Department of Commerce provides copies of the proposed agreement to the U.S. Q producers, who jointly advise the Department that they do not object to the suspension of the investigation on the terms proposed. The Department also determines that suspension of the investigation would be in the public interest. As a result of the suspension agreement, prices in the United States of Q imported from Sigma rise by an average of 25 percent from the prices that prevailed before the antidumping action was initiated.

Discussion:
While an unsupervised agreement among foreign firms to raise their U.S. sales prices ordinarily would violate the Sherman Act, the suspension

[103] See, e.g., Letter from Charles F. Rule, Acting Assistant Attorney General, Antitrust Division, Department of Justice, to Mr. Makoto Kuroda, Vice-Minister for International Affairs, Japanese Ministry of International Trade and Industry, July 30, 1986 (concluding that a suspension agreement did not violate U.S. antitrust laws on the basis of factual representations that the agreement applied only to products under investigation, that it did not require pricing above levels needed to eliminate sales below foreign market value, and that assigning weighted-average foreign market values to exporters who were not respondents in the investigation was necessary to achieve the purpose of the antidumping law).

[104] Cf. United States v. Socony-Vacuum Oil Co., 310 U.S. 150, 226 (1940) ("Though employees of the government may have known of those programs and winked at them or tacitly approved them, no immunity would have thereby been obtained. For Congress had specified the precise manner and method of securing immunity [in the National Industrial Recovery Act]. None other would suffice. . . ."); see also Otter Tail Power Co. v. United States, 410 U.S. 366, 378–79 (1973).

agreement outlined above qualifies for an implied immunity from the antitrust laws. As demonstrated here, the parties have engaged only in conduct contemplated by the Tariff Act and none of the participants have engaged in conduct beyond what is necessary to implement that statutory scheme.

ILLUSTRATIVE EXAMPLE N

Situation:
The Export Association is a Webb-Pomerene association that has filed the appropriate certificates and reports with the Commission. The Association exports a commodity to markets around the world, and fixes the price at which all of its members sell the commodity in the foreign markets. Nearly 80 percent of all U.S. producers of the commodity belong to the Association, and on a world-wide level, the Association's members account for approximately 40 percent of annual sales.

Discussion:
The Webb-Pomerene Act addresses only the question of antitrust liability under U.S. law. Although the U.S. antitrust laws confer an immunity on such associations, the Act does not purport to confer immunity under the law of any foreign country, nor does the Act compel the members of a Webb-Pomerene association to act in any particular way. Thus, a foreign government retains the ability to initiate proceedings if such an association allegedly violates that country's competition law.

---

4. PERSONAL JURISDICTION AND PROCEDURAL RULES

4.1 Personal Jurisdiction and Venue

The Agencies will bring suit only if they conclude that personal jurisdiction exists under the due process clause of the U.S. Constitution.[105] The Constitution requires that the defendant have affiliating or minimum contacts with the United States, such that the proceeding comports with "fair play and substantial justice."[106]

Section 12 of the Clayton Act, 15 U.S.C. 22, provides that any suit under the antitrust laws against a corporation may be brought in the judicial district where it is an inhabitant, where it may be found, or where it transacts business. The concept of transacting business is interpreted pragmatically by the Agencies. Thus, a company may transact business in a particular district directly through an agent, or through a related corporation that is actually the "alter ego" of the foreign party.[107]

---

[105] See also International Shoe Co. v. Washington, 326 U.S. 310 (1945); Asahi Metal Industry Co. Ltd. v. Superior Court, 480 U.S. 102 (1987).

[106] Go-Video, Inc. v. Akai Elec. Co., Ltd., 885 F.2d 1406, 1414 (9th Cir. 1989); Wells Fargo & Co. v. Wells Fargo Express Co., 556 F.2d 406, 418 (9th Cir. 1977). To establish jurisdiction, parties must also be served in accordance with the Federal Rules of Civil Procedure or other relevant authority. Fed. R. Civ. P. 4(k); 15 U.S.C. 22, 44.

[107] See, e.g., Letter from Donald S. Clark, Secretary of the Federal Trade Commission, to Caswell O. Hobbs, Esq., Morgan, Lewis & Bockius, Jan. 17, 1990 (Re: Petition to Quash Subpoena Nippon Sheet Glass, et al., File No. 891-0088, at page 3) ("The Commission . . . may exercise jurisdiction over and serve process on, a foreign entity that has a related company in the United States acting as its agent or alter ego."); see also Fed. R. Civ. P. 4; Volkswagenwerk AG v. Schlunk, 486 U.S. 694, 707–708 (1988); United States v. Scophony Corp., 333 U.S. 795, 810–818 (1948).

4.2 Investigatory Practice Relating to Foreign Nations

In conducting investigations that require documents that are located outside the United States, or contacts with persons located outside the United States, the Agencies first consider requests for voluntary cooperation when practical and consistent with enforcement objectives. When compulsory measures are needed, they seek whenever possible to work with the foreign government involved. U.S. law also provides authority in some circumstances for the use of compulsory measures directed to parties over whom the courts have personal jurisdiction, which the Agencies may use when other efforts to obtain information have been exhausted or would be unavailing.[108]

Conflicts can arise, however, where foreign statutes purport to prevent persons from disclosing documents or information for use in U.S. proceedings. However, the mere existence of such statutes does not excuse noncompliance with a request for information from one of the Agencies.[109] To enable the Agencies to obtain evidence located abroad more effectively, as noted in Section 2.91 above, Congress recently has enacted legislation authorizing the Agencies to negotiate bilateral agreements with foreign governments or antitrust enforcement agencies to facilitate the exchange of documents and evidence in civil and criminal investigations.[110]

4.22 Hart-Scott-Rodino: Special Foreign Commerce Rules

As noted above in Section 2.4, qualifying mergers and acquisitions, defined both in terms of size of party and size of transaction, must be reported to the Agencies, along with certain information about the parties and the transaction, prior to their consummation, pursuant to the HSR Amendments to the Clayton Act, 15 U.S.C. 18a.

In some instances, the HSR implementing regulations exempt otherwise reportable foreign transactions.[111] First, some acquisitions by U.S. persons are exempt. Acquisitions of foreign assets by a U.S. person are exempt when

i. no sales in or into the United States are attributable to those assets, or

ii. some sales in or into the United States are attributable to those assets, but the acquiring person would not hold assets of the acquired person to which $25 million or more of such sales in the acquired person's most recent fiscal year were attributable.[112]

Acquisitions by a U.S. person of voting securities of a foreign issuer are exempt unless the issuer holds assets in the United States having an aggregate book value of $15 million or more, or made aggregate sales in or

---

[108] For example, 28 U.S.C. 1783(a) (1988) authorizes a U.S. court to order the issuance of a subpoena "requiring the appearance as a witness before it, or before a person or body designated by it, of a national or resident of the United States who is in a foreign country, or requiring the production of a specified document or other thing by him," under circumstances spelled out in the statute.

[109] See Societe Internationale pour Participations Industrielles et Commerciales, S.A. v. Rogers, 357 U.S. 197 (1958).

[110] International Antitrust Enforcement Assistance Act of 1994, Pub. L. No. 103-438, 108 Stat. 4597 (1994).

[111] See 16 C.F.R. 802.50–52 (1994).

[112] See 16 C.F.R. 802.50(a) (1994).

into the United States of $25 million or more in its most recent fiscal year. [113]

Second, some acquisitions by foreign persons are exempt. An exemption exists for acquisitions by foreign persons if

i. the acquisition is of voting securities of a foreign issuer and would not confer control of a U.S. issuer having annual net sales or total assets of $25 million or more, or of any issuer with assets located in the United States having a book value of $15 million or more; or

ii. the acquired person is also a foreign person and the aggregate annual net sales of the merging firms in or into the United States is less than $110 million and their aggregate total assets in the United States are less than $110 million.[114]

In addition, an acquisition by a foreign person of assets located outside the United States is exempt. Acquisitions by foreign persons of U.S. issuers or assets are not exempt.

Finally, acquisitions are exempt if the ultimate parent entity of either the acquiring or the acquired person is controlled by a foreign state, and the acquisition is of assets located within that foreign state, or of voting securities of an issuer organized under its laws.[115] The HSR rules are necessarily technical, and should be consulted rather than relying on the summary description herein.

---

[113] See 16 C.F.R. 802.50(b) (1994).

[114] See 16 C.F.R. 802.51 (1994).

[115] See 16 C.F.R. 802.52 (1994).

11

ANTITRUST GUIDELINES FOR THE LICENSING OF INTELLECTUAL PROPERTY

U.S. DEPARTMENT OF JUSTICE AND FEDERAL TRADE COMMISSION[1]

April 6, 1995

TABLE OF CONTENTS

---

[1] [Authors' footnote] The Patent Code contains licensing provisions which should be considered with these Guidelines. Section 271 of the Patent Code, 35 U.S.C. § 271, defining the meaning of "infringement," contains a subsection dealing with the scope of the invalidity and misuse defenses to an infringement action for patent licensing practices. 35 U.S.C. § 271(d) provides:

"(d) No patent owner otherwise entitled to relief for infringement or contributory infringement of a patent shall be denied relief or deemed guilty of misuse or illegal extension of the patent right by reason of his having done one or more of the following: (1) derived revenue from acts which if performed by another without his consent would constitute contributory infringement of the patent; (2) licensed or authorized another to perform acts which if performed without his consent would constitute contributory infringement of the patent; (3) sought to enforce his patent rights against infringement or contributory infringement; (4) refused to license or use any rights to the patent; or (5) conditioned the license of any rights to the patent or the sale of the patented product on the acquisition of a license to rights in another patent or purchase of a separate product, unless, in view of the circumstances, the patent owner has market power in the relevant market for the patent or patented product on which the license or sale is conditioned."

ANTITRUST GUIDELINES FOR LICENSING OF
INTELLECTUAL PROPERTY

---

1. Intellectual property protection and the antitrust laws

1.0 These Guidelines state the antitrust enforcement policy of the U.S. Department of Justice and the Federal Trade Commission (individually, "the Agency," and collectively, "the Agencies") with respect to the licensing of intellectual property protected by patent, copyright, and trade secret law, and of know-how.[2] By stating their general policy, the Agencies hope to assist those who need to predict whether the Agencies will challenge a practice as anticompetitive. However, these Guidelines cannot remove judgment and discretion in antitrust law enforcement. Moreover, the standards set forth in these Guidelines must be applied in unforeseeable circumstances. Each case will be evaluated in light of its own facts, and these Guidelines will be applied reasonably and flexibly.[3]

In the United States, patents confer rights to exclude others from making, using, or selling in the United States the invention claimed by the patent for a period of seventeen years from the date of issue.[4] To gain patent

[2] These Guidelines do not cover the antitrust treatment of trademarks. Although the same general antitrust principles that apply to other forms of intellectual property apply to trademarks as well, these Guidelines deal with technology transfer and innovation-related issues that typically arise with respect to patents, copyrights, trade secrets, and know-how agreements, rather than with product-differentiation issues that typically arise with respect to trademarks.

[3] As is the case with all guidelines, users should rely on qualified counsel to assist them in evaluating the antitrust risk associated with any contemplated transaction or activity. No set of guidelines can possibly indicate how the Agencies will assess the particular facts of every case. Parties who wish to know the Agencies' specific enforcement intentions with respect to any particular transaction should consider seeking a Department of Justice business review letter pursuant to 28 C.F.R. § 50.6 or a Federal Trade Commission Advisory Opinion pursuant to 16 C.F.R. §§ 1.1–1.4.

[4] *See* 35 U.S.C. § 154 (1988). Section 532(a) of the Uruguay Round Agreements Act, Pub. L. No. 103-465, 108 Stat. 4809, 4983 (1994) would change the length of patent

protection, an invention (which may be a product, process, machine, or composition of matter) must be novel, nonobvious, and useful. Copyright protection applies to original works of authorship embodied in a tangible medium of expression.[5] A copyright protects only the expression, not the underlying ideas.[6] Unlike a patent, which protects an invention not only from copying but also from independent creation, a copyright does not preclude others from independently creating similar expression. Trade secret protection applies to information whose economic value depends on its not being generally known.[7] Trade secret protection is conditioned upon efforts to maintain secrecy and has no fixed term. As with copyright protection, trade secret protection does not preclude independent creation by others.

The intellectual property laws and the antitrust laws share the common purpose of promoting innovation and enhancing consumer welfare.[8] The intellectual property laws provide incentives for innovation and its dissemination and commercialization by establishing enforceable property rights for the creators of new and useful products, more efficient processes, and original works of expression. In the absence of intellectual property rights, imitators could more rapidly exploit the efforts of innovators and investors without compensation. Rapid imitation would reduce the commercial value of innovation and erode incentives to invest, ultimately to the detriment of consumers. The antitrust laws promote innovation and consumer welfare by prohibiting certain actions that may harm competition with respect to either existing or new ways of serving consumers.

---

2. General principles

2.0 These Guidelines embody three general principles:

a. for the purpose of antitrust analysis, the Agencies regard intellectual property as being essentially comparable to any other form of property;

b. the Agencies do not presume that intellectual property creates market power in the antitrust context; and

c. the Agencies recognize that intellectual property licensing allows firms to combine complementary factors of production and is generally procompetitive.

---

protection to a term beginning on the date at which the patent issues and ending twenty years from the date on which the application for the patent was filed.

5 *See* 17 U.S.C. § 102 (1988 & Supp. V 1993). Copyright protection lasts for the author's life plus 50 years, or 75 years from first publication (or 100 years from creation, whichever expires first) for works made for hire. *See* 17 U.S.C. § 302 (1988). The principles stated in these Guidelines also apply to protection of mask works fixed in a semiconductor chip product (*see* 17 U.S.C. § 901 *et seq.* (1988)), which is analogous to copyright protection for works of authorship.

6 *See* 17 U.S.C. § 102(b) (1988).

7 Trade secret protection derives from state law. *See generally Kewanee Oil Co. v. Bicron Corp.*, 416 U.S. 470 (1974).

8 "[T]he aims and objectives of patent and antitrust laws may seem, at first glance, wholly at odds. However, the two bodies of law are actually complementary, as both are aimed at encouraging innovation, industry and competition." *Atari Games Corp. v. Nintendo of America, Inc.*, 897 F.2d 1572, 1576 (Fed. Cir. 1990).

2.1 Standard antitrust analysis applies to intellectual property

The Agencies apply the same general antitrust principles to conduct involving intellectual property that they apply to conduct involving any other form of tangible or intangible property. That is not to say that intellectual property is in all respects the same as any other form of property. Intellectual property has important characteristics, such as ease of misappropriation, that distinguish it from many other forms of property. These characteristics can be taken into account by standard antitrust analysis, however, and do not require the application of fundamentally different principles.[9]

Although there are clear and important differences in the purpose, extent, and duration of protection provided under the intellectual property regimes of patent, copyright, and trade secret, the governing antitrust principles are the same. Antitrust analysis takes differences among these forms of intellectual property into account in evaluating the specific market circumstances in which transactions occur, just as it does with other particular market circumstances.

Intellectual property law bestows on the owners of intellectual property certain rights to exclude others. These rights help the owners to profit from the use of their property. An intellectual property owner's rights to exclude are similar to the rights enjoyed by owners of other forms of private property. As with other forms of private property, certain types of conduct with respect to intellectual property may have anticompetitive effects against which the antitrust laws can and do protect. Intellectual property is thus neither particularly free from scrutiny under the antitrust laws, nor particularly suspect under them.

The Agencies recognize that the licensing of intellectual property is often international. The principles of antitrust analysis described in these Guidelines apply equally to domestic and international licensing arrangements. However, as described in the 1995 Department of Justice and Federal Trade Commission Antitrust Enforcement Guidelines for International Operations, considerations particular to international operations, such as jurisdiction and comity, may affect enforcement decisions when the arrangement is in an international context.

2.2 Intellectual property and market power

Market power is the ability profitably to maintain prices above, or output below, competitive levels for a significant period of time.[10] The Agencies will not presume that a patent, copyright, or trade secret necessarily confers market power upon its owner. Although the intellectual property right confers the power to exclude with respect to the specific product, process, or work in question, there will often be sufficient actual or potential close substitutes for such product, process, or work to prevent the

[9] As with other forms of property, the power to exclude others from the use of intellectual property may vary substantially, depending on the nature of the property and its status under federal or state law. The greater or lesser legal power of an owner to exclude others is also taken into account by standard antitrust analysis.

[10] Market power can be exercised in other economic dimensions, such as quality, service, and the development of new or improved goods and processes. It is assumed in this definition that all competitive dimensions are held constant except the ones in which market power is being exercised; that a seller is able to charge higher prices for a higher-quality product does not alone indicate market power. The definition in the text is stated in terms of a seller with market power. A buyer could also exercise market power (e.g., by maintaining the price below the competitive level, thereby depressing output).

exercise of market power.[11] If a patent or other form of intellectual property does confer market power, that market power does not by itself offend the antitrust laws. As with any other tangible or intangible asset that enables its owner to obtain significant supracompetitive profits, market power (or even a monopoly) that is solely "a consequence of a superior product, business acumen, or historic accident" does not violate the antitrust laws.[12] Nor does such market power impose on the intellectual property owner an obligation to license the use of that property to others. As in other antitrust contexts, however, market power could be illegally acquired or maintained, or, even if lawfully acquired and maintained, would be relevant to the ability of an intellectual property owner to harm competition through unreasonable conduct in connection with such property.

2.3 Procompetitive benefits of licensing

Intellectual property typically is one component among many in a production process and derives value from its combination with complementary factors. Complementary factors of production include manufacturing and distribution facilities, workforces, and other items of intellectual property. The owner of intellectual property has to arrange for its combination with other necessary factors to realize its commercial value. Often, the owner finds it most efficient to contract with others for these factors, to sell rights to the intellectual property, or to enter into a joint venture arrangement for its development, rather than supplying these complementary factors itself.

Licensing, cross-licensing, or otherwise transferring intellectual property (hereinafter "licensing") can facilitate integration of the licensed property with complementary factors of production. This integration can lead to more efficient exploitation of the intellectual property, benefiting consumers through the reduction of costs and the introduction of new products. Such arrangements increase the value of intellectual property to consumers and to the developers of the technology. By potentially increasing the expected returns from intellectual property, licensing also can increase the incentive for its creation and thus promote greater investment in research and development.

Sometimes the use of one item of intellectual property requires access to another. An item of intellectual property "blocks" another when the second cannot be practiced without using the first. For example, an improvement on a patented machine can be blocked by the patent on the machine. Licensing may promote the coordinated development of technologies that are in a blocking relationship.

Field-of-use, territorial, and other limitations on intellectual property licenses may serve procompetitive ends by allowing the licensor to exploit

---

[11] The Agencies note that the law is unclear on this issue. *Compare Jefferson Parish Hospital District No. 2 v. Hyde*, 466 U.S. 2, 16 (1984) (expressing the view in dictum that if a product is protected by a patent, "it is fair to presume that the inability to buy the product elsewhere gives the seller market power") *with id.* at 37 n.7 (O'Connor, J., concurring) ("[A] patent holder has no market power in any relevant sense if there are close substitutes for the patented product."). *Compare also Abbott Laboratories v. Brennan*, 952 F.2d 1346, 1354–55 (Fed. Cir. 1991) (no presumption of market power from intellectual property right), *cert. denied*, 112 S. Ct. 2993 (1992) with *Digidyne Corp. v. Data General Corp.*, 734 F.2d 1336, 1341–42 (9th Cir. 1984) (requisite economic power is presumed from copyright), *cert. denied*, 473 U.S. 908 (1985).

[12] *United States v. Grinnell Corp.*, 384 U.S. 563, 571 (1966); *see also United States v. Aluminum Co. of America*, 148 F.2d 416, 430 (2d Cir. 1945) (Sherman Act is not violated by the attainment of market power solely through "superior skill, foresight and industry").

its property as efficiently and effectively as possible. These various forms of exclusivity can be used to give a licensee an incentive to invest in the commercialization and distribution of products embodying the licensed intellectual property and to develop additional applications for the licensed property. The restrictions may do so, for example, by protecting the licensee against free-riding on the licensee's investments by other licensees or by the licensor. They may also increase the licensor's incentive to license, for example, by protecting the licensor from competition in the licensor's own technology in a market niche that it prefers to keep to itself. These benefits of licensing restrictions apply to patent, copyright, and trade secret licenses, and to know-how agreements.

EXAMPLE 1[13]

Situation:

ComputerCo develops a new, copyrighted software program for inventory management. The program has wide application in the health field. ComputerCo licenses the program in an arrangement that imposes both field of use and territorial limitations. Some of ComputerCo's licenses permit use only in hospitals; others permit use only in group medical practices. ComputerCo charges different royalties for the different uses. All of ComputerCo's licenses permit use only in specified portions of the United States and in specified foreign countries.[14] The licenses contain no provisions that would prevent or discourage licensees from developing, using, or selling any other program, or from competing in any other good or service other than in the use of the licensed program. None of the licensees are actual or likely potential competitors of ComputerCo in the sale of inventory management programs.

Discussion:

The key competitive issue raised by the licensing arrangement is whether it harms competition among entities that would have been actual or likely potential competitors in the absence of the arrangement. Such harm could occur if, for example, the licenses anticompetitively foreclose access to competing technologies (in this case, most likely competing computer programs), prevent licensees from developing their own competing technologies (again, in this case, most likely computer programs), or facilitate market allocation or price-fixing for any product or service supplied by the licensees. (See section 3.1.) If the license agreements contained such provisions, the Agency evaluating the arrangement would analyze its likely competitive effects as described in parts 3–5 of these Guidelines. In this hypothetical, there are no such provisions and thus the arrangement is merely a subdivision of the licensor's intellectual property among different fields of use and territories. The licensing arrangement does not appear likely to harm competition among entities that would have been actual or likely potential competitors if ComputerCo had chosen not to license the software program. The Agency therefore would be unlikely to object to this arrangement. Based on these facts, the result of the antitrust analysis would be the same whether the technology was protected by patent, copyright, or trade secret. The Agency's conclusion as to likely

---

[13] The examples in these Guidelines are hypothetical and do not represent judgments about, or analysis of, any actual market circumstances of the named industries.

[14] These Guidelines do not address the possible application of the antitrust laws of other countries to restraints such as territorial restrictions in international licensing arrangements.

competitive effects could differ if, for example, the license barred licensees from using any other inventory management program.

---

3. Antitrust concerns and modes of analysis

3.1 Nature of the concerns

While intellectual property licensing arrangements are typically welfare-enhancing and procompetitive, antitrust concerns may nonetheless arise. For example, a licensing arrangement could include restraints that adversely affect competition in goods markets by dividing the markets among firms that would have competed using different technologies. See, e.g., Example 7. An arrangement that effectively merges the research and development activities of two of only a few entities that could plausibly engage in research and development in the relevant field might harm competition for development of new goods and services. See section 3.2.3. An acquisition of intellectual property may lessen competition in a relevant antitrust market. See section 5.7. The Agencies will focus on the actual effects of an arrangement, not on its formal terms.

The Agencies will not require the owner of intellectual property to create competition in its own technology. However, antitrust concerns may arise when a licensing arrangement harms competition among entities that would have been actual or likely potential competitors[15] in a relevant market in the absence of the license (entities in a "horizontal relationship"). A restraint in a licensing arrangement may harm such competition, for example, if it facilitates market division or price-fixing. In addition, license restrictions with respect to one market may harm such competition in another market by anticompetitively foreclosing access to, or significantly raising the price of, an important input,[16] or by facilitating coordination to increase price or reduce output. When it appears that such competition may be adversely affected, the Agencies will follow the analysis set forth below. See generally sections 3.4 and 4.2.

3.2 Markets affected by licensing arrangements

Licensing arrangements raise concerns under the antitrust laws if they are likely to affect adversely the prices, quantities, qualities, or varieties of goods and services[17] either currently or potentially available. The competitive effects of licensing arrangements often can be adequately assessed within the relevant markets for the goods affected by the arrangements. In such instances, the Agencies will delineate and analyze only goods markets. In other cases, however, the analysis may require the delineation of markets for technology or markets for research and development (innovation markets).

3.2.1 Goods markets

A number of different goods markets may be relevant to evaluating the effects of a licensing arrangement. A restraint in a licensing arrangement may have competitive effects in markets for final or intermediate goods

---

[15] A firm will be treated as a likely potential competitor if there is evidence that entry by that firm is reasonably probable in the absence of the licensing arrangement.

[16] As used herein, "input" includes outlets for distribution and sales, as well as factors of production. *See, e.g.*, sections 4.1.1 and 5.3–5.5 for further discussion of conditions under which foreclosing access to, or raising the price of, an input may harm competition in a relevant market.

[17] Hereinafter, the term "goods" also includes services.

made using the intellectual property, or it may have effects upstream, in markets for goods that are used as inputs, along with the intellectual property, to the production of other goods. In general, for goods markets affected by a licensing arrangement, the Agencies will approach the delineation of relevant market and the measurement of market share in the intellectual property area as in section 1 of the U.S. Department of Justice and Federal Trade Commission Horizontal Merger Guidelines.[18]

3.2.2 Technology markets

Technology markets consist of the intellectual property that is licensed (the "licensed technology") and its close substitutes—that is, the technologies or goods that are close enough substitutes significantly to constrain the exercise of market power with respect to the intellectual property that is licensed.[19] When rights to intellectual property are marketed separately from the products in which they are used,[20] the Agencies may rely on technology markets to analyze the competitive effects of a licensing arrangement.

EXAMPLE 2

Situation:

Firms Alpha and Beta independently develop different patented process technologies to manufacture the same off-patent drug for the treatment of a particular disease. Before the firms use their technologies internally or license them to third parties, they announce plans jointly to manufacture the drug, and to assign their manufacturing processes to the new manufacturing venture. Many firms are capable of using and have the incentive to use the licensed technologies to manufacture and distribute the drug; thus, the market for drug manufacturing and distribution is competitive. One of the Agencies is evaluating the likely competitive effects of the planned venture.

Discussion:

The Agency would analyze the competitive effects of the proposed joint venture by first defining the relevant markets in which competition may be affected and then evaluating the likely competitive effects of the joint venture in the identified markets. (See Example 4 for a discussion of the Agencies' approach to joint venture analysis.) In this example, the structural effect of the joint venture in the relevant goods market for the manufacture and distribution of the drug is unlikely to be significant, because many firms in addition to the joint venture compete in that market. The joint venture might, however, increase the prices of the drug

---

18 U.S. Department of Justice and Federal Trade Commission, Horizontal Merger Guidelines (April 2, 1992) (hereinafter "1992 Horizontal Merger Guidelines"). As stated in section 1.41 of the 1992 Horizontal Merger Guidelines, market shares for goods markets "can be expressed either in dollar terms through measurement of sales, shipments, or production, or in physical terms through measurement of sales, shipments, production, capacity or reserves."

19 For example, the owner of a process for producing a particular good may be constrained in its conduct with respect to that process not only by other processes for making that good, but also by other goods that compete with the downstream good and by the processes used to produce those other goods.

20 Intellectual property is often licensed, sold, or transferred as an integral part of a marketed good. An example is a patented product marketed with an implied license permitting its use. In such circumstances, there is no need for a separate analysis of technology markets to capture relevant competitive effects.

produced using Alpha's or Beta's technology by reducing competition in the relevant market for technology to manufacture the drug.

The Agency would delineate a technology market in which to evaluate likely competitive effects of the proposed joint venture. The Agency would identify other technologies that can be used to make the drug with levels of effectiveness and cost per dose comparable to that of the technologies owned by Alpha and Beta. In addition, the Agency would consider the extent to which competition from other drugs that are substitutes for the drug produced using Alpha's or Beta's technology would limit the ability of a hypothetical monopolist that owned both Alpha's and Beta's technology to raise its price.

To identify a technology's close substitutes and thus to delineate the relevant technology market, the Agencies will, if the data permit, identify the smallest group of technologies and goods over which a hypothetical monopolist of those technologies and goods likely would exercise market power—for example, by imposing a small but significant and nontransitory price increase.[21] The Agencies recognize that technology often is licensed in ways that are not readily quantifiable in monetary terms. [22] In such circumstances, the Agencies will delineate the relevant market by identifying other technologies and goods which buyers would substitute at a cost comparable to that of using the licensed technology.

In assessing the competitive significance of current and likely potential participants in a technology market, the Agencies will take into account all relevant evidence. When market share data are available and accurately reflect the competitive significance of market participants, the Agencies will include market share data in this assessment. The Agencies also will seek evidence of buyers' and market participants' assessments of the competitive significance of technology market participants. Such evidence is particularly important when market share data are unavailable, or do not accurately represent the competitive significance of market participants. When market share data or other indicia of market power are not available, and it appears that competing technologies are comparably efficient,[23] the Agencies will assign each technology the same market share. For new technologies, the Agencies generally will use the best available information to estimate market acceptance over a two-year period, beginning with commercial introduction.

3.2.3 Research and development: innovation markets

If a licensing arrangement may adversely affect competition to develop new or improved goods or processes, the Agencies will analyze such an impact either as a separate competitive effect in relevant goods or technology markets, or as a competitive effect in a separate innovation market. A licensing arrangement may have competitive effects on innovation that cannot be adequately addressed through the analysis of goods or technology markets. For example, the arrangement may affect the

[21] This is conceptually analogous to the analytical approach to goods markets under the 1992 Horizontal Merger Guidelines. *Cf.* § 1.11. Of course, market power also can be exercised in other dimensions, such as quality, and these dimensions also may be relevant to the definition and analysis of technology markets.

[22] For example, technology may be licensed royalty-free in exchange for the right to use other technology, or it may be licensed as part of a package license.

[23] The Agencies will regard two technologies as "comparably efficient" if they can be used to produce close substitutes at comparable costs.

development of goods that do not yet exist.[24] Alternatively, the arrangement may affect the development of new or improved goods or processes in geographic markets where there is no actual or likely potential competition in the relevant goods.[25]

An innovation market consists of the research and development directed to particular new or improved goods or processes, and the close substitutes for that research and development. The close substitutes are research and development efforts, technologies, and goods[26] that significantly constrain the exercise of market power with respect to the relevant research and development, for example by limiting the ability and incentive of a hypothetical monopolist to retard the pace of research and development. The Agencies will delineate an innovation market only when the capabilities to engage in the relevant research and development can be associated with specialized assets or characteristics of specific firms.

In assessing the competitive significance of current and likely potential participants in an innovation market, the Agencies will take into account all relevant evidence. When market share data are available and accurately reflect the competitive significance of market participants, the Agencies will include market share data in this assessment. The Agencies also will seek evidence of buyers' and market participants' assessments of the competitive significance of innovation market participants. Such evidence is particularly important when market share data are unavailable or do not accurately represent the competitive significance of market participants. The Agencies may base the market shares of participants in an innovation market on their shares of identifiable assets or characteristics upon which innovation depends, on shares of research and development expenditures, or on shares of a related product. When entities have comparable capabilities and incentives to pursue research and development that is a close substitute for the research and development activities of the parties to a licensing arrangement, the Agencies may assign equal market shares to such entities.

EXAMPLE 3

Situation:

Two companies that specialize in advanced metallurgy agree to cross-license future patents relating to the development of a new component for aircraft jet turbines. Innovation in the development of the component requires the capability to work with very high tensile strength materials for jet turbines. Aspects of the licensing arrangement raise the possibility that competition in research and development of this and related

---

[24] *E.g., Sensormatic*, FTC Inv. No. 941-0126, 60 Fed. Reg. 5428 (accepted for comment Dec. 28, 1994); *Wright Medical Technology, Inc.*, FTC Inv. No. 951-0015, 60 Fed. Reg. 460 (accepted for comment Dec. 8, 1994); *American Home Products*, FTC Inv. No. 941-0116, 59 Fed. Reg. 60,807 (accepted for comment Nov. 28, 1994); *Roche Holdings Ltd.*, 113 F.T.C. 1086 (1990); *United States v. Automobile Mfrs. Ass'n*, 307 F. Supp. 617 (C.D. Cal. 1969), *appeal dismissed sub nom. City of New York v. United States*, 397 U.S. 248 (1970), *modified sub nom. United States v. Motor Vehicles Mfrs. Ass'n*, 1982–83 Trade Cas. (CCH) ¶ 65,088 (C.D. Cal. 1982).

[25] *See* Complaint, *United States v. General Motors Corp.*, Civ. No. 93-530 (D. Del., filed Nov. 16, 1993).

[26] For example, the licensor of research and development may be constrained in its conduct not only by competing research and development efforts but also by other existing goods that would compete with the goods under development.

components will be lessened. One of the Agencies is considering whether to define an innovation market in which to evaluate the competitive effects of the arrangement.

Discussion:

If the firms that have the capability and incentive to work with very high tensile strength materials for jet turbines can be reasonably identified, the Agency will consider defining a relevant innovation market for development of the new component. If the number of firms with the required capability and incentive to engage in research and development of very high tensile strength materials for aircraft jet turbines is small, the Agency may employ the concept of an innovation market to analyze the likely competitive effects of the arrangement in that market, or as an aid in analyzing competitive effects in technology or goods markets. The Agency would perform its analysis as described in parts 3–5.

If the number of firms with the required capability and incentive is large (either because there are a large number of such firms in the jet turbine industry, or because there are many firms in other industries with the required capability and incentive), then the Agency will conclude that the innovation market is competitive. Under these circumstances, it is unlikely that any single firm or plausible aggregation of firms could acquire a large enough share of the assets necessary for innovation to have an adverse impact on competition.

If the Agency cannot reasonably identify the firms with the required capability and incentive, it will not attempt to define an innovation market.

EXAMPLE 4

Situation:

Three of the largest producers of a plastic used in disposable bottles plan to engage in joint research and development to produce a new type of plastic that is rapidly biodegradable. The joint venture will grant to its partners (but to no one else) licenses to all patent rights and use of know-how. One of the Agencies is evaluating the likely competitive effects of the proposed joint venture.

Discussion:

The Agency would analyze the proposed research and development joint venture using an analysis similar to that applied to other joint ventures.[27] The Agency would begin by defining the relevant markets in which to analyze the joint venture's likely competitive effects. In this case, a relevant market is an innovation market—research and development for biodegradable (and other environmentally friendly) containers. The Agency would seek to identify any other entities that would be actual or likely potential competitors with the joint venture in that relevant market. This would include those firms that have the capability and incentive to undertake research and development closely substitutable for the research and development proposed to be undertaken by the joint venture, taking into account such firms' existing technologies and technologies under

[27] *See, e.g.*, U.S. Department of Justice and Federal Trade Commission, Statements of Enforcement Policy and Analytical Principles Relating to Health Care and Antitrust 20–23, 37–40, 72–74 (September 27, 1994). This type of transaction may qualify for treatment under the National Cooperative Research and Production Act of 1993, 15 U.S.C.A §§ 4301–05.

development, R&D facilities, and other relevant assets and business circumstances. Firms possessing such capabilities and incentives would be included in the research and development market even if they are not competitors in relevant markets for related goods, such as the plastics currently produced by the joint venturers, although competitors in existing goods markets may often also compete in related innovation markets.

Having defined a relevant innovation market, the Agency would assess whether the joint venture is likely to have anticompetitive effects in that market. A starting point in this analysis is the degree of concentration in the relevant market and the market shares of the parties to the joint venture. If, in addition to the parties to the joint venture (taken collectively), there are at least four other independently controlled entities that possess comparable capabilities and incentives to undertake research and development of biodegradable plastics, or other products that would be close substitutes for such new plastics, the joint venture ordinarily would be unlikely to adversely affect competition in the relevant innovation market (cf. section 4.3). If there are fewer than four other independently controlled entities with similar capabilities and incentives, the Agency would consider whether the joint venture would give the parties to the joint venture an incentive and ability collectively to reduce investment in, or otherwise to retard the pace or scope of, research and development efforts. If the joint venture creates a significant risk of anticompetitive effects in the innovation market, the Agency would proceed to consider efficiency justifications for the venture, such as the potential for combining complementary R&D assets in such a way as to make successful innovation more likely, or to bring it about sooner, or to achieve cost reductions in research and development.

The Agency would also assess the likelihood that the joint venture would adversely affect competition in other relevant markets, including markets for products produced by the parties to the joint venture. The risk of such adverse competitive effects would be increased to the extent that, for example, the joint venture facilitates the exchange among the parties of competitively sensitive information relating to goods markets in which the parties currently compete or facilitates the coordination of competitive activities in such markets. The Agency would examine whether the joint venture imposes collateral restraints that might significantly restrict competition among the joint venturers in goods markets, and would examine whether such collateral restraints were reasonably necessary to achieve any efficiencies that are likely to be attained by the venture.

3.3 Horizontal and vertical relationships

As with other property transfers, antitrust analysis of intellectual property licensing arrangements examines whether the relationship among the parties to the arrangement is primarily horizontal or vertical in nature, or whether it has substantial aspects of both. A licensing arrangement has a vertical component when it affects activities that are in a complementary relationship, as is typically the case in a licensing arrangement. For example, the licensor's primary line of business may be in research and development, and the licensees, as manufacturers, may be buying the rights to use technology developed by the licensor. Alternatively, the licensor may be a component manufacturer owning intellectual property rights in a product that the licensee manufactures by combining the component with other inputs, or the licensor may manufacture the product, and the licensees may operate primarily in distribution and marketing.

In addition to this vertical component, the licensor and its licensees may also have a horizontal relationship. For analytical purposes, the Agencies ordinarily will treat a relationship between a licensor and its licensees, or between licensees, as horizontal when they would have been actual or likely potential competitors in a relevant market in the absence of the license.

The existence of a horizontal relationship between a licensor and its licensees does not, in itself, indicate that the arrangement is anticompetitive. Identification of such relationships is merely an aid in determining whether there may be anticompetitive effects arising from a licensing arrangement. Such a relationship need not give rise to an anticompetitive effect, nor does a purely vertical relationship assure that there are no anticompetitive effects.

The following examples illustrate different competitive relationships among a licensor and its licensees.

EXAMPLE 5

Situation:

AgCo, a manufacturer of farm equipment, develops a new, patented emission control technology for its tractor engines and licenses it to FarmCo, another farm equipment manufacturer. AgCo's emission control technology is far superior to the technology currently owned and used by FarmCo, so much so that FarmCo's technology does not significantly constrain the prices that AgCo could charge for its technology. AgCo's emission control patent has a broad scope. It is likely that any improved emissions control technology that FarmCo could develop in the foreseeable future would infringe AgCo's patent.

Discussion:

Because FarmCo's emission control technology does not significantly constrain AgCo's competitive conduct with respect to its emission control technology, AgCo's and FarmCo's emission control technologies are not close substitutes for each other. FarmCo is a consumer of AgCo's technology and is not an actual competitor of AgCo in the relevant market for superior emission control technology of the kind licensed by AgCo. Furthermore, FarmCo is not a likely potential competitor of AgCo in the relevant market because, even if FarmCo could develop an improved emission control technology, it is likely that it would infringe AgCo's patent. This means that the relationship between AgCo and FarmCo with regard to the supply and use of emissions control technology is vertical. Assuming that AgCo and FarmCo are actual or likely potential competitors in sales of farm equipment products, their relationship is horizontal in the relevant markets for farm equipment.

EXAMPLE 6

Situation:

FarmCo develops a new valve technology for its engines and enters into a cross-licensing arrangement with AgCo, whereby AgCo licenses its emission control technology to FarmCo and FarmCo licenses its valve technology to AgCo. AgCo already owns an alternative valve technology that can be used to achieve engine performance similar to that using FarmCo's valve technology and at a comparable cost to consumers. Before adopting FarmCo's technology, AgCo was using its own valve technology in its production of engines and was licensing (and continues to license) that technology for use by others. As in Example 5, FarmCo does not own or control an emission control technology that is a close substitute for the technology licensed from AgCo. Furthermore, as in Example 5, FarmCo is not likely to develop an improved emission control technology that would be a close substitute for AgCo's technology, because of AgCo's blocking patent.

Discussion:

FarmCo is a consumer and not a competitor of AgCo's emission control technology. As in Example 5, their relationship is vertical with regard to this technology. The relationship between AgCo and FarmCo in the relevant market that includes engine valve technology is vertical in part and horizontal in part. It is vertical in part because AgCo and FarmCo stand in a complementary relationship, in which AgCo is a consumer of a technology supplied by FarmCo. However, the relationship between AgCo and FarmCo in the relevant market that includes engine valve technology is also horizontal in part, because FarmCo and AgCo are actual competitors in the licensing of valve technology that can be used to achieve similar engine performance at a comparable cost. Whether the firms license their valve technologies to others is not important for the conclusion that the firms have a horizontal relationship in this relevant market. Even if AgCo's use of its valve technology were solely captive to its own production, the fact that the two valve technologies are substitutable at comparable cost means that the two firms have a horizontal relationship.

As in Example 5, the relationship between AgCo and FarmCo is horizontal in the relevant markets for farm equipment.

3.4 Framework for evaluating licensing restraints

In the vast majority of cases, restraints in intellectual property licensing arrangements are evaluated under the rule of reason. The Agencies' general approach in analyzing a licensing restraint under the rule of reason is to inquire whether the restraint is likely to have anticompetitive effects and, if so, whether the restraint is reasonably necessary to achieve procompetitive benefits that outweigh those anticompetitive effects. See Federal Trade Commission v. Indiana Federation of Dentists, 476 U.S. 447 (1986); NCAA v. Board of Regents of the University of Oklahoma, 468 U.S. 85 (1984); Broadcast Music, Inc. v. Columbia Broadcasting System, Inc., 441 U.S. 1 (1979); 7 Phillip E. Areeda, Antitrust Law § 1502 (1986). See also part 4.

In some cases, however, the courts conclude that a restraint's "nature and necessary effect are so plainly anticompetitive" that it should be treated as unlawful per se, without an elaborate inquiry into the restraint's likely competitive effect. Federal Trade Commission v. Superior Court Trial Lawyers Association, 493 U.S. 411, 433 (1990); National Society of Professional Engineers v. United States, 435 U.S. 679, 692 (1978). Among the restraints that have been held per se unlawful are naked price-fixing, output restraints, and market division among horizontal competitors, as well as certain group boycotts and resale price maintenance.

To determine whether a particular restraint in a licensing arrangement is given per se or rule of reason treatment, the Agencies will assess whether the restraint in question can be expected to contribute to an efficiency-enhancing integration of economic activity. See Broadcast Music, 441 U.S. at 16–24. In general, licensing arrangements promote such integration because they facilitate the combination of the licensor's intellectual property with complementary factors of production owned by the licensee. A restraint in a licensing arrangement may further such integration by, for example, aligning the incentives of the licensor and the licensees to promote the development and marketing of the licensed technology, or by substantially reducing transactions costs. If there is no efficiency-enhancing integration of economic activity and if the type of restraint is one that has been accorded per se treatment, the Agencies will challenge the restraint under the per se rule. Otherwise, the Agencies will apply a rule of reason analysis.

Application of the rule of reason generally requires a comprehensive inquiry into market conditions. (See sections 4.1–4.3.) However, that inquiry may be truncated in certain circumstances. If the Agencies conclude that a restraint has no likely anticompetitive effects, they will treat it as reasonable, without an elaborate analysis of market power or the justifications for the restraint. Similarly, if a restraint facially appears to be of a kind that would always or almost always tend to reduce output or increase prices,[28] and the restraint is not reasonably related to efficiencies, the Agencies will likely challenge the restraint without an elaborate analysis of particular industry circumstances.[29] See Indiana Federation of Dentists, 476 U.S. at 459–60; NCAA, 468 U.S. at 109.

EXAMPLE 7

Situation:

Gamma, which manufactures Product X using its patented process, offers a license for its process technology to every other manufacturer of Product X, each of which competes world-wide with Gamma in the manufacture and sale of X. The process technology does not represent an economic improvement over the available existing technologies. Indeed, although most manufacturers accept licenses from Gamma, none of the licensees actually uses the licensed technology. The licenses provide that each manufacturer has an exclusive right to sell Product X manufactured using the licensed technology in a designated geographic area and that no manufacturer may sell Product X, however manufactured, outside the designated territory.

Discussion:

The manufacturers of Product X are in a horizontal relationship in the goods market for Product X. Any manufacturers of Product X that control technologies that are substitutable at comparable cost for Gamma's process are also horizontal competitors of Gamma in the relevant technology market. The licensees of Gamma's process technology are technically in a

---

[28] Details about the Federal Trade Commission's approach are set forth in *Massachusetts Board of Registration in Optometry*, 110 F.T.C. 549, 604 (1988). In applying its truncated rule of reason inquiry, the FTC uses the analytical category of "inherently suspect" restraints to denote facially anticompetitive restraints that would always or almost always tend to decrease output or increase prices, but that may be relatively unfamiliar or may not fit neatly into traditional per se categories.

[29] Under the FTC's *Mass. Board* approach, asserted efficiency justifications for inherently suspect restraints are examined to determine whether they are plausible and, if so, whether they are valid in the context of the market at issue. *Mass. Board*, 110 F.T.C. at 604.

vertical relationship, although that is not significant in this example because they do not actually use Gamma's technology.

The licensing arrangement restricts competition in the relevant goods market among manufacturers of Product X by requiring each manufacturer to limit its sales to an exclusive territory. Thus, competition among entities that would be actual competitors in the absence of the licensing arrangement is restricted. Based on the facts set forth above, the licensing arrangement does not involve a useful transfer of technology, and thus it is unlikely that the restraint on sales outside the designated territories contributes to an efficiency-enhancing integration of economic activity. Consequently, the evaluating Agency would be likely to challenge the arrangement under the per se rule as a horizontal territorial market allocation scheme and to view the intellectual property aspects of the arrangement as a sham intended to cloak its true nature.

If the licensing arrangement could be expected to contribute to an efficiency-enhancing integration of economic activity, as might be the case if the licensed technology were an advance over existing processes and used by the licensees, the Agency would analyze the arrangement under the rule of reason applying the analytical framework described in this section.

In this example, the competitive implications do not generally depend on whether the licensed technology is protected by patent, is a trade secret or other know-how, or is a computer program protected by copyright; nor do the competitive implications generally depend on whether the allocation of markets is territorial, as in this example, or functional, based on fields of use.

---

4. General principles concerning the Agencies' evaluation of licensing arrangements under the rule of reason

4.1 Analysis of anticompetitive effects

The existence of anticompetitive effects resulting from a restraint in a licensing arrangement will be evaluated on the basis of the analysis described in this section.

4.1.1 Market structure, coordination, and foreclosure

When a licensing arrangement affects parties in a horizontal relationship, a restraint in that arrangement may increase the risk of coordinated pricing, output restrictions, or the acquisition or maintenance of market power. Harm to competition also may occur if the arrangement poses a significant risk of retarding or restricting the development of new or improved goods or processes. The potential for competitive harm depends in part on the degree of concentration in, the difficulty of entry into, and the responsiveness of supply and demand to changes in price in the relevant markets. Cf. 1992 Horizontal Merger Guidelines §§ 1.5, 3.

When the licensor and licensees are in a vertical relationship, the Agencies will analyze whether the licensing arrangement may harm competition among entities in a horizontal relationship at either the level of the licensor or the licensees, or possibly in another relevant market. Harm to competition from a restraint may occur if it anticompetitively forecloses access to, or increases competitors' costs of obtaining, important inputs, or facilitates coordination to raise price or restrict output. The risk of anticompetitively foreclosing access or increasing competitors' costs is related to the proportion of the markets affected by the licensing restraint;

other characteristics of the relevant markets, such as concentration, difficulty of entry, and the responsiveness of supply and demand to changes in price in the relevant markets; and the duration of the restraint. A licensing arrangement does not foreclose competition merely because some or all of the potential licensees in an industry choose to use the licensed technology to the exclusion of other technologies. Exclusive use may be an efficient consequence of the licensed technology having the lowest cost or highest value.

Harm to competition from a restraint in a vertical licensing arrangement also may occur if a licensing restraint facilitates coordination among entities in a horizontal relationship to raise prices or reduce output in a relevant market. For example, if owners of competing technologies impose similar restraints on their licensees, the licensors may find it easier to coordinate their pricing. Similarly, licensees that are competitors may find it easier to coordinate their pricing if they are subject to common restraints in licenses with a common licensor or competing licensors. The risk of anticompetitive coordination is increased when the relevant markets are concentrated and difficult to enter. The use of similar restraints may be common and procompetitive in an industry, however, because they contribute to efficient exploitation of the licensed property.

4.1.2 Licensing arrangements involving exclusivity

A licensing arrangement may involve exclusivity in two distinct respects. First, the licensor may grant one or more exclusive licenses, which restrict the right of the licensor to license others and possibly also to use the technology itself. Generally, an exclusive license may raise antitrust concerns only if the licensees themselves, or the licensor and its licensees, are in a horizontal relationship. Examples of arrangements involving exclusive licensing that may give rise to antitrust concerns include cross-licensing by parties collectively possessing market power (see section 5.5), grantbacks (see section 5.6), and acquisitions of intellectual property rights (see section 5.7).

A non-exclusive license of intellectual property that does not contain any restraints on the competitive conduct of the licensor or the licensee generally does not present antitrust concerns even if the parties to the license are in a horizontal relationship, because the non-exclusive license normally does not diminish competition that would occur in its absence.

A second form of exclusivity, exclusive dealing, arises when a license prevents or restrains the licensee from licensing, selling, distributing, or using competing technologies. See section 5.4. Exclusivity may be achieved by an explicit exclusive dealing term in the license or by other provisions such as compensation terms or other economic incentives. Such restraints may anticompetitively foreclose access to, or increase competitors' costs of obtaining, important inputs, or facilitate coordination to raise price or reduce output, but they also may have procompetitive effects. For example, a licensing arrangement that prevents the licensee from dealing in other technologies may encourage the licensee to develop and market the licensed technology or specialized applications of that technology. See, e.g., Example 8. The Agencies will take into account such procompetitive effects in evaluating the reasonableness of the arrangement. See section 4.2.

The antitrust principles that apply to a licensor's grant of various forms of exclusivity to and among its licensees are similar to those that apply to comparable vertical restraints outside the licensing context, such as exclusive territories and exclusive dealing. However, the fact that intellectual property may in some cases be misappropriated more easily than other forms of property may justify the use of some restrictions that might be anticompetitive in other contexts.

As noted earlier, the Agencies will focus on the actual practice and its effects, not on the formal terms of the arrangement. A license denominated as non-exclusive (either in the sense of exclusive licensing or in the sense of exclusive dealing) may nonetheless give rise to the same concerns posed by formal exclusivity. A non-exclusive license may have the effect of exclusive licensing if it is structured so that the licensor is unlikely to license others or to practice the technology itself. A license that does not explicitly require exclusive dealing may have the effect of exclusive dealing if it is structured to increase significantly a licensee's cost when it uses competing technologies. However, a licensing arrangement will not automatically raise these concerns merely because a party chooses to deal with a single licensee or licensor, or confines his activity to a single field of use or location, or because only a single licensee has chosen to take a license.

EXAMPLE 8

Situation:

NewCo, the inventor and manufacturer of a new flat panel display technology, lacking the capability to bring a flat panel display product to market, grants BigCo an exclusive license to sell a product embodying NewCo's technology. BigCo does not currently sell, and is not developing (or likely to develop), a product that would compete with the product embodying the new technology and does not control rights to another display technology. Several firms offer competing displays, BigCo accounts for only a small proportion of the outlets for distribution of display products, and entry into the manufacture and distribution of display products is relatively easy. Demand for the new technology is uncertain and successful market penetration will require considerable promotional effort. The license contains an exclusive dealing restriction preventing BigCo from selling products that compete with the product embodying the licensed technology.

Discussion:

This example illustrates both types of exclusivity in a licensing arrangement. The license is exclusive in that it restricts the right of the licensor to grant other licenses. In addition, the license has an exclusive dealing component in that it restricts the licensee from selling competing products.

The inventor of the display technology and its licensee are in a vertical relationship and are not actual or likely potential competitors in the manufacture or sale of display products or in the sale or development of technology. Hence, the grant of an exclusive license does not affect competition between the licensor and the licensee. The exclusive license may promote competition in the manufacturing and sale of display products by encouraging BigCo to develop and promote the new product in the face of uncertain demand by rewarding BigCo for its efforts if they lead to large sales. Although the license bars the licensee from selling competing products, this exclusive dealing aspect is unlikely in this example to harm competition by anticompetitively foreclosing access, raising competitors' costs of inputs, or facilitating anticompetitive pricing because the relevant product market is unconcentrated, the exclusive dealing restraint affects only a small proportion of the outlets for distribution of display products, and entry is easy. On these facts, the evaluating Agency would be unlikely to challenge the arrangement.

4.2 Efficiencies and justifications

If the Agencies conclude, upon an evaluation of the market factors described in section 4.1, that a restraint in a licensing arrangement is unlikely to have an anticompetitive effect, they will not challenge the restraint. If the Agencies conclude that the restraint has, or is likely to have, an anticompetitive effect, they will consider whether the restraint is reasonably necessary to achieve procompetitive efficiencies. If the restraint is reasonably necessary, the Agencies will balance the procompetitive efficiencies and the anticompetitive effects to determine the probable net effect on competition in each relevant market.

The Agencies' comparison of anticompetitive harms and procompetitive efficiencies is necessarily a qualitative one. The risk of anticompetitive effects in a particular case may be insignificant compared to the expected efficiencies, or vice versa. As the expected anticompetitive effects in a particular licensing arrangement increase, the Agencies will require evidence establishing a greater level of expected efficiencies.

The existence of practical and significantly less restrictive alternatives is relevant to a determination of whether a restraint is reasonably necessary. If it is clear that the parties could have achieved similar efficiencies by means that are significantly less restrictive, then the Agencies will not give weight to the parties' efficiency claim. In making this assessment, however, the Agencies will not engage in a search for a theoretically least restrictive alternative that is not realistic in the practical prospective business situation faced by the parties.

When a restraint has, or is likely to have, an anticompetitive effect, the duration of that restraint can be an important factor in determining whether it is reasonably necessary to achieve the putative procompetitive efficiency. The effective duration of a restraint may depend on a number of factors, including the option of the affected party to terminate the arrangement unilaterally and the presence of contract terms (e.g., unpaid balances on minimum purchase commitments) that encourage the licensee to renew a license arrangement. Consistent with their approach to less restrictive alternative analysis generally, the Agencies will not attempt to draw fine distinctions regarding duration; rather, their focus will be on situations in which the duration clearly exceeds the period needed to achieve the procompetitive efficiency.

The evaluation of procompetitive efficiencies, of the reasonable necessity of a restraint to achieve them, and of the duration of the restraint, may depend on the market context. A restraint that may be justified by the needs of a new entrant, for example, may not have a procompetitive efficiency justification in different market circumstances. Cf. United States v. Jerrold Electronics Corp., 187 F. Supp. 545 (E.D. Pa. 1960), aff'd per curiam, 365 U.S. 567 (1961).

4.3 Antitrust "safety zone"

Because licensing arrangements often promote innovation and enhance competition, the Agencies believe that an antitrust "safety zone" is useful in order to provide some degree of certainty and thus to encourage such activity.[30] Absent extraordinary circumstances, the Agencies will not challenge a restraint in an intellectual property licensing arrangement if (1) the restraint is not facially anticompetitive[31] and (2) the licensor and its licensees collectively account for no more than twenty percent of each relevant market significantly affected by the restraint. This "safety zone" does not apply to those transfers of intellectual property rights to which a merger analysis is applied. See section 5.7.

Whether a restraint falls within the safety zone will be determined by reference only to goods markets unless the analysis of goods markets alone would inadequately address the effects of the licensing arrangement on competition among technologies or in research and development.

If an examination of the effects on competition among technologies or in research development is required, and if market share data are unavailable or do not accurately represent competitive significance, the following safety zone criteria will apply. Absent extraordinary circumstances, the Agencies will not challenge a restraint in an intellectual property licensing arrangement that may affect competition in a technology market if (1) the restraint is not facially anticompetitive and (2) there are four or more independently controlled technologies in addition to the technologies controlled by the parties to the licensing arrangement that may be substitutable for the licensed technology at a comparable cost to the user. Absent extraordinary circumstances, the Agencies will not challenge a restraint in an intellectual property licensing arrangement that may affect competition in an innovation market if (1) the restraint is not facially anticompetitive and (2) four or more independently controlled entities in addition to the parties to the licensing arrangement possess the required specialized assets or characteristics and the incentive to engage in research and development that is a close substitute of the research and development activities of the parties to the licensing agreement.[32]

The Agencies emphasize that licensing arrangements are not anticompetitive merely because they do not fall within the scope of the safety zone. Indeed, it is likely that the great majority of licenses falling outside the safety zone are lawful and procompetitive. The safety zone is designed to provide owners of intellectual property with a degree of certainty in those situations in which anticompetitive effects are so unlikely that the arrangements may be presumed not to be anticompetitive without an inquiry into particular industry circumstances. It is not intended to suggest that parties should conform to the safety zone or to discourage parties falling outside the safety zone from adopting restrictions in their license arrangements that are reasonably necessary to achieve an efficiency-enhancing integration of economic activity. The Agencies will analyze arrangements falling outside the safety zone based on the considerations outlined in parts 3–5.

---

[30] The antitrust "safety zone" does not apply to restraints that are not in a licensing arrangement, or to restraints that are in a licensing arrangement but are unrelated to the use of the licensed intellectual property.

[31] "Facially anticompetitive" refers to restraints that normally warrant per se treatment, as well as other restraints of a kind that would always or almost always tend to reduce output or increase prices. *See* section 3.4.

[32] This is consistent with congressional intent in enacting the National Cooperative Research Act. *See* H.R. Conf. Rpt. No. 1044, 98th Cong., 2d Sess., 10, *reprinted in* 1984 U.S.C.C.A.N. 3105, 3134–35.

The status of a licensing arrangement with respect to the safety zone may change over time. A determination by the Agencies that a restraint in a licensing arrangement qualifies for inclusion in the safety zone is based on the factual circumstances prevailing at the time of the conduct at issue.[33]

5. Application of general principles

5.0 This section illustrates the application of the general principles discussed above to particular licensing restraints and to arrangements that involve the cross-licensing, pooling, or acquisition of intellectual property. The restraints and arrangements identified are typical of those that are likely to receive antitrust scrutiny; however, they are not intended as an exhaustive list of practices that could raise competitive concerns.

5.1 Horizontal restraints

The existence of a restraint in a licensing arrangement that affects parties in a horizontal relationship (a "horizontal restraint") does not necessarily cause the arrangement to be anticompetitive. As in the case of joint ventures among horizontal competitors, licensing arrangements among such competitors may promote rather than hinder competition if they result in integrative efficiencies. Such efficiencies may arise, for example, from the realization of economies of scale and the integration of complementary research and development, production, and marketing capabilities.

Following the general principles outlined in section 3.4, horizontal restraints often will be evaluated under the rule of reason. In some circumstances, however, that analysis may be truncated; additionally, some restraints may merit per se treatment, including price fixing, allocation of markets or customers, agreements to reduce output, and certain group boycotts.

EXAMPLE 9

Situation:

Two of the leading manufacturers of a consumer electronic product hold patents that cover alternative circuit designs for the product. The manufacturers assign their patents to a separate corporation wholly owned by the two firms. That corporation licenses the right to use the circuit designs to other consumer product manufacturers and establishes the license royalties. None of the patents is blocking; that is, each of the patents can be used without infringing a patent owned by the other firm. The different circuit designs are substitutable in that each permits the manufacture at comparable cost to consumers of products that consumers consider to be interchangeable. One of the Agencies is analyzing the licensing arrangement.

Discussion:

In this example, the manufacturers are horizontal competitors in the goods market for the consumer product and in the related technology markets. The competitive issue with regard to a joint assignment of patent rights is whether the assignment has an adverse impact on competition in technology and goods markets that is not outweighed by procompetitive efficiencies, such as benefits in the use or dissemination of the technology. Each of the patent owners has a right to exclude others from using its patent. That right does not extend, however, to the agreement to assign

[33] The conduct at issue may be the transaction giving rise to the restraint or the subsequent implementation of the restraint.

rights jointly. To the extent that the patent rights cover technologies that are close substitutes, the joint determination of royalties likely would result in higher royalties and higher goods prices than would result if the owners licensed or used their technologies independently. In the absence of evidence establishing efficiency-enhancing integration from the joint assignment of patent rights, the Agency may conclude that the joint marketing of competing patent rights constitutes horizontal price fixing and could be challenged as a per se unlawful horizontal restraint of trade. If the joint marketing arrangement results in an efficiency-enhancing integration, the Agency would evaluate the arrangement under the rule of reason. However, the Agency may conclude that the anticompetitive effects are sufficiently apparent, and the claimed integrative efficiencies are sufficiently weak or not reasonably related to the restraints, to warrant challenge of the arrangement without an elaborate analysis of particular industry circumstances (see section 3.4).

5.2 Resale price maintenance

Resale price maintenance is illegal when "commodities have passed into the channels of trade and are owned by dealers." Dr. Miles Medical Co. v. John D. Park & Sons Co., 220 U.S. 373, 408 (1911). It has been held per se illegal for a licensor of an intellectual property right in a product to fix a licensee's resale price of that product. United States v. Univis Lens Co., 316 U.S. 241 (1942); Ethyl Gasoline Corp. v. United States, 309 U.S. 436 (1940).[34] Consistent with the principles set forth in section 3.4, the Agencies will enforce the per se rule against resale price maintenance in the intellectual property context.[35]

5.3 Tying arrangements

A "tying" or "tie-in" or "tied sale" arrangement has been defined as "an agreement by a party to sell one product . . . on the condition that the buyer also purchases a different (or tied) product, or at least agrees that he will not purchase that [tied] product from any other supplier." Eastman Kodak Co. v. Image Technical Services, Inc., 112 S. Ct. 2072, 2079 (1992). Conditioning the ability of a licensee to license one or more items of intellectual property on the licensee's purchase of another item of intellectual property or a good or a service has been held in some cases to constitute illegal tying.[36] Although tying arrangements may result in anticompetitive effects, such arrangements can also result in significant

---

[34] *But cf. United States v. General Electric Co.*, 272 U.S. 476 (1926) (holding that an owner of a product patent may condition a license to manufacture the product on the fixing of the *first* sale price of the patented product). Subsequent lower court decisions have distinguished the *GE* decision in various contexts. *See, e.g., Royal Indus. v. St. Regis Paper Co.*, 420 F.2d 449, 452 (9th Cir. 1969) (observing that *GE* involved a restriction by a patentee who also manufactured the patented product and leaving open the question whether a nonmanufacturing patentee may fix the price of the patented product); *Newburgh Moire Co. v. Superior Moire Co.*, 237 F.2d 283, 293–94 (3rd Cir. 1956) (grant of multiple licenses each containing price restrictions does not come within the *GE* doctrine); *Cummer-Graham Co. v. Straight Side Basket Corp.*, 142 F.2d 646, 647 (5th Cir.) (owner of an intellectual property right in a process to manufacture an unpatented product may not fix the sale price of that product), *cert. denied*, 323 U.S. 726 (1944); *Barber-Colman Co. v. National Tool Co.*, 136 F.2d 339, 343–44 (6th Cir. 1943) (same).

[35] [Editor's Footnote]: Leegin Creative Leather Products, Inc. v. PSKS, Inc., 551 U.S. 877 (2007) directly overruled Dr. Miles.

[36] *See, e.g., United States v. Paramount Pictures, Inc.*, 334 U.S. 131, 156–58 (1948) (copyrights); *International Salt Co. v. United States*, 332 U.S. 392 (1947) (patent and related product).

efficiencies and procompetitive benefits. In the exercise of their prosecutorial discretion, the Agencies will consider both the anticompetitive effects and the efficiencies attributable to a tie-in. The Agencies would be likely to challenge a tying arrangement if: (1) the seller has market power in the tying product,[37] (2) the arrangement has an adverse effect on competition in the relevant market for the tied product, and (3) efficiency justifications for the arrangement do not outweigh the anticompetitive effects.[38] The Agencies will not presume that a patent, copyright, or trade secret necessarily confers market power upon its owner.

Package licensing—the licensing of multiple items of intellectual property in a single license or in a group of related licenses—may be a form of tying arrangement if the licensing of one product is conditioned upon the acceptance of a license of another, separate product. Package licensing can be efficiency enhancing under some circumstances. When multiple licenses are needed to use any single item of intellectual property, for example, a package license may promote such efficiencies. If a package license constitutes a tying arrangement, the Agencies will evaluate its competitive effects under the same principles they apply to other tying arrangements.

5.4 Exclusive dealing

In the intellectual property context, exclusive dealing occurs when a license prevents the licensee from licensing, selling, distributing, or using competing technologies. Exclusive dealing arrangements are evaluated under the rule of reason. See Tampa Electric Co. v. Nashville Coal Co., 365 U.S. 320 (1961) (evaluating legality of exclusive dealing under section 1 of the Sherman Act and section 3 of the Clayton Act); Beltone Electronics Corp., 100 F.T.C. 68 (1982) (evaluating legality of exclusive dealing under section 5 of the Federal Trade Commission Act). In determining whether an exclusive dealing arrangement is likely to reduce competition in a relevant market, the Agencies will take into account the extent to which the arrangement (1) promotes the exploitation and development of the licensor's technology and (2) anticompetitively forecloses the exploitation and development of, or otherwise constrains competition among, competing technologies.

The likelihood that exclusive dealing may have anticompetitive effects is related, inter alia, to the degree of foreclosure in the relevant market, the duration of the exclusive dealing arrangement, and other characteristics of the input and output markets, such as concentration, difficulty of entry, and the responsiveness of supply and demand to changes in price in the relevant markets. (See sections 4.1.1 and 4.1.2.) If the Agencies determine that a particular exclusive dealing arrangement may have an anticompetitive effect, they will evaluate the extent to which the restraint encourages licensees to develop and market the licensed technology (or specialized applications of that technology), increases licensors' incentives to develop or refine the licensed technology, or otherwise increases competition and enhances output in a relevant market. (See section 4.2 and Example 8.)

---

[37] *Cf.* 35 U.S.C. § 271(d) (1988 & Supp. V 1993) (requirement of market power in patent misuse cases involving tying).

[38] As is true throughout these Guidelines, the factors listed are those that guide the Agencies' internal analysis in exercising their prosecutorial discretion. They are not intended to circumscribe how the Agencies will conduct the litigation of cases that they decide to bring.

5.5 Cross-licensing and pooling arrangements

Cross-licensing and pooling arrangements are agreements of two or more owners of different items of intellectual property to license one another or third parties. These arrangements may provide procompetitive benefits by integrating complementary technologies, reducing transaction costs, clearing blocking positions, and avoiding costly infringement litigation. By promoting the dissemination of technology, cross-licensing and pooling arrangements are often procompetitive.

Cross-licensing and pooling arrangements can have anticompetitive effects in certain circumstances. For example, collective price or output restraints in pooling arrangements, such as the joint marketing of pooled intellectual property rights with collective price setting or coordinated output restrictions, may be deemed unlawful if they do not contribute to an efficiency-enhancing integration of economic activity among the participants. Compare NCAA 468 U.S. at 114 (output restriction on college football broadcasting held unlawful because it was not reasonably related to any purported justification) with Broadcast Music, 441 U.S. at 23 (blanket license for music copyrights found not per se illegal because the cooperative price was necessary to the creation of a new product). When cross-licensing or pooling arrangements are mechanisms to accomplish naked price fixing or market division, they are subject to challenge under the per se rule. See United States v. New Wrinkle, Inc., 342 U.S. 371 (1952) (price fixing).

Settlements involving the cross-licensing of intellectual property rights can be an efficient means to avoid litigation and, in general, courts favor such settlements. When such cross-licensing involves horizontal competitors, however, the Agencies will consider whether the effect of the settlement is to diminish competition among entities that would have been actual or likely potential competitors in a relevant market in the absence of the cross-license. In the absence of offsetting efficiencies, such settlements may be challenged as unlawful restraints of trade. Cf. United States v. Singer Manufacturing Co., 374 U.S. 174 (1963) (cross-license agreement was part of broader combination to exclude competitors).

Pooling arrangements generally need not be open to all who would like to join. However, exclusion from cross-licensing and pooling arrangements among parties that collectively possess market power may, under some circumstances, harm competition. Cf. Northwest Wholesale Stationers, Inc. v. Pacific Stationery & Printing Co., 472 U.S. 284 (1985) (exclusion of a competitor from a purchasing cooperative not per se unlawful absent a showing of market power). In general, exclusion from a pooling or cross-licensing arrangement among competing technologies is unlikely to have anticompetitive effects unless (1) excluded firms cannot effectively compete in the relevant market for the good incorporating the licensed technologies and (2) the pool participants collectively possess market power in the relevant market. If these circumstances exist, the Agencies will evaluate whether the arrangement's limitations on participation are reasonably related to the efficient development and exploitation of the pooled technologies and will assess the net effect of those limitations in the relevant market. See section 4.2.

Another possible anticompetitive effect of pooling arrangements may occur if the arrangement deters or discourages participants from engaging in research and development, thus retarding innovation. For example, a pooling arrangement that requires members to grant licenses to each other for current and future technology at minimal cost may reduce the incentives of its members to engage in research and development because members of the pool have to share their successful research and development and each of the members can free ride on the accomplishments of other pool members. See generally United States v. Mfrs. Aircraft Ass'n, Inc., 1976-1 Trade Cas. (CCH) ¶ 60,810 (S.D.N.Y. 1975); United States v. Automobile Mfrs. Ass'n, 307 F. Supp. 617 (C.D. Cal 1969), appeal dismissed sub nom. City of New York v. United States, 397 U.S. 248 (1970), modified sub nom. United States v. Motor Vehicle Mfrs. Ass'n, 1982–83 Trade Cas. (CCH) ¶ 65,088 (C.D. Cal. 1982). However, such an arrangement can have procompetitive benefits, for example, by exploiting economies of scale and integrating complementary capabilities of the pool members, (including the clearing of blocking positions), and is likely to cause competitive problems only when the arrangement includes a large fraction of the potential research and development in an innovation market. See section 3.2.3 and Example 4.

EXAMPLE 10

Situation:

As in Example 9, two of the leading manufacturers of a consumer electronic product hold patents that cover alternative circuit designs for the product. The manufacturers assign several of their patents to a separate corporation wholly owned by the two firms. That corporation licenses the right to use the circuit designs to other consumer product manufacturers and establishes the license royalties. In this example, however, the manufacturers assign to the separate corporation only patents that are blocking. None of the patents assigned to the corporation can be used without infringing a patent owned by the other firm.

Discussion:

Unlike the previous example, the joint assignment of patent rights to the wholly owned corporation in this example does not adversely affect competition in the licensed technology among entities that would have been actual or likely potential competitors in the absence of the licensing arrangement. Moreover, the licensing arrangement is likely to have procompetitive benefits in the use of the technology. Because the manufacturers' patents are blocking, the manufacturers are not in a horizontal relationship with respect to those patents. None of the patents can be used without the right to a patent owned by the other firm, so the patents are not substitutable. As in Example 9, the firms are horizontal competitors in the relevant goods market. In the absence of collateral restraints that would likely raise price or reduce output in the relevant goods market or in any other relevant antitrust market and that are not reasonably related to an efficiency-enhancing integration of economic activity, the evaluating Agency would be unlikely to challenge this arrangement.

5.6 Grantbacks

A grantback is an arrangement under which a licensee agrees to extend to the licensor of intellectual property the right to use the licensee's improvements to the licensed technology. Grantbacks can have procompetitive effects, especially if they are nonexclusive. Such arrangements provide a means for the licensee and the licensor to share risks and reward the licensor for making possible further innovation based on or informed by the licensed technology, and both promote innovation in the first place and promote the subsequent licensing of the results of the innovation. Grantbacks may adversely affect competition, however, if they substantially reduce the licensee's incentives to engage in research and development and thereby limit rivalry in innovation markets.

A non-exclusive grantback allows the licensee to practice its technology and license it to others. Such a grantback provision may be necessary to ensure that the licensor is not prevented from effectively competing because it is denied access to improvements developed with the aid of its own technology. Compared with an exclusive grantback, a non-exclusive grantback, which leaves the licensee free to license improvements technology to others, is less likely to have anticompetitive effects.

The Agencies will evaluate a grantback provision under the rule of reason, see generally Transparent-Wrap Machine Corp. v. Stokes & Smith Co., 329 U.S. 637, 645–48 (1947) (grantback provision in technology license is not per se unlawful), considering its likely effects in light of the overall structure of the licensing arrangement and conditions in the relevant markets. An important factor in the Agencies' analysis of a grantback will be whether the licensor has market power in a relevant technology or innovation market. If the Agencies determine that a particular grantback provision is likely to reduce significantly licensees' incentives to invest in improving the licensed technology, the Agencies will consider the extent to which the grantback provision has offsetting procompetitive effects, such as (1) promoting dissemination of licensees' improvements to the licensed technology, (2) increasing the licensors' incentives to disseminate the licensed technology, or (3) otherwise increasing competition and output in a relevant technology or innovation market. See section 4.2. In addition, the Agencies will consider the extent to which grantback provisions in the relevant markets generally increase licensors' incentives to innovate in the first place.

5.7 Acquisition of intellectual property rights

Certain transfers of intellectual property rights are most appropriately analyzed by applying the principles and standards used to analyze mergers, particularly those in the 1992 Horizontal Merger Guidelines. The Agencies will apply a merger analysis to an outright sale by an intellectual property owner of all of its rights to that intellectual property and to a transaction in which a person obtains through grant, sale, or other transfer an exclusive license for intellectual property (i.e., a license that precludes all other persons, including the licensor, from using the licensed intellectual property).[39] Such transactions may be assessed under section 7 of the Clayton Act, sections 1 and 2 of the Sherman Act, and section 5 of the Federal Trade Commission Act.

EXAMPLE 11

Situation:

Omega develops a new, patented pharmaceutical for the treatment of a particular disease. The only drug on the market approved for the treatment of this disease is sold by Delta. Omega's patented drug has almost completed regulatory approval by the Food and Drug

[39] The safety zone of section 4.3 does not apply to transfers of intellectual property such as those described in this section.

Administration. Omega has invested considerable sums in product development and market testing, and initial results show that Omega's drug would be a significant competitor to Delta's. However, rather than enter the market as a direct competitor of Delta, Omega licenses to Delta the right to manufacture and sell Omega's patented drug. The license agreement with Delta is nominally nonexclusive. However, Omega has rejected all requests by other firms to obtain a license to manufacture and sell Omega's patented drug, despite offers by those firms of terms that are reasonable in relation to those in Delta's license.

Discussion:

Although Omega's license to Delta is nominally nonexclusive, the circumstances indicate that it is exclusive in fact because Omega has rejected all reasonable offers by other firms for licenses to manufacture and sell Omega's patented drug. The facts of this example indicate that Omega would be a likely potential competitor of Delta in the absence of the licensing arrangement, and thus they are in a horizontal relationship in the relevant goods market that includes drugs for the treatment of this particular disease. The evaluating Agency would apply a merger analysis to this transaction, since it involves an acquisition of a likely potential competitor.

---

6. Enforcement of invalid intellectual property rights

The Agencies may challenge the enforcement of invalid intellectual property rights as antitrust violations. Enforcement or attempted enforcement of a patent obtained by fraud on the Patent and Trademark Office or the Copyright Office may violate section 2 of the Sherman Act, if all the elements otherwise necessary to establish a section 2 charge are proved, or section 5 of the Federal Trade Commission Act. Walker Process Equipment, Inc. v. Food Machinery & Chemical Corp., 382 U.S. 172 (1965) (patents); American Cyanamid Co., 72 F.T.C. 623, 684–85 (1967), aff'd sub. nom. Charles Pfizer & Co., 401 F.2d 574 (6th Cir. 1968), cert. denied, 394 U.S. 920 (1969) (patents); Michael Anthony Jewelers, Inc. v. Peacock Jewelry, Inc., 795 F. Supp. 639, 647 (S.D.N.Y. 1992) (copyrights). Inequitable conduct before the Patent and Trademark Office will not be the basis of a section 2 claim unless the conduct also involves knowing and willful fraud and the other elements of a section 2 claim are present. Argus Chemical Corp. v. Fibre Glass-Evercoat, Inc., 812 F.2d 1381, 1384–85 (Fed. Cir. 1987). Actual or attempted enforcement of patents obtained by inequitable conduct that falls short of fraud under some circumstances may violate section 5 of the Federal Trade Commission Act, American Cyanamid Co., supra. Objectively baseless litigation to enforce invalid intellectual property rights may also constitute an element of a violation of the Sherman Act. See Professional Real Estate Investors, Inc. v. Columbia Pictures Industries, Inc., 113 S. Ct. 1920, 1928 (1993) (copyrights); Handgards, Inc. v. Ethicon, Inc., 743 F.2d 1282, 1289 (9th Cir. 1984), cert. denied, 469 U.S. 1190 (1985) (patents); Handgards, Inc. v. Ethicon, Inc., 601 F.2d 986, 992–96 (9th Cir. 1979), cert. denied, 444 U.S. 1025 (1980) (patents); CVD, Inc. v. Raytheon Co., 769 F.2d 842 (1st Cir. 1985) (trade secrets), cert. denied, 475 U.S. 1016 (1986).

12

HORIZONTAL MERGER GUIDELINES OF THE NATIONAL ASSOCIATION OF ATTORNEYS GENERAL

Adopted and Published on March 30, 1993

Table of Contents

1. PURPOSE AND SCOPE OF THE GUIDELINES

These guidelines explain the general enforcement policy of the state and territorial attorneys general ("the Attorneys General") who comprise the National Association of Attorneys General[1] ("NAAG") concerning horizontal acquisitions and mergers[2] (collectively "mergers") subject to section 7 of the Clayton Act,[3] sections 1 and 2 of the Sherman Act[4] and analogous provisions of the antitrust laws of those states which have enacted them.[5]

The state attorney general is the primary or exclusive public enforcer of the antitrust law in most states. The Attorneys General also represent their

[1] The Attorneys General of American Samoa, Guam, The Commonwealth of Northern Marianas Islands, The Commonwealth of Puerto Rico and the Virgin Islands are members of NAAG.

[2] A horizontal merger involves firms that are actually or potentially in both the same product and geographic markets, as those markets are defined in Section 3 of these guidelines.

[3] Section 7 of the Clayton Act, 15 U.S.C. Section 18, prohibits mergers if their effect "may be substantially to lessen competition or to tend to create a monopoly."

[4] Section 1 of the Sherman Act, 15 U.S.C. Section 1, prohibits mergers which constitute an unreasonable "restraint of trade." Section 2 of the Sherman Act, 15 U.S.C. Section 2, prohibits mergers which create a monopoly or constitute an attempt, combination or conspiracy to monopolize.

[5] The antitrust laws of the states are set forth in 6 TRADE REG. REP. (CCH) p 30,000 et seq.

states and the natural person citizens of their states in federal antitrust litigation.[6]

These guidelines embody the general enforcement policy of the Attorneys General. Individual attorneys general may vary or supplement this general policy in recognition of variations in precedents among the federal circuits and differences in state antitrust laws and in the exercise of their individual prosecutorial discretion.

These guidelines serve three principal purposes. First, they provide a uniform framework for the states to evaluate the facts of a particular horizontal merger and the dynamic conditions of an industry. Second, they inform businesses of the substantive standards used by the Attorneys General to review, and when appropriate, challenge specific mergers. They help businesses to assess the legality of potential transactions and therefore are useful as a business planning tool. Third, the guidelines are designed primarily to articulate the analytical framework the states apply in determining whether a merger is likely substantially to lessen competition, not to describe how the states will conduct litigation. As such, the Guidelines do not purport to provide a complete restatement of existing merger law. Rather, the Guidelines put forward a framework for the analysis of horizontal mergers which relies upon an accurate characterization of relevant markets and which is grounded in and consistent with the purposes and meaning of section 7 of the Clayton Act, as amended by the Celler-Kefauver Act of 1950 ("section 7"), and as reflected in its legislative history and interpretation by the United States Supreme Court.

The organizing principle of the guidelines is the application of facts concerning the marketplace and widely accepted economic theory to these authoritative sources of the law's meaning.

2. POLICIES UNDERLYING THESE GUIDELINES

The federal antitrust law provisions relevant to horizontal mergers, most specifically section 7 and analogous state law provisions,[7] have one primary and several subsidiary purposes. The central purpose of the law is to prevent firms from attaining either market or monopoly power,[8] because firms possessing such power can raise prices to consumers above competitive levels, thereby effecting a transfer of wealth from consumers to such firms.[9]

---

6 The authority of the Attorneys General to invoke section 7 of the Clayton Act to enjoin a merger injurious to the general welfare and economy of the State was first articulated in Georgia v. Pennsylvania R.R., 324 U.S. 439 (1945). California v. American Stores, 110 S. Ct. 1853 (1990), confirms Attorneys General's authority to enforce Section 7 and confirms the availability of the divestiture remedy to Attorneys General.

7 For example, *see* statutes of Hawaii, Maine, Mississippi, Nebraska, New Jersey, Ohio, Oklahoma, Texas, Washington and Puerto Rico for provisions analogous to section 7. *See* 6 TRADE REG. REP. (CCH) p 30,000 et seq. However, all states with a provision analogous to section 1 of the Sherman Act may also challenge mergers under such authority. *See* note 6 concerning state enforcement of section 7. Appendix A contains copies of the NAAG Voluntary Pre-Merger Disclosure Compact, the Protocol for Coordinating Federal-State Merger Probes and the FTC's Implementation of Program for Federal-State Cooperation in Merger Enforcement.

8 Market power is the ability of one or more firms to maintain prices above a competitive level, or to prevent prices from decreasing to a lower competitive level, or to limit output or entry.

9 A buyer or group of buyers may similarly attain and exercise the power to drive prices below a competitive level for a significant period of time. This is usually

Congress determined that highly concentrated industries were characterized by and conducive to the exercise of market power and prohibited mergers which may substantially lessen competition. Such mergers were prohibited even prior to the parties actual attainment or exercise of market power, that is, when the trend to harmful concentration was incipient.

These guidelines deal only with these competitive consequences of horizontal mergers, and challenges will be instituted only against mergers that may lead to detrimental economic effects. Mergers may also have other consequences that are relevant to the social and political goals of section 7. For example, mergers may affect the opportunities for small and regional business to survive and compete. Although such consequences are beyond the scope of these guidelines, they may affect the Attorneys General's ultimate exercise of prosecutorial discretion and may help the states decide which of the possible challenges that are justified on economic grounds should be instituted.

Goals such as productive and allocative efficiency are generally consistent with, though subsidiary to, the central goal of preventing wealth transfers from consumers to firms possessing market power. When the productive efficiency of a firm increases (its cost of production is lowered), a firm in a highly competitive industry may pass on some of the savings to consumers in the form of lower prices. However, to the extent that a merger increases market power, there is less likelihood that any productive efficiencies would be passed along to consumers.

To the extent that Congress was concerned with productive efficiency in enacting these laws, it prescribed the prevention of high levels of market concentration as the means to this end.[10] Furthermore, the Supreme Court has clearly ruled that any conflict between the goal of preventing anticompetitive mergers and that of increasing efficiency must be resolved in favor of the former explicit and predominant concern of the Congress.[11]

---

termed an exercise of "monopsony power." When the terms "buyer(s)" or "groups of buyers" are used herein they are deemed to include "seller(s)" or "groups of sellers" adversely affected by the exercise of market or monopsony power.

[10] There is vigorous debate whether firms in industries with high concentration are on average more or less efficient than those in industries with moderate or low levels of concentration.

The theory of "x-inefficiency" predicts that firms constrained by vigorous competition have lower production costs than firms in an industry with little or no competition. Various economists have attempted to quantify production cost increases due to x-inefficiency and the theory is the subject of ongoing debate.

[11] In *FTC v. Procter & Gamble Co.*, 386 U.S. 568, 580 (1967), the Court stated: "Possible economies cannot be used as a defense to illegality. Congress was aware that some mergers which lessen competition may also result in economies but it struck the balance in favor of protecting competition."

> In *United States v. Philadelphia National Bank*, 374 U.S. 321, 371 (1963), the Court stated:
>
> We are clear, however, that a merger the effect of which "may be substantially to lessen competition" is not saved because, on some ultimate reckoning of social or economic debits and credits, it may be deemed beneficial. A value choice of such magnitude is beyond the ordinary limits of judicial competence, and in any event has been made for us already, by Congress when it enacted the amended Section 7. Congress determined to preserve our traditionally competitive economy. It therefore proscribed anticompetitive mergers, the

Although Congress was apparently unaware of allocative efficiency when it enacted section 7 and the other antitrust laws,[12] preserving allocative efficiency is generally considered an additional benefit realized by the prevention of market power, because the act of restricting output has the concomitant effect of raising prices to consumers.[13]

2.1 THE ECONOMIC EFFECTS OF MERGERS

Mergers may have negative or positive competitive consequences. The following is a summary description of the most common competitive effects of mergers relevant to enforcement of section 7.

2.11 ACQUISITION OF MARKET POWER AND WEALTH TRANSFERS

When two firms, neither possessing market power, cease competing and merge, the inevitable consequence is the elimination of the competition between them. More significantly, however, the merged entity may now possess market power, an anticompetitive outcome.

A merger may also increase the concentration level in an industry to a point at which the remaining firms can effectively engage in active collusion or implicitly coordinate their actions and thus collectively exercise market power.

When a firm or firms exercise market power by profitably maintaining prices above competitive levels for a significant period of time, a transfer of wealth from consumers to those firms occurs.[14] This transfer of wealth is the major evil sought to be addressed by section 7.[15]

---

benign and the malignant alike, fully aware, we must assume, that some price might have to be paid.

[12] Perfect "allocative efficiency" or "pareto optimality" is a state of equilibrium on the "utility-possibility frontier" in which no person can be made better off without making someone else worse off. Allocative efficiency can be achieved in an economy with massive inequalities of income and distribution, e.g., one percent of the population can receive ninety-nine percent of the economy's wealth and ninety-nine percent of the population can receive one percent. A massive transfer of wealth from consumers to a monopolist does not of itself decrease allocative efficiency. However, when a monopolist restricts its output, the total wealth of society is diminished, thereby reducing allocative efficiency. Economists term this loss of society's wealth the "deadweight loss." The term of art "consumer welfare," often used when discussing the efficiency effects of mergers and restraints of trade, refers to the concept of allocative efficiency, not the welfare of consumers who purchase the monopolist's product. Consumer welfare is diminished when a monopolist restricts output.

[13] In most mergers creating market power, the dollar magnitude of the wealth transfer from consumers would be greater than the monetary measure of loss in allocative efficiency (dead weight loss). See note 12. It is, moreover, important to understand that a transfer of wealth from consumers to firms with market power can decrease the well-being of consumers without any decrease in so-called "consumer welfare."

[14] Tacit or active collusion on terms of trade other than price also produces wealth transfer effects. This would include, for example, an agreement to eliminate rivalry on service features or to limit the choices otherwise available to consumers.

[15] The predominant concern with wealth transfers was evidenced in the statements of both supporters and opponents of the Celler-Kefauver amendments. *See, e.g.*, 95 Cong. Rec. 11,506 (1949) (remarks of Rep. Bennett); Id . at 11,492 (remarks of Rep. Carroll); Id. at 11,506 (remarks of Rep. Byrne); Hearings before the Subcom. on the Judiciary, 81st Cong., lst and 2d Sess., note 260 at 180 (remarks of Sen. Kilgore); 95 Cong . Rec. 11,493 (1949) (remarks of Rep. Yates); Id. at 11,490–91 (remarks of Rep. Goodwin); 95 Cong. Rec. 16,490 (1949) (colloquy of Sen. Kefauver and Sen. Wiley).

The wealth transfer orientation of section 7 is the same as that of the Sherman Act. The major difference between the two provisions, and reason for the enactment of section 7, is the "incipiency" standard of section 7, which permits antitrust intervention at a point when the anticompetitive consequences of a merger are not manifest but are likely to occur absent intervention. The Celler-Kefauver amendments retained and strengthened the "incipiency" standard by extending the coverage of the law to acquisitions of assets. In section 4 of these guidelines the Attorneys General specifically attempt to give expression to the statutory concern of "incipiency."

2.12 PRODUCTIVE EFFICIENCY

A merger may increase or decrease the costs of the parties to the merger and thus increase or decrease productive efficiency. A merger which increases productive efficiency and does not produce a firm or firms capable of exercising market power should lower prices paid by consumers. An inefficient merger in an unconcentrated industry is generally of no competitive concern. The efficiency effects of mergers are easy to speculate about but hard to accurately predict. There is much disagreement among economists as to whether merged firms usually perform well and whether, on average, mergers have been shown to produce significant efficiencies. However, most efficiencies and those most quantitatively significant will be realized in mergers involving small firms. Such mergers do not raise any concern under the enforcement standards adopted in section 4 of these guidelines. Furthermore, the concentration thresholds adopted in section 4 are usually sufficient to enable firms to obtain the most significant efficiencies likely to result from growth through merger as opposed to growth through internal expansion.[16]

2.13 ALLOCATIVE EFFICIENCY

A merger which facilitates the exercise of market power results in a decrease in allocative efficiency. When firms with market power restrict their output, the total wealth of society diminishes. This effect is universally condemned by economists, and its prevention, while not a concern of the Congress which enacted section 7, is a goal consistent with the purposes of the antitrust laws.

2.14 RAISING RIVALS' COSTS

In certain circumstances, a merger may raise the costs of the competitors of the parties to the merger. For example, a merger could increase the power of a firm to affect the price that rivals must pay for inputs or the conditions under which they must operate, in a manner that creates a relative disadvantage for the rivals. If the market structure is such that these increased costs can be passed on to consumers, then the prevention of this effect is consistent with the goals of the antitrust laws. Preventing such effect will also prevent a decrease in allocative and productive efficiency.

3. MARKET DEFINITION

These guidelines are concerned with horizontal mergers, that is, mergers involving firms that are actual or potential competitors in the same product and geographic markets. The primary analytical tool utilized in the guidelines is the measurement of concentration in a particular market and increase in concentration in that market resulting from a merger. The

---

[16] There may be rare instances where the minimum efficient scale of production and output constitutes a significant percentage of the relevant market.

market shares used to compute these concentration factors will depend upon the market definition adopted.[17] The reasonable delineation of these market boundaries is critical to realizing the objectives of the guidelines and the antitrust laws. If the market boundaries chosen are seriously distorted in relation to the actual workings of the marketplace, an enforcement error is likely.[18] An overly restricted product or geographic market definition may trigger antitrust intervention when the merger would not significantly harm competition or in other circumstances result in the failure to challenge an anticompetitive merger. An overly expansive market definition, on the other hand, may result in the failure to challenge a merger with serious anticompetitive consequences.[19] Markets should be defined from the perspective of those interests section 7 was primarily enacted to protect, *i.e.*, the classes of consumers (or suppliers) who may be adversely affected by an anticompetitive merger. The Attorneys General will utilize historical data to identify these classes of consumers ("the protected interest group"), their sources of supply, suitable substitutes for the product and alternative sources of the product and its substitutes. The market thus defined will be presumed correct unless rebutted by empirical evidence that supply responses within a reasonable period of time will render unprofitable an attempted exercise of market power.[20]

The following sections detail how these general principles will be applied to define product and geographic markets and to calculate the market shares of firms determined to be within the relevant market.

---

[17] For example, consider the proposed merger of two firms producing the same product. Each has a fifty percent share of the sales of this product in a certain state but only one percent of national sales. If the proper geographic market is the state, then the competitive consequences of the merger will be far different than if the geographic market is the entire country.

[18] Governmental challenge of a merger which is not likely to lessen competition substantially is frequently termed "Type I error." The failure to challenge a merger which is likely to lessen competition substantially is termed "Type II error." Type I error can be corrected by the court which determines the validity of the challenge. Type II error will most likely go uncorrected, since the vast majority of merger challenges are mounted by the government. In other areas of antitrust law, private actions predominate and can correct Type II error. Consumers, whose interests were paramount in the enactment of section 7 and section 1 of the Sherman Act, suffer the damage of Type II error.

[19] Consider, for example, the market(s) for flexible wrapping materials. These materials include clear plastic, metallic foils, waxed paper and others. Firms A and B each produce thirty percent of the clear plastic wrap and five percent of all flexible wrapping material in a relevant geographic market. Firm C produces seventy percent of the metallic foil and sixty percent of all flexible wrap. If the proper market definition is all flexible wrapping materials, then treating clear plastic and metallic foils as separate markets may lead to an unwarranted challenge to a merger between firms A and B. The same incorrect market definition may also result in the failure to challenge a merger between Firm C and either Firm A or Firm B because of the incorrect assumption that metallic foil and clear plastic wrap do not compete. However, if the correct market definition is clear plastic wrap but the more expansive market definition of all flexible materials is chosen, this may result in the failure to challenge an anticompetitive merger of firms A and B.

[20] Empirical evidence, as contrasted with expert opinion, speculation, or economic theories, is generally grounded in demonstrable, historical fact. Empirical evidence of a probable supply response would include a factual showing that this response had occurred in the past when prices increased significantly. A mere prediction based on a theoretical possibility that a manufacturer would or could shift his production from one product to another to capitalize on a price increase, when unsupported by evidence of previous similar responses or other factual information of comparable probative weight, is not considered "empirical evidence."

3.1 PRODUCT MARKET DEFINITION

The Attorneys General will determine the customers who purchase the products or services ("products") of the merging firms. Each product produced in common by the merging parties will constitute a provisional product market. However, if a market is incorrectly defined too narrowly, the merger may appear to be not horizontal when there may be a horizontal anticompetitive effect in a broader market.[21] In short, the provisional product market will be expanded to include suitable substitutes for the product which are comparably priced.[22] A comparably priced substitute will be deemed suitable and thereby expand the product market definition if, and only if, considered suitable by customers accounting for seventy-five percent of the purchases.

Actual substitution by customers in the past will presumptively establish that a product is considered a suitable substitute for the provisionally defined product. However, other evidence offered by the parties probative of the assertion that customers deem a product to be a suitable substitute will also be considered.[23]

3.11 CONSUMERS WHO MAY BE VULNERABLE TO PRICE DISCRIMINATION

Notwithstanding the determination in Section 3.1 that a product is a suitable substitute for the provisional product pursuant to application of the seventy-five percent rule, there may be small, but significant, groups of consumers who cannot substitute or can do so only with great difficulty. These consumers may be subject to price discrimination and thus may be particularly adversely affected by a merger. In addition, some markets may contain differentiated products which are not perfect substitutes for one another but are not sufficiently differentiated to warrant separate markets. If the products of the merging firms are closer substitutes, *i.e.*, the more the buyers of one product consider the other product to be their next choice, the consumers of these products may be more subject to an exercise of market power. Similarly, the existence of distinct prices, unique production facilities, a product's peculiar characteristics and uses, distinct customers,

---

[21] For example, suppose there are two beer producers and two malt liquor producers and the merger involves the acquisition of one of the malt liquor firms by one of the beer producers. If the relevant market is defined as "beer," the merger would not be horizontal. The provisional market should be defined as "beverages containing X percent alcohol."

[22] The existence of a functionally suitable substitute which is significantly more expensive than the relevant product will not discipline an exercise of market power until the price of the relevant product has been raised to a level comparable to the substitute. The Attorneys General will also seek to ascertain whether current price comparability of two products resulted from an exercise of market power. For example, suppose that the provisionally defined product recently cost twenty percent less than a possible substitute, but its price has recently risen twenty percent as a result of the exercise of market power. Rather than serving as a basis for broadening the product market to include the possible substitute, this finding will provide compelling evidence that any further concentration through merger will only exacerbate the market power which already exists. To ascertain whether the price comparability of two possibly interchangeable products was the result of an exercise of market power over one product, the appropriate question to ask may be "what would happen if the price of the product in question dropped?" If a significant price decrease does not substantially increase sales, then a previous exercise of market power has likely been detected, and the two products should probably be considered to be in separate product markets. *See United States v. E.I. duPont de Nemours & Co.*, 351 U.S. 377, 399–400 (1956).

[23] Recycled or reconditioned goods will be considered suitable substitutes if they meet the requirements of this section.

and specialized vendors may support the definition of narrower product markets.[24]

Evidence of the commercial reality of such a market includes price discrimination, inelasticity of demand and industry or public recognition of a distinct market.

3.2 GEOGRAPHIC MARKET DEFINITION

Utilizing the product market(s) defined in Section 3.1, the Attorneys General will define the relevant geographic market. First, the Attorneys General will determine the sources and locations where the customers of the merging parties readily turn for their supply of the relevant product. These will include the merging parties and other sources of supply. To this group of suppliers and their locations will be added suppliers or buyers closely proximate to the customers of the merging parties. In determining those suppliers to whom the protected interest group readily turn for supply of the relevant product, the Attorneys General will include all sources of supply within the past two years still present in the market.

Utilizing the locations from which supplies of the relevant product are obtained by members of the protected interest group, the geographic market will be defined as the area encompassing the production locations from which this group purchases seventy-five percent of their supplies of the relevant product.

The product and geographic markets as defined above will be utilized in calculating market shares and concentration levels unless additional sources of supply are recognized by application of the procedures specified in Section 3.3.

3.21 GEOGRAPHIC MARKETS SUBJECT TO PRICE DISCRIMINATION

The Attorneys General may define additional narrower geographic markets when there is strong evidence that sellers are able to discriminate among buyers in separate locations within the geographic market(s) defined in Section 3.2. The Attorneys General will evaluate evidence concerning discrimination on price, terms of credit and delivery, and priority of shipment.[25]

3.3 PRINCIPLES FOR RECOGNIZING POTENTIAL COMPETITION

Where there is relevant empirical evidence of profitable supply and demand responses which will be likely to occur within one year of any attempted exercise of market power, the Attorneys General will calculate market shares and concentration levels, incorporating both sources of potential supply and the firms identified as being in the market defined by the procedures outlined in Sections 3.1 and 3.11.

The Attorneys General will evaluate empirical evidence of the following sources of potential competition:

1) That current suppliers of the product will produce additional supplies for the relevant market by utilizing excess capacity;

---

[24] *See Brown Shoe Co. v. United States*, 370 U.S. 294, 325 (1962).

[25] The Attorneys General welcome submissions by buyers concerning such discrimination or any other non-speculative evidence that a proposed merger will adversely affect them.

2) That new sources of the product will be readily available from firms outside the geographic market with excess capacity.

3.31 EXPANSION OF OUTPUT

The Attorneys General will identify current suppliers of the product that will expand their output by utilization of excess capacity within one year of any attempted exercise of market power. Proof of probable utilization of excess capacity addresses the issues of: (i) The cost of bringing the excess capacity on line; (ii) the amount of excess capacity; (iii) prior history of supplying this market or present intention to do so; and (iv) how much prices would have to rise to likely induce this supply response.

3.32 NEW SOURCES OF ADDITIONAL SUPPLY

The Attorneys General will identify firms not currently supplying the product in the geographic market but which will expand their output by utilization of excess capacity within one year of any attempted exercise of market power. Proof of probable utilization of excess capacity addresses the issues of: (i) The cost of bringing the excess capacity on line; (ii) the amount of excess capacity; (iii) prior history of supplying this market or present intention to do so; and (iv) how much prices would have to rise to likely induce this supply response.

3.4 CALCULATING MARKET SHARES

Using the product and geographic markets defined in Sections 3.1 and 3.2, the firms supplying the market and any additional sources of supply recognized under Section 3.3, the shares of all firms determined to be in the market will be calculated.[26]

The market shares of firms presently supplying the market shall be based upon actual data from the relevant market. If there has been a demonstration of a probable supply response as defined in Section 3.3, the market shares of firms already selling in the market will be adjusted to account for the proven probable supply response. Similarly, market shares will be assigned to firms not currently supplying the market who have been shown to be likely to expand output to provide additional sources of supply as discussed in Sections 3.32 and 3.33. The assigned market shares of such firms will be based upon the amount of the product these firms would supply. The Attorneys General will utilize dollar sales, unit sales, capacity measures or other appropriate sales measurements to quantify actual market activity.

3.41 FOREIGN FIRMS

Foreign firms presently supplying the relevant market will be assigned market shares in the same manner as domestic firms, according to their actual current sales in the relevant market. Foreign firms and their productive capacity are inherently a less reliable check on market power by domestic firms because foreign firms face a variety of barriers to continuing sales or increasing their sales. These barriers include import quotas, voluntary quantitative restrictions, tariffs and fluctuations in exchange

---

[26] In some situations, market share and market concentration data may either understate or overstate the likely future competitive significance of a firm or firms in the market or the impact of a merger. The Attorneys General will consider empirical evidence of recent or ongoing changes in market conditions or in a particular firm and may make appropriate adjustments to the market concentration and market share data. *See United States v. General Dynamics Corp.*, 415 U.S. 486 (1974).

rates. When such barriers exist, market share based upon historical sales data will be reduced appropriately.

A single market share will be assigned to the firms of any foreign country or group of countries which in fact coordinate their sales.[27]

3A ALTERNATIVE METHOD FOR DEFINING MARKETS UTILIZING THE METHODOLOGY OF THE UNITED STATES DEPARTMENT OF JUSTICE/FEDERAL TRADE COMMISSION MERGER GUIDELINES

Any party presenting a position concerning the likely competitive consequences of a merger to one or more Attorneys General may present its position and analysis using the market definition principles and methodology set forth in the Merger Guidelines of the United States Department of Justice and the Federal Trade Commission, released on April 2, 1992 (DOJ/FTC Guidelines), 62 Antitrust & Trade Reg.Rep. Special Supp. (April 2, 1992). This method will only be considered where, in the opinion of the state Attorney General, sufficient evidence is available to implement the methodology workably and without speculation. In most situations, both the NAAG and DOJ/FTC market definition methodologies will produce the same result. In the event that the two tests produce different results, the Attorneys General will rely on the test that appears most accurately to reflect the market and is based on the most reliable evidence.

There are two purposes for permitting such alternative method for defining markets. First, many of the mergers which the Attorneys General may analyze using these guidelines will also be subject to scrutiny by either the Antitrust Division of the United States Department of Justice or the Federal Trade Commission. Parties may desire to present positions concerning the likely competitive consequences of a particular transaction to both federal and state antitrust enforcement agencies. Such parties will benefit from the ability to utilize a single market definition methodology in presenting their position concerning a particular transaction. Second, the Attorneys General seek to facilitate the joint or coordinated analysis of mergers by state and federal enforcement agencies.

Consistent with these principles, the Attorneys General may utilize the market definition methodology set forth in the DOJ/FTC Guidelines as an additional or alternative method in analyzing the competitive consequences of particular transactions.

4. MEASUREMENT OF CONCENTRATION

The primary tool utilized by the Attorneys General to determine whether a specific horizontal merger is likely to substantially harm competition is a measurement of the level of concentration in each market defined in Section 3 or 3A. Concentration is a measurement of the number of firms in a market and their market shares. The guidelines employ the Herfindahl-Hirschman Index ("HHI") to calculate the level of concentration in an industry before and after a merger and, therefore, the increase in concentration which would result from the merger.[28]

---

[27] For example, an import quota may be established for a particular foreign country and the foreign government may then apportion the quota among firms engaged in the import of the relevant product.

[28] The HHI is computed by summing the numerical squares of the market shares of all the firms in the market. For example, a market with four firms each having a market

Unlike the traditional four firm concentration ratio ("CR4") which was formerly used by enforcement agencies and courts to measure market concentration,[29] the HHI reflects both the distribution of the market shares of all the leading firms in the market and the composition of the market beyond the leading firms.[30]

The predominant concern of the Congress in enacting section 7 was the prevention of high levels of industrial concentration because it believed that such structure was likely to produce anticompetitive consequences. Foremost among these expected anticompetitive effects of high concentration is the exercise of market power by one or more firms. The HHI levels which trigger presumptions that mergers are likely to create or enhance market power should be set at the concentration levels likely to predict a substantial lessening of competition.[31]

Furthermore, an important component of the scholarly economic inquiry into the competitive consequences of mergers has been the correlation of concentration levels with various indicia of competition. Other theories which predict the competitive effects of mergers based upon factors other than market concentration are valuable adjuncts to market concentration analysis. The most important of the supplemental inquiries concerns "ease of entry" into the markets affected by the merger.[32]

The Attorneys General divide the spectrum of market concentration into the same three numerical regions utilized by the United States Department of Justice. They are characterized in these guidelines as "unconcentrated" (HHI below 1000) "moderately concentrated" (HHI between 1000 and 1800) and "highly concentrated" (HHI above 1800).[33]

4.1 GENERAL STANDARDS

The Attorneys General will calculate the post-merger concentration level in the market and the increase in concentration caused by the merger.

---

share of 25% has an HHI of 2500 calculated as follows: $25^2 + 25^2 + 25^2 + 25^2 = 2500$. A market with a pure monopolist, *i.e.*, a firm with 100 percent of the market has an HHI of 10,000 calculated as $100^2 = 10{,}000$. If the market has four firms, each having a market share of twenty-five percent and two of these four firms merge, the increase in the HHI is computed as follows: Pre-merger $25^2 + 25^2 + 25^2 + 25^2 = 2500$. Post-merger $50^2 + 25^2 + 25^2 = 3750$. The increase in the HHI due to the merger is 1250, *i.e.*, $3750 - 2500 = 1250$. The increase is also equivalent to twice the product of the market shares of the merging firms, *i.e.*, $25 \times 25 \times 2 = 1250$.

[29] The CR4 is the sum of the market shares of the top four firms in the market. A CR4 cannot be converted into any single HHI but rather includes a possible range of HHI levels. For example, consider two markets with CR4 of 100 percent. The first is comprised of four firms; each with a market share of twenty-five percent. This yields an HHI of 2500, *i.e.*, $25^2 + 25^2 + 25^2 + 25^2 = 2500$. The second market is comprised of four firms with market shares of 70%, 10%, 10% and 10%. This yields an HHI of 5200, *i.e.*, $70^2 + 10^2 + 10^2 + 10^2 = 5200$.

[30] The HHI also gives significantly greater weight to the market shares of the largest firms, which properly reflects the leading roles which such firms are likely to play in a collusive agreement or other exercise of market power. A single dominant firm's likely role as the price leader in an oligopolistic market is also reflected in the HHI. For these reasons, the HHI is now the generally preferred measure of concentration.

[31] Other characteristics of the particular industry, such as barriers to entry, may indicate that concentration measures either overstate or understate the competitive significance of the merger.

[32] *See* Section 5.1.

[33] Mergers resulting in a post-merger HHI of less than 1,000 do not create a presumption that the merger will have significant anticompetitive impact.

While it may be justifiable to challenge any merger above the threshold of market concentration where successful tacit or express collusion and interdependent behavior are significantly facilitated (HHI 1000) the Attorneys General are unlikely to challenge mergers which do not significantly increase concentration. This policy recognizes section 7's prohibition of mergers whose effect "may be substantially to lessen competition." When the threshold of very high concentration is exceeded (HHI 1800), the likelihood of anticompetitive effects are greatly increased and the increase in concentration likely to substantially lessen competition concomitantly reduced. The concentration increases which trigger presumptions that mergers are likely to create or enhance market power have been adopted in reasonable accommodation of both the "substantiality" requirement of section 7 and the need objectively to factor in the dynamic conditions in an industry.[34]

4.2 POST-MERGER HHI BETWEEN 1000 AND 1800

A merger that increases the HHI by more than 100 to a level in excess of 1,000 creates a presumption that the merger will result in significant anticompetitive effects. This presumption may be overcome if the merging parties are able to demonstrate, upon consideration of all of the other factors contained in these guidelines, that the merger is not likely to significantly lessen competition. The greater the HHI increase and level, the less likely that these factors will overcome this presumption.

4.3 POST-MERGER HHI ABOVE 1800

A merger that increases the HHI by more than fifty to a level in excess of 1,800 creates a presumption that the merger will result in significant anticompetitive effects. This presumption may be overcome if the merging parties are able to demonstrate, upon consideration of all of the other factors contained in these guidelines, that the merger is not likely significantly to lessen competition. The greater the HHI increase and level, the less likely that these factors will overcome this presumption.[35]

4.4 MERGERS INVOLVING THE LEADING FIRM OR A NEW, INNOVATIVE FIRM IN A MARKET

The merger of a dominant firm with a small firm in the market may create or increase the market power of the dominant firm yet increase the HHI by an amount less than the levels set forth in Sections 4.2 and 4.3. Similarly, the merger of a new, innovative firm with an existing significant competitor in the market may substantially reduce competition yet increase the HHI by an amount less than the levels set forth in Sections 4.2 and 4.3. Therefore, mergers presumptively create or enhance market power if the proposed merger involves either a leading firm with a market share of at least thirty-five percent and a firm with a market share of one percent or more, or a firm with a market share of twenty percent or more and a new, innovative firm in a market or attempting to enter a market that is

[34] The decision whether or not to bring suit is ultimately within the sole discretion of each Attorney General. In addition to the economic impact of a merger on a state, Attorneys General may consider numerous other factors in deciding whether to challenge a merger that raises competitive concerns. For example, Attorneys General are more likely to be concerned about mergers in industries exhibiting a significant trend towards concentration. The existence of an in-depth examination of the merger by other antitrust enforcement agencies may be relevant to the action of an Attorney General with respect to a merger that otherwise raises competitive concerns.

[35] For example, this presumption will be rarely overcome if the increase exceeds 200 and the resulting HHI level exceeds 2,500.

moderately or highly concentrated, unless assessment of the factors discussed in Sections 5.1 and/or 5.3 clearly compels the conclusion that the merger is not likely substantially to lessen competition.

5. ADDITIONAL FACTORS THAT MAY BE CONSIDERED IN DETERMINING WHETHER TO CHALLENGE A MERGER

There are additional factors aside from market share and market concentration that may make a merger more or less likely substantially to lessen competition. While the assessment of these factors would increase the flexibility of these guidelines, overemphasis on these other factors, given the current state of economic knowledge, would significantly vitiate the predictability and the consistency of enforcement under the guidelines and would greatly reduce their value as a planning and risk assessment tool for the business community.

The present state of economic theory, especially where there is an absence of supporting empirical work, is generally insufficient to overcome the usual presumption that increases in market concentration will increase the likelihood and degree to which industry performance is adversely affected. Increased concentration may allow the industry's constituent firms to coordinate pricing in a variety of ways, to neutralize the potential benefits of increased efficiency through output reduction and to forestall entry.

For example, many theories have been offered regarding the extent to which a particular factor may tend to increase or decrease the likelihood of collusion. In an actual merger analysis, however, a relevant market is likely to be characterized by several of these factors pointing in opposite directions, and economics offers little guidance on how the individual factors should be judged in combination. Even the significance of isolated factors remains in doubt. Many states have discovered bid-rigging among highway contractors, for example, when the characteristics of the industry might lead some to predict theoretically that collusion would be extremely difficult, if not impossible.

Because of this, the merging parties will bear a heavy burden of showing that the normal presumption of anticompetitive effect should not be applied in a particular case. This heavy burden will increase further with higher levels of concentration and increases in concentration, particularly to the extent the post-merger HHI would be greater than 1800 and the increase in HHI greater than 50.

While maintaining primary reliance on the concentration and market share analysis discussed in Section 4, the Attorneys General will, in appropriate circumstances, assess four additional factors. These are ease of entry, collusive behavior, powerful or sophisticated buyers and efficiencies.

5.1 EASE OF ENTRY

5.11 OVERVIEW

A merger is not likely to create or enhance market power or to facilitate its exercise if entry into the market is so easy that market participants, after the merger, either collectively or unilaterally could not profitably maintain a price increase above premerger levels. Such entry likely will deter an anticompetitive merger in its incipiency, or deter or counteract the competitive effects of concern.

Entry is that easy if entry would be timely, likely and sufficient in its magnitude, character and scope to deter or counteract the competitive effects of concern. In markets where entry is that easy (*i.e.*, where entry passes these tests of timeliness, likelihood, and sufficiency), the merger raises no antitrust concern and ordinary requires no further analysis.

The entry treated in this section is defined as new competition that requires expenditure of significant sunk costs of entry and exit ("committed entry"). The Attorneys General will employ a three-step methodology to assess whether committed entry would deter or counteract a competitive effect of concern.

This first step assesses whether entry can achieve significant market impact within a timely period. If significant market impact would require a longer period, entry will not deter or counteract the competitive effect of concern.

The second step assesses whether committed entry would be a profitable and, hence, a likely response to a merger having competitive effects of concern. Firms considering entry that requires significant sunk costs must evaluate that profitability of the entry on the basis of long-term participation in the market, because the underlying assets will be committed to the market until they are economically depreciated. Entry that is sufficient to counteract the competitive effects of concern will cause prices to fall to their premerger levels or lower. Thus, the profitability of such committed entry must be determined on the basis of pre-merger market prices over the long term.

A merger having anticompetitive effects can attract committed entry, profitable at premerger prices, that would not have occurred premerger at these same prices. But following the merger, the reduction in industry output and increase in prices associated with the competitive effect of concern may allow the same entry to occur without driving market prices below premerger levels. After a merger that results in decreased output and increased prices, the likely sales opportunities available to entrants at premerger prices will be larger than they were premerger, larger by the output reduction caused by the merger. If entry could be profitable at premerger prices without exceeding the likely sales opportunities—opportunities that include pre-existing pertinent factors as well as the merger-induced output reduction—then such entry is likely in response to the merger.

The third step assesses whether timely and likely entry would be sufficient to return market prices to their premerger levels. This end may be accomplished either through multiple entry or individual entry at a sufficient scale. Entry may not be sufficient, even though timely and likely, where the constraints on availability of essential assets, due to incumbent control, make it impossible for entry profitably to achieve the necessary level of sales. Also, the character and scope of entrants' products might not be fully responsive to the localized sales opportunities created by the removal of direct competition among sellers of differentiated products. In assessing whether entry will be timely, likely, and sufficient, the Attorneys General recognize that precise and detailed information may be difficult or impossible to obtain. In such instances, the Attorneys General will rely on all available evidence bearing on whether entry will satisfy the conditions of timeliness, likelihood, and sufficiency.

5.12 TIMELINESS OF ENTRY

In order to deter or counteract the competitive effects of concern, entrants quickly must achieve a significant impact on price in the relevant market.

The Attorneys General generally will consider timely only those committed entry alternatives that can be achieved within two years from initial planning to significant market impact.[36] Where the relevant product is a durable good, consumers, in response to a significant commitment to entry, may defer purchases by making additional investments to extend the useful life of previously purchased goods and in this way deter or counteract for a time the competitive effects of concern. In these circumstances, if entry only can occur outside of the two year period, the Attorneys General will consider entry to be timely so long as it would deter or counteract the competitive effects of concern within the two year period and subsequently.

5.13 LIKELIHOOD OF ENTRY

An entry alternative is likely if it would be profitable at premerger prices, and if such prices could be secured by the entrant.[37] The committed entrant will be unable to secure prices at premerger levels if its output is too large for the market to absorb without depressing prices further. Thus, entry is unlikely if the minimum viable scale is larger than the likely sales opportunity available to entrants.

Minimum viable scale is the smallest average annual level of sales that the committed entrant must persistently achieve for profitability at premerger prices.[38] Minimum viable scale is a function of expected revenues, based upon premerger prices,[39] and all categories of costs associated with the entry alternative, including an appropriate rate of return on invested capital given that entry could fail and sunk costs, if any, will be lost.[40]

Sources of sales opportunities available to entrants include: (a) The output reduction associated with the competitive effect of concern;[41] (b) entrants' ability to capture a share of reasonably expected growth in market demand;[42] (c) entrants' ability securely to divert sales from incumbents, for example, through vertical integration or through forward contracting; and (d) any additional anticipated contraction in incumbents' output in response to entry.[43] Factors that reduce the sales opportunities available to entrants

---

[36] Firms which have committed to entering the market prior to the merger generally will be included in the measurement of the market. Only committed entry or adjustments to pre-existing entry plans that are induced by the merger will be considered as possibly deterring or counteracting the competitive effects of concern.

[37] Where conditions indicate that entry may be profitable at prices below premerger levels, the Attorneys General will assess the likelihood of entry at the lowest price at which such entry would be profitable.

[38] The concept of minimum viable scale ("MVS") differs from the concept of minimum efficient scale ("MES"). While MES is the smallest scale at which average costs are minimized, MVS is the smallest scale at which average costs equal the premerger price.

[39] The expected path of future prices, absent the merger, may be used if future price changes can be predicted with reasonable reliability.

[40] The minimum viable scale of an entry alternative will be relatively large when the fixed costs of entry are large, when the fixed costs of entry are largely sunk, when the marginal costs of production are high at low levels of output, and when a plant is underutilized for a long time because of delays in achieving market acceptance.

[41] Five percent of total market sales typically is used because where a monopolist profitability would raise price by five percent or more across the entire relevant market, it is likely that the accompanying reduction in sales would be no less than five percent.

[42] Entrant's anticipated share of growth in demand depends on incumbents' capacity constraints and irreversible investments in capacity expansion, as well as on the relative appeal, acceptability and reputation of incumbents' and entrants' products to the new demand.

[43] For example, in a bidding market where all bidders are on equal footing, the market share of incumbents will contract as a result of entry.

include: (a) The prospect that an entrant will share in a reasonably expected decline in market demand; (b) the exclusion of an entrant from a portion of the market over the long term because of vertical integration or forward contracting by incumbents; and (c) any anticipated strategic reaction, including but not limited to, sales expansion by incumbents in reaction to entry, either generalized or targeted at customers approached by the entrant, that utilized prior irreversible investments in excess production capacity. Demand growth or decline will be viewed as relevant only if total market demand is projected to experience long-lasting change during at least the two year period following the competitive effect of concern.

5.14 SUFFICIENCY OF ENTRY

Inasmuch as multiple entry generally is possible and individual entrants may flexibly choose their scale, committed entry generally will be sufficient to deter or counteract the competitive effects of concern whenever entry is likely under the analysis of Section 5.1. However, entry, although likely, will not be sufficient if, as a result of incumbent control, the tangible and intangible assets required for entry are not adequately available for entrants to respond fully to their sales opportunities. In addition, where the competitive effect of concern is not uniform across the relevant market, in order for entry to be sufficient, the character and scope of entrants' products must be responsive to the localized sales opportunities that include the output reduction associated with the competitive effect of concern. For example, where the concern is unilateral price elevation as a result of a merger between producers of differentiated products, entry, in order to be sufficient, must involve a product so close to the products of the merging firms that the merged firm will be unable to internalize enough of the sales loss due to the price rise, rendering the price increase unprofitable.

5.15 ENTRY ALTERNATIVES

The Attorneys General will examine the timeliness, likelihood, and sufficiency of the means of entry (entry alternatives) a potential entrant might practically employ, without attempting to identify who might be potential entrants. An entry alternative is defined by the actions the firm must take in order to produce and sell in the market. All phases of the entry effort will be considered, including, where relevant, planning, design, and management; permitting, licensing, and other approvals, construction, debugging, and operation of production facilities; and promotion (including necessary introductory discounts), marketing, distribution and satisfaction of customer testing and qualification requirements.[44] Recent examples of entry, whether successful or unsuccessful, may provide a useful starting point for identifying the necessary actions, time requirements, and characteristics of possible entry alternatives. Entry may be by diversion of existing supplies into the market or by new production sources of supply. The Attorneys General will evaluate empirical evidence of the following sources of entry.

5.15A DIVERSION OF EXISTING SUPPLIES INTO THE MARKET

The parties to a merger may produce evidence that firms will divert supplies of the product into the market in response to a price increase or restriction of output. The Attorneys General will analyze proof concerning such probable diversions of supplies currently exported from the relevant market, supplies internally consumed by vertically integrated firms in the

[44] Many of these phases may be undertaken simultaneously.

market and additional supplies from firms currently shipping part of their production into the market.

5.15A(1) EXPORTS

A firm currently exporting the product from the relevant market may divert the supply back into the market in response to a price increase or restriction of output.

This response is unlikely from an exporter who is a party to the merger, since it is unlikely to discipline its own attempted exercise of market power. It is also unlikely if the exporter is an oligopolist likely to benefit from the collective exercise of market power.

Although parties wishing to prove this supply response are free to produce any empirical evidence, the most persuasive proof will be historical shipping patterns showing past diversion of exports in response to price increases or restricted supply. In addition, the parties should, at a minimum, address the following questions: Are the exports contractually committed and for what term? Are the exports otherwise obligated to current buyers?

5.15A(2) INTERNAL CONSUMPTION

A vertically integrated firm producing the product for internal consumption may divert this supply to the open market. Diversion is unlikely if there are no suitable and economical substitutes for the product and/or the firm has contractual or other obligations for the goods utilizing the relevant product. The most persuasive proof of such diversion will be evidence that a vertically integrated firm already sells some of the product on the open market and has a history of transferring production intended for internal consumption to the open market.

5.15A(3) INCREASED IMPORTATION

A firm shipping part of its output of the product into the relevant market may respond to an attempted exercise of market power by diverting additional production into the relevant market. In order to address the impact of such a response, the parties should, at a minimum, address the factual issues of whether and for what terms these additional supplies are contractually or otherwise obligated to buyers outside the relevant market, the percentage of the suppliers' production now sent into the market and their historical shipping patterns.

5.15B NEW PRODUCTION SOURCES OF ADDITIONAL SUPPLY

The parties to a merger may produce evidence that firms not currently supplying the product will do so within two years of any attempted exercise of market power. This might be shown for firms with production flexibility, firms who will erect new production facilities and firms engaging in arbitrage.

5.15B(1) PRODUCTION FLEXIBILITY

The Attorneys General will evaluate proof concerning firms with flexible production facilities that are capable of switching to the production of the relevant product within two years and are likely to do so. A history of such switching in the past will be the most persuasive evidence that this response is probable.

5.15B(2) CONSTRUCTION OF NEW FACILITIES

A party may attempt to demonstrate that firms not presently supplying the product will erect new plant facilities (or establish new service facilities) within two years of an attempted exercise of market power.

5.15B(3) ARBITRAGE

Firms proximate to the relevant market may respond to an exercise of market power by buying the product outside the market and reselling it inside the market. This potential source of supply is unlikely if the relevant product is a service or combined product and service. A history of arbitrage in the industry will be most probative that this potential response is probable.

5.2 COLLUSION AND OLIGOPOLISTIC BEHAVIOR

If there is evidence of past collusion or anticompetitive behavior,[45] the presumptions set forth in Section 4 will rarely be overcome and a proposed merger falling below the numerical thresholds set forth in Section 4 may also be examined more closely where such evidence is present. In the face of indications that collusion or oligopolistic behavior is likely to be presently occurring, the Attorneys General will not consider other factors offered for the purpose of showing that the presumptions in Section 4 are overcome.

The absence of current or past collusion or oligopolistic behavior will not diminish the presumptions set forth in Section 4.

5.3 EFFICIENCIES

To the extent that efficiency was a concern of the Congress in enacting section 7, that concern was expressed in the legislative finding that less industrial concentration would further that goal.[46] The Attorneys General find that there is no substantial empirical support for the assertion that mergers involving firms of sufficient size to raise concerns under the standards set forth in Section 4, usually or on average result in substantial efficiencies. Furthermore, the concentration thresholds adopted in Section 4 are generally high enough to enable firms to obtain the most significant efficiencies likely to result from growth through merger.

Even in those rare situations where significant efficiencies can be demonstrated, rather than merely predicted, this showing cannot constitute a defense to an otherwise unlawful merger.[47] Accordingly, efficiencies will only be considered when the merging parties can demonstrate by clear and convincing evidence that the merger will lead to significant efficiencies. Moreover, the merging parties must demonstrate that the efficiencies will ensure that consumer prices will not increase despite any increase in market power due to the merger. In highly concentrated markets, even a merger which produces efficiencies will tend to create or enhance market

---

[45] An oligopolistic market will usually be moderately to highly concentrated or very highly concentrated and will exhibit one or more of the following practices: (1) Price leadership; (2) preannounced price changes; (3) relative price rigidity in response to excess capacity or diminished demand; (4) public pronouncements regarding price; and (5) price discrimination.

[46] For example, *see* 95 Cong. Rec. 11,487 (1949) (statement of Rep. Celler, co-author of legislation). "Bigness does not mean efficiency, a better product, or lower prices." 95 Cong. Rec. 11,495–98 (1949) (statement of Rep. Boggs); Corporate Mergers and Acquisitions: Hearings on H.R. 2734 before a Subcomm. of the Senate Comm. on the Judiciary, 81st Cong. lst & 2nd Sess. 206, 308 (1950) (statement of James L. Donnelly).

[47] *See* Note 11.

power and will likely increase consumer prices. In addition, the Attorneys General will reject claims of efficiencies unless the merging parties can demonstrate that equivalent or comparable savings can not be achieved through other means and that such cost savings will persist over the long run.[48]

5.4 POWERFUL OR SOPHISTICATED BUYERS

Tacit or express collusion can be frustrated by the presence of powerful and sophisticated buyers if these are appropriately situated to force firms in the primary market to negotiate secretly or offer substantial concessions for large purchasers. In most circumstances, however, the Attorneys General find that the presence of powerful or sophisticated buyers is unlikely to prevent anticompetitive effects from occurring.[49] Thus, the presence of powerful or sophisticated buyers will only be considered when the buyers are uniquely positioned to enter the primary market in response to collusive pricing, or to finance or otherwise facilitate the entry of others.

6. FAILING FIRM DEFENSE

The failing firm doctrine, which has been recognized by the United States Supreme Court, may be a defense to an otherwise unlawful merger.[50] Because it may allow anticompetitive mergers, the defense will be strictly construed.

The Attorneys General will only consider a failing firm defense to an anticompetitive merger where the proponents of the merger satisfy their burden of showing the following three elements: (1) That the resources of the allegedly failing firm are so depleted and the prospect of rehabilitation is so remote that the firm faces a high probability of a business failure; [51](2) that it had made reasonable good faith efforts and had failed to find another reasonable prospective purchaser; and (3) that there is no less anticompetitive alternative available.[52]

---

[48] Example: In an industry with a one percent profit margin, proven cost savings of three percent would be significant. If a merger which produces cost savings of the magnitude specified does not simultaneously facilitate the exercise of market power, these savings should reduce consumer prices, an effect consistent with the purposes of section 7. However, if the merger simultaneously produces these efficiencies and creates or enhances market power, there is less likelihood that consumer prices will be reduced. In such circumstances consumer prices likely will rise as a result of the exercise of market power.

[49] For example, if some but not all of the buyers in a market are powerful and sophisticated, the former may be able to achieve price concessions while the less powerful buyers will not. In that case the merger should be evaluated by its impact on the less powerful buyers. Similarly, powerful buyers may often find it more profitable to preserve the monopoly in the primary market and share in its profits than to force competition there. This is most likely when both buyer and seller market levels are highly concentrated and each side has significant power to force the other side to behave competitively. In that case forbearance on both sides, which results in preservation of the monopoly and sharing of its profits, is a more profitable result than aggressive behavior that will eliminate monopoly profits at both levels.

[50] *U.S. v. General Dynamics Corp.*, 415 U.S. 486, 507 (1974); *U.S. v. Greater Buffalo Press, Inc.*, 402 U.S. 549, 555 (1971).

[51] Evidence showing that the putative failing firm would not be able to reorganize successfully under Chapter 11 of the Bankruptcy Act, 11 U.S.C. Section 1101–1174 (1988), would be highly relevant.

[52] The Attorneys General may exercise their prosecutorial discretion by declining to challenge a merger which will sustain a failing division of an otherwise viable firm. Since the failing division claim is highly susceptible to manipulation and abuse, the Attorneys General will require the three elements of the "failing firm" defense to be proven by clear and convincing evidence.

13

NATIONAL ASSOCIATION OF ATTORNEYS GENERAL VOLUNTARY PRE-MERGER DISCLOSURE COMPACT

Last Updated: March 1994

The undersigned state and territorial Attorneys General who are empowered under federal and/or state antitrust law to enjoin corporate mergers and acquisitions which are likely substantially to lessen competition or tend to create a monopoly in any line of commerce in any section of the country hereby institute the "NAAG Voluntary Pre-Merger Disclosure Compact" (The Compact") which shall be governed according to the following rules and principles:

First, that the Attorney General members of The Compact agree that it is in the interests of the business community, the general welfare and economy and citizens of their states and the harmonious and orderly administration of state and federal antitrust law that state and federal government officials invested with authority to enforce the antitrust laws as they related to mergers and acquisitions ("mergers") analyze the same factual information when determining whether a merger is anticompetitive, and further that such information is now disclosed to the federal antitrust enforcement agencies pursuant to certain provisions of the Hart-Scott-Rodino Antitrust Improvements Act of 1976 codified in Section 7A of the Clayton Act, 15 U.S.C. Section 18a ("H.S.R. filing"), and implemented in Subchapter H of Title 16 of the Code of Federal Regulations, 16 C.F.R. Section 800 *et seq.*;

Second, that the parties to any proposed merger subject to the filing requirements of 15 U.S.C. § 18a may voluntarily file a photocopy of the first filing with the "liaison state" member of The Compact, as defined in the Third Proviso herein, simultaneous with the filing of the original with the federal enforcement agency. The liaison state shall thereafter forthwith notify all signatories of The Compact of the filing and identity of the merging parties;

Third, the "liaison state" upon whom the voluntary filing specified in the Second Proviso herein shall be made, shall be a member of The Compact determined in the following order of preference: First the Attorney General of the state which is the principal place of business of the acquiring party to the merger, next to the Attorney General of the state which is the principal place of business of the acquired party,[1] next to the Attorney General of the state of incorporation of the acquired party. If no member of The Compact falls within the foregoing four preferences, the parties may make the voluntary filing upon any member of The Compact, who shall act as the liaison state for such transaction;

[1] Acquiring and acquired party are defined in subchapter H of Title 16 of the Code of Federal Regulations for use by the parties to the merger in preparing the H.S.R. filing. Therefore, the parties will already have determined the identity of the acquiring and acquired firms.

Fourth, the parties to The Compact agree to serve no other or further investigative subpoenae, Civil Investigative Demands or other compulsory pre-complaint demands for disclosure upon the merging party that makes the voluntary filing specified in the Second Proviso during the pendency of the Hart-Scott-Rodino waiting period, (including any extension of the waiting period as permitted under the statute), provided, however, that the merging parties shall additionally and contemporaneously file with the liaison state a single photocopy of any other materials that may be supplied to the federal agencies in connection with their review of the transaction, including without limitation, any "second" and subsequent requests for additional material requested by the federal enforcement agencies under the provisions of 15 U.S.C. § 18a(e) and, provided further, however, that nothing contained herein shall preclude the parties to The Compact from serving investigative subpoenae, Civil Investigative Demands or compulsory pre-complaint demands for disclosure upon the merging parties for any additional material which any party to The Compact has requested be voluntarily supplied by any such merging party during such waiting period or any extension(s) thereof and which such merging party has refused to provide within a time period that is reasonable under the circumstances;

Fifth, that The Compact shall apply to "hostile" transactions, but only to those parties to the hostile transaction that make the voluntary filings specified in the Second and Fourth Provisos, herein;

Sixth, that The Compact shall not preclude any member of The Compact from serving investigative subpoenae, Civil Investigative Demands or other pre-complaint demands for disclosure, at any time, upon any person that does not make the voluntary filing specified in the Second Proviso;

Seventh, that a party, by making the voluntary filings specified in the Second and Fourth Provisos herein, agrees and consents to allow the members of the Compact to have access to such filings in the hands of the federal antitrust enforcement agencies and will, at the request of any party to The Compact, so advise the federal agencies in writing in the form, if any, that may be reasonably required by any such federal agencies;

Eighth, that the members of The Compact agree to keep confidential the H.S.R. filing, not to make any portion of such filing public except as may be relevant to instituting a judicial action to enjoin the merger or file comments with regard to the merger with the federal enforcement agencies and to limit the use of such information solely to instituting an action to enjoin the merger under federal or state antitrust law or commenting upon the merger in writing to the federal enforcement agencies;

Ninth, that the members of The Compact may inspect the H.S.R. filing at the headquarters of the liaison state or direct the liaison state to furnish a photocopy of the filing, providing that a member requesting a copy of the filing will reimburse the liaison state for the costs of photocopying;

Tenth, that the members of The Compact agree, to the extent permitted by law, to return the H.S.R. filing to the merging parties after the uses specified in the Eighth Proviso are completed or to destroy the H.S.R. filing, at the option of the merging parties;

Eleventh, that any state or territorial Attorney General may become a member of The Compact or resign from membership at any time upon duly notifying the General Counsel of NAAG in writing of such action, provided, however, that the resignation from The Compact shall not relieve the resigning member from any obligation that a member of The Compact has to the parties to a particular merger under this Compact when such parties have duly filed the H.S.R. material with the liaison state prior to the resignation;

Twelfth, that the General Counsel of NAAG shall request and cause a copy of The Compact and the identity of its members to be published in the Antitrust Report of NAAG, the Antitrust and Trade Regulation Report of the Bureau of National Affairs, the Trade Regulation Reports of the Commerce Clearing House, the Antitrust Report of Matthew Bender and other appropriate publications and will further inform such publications of each instance when an Attorney General joins or resigns from The Compact.

SIGNATORIES:

NAAG VOLUNTARY PRE-MERGER DISCLOSURE COMPACT

ELECTION FORM

NAAG VOLUNATRY PRE-MERGER DISCLOSURE COMPACT

In accordance with the Eighth Principle of the Voluntary Pre-Merger Disclosure Compact adopted by the National Association of Attorneys General on December 12, 1987, I, ______________________ (insert name of Attorney General), Attorney General of ______ (state), hereby resign from the Pre-Merger Compact. This resignation is effective immediately.

I hereby declare my intention [to adhere] [not to adhere]* to the NAAG Voluntary Pre-Merger Disclosure Compact as revised and approved by the NAAG Antitrust Committee on March 22, 1994. Regardless of my present intention, I reserve the right to resign from or adhere to the Compact at any time in the future, upon written notification to the Executive Director of NAAG.

ATTORNEY GENERAL OR DESIGNEE

Dated: ______________,1996

* Please cross out one

PLEASE MAIL TO:
Saira Nayak-Lieb
Counsel for Antitrust & Health
NAAG
444 North Capitol Street, Suite 339
Washington, D.C. 20001

NAAG VOLUNTARY PRE-MERGER DISCLOSURE COMPACT

MODEL CERTIFICATE FOR STATES

General Counsel
Federal Trade Commission
Washington, DC 20530

Re: Participation in Program for Federal-State Cooperation in Merger Enforcement: Certification of Intent to Maintain Confidentiality.

On behalf of the Attorney General of [name of state or jurisdiction], I certify that the [name of jurisdiction] will maintain the confidentiality of all information and analysis (hereafter "information") obtained directly from the Commission under the captioned program, as well as all information obtained indirectly from the Commission through another state participating in the program. All information obtained under the program will be used only for official law enforcement purposes.

If any such information is subject to a discovery request in litigation or an access request under a public access law, the [name of jurisdiction] will advise the General Counsel of the Federal Trade Commission ("General Counsel") of the request, and will vigorously assert any privilege or exemption claimed by the General Counsel, or assist the General Counsel in intervening in a state or federal proceeding to protect the information in question. In no event will any action be taken, or any statement be made, that will compromise the Commission's claim of confidentiality.

I understand that information obtained pursuant to this certification may be share with other state Attorney General offices only if they have filed a certification with the General Counsel.

Signed: ______________________________

Position: ______________________________

Telephone: ____________________________

NAAG VOLUNTARY PRE-MERGER DISCLOSURE COMPACT

MODEL WAIVER FOR SUBMITTERS

To: Assistant Director for Premerger Notification
Bureau of Competition
Federal Trade Commission
Washington, DC 20580.

With respect to [the proposed acquisition of X Corp. by Y Corp.], the undersigned attorney or corporate officer, acting on behalf of [indicate entity], hereby waives confidentiality protections under the Federal Trade Commission Act, 15 U.S.C. § 41 *et seq.*, the Hart-Scott-Rodino Act, 15 U.S.C. § 18a(h), and the Federal Trade Commissions Rules of Practice, 16 CFR § 4.9 *et seq.*, insofar as these protections in any way limit discussions about [identity of transaction] between the Federal Trade Commission and members of the NAAG Voluntary Pre-Merger Disclosure Compact ("Compact").

I understand that the Commission will not provide the states with copies of filings by [indicate entity] under the Hart-Scott-Rodino Act. Rather, these materials will be provided to the states by [indicate entity] pursuant to the Compact, and will be provided only with such confidentiality protections as are accorded by the Compact and its members.

Signed: ______________________________

Position: ______________________________

14

1992 HORIZONTAL MERGER GUIDELINES

U.S. DEPARTMENT OF JUSTICE AND FEDERAL TRADE COMMISSION

(Revised April 8, 1997)

The U.S. Department of Justice ("Department") and Federal Trade Commission ("Commission") today jointly issued Horizontal Merger Guidelines revising the Department's 1984 Merger Guidelines and the Commission's 1982 Statement Concerning Horizontal Merger Guidelines. The release marks the first time that the two federal agencies that share antitrust enforcement jurisdiction have issued joint guidelines.

Central to the 1992 Department of Justice and Federal Trade Commission Horizontal Merger Guidelines is a recognition that sound merger enforcement is an essential component of our free enterprise system benefitting the competitiveness of American firms and the welfare of American consumers. Sound merger enforcement must prevent anticompetitive mergers yet avoid deterring the larger universe of procompetitive or competitively neutral mergers. The 1992 Horizontal Merger Guidelines implement this objective by describing the analytical foundations of merger enforcement and providing guidance enabling the business community to avoid antitrust problems when planning mergers. The Department first released Merger Guidelines in 1968 in order to inform the business community of the analysis applied by the Department to mergers under the federal antitrust laws. The 1968 Merger Guidelines eventually fell into disuse, both internally and externally, as they were eclipsed by developments in legal and economic thinking about mergers.

In 1982, the Department released revised Merger Guidelines which, reflecting those developments, departed dramatically from the 1968 version. Relative to the Department's actual practice, however, the 1982 Merger Guidelines represented an evolutionary not revolutionary change. On the same date, the Commission released its Statement Concerning Horizontal Mergers highlighting the principal considerations guiding the Commission's horizontal merger enforcement and noting the "considerable weight" given by the Commission to the Department's 1982 Merger Guidelines.

The Department's current Merger Guidelines, released in 1984, refined and clarified the analytical framework of the 1982 Merger Guidelines. Although the agencies' experience with the 1982 Merger Guidelines reaffirmed the soundness of its underlying principles, the Department concluded that there remained room for improvement.

The revisions embodied in the 1992 Horizontal Merger Guidelines reflect the next logical step in the development of the agencies' analysis of mergers. They reflect the Department's experience in applying the 1982 and 1984 Merger Guidelines as well as the Commission's experience in applying those guidelines and the Commission's 1982 Statement. Both the Department and the Commission believed that their respective Guidelines and Statement presented sound frameworks for antitrust analysis of mergers, but that improvements could be made to reflect advances in legal and economic thinking. The 1992 Horizontal Merger Guidelines accomplish this objective and also clarify certain aspects of the Merger Guidelines that proved to be ambiguous or were interpreted by observers in ways that were inconsistent with the actual policy of the agencies.

The 1992 Horizontal Merger Guidelines do not include a discussion of horizontal effects from non-horizontal mergers (e.g., elimination of specific potential entrants and competitive problems from vertical mergers). Neither agency has changed its policy with respect to non-horizontal mergers. Specific guidance on non-horizontal mergers is provided in Section 4 of the Department's 1984 Merger Guidelines, read in the context of today's revisions to the treatment of horizontal mergers.

A number of today's revisions are largely technical or stylistic. One major objective of the revisions is to strengthen the document as an analytical road map for the evaluation of mergers. The language, therefore, is intended to be burden-neutral, without altering the burdens of proof or burdens of coming forward as those standards have been established by the courts. In addition, the revisions principally address two areas.

The most significant revision to the Merger Guidelines is to explain more clearly how mergers may lead to adverse competitive effects and how particular market factors relate to the analysis of those effects. These revisions are found in Section 2 of the Horizontal Merger Guidelines. The second principal revision is to sharpen the distinction between the treatment of various types of supply responses and to articulate the framework for analyzing the timeliness, likelihood and sufficiency of entry. These revisions are found in Sections 1.3 and 3.

The new Horizontal Merger Guidelines observe, as did the 1984 Guidelines, that because the specific standards they set out must be applied in widely varied factual circumstances, mechanical application of those standards could produce misleading results. Thus, the Guidelines state that the agencies will apply those standards reasonably and flexibly to the particular facts and circumstances of each proposed merger.

TABLE OF CONTENTS

0. Purpose, Underlying Policy Assumptions and Overview

These Guidelines outline the present enforcement policy of the Department of Justice and the Federal Trade Commission (the "Agency") concerning horizontal acquisitions and mergers ("mergers") subject to section 7 of the Clayton Act,[1] to section 1 of the Sherman Act,[2] or to section 5 of the FTC Act.[3] They describe the analytical framework and specific standards normally used by the Agency in analyzing mergers.[4] By stating its policy as simply and clearly as possible, the Agency hopes to reduce the uncertainty associated with enforcement of the antitrust laws in this area.

Although the Guidelines should improve the predictability of the Agency's merger enforcement policy, it is not possible to remove the exercise of judgment from the evaluation of mergers under the antitrust laws. Because the specific standards set forth in the Guidelines must be applied to a broad range of possible factual circumstances, mechanical application of those standards may provide misleading answers to the economic questions raised under the antitrust laws. Moreover, information is often incomplete and the picture of competitive conditions that develops from historical evidence may provide an incomplete answer to the forward-looking inquiry of the Guidelines. Therefore, the Agency will apply the standards of the Guidelines reasonably and flexibly to the particular facts and circumstances of each proposed merger.

---

[1] 15 U.S.C. Section 18 (1988). Mergers subject to section 7 are prohibited if their effect "may be substantially to lessen competition, or to tend to create a monopoly."

[2] 15 U.S.C. Section 1 (1988). Mergers subject to section 1 are prohibited if they constitute a "contract, combination or conspiracy in restraint of trade."

[3] 15 U.S.C. Section 45 (1988). Mergers subject to section 5 are prohibited if they constitute an "unfair method of competition."

[4] These Guidelines update the Merger Guidelines issued by the U.S. Department of Justice in 1984 and the Statement of Federal Trade Commission Concerning Horizontal Mergers issued in 1982. The Merger Guidelines may be revised from time to time as necessary to reflect any significant changes in enforcement policy or to clarify aspects of existing policy.

0.1 Purpose and Underlying Policy Assumptions of the Guidelines

The Guidelines are designed primarily to articulate the analytical framework the Agency applies in determining whether a merger is likely substantially to lessen competition, not to describe how the Agency will conduct the litigation of cases that it decides to bring. Although relevant in the latter context, the factors contemplated in the Guidelines neither dictate nor exhaust the range of evidence that the Agency must or may introduce in litigation. Consistent with their objective, the Guidelines do not attempt to assign the burden of proof, or the burden of coming forward with evidence, on any particular issue. Nor do the Guidelines attempt to adjust or reapportion burdens of proof or burdens of coming forward as those standards have been established by the courts.[5] Instead, the Guidelines set forth a methodology for analyzing issues once the necessary facts are available. The necessary facts may be derived from the documents and statements of both the merging firms and other sources.

Throughout the Guidelines, the analysis is focused on whether consumers or producers "likely would" take certain actions, that is, whether the action is in the actor's economic interest. References to the profitability of certain actions focus on economic profits rather than accounting profits. Economic profits may be defined as the excess of revenues over costs where costs include the opportunity cost of invested capital.

Mergers are motivated by the prospect of financial gains. The possible sources of the financial gains from mergers are many, and the Guidelines do not attempt to identify all possible sources of gain in every merger. Instead, the Guidelines focus on the one potential source of gain that is of concern under the antitrust laws: market power.

The unifying theme of the Guidelines is that mergers should not be permitted to create or enhance market power or to facilitate its exercise. Market power to a seller is the ability profitably to maintain prices above competitive levels for a significant period of time.[6] In some circumstances, a sole seller (a "monopolist") of a product with no good substitutes can maintain a selling price that is above the level that would prevail if the market were competitive. Similarly, in some circumstances, where only a few firms account for most of the sales of a product, those firms can exercise market power, perhaps even approximating the performance of a monopolist, by either explicitly or implicitly coordinating their actions. Circumstances also may permit a single firm, not a monopolist, to exercise market power through unilateral or non-coordinated conduct—conduct the success of which does not rely on the concurrence of other firms in the market or on coordinated responses by those firms. In any case, the result of the exercise of market power is a transfer of wealth from buyers to sellers or a misallocation of resources.

Market power also encompasses the ability of a single buyer (a "monopsonist"), a coordinating group of buyers, or a single buyer, not a monopsonist, to depress the price paid for a product to a level that is below the competitive price and thereby depress output. The exercise of market power by buyers ("monopsony power") has adverse effects comparable to

---

5 For example, the burden with respect to efficiency and failure continues to reside with the proponents of the merger.

6 Sellers with market power also may lessen competition on dimensions other than price, such as product quality, service, or innovation.

those associated with the exercise of market power by sellers. In order to assess potential monopsony concerns, the Agency will apply an analytical framework analogous to the framework of these Guidelines.

While challenging competitively harmful mergers, the Agency seeks to avoid unnecessary interference with the larger universe of mergers that are either competitively beneficial or neutral. In implementing this objective, however, the Guidelines reflect the congressional intent that merger enforcement should interdict competitive problems in their incipiency.

0.2 Overview

The Guidelines describe the analytical process that the Agency will employ in determining whether to challenge a horizontal merger. First, the Agency assesses whether the merger would significantly increase concentration and result in a concentrated market, properly defined and measured. Second, the Agency assesses whether the merger, in light of market concentration and other factors that characterize the market, raises concern about potential adverse competitive effects. Third, the Agency assesses whether entry would be timely, likely and sufficient either to deter or to counteract the competitive effects of concern. Fourth, the Agency assesses any efficiency gains that reasonably cannot be achieved by the parties through other means. Finally the Agency assesses whether, but for the merger, either party to the transaction would be likely to fail, causing its assets to exit the market. The process of assessing market concentration, potential adverse competitive effects, entry, efficiency and failure is a tool that allows the Agency to answer the ultimate inquiry in merger analysis: whether the merger is likely to create or enhance market power or to facilitate its exercise.

1. MARKET DEFINITION, MEASUREMENT AND CONCENTRATION

1.0 Overview

A merger is unlikely to create or enhance market power or to facilitate its exercise unless it significantly increases concentration and results in a concentrated market, properly defined and measured. Mergers that either do not significantly increase concentration or do not result in a concentrated market ordinarily require no further analysis.

The analytic process described in this section ensures that the Agency evaluates the likely competitive impact of a merger within the context of economically meaningful markets—i.e., markets that could be subject to the exercise of market power. Accordingly, for each product or service (hereafter "product") of each merging firm, the Agency seeks to define a market in which firms could effectively exercise market power if they were able to coordinate their actions.

Market definition focuses solely on demand substitution factors—i.e., possible consumer responses. Supply substitution factors—i.e., possible production responses—are considered elsewhere in the Guidelines in the identification of firms that participate in the relevant market and the analysis of entry. See Sections 1.3 and 3. A market is defined as a product or group of products and a geographic area in which it is produced or sold such that a hypothetical profit-maximizing firm, not subject to price regulation, that was the only present and future producer or seller of those products in that area likely would impose at least a "small but significant and nontransitory" increase in price, assuming the terms of sale of all other products are held constant. A relevant market is a group of products and a geographic area that is no bigger than necessary to satisfy this test. The "small but significant and non-transitory" increase in price is employed solely as a methodological tool for the analysis of mergers: it is not a tolerance level for price increases.

Absent price discrimination, a relevant market is described by a product or group of products and a geographic area. In determining whether a hypothetical monopolist would be in a position to exercise market power, it is necessary to evaluate the likely demand responses of consumers to a price increase. A price increase could be made unprofitable by consumers either switching to other products or switching to the same product produced by firms at other locations. The nature and magnitude of these two types of demand responses respectively determine the scope of the product market and the geographic market.

In contrast, where a hypothetical monopolist likely would discriminate in prices charged to different groups of buyers, distinguished, for example, by their uses or locations, the Agency may delineate different relevant markets corresponding to each such buyer group. Competition for sales to each such group may be affected differently by a particular merger and markets are delineated by evaluating the demand response of each such buyer group. A relevant market of this kind is described by a collection of products for sale to a given group of buyers.

Once defined, a relevant market must be measured in terms of its participants and concentration. Participants include firms currently producing or selling the market's products in the market's geographic area. In addition, participants may include other firms depending on their likely supply responses to a "small but significant and nontransitory" price increase. A firm is viewed as a participant if, in response to a "small but significant and nontransitory" price increase, it likely would enter rapidly into production or sale of a market product in the market's area, without incurring significant sunk costs of entry and exit. Firms likely to make any of these supply responses are considered to be "uncommitted" entrants because their supply response would create new production or sale in the relevant market and because that production or sale could be quickly terminated without significant loss.[7]

Uncommitted entrants are capable of making such quick and uncommitted supply responses that they likely influenced the market premerger, would influence it post-merger, and accordingly are considered as market participants at both times. This analysis of market definition and market measurement applies equally to foreign and domestic firms.

If the process of market definition and market measurement identifies one or more relevant markets in which the merging firms are both participants, then the merger is considered to be horizontal. Sections 1.1 through 1.5 describe in greater detail how product and geographic markets will be defined, how market shares will be calculated and how market concentration will be assessed.

---

[7] Probable supply responses that require the entrant to incur significant sunk costs of entry and exit are not part of market measurement, but are included in the analysis of the significance of entry. See Section 3. Entrants that must commit substantial sunk costs are regarded as "committed" entrants because those sunk costs make entry irreversible in the short term without foregoing that investment; thus the likelihood of their entry must be evaluated with regard to their long-term profitability.

1.1 Product Market Definition

The Agency will first define the relevant product market with respect to each of the products of each of the merging firms.[8]

1.11 General Standards

Absent price discrimination, the Agency will delineate the product market to be a product or group of products such that a hypothetical profit-maximizing firm that was the only present and future seller of those products ("monopolist") likely would impose at least a "small but significant and nontransitory" increase in price. That is, assuming that buyers likely would respond to an increase in price for a tentatively identified product group only by shifting to other products, what would happen? If the alternatives were, in the aggregate, sufficiently attractive at their existing terms of sale, an attempt to raise prices would result in a reduction of sales large enough that the price increase would not prove profitable, and the tentatively identified product group would prove to be too narrow.

Specifically, the Agency will begin with each product (narrowly defined) produced or sold by each merging firm and ask what would happen if a hypothetical monopolist of that product imposed at least a "small but significant and nontransitory" increase in price, but the terms of sale of all other products remained constant. If, in response to the price increase, the reduction in sales of the product would be large enough that a hypothetical monopolist would not find it profitable to impose such an increase in price, then the Agency will add to the product group the product that is the next-best substitute for the merging firm's product.[9]

In considering the likely reaction of buyers to a price increase, the Agency will take into account all relevant evidence, including, but not limited to, the following:

(1) evidence that buyers have shifted or have considered shifting purchases between products in response to relative changes in price or other competitive variables;

(2) evidence that sellers base business decisions on the prospect of buyer substitution between products in response to relative changes in price or other competitive variables;

(3) the influence of downstream competition faced by buyers in their output markets; and

(4) the timing and costs of switching products.

The price increase question is then asked for a hypothetical monopolist controlling the expanded product group. In performing successive iterations of the price increase test, the hypothetical monopolist will be assumed to pursue maximum profits in deciding whether to raise the prices of any or all of the additional products under its control. This process will continue until a group of products is identified such that a hypothetical monopolist over

---

[8] Although discussed separately, product market definition and geographic market definition are interrelated. In particular, the extent to which buyers of a particular product would shift to other products in the event of a "small but significant and nontransitory" increase in price must be evaluated in the context of the relevant geographic market.

[9] Throughout the Guidelines, the term "next best substitute" refers to the alternative which, if available in unlimited quantities at constant prices, would account for the greatest value of diversion of demand in response to a "small but significant and nontransitory" price increase.

that group of products would profitably impose at least a "small but significant and nontransitory" increase, including the price of a product of one of the merging firms. The Agency generally will consider the relevant product market to be the smallest group of products that satisfies this test.

In the above analysis, the Agency will use prevailing prices of the products of the merging firms and possible substitutes for such products, unless premerger circumstances are strongly suggestive of coordinated interaction, in which case the Agency will use a price more reflective of the competitive price.[10]

However, the Agency may use likely future prices, absent the merger, when changes in the prevailing prices can be predicted with reasonable reliability. Changes in price may be predicted on the basis of, for example, changes in regulation which affect price either directly or indirectly by affecting costs or demand.

In general, the price for which an increase will be postulated will be whatever is considered to be the price of the product at the stage of the industry being examined.[11] In attempting to determine objectively the effect of a "small but significant and nontransitory" increase in price, the Agency, in most contexts, will use a price increase of five percent lasting for the foreseeable future. However, what constitutes a "small but significant and nontransitory" increase in price will depend on the nature of the industry, and the Agency at times may use a price increase that is larger or smaller than five percent.

1.12 Product Market Definition in the Presence of Price Discrimination

The analysis of product market definition to this point has assumed that price discrimination—charging different buyers different prices for the same product, for example—would not be profitable for a hypothetical monopolist. A different analysis applies where price discrimination would be profitable for a hypothetical monopolist.

Existing buyers sometimes will differ significantly in their likelihood of switching to other products in response to a "small but significant and nontransitory" price increase. If a hypothetical monopolist can identify and price differently to those buyers ("targeted buyers") who would not defeat the targeted price increase by substituting to other products in response to a "small but significant and nontransitory" price increase for the relevant product, and if other buyers likely would not purchase the relevant product and resell to targeted buyers, then a hypothetical monopolist would profitably impose a discriminatory price increase on sales to targeted buyers. This is true regardless of whether a general increase in price would cause such significant substitution that the price increase would not be profitable. The Agency will consider additional relevant product markets consisting of a particular use or uses by groups of buyers of the product for which a hypothetical monopolist would profitably and separately impose at least a "small but significant and nontransitory" increase in price.

---

[10] The terms of sale of all other products are held constant in order to focus market definition on the behavior of consumers. Movements in the terms of sale for other products, as may result from the behavior of producers of those products, are accounted for in the analysis of competitive effects and entry. See Sections 2 and 3.

[11] For example, in a merger between retailers, the relevant price would be the retail price of a product to consumers. In the case of a merger among oil pipelines, the relevant price would be the tariff—the price of the transportation service.

1.2 Geographic Market Definition

For each product market in which both merging firms participate, the Agency will determine the geographic market or markets in which the firms produce or sell. A single firm may operate in a number of different geographic markets.

1.21 General Standards

Absent price discrimination, the Agency will delineate the geographic market to be a region such that a hypothetical monopolist that was the only present or future producer of the relevant product at locations in that region would profitably impose at least a "small but significant and nontransitory" increase in price, holding constant the terms of sale for all products produced elsewhere. That is, assuming that buyers likely would respond to a price increase on products produced within the tentatively identified region only by shifting to products produced at locations of production outside the region, what would happen? If those locations of production outside the region were, in the aggregate, sufficiently attractive at their existing terms of sale, an attempt to raise price would result in a reduction in sales large enough that the price increase would not prove profitable, and the tentatively identified geographic area would prove to be too narrow.

In defining the geographic market or markets affected by a merger, the Agency will begin with the location of each merging firm (or each plant of a multiplant firm) and ask what would happen if a hypothetical monopolist of the relevant product at that point imposed at least a "small but significant and nontransitory" increase in price, but the terms of sale at all other locations remained constant. If, in response to the price increase, the reduction in sales of the product at that location would be large enough that a hypothetical monopolist producing or selling the relevant product at the merging firm's location would not find it profitable to impose such an increase in price, then the Agency will add the location from which production is the next-best substitute for production at the merging firm's location.

In considering the likely reaction of buyers to a price increase, the Agency will take into account all relevant evidence, including, but not limited to, the following:

(1) evidence that buyers have shifted or have considered shifting purchases between different geographic locations in response to relative changes in price or other competitive variables;

(2) evidence that sellers base business decisions on the prospect of buyer substitution between geographic locations in response to relative changes in price or other competitive variables;

(3) the influence of downstream competition faced by buyers in their output markets; and

(4) the timing and costs of switching suppliers.

The price increase question is then asked for a hypothetical monopolist controlling the expanded group of locations. In performing successive iterations of the price increase test, the hypothetical monopolist will be assumed to pursue maximum profits in deciding whether to raise the price at any or all of the additional locations under its control. This process will continue until a group of locations is identified such that a hypothetical monopolist over that group of locations would profitably impose at least a "small but significant and nontransitory" increase, including the price charged at a location of one of the merging firms.

The "smallest market" principle will be applied as it is in product market definition. The price for which an increase will be postulated, what constitutes a "small but significant and nontransitory" increase in price, and the substitution decisions of consumers all will be determined in the same way in which they are determined in product market definition.

1.22 Geographic Market Definition in the Presence of Price Discrimination

The analysis of geographic market definition to this point has assumed that geographic price discrimination—charging different prices net of transportation costs for the same product to buyers in different areas, for example—would not be profitable for a hypothetical monopolist. However, if a hypothetical monopolist can identify and price differently to buyers in certain areas ("targeted buyers") who would not defeat the targeted price increase by substituting to more distant sellers in response to a "small but significant and nontransitory" price increase for the relevant product, and if other buyers likely would not purchase the relevant product and resell to targeted buyers,[12] then a hypothetical monopolist would profitably impose a discriminatory price increase. This is true even where a general price increase would cause such significant substitution that the price increase would not be profitable. The Agency will consider additional geographic markets consisting of particular locations of buyers for which a hypothetical monopolist would profitably and separately impose at least a "small but significant and nontransitory" increase in price.

1.3 Identification of Firms that Participate in the Relevant Market

1.31 Current Producers or Sellers

The Agency's identification of firms that participate in the relevant market begins with all firms that currently produce or sell in the relevant market. This includes vertically integrated firms to the extent that such inclusion accurately reflects their competitive significance in the relevant market prior to the merger. To the extent that the analysis under Section 1.1 indicates that used, reconditioned or recycled goods are included in the relevant market, market participants will include firms that produce or sell such goods and that likely would offer those goods in competition with other relevant products.

1.32 Firms That Participate Through Supply Response

In addition, the Agency will identify other firms not currently producing or selling the relevant product in the relevant area as participating in the relevant market if their inclusion would more accurately reflect probable supply responses. These firms are termed "uncommitted entrants." These supply responses must be likely to occur within one year and without the expenditure of significant sunk costs of entry and exit, in response to a "small but significant and nontransitory" price increase. If a firm has the technological capability to achieve such an uncommitted supply response, but likely would not (e.g., because difficulties in achieving product acceptance, distribution, or production would render such a response

---

[12] This arbitrage is inherently impossible for many services and is particularly difficult where the product is sold on a delivered basis and where transportation costs are a significant percentage of the final cost.

unprofitable), that firm will not be considered to be a market participant. The competitive significance of supply responses that require more time or that require firms to incur significant sunk costs of entry and exit will be considered in entry analysis. See Section 3.[13]

Sunk costs are the acquisition costs of tangible and intangible assets that cannot be recovered through the redeployment of these assets outside the relevant market, i.e., costs uniquely incurred to supply the relevant product and geographic market. Examples of sunk costs may include market-specific investments in production facilities, technologies, marketing (including product acceptance), research and development, regulatory approvals, and testing. A significant sunk cost is one which would not be recouped within one year of the commencement of the supply response, assuming a "small but significant and nontransitory" price increase in the relevant market. In this context, a "small but significant and nontransitory" price increase will be determined in the same way in which it is determined in product market definition, except the price increase will be assumed to last one year. In some instances, it may be difficult to calculate sunk costs with precision. Accordingly, when necessary, the Agency will make an overall assessment of the extent of sunk costs for firms likely to participate through supply responses.

These supply responses may give rise to new production of products in the relevant product market or new sources of supply in the relevant geographic market. Alternatively, where price discrimination is likely so that the relevant market is defined in terms of a targeted group of buyers, these supply responses serve to identify new sellers to the targeted buyers. Uncommitted supply responses may occur in several different ways: by the switching or extension of existing assets to production or sale in the relevant market; or by the construction or acquisition of assets that enable production or sale in the relevant market.

1.321 Production Substitution and Extension: The Switching or Extension of Existing Assets to Production or Sale in the Relevant Market

The productive and distributive assets of a firm sometimes can be used to produce and sell either the relevant products or products that buyers do not regard as good substitutes. Production substitution refers to the shift by a firm in the use of assets from producing and selling one product to producing and selling another. Production extension refers to the use of those assets, for example, existing brand names and reputation, both for their current production and for production of the relevant product. Depending upon the speed of that shift and the extent of sunk costs incurred in the shift or extension, the potential for production substitution or extension may necessitate treating as market participants firms that do not currently produce the relevant product.[14]

---

[13] If uncommitted entrants likely would also remain in the market and would meet the entry tests of timeliness, likelihood and sufficiency, and thus would likely deter anticompetitive mergers or deter or counteract the competitive effects of concern (see Section 3, infra), the Agency will consider the impact of those firms in the entry analysis.

[14] Under other analytical approaches, production substitution sometimes has been reflected in the description of the product market. For example, the product market for stamped metal products such as automobile hub caps might be described as "light metal stamping," a production process rather than a product. The Agency believes that the approach described in the text provides a more clearly focused method of incorporating this factor in merger analysis. If production substitution among a group of products is

If a firm has existing assets that likely would be shifted or extended into production and sale of the relevant product within one year, and without incurring significant sunk costs of entry and exit, in response to a "small but significant and nontransitory" increase in price for only the relevant product, the Agency will treat that firm as a market participant. In assessing whether a firm is such a market participant, the Agency will take into account the costs of substitution or extension relative to the profitability of sales at the elevated price, and whether the firm's capacity is elsewhere committed or elsewhere so profitably employed that such capacity likely would not be available to respond to an increase in price in the market.

1.322 Obtaining New Assets for Production or Sale of the Relevant Product

A firm may also be able to enter into production or sale in the relevant market within one year and without the expenditure of significant sunk costs of entry and exit, in response to a "small but significant and nontransitory" increase in price for only the relevant product, even if the firm is newly organized or is an existing firm without products or productive assets closely related to the relevant market. If new firms, or existing firms without closely related products or productive assets, likely would enter into production or sale in the relevant market within one year without the expenditure of significant sunk costs of entry and exit, the Agency will treat those firms as market participants.

1.4 Calculating Market Shares

1.41 General Approach

The Agency normally will calculate market shares for all firms (or plants) identified as market participants in Section 1.3 based on the total sales or capacity currently devoted to the relevant market together with that which likely would be devoted to the relevant market in response to a "small but significant and nontransitory" price increase. Market shares can be expressed either in dollar terms through measurement of sales, shipments, or production, or in physical terms through measurement of sales, shipments, production, capacity, or reserves.

Market shares will be calculated using the best indicator of firms' future competitive significance. Dollar sales or shipments generally will be used if firms are distinguished primarily by differentiation of their products. Unit sales generally will be used if firms are distinguished primarily on the basis of their relative advantages in serving different buyers or groups of buyers. Physical capacity or reserves generally will be used if it is these measures that most effectively distinguish firms.[15] Typically, annual data are used, but where individual sales are large and infrequent so that annual data may be unrepresentative, the Agency may measure market shares over a longer period of time.

In measuring a firm's market share, the Agency will not include its sales or capacity to the extent that the firm's capacity is committed or so profitably employed outside the relevant market that it would not be available to respond to an increase in price in the market.

---

nearly universal among the firms selling one or more of those products, however, the Agency may use an aggregate description of those markets as a matter of convenience.

[15] Where all firms have, on a forward-looking basis, an equal likelihood of securing sales, the Agency will assign firms equal shares.

1.42 Price Discrimination Markets

When markets are defined on the basis of price discrimination (Sections 1.12 and 1.22), the Agency will include only sales likely to be made into, or capacity likely to be used to supply, the relevant market in response to a "small but significant and nontransitory" price increase.

1.43 Special Factors Affecting Foreign Firms

Market shares will be assigned to foreign competitors in the same way in which they are assigned to domestic competitors. However, if exchange rates fluctuate significantly, so that comparable dollar calculations on an annual basis may be unrepresentative, the Agency may measure market shares over a period longer than one year.

If shipments from a particular country to the United States are subject to a quota, the market shares assigned to firms in that country will not exceed the amount of shipments by such firms allowed under the quota.[16]

In the case of restraints that limit imports to some percentage of the total amount of the product sold in the United States (i.e., percentage quotas), a domestic price increase that reduced domestic consumption also would reduce the volume of imports into the United States. Accordingly, actual import sales and capacity data will be reduced for purposes of calculating market shares. Finally, a single market share may be assigned to a country or group of countries if firms in that country or group of countries act in coordination.

1.5 Concentration and Market Shares

Market concentration is a function of the number of firms in a market and their respective market shares. As an aid to the interpretation of market data, the Agency will use the Herfindahl-Hirschman Index ("HHI") of market concentration. The HHI is calculated by summing the squares of the individual market shares of all the participants.[17] Unlike the four-firm concentration ratio, the HHI reflects both the distribution of the market shares of the top four firms and the composition of the market outside the top four firms. It also gives proportionately greater weight to the market shares of the larger firms, in accord with their relative importance in competitive interactions.

The Agency divides the spectrum of market concentration as measured by the HHI into three regions that can be broadly characterized as unconcentrated (HHI below 1000), moderately concentrated (HHI between 1000 and 1800), and highly concentrated (HHI above 1800). Although the resulting regions provide a useful framework for merger analysis, the numerical divisions suggest greater precision than is possible with the available economic tools and information. Other things being equal, cases falling just above and just below a threshold present comparable competitive issues.

---

[16] The constraining effect of the quota on the importer's ability to expand sales is relevant to the evaluation of potential adverse competitive effects. See Section 2.

[17] For example, a market consisting of four firms with market shares of 30 percent, 30 percent, 20 percent and 20 percent has an HHI of 2600 ($30^2 + 30^2 + 20^2 + 20^2 = 2600$). The HHI ranges from 10,000 (in the case of a pure monopoly) to a number approaching zero (in the case of an atomistic market). Although it is desirable to include all firms in the calculation, lack of information about small firms is not critical because such firms do not affect the HHI significantly.

1.51 General Standards

In evaluating horizontal mergers, the Agency will consider both the post-merger market concentration and the increase in concentration resulting from the merger.[18]

Market concentration is a useful indicator of the likely potential competitive effect of a merger. The general standards for horizontal mergers are as follows:

a) Post-Merger HHI Below 1000. The Agency regards markets in this region to be unconcentrated. Mergers resulting in unconcentrated markets are unlikely to have adverse competitive effects and ordinarily require no further analysis.

b) Post-Merger HHI Between 1000 and 1800. The Agency regards markets in this region to be moderately concentrated. Mergers producing an increase in the HHI of less than 100 points in moderately concentrated markets post-merger are unlikely to have adverse competitive consequences and ordinarily require no further analysis. Mergers producing an increase in the HHI of more than 100 points in moderately concentrated markets post-merger potentially raise significant competitive concerns depending on the factors set forth in Sections 2–5 of the Guidelines.

c) Post-Merger HHI Above 1800. The Agency regards markets in this region to be highly concentrated. Mergers producing an increase in the HHI of less than 50 points, even in highly concentrated markets post-merger, are unlikely to have adverse competitive consequences and ordinarily require no further analysis. Mergers producing an increase in the HHI of more than 50 points in highly concentrated markets post-merger potentially raise significant competitive concerns, depending on the factors set forth in Sections 2–5 of the Guidelines. Where the post-merger HHI exceeds 1800, it will be presumed that mergers producing an increase in the HHI of more than 100 points are likely to create or enhance market power or facilitate its exercise. The presumption may be overcome by a showing that factors set forth in Sections 2–5 of the Guidelines make it unlikely that the merger will create or enhance market power or facilitate its exercise, in light of market concentration and market shares.

1.52 Factors Affecting the Significance of Market Shares and Concentration

The post-merger level of market concentration and the change in concentration resulting from a merger affect the degree to which a merger raises competitive concerns. However, in some situations, market share and market concentration data may either understate or overstate the likely future competitive significance of a firm or firms in the market or the impact of a merger. The following are examples of such situations.

---

[18] The increase in concentration as measured by the HHI can be calculated independently of the overall market concentration by doubling the product of the market shares of the merging firms. For example, the merger of firms with shares of 5 percent and 10 percent of the market would increase the HHI by 100 (5 x 10 x 2 = 100). The explanation for this technique is as follows: In calculating the HHI before the merger, the market shares of the merging firms are squared individually:

$(a)^2 + (b)^2$. After the merger, the sum of those shares would be squared: $(a + b)^2$, which equals $a^2 + 2ab + b^2$. The increase in the HHI therefore is represented by 2ab.

1.521 Changing Market Conditions

Market concentration and market share data of necessity are based on historical evidence. However, recent or ongoing changes in the market may indicate that the current market share of a particular firm either understates or overstates the firm's future competitive significance. For example, if a new technology that is important to long-term competitive viability is available to other firms in the market, but is not available to a particular firm, the Agency may conclude that the historical market share of that firm overstates its future competitive significance. The Agency will consider reasonably predictable effects of recent or ongoing changes in market conditions in interpreting market concentration and market share data.

1.522 Degree of Difference Between the Products and Locations in the Market and Substitutes Outside the Market

All else equal, the magnitude of potential competitive harm from a merger is greater if a hypothetical monopolist would raise price within the relevant market by substantially more than a "small but significant and nontransitory" amount. This may occur when the demand substitutes outside the relevant market, as a group, are not close substitutes for the products and locations within the relevant market. There thus may be a wide gap in the chain of demand substitutes at the edge of the product and geographic market. Under such circumstances, more market power is at stake in the relevant market than in a market in which a hypothetical monopolist would raise price by exactly five percent.

2. THE POTENTIAL ADVERSE COMPETITIVE EFFECTS OF MERGERS

2.0 Overview

Other things being equal, market concentration affects the likelihood that one firm, or a small group of firms, could successfully exercise market power. The smaller the percentage of total supply that a firm controls, the more severely it must restrict its own output in order to produce a given price increase, and the less likely it is that an output restriction will be profitable. If collective action is necessary for the exercise of market power, as the number of firms necessary to control a given percentage of total supply decreases, the difficulties and costs of reaching and enforcing an understanding with respect to the control of that supply might be reduced. However, market share and concentration data provide only the starting point for analyzing the competitive impact of a merger. Before determining whether to challenge a merger, the Agency also will assess the other market factors that pertain to competitive effects, as well as entry, efficiencies and failure.

This section considers some of the potential adverse competitive effects of mergers and the factors in addition to market concentration relevant to each. Because an individual merger may threaten to harm competition through more than one of these effects, mergers will be analyzed in terms of as many potential adverse competitive effects as are appropriate. Entry, efficiencies, and failure are treated in Sections 3–5.

2.1 Lessening of Competition Through Coordinated Interaction

A merger may diminish competition by enabling the firms selling in the relevant market more likely, more successfully, or more completely to engage in coordinated interaction that harms consumers. Coordinated interaction is comprised of actions by a group of firms that are profitable for each of them only as a result of the accommodating reactions of the others. This behavior includes tacit or express collusion, and may or may not be lawful in and of itself.

Successful coordinated interaction entails reaching terms of coordination that are profitable to the firms involved and an ability to detect and punish deviations that would undermine the coordinated interaction. Detection and punishment of deviations ensure that coordinating firms will find it more profitable to adhere to the terms of coordination than to pursue short-term profits from deviating, given the costs of reprisal. In this phase of the analysis, the Agency will examine the extent to which post-merger market conditions are conducive to reaching terms of coordination, detecting deviations from those terms, and punishing such deviations. Depending upon the circumstances, the following market factors, among others, may be relevant: the availability of key information concerning market conditions, transactions and individual competitors; the extent of firm and product heterogeneity; pricing or marketing practices typically employed by firms in the market; the characteristics of buyers and sellers; and the characteristics of typical transactions.

Certain market conditions that are conducive to reaching terms of coordination also may be conducive to detecting or punishing deviations from those terms. For example, the extent of information available to firms in the market, or the extent of homogeneity, may be relevant to both the ability to reach terms of coordination and to detect or punish deviations from those terms. The extent to which any specific market condition will be relevant to one or more of the conditions necessary to coordinated interaction will depend on the circumstances of the particular case.

It is likely that market conditions are conducive to coordinated interaction when the firms in the market previously have engaged in express collusion and when the salient characteristics of the market have not changed appreciably since the most recent such incident. Previous express collusion in another geographic market will have the same weight when the salient characteristics of that other market at the time of the collusion are comparable to those in the relevant market.

In analyzing the effect of a particular merger on coordinated interaction, the Agency is mindful of the difficulties of predicting likely future behavior based on the types of incomplete and sometimes contradictory information typically generated in merger investigations. Whether a merger is likely to diminish competition by enabling firms more likely, more successfully or more completely to engage in coordinated interaction depends on whether market conditions, on the whole, are conducive to reaching terms of coordination and detecting and punishing deviations from those terms.

2.11 Conditions Conducive to Reaching Terms of Coordination

Firms coordinating their interactions need not reach complex terms concerning the allocation of the market output across firms or the level of the market prices but may, instead, follow simple terms such as a common price, fixed price differentials, stable market shares, or customer or territorial restrictions. Terms of coordination need not perfectly achieve the monopoly outcome in order to be harmful to consumers. Instead, the terms of coordination may be imperfect and incomplete—inasmuch as they omit some market participants, omit some dimensions of competition, omit some customers, yield elevated prices short of monopoly levels, or lapse into episodic price wars—and still result in significant competitive harm. At some point, however, imperfections cause the profitability of abiding by the terms of coordination to decrease and, depending on their extent, may make coordinated interaction unlikely in the first instance.

Market conditions may be conducive to or hinder reaching terms of coordination. For example, reaching terms of coordination may be facilitated by product or firm homogeneity and by existing practices among firms, practices not necessarily themselves antitrust violations, such as standardization of pricing or product variables on which firms could compete. Key information about rival firms and the market may also facilitate reaching terms of coordination. Conversely, reaching terms of coordination may be limited or impeded by product heterogeneity or by firms having substantially incomplete information about the conditions and prospects of their rival's businesses, perhaps because of important differences among their current business operations. In addition, reaching terms of coordination may be limited or impeded by firm heterogeneity, for example, differences in vertical integration or the production of another product that tends to be used together with the relevant product.

2.12 Conditions Conducive to Detecting and Punishing Deviations

Where market conditions are conducive to timely detection and punishment of significant deviations, a firm will find it more profitable to abide by the terms of coordination than to deviate from them. Deviation from the terms of coordination will be deterred where the threat of punishment is credible. Credible punishment, however, may not need to be any more complex than temporary abandonment of the terms of coordination by other firms in the market.

Where detection and punishment likely would be rapid, incentives to deviate are diminished and coordination is likely to be successful. The detection and punishment of deviations may be facilitated by existing practices among firms, themselves not necessarily antitrust violations, and by the characteristics of typical transactions. For example, if key information about specific transactions or individual price or output levels is available routinely to competitors, it may be difficult for a firm to deviate secretly. If orders for the relevant product are frequent, regular and small relative to the total output of a firm in a market, it may be difficult for the firm to deviate in a substantial way without the knowledge of rivals and without the opportunity for rivals to react. If demand or cost fluctuations are relatively infrequent and small, deviations may be relatively easy to deter.

By contrast, where detection or punishment is likely to be slow, incentives to deviate are enhanced and coordinated interaction is unlikely to be successful. If demand or cost fluctuations are relatively frequent and large, deviations may be relatively difficult to distinguish from these other sources of market price fluctuations, and, in consequence, deviations may be relatively difficult to deter.

In certain circumstances, buyer characteristics and the nature of the procurement process may affect the incentives to deviate from terms of coordination. Buyer size alone is not the determining characteristic. Where large buyers likely would engage in long-term contracting, so that the sales covered by such contracts can be large relative to the total output of a firm in the market, firms may have the incentive to deviate. However, this only can be accomplished where the duration, volume and profitability of the business covered by such contracts are sufficiently large as to make deviation more profitable in the long term than honoring the terms of coordination, and buyers likely would switch suppliers.

In some circumstances, coordinated interaction can be effectively prevented or limited by maverick firms—firms that have a greater economic incentive to deviate from the terms of coordination than do most of their rivals (e.g., firms that are unusually disruptive and competitive influences in the market). Consequently, acquisition of a maverick firm is one way in which a merger may make coordinated interaction more likely, more successful, or more complete. For example, in a market where capacity constraints are significant for many competitors, a firm is more likely to be a maverick the greater is its excess or divertable capacity in relation to its sales or its total capacity, and the lower are its direct and opportunity costs of expanding sales in the relevant market.[19]

This is so because a firm's incentive to deviate from price-elevating and output-limiting terms of coordination is greater the more the firm is able profitably to expand its output as a proportion of the sales it would obtain if it adhered to the terms of coordination and the smaller is the base of sales on which it enjoys elevated profits prior to the price cutting deviation.[20] A firm also may be a maverick if it has an unusual ability secretly to expand its sales in relation to the sales it would obtain if it adhered to the terms of coordination. This ability might arise from opportunities to expand captive production for a downstream affiliate.

2.2 Lessening of Competition Through Unilateral Effects

A merger may diminish competition even if it does not lead to increased likelihood of successful coordinated interaction, because merging firms may find it profitable to alter their behavior unilaterally following the acquisition by elevating price and suppressing output. Unilateral competitive effects can arise in a variety of different settings. In each setting, particular other factors describing the relevant market affect the likelihood of unilateral competitive effects. The settings differ by the primary characteristics that distinguish firms and shape the nature of their competition.

2.21 Firms Distinguished Primarily by Differentiated Products

In some markets the products are differentiated, so that products sold by different participants in the market are not perfect substitutes for one another. Moreover, different products in the market may vary in the degree

[19] But excess capacity in the hands of non-maverick firms may be a potent weapon with which to punish deviations from the terms of coordination.

[20] Similarly, in a market where product design or quality is significant, a firm is more likely to be an effective maverick the greater is the sales potential of its products among customers of its rivals, in relation to the sales it would obtain if it adhered to the terms of coordination. The likelihood of expansion responses by a maverick will be analyzed in the same fashion as uncommitted entry or committed entry (see Sections 1.3 and 3) depending on the significance of the sunk costs entailed in expansion.

of their substitutability for one another. In this setting, competition may be non-uniform (i.e., localized), so that individual sellers compete more directly with those rivals selling closer substitutes.[21]

A merger between firms in a market for differentiated products may diminish competition by enabling the merged firm to profit by unilaterally raising the price of one or both products above the premerger level. Some of the sales loss due to the price rise merely will be diverted to the product of the merger partner and, depending on relative margins, capturing such sales loss through merger may make the price increase profitable even though it would not have been profitable premerger. Substantial unilateral price elevation in a market for differentiated products requires that there be a significant share of sales in the market accounted for by consumers who regard the products of the merging firms as their first and second choices, and that repositioning of the non-parties' product lines to replace the localized competition lost through the merger be unlikely. The price rise will be greater the closer substitutes are the products of the merging firms, i.e., the more the buyers of one product consider the other product to be their next choice.

2.211 Closeness of the Products of the Merging Firms

The market concentration measures articulated in Section 1 may help assess the extent of the likely competitive effect from a unilateral price elevation by the merged firm notwithstanding the fact that the affected products are differentiated. The market concentration measures provide a measure of this effect if each product's market share is reflective of not only its relative appeal as a first choice to consumers of the merging firms' products but also its relative appeal as a second choice, and hence as a competitive constraint to the first choice.[22] Where this circumstance holds, market concentration data fall outside the safeharbor regions of Section 1.5, and the merging firms have a combined market share of at least thirty-five percent, the Agency will presume that a significant share of sales in the market are accounted for by consumers who regard the products of the merging firms as their first and second choices.

Purchasers of one of the merging firms, products may be more or less likely to make the other their second choice than market shares alone would indicate. The market shares of the merging firms, products may understate the competitive effect of concern, when, for example, the products of the merging firms are relatively more similar in their various attributes to one another than to other products in the relevant market. On the other hand, the market shares alone may overstate the competitive effects of concern

[21] Similarly, in some markets sellers are primarily distinguished by their relative advantages in serving different buyers or groups of buyers, and buyers negotiate individually with sellers. Here, for example, sellers may formally bid against one another for the business of a buyer, or each buyer may elicit individual price quotes from multiple sellers. A seller may find it relatively inexpensive to meet the demands of particular buyers or types of buyers, and relatively expensive to meet others' demands. Competition, again, may be localized: sellers compete more directly with those rivals having similar relative advantages in serving particular buyers or groups of buyers. For example, in open outcry auctions, price is determined by the cost of the second lowest-cost seller. A merger involving the first and second lowest-cost sellers could cause prices to rise to the constraining level of the next lowest-cost seller.

[22] Information about consumers' actual first and second product choices may be provided by marketing surveys, information from bidding structures, or normal course of business documents from industry participants.

when, for example, the relevant products are less similar in their attributes to one another than to other products in the relevant market.

Where market concentration data fall outside the safeharbor regions of Section 1.5, the merging firms have a combined market share of at least thirty-five percent, and where data on product attributes and relative product appeal show that a significant share of purchasers of one merging firm's product regard the other as their second choice, then market share data may be relied upon to demonstrate that there is a significant share of sales in the market accounted for by consumers who would be adversely affected by the merger.

2.212 Ability of Rival Sellers to Replace Lost Competition

A merger is not likely to lead to unilateral elevation of prices of differentiated products if, in response to such an effect, rival sellers likely would replace any localized competition lost through the merger by repositioning their product lines.[23]

In markets where it is costly for buyers to evaluate product quality, buyers who consider purchasing from both merging parties may limit the total number of sellers they consider. If either of the merging firms would be replaced in such buyers, consideration by an equally competitive seller not formerly considered, then the merger is not likely to lead to a unilateral elevation of prices.

2.22 Firms Distinguished Primarily by Their Capacities

Where products are relatively undifferentiated and capacity primarily distinguishes firms and shapes the nature of their competition, the merged firm may find it profitable unilaterally to raise price and suppress output. The merger provides the merged firm a larger base of sales on which to enjoy the resulting price rise and also eliminates a competitor to which customers otherwise would have diverted their sales. Where the merging firms have a combined market share of at least thirty-five percent, merged firms may find it profitable to raise price and reduce joint output below the sum of their premerger outputs because the lost markups on the foregone sales may be outweighed by the resulting price increase on the merged base of sales.

This unilateral effect is unlikely unless a sufficiently large number of the merged firm's customers would not be able to find economical alternative sources of supply, i.e., competitors of the merged firm likely would not respond to the price increase and output reduction by the merged firm with increases in their own outputs sufficient in the aggregate to make the unilateral action of the merged firm unprofitable. Such non-party expansion is unlikely if those firms face binding capacity constraints that could not be economically relaxed within two years or if existing excess capacity is significantly more costly to operate than capacity currently in use.[24]

---

[23] The timeliness and likelihood of repositioning responses will be analyzed using the same methodology as used in analyzing uncommitted entry or committed entry (see Sections 1.3 and 3), depending on the significance of the sunk costs entailed in repositioning.

[24] The timeliness and likelihood of non-party expansion will be analyzed using the same methodology as used in analyzing uncommitted or committed entry (see Sections 1.3 and 3) depending on the significance of the sunk costs entailed in expansion.

3. ENTRY ANALYSIS

3.0 Overview

A merger is not likely to create or enhance market power or to facilitate its exercise, if entry into the market is so easy that market participants, after the merger, either collectively or unilaterally could not profitably maintain a price increase above premerger levels. Such entry likely will deter an anticompetitive merger in its incipiency, or deter or counteract the competitive effects of concern.

Entry is that easy if entry would be timely, likely, and sufficient in its magnitude, character and scope to deter or counteract the competitive effects of concern. In markets where entry is that easy (i.e., where entry passes these tests of timeliness, likelihood, and sufficiency), the merger raises no antitrust concern and ordinarily requires no further analysis.

The committed entry treated in this Section is defined as new competition that requires expenditure of significant sunk costs of entry and exit.[25] The Agency employs a three step methodology to assess whether committed entry would deter or counteract a competitive effect of concern.

The first step assesses whether entry can achieve significant market impact within a timely period. If significant market impact would require a longer period, entry will not deter or counteract the competitive effect of concern.

The second step assesses whether committed entry would be a profitable and, hence, a likely response to a merger having competitive effects of concern. Firms considering entry that requires significant sunk costs must evaluate the profitability of the entry on the basis of long term participation in the market, because the underlying assets will be committed to the market until they are economically depreciated. Entry that is sufficient to counteract the competitive effects of concern will cause prices to fall to their premerger levels or lower. Thus, the profitability of such committed entry must be determined on the basis of premerger market prices over the long-term.

A merger having anticompetitive effects can attract committed entry, profitable at premerger prices, that would not have occurred premerger at these same prices. But following the merger, the reduction in industry output and increase in prices associated with the competitive effect of concern may allow the same entry to occur without driving market prices below premerger levels. After a merger that results in decreased output and increased prices, the likely sales opportunities available to entrants at premerger prices will be larger than they were premerger, larger by the output reduction caused by the merger. If entry could be profitable at premerger prices without exceeding the likely sales opportunities—opportunities that include pre-existing pertinent factors as well as the merger-induced output reduction—then such entry is likely in response to the merger.

The third step assesses whether timely and likely entry would be sufficient to return market prices to their premerger levels. This end may be accomplished either through multiple entry or individual entry at a sufficient scale. Entry may not be sufficient, even though timely and likely, where the constraints on availability of essential assets, due to incumbent control, make it impossible for entry profitably to achieve the necessary

[25] Supply responses that require less than one year and insignificant sunk costs to effectuate are analyzed as uncommitted entry in Section 1.3.

level of sales. Also, the character and scope of entrants' products might not be fully responsive to the localized sales opportunities created by the removal of direct competition among sellers of differentiated products. In assessing whether entry will be timely, likely, and sufficient, the Agency recognizes that precise and detailed information may be difficult or impossible to obtain. In such instances, the Agency will rely on all available evidence bearing on whether entry will satisfy the conditions of timeliness, likelihood, and sufficiency.

3.1 Entry Alternatives

The Agency will examine the timeliness, likelihood, and sufficiency of the means of entry (entry alternatives) a potential entrant might practically employ, without attempting to identify who might be potential entrants. An entry alternative is defined by the actions the firm must take in order to produce and sell in the market. All phases of the entry effort will be considered, including, where relevant, planning, design, and management; permitting, licensing, and other approvals; construction, debugging, and operation of production facilities; and promotion (including necessary introductory discounts), marketing, distribution, and satisfaction of customer testing and qualification requirements.[26]

Recent examples of entry, whether successful or unsuccessful, may provide a useful starting point for identifying the necessary actions, time requirements, and characteristics of possible entry alternatives.

3.2 Timeliness of Entry

In order to deter or counteract the competitive effects of concern, entrants quickly must achieve a significant impact on price in the relevant market. The Agency generally will consider timely only those committed entry alternatives that can be achieved within two years from initial planning to significant market impact.[27] Where the relevant product is a durable good, consumers, in response to a significant commitment to entry, may defer purchases by making additional investments to extend the useful life of previously purchased goods and in this way deter or counteract for a time the competitive effects of concern. In these circumstances, if entry only can occur outside of the two year period, the Agency will consider entry to be timely so long as it would deter or counteract the competitive effects of concern within the two year period and subsequently.

3.3 Likelihood of Entry

An entry alternative is likely if it would be profitable at premerger prices, and if such prices could be secured by the entrant.[28] The committed entrant will be unable to secure prices at premerger levels if its output is too large for the market to absorb without depressing prices further. Thus, entry is unlikely if the minimum viable scale is larger than the likely sales opportunity available to entrants.

---

[26] Many of these phases may be undertaken simultaneously.

[27] Firms which have committed to entering the market prior to the merger generally will be included in the measurement of the market. Only committed entry or adjustments to pre-existing entry plans that are induced by the merger will be considered as possibly deterring or counteracting the competitive effects of concern.

[28] Where conditions indicate that entry may be profitable at prices below premerger levels, the Agency will assess the likelihood of entry at the lowest price at which such entry would be profitable.

Minimum viable scale is the smallest average annual level of sales that the committed entrant must persistently achieve for profitability at premerger prices.[29] Minimum viable scale is a function of expected revenues, based upon premerger prices,[30] and all categories of costs associated with the entry alternative, including an appropriate rate of return on invested capital given that entry could fail and sunk costs, if any, will be lost.[31]

Sources of sales opportunities available to entrants include: (a) the output reduction associated with the competitive effect of concern,[32] (b) entrants' ability to capture a share of reasonably expected growth in market demand,[33] (c) entrants' ability securely to divert sales from incumbents, for example, through vertical integration or through forward contracting, and (d) any additional anticipated contraction in incumbents' output in response to entry.[34] Factors that reduce the sales opportunities available to entrants include: (a) the prospect that an entrant will share in a reasonably expected decline in market demand, (b) the exclusion of an entrant from a portion of the market over the long term because of vertical integration or forward contracting by incumbents, and (c) any anticipated sales expansion by incumbents in reaction to entry, either generalized or targeted at customers approached by the entrant, that utilizes prior irreversible investments in excess production capacity. Demand growth or decline will be viewed as relevant only if total market demand is projected to experience long-lasting change during at least the two year period following the competitive effect of concern.

3.4 Sufficiency of Entry

Inasmuch as multiple entry generally is possible and individual entrants may flexibly choose their scale, committed entry generally will be sufficient to deter or counteract the competitive effects of concern whenever entry is likely under the analysis of Section 3.3. However, entry, although likely, will not be sufficient if, as a result of incumbent control, the tangible and intangible assets required for entry are not adequately available for entrants to respond fully to their sales opportunities. In addition, where the competitive effect of concern is not uniform across the relevant market, in order for entry to be sufficient, the character and scope of entrants' products must be responsive to the localized sales opportunities that include the output reduction associated with the competitive effect of concern. For example, where the concern is unilateral price elevation as a result of a merger between producers of differentiated products, entry, in order to be

---

[29] The concept of minimum viable scale ("MVS") differs from the concept of minimum efficient scale ("MES"). While MES is the smallest scale at which average costs are minimized, MVS is the smallest scale at which average costs equal the premerger price.

[30] The expected path of future prices, absent the merger, may be used if future price changes can be predicted with reasonable reliability.

[31] The minimum viable scale of an entry alternative will be relatively large when the fixed costs of entry are large, when the fixed costs of entry are largely sunk, when the marginal costs of production are high at low levels of output, and when a plant is underutilized for a long time because of delays in achieving market acceptance.

[32] Five percent of total market sales typically is used because where a monopolist profitably would raise price by five percent or more across the entire relevant market, it is likely that the accompanying reduction in sales would be no less than five percent.

[33] Entrants' anticipated share of growth in demand depends on incumbents' capacity constraints and irreversible investments in capacity expansion, as well as on the relative appeal, acceptability and reputation of incumbents' and entrants' products to the new demand.

[34] For example, in a bidding market where all bidders are on equal footing, the market share of incumbents will contract as a result of entry.

sufficient, must involve a product so close to the products of the merging firms that the merged firm will be unable to internalize enough of the sales loss due to the price rise, rendering the price increase unprofitable.

4. Efficiencies

Competition usually spurs firms to achieve efficiencies internally. Nevertheless, mergers have the potential to generate significant efficiencies by permitting a better utilization of existing assets, enabling the combined firm to achieve lower costs in producing a given quantity and quality than either firm could have achieved without the proposed transaction. Indeed, the primary benefit of mergers to the economy is their potential to generate such efficiencies.

Efficiencies generated through merger can enhance the merged firm's ability and incentive to compete, which may result in lower prices, improved quality, enhanced service, or new products. For example, merger-generated efficiencies may enhance competition by permitting two ineffective (e.g., high cost) competitors to become one effective (e.g., lower cost) competitor. In a coordinated interaction context (see Section 2.1), marginal cost reductions may make coordination less likely or effective by enhancing the incentive of a maverick to lower price or by creating a new maverick firm. In a unilateral effects context (see Section 2.2), marginal cost reductions may reduce the merged firm's incentive to elevate price. Efficiencies also may result in benefits in the form of new or improved products, and efficiencies may result in benefits even when price is not immediately and directly affected. Even when efficiencies generated through merger enhance a firm's ability to compete, however, a merger may have other effects that may lessen competition and ultimately may make the merger anticompetitive.

The Agency will consider only those efficiencies likely to be accomplished with the proposed merger and unlikely to be accomplished in the absence of either the proposed merger or another means having comparable anticompetitive effects. These are termed merger-specific efficiencies.[35] Only alternatives that are practical in the business situation faced by the merging firms will be considered in making this determination; the Agency will not insist upon a less restrictive alternative that is merely theoretical.

Efficiencies are difficult to verify and quantify, in part because much of the information relating to efficiencies is uniquely in the possession of the merging firms. Moreover, efficiencies projected reasonably and in good faith by the merging firms may not be realized. Therefore, the merging firms must substantiate efficiency claims so that the Agency can verify by reasonable means the likelihood and magnitude of each asserted efficiency, how and when each would be achieved (and any costs of doing so), how each would enhance the merged firm's ability and incentive to compete, and why each would be merger-specific. Efficiency claims will not be considered if they are vague or speculative or otherwise cannot be verified by reasonable means.

Cognizable efficiencies are merger-specific efficiencies that have been verified and do not arise from anticompetitive reductions in output or service. Cognizable efficiencies are assessed net of costs produced by the merger or incurred in achieving those efficiencies.

---

[35] The Agency will not deem efficiencies to be merger-specific if they could be preserved by practical alternatives that mitigate competitive concerns, such as divestiture or licensing. If a merger affects not whether but only when an efficiency would be achieved, only the timing advantage is a merger-specific efficiency.

The Agency will not challenge a merger if cognizable efficiencies are of a character and magnitude such that the merger is not likely to be anticompetitive in any relevant market.[36] To make the requisite determination, the Agency considers whether cognizable efficiencies likely would be sufficient to reverse the merger's potential to harm consumers in the relevant market, e.g., by preventing price increases in that market. In conducting this analysis,[37] the Agency will not simply compare the magnitude of the cognizable efficiencies with the magnitude of the likely harm to competition absent the efficiencies. The greater the potential adverse competitive effect of a merger—as indicated by the increase in the HHI and post-merger HHI from Section 1, the analysis of potential adverse competitive effects from Section 2, and the timeliness, likelihood, and sufficiency of entry from Section 3—the greater must be cognizable efficiencies in order for the Agency to conclude that the merger will not have an anticompetitive effect in the relevant market. When the potential adverse competitive effect of a merger is likely to be particularly large, extraordinarily great cognizable efficiencies would be necessary to prevent the merger from being anticompetitive.

In the Agency's experience, efficiencies are most likely to make a difference in merger analysis when the likely adverse competitive effects, absent the efficiencies, are not great. Efficiencies almost never justify a merger to monopoly or near-monopoly.

The Agency has found that certain types of efficiencies are more likely to be cognizable and substantial than others. For example, efficiencies resulting from shifting production among facilities formerly owned separately, which enable the merging firms to reduce the marginal cost of production, are more likely to be susceptible to verification, merger-specific, and substantial, and are less likely to result from anticompetitive reductions in output. Other efficiencies, such as those relating to research and development, are potentially substantial but are generally less susceptible to verification and may be the result of anticompetitive output reductions. Yet others, such as those relating to procurement, management, or capital cost are less likely to be merger-specific or substantial, or may not be cognizable for other reasons.

---

[36] Section 7 of the Clayton Act prohibits mergers that may substantially lessen competition "in any line of commerce . . . in any section of the country." Accordingly, the Agency normally assesses competition in each relevant market affected by a merger independently and normally will challenge the merger if it is likely to be anticompetitive in any relevant market. In some cases, however, the Agency in its prosecutorial discretion will consider efficiencies not strictly in the relevant market, but so inextricably linked with it that a partial divestiture or other remedy could not feasibly eliminate the anticompetitive effect in the relevant market without sacrificing the efficiencies in the other market(s). Inextricably linked efficiencies rarely are a significant factor in the Agency's determination not to challenge a merger. They are most likely to make a difference when they are great and the likely anticompetitive effect in the relevant market(s) is small.

[37] The result of this analysis over the short term will determine the Agency's enforcement decision in most cases. The Agency also will consider the effects of cognizable efficiencies with no short-term, direct effect on prices in the relevant market. Delayed benefits from efficiencies (due to delay in the achievement of, or the realization of consumer benefits from, the efficiencies) will be given less weight because they are less proximate and more difficult to predict.

5. FAILURE AND EXITING ASSETS

5.0 Overview

Notwithstanding the analysis of Sections 1–4 of the Guidelines, a merger is not likely to create or enhance market power or to facilitate its exercise, if imminent failure, as defined below, of one of the merging firms would cause the assets of that firm to exit the relevant market. In such circumstances, post-merger performance in the relevant market may be no worse than market performance had the merger been blocked and the assets left the market.

5.1 Failing Firm

A merger is not likely to create or enhance market power or facilitate its exercise if the following circumstances are met: 1) the allegedly failing firm would be unable to meet its financial obligations in the near future; 2) it would not be able to reorganize successfully under Chapter 11 of the Bankruptcy Act;[38] 3) it has made unsuccessful good-faith efforts to elicit reasonable alternative offers of acquisition of the assets of the failing firm[39] that would both keep its tangible and intangible assets in the relevant market and pose a less severe danger to competition than does the proposed merger; and 4) absent the acquisition, the assets of the failing firm would exit the relevant market.

5.2 Failing Division

A similar argument can be made for "failing" divisions as for failing firms. First, upon applying appropriate cost allocation rules, the division must have a negative cash flow on an operating basis. Second, absent the acquisition, it must be that the assets of the division would exit the relevant market in the near future if not sold. Due to the ability of the parent firm to allocate costs, revenues, and intracompany transactions among itself and its subsidiaries and divisions, the Agency will require evidence, not based solely on management plans that could be prepared solely for the purpose of demonstrating negative cash flow or the prospect of exit from the relevant market. Third, the owner of the failing division also must have complied with the competitively-preferable purchaser requirement of Section 5.1.

---

[38] 11 U.S.C. Sections 1101–1174 (1988).

[39] Any offer to purchase the assets of the failing firm for a price above the liquidation value of those assets—the highest valued use outside the relevant market or equivalent offer to purchase the stock of the failing firm—will be regarded as a reasonable alternative offer.

15

COMMENTARY ON THE HORIZONTAL MERGER GUIDELINES

U.S. DEPARTMENT OF JUSTICE AND FEDERAL TRADE COMMISSION

March 2006

Table of Contents

Foreword

Mergers between competing firms, i.e., "horizontal" mergers, are a significant dynamic force in the American economy. The vast majority of mergers pose no harm to consumers, and many produce efficiencies that benefit consumers in the form of lower prices, higher quality goods or services, or investments in innovation. Efficiencies such as these enable companies to compete more effectively, both domestically and overseas.

Fourteen years ago, to describe their application of the antitrust laws to horizontal mergers, the Federal Trade Commission and the U.S. Department of Justice (collectively, the "Agencies")—the two federal Agencies responsible for U.S. antitrust law enforcement—jointly issued the 1992 Horizontal Merger Guidelines (the "Guidelines"). In 1997, the Agencies jointly issued revisions to the Guidelines' section on Efficiencies. Since these publications were issued, the Agencies have consistently applied the Guidelines' analytical framework to the horizontal mergers under their review.

Today, to provide greater transparency and foster deeper understanding regarding antitrust law enforcement, the Agencies jointly issue this Commentary on the Guidelines.

The Commentary continues the Agencies' ongoing efforts to increase the transparency of their decision-making processes. These efforts include the Agencies' joint publication of Merger Challenges Data, Fiscal Years 1999–2003 (issued December 18, 2003), the Commission's subsequent publication of Horizontal Merger Investigation Data, Fiscal Years 1996–2003 (issued February 2, 2004 and revised August 31, 2004), the Department's Merger Review Process Initiative (issued October 12, 2001 and revised August 4, 2004 and December 14, 2006), the Reforms to the Merger Review Process at the Commission (issued February 16, 2006), and the Department's and Commission's increased use of explanatory closing statements following merger investigations.

The Commentary follows on the Agencies' February 2004 Merger Enforcement Workshop. Over three days, leading antitrust practitioners and economists who have examined merger policy and the Guidelines' analytical framework discussed in detail all sections of the Guidelines. The Workshop focused on whether the analytical framework set forth by the Guidelines adequately serves the dual purposes of leading to appropriate enforcement decisions on proposed horizontal mergers, and providing the antitrust bar and the business community with reasonably clear guidance from which to assess the antitrust enforcement risks of proposed transactions.

Workshop participants generally agreed that the analytical framework set out in the Guidelines is effective in yielding the right results in individual cases and in providing advice to parties considering a merger. Thus, the Agencies concluded that a revamping of the Guidelines is neither needed nor widely desired at this time. Rather, the Guidelines' analytic framework has proved both robust and sufficiently flexible to allow the Agencies properly to account for the particular facts presented in each merger investigation.

The Agencies also have observed that the antitrust bar and business community would find useful and beneficial an explication of how the Agencies apply the Guidelines in particular investigations. This Commentary is intended to respond to this important public interest by enhancing the transparency of the analytical process by which the Agencies apply the antitrust laws to horizontal mergers.

Deborah Platt Majoras
Chairman, Federal Trade Commission

Thomas O. Barnett
Assistant Attorney General for Antitrust, U.S. Department of Justice

March 2006

Introduction

Governing Legal Principles

The principal federal antitrust laws applicable to mergers are section 7 of the Clayton Act, section 1 of the Sherman Act, and section 5 of the Federal Trade Commission Act. Section 7 proscribes a merger the effects of which "may be substantially to lessen competition." Section 1 prohibits an agreement that constitutes an unreasonable "restraint of trade." Section 5, which the Federal Trade Commission enforces, proscribes "unfair methods of competition." Over many decades, the federal courts have provided an expansive body of case law interpreting these statutes within the factual and economic context of individual cases.

The core concern of the antitrust laws, including as they pertain to mergers between rivals, is the creation or enhancement of market power. In the context of sellers of goods or services, "market power" may be defined as the ability profitably to maintain prices above competitive levels for a significant period of time. Market power may be exercised, however, not only by raising price, but also, for example, by reducing quality or slowing innovation. In addition, mergers also can create market power on the buying side of a market. Most mergers between rivals do not create or enhance market power. Many mergers, moreover, enable the merged firm to reduce its costs and become more efficient, which, in turn, may lead to lower prices, higher quality products, or investments in innovation. However, the Agencies challenge mergers that are likely to create or enhance the merged firm's ability—either unilaterally or through coordination with rivals—to exercise market power.

Following their mandate under the antitrust statutory and case law, the Agencies focus their horizontal merger analysis on whether the transactions under review are likely to create or enhance market power. The Guidelines set forth the analytical framework and standards, consistent with the law and with economic learning, that the Agencies use to assess whether an anticompetitive outcome is likely. The unifying theme of that assessment is "that mergers should not be permitted to create or enhance market power or to facilitate its exercise." Guidelines § 0.1. The Guidelines are flexible, allowing the Agencies' analysis to adapt as business practices and economic learning evolve.

In applying the Guidelines to the transactions that each separately reviews, the Agencies strive to allow transactions unlikely substantially to lessen competition to proceed as expeditiously as possible. The Agencies focus their attention on quickly identifying those transactions that could violate the antitrust laws, subjecting those mergers to greater scrutiny. Most mergers that pose significant risk to competition come to the Agencies' attention before they are consummated under the premerger notification and reporting requirements of the Hart-Scott-Rodino Antitrust Improvements Act of 1976, 15 U.S.C. § 18a ("HSR"). HSR requires that the parties to a transaction above a certain size notify the Agencies before consummation and prohibits consummation of the transaction until expiration of one or more waiting periods during which one of the Agencies reviews the transaction. The waiting periods provide the Agencies time to review a transaction before consummation.

For more than 95% of the transactions reported under HSR, the Agencies promptly determine—i.e., within the initial fifteen- or thirty-day waiting period that immediately follows HSR filings—that a substantial lessening of competition is unlikely. The Agencies base such expeditious determinations on material provided as part of the HSR notification, experience from prior investigations, and other market information. For many industries, a wealth of information is available from government reports, trade directories and publications, and Internet resources. For some transactions, the parties volunteer additional information, and for some, the Agencies obtain information from non-public sources. The most important non-public sources are market participants, especially the parties' customers, who typically provide information voluntarily when the Agencies solicit their cooperation.

Evidence that the merged firm would have a relatively high share of sales (or of capacity, or of units, or of another relevant basis for measurement) or that the market is relatively highly concentrated may be particularly significant to a decision by either of the Agencies to extend a pre-merger investigation pursuant to HSR by issuing a request for additional information (commonly referred to as a "second request"). A decision to issue a second request must be made within the initial HSR thirty-day waiting period (fifteen days for cash tender offers), or the parties will no longer be prevented under HSR from consummating their merger. A second request may be necessary when it is not possible within thirty days to gather and analyze the facts necessary to address appropriately the competitive concerns that may arise at the threshold of the investigation, such as when parties to a merger appear to have relatively high shares in the market or markets in which they compete. Although the ultimate decision of whether a merger likely will be anticompetitive is based heavily on evidence of potential anticompetitive effects, the Agencies find that only in extraordinary circumstances can they conduct an extensive competitive effects analysis within thirty days. That is why market shares and concentration levels, which have some predictive value, frequently are used as at least a starting point during the initial waiting period.

Sometimes the Agencies also investigate consummated mergers, especially when evidence suggests that anticompetitive effects may have resulted from them. The Agencies apply Guidelines analysis to consummated mergers as well as to mergers under review pursuant to HSR.

Overview of Guidelines Analysis

The Guidelines' five-part organizational structure has become deeply embedded in mainstream merger analysis. These parts are: (1) market definition and concentration; (2) potential adverse competitive effects; (3) entry analysis; (4) efficiencies; and (5) failing and exiting assets.

Each of the Guidelines' sections identifies a distinct analytical element that the Agencies apply in an integrated approach to merger review. The ordering of these elements in the Guidelines, however, is not itself analytically significant, because the Agencies do not apply the Guidelines as a linear, step-by-step progression that invariably starts with market definition and ends with efficiencies or failing assets. Analysis of efficiencies, for example, does not occur "after" competitive effects or market definition in the Agencies' analysis of proposed mergers, but rather is part of an integrated approach. If the conditions necessary for an anticompetitive effect are not present—for example, because entry would reverse that effect before significant time elapsed—the Agencies terminate their review because it would be unnecessary to address all of the analytical elements.

The chapters that follow, in the context of specific analytical elements such as market definition or entry, describe many principles of Guidelines analysis that the Agencies apply in the course of investigating mergers. Three significant principles are generally applicable throughout.

The Agencies' Focus Is on Competitive Effects

The Guidelines' integrated process is "a tool that allows the Agency to answer the ultimate inquiry in merger analysis: whether the merger is likely to create or enhance market power or facilitate its exercise." Guidelines § 0.2. At the center of the Agencies' application of the

Guidelines, therefore, is competitive effects analysis. That inquiry directly addresses the key question that the Agencies must answer: Is the merger under review likely substantially to lessen competition? To this end, the Agencies examine whether the merger of two particular rivals matters, that is, whether the merger is likely to affect adversely the competitive process, resulting in higher prices, lower quality, or reduced innovation.

The Guidelines identify two broad analytical frameworks for assessing whether a merger between competing firms may substantially lessen competition. These frameworks require that the Agencies ask whether the merger may increase market power by facilitating coordinated interaction among rival firms and whether the merger may enable the merged firm unilaterally to raise price or otherwise exercise market power. Together, these two frameworks are intended to embrace every competitive effect of any form of horizontal merger. The Guidelines were never intended to detail how the Agencies would assess every set of circumstances that a proposed merger may present. As the Guidelines themselves note, the specific standards set forth therein must be applied to a broad range of possible factual circumstances.

Investigations Are Intensively Fact-Driven, Iterative Processes

Merger analysis depends heavily on the specific facts of each case. At the outset of an investigation, when Agency staff may know relatively little about the merging firms, their products, their rivals, or the applicable relevant markets, staff typically contemplates several broad hypotheses of possible harm.

For example, based on initial information, staff may hypothesize that a merger would reduce the number of competitors from four to three and, in so doing, may foster or enhance coordination by enabling the remaining firms profitably to allocate customers based on prior sales. Staff also might hypothesize that the products of the merging firms are particularly close substitutes with respect to product characteristics or geographic location such that unilateral anticompetitive effects are likely.

Staff evaluates potential competitive factors of this sort by gathering additional information and conducting intensive factual analysis to assess both the applicability of individual analytical frameworks and their implications for the likely competitive effects of the merger. As it learns more about the merging firms and the market environment in which they compete, staff rejects or refines its hypotheses of probable relevant markets and competitive effects, ultimately resulting in a conclusion about likelihood of harm. If the facts do not point to such a likelihood, the merger investigation is closed.

In testing a particular postulated risk of competitive harm arising from a merger, the Agencies take into account pertinent characteristics of the market's competitive process using data, documents, and other information obtained from the parties, their competitors, their customers, databases of various sorts, and academic literature or private industry studies. The Agencies carefully consider the views of informed customers on market structure, the competitive process, and anticipated effects from the merger. The Agencies further consider any information voluntarily provided by the parties, which may include extensive analyses prepared by economists or in consultation with economists. The Agencies also carefully consider prospects for efficiencies that the proposed transaction may generate and evaluate the effects of any efficiencies on the outcome of the competitive process.

The Same Evidence Often Is Relevant to Multiple Elements of the Analysis

A single piece of evidence often is relevant to several issues in the assessment of a proposed merger. For example, mergers frequently occur in markets that have experienced prior mergers. Sometimes evidence exists concerning the effects of prior mergers on various attributes of competition. Such evidence may be probative, for example, of the scope of the relevant product and geographic markets, of the likely competitive effects of the proposed merger, and of the likelihood that entry would deter or counteract any attempted exercise of market power following the merger under review. Similarly, evidence of actual or likely anticompetitive effects from a merger could be used in addressing the scope of the market or entry conditions.

An investigation involving potential coordinated effects may uncover evidence of past collusion and sustained supra-competitive prices in the market. This information can be relevant to several elements of the analysis. The product and geographic markets that were subject to collusion in the past may be probative of the relevant product and geographic markets today. That entry failed to undermine collusion in the past may be probative of whether entry is likely today. Of course, during its investigation, the Agency may discover facts that tend to negate these possibilities. For example, since collusion occurred, new production technologies may have emerged that have altered the ability or incentives of firms to coordinate their actions. Similarly, innovation may have led to the introduction of new products that compete with the incumbent products and constrain the ability of the merging firms and their rivals to coordinate successfully in the future.

Commentary Outline

In the chapters that follow, the Commentary explains how the Agencies have applied particular Guidelines' provisions relating to market definition and concentration, competitive effects (including coordinated interaction and unilateral effects analysis), entry conditions, and efficiencies. Application of the Guidelines' provisions relating to failure and exiting assets is not discussed in the Commentary because those provisions are very infrequently applied. For convenience, the order of these chapters follows the order of the issues set forth in the Guidelines.

Included throughout the Commentary are short summaries of matters that the Agencies have investigated. They have been included to further understanding of the principles under discussion at that point in the narrative. None of the summaries exhaustively addresses all the pertinent facts or issues that arose in the investigation. No other significance should be attributed to the selection of the matters used as examples. (In some instances in the Efficiencies chapter, names and other key facts of actual matters are changed to protect the confidentiality of business and proprietary information. Each is noted as a "Disguised Example.") An Index at the end of the Commentary lists all of the mergers discussed in these case examples and provides citations to additional public information.

For the reader's convenience, the case examples briefly state how each investigation ended, i.e., whether it was closed because the Agency determined not to challenge the merger or because the parties abandoned the merger in response to imminent Agency challenge, or whether the investigation proceeded to a consent agreement or to litigation. The discussion within each case example pertains solely to the relevant Agency's analysis of the merger, and does not elaborate on any subsequent judicial or administrative proceedings.

---

1. Market Definition and Concentration

The Agencies evaluate a merger's likely competitive effects "within the context of economically significant markets—i.e., markets that could be subject to the exercise of market power." Guidelines § 1.0. The purpose of merger analysis under the Guidelines is to identify those mergers that are likely to create or enhance market power in any market. The Agencies therefore examine all plausible markets to determine whether an adverse competitive effect is likely to occur in any of them. The market definition process is not isolated from the other analytic components in the Guidelines. The Agencies do not settle on a relevant market definition before proceeding to address other issues. Rather, market definition is part of the integrated process by which the Agencies apply Guidelines principles, iterated as new facts are learned, to reach an understanding of the merger's likely effect on competition.

The mechanics of how the Agencies define markets using the Guidelines method has been the subject of extensive discussion in legal and economic literature and appears to be well understood in the antitrust community. This Commentary, accordingly, provides only a brief overview of the mechanics. The remainder of this chapter addresses a number of discrete topics concerning market definition issues that frequently arise in merger investigations.

Mechanics of Market Definition

The Guidelines define a market as "a product or group of products and a geographic area in which it is produced or sold such that a hypothetical profit-maximizing firm, not subject to price regulation, that was the only present and future producer or seller of those products in that area likely would impose at least a 'small but significant and nontransitory' increase in price, assuming the terms of sale of all other products are held constant." Guidelines § 1.0.

This approach to market definition is referred to as the "hypothetical monopolist" test. To determine the effects of this " 'small but significant and nontransitory' increase in price" (commonly referred to as a "SSNIP"), the Agencies generally use a price increase of five percent. This test identifies which product(s) in which geographic locations significantly constrain the price of the merging firms' products.

The Guidelines' method for implementing the hypothetical monopolist test starts by identifying each product produced or sold by each of the merging firms. Then, for each product, it iteratively broadens the candidate market by adding the next-best substitute. A relevant product market emerges as the smallest group of products that satisfies the hypothetical monopolist test. Product market definition depends critically upon demand-side substitution—i.e., consumers' willingness to switch from one product to another in reaction to price changes. The Guidelines' approach to market definition reflects the separation of demand substitutability from supply substitutability—i.e., the ability and willingness, given existing capacity, of firms to substitute from making one product to producing another in reaction to a price change. Under this approach, demand substitutability is the concern of market delineation, while supply substitutability and entry are concerned with current and future market participants.

Definition of the relevant geographic market is undertaken in much the same way as product market definition—by identifying the narrowest possible market and then broadening it by iteratively adding the next-best substitutes. Thus, for geographic market definition, the Agencies begin with the area(s) in which the merging firms compete respecting each relevant product, and extend the boundaries of those areas until an area is determined within which a hypothetical monopolist would raise prices by at least a small but significant and non-transitory amount.

> ***DaVita-Gambro* (FTC 2005)** DaVita Inc., proposed to acquire Gambro Healthcare, Inc. The firms competed across the United States in the provision of outpatient dialysis services for persons with end stage renal disease ("ESRD"). Commission staff found that the relevant geographic markets within which to analyze the transaction's likely competitive effects were local. Most ESRD patients receive treatments about 3 times per week, in sessions lasting 3–5 hours, and in general either are unwilling or unable to travel more than 30 miles or 30 minutes to receive kidney dialysis treatment. In the process of defining the geographic market, staff identified the Metropolitan Statistical Areas ("MSAs") within which both firms had outpatient dialysis clinics, then examined each area to determine if geographic factors such as mountains, rivers, and bays, and travel conditions, were such that the scope of the relevant market differed from the MSA's boundaries.
>
> Within each such MSA, staff isolated the area immediately surrounding each dialysis clinic of both merging parties, and assessed whether a hypothetical monopolist within that area would impose a significant price increase. Staff expanded the boundaries of each area until the evidence showed that such a hypothetical monopolist would impose a significant price increase. From interviews with industry participants and analysis of documents, staff found that, in general, dialysis patients tend to travel greater distances in rural and suburban areas than in dense urban areas, where travel distances as small as 5–10 miles may take significantly more than 30 minutes, due to congestion, road conditions, reliance on public transportation, and other factors. Maps indicating the locations from which each clinic drew its patients were particularly useful. Thus, some MSAs included within their respective boundaries many distinct areas over which a hypothetical monopolist would exercise market power. The Commission entered into a consent agreement with the parties to resolve the concern that the transaction would likely lead to anticompetitive effects in 35 local markets. In an order issued with the consent agreement, the Commission required, among other things, the divestiture of dialysis clinics in the 35 markets at issue.

The Breadth of Relevant Markets

Defining markets under the Guidelines' method does not necessarily result in markets that include the full range of functional substitutes from which customers choose. That is because, as the Guidelines provide, a "relevant market is a group of products and a geographic area that is no bigger than necessary to satisfy [the hypothetical monopolist] test." Guidelines § 1.0. This is one of several points at which the Guidelines articulate what is referred to in section 1.21 as the " 'smallest market' principle" for determining the relevant market. The Agencies frequently conclude that a relatively narrow range of products or geographic space within a larger group describes the competitive arena within which significant anticompetitive effects are possible.

Nestle-Dreyer's **(FTC 2003)** Nestle Holdings, Inc., proposed to merge with Dreyer's Grand Ice Cream, Inc. The firms were rivals in the sale of superpremium ice cream. Ice cream is differentiated on the basis of the quality of ingredients. Compared to premium and non-premium ice cream, superpremium ice cream contains more butterfat, less air, and more costly ingredients. Superpremium ice cream sells at a substantially higher price than premium ice cream. Using scanner data, Commission staff estimated demand elasticities for the superpremium, premium, and economy ice cream segments. Staff's analysis showed that a hypothetical monopolist of superpremium ice cream would increase prices significantly. This, together with other documentary and testimonial evidence, indicated that the relevant market in which to analyze the transaction was superpremium ice cream. The Commission entered into a consent agreement with the merging firms, requiring divestiture of two brands and of key distribution assets.

UPM-MACtac **(DOJ 2003)** UPM-Kymmene Oyj sought to acquire (from Bemis Co.) Morgan Adhesives Co. ("MACtac"). They were two of the three largest producers of paper pressure-sensitive labelstock, from which "converters" make pressure-sensitive labels. End users peel pressure-sensitive labels off a silicon-coated base material and directly apply them to items being labeled. The Department challenged the acquisition on the basis of likely anticompetitive effects in two relevant product markets. One was paper labelstock used to make pressure sensitive labels for "variable information printing" ("VIP"). Some or all of the printing on VIP labels is done by end users as the label is applied. A familiar example is the price labeling of fresh meat sold in supermarkets. Although paper labelstock for VIP labels competes with plastic film labelstock, the Department found that film labels are of sufficiently higher cost that a hypothetical monopolist of paper labelstock for VIP labels would raise price significantly. The other relevant product market was paper labelstock used for "prime" labels. Prime labels are used for product identification and are printed in advance of application. Paper labelstock for prime labels, competes not just with film labelstock, but also with pre-printed packaging and other means of product identification. Nevertheless, the Department found that a hypothetical monopolist of paper labelstock for prime labels would raise price significantly because users of pressure-sensitive paper labels find them the least-cost alternative for their particular applications and because they would have to incur significant switching costs if they adopted an alternative means of product identification. After trial, the court enjoined the consummation of the acquisition.

Tenet-Slidell **(FTC 2003)** Tenet Health Care Systems owned a hospital in Slidell, Louisiana (near New Orleans), and proposed to acquire Slidell's only other full-service hospital. There were many other full-service hospitals in the New Orleans area but all were outside of Slidell. Commission staff found that a significant number of Slidell residents and their employers required access to either of the two Slidell hospitals in their private health insurance plans. The Slidell hospitals competed against each other for inclusion in health plan networks. After merging, the combined hospital would have had no rival with "must have" network status among Slidell residents and employers. A hypothetical monopolist of the Slidell hospitals likely would have imposed a small but significant and non-transitory price increase on health plans selling coverage in Slidell, because neighboring hospitals outside of Slidell were not effective substitutes for network inclusion. The relevant geographic market, therefore, was limited to hospitals located in Slidell. Under Louisiana law, proposed acquisitions of not-for-profit hospitals must be approved by the Louisiana Attorney General. By invitation of the state Attorney General, Commission staff, in a public letter authorized by the Commission, advised the Attorney General of the staff's view that, based on the facts gathered in its then-ongoing investigation, the proposed acquisition raised serious competitive concerns. In a vote authorized by local law, parish residents subsequently rejected the proposed transaction, which never was consummated.

In sections 1.12 and 1.22, the Guidelines explain that the Agencies may define relevant markets on the basis of price discrimination if a hypothetical monopolist likely would exercise market power only, or especially, in sales to particular customers or in particular geographic areas. The Agencies address the same basic issues for any form of discrimination: Would price discrimination, if feasible, permit a significantly greater exercise of market power? Could competitors successfully identify the transactions to be discriminated against? Would customers or third parties be able to undermine substantially the discrimination through some form of arbitrage in which a product sold at lower prices to some customer groups is resold to customer groups intended by the firms to pay higher prices? In cases in which a hypothetical monopolist is likely to target only a subset of customers for anticompetitive price increases, the Agencies are likely to identify relevant markets based on the ability of sellers to price discriminate.

***Quest-Unilab* (FTC 2003)** Quest Diagnostics, Inc. and Unilab Corp., the two leading providers of clinical laboratory testing services to physician groups in Northern California, proposed to merge. Their combined market share would have exceeded 70%; the next largest rival had a market share of 4%. Clinical laboratory testing services are marketed and sold to various groups of customers, including physicians, health insurers, and hospitals. Commission staff determined that purchasers of these services cannot economically resell them to other customers, and that suppliers of the services can potentially identify the competitive alternatives available to physician group customers according to the group's base of physicians and geographic coverage. This information indicated that a hypothetical monopolist could discriminate on price among customer types. Suppliers' ability to price discriminate, combined with the fact that some types of customers had few competitive alternatives to contracting with suppliers that had a network of locations, led staff to define markets based on customer categories. The Commission issued a complaint alleging that the transaction would lessen competition substantially in one of the customer categories: the provision of clinical laboratory testing services to physician groups in Northern California. An accompanying consent order required divestiture of assets used to provide clinical laboratory testing services to physician groups in Northern California.

***Ingersoll-Dresser-Flowserve* (DOJ 2000)** Flowserve Corp. agreed to acquire Ingersoll-Dresser Pump Co. Both firms produced a broad array of pumps used in industrial processes. The Department challenged the proposed acquisition on the basis of likely anticompetitive effects in

"API 610" pumps, which are used by oil refineries, and pumps used in electric power plants. Both sorts of pumps are customized according to the specifications of the particular buyer and are sold through bidding mechanisms. Customization of the pumps made arbitrage infeasible. The Department concluded that the competition in each procurement was entirely distinct and therefore that each procurement took place in a separate and distinct relevant market. The Department's challenge to the merger was resolved by consent decree.

***Interstate Bakeries-Continental* (DOJ 1995)** The Department challenged Interstate Bakeries Corp.'s purchase of Continental Baking Co. from Ralston Purina Co. The challenge focused on white pan bread, and the Department found that the purchase likely would have produced significant price increases in five metropolitan areas—Chicago, Milwaukee, Central Illinois, Los Angeles, and San Diego. Among the reasons the Department concluded that competition was localized to these metropolitan areas were that bakers charged different prices for the same brands produced in the same bakeries, depending on where the bread was sold, and that arbitrage was infeasible. Arbitrage was exceptionally costly because the bakers themselves placed their bread on the supermarket shelves, so arbitrage required removing bread from the shelves, reshipping it, and reshelving it. This process also would consume a significant portion of the brief period during which the bread is fresh. The Department settled its challenge to the proposed merger by a consent decree requiring divestiture of brands and related assets in the five metropolitan areas.

The Guidelines indicate that the relevant market is the smallest collection of products and geographic areas within which a hypothetical monopolist would raise price significantly. At times, the Agencies may act conservatively and focus on a market definition that might not be the smallest possible relevant market. For example, the Agencies may focus initially on a bright line identifying a group of products or areas within which it is clear that a hypothetical monopolist would raise price significantly and seek to determine whether anticompetitive effects are—or are not—likely to result from the transaction in such a candidate market. If the answer for the broader market is likely to be the same as for any plausible smaller relevant market, there is no need to pinpoint the smallest market as the precise line drawn does not affect the determination of whether a merger is anticompetitive. Also, when the analysis is identical across products or geographic areas that could each be defined as separate relevant markets using the smallest market principle, the Agencies may elect to employ a broader market definition that encompasses many products or geographic areas to avoid redundancy in presentation. The Guidelines describe this practice of aggregation "as a matter of convenience." Guidelines § 1.321 n.14.

Evidentiary Sources for Market Definition

The Importance of Evidence from and about Customers

Customers typically are the best source, and in some cases they may be the only source, of critical information on the factors that govern their ability and willingness to substitute in the event of a price increase. The Agencies routinely solicit information from customers regarding their product and supplier selections. In selecting their suppliers, customers typically evaluate the alternatives available to them and can often provide the

Agencies with information on their functional needs as well as on the cost and availability of substitutes. Customers also provide relevant information that they uniquely possess on how they choose products and suppliers. In some investigations, customers provide useful information on how they have responded to previous significant changes in circumstances. In some investigations, the Agencies are able to explore consumer preferences with the aid of price and quantity data that allow econometric estimation of the relevant elasticities of demand.

> ***Dairy Farmers-SODIAAL* (DOJ 2000)** The Department challenged the proposed acquisition by Dairy Farmers of America, Inc. of SODIAAL North America Corp. on the basis of likely anticompetitive effects in the sale of "branded stick and whipped butter in the Philadelphia and New York metropolitan areas." DFA sold the Breakstone brand, and SODIAAL sold the Keller's and Hotel Bar brands. The Department concluded that consumers of branded butter in these metropolitan areas so preferred it over private-label butter, as well as margarine and other substitutes, that a hypothetical monopolist over just branded butter in each of those areas would raise price significantly. This conclusion was supported by econometric evidence, derived from data collected from supermarkets, on the elasticity of demand for branded butter in Philadelphia and New York. The Department's complaint was resolved by a consent decree transferring the SODIAAL assets to a new company not wholly owned by DFA and containing additional injunctive provisions.

In the vast majority of cases, the Agencies largely rely on non-econometric evidence, obtained primarily from customers and from business documents.

> ***Cemex-RMC* (FTC 2005)** The proposed acquisition of RMC Group PLC by Cemex, S.A. de C.V. would have combined two of the three independent ready-mix concrete suppliers in Tucson, Arizona. Ready-mix concrete is a precise mixture of cement, aggregates, and water. It is produced at local plants and delivered as a slurry in trucks with revolving drums to construction sites, where it is poured and formed into its final shape. Commission staff determined from information received from customers that a hypothetical monopolist over ready-mix concrete would raise price significantly in the relevant area. Asphalt and other building materials were found not to be good substitutes for ready-mix concrete, due in significant part to concrete's pliability when freshly mixed and strength and permanence when hardened. Concerned that the transaction likely would result in coordinated interaction in the Tucson area, the Commission, pursuant to a consent agreement, ordered Cemex, among other things, to divest RMC's Tucson-area ready-mix concrete assets.

> ***Swedish Match-National* (FTC 2000)** Swedish Match North America, Inc. proposed to acquire National Tobacco Company, L.P. The acquisition would have combined the first- and third-largest producers of loose leaf chewing tobacco in the United States. Commission staff evaluated whether, as the merging firms contended, moist snuff should be included in the relevant market for loose leaf chewing tobacco. Swedish Match's own market research revealed that consumers would substitute less expensive loose leaf, but not more expensive snuff, if loose leaf prices increased slightly. Additional evidence from the firms' own business documents, and customer testimony from distributors that purchase and resell the products to retailers, demonstrated that loose leaf chewing tobacco constitutes a distinct product market that

does not include moist snuff. The acquisition would therefore have resulted in a merged firm with a high share of the relevant market for loose leaf chewing tobacco. The Commission successfully challenged the merger in federal district court.

In determining whether to challenge a transaction, the Agencies do not simply tally the number of customers that oppose a transaction and the number of customers that support it. The Agencies take into account that all customers in a relevant market are not necessarily situated similarly in terms of their incentives. For example, intermediate resellers' views about a proposed merger between two suppliers may be influenced by the resellers' ability profitably to pass along a price increase. If resellers can profitably pass along a price increase, they may have no objection to the merger. End-users, by contrast, generally lack such an incentive because they must absorb higher prices. In all cases, the Agencies credit customer testimony only to the extent the Agencies conclude that there is a sound foundation for the testimony.

Evidence of Effects May Be the Analytical Starting Point

In some investigations, before having determined the relevant market boundaries, the Agencies may have evidence that more directly answers the "ultimate inquiry in merger analysis," i.e., "whether the merger is likely to create or enhance market power or facilitate its exercise." Guidelines § 0.2. Evidence pointing directly toward competitive effects may arise from statistical analysis of price and quantity data related to, among other things, incumbent responses to prior events (sometimes called "natural experiments") such as entry or exit by rivals. For example, it may be that one of the merging parties recently entered and that econometric tools applied to pricing data show that the other merging party responded to that entry by reducing price by a significant amount and on a nontransitory basis while the prices of some other sellers that might be in the relevant market did not.

To be probative, of course, such data analyses must be based on accepted economic principles, valid statistical techniques, and reliable data. Moreover, the Agencies accord weight to such analyses only within the context of the full investigatory record, including information and testimony received from customers and other industry participants and from business documents.

Evidence pertaining more directly to a merger's actual or likely competitive effects also may be useful in determining the relevant market in which effects are likely. Such evidence may identify potential relevant markets and significantly reinforce or undermine other evidence relating to market definition.

***Staples-Office Depot* (FTC 1997)** Staples, Inc. proposed to acquire Office Depot, Inc., a merger that would have combined two of the three national retail chains of office supply superstores. The Commission found that in metropolitan areas where Staples faced no office superstore rival, it charged significantly higher prices than in metropolitan areas where it faced competition from Office Depot or the other office supply superstore chain, OfficeMax. Office Depot data showed a similar pattern: its prices were lowest where Staples and OfficeMax also operated, and highest where they did not. These patterns held regardless of how many non-superstore sellers of office supplies operated in the metropolitan area under review.

The Commission also found that evidence relating to entry showed that local rivalry from office supply superstores acted as the principal competitive constraint on Staples and Office Depot. Each firm regularly dropped prices in areas where they confronted entry by another office supply superstore, but did not do so in response to entry by other sellers of office supplies, such as Wal-Mart. Newspaper advertising and other promotional materials likewise reflected greater price competition in those areas in which Staples and Office Depot faced local rivalry from one another or from OfficeMax. Such evidence provided direct support for the conclusion that the acquisition would cause anticompetitive effects in the relevant product market defined as the sale of consumable office supplies through office supply superstores, in those metropolitan areas where Staples and Office Depot competed prior to the merger. The Commission successfully challenged the merger in federal district court.

In some cases, competitive effects analysis may eliminate the need to identify with specificity the appropriate relevant market definition, because, for example, the analysis shows that anticompetitive effects are unlikely in any plausibly defined market.

Federated-May **(FTC 2005)** Federated Department Stores, Inc. proposed to acquire The May Department Stores Co., thereby combining the two largest chains in the United States of so-called "traditional" or "conventional" department stores. Conventional department stores typically anchor enclosed shopping malls, feature products in the mid-range of price and quality, and sell a wide range of products. The transaction would create high levels of concentration among conventional department stores in many metropolitan areas of the United States, and the merged firm would become the only conventional department store at certain of the 1,200 malls in the United States.

If the relevant product market included only conventional department stores, then before the merger Federated had a market share greater than 90% in the New York-New Jersey metropolitan area. If the relevant product market also included, for example, specialty stores, then Federated's share in that geographic area was much smaller. The evidence that Commission staff obtained indicated that the relevant product market was broader than conventional department stores. For example, in the New York-New Jersey metropolitan area, Federated charged consumers the same prices that it charged throughout much of the eastern region of the United States, including where Federated faced larger numbers of traditional department store rivals. May and other department store chains, like Federated, also set prices to consumers that were uniform over very broad geographic areas and did not appear to vary local prices based on the number or identity of conventional department stores in malls or metropolitan areas.

This evidence provided support for the conclusion that the acquisition likely would not create anticompetitive effects. Staff also found no evidence that competitive constraints, e.g., rivalry from retailers other than department stores, in New York-New Jersey were not representative of other markets in which Federated and May competed. Further, evidence pertaining both to which firms the parties monitored for pricing and to consumer purchasing behavior also supported the conclusion that the relevant market was sufficiently broad that the merger was not likely to cause anticompetitive effects. The Commission closed the investigation.

Industry Usage of the Word "Market" Is Not Controlling

Relevant market definition is, in the antitrust context, a technical exercise involving analysis of customer substitution in response to price increases; the "markets" resulting from this definition process are specifically designed to analyze market power issues. References to a "market" in business documents may provide important insights into the identity of firms, products, or regions that key industry participants consider to be sources of rivalry, which in turn may be highly probative evidence upon which to define the "relevant market" for antitrust purposes. The Agencies are careful, however, not to assume that a "market" identified for business purposes is the same as a relevant market defined in the context of a merger analysis. When businesses and their customers use the word "market," they generally are not referring to a product or geographic market in the precise sense used in the Guidelines, although what they term a "market" may be congruent with a Guidelines' market.

> ***Staples-Office Depot*** **(FTC 1997)** In the blocked Staples-Office Depot transaction described above in this Chapter, the Commission alleged, and the district court found, that the relevant product market was "the sale of consumable office supplies through office supply superstores," with "consumable" meaning products that consumers buy recurrently, like pens, paper, and file folders. Industry members in the ordinary course of business did not describe the "market" using this phrase. The facts showed that a hypothetical monopolist office supply superstore would raise price significantly on consumable office supplies. Many retail firms that are not office supply superstores—such as discount and general merchandise stores—sold consumable office supplies in areas near the merging firms. Despite the existence of such other sellers, evidence, including the facts identified above, justified definition of the relevant product market as one limited to the sale of consumable office products solely through office supply superstores.

It is unremarkable that "markets" in common business usage do not always coincide with "markets" in an antitrust context, inasmuch as the terms are used for different purposes. The description of an "antitrust market" sometimes requires several qualifying words and as such does not reflect common business usage of the word "market." Antitrust markets are entirely appropriate to the extent that they realistically describe the range of products and geographic areas within which a hypothetical monopolist would raise price significantly and in which a merger's likely competitive effects would be felt.

> ***Waste Management-Allied*** **(DOJ 2003)** Waste Management, Inc. agreed to acquire assets from Allied Waste Industries, Inc. that were used in its municipal solid waste collection operations in Broward County, Florida. The Department challenged the proposed acquisition on the basis of anticompetitive effects in "small container commercial hauling." Commercial haulers serve customers such as office buildings, apartment buildings, and retail establishments. Small containers have capacities of 1–10 cubic yards, and waste from them is collected using specialized, front-end loading vehicles. The Department found that this market was separate and distinct from markets for other municipal solid waste collection services. The Department concluded that a hypothetical monopolist in just small container commercial hauling

would have raised prices significantly because it was uneconomical for homeowners to use the much larger containers used by commercial customers and uneconomical for commercial customers using large "roll-off" containers to switch to small commercial containers. The Department's challenge to the merger was resolved by a consent decree requiring divestiture of specified collection routes and the assets used on them.

***Pacific Enterprises-Enova* (DOJ 1998)** Pacific Enterprises (which owned Southern California Gas Co.) and Enova Corp. (which owned San Diego Gas & Electric Co.) agreed to combine the companies under a common holding company. The Department challenged the combination on the basis of likely anticompetitive effects arising from the ability of the combined companies to raise electricity prices by restricting the supply of natural gas. The Department concluded that the relevant market was the sale of electricity in California during periods of high demand. In high-demand periods, limitations on transmission capacity cause prices in California to be determined by power plants in California. Inter-temporal arbitrage was infeasible because there is only a very limited opportunity to store electric power. Thus, the Department concluded that a hypothetical electricity monopolist during just periods of high demand would raise prices significantly. The Department's complaint was resolved by a consent decree requiring divestiture of generating facilities and associated assets.

Market Definition and Integrated Analysis

Market Definition Is Linked to Competitive Effects Analysis

The process of defining the relevant market is directly linked to competitive effects analysis. In analyzing mergers, the Agencies identify specific risks of potential anticompetitive harm, and delineate the appropriate markets within which to evaluate the likelihood of such potential harm. This process could lead to different conclusions about the relevant markets likely to experience competitive harm for two similar mergers within the same industry.

***Thrifty-PayLess* (FTC 1994)** A proposed merger of Thrifty Drug Stores and PayLess Drug Stores would have combined retail drug store chains with store locations near one another in towns in California, Oregon, and Washington. Commission staff identified two potential anticompetitive effects from the merger: (1) that "cash" customers, i.e., individual consumers who pay out of pocket for prescription drugs, likely would pay higher prices; and (2) that third-party payers, such as health plans and pharmacy benefit managers ("PBMs"), likely would pay higher dispensing fees to chain pharmacy firms to obtain their participation in provider networks.

Cash customers tend to shop close to home or place of employment, suggesting small geographic markets for those customers. Third-party payers need network participation from chains having wide territorial coverage. The staff assessed different relevant markets for the two risks of competitive harm. In its complaint accompanying a consent agreement, the Commission alleged that the sale of prescription drugs in retail stores (i.e., sales to cash customers) was a relevant product market and that anticompetitive effects from the merger were likely in this market. The Commission did not allege a diminution in competition regarding the process by which pharmacies negotiate for inclusion in health plan provider networks and sought no relief in that market. The Commission ordered Thrifty, among other things, to divest retail pharmacies in the geographic markets of concern.

Rite Aid-Revco **(FTC 1996)** The nation's two largest retail drug store chains, Rite Aid Corp. and Revco D.S., Inc., proposed to merge. They competed in many local markets, including in 15 metropolitan areas in which the merged firm would have had more than 35% of the retail pharmacies. As in the foregoing *Thrifty-PayLess* matter, Commission staff defined two markets in which harm potentially may have resulted: retail sales made to cash customers, and sales through PBMs, which contract with multiple pharmacy firms to form networks offering pharmacy benefits as part of health insurance coverage. Pharmacy networks often include a high percentage of local pharmacies because access to many participating pharmacies is often important to plan enrollees.

Rite Aid and Revco constrained one another's pricing leverage with PBMs in bargaining for inclusion in PBM networks. Each merging firm offered rival broad local coverage of pharmacy locations, such that PBMs could assemble marketable networks with just one of the firms included. A high proportion of PBM plan enrollees would have considered the merged entity to be their preferred pharmacy chain, leaving PBMs with less attractive options for assembling networks that did not include the merged firm. This would have empowered the merged firm successfully to charge higher dispensing fees as a condition of participating in a network.

Commission staff determined that the merger was likely substantially to lessen competition in the relevant market of sales to PBMs and similar customers who needed a network of pharmacies. The Commission voted to challenge the merger, stating that "the proposed Rite Aid-Revco merger is the first drug store merger where the focus has been on anticompetitive price increases to the growing numbers of employees covered by these pharmacy benefit plans, rather than exclusively focusing on the cash paying customer." The parties subsequently abandoned the deal.

Many mergers, in a wide variety of industries, potentially have effects in more than one relevant geographic market or product market and require independent competitive assessments for each market.

Suiza-Broughton **(DOJ 1998)** The Department challenged the proposed acquisition of Broughton Foods Co. by Suiza Foods Corp. Suiza was a nationwide operator of milk processing plants with four dairies in Kentucky and Tennessee. Broughton operated two dairies, including the Southern Belle Dairy in Pulaski County, Kentucky. The two companies competed in the sale of milk and other dairy products to grocery stores, convenience stores, schools, and institutions. The Department's investigation focused on schools, many of which require daily, or every-other-day, delivery. School districts procured the milk through annual contracts, each of which the Department found to be an entirely separate competition. Thus, the Department defined 55 relevant markets, each consisting of a school district in south central Kentucky in which the proposed merger threatened competition. The Department's complaint was resolved by a consent decree requiring divestiture of the Southern Belle Dairy.

NAT, L.C.-D.R. Partners **(DOJ 1995)** The Department and private plaintiffs challenged the consummated acquisition of the Northwest Arkansas Times by interests owning the competing Morning News of Northwest Arkansas. The Department concluded that the acquisition likely would harm subscribers of these newspapers as well as local advertisers, and defined separate relevant markets for readers and local advertisers. The Department found that both markets included only daily newspapers because of unique characteristics valued by readers and local advertisers, and concluded that the acquisition likely would harm both groups of customers. The courts required rescission of the acquisition.

Market Definition and Competitive Effects Analysis May Involve the Same Facts

Often the same information is relevant to multiple aspects of the analysis. For example, regarding mergers that raise the concern that the merged firm would be able to exercise unilateral market power, the Agencies often use the same data and information both to define the relevant market and to ascertain whether the merger is likely to have a significant unilateral anticompetitive effect.

General Mills-Pillsbury **(FTC 2001)** General Mills, Inc. proposed to acquire The Pillsbury Co. General Mills owned the Betty Crocker brand of pancake mix and the Bisquick brand of all-purpose baking mix, a product that can be used to make pancakes as well as other products. Pillsbury owned the Hungry Jack pancake mix brand. An issue was whether the relevant product market for pancake mixes included Bisquick. General Mills' Betty Crocker pancake mix had a relatively small share of a candidate pancake mix market that excluded Bisquick, suggesting that the merger likely would not raise significant antitrust concerns in the candidate pancake mix market should the relevant market exclude Bisquick.

In addition to obtaining information from industry documents and interviews with industry participants on the correct contours of the relevant product market, FTC staff analyzed scanner data to address whether Bisquick competed with pancake mixes. Demand estimation revealed significant cross-price elasticities of demand between Bisquick and most of the individual pancake mix brands, suggesting that Bisquick competed in the same relevant market as pancake mixes. Merger simulation based on the elasticities calculated from the scanner data showed that if General Mills acquired Pillsbury it likely would unilaterally raise prices. All of the evidence taken together further confirmed that Pillsbury's Hungry Jack and Bisquick were significant substitutes, and the staff concluded that the relevant market included both pancake mixes and Bisquick. The parties resolved the competitive concerns in this market by selling Pillsbury's baking product line. No Commission action was taken.

Interstate Bakeries-Continental **(DOJ 1995)** The Department challenged Interstate Bakeries Corp.'s purchase of Continental Baking Co. from Ralston Purina Co. on the basis of likely unilateral effects in the sale of white pan bread. Econometric analysis determined that there were substantial cross-elasticities of demand between the Continental and Interstate brands of white pan bread. The Department used the estimated cross-elasticities in a merger simulation, which predicted that the merger was likely to result in price increases for those brands of 5–10%. The data used to estimate these elasticities also were used to estimate the elasticity of demand for white pan bread in the aggregate and for just "premium" brands of white pan bread. The latter estimation indicated that the relevant market was no broader than all white pan bread, despite some limited competition from other bread products and other sources of carbohydrates. The Department's challenge to the proposed merger was settled by a consent decree requiring divestiture of brands and related assets in the five metropolitan areas.

Integrated Analysis Takes into Account that Defined Market Boundaries Are Not Necessarily Precise or Rigid

For mergers involving relatively homogeneous products and distinct, identifiable geographic areas, with no substitute products or locations just outside the market boundaries, market definition is likely to be relatively easy and uncontroversial. The boundaries of a market are less clear-cut in merger cases that involve products or geographic areas for which substitutes exist along a continuum. The simple dichotomy of "in the market" or "out of the market" may not adequately capture the competitive interaction either of particularly close substitutes or of relatively distant substitutes.

Even when no readily apparent gap exists in the chain of substitutes, drawing a market boundary within the chain may be entirely appropriate when a hypothetical monopolist over just a segment of the chain of substitutes would raise prices significantly. Whenever the Agencies draw such a boundary, they recognize and account for the fact that an increase in prices within just that segment could cause significant sales to be lost to products or geographic areas outside the segment. Although these lost sales may be insufficient to deter a hypothetical monopolist from raising price significantly, combined with other factors, they may be sufficient to make anticompetitive effects an unlikely result of the merger.

Significance of Concentration and Market Share Statistics

Section 2 of the Guidelines explains that "market share and concentration data provide only the starting point for analyzing the competitive impact of a merger." Indeed, the Agencies do not make enforcement decisions solely on the basis of market shares and concentration, but both measures nevertheless play an important role in the analysis. A merger in an industry in which all participants have low shares—especially low shares in all plausible relevant markets—usually requires no significant investigation, because experience shows that such mergers normally pose no real threat to lessen competition substantially. For example, if the merging parties are small producers of a homogeneous product, operating in a geographic area where many other producers of the same homogeneous product also are located, the Agencies may conclude that the merger likely raises no competition concerns without ever determining the precise contours of the market. By contrast, mergers occurring in industries characterized by high shares in at least one plausible relevant market usually require additional analysis and consideration of factors in addition to market share.

Section 1.51 of the Guidelines sets out the general standards, based on market shares and concentration, that the Agencies use to determine whether a proposed merger ordinarily requires further analysis. The Agencies use the Herfindahl-Hirschman Index ("HHI"), which is the sum of the squares of the market shares of all market participants, as the measure of market concentration. In particular, the Agencies rely on the "change in the HHI," which is twice the product of the market shares of the merging firms, and the "post-merger HHI," which is the HHI before the merger plus the change in the HHI. Section 1.51 sets out zones defined by the HHI and the change in the HHI within which mergers ordinarily will not require additional analysis. Proposed mergers ordinarily require no further analysis if (a) the post-merger HHI is under 1000; (b) the post-merger HHI falls between 1000 and 1800, and the change in the HHI is less than 100; or (c) the post-merger HHI is above 1800, and the change in the HHI is less than 50.

The Agencies' joint publication of Merger Challenges Data, Fiscal Years 1999–2003 (issued December 18, 2003), and the Commission's publication of Horizontal Merger Investigation Data, Fiscal Years 1996–2003 (issued February 2, 2004 and revised August 31, 2004), document that the Agencies have often not challenged mergers involving market shares and concentration that fall outside the zones set forth in Guidelines section 1.51. This does not mean that the zones are not meaningful, but rather that market shares and concentration are but a "starting point" for the analysis, and that many mergers falling outside these three zones nevertheless, upon full consideration of the factual and economic evidence, are found unlikely substantially to lessen competition. Application of the Guidelines as an integrated whole to case-specific facts—not undue emphasis on market share and concentration statistics—determines whether the Agency will challenge a particular merger. As discussed in section 1.521 of the Guidelines, historical market shares may not reflect a firm's future competitive significance.

> ***Boeing-McDonnell Douglas*** **(FTC 1997)** The Boeing Co., the world's largest producer of large commercial aircraft with 60% of that market, proposed to acquire McDonnell Douglas Corp., which through Douglas Aircraft had a share of nearly 5% in that market. Airbus S.A.S. was the only other significant rival, and obstacles to entry were exceptionally high. Although McDonnell Douglas was not a failing firm, staff determined that McDonnell Douglas' significance as an independent supplier of commercial aircraft had deteriorated to the point that it was no longer a competitive constraint on the pricing of Boeing and Airbus for large commercial aircraft. Many purchasers of aircraft indicated that McDonnell Douglas' prospects for future aircraft sales were close to zero. McDonnell Douglas' decline in competitive significance stemmed from the fact that it had not made the continuing investments in new aircraft technology necessary to compete successfully against Boeing and Airbus. Staff's investigation failed to turn up any evidence that this situation could be expected to be reversed. The Commission closed the investigation without taking any action.

Indeed, market concentration may be unimportant under a unilateral effects theory of competitive harm. As discussed in more detail in Chapter 2's discussion of Unilateral Effects, the question in a unilateral effects analysis is whether the merged firm likely would exercise market power absent any coordinated response from rival market incumbents. The concentration of the remainder of the market often has little impact on the answer to that question.

2. The Potential Adverse Competitive Effects of Mergers

Section 2 of the Guidelines identifies two broad analytical frameworks for assessing whether a merger between rival firms may substantially lessen competition: "coordinated interaction" and "unilateral effects." A horizontal merger is likely to lessen competition substantially through coordinated interaction if it creates a likelihood that, after the merger, competitors would coordinate their pricing or other competitive actions, or would coordinate them more completely or successfully than before the merger. A merger is likely to lessen competition substantially through unilateral effects if it creates a likelihood that the merged firm, without any coordination with non-merging rivals, would raise its price or otherwise exercise market power to a greater degree than before the merger.

Normally, the likely effects of a merger within a particular market are best characterized as either coordinated or unilateral, but it is possible to have both sorts of competitive effects within a single relevant market. This possibility may be most likely if the coordinated and unilateral effects relate to different dimensions of competition or would manifest themselves at different times.

Although these two broad analytical frameworks provide guidance on how the Agencies analyze competitive effects, the particular labels are not the focus. What matters is not the label applied to a competitive effects analysis, but rather whether the analysis is clearly articulated and grounded in both sound economics and the facts of the particular case. These frameworks embrace every competitive effect of any form of horizontal merger. The Agencies do not recognize or apply narrow readings of the Guidelines that could cause anticompetitive transactions to fall outside of, or fall within a perceived gap between, the coordinated and unilateral effects frameworks.

In evaluating the likely competitive effects of a proposed merger, the Agencies assess the full range of qualitative and quantitative evidence obtained from the merging parties, their competitors, their customers, and a variety of other sources. By carefully evaluating this evidence, the Agencies gain an understanding of the setting in which the proposed merger would occur and how best to analyze competition. This understanding draws heavily on the qualitative evidence from documents and first-hand observations of the industry by customers and other market participants. In some cases, this understanding is enhanced significantly by quantitative analyses of various sorts. One type of quantitative analysis is, as explained in Chapter 1, the "natural experiment" in which variation in market structure (e.g., from past mergers) can be empirically related to changes in market performance.

The Agencies examine whatever evidence is available and apply whatever tools of economics would be productive in an effort to arrive at the most reliable assessment of the likely effects of proposed mergers. Because the facts of merger investigations commonly are complex, some bits of evidence may appear inconsistent with the Agencies' ultimate assessments. The Agencies challenge a merger if the weight of the evidence establishes a likelihood that the merger would be anticompetitive. The type of evidence that is most telling varies from one merger to the next, as do the most productive tools of economics.

In assessing a merger between rival sellers, the Agencies consider whether buyers are likely able to defeat any attempts by sellers after the merger to exercise market power. Large buyers rarely can negate the likelihood that an otherwise anticompetitive merger between sellers would harm at least some buyers. Most markets with large buyers also have other buyers against which market power can be exercised even if some large buyers could protect themselves. Moreover, even very large buyers may be unable to thwart the exercise of market power.

Although they generally focus on the likely effects of proposed mergers on prices paid by consumers, the Agencies also evaluate the effects of mergers in other dimensions of competition. The Agencies may find that a proposed merger would be likely to cause significant anticompetitive effects with respect to innovation or some other form of non-price rivalry. Such effects may occur in addition to, or instead of, price effects.

The sections that follow address in greater detail the Agencies' application of the Guidelines' coordinated interaction and unilateral effects frameworks.

Coordinated Interaction

A horizontal merger changes an industry's structure by removing a competitor and combining its assets with those of the acquiring firm. Such a merger may change the competitive environment in such a way that the remaining firms—both the newly merged entity and its competitors—would engage in some form of coordination on price, output, capacity, or other dimensions of competition. The coordinated effects section of the Guidelines addresses this potential competitive concern. In particular, the Agencies seek to identify those mergers that are likely either to increase the likelihood of coordination among firms in the relevant market when no coordination existed prior to the merger, or to increase the likelihood that any existing coordinated interaction among the remaining firms in the relevant market would be more successful, complete, or sustainable.

A merger could reduce competition substantially through coordinated interaction and run afoul of section 7 of the Clayton Act without an agreement or conspiracy within the meaning of the Sherman Act. Even if a merger is likely to result in coordinated interaction, or more successful coordinated interaction, and violates section 7 of the Clayton Act, that coordination, depending on the circumstances, may not constitute a violation of the Sherman Act. As section 2.1 of the Guidelines states, coordinated interaction "includes tacit or express collusion, and may or may not be lawful in and of itself."

Most mergers have no material effect on the potential for coordination. Some may even lessen the likelihood of coordination. To identify those mergers that enhance the likelihood or effectiveness of coordination, the Agencies typically evaluate whether the industry in which the merger would occur is one that is conducive to coordinated behavior by the market participants. The Agencies also evaluate how the merger changes the environment to determine whether the merger would make it more likely that firms successfully coordinate.

In conducting this analysis, the Agencies attempt to identify the factors that constrain rivals' ability to coordinate their actions before the merger. The Agencies also consider whether the merger would sufficiently alter competitive conditions such that the remaining rivals after the merger would be significantly more likely to overcome any pre-existing obstacles to coordination. Thus, the Agencies not only assess whether the market conditions for viable coordination are present, but also ascertain specifically whether and how the merger would affect market conditions to make successful coordination after the merger significantly more likely. This analysis includes an assessment of whether a merger is likely to foster a set of common incentives among remaining rivals, as well as to foster their ability to coordinate successfully on price, output, or other dimensions of competition.

Successful coordination typically requires rivals (1) to reach terms of coordination that are profitable to each of the participants in the coordinating group, (2) to have a means to detect deviations that would undermine the coordinated interaction, and (3) to have the ability to punish deviating firms, so as to restore the coordinated status quo and diminish the risk of deviations. Guidelines § 2.1. Punishment may be possible, for example, through strategic price-cutting to the deviating rival's customers, so as effectively to erase the rival's profits from its deviation and make the rival less likely to "cheat" again. Coordination on prices tends to be easier the more transparent are rivals' prices, and coordination through allocation of customers tends to be easier the more transparent are the identities of particular customers' suppliers. It may be relatively more difficult for firms to coordinate on multiple dimensions of competition in markets with complex product characteristics or terms of trade. Such complexity, however, may not affect the ability to coordinate in particular ways, such as through customer allocation. Under Guidelines analysis, likely coordination need not be perfect. To the contrary, the Agencies assess whether, for example, it is likely that coordinated interaction will be sufficiently successful following the merger to result in anticompetitive effects.

> ***LaFarge-Blue Circle* (FTC 2001)** A merger of LaFarge S.A. and Blue Circle Industries PLC raised coordinated interaction concerns in several relevant markets, including that for cement in the Great Lakes region. In that market, the merger would have created a firm with a combined market share exceeding 40% and a market in which the top four firms would control approximately 90% of the supply. The post-merger HHI would have been greater than 3,000, with a change in the HHI of over 1,000. Cement is widely viewed as a homogeneous, highly standardized commodity product over which producers compete principally on price. Industry practice was that suppliers informed customers of price increases months before they were to take effect, making prices across rival suppliers relatively transparent.
>
> Sales transactions tended to be frequent, regular, and relatively small. These factors heightened concern that, after the merger, incumbents were not only likely to coordinate profitably on price terms, but also that the firms would have little incentive to deviate from the consensus price. That possibility existed because the profit to be gained from deviation would be less than the potential losses that would result if rivals retaliated. The Commission challenged the merger, resolving it by a consent order that required, among other things, divestiture of cement-related assets in the Great Lakes region.
>
> ***R.J. Reynolds-British American* (FTC 2004)** In a merger of the second- and third-largest marketers of cigarettes, R.J. Reynolds Tobacco Holdings, Inc. proposed to acquire Brown & Williamson Tobacco Corporation from British American Tobacco plc. Within the market for all cigarettes, the merger would have increased the HHI from 2,735 to 3,113. The Commission assessed whether the cigarette market was susceptible to coordinated interaction. Concluding that "the market for cigarettes is subject to many complexities, continual changes, and uncertainties that would severely complicate the tasks of reaching and monitoring a consensus," the Commission closed the

> investigation without challenging the merger. The Commission's closing statement points to the high degree of differentiation among cigarette brands, as well as sizable variation in firm sizes, product portfolios, and market positions among the manufacturers as factors that created different incentives for the different manufacturers to participate in future coordination. These factors made future coordination more difficult to manage and therefore unlikely.
>
> Both RJR and Brown & Williamson had portfolios of cigarette brands that included a smaller proportion of strong premium brands and a larger proportion of vulnerable and declining discount brands than the other major cigarette competitors. At the time of the merger, both companies were investing in growing a smaller number of premium equity brands to maintain sales and market share. There was uncertainty about the results of these strategic changes. The Commission concluded that uncertainties of these types greatly increased the difficulty of engaging in coordinated behavior. The Commission also noted that competition in the market was driven by discount brands and by equity investment in select premium brands among the four leading rivals, and there was little evidence that Brown & Williamson's continued autonomy was critical to the preservation of either form of competition. Brown & Williamson had been reducing, not increasing, its commitment in the discount segment, and was a very small factor in equity brands.
>
> The Commission also described variations in the marketing environment for cigarettes from state to state and between rural and urban areas. These variations made it more difficult and costly for firms to monitor their rival's activities and added to the complexity of coordination.

Coordination that reduces competition and consumer welfare could be accomplished using many alternative mechanisms. Coordinated interaction can occur on one or more competitive dimensions, such as price, output, capacity, customers served, territories served, and new product introduction. Coordination on price and coordination on output are essentially equivalent in their effects. When rivals successfully coordinate to restrict output, price rises. Similarly, when rivals successfully coordinate on price—that is, they maintain price above the level it would be absent the coordination—the rate of output declines because consumers buy fewer units.

Coordination on either price or output may pose difficulties that can be avoided by coordinating on customers or territories served. Rivals may coordinate on the specific customers with which each does business, or on the general types of customers with which they seek to do business. They also may coordinate on the particular geographic areas in which they operate or concentrate their efforts. Coordination also can occur with respect to aspects of rivalry, such as new product introduction. Rivals are likely to adopt the form of coordination for which it is easiest to spot deviations from the agreed terms of coordination and easiest to punish firms that deviate from those terms. Industry-specific factors thus are likely to influence firms' choices on how to coordinate their activities.

Concentration

The number of rival firms remaining after a merger, their market shares, and market concentration are relevant factors in determining the effect of a merger on the likelihood of coordinated interaction. The presence of many competitors tends to make it more difficult to achieve and sustain coordination on competitive terms and also reduces the incentive to participate in coordination. Guidelines § 2.0. The Guidelines' market share and concentration thresholds reflect this reality.

The Agencies do not automatically conclude that a merger is likely to lead to coordination simply because the merger increases concentration above a certain level or reduces the number of remaining firms below a certain level. Although the Agencies recently have challenged mergers when four or more competitors would have remained in the market, see, e.g., LaFarge-Blue Circle, described above, when the evidence does not show that the merger will change the likelihood of coordination among the market participants or of other anticompetitive effects, the Agencies regularly close merger investigations, including those involving markets that would have fewer than four firms.

As discussed in Chapter 1, enforcement data released by the Agencies show that market shares and concentration alone are not good predictors of enforcement challenges, except at high levels. Market shares and concentration nevertheless are important in the Agencies' evaluation of the likely competitive effects of a merger. Investigations are almost always closed when concentration levels are below the thresholds set forth in section 1.51 of the Guidelines. In addition, the larger the market shares of the merging firms, and the higher the market concentration after the merger, the more disposed are the Agencies to concluding that significant anticompetitive effects are likely.

Additional Market Characteristics Relevant to Competitive Analysis

Section 2.1 of the Guidelines sets forth several general market characteristics that may be relevant to the analysis of the likelihood of coordinated interaction following a merger: "the availability of key information concerning market conditions, transactions and individual competitors; the extent of firm and product heterogeneity; pricing or market practices typically employed by firms in the market; the characteristics of buyers and sellers; and the characteristics of typical transactions." Section 2.11 of the Guidelines states that the ability of firms to reach terms of coordination "may be facilitated by product or firm homogeneity and by existing practices among firms, practices not necessarily themselves antitrust violations, such as standardization of pricing or product variables on which firms could compete." Further, "[k]ey information about rival firms and the market may also facilitate reaching terms of coordination." Id.

These market characteristics may illuminate the degree of transparency and complexity in the competitive environment. The existence or absence of any particular characteristic (e.g., product homogeneity or transparency in prices) in a relevant market, however, is neither a necessary nor a sufficient basis for the Agencies to determine whether successful coordination is likely following a merger. In other words, these factors are not simply put on the left or right side of a ledger and balanced against one another. Rather, the Agencies identify the specific factors relevant to the particular mechanism for coordination being assessed and focus on how those factors affect whether the merger would alter the likelihood of successful coordination.

> ***Formica-International Paper*** **(DOJ 1999)** Formica Corp. and International Paper Co. were two producers of high-pressure laminates used to make durable surfaces such as countertops, work surfaces, doors, and other interior building products. Formica sought to acquire the high-pressure laminates business of International Paper Co. There

were just four competitors in the United States, and the acquisition of International Paper Co.'s business would have given Formica and its largest remaining competitor almost 90% of total sales between them. The market appeared to have been performing reasonably competitively, but the Department was concerned that two dominant competitors would coordinate pricing and output after the acquisition.

One reason for this concern was that the small competitors remaining after the merger had relatively high costs and were unable to expand output significantly, so they would not have been able to undermine that coordination. In addition, the Department concluded that International Paper, with significant excess capacity, had the ability to undermine coordination and had done so. The Department also found that major competitors had very good information on each others' pricing and would be able to detect deviations from coordinated price levels. After the Department announced its intention to challenge the merger, the parties abandoned the deal.

Although coordination may be less likely the greater the extent of product heterogeneity, mergers in markets with differentiated products nonetheless can facilitate coordination. Although a merger resulting in closer portfolio conformity may prompt more intense, head-to-head competition among rivals that benefits consumers, an enhanced mutual understanding of the production and marketing variables that each rival faces also may result. Better mutual understanding can increase the ability to coordinate successfully, thus diminishing the benefits to consumers that the more intense competition otherwise would have provided. Sellers of differentiated products also may coordinate in non-price dimensions of competition by limiting their product portfolios, thereby limiting the extent of competition between the products of rival sellers. They also may coordinate on customers or territories rather than on prices.

Diageo-Vivendi **(FTC 2001)** The Commission challenged a merger between Diageo plc and Vivendi Universal S.A., competitors in the manufacture and sale of premium rum—a product that is heterogeneous as to brand name and the type of rum, e.g., light or gold, flavored or unflavored—on the grounds, among others, that the transaction was likely to lead to coordinated interaction among premium rum rivals. Diageo, which owned the Malibu Rum brand with about an 8% share, was seeking to acquire Seagram's, which marketed Captain Morgan Original Spiced Rum and Captain Morgan Parrot Bay Rum brands and had about a 33% share. Bacardi USA, with its Bacardi Light and Bacardi Limon brands, was the largest competitor with about a 54% share. Thus, after the acquisition, Diageo and Bacardi USA would have had a combined share of about 95% in the U.S. premium rum market.

Significant differentiation among major brands of rum reduces the closeness of substitution among them. Nonetheless, the Commission had reason to believe that the acquisition would increase the likelihood and extent of coordinated interaction to raise prices. Having a single owner of both the Seagram's rum products and the Malibu brand created the substantial concern that coordination that was not profitable for Bacardi and Seagram's before the merger likely would have become profitable after the merger. Although a smaller rival before the merger, Diageo's Malibu imposed a significant competitive constraint on Seagram's and Bacardi. The Commission challenged the merger and agreed to a settlement with the parties that required Diageo to divest its worldwide Malibu rum business to a third party.

Role of Evidence of Past Coordination

Facts showing that rivals in the relevant market have coordinated in the past are probative of whether a market is conducive to coordination. Guidelines § 2.1. Such facts are probative because they demonstrate the feasibility of coordination under past market conditions. Other things being equal, the removal of a firm via merger, in a market in which incumbents already have engaged in coordinated behavior, generally raises the risk that future coordination would be more successful, durable, or complete. Accordingly, the Agencies investigate whether the relevant market at issue has experienced such behavior and, if so, whether market conditions that existed when the coordination took place—and thus were conducive to coordination—are still in place. A past history of coordination found unlawful can provide strong evidence of the potential for coordination after a merger.

***Air Products-L'Air Liquide* (FTC 2000)** Two of the four largest industrial gas suppliers, Air Products and Chemicals, Inc. and L'Air Liquide S.A., proposed acquisitions that would result in splitting between them the assets of a third large rival, The BOC Group plc. The proposed asset split would have resulted in three remaining industrial gas suppliers that were nearly the same in size, cost structure, and geographic service areas. Products involved in the asset split included bulk liquid oxygen, bulk liquid nitrogen, and bulk liquid argon (together referred to as atmospheric gases), various electronic specialty gases, and helium—each of which is a homogeneous product. Bulk liquid oxygen and nitrogen trade in regional markets, and the transactions would have affected multiple regional areas. In these areas, the four largest producers accounted for between 70% and 100% of the markets. The four suppliers also accounted for about 90% of the national market for bulk liquid argon.

The staff found evidence of past coordination. In 1991, the four major industrial air gas suppliers pled guilty in Canada to a charge of conspiring to eliminate competition for a wide range of industrial gases, including bulk liquid oxygen, nitrogen, and argon. Industrial gas technology is well-established, market institutions in the U.S. were similar to those in Canada, and nothing had changed significantly during the intervening period to suggest that coordination had become more difficult or less likely.

Other evidence also indicated that the markets were susceptible to coordinated behavior: firms announced price changes publicly, and industry-wide price increases tended to follow such announcements; a number of joint ventures, swap agreements, and other relationships among the suppliers provided opportunities for information sharing; and incumbents tended not to bid aggressively for rivals' current customers. Neither fringe expansion nor new entry was likely to defeat future coordination. Staff concluded that the proposed asset split would likely enable the remaining firms to engage in coordination more effectively. The parties abandoned the proposed transactions.

***Suiza-Broughton* (DOJ 1999)** Suiza Foods Corp. and Broughton Foods Co. proposed to merge. Broughton owned the Southern Belle dairy in Somerset, Kentucky, and Suiza operated several dairies in Kentucky, including the Flav-O-Rich dairy in London, Kentucky. Six years earlier, when Flav-O-Rich and Southern Belle were independently owned, both pleaded guilty to criminal charges of rigging bids in the sale of milk to schools. The Department found that the proposed merger would have reduced from three to two the number of dairies competing to supply milk to thirty-two school districts in South Central Kentucky, including many that had been victimized by the prior bid rigging. The Department challenged the merger on the basis that it likely would lead to coordinated anticompetitive effects, and the demonstrated ability of these particular dairies to coordinate was a significant factor in the Department's decision. The Department's complaint was resolved by a consent decree requiring divestiture of the Southern Belle Dairy.

***Degussa-DuPont* (FTC 1998)** Degussa Aktiengesellschaft, a producer of hydrogen peroxide, proposed to acquire rival E.I. du Pont de Nemours & Co.'s hydrogen peroxide manufacturing assets. The Commission found that the relevant U.S. market was conducive to coordinated interaction based on evidence that showed, among other things, high concentration levels, product homogeneity, and the ready availability of reliable competitive information. Moreover, the same firms that would have been the leading U.S. producers after the merger had recently been found to have engaged in market division in Europe for several years. The Commission identified this history of collusion as a factor supporting its conclusion that the proposed transaction likely would result in anticompetitive effects from coordinated interaction. Under the terms of a consent agreement to resolve these competitive concerns, the acquirer was permitted to purchase one plant but not the entirety of the seller's hydrogen peroxide manufacturing assets.

Even when firms have no prior record of antitrust violations, evidence that firms have coordinated at least partially on competitive terms suggests that market characteristics are conducive to coordination.

***Rhodia-Albright & Wilson* (FTC 2000)** Rhodia entered into an agreement to acquire Albright & Wilson PLC, a wholly owned subsidiary of Donau Chemie AG. The merging firms were industrial phosphoric acid producers. The Commission developed evidence that the market was highly concentrated, that the relevant product was homogenous, and that timely competitive intelligence was readily available—all conditions that are generally conducive to coordination. Incumbent marketing strategies suggested a tendency to curb aggressive price competition and suggested a lack of competition.

The Commission found that industrial phosphoric acid pricing, unlike the pricing of other similar chemical products, had not historically responded significantly to changes in the rate of capacity utilization among producers. In most chemical product markets, when capacity utilization declines, prices often decline as well. In this market, however, during periods of decline in capacity utilization among industrial phosphoric acid producers, prices often remained relatively stable. All of these factors established that the relevant market—even before the proposed merger—was performing in a manner consistent with coordination. The Commission entered into a consent order requiring, among other things, divestiture of phosphoric acid assets.

When investigating mergers in industries characterized by collusive behavior or previous coordinated interaction, the Agencies focus on how the mergers affect the likelihood of successful coordination in the future. In some instances, a simple reduction in the number of firms may increase the likelihood of effective coordinated interaction. Evidence of past coordination is less probative if the conduct preceded significant changes in the competitive environment that made coordination more difficult or otherwise less likely. Such changes might include, for example, entry, changes in the manufacturing processes of some competitors, or changes in the characteristics in the relevant product itself. Events such as these may have altered the incumbents' incentives or ability to coordinate successfully.

Although a history of past collusion may be probative as to whether the market currently is conducive to coordination, the converse is not necessarily true, i.e., a lack of evidence of past coordination does not imply that future coordination is unlikely. When the Agencies conclude that previous episodes of coordinated interaction are not probative in the context of current market conditions—or when they find no evidence that rivals coordinated in the past—an important focus of the investigation becomes whether the merger is likely to cause the relevant market to change from one in which coordination did not occur to one in which such coordination is likely.

> ***Premdor-Masonite* (DOJ 2001)** Premdor Inc. sought to acquire (from International Paper Co.) Masonite Corp., one of two large producers of "interior molded doorskins," which form the front and back of "interior molded doors." Interior molded doors provide much the same appearance as solid wood doors but at a much lower cost, and Premdor was the world's largest producer. Premdor also held a substantial equity stake in a firm that supplied some of its doorskins. The vast majority of doorskins, however, were produced by Masonite and by a third party that was also Premdor's only large rival in the sale of interior molded doors. The Department concluded that the upstream and downstream markets for interior molded doorskins and interior molded doors were highly concentrated and that the proposed acquisition would have removed significant impediments to coordination.
>
> The Department found that the most significant impediment to upstream coordination was Premdor's ability, in the event of an upstream price increase, to expand production of doorskins, both for its own use and for sale to other door producers. The proposed acquisition, however, would have eliminated Premdor's incentive to undermine upstream coordination. The Department also found that a significant impediment to downstream coordination was Masonite's incentive and ability to support output increases by smaller downstream competitors. The proposed acquisition, however, would have eliminated Masonite's incentive to do so.
>
> Finally, the Department found that the acquisition would have facilitated coordination by bringing the cost structures of the principal competitors into alignment, both upstream and downstream, and by making it easier to monitor departures from any coordination. The Department's challenge of the acquisition was resolved by a consent decree requiring, among other things, divestiture of a Masonite manufacturing facility.

Maverick and Capacity Factors in Coordination

A merger may make coordination more likely or more effective when it involves the acquisition of a firm or asset that is competitively unique. In this regard, section 2.12 of the Guidelines addresses the acquisition of "maverick" firms, i.e., "firms that have a greater economic incentive to deviate from the terms of coordination than do most of their rivals (e.g., firms that are unusually disruptive and competitive influences in the market)." If the acquired firm is a maverick, its acquisition may make coordination more likely because the nature and intensity of competition may change significantly as a result of the merger. In such a case, the Agency's investigation examines whether the acquired firm has behaved as a maverick and whether the incentives that are expected to guide the merged firm's behavior likely would be different.

Similarly, a merger might lead to anticompetitive coordination if assets that might constrain coordination are acquired by one of a limited number of larger incumbents. For example, coordination could result if, prior to the acquisition, the capacity of fringe firms to expand output was sufficient to defeat the larger firms' attempts to coordinate price, but the acquisition would shift enough of the fringe capacity to a major firm (or otherwise eliminate it as a competitive threat) so that insufficient fringe capacity would remain to undermine a coordinated price increase.

***Arch Coal-Triton* (FTC 2004)** The Commission challenged Arch Coal, Inc.'s acquisition of Triton Coal Co., LLC's North Rochelle mine in the Southern Powder River Basin of Wyoming ("SPRB"). Prior to the acquisition, three large companies—Arch, Kennecott, and Peabody (the "Big Three")—owned a large majority of SPRB mining capacity. The remaining capacity, including the North Rochelle mine, was owned by fringe companies with smaller market shares. The Commission's competitive concern was that, by transferring ownership of the North Rochelle mine from the fringe to a member of the Big Three, the acquisition would significantly reduce the supply elasticity of the fringe and increase the likelihood of coordination to reduce Big Three output. As a result of the reduction in fringe supply elasticity, a given reduction in output by the Big Three would be more profitable to each member of that group after the acquisition than would have been the case before the acquisition. Mine operators had, in the past, announced their future intentions with regard to production and had publicly encouraged "production discipline." The court denied the Commission's preliminary injunction request and, after further investigation, the Commission decided not to pursue further administrative litigation.

***UPM-MACtac* (DOJ 2003)** UPM-Kymmene Oyj sought to acquire (from Bemis Co.) Morgan Adhesives Co. ("MACtac"). Three firms—MACtac, UPM's Raflatac, Inc. subsidiary, and Avery Dennison Corp.—were the only large producers of paper pressure-sensitive labelstock, which is used by "converters" to make paper self-adhesive labels for a range of consumer and commercial applications. The Department found that the proposed acquisition would result in UPM and Avery controlling over 70% of sales in the relevant market, and in smaller rivals having insufficient capacity to undermine a price increase by UPM and Avery. Prior to the announcement of its proposed acquisition of MACtac, UPM and Avery had exchanged communications about their mutual concerns regarding intense price competition, and there was evidence that they had reached an understanding to hold the line on further price cuts. MACtac, however, was not a party to this understanding, and it had both substantial excess capacity and the incentive to expand sales by cutting price.

> The Department concluded that the proposed acquisition would eliminate the threat to coordination from MACtac and that no other competitor posed such a threat. Also significant was the fact that UPM was a major input supplier for Avery both because this relationship created opportunities for communication between the two and because it made possible mutual threats that could be used to induce or enforce coordination. The Department, therefore, concluded that Avery and UPM would be likely to coordinate after the acquisition and challenged the transaction on that basis. After trial, the district court enjoined the consummation of the acquisition.

Unilateral Effects

Section 2.2 of the Guidelines states that "merging firms may find it profitable to alter their behavior unilaterally following the acquisition by elevating price and suppressing output." The manner in which a horizontal merger may generate unilateral competitive effects is straightforward: By eliminating competition between the merging firms, a merger gives the merged firm incentives different from those of the merging firms. The simplest unilateral effect arises from merger to monopoly, which eliminates all competition in the relevant market. Since the issuance of the Guidelines in 1992, a substantial proportion of the Agencies' merger challenges have been predicated at least in part on a conclusion that the proposed mergers were likely to generate anticompetitive unilateral effects.

Section 2.2 of the Guidelines explains: "Unilateral competitive effects can arise in a variety of different settings. In each setting, particular other factors describing the relevant market affect the likelihood of unilateral competitive effects. The settings differ by the primary characteristics that distinguish firms and shape the nature of their competition." Section 2.2 does not articulate, much less detail, every particular unilateral effects analysis the Agencies may apply.

The Agencies' analysis of unilateral competitive effects draws on many models developed by economists. The simplest is the model of monopoly, which applies to a merger involving the only two competitors in the relevant market. One step removed from monopoly is the dominant firm model. That model posits that all competitors but one in an industry act as a "competitive fringe," which can economically satisfy only part of total market demand. The remaining competitor acts as a monopolist with respect to the portion of total industry demand that the competitive fringe does not elect to supply. This model might apply, for example, in a homogeneous product industry in which the fringe competitors are unable to expand output significantly.

In other models, two or more competitors interact strategically. These models differ with respect to how competitors interact. In the Bertrand model, for example, competitors interact in the choice of the prices they charge. Similar to the Bertrand model are auction models, in which firms interact by bidding. There are many auction models with many different bidding procedures. In the Cournot model, competitors interact in the choice of the quantities they sell. And in bargaining models, competitors interact through their choices of terms on which they will deal with their customers.

Formal economic modeling can be useful in interpreting the available data (even with natural experiments). One type of modeling the Agencies use is "merger simulation," which "calibrates" a model to match quantitative aspects (e.g., demand elasticities) of the industry in which the merger occurs and uses the calibrated model to predict the outcome of the competitive process after the merger. Merger simulation can be a useful tool in determining whether unilateral effects are likely to constitute a substantial lessening of competition when a particular model mentioned above fits the facts of the industry under review and suitable data can be found to calibrate the model. The fit of a model is evaluated on the basis of the totality of the evidence.

Section 2.2 of the Guidelines does not establish a special safe harbor applicable to the Agencies' consideration of possible unilateral effects. Section 2.2.1 provides that significant unilateral effects are likely with differentiated products when the combined market share of the merging firms exceeds 35% and other market characteristics indicate that market share is a reasonable proxy for the relative appeal of the merging products as second choices as well as first choices. Section 2.2.2 provides that significant unilateral effects are likely with undifferentiated products when the combined market share of the merging firms exceeds 35% and other market characteristics indicate that non-merging firms would not expand output sufficiently to frustrate an effort to reduce total market output.

As an empirical matter, the unilateral effects challenges made by the Agencies nearly always have involved combined shares greater than 35%. Nevertheless, the Agencies may challenge mergers when the combined share falls below 35% if the analysis of the mergers' particular unilateral competitive effects indicates that they would be likely substantially to lessen competition. Combined shares less than 35% may be sufficiently high to produce a substantial unilateral anticompetitive effect if the products are differentiated and the merging products are especially close substitutes or if the product is undifferentiated and the non-merging firms are capacity constrained.

Unilateral Effects from Merger to Monopoly

The Agencies are likely to challenge a proposed merger of the only two firms in a relevant market. The case against such a merger would rest upon the simplest of all unilateral effects models. Relatively few mergers to monopoly are proposed. Some proposed mergers affecting many markets would have resulted in monopolies in one or more of these markets.

> ***Franklin Electric-United Dominion*** **(DOJ 2000)** Subsidiaries of Franklin Electric Co. and United Dominion Industries were the only two domestic producers of submersible turbine pumps used for pumping gasoline from underground storage tanks at retail stations. The parent companies entered into a joint venture agreement that would have combined those subsidiaries. The Department found that entry was difficult and that other pumps, including foreign-produced pumps, were not good substitutes. Hence, the Department concluded that the formation of the joint venture likely would create a monopoly and thus give rise to a significant unilateral anticompetitive effect. After trial, the district court granted the Department's motion for a permanent injunction.

> ***Glaxo Wellcome-SmithKline Beecham*** **(FTC 2000)** When Glaxo Wellcome plc and SmithKline Beecham plc proposed to merge, each manufactured and marketed numerous pharmaceutical products. For most products, the transaction raised no significant competition issues, but it did raise concerns in several product lines. Among them was the market for research, development, manufacture, and sale of second generation oral and intravenous antiviral drugs used in the treatment of herpes. Glaxo Wellcome's Valtrex and SmithKline Beecham's

Famvir were the only such drugs sold in the United States. Having concern both for the market for currently approved drugs and the market for new competing drugs, the Commission alleged that the merger would have prompted a unilateral increase in prices and reduction in innovation in this monopolized market. The matter was resolved by a consent order, pursuant to which the merged firm was required, among other things, to divest SmithKline's Famvir-related assets.

***Suiza-Broughton* (DOJ 1999)** Suiza Foods Corp. and Broughton Foods Co. competed in the sale of milk to school districts, which procured the milk through annual contracts entered into after taking bids. The Department found that competition for each of the school districts was entirely separate from the others, so each constituted a separate geographic market. The Department sought to enjoin the proposed merger of the two companies after finding that it threatened competition in 55 school districts in south central Kentucky and would have created a monopoly in 23 of those districts. The matter was resolved by a consent order, pursuant to which the merged firm was required to divest the dairy in Kentucky owned by Broughton.

Unilateral Effects Relating to Capacity and Output for Homogeneous Products

In markets for homogeneous products, the Agencies consider whether proposed mergers would, once consummated, likely provide the incentive to restrict capacity or output significantly and thereby drive up prices.

***Georgia-Pacific-Fort James* (DOJ 2000)** Georgia-Pacific Corp. and Fort James Corp. were the two largest producers in the United States of "away-from-home" tissue products (i.e., paper napkins, towels, and toilet tissue used in commercial establishments). These products are produced in a two-stage process, the first stage of which is the production of massive parent rolls, which also are used to make at-home tissue products. Georgia-Pacific's proposed acquisition of Fort James would have increased Georgia-Pacific's share of North American parent roll capacity to 36%. Investigation revealed that the industry was operating at nearly full capacity, that capacity could not be quickly expanded, and that demand was relatively inelastic. These factors combined to create a danger that, after the merger, Georgia-Pacific would act as a dominant firm by restricting production of parent rolls and thereby forcing up prices for away-from-home tissue products. Merger simulation indicated that the acquisition would cause a significant price increase. The Department's challenge to the acquisition was settled by a consent decree requiring the divestiture of Georgia-Pacific's away-from-home tissue business.

Unilateral Effects Relating to the Pricing of Differentiated Products

In analyzing a merger of two producers of differentiated consumer products, the Agencies examine whether the merger will alter the merged firm's incentives in a way that leads to higher prices. The seller of a differentiated consumer product raises price above marginal cost to the point at which the profit gain from higher prices is balanced by the loss in sales. Merging two sellers of competing differentiated products may create an incentive for the merged firm to increase the price of either or both products because some of the sales lost as a result of the increase in the price of either of the two products would be "recaptured" by the other.

As section 2.21 of the Guidelines explains, what matters in determining the unilateral effect of a differentiated products merger is whether "a significant share of sales in the market [is] accounted for by consumers who regard the products of the merging firms as their first and second choices." Consumers typically differ widely with respect to both their most preferred products and their second choices. If a significant share of consumers view the products combined by the merger as their first and second choices, the merger may result in a significant unilateral effect.

In all merger cases, the Agencies focus on the particular competitive relationship between the merging firms, and for mergers involving differentiated products, the "diversion ratios" between products combined by the merger are of particular importance. An increase in the price of a differentiated product causes a decrease in the quantity sold for that product and an increase in the quantities sold of products to which consumers switch. The diversion ratio from one product to another is the proportion of the decrease in the quantity of the first product purchased resulting from a small increase in its price that is accounted for by the increase in quantity purchased for the other product. In general, for any two products brought under common control by a transaction, the higher the diversion ratios, the more likely is significant harm to competition.

A merger may produce significant unilateral effects even though a large majority of the substitution away from each merging product goes to non-merging products. The products of the merging firms need only be sufficiently close to each other (that is, have sufficiently high diversion ratios) that recapturing the portion of the lost sales indicated by the diversion ratios provides a significant incentive to raise prices. Significant unilateral effects are unlikely if the diversion ratios between pairs of products brought together by a merger are sufficiently low.

A merger may produce significant unilateral effects even though a non-merging product is the "closest" substitute for every merging product in the sense that the largest diversion ratio for every product of the merged firm is to a non-merging firm's product. The unilateral effects of a merger of differentiated consumer products are largely determined by the diversion ratios between pairs of products combined by the merger, and the diversion ratios between those products and the products of non-merging firms have at most a secondary effect.

In ascertaining the competitive relationships in mergers involving differentiated products, the Agencies look to both qualitative and quantitative evidence bearing on the intensity or nature of competition. The Agencies make use of any available data that can shed light on diversion ratios, and when possible estimate them using statistical methods. Often, however, the available data are insufficient for reliable estimation of the diversion ratios. The absence of data suitable for such estimation does not preclude a challenge to a merger. The Agencies also rely on traditional sources of evidence, including documentary and testimonial evidence from market participants. Even when the Agencies estimate diversion ratios, documentary and testimonial evidence typically are used to corroborate the estimates.

> ***General Electric-Agfa NDT* (FTC 2003)** General Electric Co. proposed to acquire Agfa NDT Inc. from Agfa-Gevaert N.V. Through their subsidiaries, the firms were the two largest suppliers of ultrasonic non-destructive testing ("NDT") equipment in the United States. NDT equipment is used to inspect the structure and tolerance

of materials without damaging them or impairing their future usefulness. Manufacturers and end users in a variety of industries use ultrasonic NDT equipment for quality control and safety purposes. Unilateral concerns arose in three relevant product markets: portable flaw detectors, corrosion thickness gauges, and precision thickness gauges. In each of these markets, the merging parties were the two largest firms, and the combined firm would have had a market share of greater than 70% in each of the markets. Documents and testimonial evidence indicated that the rivalry between GE and Agfa was particularly close, and that, for a wide variety of industry participants, the products of the two firms were their first and second choices. The evidence also showed that the two firms frequently were head-to-head rivals and that this competition benefitted consumers through aggressive price competition and innovation. Evidence also suggested that the remaining fringe manufacturers would not be able to constrain a unilateral price increase by the merged firm. The Commission obtained a consent order requiring divestiture of GE's NDT business.

In many matters involving differentiated consumer products, the Agencies have analyzed price and quantity data generated at the point of sale, particularly by scanners at supermarket checkouts, to assess the likely effect of the merger on prices.

***Nestle-Dreyer's* (FTC 2003)** Nestle Holdings, Inc., proposed to merge with Dreyer's Grand Ice Cream, Inc. The firms were rivals in the sale of "superpremium ice cream." Compared to premium and non-premium ice cream, superpremium ice cream contains more butterfat, less air, and more costly ingredients, and sells at a substantially higher price. Nestle sold the Haagen-Dazs brand in competition with the Dreyer's Dreamery, Godiva, and Starbucks brands. Together Nestle and Dreyer's accounted for about 55% of superpremium ice cream sales, and Unilever, through its Ben & Jerry's brand, accounted for nearly all of the rest. Commission staff developed evidence showing that the merger was likely to result in unilateral anticompetitive effects, reflecting the close rivalry between the merging firms. Dreyer's recently had expanded on a large scale into superpremium ice cream production and increased its share in this relatively mature market to above 20%. Analysis suggested that, by expanding, Dreyer's induced increased competition from incumbent superpremium firms. Econometric analysis showed that the diversion ratios between the Nestle and Dreyer's superpremium brands were sufficient to make a significant unilateral price increase by the merged firm likely. The diversion ratios with Unilever's superpremium brands also were high. The analysis implied that the merged firm would be likely to raise its prices anticompetitively and that Unilever would also likely raise its Ben & Jerry's prices in the post-merger environment. The Commission entered into a consent agreement with the merging firms requiring divestiture of two brands and key distribution assets.

***General Mills-Pillsbury* (FTC 2001)** General Mills, Inc.'s proposed purchase of The Pillsbury Co. from Diageo plc, involved the sale of some of the most widely recognized food products in the United States. Most of the products involved in the transaction did not raise antitrust concerns, but there were overlaps of potential concern in a handful of product lines, including flour. The Pillsbury and General Mills (Gold Medal) brands were the only two national flour brands, and after the merger General Mills would account for over half of total U.S. retail flour sales. Private label sales comprised less than 25% of sales nationwide, with the balance accounted for by numerous regional firms. Evidence tended to indicate that regional brands were not a significant constraint on General Mills and Pillsbury. The regional brands generally were highly differentiated, specialty brands and were not viewed as close substitutes for the more commodity-like General Mills and Pillsbury brands. The degree of constraint provided by private label brands was mixed, with some evidence suggesting that private label brands were a significant constraint but other evidence suggesting otherwise.

Commission staff used scanner data to estimate demand elasticities. Because the strength of private label and regional flour brands varied across geographic regions, staff estimated elasticities for groups of markets defined according to the presence of regional brands. The cross-price elasticities between Gold Medal and Pillsbury brands and between these brands and private label and regional brands differed across regions. For example, the results suggested that Gold Medal and Pillsbury were the closest substitutes in some markets, while private label alternatives were an equally close substitute in other markets. Some regional brands also were found to be relatively close substitutes for Gold Medal and Pillsbury, while others were not. Commission staff used the estimated elasticities to simulate the expected price effect from the merger using the Bertrand model. The results suggested that the merging parties would raise their prices more than 10% even in markets where private label and regional brands were estimated to be equally close substitutes for Gold Medal and Pillsbury.

Commission staff also examined whether pricing for flour varied across markets in relation to the amount of competition from private label or other brands. In particular, staff compared prices in geographic markets that were supplied predominantly by Gold Medal and private label, with prices in markets where Pillsbury or another brand was also strong. The results indicated that Pillsbury generally played an important role in constraining Gold Medal prices. These results were consistent with the elasticity results discussed above, and both suggested that the proposed merger would lead to price increases for flour. The parties resolved the competitive concerns in this market by selling Pillsbury's product line. No Commission action was taken.

***Kimberly-Clark-Scott* (DOJ 1995)** Kimberly-Clark Corp. and Scott Paper Co. were two of the nation's leading producers of consumer paper products when they announced their intention to merge. In facial tissue, Kimberly-Clark and Scott, together with Procter & Gamble, accounted for nearly 90% of all sales, and Kimberly-Clark's Kleenex brand itself accounted for over half of sales. By estimating the relevant demand elasticities using scanner data, the Department determined that Scott's facial tissue products, which were "value" products (sold at relatively low prices) and accounted for only 7% of sales, imposed a significant constraint on Kimberly-Clark's prices. Likewise, in baby wipes, in which Kimberly-Clark and Scott's brands together accounted for approximately 56% of sales, the Department's analysis indicated that each was the other's most significant competitive constraint. Hence, the Department concluded that acquiring Scott's facial tissue and baby wipes businesses likely would give Kimberly-Clark an incentive to increase prices significantly for the merging brands. The Department's challenge to the proposed merger was settled by a consent decree requiring the divestiture of assets relating to facial tissue and baby wipes.

***Interstate Bakeries-Continental* (DOJ 1995)** The Department undertook significant analysis of scanner data in evaluating Interstate Bakeries Corp.'s purchase of Continental Baking Co. from Ralston Purina Co. At the time, Continental, with its Wonder brand, was the largest baker of fresh bread in the United States, and Interstate was the third-largest. The Department's investigation focused on white pan bread. White pan bread is the primary sandwich and toasting bread in the United States, and market participants viewed it as a highly differentiated product. Price differences were a clear indication of consumer preference for premium brands over supermarket private label brands; the price of the premium brands was at least twice the price of the private label products. Econometric evidence confirmed that there was only limited competitive interaction between premium and private label brands. Marketing, econometric, and other evidence also indicated that there were significant preferences among individual premium brands. The Department's investigation focused on five metropolitan areas (Chicago, Milwaukee, Central Illinois, Los Angeles, and San Diego) in which Continental and Interstate had the two largest-selling premium brands, or two of the three largest-selling brands.

Econometric analysis determined that there were substantial cross-elasticities of demand between the Continental and Interstate brands of white pan bread, consistent with a likelihood of significant unilateral anticompetitive effects following the merger. The Department used the estimated cross elasticities in a Bertrand merger simulation, which predicted that the merger was likely to result in price increases of 5–10% for those brands. The Bertrand model was considered reliable for several reasons, including that it accurately predicted pre-merger price-cost margins. In addition, retailers marked up every wholesale price by the same percentage, so estimated retail-level demand elasticities were the same as those at the wholesale level. The Department concluded that the proposed acquisition likely would result in significant price increases for premium white pan bread in five metropolitan areas. The Department's challenge to the proposed merger was settled by a consent decree requiring divestiture of brands and related assets in the five metropolitan areas.

The Agencies challenge only a tiny fraction of proposed mergers. (In fiscal years 1999–2003, over 14,000 transactions were notified to the Agencies under HSR; the Agencies collectively challenged fewer than 200.) The following matters illustrate, for differentiated consumer products, the sort of evidence that has formed the basis of decisions not to challenge particular transactions.

***Fortune Brands-Allied Domecq* (FTC 2005)** Fortune Brands, Inc., owner of the Knob Creek brand of bourbon, proposed to acquire Allied Domecq's Maker's Mark brand of bourbon. Commission staff analyzed whether the acquisition would create or enhance unilateral market power for premium bourbon. Staff analysis of information discovered in the investigation suggested that several other large whiskey brands, including bourbons, competed strongly with Maker's Mark and with Knob Creek. Econometric analysis of retail scanner pricing data indicated substantial cross-price elasticities among the several whiskey brands. Using these cross-price elasticities staff estimated the diversion ratios involving Maker's Mark and Knob Creek. The results showed that, in the event of a Maker's Mark price increase, very few of the sales lost would go to Knob Creek. The analysis also found no support for the proposition that Maker's Mark would receive a substantial proportion of the substitution away from Knob Creek in the event of an increase in the price of the latter. The staff closed the investigation.

***Maybelline-Cosmair* (DOJ 1996)** The Department investigated and decided not to challenge the proposed merger of Maybelline, Inc., a leading U.S. cosmetics company, and Cosmair, Inc., the U.S. subsidiary of French cosmetics giant L'Oreal S.A. Maybelline and L'Oreal were leading brands, and both were sold almost exclusively through mass-market outlets. Although the merger involved many products, the investigation focused largely on mascara, in which Maybelline had the leading share among brands sold through mass-market outlets, and L'Oreal ranked third. They combined to account for 52% of sales. Some evidence suggested that the images associated with the merging brands were quite different, and demand estimation was employed to determine whether there was substantial direct competition between them.

As in many other investigations involving differentiated consumer products, the Department relied on weekly data generated by scanners at the point of retail sale. Estimated demand elasticities were used to simulate the effects of the proposed merger using the Bertrand model. The analysis indicated that a significant anticompetitive effect was not likely, and the Department decided not to challenge the proposed merger.

Although the Agencies commonly use scanner data in analyzing the likely competitive effects of mergers involving differentiated products, such data do not exist for many such products. When scanner data do not exist, if feasible, it may be useful to conduct a consumer survey.

***Vail Resorts-Ralston Resorts* (DOJ 1997)** Vail Resorts, Inc. and Ralston Resorts, Inc. were the two largest owner-operators of ski resorts in Colorado. In 1996, Vail proposed to acquire three ski areas operated by Ralston, which would have given Vail control of five ski areas in the "front range" area west of Denver, accounting for 38–50% of front range skier-days. Relying in part on a survey of skiers, the Department found that the Vail and Ralston facilities were close, premium-quality competitors and that skiers were likely to switch from one to the other on the basis of small changes in price, whereas consumers were much less likely to switch to several other resorts considered to be of lesser quality.

Bertrand merger simulation based on the survey data suggested the merger likely would cause a significant increase in lift-ticket prices at the acquiring firm's resorts. The Department therefore challenged the merger. The merger simulation also indicated that divestiture of Ralston's Arapahoe Basin resort would substantially prevent price increases, and that remedy was implemented through a consent decree.

Before challenging a merger involving differentiated consumer products, the Agencies consider the possibility of product repositioning by non-merging firms in accord with section 2.212 of the Guidelines. Consideration of repositioning closely parallels the consideration of entry, discussed below, and also focuses on timeliness, likelihood, and sufficiency. The Agencies rarely find evidence that repositioning would be sufficient to prevent or reverse what otherwise would be significant anticompetitive unilateral effects from a differentiated products merger. Repositioning of a differentiated product entails altering consumers' perceptions instead of, or in addition to, altering its physical properties. The former can be difficult, especially with well-established brands, and expensive efforts at doing so typically pose a significant risk of failure and thus may not be undertaken.

Unilateral Effects Relating to Auctions

In some markets, buyers conduct formal auctions to select suppliers and set prices. In such markets, the Agencies account for the fact that competition takes place through an auction. To an extent, the effects of a merger may depend on the specific auction format employed, and the Agencies also account for the specific format of the auction. The basic effects of mergers, however, may be quite similar in different auction formats.

Procurement through an auction tends to be simple for a homogeneous industrial product.

> ***Cargill-Akzo Nobel* (DOJ 1997)** Cargill, Inc. proposed to acquire the western hemisphere salt-producing assets of Akzo Nobel, N.V. Cargill and Akzo Nobel were two of only four competitors engaged in the production of rock salt used for de-icing purposes in an area of the United States centered on the eastern portion of Lake Erie, and de-icing salt was sold primarily to government agencies through formal sealed bid auctions. To gauge the likely unilateral effect of the merger, the Department conducted an econometric analysis of data on winning bids in the area of interest and found that bids had been significantly lower when there were four bids than when there were three. Partly on the strength of that evidence, the Department challenged the merger on the basis of a likely unilateral price increase, and the case was settled by a consent decree requiring divestitures.

Procurement using an auction is also observed with more complex and customized products. With customized products, arbitrage between customers is likely to be infeasible, and the Agencies have sometimes found that there was a separate competition in each auction because vendors tailored their prices and other terms to the particular situation of each customer.

> ***Chicago Bridge-Pitt-Des Moines* (FTC 2005)** The Commission issued an administrative ruling that the consummated acquisition by Chicago Bridge & Iron Co. of certain assets from Pitt-Des Moines, Inc., violated section 7 of the Clayton Act and section 5 of the FTC Act. The companies designed, engineered, and built storage tanks for liquified natural gas ("LNG"), liquified petroleum gas ("LPG"), and liquid atmospheric gases such as nitrogen, oxygen, and argon ("LIN/LOX"); they also designed, engineered, and built thermal vacuum chambers ("TVC"). It was uncontested that each of these "field-erected" products was a distinct relevant market. The Commission found that, in all four markets, respondents were each other's closest pre-acquisition rival and that together they largely had dominated sales since 1990. Field-erected tanks for LNG, LPG, and LIN/LOX, and TVCs are custom-made to suit each purchaser's needs, and customers place great emphasis upon a supplier's reputation for quality and service.

For each of the relevant products, customers generally seek competitive bids from several suppliers. Customers in the tank markets use a second round of bidding to negotiate price, and sometimes inform bidders of the existence of competition to reduce the prices that are bid. TVC customers select one bidder with which to negotiate a best and final offer, or they negotiate such offers from multiple bidders. Chicago Bridge exerted substantial competitive pressure on Pitt-Des Moines, and vice-versa. The companies closely monitored each other's activities, and customers frequently were able to play one firm against the other in order to obtain lower prices. Although other firms sometimes were awarded bids, the Commission found that most pre-merger competition was between Chicago Bridge and Pitt-Des Moines.

The bidding evidence also showed that the markets were not characterized by easy entry and expansion and that Chicago Bridge and Pitt-Des Moines would have continued to dominate the competition for years. The Commission considered specific instances of bidding by entrants into the relevant markets but concluded that these instances of bidding did not demonstrate that the entrants would be able to gain enough market share to affect prices and provide sufficient competition to replace the competition that was lost through the merger. In most instances, entrants' bids were rejected because the entrants lacked requisite reputation and experience. To remedy the transaction's anticompetitive effects, the Commission ordered Chicago Bridge, among other things, to reorganize its business into two stand-alone divisions, and divest one of them.

***Metso Oyj-Svedala* (FTC 2001)** In a merger involving producers of rock-crushing equipment, Metso Oyj proposed acquiring Svedala Industri AB. Rock-crushing equipment is used in mining and aggregate production to make small rocks out of big rocks. Rock-crushing equipment includes cone crushers, jaw crushers, primary gyratory crushers, and grinding mills. Each of these types of equipment was determined to be a separate relevant product market. In some of these markets, Metso and Svedala were the largest and second largest competitors, and the combined firm would have had a market share many times higher than any other competitor. Competition in these markets was analyzed in an auction model. Metso and Svedala regularly bid against each other for rock-crushing equipment sales in each of the relevant markets. By eliminating competition between these two leading suppliers, the proposed acquisition would have allowed Metso to raise prices unilaterally for certain bids and to reduce innovation. The Commission resolved the competitive concerns by requiring divestitures in the relevant markets of concern.

***Ingersoll-Dresser-Flowserve* (DOJ 2001)** Flowserve Corp. proposed to acquire Ingersoll-Dresser Pump Co. These companies were two of the largest U.S. manufacturers of specialized, highly engineered pumps used in oil refining ("API 610 pumps") and electrical generation facilities ("power plant pumps"), and only two other suppliers competed to sell these pumps in the United States. These pumps are procured through formal sealed-bid auctions and then manufactured to meet the buyers' specifications. The Department found that each of these auctions was an entirely separate competition, and therefore each constituted a distinct relevant market. The Department also found that there were only four competitors in these markets and concluded that the merger likely would cause the remaining competitors unilaterally to increase their bids significantly. Each competitor would realize that eliminating a bidder in these auctions would increase the probability of winning the auction associated with any given bid. The Department's challenge to the acquisition was settled by a consent decree requiring divestiture of Flowserve brands as well as manufacturing and repair facilities.

The procurement process for many complex products tends to be rather involved, and competition may occur in several distinct stages with extensive discussions between buyer and seller at such stages. The Agencies have often found that such competition could be understood in terms of an auction model with the procurement process working much like multiple rounds of bidding in an oral auction.

Arch Wireless-Metrocall **(DOJ 2004)** The Department investigated and decided not to challenge the proposed acquisition of Metrocall Holdings, Inc. by Arch Wireless, Inc. The two firms were the two largest providers of paging services in the United States. The Department focused on possible unilateral anticompetitive effects in the sale of one-way paging services to businesses in many individual metropolitan areas within the United States. In these areas, the combined firm would have accounted for a share of all pager units in service from less than 15% to over 80%. Because many paging customers had switched to other technologies, such as cellular or PCS telephony, the Department focused on the customers least likely to switch, notably many hospitals and emergency "first responders."

The Department observed that the competition at any one hospital was separate from the competition at any other, and that each hospital paid a price determined by that hospital's particular needs and the local rivalry among alternative technologies. This suggested that competition was best analyzed as an oral auction. The Department ultimately concluded that the merger likely would not substantially lessen competition primarily because most customers have sufficient alternatives to Arch and Metrocall. These alternatives included other paging providers, self-provision of paging services, and emerging technologies, such as wireless local area networks. Although some customers may not have sufficient alternatives, the Department concluded that service providers competing for their business would not be able to identify such customers and therefore likely would act as if they faced substantial competition.

Quest Diagnostics-Unilab **(FTC 2003)** Quest Diagnostics, Inc. and Unilab Corp. were the two leading providers of clinical laboratory testing services to physician groups in Northern California, with a combined market share of approximately 70% (the next largest competitor had approximately 4%). Delivery of health care in California was distinguished by high penetration by managed care organizations, which often delegated the financial risk for providing health care services to physician groups. Independent physician associations ("IPAs") in Northern California that assumed the financial risk for laboratory services, generally under a capitated arrangement, constituted a significant category of purchasers of laboratory services. IPA arrangements with the laboratories typically consisted of exclusive or semi-exclusive contracts, pursuant to which the physician group paid the laboratory a set amount per month for each patient affiliated with the pre-paid health plans.

An auction model best represented competition for these capitated contracts with the IPAs. Quest and Unilab were the first- and second-lowest bidders for a substantial portion of these contracts, and thus the merger was likely to cause prices to rise to the constraining level of the next-lowest-price seller. The Commission resolved by consent agreement its concern that the merger was likely to result in anticompetitive effects. Pursuant to the consent agreement, the Commission ordered, among other things, that the merged firm divest assets used to provide clinical laboratory testing services to physician groups in Northern California.

Unilateral Effects Relating to Bargaining

In some markets, individual sellers negotiate with individual buyers on a transaction-by-transaction basis to determine prices and other terms of trade. The merger of competing sellers in such markets may enhance the ability of the combined seller to bargain for a more favorable result. That may be most apt to occur if, before the merger, the buyer viewed a bargain with either of the two merging parties as significantly better than a bargain with any other seller. In that event, the merger could cause the buyer to be willing to accept worse terms from the merged seller rather than to strike no bargain at all. That willingness normally would cause a bargain to be struck on terms less favorable for the buyer.

***Aspen Technology-Hyprotech* (FTC 2004)** The Commission challenged the consummated acquisition by Aspen Technology, Inc. of Hyprotech, Ltd. Prior to the acquisition, they were two of the three significant vendors of process engineering simulation software. This software is used in the petroleum, chemical, and pharmaceutical industries to design new, and model existing, processes to produce intermediate and finished products. The combined firm accounted for between 67% and 82% of various process engineering simulation software markets, and a single other firm made virtually all other sales. The Commission's complaint alleged that the transaction may have allowed AspenTech unilaterally to exercise market power in seven global markets.

The firms' software offerings were differentiated in their respective capabilities and in how well they met customers' needs and equipment. Evidence showed that AspenTech and Hyprotech were the two closest competitors on price and on innovation in each of the markets. Evidence also showed that, prior to the merger, AspenTech and Hyprotech discounted prices to win or maintain customers, and that, due to the merger, customers would no longer be able to obtain a lower price from AspenTech by threatening to switch to Hyprotech. The third firm in the market was declining and represented a less credible threat for customers to use in price negotiations. This suggested that competition was best analyzed in a bargaining framework. Staff concluded that the transaction would have allowed AspenTech to profit by unilaterally raising prices and reducing innovation because a significant portion of the sales that may otherwise have been lost to the other merging partner as a consequence of such actions would be retained because of the acquisition. The Commission resolved these competitive concerns by issuing a consent order requiring divestiture of certain process engineering simulation software assets.

The Agencies have used bargaining theory to analyze the effects of hospital mergers on the prices they charge managed care organizations ("MCOs").

MCOs market health care plans in which subscribers' health care costs are, in whole or in part, paid for directly by the plan or reimbursed after being paid by the subscriber. MCOs negotiate with health care providers, especially hospitals, the charges they or their subscribers pay. A subscriber's out-of-pocket costs of using a particular hospital depends significantly on whether that subscriber's plan has contracted with that hospital and on what terms.

To market a plan successfully in a given area, an MCO seeks to contract on favorable terms with a wide array of hospitals so that the hospitals preferred by many potential subscribers are available to them on favorable terms. Subscribers are attracted to a plan by the ability to get care from providers they prefer on favorable terms resulting from the MCO having negotiated discounts off the providers' usual rates. The strength of a hospital's bargaining position with respect to MCOs is determined in large part by the proximity of other hospitals offering a similar or broader package of services with a similar or higher perceived quality. For example, close head-to-head competition between two hospitals allows an MCO credibly to threaten both that it will contract with, and steer its patients to, only the other. The elimination of such competition through a merger, therefore, can enable the hospitals to negotiate higher prices.

> ***Carilion-Centra* (FTC 2005)** The Commission investigated a consummated joint venture between Carilion Health System, the largest hospital system in southwest Virginia, and Centra Health, Inc. Carilion owns and operates two large hospitals in Roanoke, Virginia, while Centra owns two hospitals in Lynchburg, Virginia. Prior to the transaction, Carilion also was the sole owner of a small community hospital located in Bedford County, halfway between Roanoke and Lynchburg, about 30 miles from each city. In connection with the joint venture transaction, Carilion sold half of its interest in Bedford to Centra, so that the two hospital systems each had a 50% interest in the Bedford facility.
>
> The joint venture partners, Carilion and Centra, were the two largest hospital competitors in the Bedford area prior to the joint venture. Staff examined whether the joint venture would result in an increase in prices in Bedford County as a result of reduced competition between Carilion and Centra to attract Bedford area patients. Staff found that, after the creation of the joint venture, the Bedford hospital negotiated its prices separately from the Carilion or Centra systems and that Bedford prices either declined substantially or remained roughly the same. Staff closed the investigation.
>
> ***Slidell Memorial-Tenet* (FTC 2003)** Tenet Health Care Systems, which operated NorthShore Regional Medical Center in Slidell, Louisiana, proposed to acquire Slidell Memorial Hospital. The transaction would have combined the only full-service acute care hospitals in Slidell. Evidence suggested to Commission staff that Slidell residents and their employers demanded health insurance plans that included either Slidell Memorial or NorthShore Regional as network participants, and that a nearby small surgical hospital and cardiac specialty hospital were inadequate substitutes because they were not full-service hospitals.
>
> If Tenet purchased Slidell Memorial, health insurance companies would face the choice either of meeting Tenet's price terms, or, alternatively, excluding both NorthShore Regional and Slidell

Memorial from their provider networks. The latter action would likely make the health plan far less marketable, particularly to employers and their employees who desire access to a Slidell hospital. In addition, a health plan that did not include these hospitals could offer services only from physicians willing and able to treat the plan's patients at hospitals located outside of Slidell. Information received from local employers, residents, and health insurance plans suggested to Commission staff that health insurance companies would be unlikely to risk losing NorthShore Regional, Slidell Memorial, and the physician base of the hospitals, and instead likely would agree to a price increase. Commission staff set forth its competition analysis in public comments to the Louisiana Attorney General, subsequent to which local citizens, prior to conclusion of the Commission's investigation, voted to reject the proposed acquisition. The deal was never consummated.

***Rite Aid-Revco* (FTC 1996)** The nation's two largest retail drug store chains, Rite Aid Corp. and Revco D.S., Inc., sought to merge. The firms competed with each other in many local markets, including in 15 metropolitan areas in which the merged firm would have had more than 35% of the retail pharmacies. Commission staff analyzed the merger's effect on retail sales made through pharmacy benefit plans. Pharmacy benefit managers ("PBMs") contract with multiple pharmacy firms to form networks offering pharmacy benefits as part of health insurance coverage. Pharmacy networks often include a high percentage of local pharmacies because access to many participating pharmacies is often important to plan enrollees.

Rite Aid and Revco each offered a significant portion of the broad local coverage that payers demanded on behalf of their enrollees. Marketable networks could be assembled with just one of the firms participating. After the merger, a high proportion of plan enrollees would have considered the merged entity to be their most preferred pharmacy chain, leaving PBMs with less attractive options for assembling networks that did not include the merged firm. The merged firm as a result unilaterally could have demanded higher dispensing fees as a condition of participating in a network. The Commission voted to challenge the transaction, after which the parties abandoned it.

Mergers can create or enhance market power on the part of buyers as well as on the part of sellers. The Agencies, therefore, consider the possibility that a merger would produce a significant anticompetitive effect by eliminating competition between the merging firms in a relevant market in which they compete for an input. By eliminating an important alternative for input suppliers, a merger can lessen competition for an input significantly.

***Aetna-Prudential* (DOJ 1999)** Aetna, Inc. proposed to acquire assets relating to health insurance from The Prudential Insurance Co. of America. The acquisition would have eliminated head-to-head competition between Aetna and Prudential in the sale of health maintenance organization ("HMO") and HMO-based point-of-service health plans in Dallas and Houston. The Department challenged the proposed acquisition on the basis of likely anticompetitive effects in the purchase of physicians services for these two types of health plans and on the basis of likely anticompetitive effects in the sale of those plans. The Department concluded that the proposed merger would have allowed Aetna to reduce physician reimbursement rates because it would have significantly increased the number of patients enrolled in Aetna health plans and therefore also the number of patients a physician would have lost by terminating participation in Aetna health plans. The Department's challenge to the acquisition was settled by a consent decree requiring, among other things, the divestiture of interests Aetna had acquired in two other health plans operating in Dallas and Houston.

---

3. Entry Analysis

As explained by section 3.0 of the Guidelines, an anticompetitive merger can create "sales opportunities available to entrants," and consequently a "merger having anticompetitive effects can attract . . . entry, profitable at premerger prices, that would not have occurred" without the merger. In evaluating the competitive effects of a proposed merger, the Agencies therefore ask whether the merger would attract entry that "would be timely, likely, and sufficient in its magnitude, character and scope to deter or counteract the competitive effects" of the merger, thereby causing "prices to fall to their premerger levels or lower." To address this question, the Agencies examine industry conditions to determine whether a merger is likely to attract entry, as well as whether entry would be likely to prevent, or to reverse in a timely fashion, any anticompetitive effects of a merger.

In evaluating the likely competitive effects of a proposed merger, the Agencies distinguish among different sorts of firms that potentially would supply the relevant product in the event of an attempt to exercise market power. Section 3 of the Guidelines addresses "committed entry," which is defined as "new competition that requires expenditure of significant sunk costs." Costs associated with entry are "sunk" if they cannot be recovered by reversing the entry decision. Section 1.32 of the Guidelines addresses "uncommitted entry," which refers to supply responses not incurring significant sunk costs. Uncommitted entry normally takes the form of incumbent firms using their existing assets to make products or perform services those firms do not currently make or perform.

The focus of this chapter is Section 3 of the Guidelines, which addresses committed entry, referred to here simply as "entry." Other sections of the Guidelines separately consider three specific types of supply responses to mergers: output increases by maverick incumbent firms that potentially would frustrate coordination among the merged firm and its rivals (§ 2.12 & n.20); output increases by market incumbents with excess capacity that potentially would frustrate the unilateral exercise of market power with undifferentiated products (§ 2.22 & n.24); and product repositioning by non-merging firms that potentially would frustrate the unilateral exercise of market power with differentiated products (§ 2.212 & n.23). As with entry, the examination of these supply responses focuses on the likelihood, timeliness, and sufficiency of the supply response.

Entry may be considered successful if the entrant generates sufficient revenue to cover all costs apart from the sunk costs of entry. Such entry succeeds in the sense that the entrant becomes and remains a viable competitor in the market. Defined in this way, successful entry into some markets may require nothing more than the investment of time and money. In such a market, an anticompetitive merger nevertheless will not attract entry if the sunk cost is so great that the entry offers little prospect of a reasonable return on that investment. Significant sunk costs may be associated, for example, with building a manufacturing facility, developing a product, achieving regulatory approvals, and gaining customer acceptance. An anticompetitive merger also will not attract entry if the risk of failed entry, and the associated loss of the entry investment, is so great that potential rewards do not justify making that investment. The Agencies therefore examine the sunk costs and likely returns associated with entry.

In other markets, successful entry may not be possible despite the investment of time and money because success may depend on factors over which a potential entrant has little control. For example, an anticompetitive merger may not attract entry because entry is regulated or even legally barred, or because entrants' efforts would be stymied by the intellectual property rights of incumbents or by the unavailability of essential inputs. An anticompetitive merger also may not attract entry because entrants would suffer significant cost disadvantages in competing with incumbents. This situation can occur for a variety of reasons, but tends to be most important when entrants would be unlikely to achieve the economies of scale (i.e., reductions in average cost from operating at a higher rate of output) and scope (i.e., reductions in cost from producing several products together) already achieved by incumbents. The Agencies therefore examine obstacles to entry and possible cost disadvantages for entrants.

If a merger does attract entry, that entry still may be insufficient to deter or fully counteract the merger's anticompetitive effect, or the entrant may take so long to achieve market significance that the merger nevertheless produces sustained anticompetitive effects. The Agencies therefore examine how long entry would take and how it likely would affect the merger's competitive consequences. The discussion that follows addresses in more detail the Guidelines' concepts of likelihood, timeliness, and sufficiency of entry.

Likelihood of Entry

The Agencies do not assess merely whether firms could commit incremental resources to the relevant market, but more importantly whether the proposed merger would be likely to induce firms to do so in a timely fashion and in a sufficient magnitude to deter or counteract the merger's anticompetitive effects. Thus, information regarding such factors as technical capability, know-how, sunk costs, and other requirements for successful entry is necessary, but not sufficient, for the Agencies' evaluation of entry conditions. The Agencies must also determine whether firms would have an adequate profit incentive to enter at prices prevailing before the merger, i.e., the prices to which the market likely would return following entry sufficient to deter or counteract the merger's anticompetitive effects. In evaluating the likelihood of entry, the Agencies thus focus on the sales opportunities created by the proposed merger.

Sunk Costs and Risks Associate with Entry

Consumer Products

The Agencies commonly find that proposed mergers involving highly differentiated consumer products would not attract the entry of new brands because entry would not be profitable at pre-merger prices. In a market populated by well-established brands, successful entry usually requires a substantial investment in advertising and promotional activity over a long period of time to build share and achieve widespread distribution through retail channels. Moreover, making such investments by no means assures success.

Nestle-Dreyer's **(FTC 2003)** Nestle Holdings, Inc. proposed to merge with Dreyer's Grand Ice Cream, Inc. The firms were two of the top three rivals in the superpremium ice cream market. Those three combined for 98% of sales. Grocery retailer private label sales accounted for the remaining 2%. Evidence showed entry to be difficult, both because of the need to develop brand equity to compete effectively, and the need to obtain effective distribution, which is difficult in this market because the product must be maintained at a particular freezing temperature throughout the distribution process. The Commission determined that entry was unlikely to prevent or reverse the merged firm's likely unilateral anticompetitive price increase and challenged the merger. To resolve the competitive concerns, the Commission entered into a consent agreement with the parties requiring divestiture of two brands.

Staples-Office Depot **(FTC 1997)** The Commission successfully challenged a merger between Staples, Inc. and Office Depot, Inc., two of the three national office supply superstore retail chains. The Commission found, and the court agreed, that entry was unlikely to prevent anticompetitive effects arising from the merger. Important to this finding was that the three incumbent office superstores had saturated many of the local markets such that a new office superstore entrant would have difficulty in achieving economies of scale in, among other things, advertising and distribution.

Kimberly-Clark-Scott **(DOJ 1995)** The Department found that entry would be unlikely to be attracted by the proposed merger of Kimberly-Clark Corp. and Scott Paper Co., which the Department challenged on the basis of unilateral anticompetitive effects in facial tissue and in baby wipes. Brand recognition was very important for both products, and the Department concluded that the costs and risks associated with establishing new brands likely would prevent the sort of entry that could prevent or reverse the likely anticompetitive effects of the merger. The Department's challenge to the proposed merger was settled by a consent decree requiring the divestiture of assets relating to facial tissue and baby wipes.

Successful prior entry can provide evidence that an anticompetitive merger would attract entry despite the need to make a substantial investment in advertising and promotional activity. Successful prior entry, however, is by no means proof that entry likely would occur following a proposed merger, or that any such entry would be sufficient to prevent significant anticompetitive effects. Evidence of the severity of entry obstacles sometimes is found in an inability of past entrants to gain consumer acceptance.

L'Oreal-Carson **(DOJ 2000)** In considering L'Oreal's proposed acquisition of Carson, Inc., the Department found that several brands of hair relaxer kits introduced in recent years had been unable to generate significant sales. That evidence reinforced the Department's conclusion that the proposed merger would not attract entry sufficient to deter or counteract the likely anticompetitive effects of the merger. The Department's challenge to the merger was resolved by a consent decree requiring the divestiture of relevant brands and associated assets, including a manufacturing facility.

Swedish Match-National **(FTC 2000)** Swedish Match North America, Inc., proposed to acquire National Tobacco Company, L.P.

The companies were the first- and third-largest producers of loose leaf chewing tobacco in the United States, with shares of 42% and 18%. Swedish Match's loose leaf products included the Red Man premium brands. National Tobacco produced the Beech-Nut line of premium brands. The Commission successfully challenged the merger in district court, asserting that the transaction would result in anticompetitive effects in the U.S. market for loose leaf chewing tobacco. The evidence showed that entry would be thwarted by, among other things, the substantial sunk costs required to overcome strong brand loyalty. The evidence included prior unsuccessful efforts at introducing new brands by established rivals.

Mergers involving differentiated consumer products also may be unlikely to attract entry because no customer has an incentive to sponsor entry. Wholesale customers often are retailers, and there are circumstances under which retailers suffer little from wholesale price increases because they pass the price increases on to final consumers. Moreover, retailers can benefit from a merger of manufacturers if the retailers sell private label products in competition with the merging manufacturers. A merger involving differentiated consumer products also is unlikely to attract entry when its anticompetitive effects would be felt in just a few local markets or if there are important local brands catering to local tastes and traditions.

***Interstate Bakeries-Continental* (DOJ 1995)** The Department challenged the proposed purchase of Continental Baking Co. by Interstate Bakeries Corp. on the basis of anti-competitive effects in the sale of white pan bread within five metropolitan areas. Anticompetitive effects in these five metropolitan areas would have been unlikely to attract entry by a national brand because the overall effect of the merger on national price would have been insignificant. In each of the five metropolitan areas, only one of the leading premium brands was sold nationally, while the others were regional or strictly local. Anticompetitive effects in these areas would have been unlikely to attract local entry because the sunk costs of brand development would be spread over relatively few sales and because important media used for advertising and promotion cannot be effectively targeted at limited metropolitan areas. The Department's challenge to the proposed merger was settled by a consent decree requiring divestiture of brands and related assets in the five metropolitan areas.

Industrial Products

The sources of the sunk costs associated with entry into markets for industrial products vary from one market to the next. In many markets, the only significant sunk costs are those associated with the construction or acquisition of productive facilities, such as manufacturing plants. In other markets, substantial investments are required for product development and to establish support organizations for distribution and service. And in some markets, additional sunk costs are associated with demonstrating product performance and reliability to potential customers. The sunk costs from each of these sources can be large or small. Mergers of industrial products manufacturers may be unlikely to attract entry if customers are unwilling to purchase products without a well-established record of satisfactory performance. A merger is especially unlikely to attract entry if product failure imposes a substantial cost on customers.

***Ingersoll-Dresser-Flowserve* (DOJ 2001)** The Department challenged the proposed acquisition of Ingersoll-Dresser Pump Co. by

Flowserve Corp. on the basis of likely unilateral anticompetitive effects in markets for specialized pumps used in oil refining and electrical generation facilities. The Department found that the design and testing of an array of such pumps would entail substantial sunk costs. The Department also found that an entrant could not effectively compete in the relevant markets without incurring additional sunk costs in the establishment of a network of service and repair facilities. And because pump failure could shut down part of a refinery or electric generation plant, the Department found that many customers in the relevant markets would not purchase from a supplier that had not demonstrated the reliability and efficiency of its pumps in the particular use for which the pump was being sought. This fact added additional sunk entry costs and extended yet further the substantial time successful entry would take. The Department's challenge to the acquisition was settled by a consent decree requiring divestiture of Flowserve brands as well as manufacturing and repair facilities.

***Metso Oyj-Svedala* (FTC 2001)** The Commission investigated a proposed merger between leading manufacturers of mining equipment, Metso Oyj and Svedala Industri AB. Both firms made equipment used in mining, including gyratory crushers, jaw crushers, cone crushers, and grinding mills. Operational failure by any of these machines would require shutting down the entire mining circuit. Purchasers would deal only with well-established companies producing equipment with a proven track record of reliability. A new entrant would face significant sunk costs in developing and testing a new piece of equipment and in gaining customer acceptance. Although several potential entrants could manufacture this equipment within two years, it was unlikely that customers would purchase new and untested equipment within this period. The Commission resolved the competitive concerns by requiring divestitures in the relevant markets of concern.

***Exxon-Mobil* (FTC 1999)** Prior to merging, Exxon Corp. and Mobil Corp. were leading producers of jet turbine oil. Jet turbine engines require a specialized lubricant that can operate in an extreme environment. Failure by the lubricant could lead to engine failure, requiring the engine to be taken out of service for an extended period of time for repairs or overhaul. This lubricant, although expensive for a lubricating oil, was inexpensive relative to the cost of losing use of an engine for any period of time as well as to the cost of repairing or replacing an engine. To secure sales to customers, jet turbine oil producers submitted their products for extensive product testing, including testing on the customer's specific model engine. After developing a satisfactory lubricant, therefore, a new entrant would have to invest substantial sunk costs in product testing and incur substantial time delay in entering. The Commission, therefore, concluded that entry would not eliminate competitive concerns. The Commission and the parties entered into a settlement that required, among other things, divestiture of Exxon's jet turbine oil business.

***Precision Castparts-Wyman-Gordon* (FTC 1999)** Precision Castparts Corp. and Wyman-Gordon Co., two leading manufacturers of titanium, stainless steel, and nickel-based superalloy cast components for jet engine and airframe applications, proposed to merge. Several companies worldwide had the capability of manufacturing these types of cast parts, but customers were not likely to purchase them from companies lacking a proven, years-long track record of producing products that did not fail. The Commission concluded that entry would not be timely, likely, and sufficient to thwart anticompetitive effects from the merger. It resolved its competitive concerns in a consent order that, among other things, required divestiture of a titanium foundry and a large cast parts foundry.

The Agencies have sometimes found that sunk costs did not pose a significant entry obstacle. In such cases, expected returns justified any required investment in new productive facilities, and successful entry typically did not require the establishment of a brand or reputation for quality.

***ADS-Hancor* (FTC 2005)** The FTC closed its investigation into the acquisition by Advanced Drainage Systems, Inc. of Hancor Holding Corp. Both firms were major producers of corrugated high density polyethylene ("HDPE") pipe used for underground water drainage. Staff found that demand for HDPE was growing, that a new HDPE manufacturing plant could be constructed at relatively low cost and could be in operation within a short period, that several firms had entered de novo in the prior ten years, and that several fringe incumbents were expanding output. Also, existing manufacturers of certain other, non-HDPE pipes could enter at relatively little sunk cost. Many of them served common customers already and thus did not have to establish a new marketing organization. The Commission concluded that entry conditions were such that anticompetitive effects from the merger were unlikely.

***Omnicare-NeighborCare* (FTC 2005)** The largest provider of pharmacy services to long-term care facilities ("LTC pharmacy"), Omnicare, Inc., offered to acquire a large rival LTC pharmacy, NeighborCare, Inc. The combined firm would have under contract more than half of skilled nursing facility beds in multiple states, and the post-merger market structure would be highly concentrated in many areas. The Commission's decision not to challenge the acquisition was based in part on relatively easy entry conditions in the then-current marketplace. Sunk costs were relatively low, illustrated by many historical examples of entry, including entry by former employees of incumbent LTC pharmacies, expansion by retail pharmacies into the LTC business, and vertical integration by skilled nursing facility operators.

***Wrigley-Kraft* (FTC 2005)** Wm. Wrigley Jr. Co. proposed to acquire certain confectionary assets from Kraft Foods, Inc., including certain well-known breath mint and chewing gum brands. Commission staff assessed whether sunk costs that would have to be incurred in acquiring the capacity to produce or market breath mints or chewing gum would pose significant impediments to post-merger competitive entry. Staff found that new entrants would have relatively easy access to third-party "co-manufacturers" for the production of the relevant products and thereby could avoid costly expenditures in developing manufacturing expertise or in building a new facility. Entrants also could competitively distribute their products by outsourcing those functions to third-parties. Staff also found evidence of significant recent branded entry. Based in part on this evidence concerning entry conditions, staff closed its investigation.

***Playbill-Stagebill* (DOJ 2002)** In its analysis of the consummated acquisition of certain assets of Stagebill Media by Playbill Inc., the

Department found that sunk costs of entry were insignificant. Prior to the acquisition, Playbill was the nation's largest publisher of theater programs and Stagebill was its largest competitor in many cities. The Department found that the merger was not likely to be anticompetitive because the printing itself could be out-sourced, so an entrant did not need to incur significant sunk costs. Indeed, the Department found that entry based on out-sourcing had occurred. The Department also found that theaters could contract directly with printers and some had done so. Finally, the Department found that prices of theater programs had not increased. Consequently, the Department took no action against the acquisition.

Although many purchasers of differentiated consumer products are reluctant to switch from brands they know and trust, purchasers of industrial commodities may be more likely to switch and be willing to sponsor entry when they perceive a lack of competition.

***National Oilwell-Varco* (DOJ 2005)** Entry considerations were a major factor in the Department's decision not to challenge the acquisition by National Oilwell Inc. of Varco, Inc. Those firms were among the very few significant competitors in the sale of various products and services relating to offshore drilling for oil and gas, and that fact initially gave the Department serious concerns about the competitive effects of the acquisition. Nevertheless, the Department found that several major customers for these products and services believed that they would be able to sponsor successful entry by committing to make purchases from firms with little or no current market presence. The Department also identified sellers of related products and services interested in entering.

In some markets, it is clear that a merger would not attract entry simply because the sunk costs of entry are far too great in comparison to the likely rewards.

***General Dynamics-Newport News* (DOJ 2001)** General Dynamics Corp. proposed to acquire Newport News Shipbuilding Inc. These were the only firms that built nuclear submarines for the U.S. Navy. The manufacture of a nuclear submarine requires much highly specialized equipment, personnel, and know-how, all of which combined to make the sunk cost of entry extraordinarily high. As a result, the merger was not likely to attract entry, especially in view of the fact that an entrant might never make a single sale. The proposed acquisition was abandoned after the Department filed suit to enjoin it.

Other Significant Obstacles to Successful Entry

Entry may not be attracted by an anticompetitive merger for many reasons. In some markets, entry is explicitly regulated, and in others, government regulation can effectively bar entry. The Agencies have found legal obstacles to entry to be significant in some instances.

For example, many states have certificate of need ("CON") programs barring entry into health care markets unless a potential entrant makes an expensive and time-consuming demonstration that there is an unmet need for its services. Regulation of this sort increases sunk costs and the time it takes to enter, and it also creates a significant risk that entry ultimately will be prohibited. For several hospital mergers challenged by the Agencies, as well as a merger of outpatient surgical centers, CON regulation was a factor in the Agencies' determination that the mergers would not attract entry.

Mercy Health-Finley **(DOJ 1994)** The Department challenged the formation of a partnership between Mercy Health Services and Finley Tri-States Health Group, Inc. The companies owned the only general acute care hospitals in Dubuque, Iowa, and the Department concluded that Iowa's CON statute would prevent the construction of any new general acute care hospital in Dubuque. That no new hospital would be built was stipulated at trial, but the district court rejected the Department's challenge to the merger on other grounds. The case became moot before the Department's appeal could be decided because the parties abandoned the merger.

Environmental and zoning regulations are other examples of rules that may make entry difficult.

Florida Rock-Harper Bros. **(DOJ 1999)** Florida Rock Industries, Inc. proposed to acquire Harper Bros., Inc. These companies competed in the sale of aggregate and silica sand in southwest Florida and together accounted for at least 60% of the sales of each product. The Department concluded that the acquisition would be likely to lessen competition substantially and challenged the acquisition. The Department found many reasons why the acquisition would not attract entry, including environmental regulation at the local, state, and federal levels that made it very difficult to open a new aggregate or silica sand production facility in the area. The Department's challenge to the merger was resolved by a consent decree requiring the divestiture of a quarry and sand mine.

In the telecommunications and pharmaceutical industries, federal regulation may pose a significant obstacle to entry. Entry into some telecommunications markets is constrained by the need to have a licence from the Federal Communication Commission for use of part of the electromagnetic spectrum, while the introduction of pharmaceuticals requires approval by the Food and Drug Administration.

Cingular-AT&T Wireless **(DOJ 2004)** Cingular Wireless Corp., a joint venture of SBC Communications Inc. and BellSouth Corp., proposed to acquire AT&T Wireless Services, Inc. Both Cingular and AT&T Wireless provided mobile wireless telecommunications service ("MWTS") throughout the United States. The Department concluded that the acquisition likely would be anticompetitive in ten local MWTS markets and challenged the acquisition partly on that basis. MWTS is provided using electromagnetic spectrum, the rights to which are licensed by the Federal Communications Commission. Among the reasons the Department concluded that the acquisition would not attract entry was difficulty in obtaining licenses to the necessary spectrum. The Department's challenge to the merger was resolved by a consent decree requiring divestitures in particular locations.

Cephalon-Cima **(FTC 2004)** Cephalon, Inc. proposed to acquire Cima Labs, Inc. Cephalon was the only firm selling a breakthrough cancer pain ("BTCP") drug in the United States. Evidence suggested that Cima was the most likely first entrant with a BTCP drug to rival Cephalon's product, and that entry subsequent to Cima's was unlikely for at least the next four years. The time needed to secure FDA approval was a significant factor in reaching this conclusion. The Commission resolved its competitive concerns with a consent order that required Cephalon, among other things, to grant an irrevocable, fully paid license to a specific third party for the manufacture and sale of a generic formulation of Cephalon's BTCP drug.

Intellectual property rights such as patents can at times pose a significant entry obstacle. Intellectual property can be important in both high-tech and low-tech industries.

***3D Systems-DTM* (DOJ 2001)** 3D Systems Corp. proposed to acquire DTM Corp., a competitor in industrial rapid prototyping systems, which are used to make functional and non-functional prototypes of new products or components. The Department challenged the acquisition in part because the two companies held extensive patent portfolios that likely created an insuperable entry obstacle even for well-established competitors outside the United States. The Department's challenge to the merger was resolved by a consent decree requiring divestiture of a package of intellectual property rights.

***Franklin Electric-United Dominion* (DOJ 2000)** The Department challenged the proposed joint venture between subsidiaries of Franklin Electric Co. and United Dominion Industries because it would have eliminated competition between the only two domestic producers of submersible turbine pumps used for pumping gasoline from underground storage tanks at retail stations. The Department found that the proposed merger would be unlikely to attract entry for several reasons, including the necessity of designing around Franklin Electric's patents. After trial, a district court granted the Department's motion for a permanent injunction.

***American Home Products-Solvay* (FTC 1997)** American Home Products Corp. proposed to acquire the animal health business of Solvay S.A. The Commission found that the proposed acquisition raised serious competitive concerns in three, highly concentrated, relevant product markets for the production and sale of animal vaccines. The Commission found, moreover, that post-merger entry was unlikely to mitigate the competitive concerns because entry would not be likely, timely, or sufficient. For each relevant market, entry would require the expenditure of significant resources over a period of many years with no assurance that a viable commercial product would result. The time required to enter the relevant markets could be further lengthened by the need to obtain U.S. Department of Agriculture approvals to sell the vaccines. Significantly, the existence of broad patents governing the manufacture of each of the relevant products enhanced the difficulty of entry. As a result, the Commission issued a complaint challenging the proposed acquisition, and ultimately reached a settlement with the parties that called for, among other things, divestiture of Solvay's intellectual property rights relating to the three vaccines.

Patents need not impose a significant obstacle to entry, even in a high-tech industry with many important patents. The Agencies may find that the requisite technology is nevertheless reasonably available, for example, because required patents could easily be licensed or invented around.

***Cinram-AOL Time Warner* (DOJ 2003)** The Department decided not to challenge the acquisition by Cinram International Inc. of the DVD and CD replication assets of AOL Time Warner Inc. in part because the requisite technology was readily available for license from patent pools. The Department also found that sunk costs were relatively low and that the prospects for recovering them were good due to high demand growth.

A merger may lead to price increases without attracting entry because potential entrants would be unable to obtain a source of supply for essential inputs, for example, when entry requires access to scarce natural resources.

***Imetal-English China Clays* (DOJ 1999)** Imetal proposed to acquire English China Clays, plc, both of which produced water-washed kaolin and calcined kaolin. These products are produced from kaolin clay, which is quite scarce. Much of the world's highest quality kaolin is found in a small area within Georgia. Among the reasons why the Department concluded that the proposed merger was unlikely to attract significant entry was that an entrant would have difficulty in acquiring suitable kaolin deposits. The Department's challenge to the merger was resolved by a consent decree requiring divestiture of a plant and associated assets such as kaolin reserves.

Difficulty in securing essential inputs can impede entry in a variety of contexts, particularly when incumbents own or control access to the inputs. In some cases, an entrant might find it difficult to secure a source of supply for a manufactured input product. In other cases, gaining access to physical facilities built and owned by third parties can pose a significant entry obstacle. In addition, access to human resources may pose a significant entry obstacle in some markets.

***DaVita-Gambro* (FTC 2005)** DaVita Inc. proposed to acquire Gambro Healthcare, Inc. The firms were rivals in the provision of outpatient dialysis services. The Commission alleged that anticompetitive effects would result from the transaction in 35 local markets where the firms competed. Laws applicable to dialysis clinics required that each such clinic must have a nephrologist as its medical director. In addition, the medical director is the clinic's primary source of referrals and thus is essential to the clinic's competitiveness. A lack of available nephrologists with an established referral stream was an obstacle to entry into each of the relevant geographic markets at issue. To resolve the Commission's concerns, the parties entered into a consent agreement that required, among other things, divestiture of dialysis clinics in the markets at issue.

***Central Parking-Allright* (DOJ 1999)** The unavailability of facilities that had to be provided by others made entry unlikely after the proposed merger of Central Parking Corp. and Allright Holdings, Inc. Both companies operated off-street parking facilities in the central business districts of many U.S. cities. In these areas, land was scarce and typically had uses higher-valued than parking lots, so adding additional parking spaces typically required the construction of a new office building, and higher parking rates were not likely to spur the construction of new office buildings. The Department's challenge to the merger was resolved by a consent decree requiring divestiture of parking facilities in many cities.

Cost Disadvantages of Entrants

A merger may lead to price increases but not attract entry because entrants would suffer a significant cost disadvantage relative to incumbents. The most common reason for a cost disadvantage is the presence of significant economies of scale and scope. In other situations, entrants may be significantly disadvantaged by economies of density in route delivery systems (i.e., reductions in cost from increasing volume, holding the size of a network fixed).

***Waste Management-Allied* (DOJ 2003)** Waste Management, Inc. agreed to acquire the assets Allied Waste Industries, Inc. used in small container commercial waste hauling in Broward County, Florida. This portion of the municipal solid waste business entails the collection, transportation, and disposal of waste generated by commercial establishments. The Department challenged the acquisition in part because an entrant would be unable to operate efficiently and provide meaningful price competition. To be efficient, a competitor must achieve a high route density by contracting with a large number of commercial establishments in a relatively small area. Doing so was found to be exceptionally difficult for an entrant because incumbents had secured many existing customers through long-term contracts. The Department's challenge to the merger was resolved by a consent decree requiring divestiture of specified routes and the assets used on them.

***Federal-Mogul-T&N* (FTC 1998)** In the merger of Federal-Mogul Corp. and T&N PLC, one of the markets the staff examined was the manufacture and sale of engine bearings to the aftermarket for repairing and overhauling engines. Each engine bearing is designed for and used in a particular truck or car engine, and each engine can use only bearings designed and built to its specifications. The parties acquired the tooling for their broad line of aftermarket bearings when engines were first in production, allowing them to amortize the cost of that tooling over a longer time and over a larger number of bearings. A new entrant that attempted to match an incumbent's product line would have been able to amortize the tooling for many bearings only over a portion of the engine's life, and would necessarily have higher relative costs. This would have put any entrant in the aftermarket at a substantial cost disadvantage to the incumbent firms. Thus, the Commission found that entry would not be timely or likely to prevent anticompetitive effects. The Commission resolved the matter with a consent order that required, among other things, divestiture of T&N's engine bearing business.

Timeliness of Entry

Section 3.2 of the Guidelines states that entry generally is considered timely only if "achieved within two years from initial planning to significant market impact." Even if a proposed merger likely would attract entry that eventually reverses any likely anticompetitive effect from a merger, the Agencies nonetheless would challenge the merger if they determined the entry would not be timely. For many of the proposed mergers discussed in this chapter, the Agencies found that entry having a material effect on competition would take significantly longer than the two-year period specified by the Guidelines.

***Alcan-Pechiney* (DOJ 2003)** The Department challenged the proposed acquisition of Pechiney, S.A. by Alcan, Inc. on the basis of likely anticompetitive effects in the production and sale of a class of aluminum alloys called "brazing sheet." Manufacturing brazing sheet requires an expensive rolling mill, which the Department found would take at least three years to construct. The Department also found that successfully selling brazing sheet requires the mastery of alloy technologies and that it likely would take several additional years after a new mill commenced production to "qualify" its output with major customers and begin making significant sales. Thus, the Department concluded that entry was unlikely and would necessarily take far longer than two years if it did occur. The Department's challenge to the merger was resolved by a consent decree requiring divestiture of Alcan's brazing sheet business, including a smelting facility, rolling mill, and associated intellectual property.

***Healthtrust-Holy Cross* (FTC 1994)** In a merger between Healthtrust, Inc.-The Hospital Co. and Holy Cross Health Services of Utah, there was no CON regulation that would preclude or delay entry into the market, and prior entry of hospitals had occurred in the geographic market. Nonetheless, the Commission concluded that timely entry was unlikely to prevent anticompetitive effects from the merger under investigation because it takes many years to plan and build a new hospital. The Commission resolved its competitive concerns arising from the transaction by reaching a consent agreement with the parties that, among other things, included an order requiring divestiture of one of the acquired firm's hospitals.

In evaluating the timeliness of entry, the Agencies include the time to complete any necessary preliminary steps, such as establishing a reputation or the development of specialized inputs into the production of the product in question.

***Federal-Mogul-T&N* (FTC 1998)** Federal-Mogul Corp. and T&N PLC, which proposed to merge, competed in selling thin-wall engine bearings, light-duty engine bearings, and heavy-duty engine bearings to original equipment manufacturers ("OEMs") and to customers in the aftermarket. These bearings required specialized alloys developed for specific applications. Entry required time to develop such alloys, to design the specific bearings for particular applications, and to test and qualify in particular applications. For each type of bearing, as to both OEM and aftermarket customers, FTC staff found that timely entry would not prevent anticompetitive effects in the relevant markets. Further, in the aftermarket, effective entry required brand name recognition that took additional time to develop. The Commission resolved the matter with a consent order that required, among other things, divestiture of T&N's engine bearing business.

Sufficiency of Entry

Section 3.0 of the Guidelines states that "[e]ntry that is sufficient to counteract the competitive effects of concern will cause prices to fall to their premerger levels or lower." Thus, even if the evidence suggests that timely entry into the relevant market is likely, the entry analysis is not complete. The entry must also be of a character and magnitude that it would "deter or counteract the competitive effect of concern."

***Chicago Bridge-Pitt-Des Moines* (FTC 2005)** The Commission ruled that the consummated acquisition by Chicago Bridge & Iron Co. of certain assets from Pitt-Des Moines, Inc., violated Section 7 of the Clayton Act and Section 5 of the FTC Act. The merging parties designed, engineered, and built storage tanks for liquified natural gas ("LNG"), liquified petroleum gas ("LPG"), and liquid atmospheric gases such as nitrogen, oxygen, and argon ("LIN/LOX"). They also designed, engineered, and built thermal vacuum chambers ("TVC"). TVCs and field-erected tanks for LNG, LPG, and LIN/LOX are custom-made to suit each purchaser's needs, and customers place great emphasis upon a supplier's reputation for quality and service. For each of the relevant products, customers generally seek competitive bids from several suppliers.

The Commission found that some timely entry into each of these markets might occur, but that it was unlikely to be sufficient to prevent anticompetitive effects from the merger. Although new firms had appeared and fringe firms had the intent to compete, these firms were not found to be significant competitors capable of replacing the competition lost due to the merger. With respect to the LNG tank market, the Commission found that new entrants lacked the reputation and experience that most customers demand, and they lacked the requisite personnel skills. With respect to the LPG and the LIN/LOX tank markets, the Commission found that, although the merging parties identified a number of actual and potential entrants, entry of those firms would not prevent the anticompetitive effects of the merger because the firms would not have the attributes desired by most customers. The record evidence showed no attempted entry into the TVC tank market by any suppliers. The Commission ordered, among other things, divestiture of assets and other remedial action to restore the competition lost as a result of the transaction.

The Agencies' reasons for concluding that entry would not face significant obstacles also can be relevant to determining whether entry would be sufficient.

Sherwin-Williams-Duron **(FTC 2004)** The Sherwin-Williams Co., the nation's largest manufacturer of architectural paint, proposed to acquire Duron, Inc., a leading architectural paint manufacturer in the eastern United States. The firms were head-to-head competitors in several metropolitan areas where each had a relatively large number of store locations. A focus of the Commission's investigation was on the potential effects of the merger on professional contractors, which in significant numbers patronize architectural paint stores rather than other retailers of paint (such as home improvement stores and other big-box retailers). Staff concluded that this class of customers made purchasing decisions largely based on local market conditions that determine price and service, rather than on national or regional contracts with paint suppliers.

The investigation assessed whether entry would require a network of store locations to compete effectively for professional painters' business. Data analysis revealed that even professional painters who use numerous company stores during a year spend the vast majority of their dollars at a limited number of favored stores. Thus, the evidence showed that professional painters did not rely on an extended store network and would not likely pay a premium to do business with firms that operate a network of stores in a region. In addition, even if a network of some size were required, the requirements to open additional stores did not pose an entry barrier. Few significant obstacles appeared to prevent firms with established brand names from opening paint stores to serve professional painters. No Commission action was taken.

---

4. Efficiencies

Merging parties may reduce their costs by combining complementary assets, eliminating duplicate activities, or achieving scale economies.

Mergers also may lead to enhanced product quality or to increased innovation that results in lower costs and prices or in more rapid introduction of new products that benefit consumers.

As the Guidelines state, efficiencies "can enhance the merged firm's ability and incentive to compete, which may result in lower prices, improved quality, enhanced service, or new products." Guidelines § 4. Moreover, when a merged firm achieves such efficiencies, it may induce competitors to strive for greater efficiencies in order to compete more effectively. Consumers benefit from such increased competition.

Efficiencies may directly prevent the consumer harm that otherwise would result from a merger. The Agencies thus do not challenge a proposed merger "if cognizable efficiencies . . . likely would be sufficient to reverse the merger's potential to harm consumers in the relevant market, e.g., by preventing price increases in that market." Guidelines § 4. In analyzing mergers, including the likely effects of cost reductions, the Agencies assume that firms maximize profits. Other things equal, a reduction in any cost that depends on a firm's output rate causes a profit-maximizing firm to reduce prices. This effect may be sufficient to counteract a merger's anticompetitive effects.

For example, one potential concern is that a proposed merger would increase the likelihood that competitors will coordinate pricing and output decisions in a way that harms consumers. In the presence of other conditions conducive to coordination, uniform cost structures across incumbent competitors may facilitate coordination. Therefore, some mergers that appreciably reduce the uniformity of costs across competitors may disrupt existing coordination or otherwise make coordination less likely. As a lower-cost producer, the merged firm may find it profitable to reduce prices notwithstanding its rivals' likely reactions. Similarly, sufficiently large reductions in the marginal costs of producing and selling the products of one or both of the merging firms may eliminate the unilateral incentive to raise prices that the merger might otherwise have created. In both of these situations, the Agencies integrate efficiencies into their assessments of competitive effects. In so doing, the Agencies assess the effects of the elimination of competition between the merging firms in light of any cognizable, merger-specific efficiencies.

Efficiencies in the form of quality improvements also may be sufficient to offset anticompetitive price increases following a merger. Because a quality improvement involves a change in product attributes, a simple comparison of pre- and post-merger prices could be misleading. A careful analysis of the effects of changes in product attributes and prices on consumer welfare is likely to be necessary.

Efficiencies the Agencies Consider

Section 4 of the Guidelines provides that, to be considered by the Agencies, an efficiency must be "merger-specific" and "cognizable."

Merger-Specific Efficiencies

Efficiencies are not taken into account by the Agencies if they are not merger-specific. Merger-specific efficiencies are "those efficiencies likely to be accomplished with the proposed merger and unlikely to be accomplished in the absence of either the proposed merger or another means having comparable anticompetitive effects." The Guidelines explain that, although the Agencies ask whether the efficiencies can be achieved by means other than the merger, "[o]nly alternatives that are practical in the business situation faced by the merging firms will be considered in making this determination; the Agency will not insist upon a less restrictive alternative that is merely theoretical."

The Agencies recognize that the merging parties often have information with respect both to how they plan to integrate after the merger and to the effect of the integration on the merged firm. Accordingly, the Agencies give full consideration to the parties' reasonable and well-supported explanations of merger-specific cost savings.

Any efficiency that enables the combined firm to achieve lower costs for a given quantity and quality of product than the firms likely would achieve without the proposed merger is merger-specific. For example, if a merged firm would combine the production from two small or underutilized facilities (one from each of the merging firms) at one facility that has lower costs, and if such a cost reduction could not practically be achieved without the merger (e.g., by one of the merging firms combining two of its own underutilized facilities or through rapid internal growth), this cost reduction is merger-specific. Such a cost reduction benefits consumers to the extent that it makes the merged firm a more vigorous competitor, reduces prices, or expands output.

That an efficiency theoretically could be achieved without a merger—for example, through a joint venture or contract—does not disqualify it from consideration in the analysis. Many joint venture agreements or contracts may not be practically feasible or may impose substantial transaction costs (including monitoring costs). In their assessment of proffered efficiency claims, the Agencies accord appropriate weight to evidence that alternatives to the merger are likely to be impractical or relatively costly.

> ***Alpha-Beta* (Disguised FTC Matter)** A proposed merger of two of the largest gizmo manufacturers ("Alpha" and "Beta") would create a firm with a market share in excess of 30%. In addition to its manufacturing business, Alpha owned a subsidiary company engaged in industrial packaging. At the time of the proposed merger, Alpha's packaging subsidiary had unutilized capacity. Among the subsidiary's customers was Beta, which owned Get-To, Inc., a company that dispenses gizmos to customers located in isolated areas not otherwise served by normal distribution channels. The parties planned to combine Alpha's unused packaging capacity with Get-To's demand for packaging. The parties claimed that this combination would yield significant cost savings. Commission staff concluded that, although such an arrangement may yield savings, the savings would not be merger-specific. Beta already was an Alpha customer, and the evidence suggested that, even in the absence of the merger, Alpha and Beta were in the position readily to expand their existing packaging services contract to achieve the claimed savings. The Commission did not challenge the merger because evidence was insufficient to show that the merger was likely to cause competitive harm.
>
> ***Nucor-Birmingham Steel* (DOJ 2002)** Nucor Corp.'s acquisition of substantially all of the assets of Birmingham Steel Corp. raised competitive concerns because the firms owned two of the three mills producing certain types of steel bar in the western United States. The Department concluded, however, that the third western mill and other domestic mills would substantially constrain any post-merger price increases and that the merger likely would generate significant efficiencies. The Department found that the acquisition would allow

the merged firm to close some distribution facilities and to supply some customers from a closer mill at a lower delivered cost. The Department also found that the acquisition would provide a Nucor mill with a lower cost input supply from Birmingham, although some of the savings might have been obtainable through a contractual arrangement. Even though some of the latter efficiencies may not have been merger specific, the Department concluded that plausible merger-specific reductions in variable costs were significant relative to the worst case scenario of anticompetitive effects from the acquisition, and the Department granted early termination under HSR.

Competition spurs firms to implement cost reduction initiatives, and those likely to be implemented without a proposed merger do not yield merger-specific efficiencies. For example, the parties may believe that they can reduce costs by adopting each other's "best practices" or by modernizing outdated equipment. But, in many cases, these efficiencies can be achieved without the proposed merger. The presence of other firms in the industry unilaterally adopting similar "best practices" would suggest that such cost savings are not merger-specific. By contrast, if a "best practice" is protected by intellectual property rights, then it could be the basis for a merger-specific efficiency claim.

Merging parties also may claim cost savings from combining sales and realizing economies of scale. These types of economies, however, might be realized from internal growth. If such unilateral changes are likely without the proposed merger (for example, if they have already been planned), they are not merger-specific. Timing can be an important factor in the consideration of such claims. If a merger can be expected significantly to accelerate the achievement of economies of scale due to increased sales as compared to internal growth, the Agencies credit the merger with merger-specific acceleration of the cost reduction.

Cognizable Efficiencies

The Guidelines define cognizable efficiencies to be "merger-specific efficiencies that have been verified and do not arise from anticompetitive reductions in output or service." Moreover, "[c]ognizable efficiencies are assessed net of costs produced by the merger or incurred in achieving those efficiencies." Guidelines § 4.

The parties can facilitate the Agencies' assessment of whether efficiency claims are cognizable by providing documentation that is logical, coherent, and grounded on facts and business experience. It is in the parties' interest to provide detailed information on the likelihood, magnitude, and timing of claimed efficiencies. They may, for example, draw on a detailed business plan that describes how the merged firm intends to achieve the efficiencies. If not already included in the business plan, the parties should also consider providing supporting evidence that justifies the planning methods and shows the reasonableness of applied assumptions.

When efficiencies are an important business motive for the merger, information pertinent to verification will often exist prior to the Agencies' antitrust review of the merger. In other situations—particularly when projected efficiencies are not a principal motive for the merger and evidence to substantiate claims has not been prepared prior to the merger agreement—the parties can elect to develop and submit to the reviewing Agency evidence (e.g., documents, data, consultant reports, or evidence from past experiences) to substantiate the claimed efficiencies.

***Arch Coal-Triton* (FTC 2004)** Pursuant to a Commission action in federal district court to enjoin the proposed merger of Arch Coal, Inc. and Triton Coal Co. LLC, the parties claimed merger-specific efficiencies totaling $130 million to $140 million over a five-year period. The parties' efficiency claims included cost-savings from equipment and operator reductions, the ability to extract additional coal through redeployment of coal mining equipment, insurance premium reductions, and safety improvements. Commission staff found that Arch Coal failed to substantiate many of its claimed savings and, in some instances, employed a methodology that overstated savings. Therefore, the staff determined that a substantial portion of Arch's claimed savings were not cognizable. For example, staff found that claims related to the ability to extract additional coal through redeployment of coal mining equipment were overstated because staff believed Triton would recover the additional coal absent the merger, just not as quickly as Arch would be able to in the combined operation. The court denied the Commission's preliminary injunction request and, after further investigation, the Commission decided not to pursue further administrative litigation.

***Oracle-PeopleSoft* (DOJ 2004)** Oracle Corp. made an unsolicited tender offer for PeopleSoft, Inc. Oracle and PeopleSoft competed in the sale of Enterprise Resource Planning software, which provides tools for automating essential operating functions within large organizations. Oracle Corp. claimed that the proposed takeover would produce cost reductions of more than $1 billion per year. Although these claims were based on projections made by a high ranking executive, the Department's attempts to verify these claims revealed that they were predicated on little more than unsupported speculation with no allowance having been made for the costs of integrating the two companies. Moreover, the Department concluded that at least a significant portion of the projected cost savings were a consequence of projected reductions in sales that would be the result of eliminating the R&D and sales staffs of PeopleSoft. The Department found that, for the most part, the cost reductions would stem from anticompetitive reductions in innovation, service, and output, and therefore did not reflect cognizable efficiencies. The Department filed suit to block the transaction, but the district court declined, on other grounds, to enjoin it.

Verification of Efficiency Claims

After the parties have presented substantiation for their claimed merger-specific efficiencies, the Agencies attempt to verify those claims. The verification process usually includes, among other things, an assessment of the parties' analytical methods, including the accuracy of their data collection and measurement, an evaluation of the reasonableness of assumptions in the analysis, and scrutiny into how well the parties' conclusions stand up to modifications in any assumptions (i.e., the "robustness" of the parties' analysis). To evaluate the parties' efficiency claims, the Agencies typically review the parties' internal documents and data, as well as the statements of knowledgeable company personnel. In some cases, to evaluate further how realistic the claimed efficiencies are, the Agencies also contact third parties, for example, to learn what efficiencies others have been able to achieve and how they have achieved those efficiencies.

The Agencies recognize that assessing a proposed merger's potential efficiency benefits, like its competitive effects, necessarily involves projections about the future. The Agencies do not automatically reject a claim due to minor discrepancies uncovered in the verification process. Nor do the Agencies reject an efficiency claim solely because the efficiency has never before been accomplished. Shortcomings in the substantiation of a particular efficiency claim may cause the Agencies to reduce the magnitude of the efficiencies associated with that claim rather than to reject the claim altogether. Similarly, the fact that one stand-alone efficiency claim cannot be verified does not necessarily result in rejection of other claims.

The stronger the supporting evidence, the more credence the Agencies are likely to give the claimed efficiencies in the competitive effects analysis. Efficiency claims that are vague, speculative, or unquantifiable and, therefore, cannot be verified by reasonable means, are not credited. For example, a general claim that the acquiring firm will save 20% of the acquired firm's expenses, without substantiation, generally would not be credited.

> ***Fine Look-Snazzy* (Disguised FTC Matter)** In a proposed merger of two consumer products packagers, Fine Look and Snazzy, the parties claimed efficiencies from rationalization and consolidation of packaging facilities ("PFs"); elimination of duplicate corporate overhead; and combining specialty packaging operations. Commission staff determined that a portion, but not all, of the savings claimed through consolidation of PFs was merger-specific and cognizable, but rejected the other claims because they could not be reasonably verified and thus were not cognizable. The Commission did not challenge the merger because evidence was insufficient to show that the merger was likely to cause competitive harm. The Commission credited the portion of the parties' efficiency claims that staff found to be merger-specific and cognizable.
>
> First, the staff considered the consolidation of PFs. Fine Look operated 30 PFs and Snazzy operated 20. The parties planned to operate 35 PFs after the merger by closing 15 owned by Fine Look and 10 owned by Snazzy, and by building 10 new PFs. The parties claimed that sales from the closed Fine Look PFs would be shifted to Snazzy PFs and that this shift would result in reduced operating and delivery costs at the Snazzy PFs. Similarly, savings would derive from reduced operating costs at Fine Look PFs because of transferred sales from closed Snazzy PFs. The parties also claimed reduced inventory costs tied to reducing the number of PFs.
>
> In estimating the potential savings from closing PFs, the parties assumed that all PF costs would be eliminated except for certain variable costs that would be shifted to the remaining PFs. In the case of the 15 Fine Look PFs projected to be closed, the parties provided reasonable substantiation of these cost savings derived from Fine Look cost records. Nonetheless, the parties' estimates assumed that, in each case of a closing, the remaining post-merger PFs would retain 100% of the customers of the closed PFs. The parties provided no analysis respecting how sensitive their estimates were to this key assumption.
>
> In addition, at least some of the consolidations for which the parties claimed efficiencies were purely intra-Snazzy (i.e., closing one Snazzy PF in proximity to another Snazzy PF). Staff concluded that such consolidations would not be merger-specific. Furthermore, the claimed

savings from closings of the Snazzy PFs were not substantiated from cost records, but instead were conjecture. Staff could not accept these claims.

Based on all of the claims respecting PF consolidation, staff concluded that only savings associated with the 15 Fine Look closings for which substantiation was provided were cognizable. But because no sensitivity analysis was performed regarding the assumption on the retention of customers, staff considered the estimated savings from the closing of the Fine Look PFs to be only an upper bound on the potential savings.

Second, the staff considered the corporate savings. The parties made a very rough calculation of projected savings through consolidation of various corporate functions. They contended that 75% of one party's corporate expenses would be eliminated by this consolidation. The calculation, however, was unsubstantiated conjecture rather than an analysis based on objective data that Agency staff could evaluate. Staff thus found the claim not to be cognizable.

Third, the staff considered the specialty packaging operations. Both Fine Look and Snazzy operated specialty packaging facilities for high-end luxury widgets, independent of their other PFs. The parties planned to consolidate Fine Look's specialty business into Snazzy's specialty business. They claimed that this consolidation would reduce costs because it would yield savings of 50% in operating expenses. In deposition, a senior executive admitted that the 50% figure was merely an unsupported assumption. Staff concluded that the parties' failure to provide sufficient evidence in support of the claim made the efficiency claim unverifiable and therefore not cognizable.

The Agencies may accord less significance to shortcomings in the documentation of claimed efficiencies when the weight of evidence suggests that merger-specific efficiencies appear to be significant and likely to be achieved.

***Genzyme-Novazyme* (FTC 2004)** Genzyme Corp. acquired Novazyme Pharmaceuticals, Inc., combining the world's only firms engaged in developing the first enzyme replacement therapy ("ERT") to treat Pompe disease, a rare, fatal disease that affects about 10,000 people worldwide. Whether either firm's Pompe drug would make it to market was not certain, but the acquisition left Genzyme as the only firm engaged in developing Pompe ERT treatments. Genzyme asserted that, even without competition from Novazyme, it had the incentive to bring its Pompe product to market in the fastest possible time frame.

Genzyme also asserted that the acquisition had resulted in significant efficiencies. Genzyme claimed that each firm had unique skills and expertise, and that, by combining, the merged firm could accelerate development of Genzyme's and Novazyme's Pompe drugs. Genzyme asserted that it possessed certain unique capabilities and technologies that it was applying to Novazyme's Pompe drug. The Commission voted to close the investigation without challenging the transaction due, in part, to the evidence supporting the claim that the merger would accelerate development of the drug.

The best way to substantiate an efficiency claim is to demonstrate that similar efficiencies were achieved in the recent past from similar actions. Documentation must be based on appropriate methods and realistic assumptions, and ideally would be grounded on actual experience. For example, a firm that recently combined its own distribution centers, or consolidated distribution centers after a recent merger, could use its actual cost savings experiences in those instances as a basis for, and to substantiate claims made about, efficiency claims arising from combining distribution centers after a proposed merger.

If the parties cannot point to similar efficiencies achieved in the recent past, they should use the best information available to substantiate their efficiency claims. For example, the parties might do an internal study and analysis of expected efficiencies using recent cost records and other pertinent objective data. In addition, some parties have found outside consultants helpful in substantiating efficiency claims.

The Agencies may verify and accept part of an efficiency claim. For example, an acquiring firm might estimate a particular efficiency by assuming that all of the acquired firm's customers and sales will transfer to the merged entity when experience suggests that customers and sales are not likely to transfer completely. Or, a party may estimate the dollar value of a particular efficiency using a discount rate that is significantly different from the discount rate it normally uses, without any justification for the difference. In such cases, the differences between the parties' efficiencies estimates and ones using the more supported assumptions are not verifiable, and those portions of the efficiency claims are unlikely to be credited.

> ***A-1 Goods-Bingo* (Disguised FTC Matter)** In a proposed merger of consumer products companies, A-1 Goods, Inc. and Bingo Co., the parties claimed cost savings of several million dollars from a reduction in the sales force and a combining of certain manufacturing facilities. Commission staff concluded that the parties' estimates were exaggerated. Staff credited some, but not the entire dollar amount of the claims.
>
> First, the staff considered the sales force reduction. The parties claimed that the merger would permit the post-merger firm to eliminate the equivalent of 90% of one of the party's pre-merger sales force, representing approximately 40% of the combined pre-merger sales employees. For calculating the estimated efficiencies, the parties assumed that the combined post-merger output would be the same as that before the merger. They also assumed that pre-merger levels of marketing and selling support to customers would be maintained. Achieving these efficiencies would require one-time costs approximating almost 80% of the projected annual cost savings.
>
> These one-time costs derived from severance payments and relocation expenses. Evidence from the parties suggested that the claims were based on aggressive assumptions. For this reason, Commission staff discounted the parties' estimates. Applying more reasonable assumptions, the staff credited most of the parties' claimed cost savings, from which the one-time cost of achieving the efficiencies was subtracted.
>
> Second, the staff considered the consolidation of manufacturing facilities. The parties claimed several million dollars in projected savings from the expected consolidation of certain manufacturing facilities. The parties planned to shut down an A-1 production facility and consolidate its output into a Bingo plant. The post-merger output rate was to be the same as on a combined, pre-merger basis, but with

fewer people needed to run the consolidated manufacturing operations. To maintain the same rate of pre-merger output, the parties envisioned that 70% of A-1's manufacturing equipment in the shut-down facility would be moved to unused space at the Bingo facility, adding to the overall manufacturing capacity of that facility. In addition, a number of A-1 employees would be relocated to the Bingo plant, while other employees would be let go. Certain retooling and capital expenditures related to integrating manufacturing operations would have to be incurred.

The parties claimed that no arrangement other than the proposed merger would generate the efficiencies claimed. They contended that any non-merger arrangement would raise insurmountable issues of control, allocation of savings between owners, transfer pricing problems, and issues dealing with the sharing of proprietary knowledge. To buttress this point, the parties presented Commission staff with evidence that the parties considered entering into contract manufacturing arrangements, joint ventures, and other internal measures to save money on production, but concluded that these were impractical or could not bring about the desired level of efficiencies. Based in part on this evidence, Commission staff concluded that the claimed efficiencies were merger-specific and cognizable.

The Commission ultimately decided not to challenge the merger on the grounds that it posed no substantial threat to competition, irrespective of any efficiency claims.

When parties to a merger base an efficiency claim on past experience, the Agencies examine whether the experience is indicative of what is likely to occur with the merger. If the experience was far out of the ordinary (e.g., during bankruptcy, a worker's strike, drought, or war), the Agencies may not credit the claims.

Sufficiency of Efficiencies

As noted in section 4 of the Guidelines, the Agencies seek to determine "whether cognizable efficiencies likely would be sufficient to reverse the merger's potential to harm consumers in the relevant market, e.g., by preventing price increases in that market." Within the integrated analysis framework for evaluating competitive effects, "efficiencies are most likely to make a difference in merger analysis when the likely adverse competitive effects, absent the efficiencies, are not great." Efficiencies are a significant factor in the Agencies' decisions not to challenge some mergers that otherwise are likely to have, at most, only slight anticompetitive effects.

***Toppan-DuPont* (DOJ 2005)** Photomasks are the masters from which integrated circuits are produced. Toppan Printing Co., Ltd. was a Japanese company that had recently begun competing in the United States. Toppan was proposing to acquire DuPont Photomasks, Inc., which was one of its three competitors for U.S. sales of the highest technology photomasks. The Department found that competition was best modeled as an auction process, with each auction essentially a separate relevant market. The Department's economists used a formal auction model to estimate the likely price effects of the transaction. This exercise indicated that, even without any efficiencies, the acquisition most likely would lead to, at most, only small price increases. Incorporating the portion of the claimed efficiencies the Department determined to be merger-specific and cognizable indicated that the transaction would not lessen the welfare of U.S. customers under the assumptions considered most plausible. Accordingly, the Department did not challenge the merger.

***PayPal-eBay* (DOJ 2002)** PayPal, Inc. and eBay, Inc. provided competing person-to-person payment systems used largely to complete transactions following eBay auctions. Even though the person-to-person payment systems offered advantages over the other means of payment, the Department decided not to challenge eBay's acquisition of Pay Pal principally because other means of payment substantially constrained eBay's ability to increase fees after the acquisition. Efficiencies to be gained by integrating PayPal with eBay were also a factor in the Department's analysis. Integrating the two would make transactions more convenient for eBay buyers and also improve the detection of fraud by combining the information that had been separately amassed by the two companies.

***DirecTV-Dish Network* (DOJ 2002)** DirecTV Enterprises Inc. was owned by Hughes Electronics Corp., which was owned by General Motors Corp. DirecTV operated one of two direct broadcast satellite ("DBS") services in the United States. EchoStar Communications Corp., which operated the other DBS service, Dish Network, proposed to acquire Hughes. Economists working for the parties and economists in the Department both engaged in extensive modeling of the competition between the two DBS services and with cable television operators with which the DBS services competed in providing "multichannel video programming distribution."

The Department concluded that this modeling supported the conclusion that the acquisition would substantially harm consumers and filed suit to prevent its consummation. Shortly thereafter, the acquisition was abandoned. The Department's modeling indicated that efficiencies claimed by the parties would be insufficient to prevent the merger from creating significant anticompetitive effects.

One source of claimed efficiencies was the reduction of programming costs. Incorporating the Department's best estimate of those reductions into the modeling only slightly reduced the likely price increase from the proposed acquisition. A second source of claimed efficiencies was a quality improvement; by combining the two services, it would be possible to offer local programming in many additional metropolitan areas with the available satellite bandwidth. The Department's analysis indicated that the consumer benefits from this quality improvement were far from sufficient to prevent the merger from harming consumers and also would be realized without the merger.

***Enerco-KleenBurn* (Disguised FTC Matter)** Enerco and KleenBurn Refinery, Inc. were gasoline refining and distribution firms that proposed to merge. The transaction involved the markets for bulk supply of conventional gasoline in the "Plains Corridor" and for bulk supply of reformulated gasoline ("RFG") in Metropolis. The parties claimed that the transaction would create substantial efficiencies in refinery and pipeline operations.

Enerco asserted that the KleenBurn refinery could, with relative ease, be integrated into Enerco's nearby refinery, which, in turn, would enable Enerco to generate substantial operational efficiencies by enhancing its ability to (1) coordinate the acquisition of crude oil and lower raw material costs; (2) align more efficiently the production processes of various light petroleum products, including conventional gasoline and RFG; (3) increase available storage to permit Enerco to manufacture and sell more gasoline grades; and (4) better plan and consolidate shipments. Commission staff concluded that at least some portion of the parties' efficiency claims were likely to be cognizable.

Enerco documents showed that it based a large portion of its bid on the value of expected synergies. When the expected synergies were counted, the refinery's value was estimated to increase four-fold over the KleenBurn refinery's stand-alone value. This estimated increase was about the same amount that Enerco offered to pay. Enerco's willingness to pay upfront for these synergies lent credence to its claims.

Enerco contended that the savings from these efficiencies would enable it to continue operating the KleenBurn refinery beyond the date that the refinery otherwise would have been expected to be decommissioned. Enerco further claimed that its previous efforts to meet new low-sulphur gasoline standards would enable KleenBurn to comply with those standards sooner and at lower cost. Thus, Enerco could, with less investment, maintain or exceed Kleenburn's historical production levels. Enerco financial analyses confirmed that it planned to run the KleenBurn refinery at or above current output rates.

Enerco asserted that it would connect the KleenBurn refinery to Enerco's Metropolis-area refineries, and reallocate Kleenburn barrels for sale in neighboring states, while reserving Metropolis-area barrels for shipment west. The Plains Feeder Line Pipeline tariff was substantially higher from the KleenBurn facility than from Enerco's refineries, and Enerco claimed that it would save over $1 million in variable delivery costs.

Enerco planned to ship several million barrels per day of combined refinery output into the Plains Corridor on Plains Feeder Line under this lower tariff. Because most bulk conventional gasoline shipped into the Plains Corridor was purchased FOB refinery gate in Metropolis, the tariff savings would, in most instances, inure directly to customers in the Plains Corridor. These customers had the existing shipping rights on Plains Corridor gasoline during the summer months when the pipeline is frequently prorated.

The Commission ultimately decided not to challenge the merger on the grounds that it posed no substantial threat to competition, irrespective of any efficiency claims.

"Out-of-Market" Efficiencies

In some cases, merger efficiencies are "not strictly in the relevant market, but so inextricably linked with it that a partial divestiture or other remedy could not feasibly eliminate the anticompetitive effect in the relevant market without sacrificing the efficiencies in the other market(s)." Guidelines § 4 at n.36. If out-of-market efficiencies are not inextricably linked to the relevant market, the Agencies often find an acceptable narrowly tailored remedy that preserves the efficiencies while preventing anticompetitive effects.

***Genzyme-Ilex* (FTC 2004)** Genzyme Corp. proposed to acquire Ilex Oncology, Inc. Ilex had one FDA-approved product, Campath, an oncology product used off-label in the solid organ transplant field. Genzyme did not compete with Campath in oncology but had a drug that was Campath's closest competitor in the market for solid organ transplant acute therapy drugs. The acquisition would have eliminated direct competition between Genzyme's market-leading drug, Thymoglobulin, and Campath.

The companies asserted that the transaction would yield significant efficiencies for oncology treatment and development. The primary efficiency encompassed several diagnostic tests that could aid the expansion of Campath for treatments in leukemia and other oncology and immune-related diseases by identifying patients who are most likely to benefit from Campath treatment.

After investigation and analysis of this efficiency, Commission staff concurred that Genzyme likely would improve Campath's quality and breadth of treatment in oncology. The companies did not demonstrate, however, that credible efficiencies would result in the solid transplant organ area. In light of the efficiencies in oncology and immune-related disease areas, the Commission tailored a remedy to alleviate the competitive concern in the market for solid organ transplant drugs while allowing the merged company to realize the potential efficiencies in oncology and other areas. In a consent order, the Commission required Genzyme, among other things, to divest contractual rights to Campath for use in solid organ transplant.

Inextricably linked out-of-market efficiencies, however, can cause the Agencies, in their discretion, not to challenge mergers that would be challenged absent the efficiencies. This circumstance may arise, for example, if a merger presents large procompetitive benefits in a large market and a small anticompetitive problem in another, smaller market.

***Gai's-United States Bakery* (DOJ 1996)** United States Bakery and Gai's Seattle French Bakery Co. proposed a joint venture, which the Department viewed as a merger. The two companies sold bread products in competition with one another in the Pacific Northwest, and the Department was concerned about the competitive effects of the transaction on restaurants and institutional accounts, particularly fast food restaurants, because the two companies accounted for more than 90% of the bread sales to such customers. Supplying such customers required a higher level of service (e.g., much more frequent deliveries) than supplying retail stores, and few bakeries provided that level of service. Without entirely resolving issues relating to competitive effects and entry, the Department decided not to challenge the transaction, concluding that the efficiencies likely would cause the merger to benefit the merged firm's customers as a whole.

Critical to the Department's assessment was the fact that the merger-specific efficiencies would benefit all customers, and the restaurant and institutional customers potentially of concern accounted for only about 20% of the companies' sales. The two groups of customers were buying essentially the same products, produced with the same facilities. Because it was otherwise impossible to preserve the efficiency benefits to all customers, the Department did not challenge the merger.

Fixed-Cost Savings

Merger-specific, cognizable efficiencies are most likely to make a difference in the Agencies' enforcement decisions when the efficiencies can be expected to result in direct, short-term, procompetitive price effects. Economic analysis teaches that price reductions are expected when efficiencies reduce the merged firm's marginal costs, i.e., costs associated with producing one additional unit of each of its products. By contrast, reductions in fixed costs—costs that do not change in the short-run with changes in output rates—typically are not expected to lead to immediate price effects and hence to benefit consumers in the short term. Instead, the immediate benefits of lower fixed costs (e.g., most reductions in overhead, management, or administrative costs) usually accrue to firm profits.

Exceptions to this general rule, however, exist. For example, under certain market or sales circumstances, fixed-cost savings may result in lower prices in the short term. Selling prices that are determined on a "cost-plus basis" (e.g., cost-based contracts) can be influenced by changes in fixed costs. Contractual arrangements also may allow fixed-cost savings to be passed through.

The Agencies consider merger-specific, cognizable reductions in fixed costs, even if they cannot be expected to result in direct, short-term, procompetitive price effects because consumers may benefit from them over the longer term even if not immediately. As with any other type of efficiency, reductions in fixed costs must be substantiated by the parties and verified by reasonable means.

Verizon-MCI; SBC-AT&T **(DOJ 2005)** In 2005 Verizon Communications, Inc. and SBC Communications, Inc., the nation's two largest regional Bell operating companies, sought to acquire MCI Inc. and AT&T Corp., the nation's two largest inter-exchange (long distance) and competitive local exchange (local service) carriers. To a significant extent, the pairs of firms proposing to merge were engaged in complementary activities. Verizon and SBC dominated local exchange and access service in their respective territories but had limited long-haul networks and only moderate success with large enterprise customers. MCI and AT&T had extensive long-haul networks and were the leading providers of telecommunications services to large businesses. The Department concluded that the proposed mergers would substantially lessen competition only in the facilities-based local private line services to many buildings for which the merging pairs of firms owned the only lines.

The Department investigated the effects of the transactions on competition in residential local and long distance telephone service, internet backbone services, and a variety of other telecommunications services. A significant factor in the Department's decision not to challenge the proposed mergers was that the transactions were likely to produce substantial efficiencies. The merging inter-exchange carriers, AT&T and MCI, sell advanced retail products to enterprise customers and generally have relied on local exchange carriers, such as their merger partners, for customer access. The merging local exchange carriers, SBC and Verizon, similarly have relied on inter-exchange carriers in selling advanced retail products to multi-region and out-of-region enterprises. The merger allowed each of the firms to provide these products at a lower cost to the customers by making inputs and complementary products available at a lower cost.

IMC Global-Western Ag **(DOJ 1997)** IMC Global Inc. proposed to acquire Western Ag-Minerals Co. The two companies operated the only potash mines and processing facilities in the Carlsbad region of New Mexico, which contains the only known reserves of langbeinite in the Western Hemisphere. Langbeinite is a mineral used to produce an agricultural fertilizer supplying magnesium, potassium, and sulfur, which are important in the production of certain crops and in correcting deficiencies in certain soils. Critically, langbeinite supplies these important elements without also containing significant amounts of chlorine.

It is possible to produce a fertilizer with the same qualities from other minerals, but the Department's preliminary analysis indicated that a single owner of both langbeinite mines would find it optimal to raise prices significantly in the absence of any efficiencies from combining the mines. The Department, nevertheless, decided not to challenge the merger because of substantial merger-specific efficiencies. The parties provided the Department with studies indicating that combining the two mining and processing operations would result in substantial efficiencies that could be achieved in no other way.

To verify these claims, the Department hired a consulting mining engineer to conduct an independent study of both the benefits of combining the two operations and alternative means of achieving particular efficiencies. The independent study concluded that the parties' efficiency claims were conservative. Among other things, the study concluded that IMC would avoid substantial costs by transporting the Western-Ag ore through its mine to its processing plant at the mine mouth. Western-Ag had been shipping the ore to its off-site processing plant. The study found additional efficiencies in combining the mining and processing of the other important mineral, sylvite, found on the adjoining IMC and Western-Ag properties.

The evidence ultimately indicated that the annual dollar savings from the merger would be as much as ten times the likely annual increase in customer costs from the merger, absent any efficiencies. Because the magnitude of the merger-specific cost savings dwarfed any potential effects exclusive of factoring in these savings, the Department did not separately evaluate the extent to which the efficiencies were likely to affect fixed costs versus variable costs.

Supporting Documentation

As with the Guidelines, the Commentary addresses how the Agencies assess the likely competitive effects of horizontal mergers but not the assignment of burdens of proof or burdens of coming forward with evidence. In litigation, the parties have the burden on any efficiencies claim (Guidelines § 0.1 n.5), and it is to their advantage to present efficiency claims (including supporting documents and data) to the reviewing Agency as early as possible. The Agencies, for their part, make a serious effort to assess each efficiency claim made. Early receipt of documentation relating to the nature and size of efficiencies allows the Agencies to factor fully the cognizable efficiencies into an integrated analysis of the likely overall competitive effects of the merger. In particular, the parties may want to highlight significant documents that support their claims and to make their experts (for example, accountants, engineers, or economists) available as early as feasible to discuss specifics regarding efficiencies. Doing so helps underscore the seriousness of efficiency claims and assists the Agencies in according the appropriate weight to efficiency considerations in assessing the mergers before them.

The Agencies recognize that, in many cases, substantiation of efficiency claims requires the collection, compilation, and analysis of competitively significant data and information from both of the merging parties. The sharing between rivals of proprietary information having potential competitive significance necessarily raises concerns about violations of section 1 of the Sherman Act, 15 U.S.C. § 1, and section 5 of the Federal Trade Commission Act, 15 U.S.C. § 45. Furthermore, the Hart-Scott-Rodino Act, 15 U.S.C. § 18a, prohibits changes in beneficial ownership prior to the end of the HSR waiting period.

Although prudent firms are cognizant of so-called "gun jumping" concerns, they can adopt appropriate safeguards to enable them to collect the information necessary to substantiate their efficiency claims. Information exchanges reasonably related to due diligence and integration planning that are accompanied by safeguards that prevent any other pre-merger use of that information are unlikely to be unlawful. The Agencies are mindful of the parties' need to provide sensitive efficiencies-related information and, in that vein, the Agencies note that the antitrust laws are flexible enough to allow the parties to adopt reasonable means to achieve that end lawfully.

16

1984 NON-HORIZONTAL MERGER GUIDELINES

ANTITRUST DIVISION, U.S. DEPARTMENT OF JUSTICE

49 FED. REG. 26823-03 (SECTION 4 HORIZONTAL EFFECTS FROM NON-HORIZONTAL MERGERS)*

* * *

4. HORIZONTAL EFFECT FROM NON-HORIZONTAL MERGERS

4.0 By definition, non-horizontal mergers involve firms that do not operate in the same market. It necessarily follows that such mergers produce no immediate change in the level of concentration in any relevant market as defined in Section 2 of these Guidelines. Although non-horizontal mergers are less likely than horizontal mergers to create competitive problems, they are not invariably innocuous. This section describes the principal theories under which the Department is likely to challenge non-horizontal mergers.

4.1 Elimination of Specific Potential Entrants

4.11 The Theory of Potential Competition

In some circumstances, the non-horizontal merger[25] of a firm already in a market (the "acquired firm") with a potential entrant to that market (the "acquiring firm")[26] may adversely affect competition in the market. If the merger effectively removes the acquiring firm from the edge of the market, it could have either of the following effects.

4.111 Harm to "Perceived Potential Competition"

By eliminating a significant present competitive threat that constrains the behavior of the firms already in the market, the merger could result in an immediate deterioration in market performance. The economic theory of limit pricing suggests that monopolists and groups of colluding firms may find it profitable to restrain their pricing in order to deter new entry that is likely to push prices even lower by adding capacity to the market. If the acquiring firm had unique advantages in entering the market, the firms in the market might be able to set a new and higher price after the threat of entry by the acquiring firm was eliminated by the merger.

* [Authors' footnote]. The 1992 Merger Guidelines revised §§ 1–3 and 5 of the 1984 Merger Guidelines and incorporate by reference § 4 of the 1984 Merger Guidelines, reprinted here.

25 Under traditional usage, such a merger could be characterized as either "vertical" or "conglomerate," but the label adds nothing to the analysis.

26 The terms "acquired and "acquiring" refer to the relationship of the firms to the market of interest, not to the way the particular transaction is formally structured.

4.112 Harm to "Actual Potential Competition"

By eliminating the possibility of entry by the acquiring firm in a more procompetitive manner, the merger could result in a lost opportunity for improvement in market performance resulting form the addition of a significant competitor. The more procompetitive alternatives include both new entry and entry through a "toehold" acquisition of a present small competitor.

4.12 Relation Between Perceived and Actual Potential Competition

If it were always profit-maximizing for incumbent firms to set price in such a way that all entry was deterred and if information and coordination were sufficient to implement this strategy, harm to perceived potential competition would be the only competitive problem to address. In practice, however, actual potential competition has independent importance. Firms already in the market may not find it optimal to set price low enough to deter all entry; moreover, those firms may misjudge the entry advantages of a particular firm and, therefore, the price necessary to deter its entry.[27]

4.13 Enforcement Standards

Because of the close relationship between perceived potential competition and actual potential competition, the Department will evaluate mergers that raise either type of potential competition concern under a single structural analysis analogous to that applied to horizontal mergers. The Department first will consider a set of objective factors designed to identify cases in which harmful effects are plausible. In such cases, the Department then will conduct a more focused inquiry to determine whether the likelihood and magnitude of the possible harm justify a challenge to the merger. In this context, the Department will consider any specific evidence presented by the merging parties to show that the inferences of competitive harm drawn from the objective factors are unreliable.

The factors that the Department will consider are as follows.

4.131 Market Concentration

Barriers to entry are unlikely to affect market performance if the structure of the market is otherwise not conducive to monopolization of collusion. Adverse competitive effects are likely only if overall concentration, or the largest firm's market share, is high. The Department is unlikely to challenge a potential competition merger unless overall concentration of the acquired firm's market is above 1800 HHI (a somewhat lower concentration will suffice if one or more of the factors discussed in Section 3.4 indicate that effective collusion in the market is particularly likely). Other things being equal, the Department is increasingly likely to challenge a merger as this threshold is exceeded.

4.132 Conditions of Entry Generally

If entry to the market is generally easy, the fact that entry is marginally easier for one or more firms is unlikely to affect the behavior of the firms in the market. The Department is unlikely to challenge a potential competition merger when new entry into the acquiring firm's market can be accomplished by firms without any specific entry advantages under the conditions stated in Section 3.3. Other things being equal, the Department

---

[27] When collusion is only tacit, the problem of arriving at and enforcing the correct limit price is likely to be particularly difficult.

is increasingly likely to challenge a merger as the difficulty of entry increase above that threshold.

4.133 The Acquiring Firm's Entry Advantage

If more than a few firms have the same or a comparable advantage in entering the acquired firm's market, the elimination of one firm is unlikely to have any adverse competitive effect. The other similarly situated firm or firms would continue to exert a present restraining influence, or, if entry would be profitable, would recognize the opportunity and enter. The Department is unlikely to challenge a potential competition merger if the entry advantage ascribed to the acquiring firm (or another advantage of comparable importance) is also possessed by three or more other firms. Other things being equal, the Department is increasingly likely to challenge a merger as the number of other similarly situated firms decreases below three and as the extent of the entry advantage over non-advantaged firms increases.

If the evidence of likely actual entry by the acquiring firm is particularly strong,[28] however, the Department may challenge a potential competition merger, notwithstanding the presence of three of more firms that are objectively similarly situated. In such cases, the Department will determine the likely scale of entry, using either the firm's own documents or the minimum efficient scale in the industry. The Department will then evaluate the merger much as it would a horizontal merger between a firm the size of the likely scale of entry and the acquired firm.

4.134 The Market Share of the Acquired Firm

Entry through the acquisition of a relatively small firm in the market may have a competitive effect comparable to new entry. Small firms frequently play peripheral roles in collusive interactions, and the particular advantages of the acquiring firm may convert a fringe firm into a significant factor in the market.[29] The Department is unlikely to challenge a potential competition merger when the acquired firm has a market share of five percent or less. Other things being equal, the Department is increasingly likely to challenge a merger as the market share of the acquired firm increases above the threshold. The Department is likely to challenge any merger satisfying the other conditions in which the acquired firm has a market share of 20 percent of more.

4.135 Efficiencies

As in the case of horizontal mergers, the Department will consider expected efficiencies in determining whether to challenge a potential competition merger. See Section 3.5 (Efficiencies).

4.2 Competitive Problems from Vertical Mergers

4.21 Barriers to Entry from Vertical Mergers

In certain circumstances, the vertical integration resulting from vertical mergers could create competitively objectionable barriers to entry. Stated generally, three conditions are necessary (but not sufficient) for this

[28] For example, the firm already may have moved beyond the stage of consideration and have made significant investments demonstrating an actual decision to enter.

[29] Although a similar effect is possible with the acquisition of larger firms, there is an increased danger that the acquiring firm will choose to acquiesce in monopolization or collusion because of the enhanced profits that would result from its own disappearance from the edge of the market.

problem to exist. First, the degree of vertical integration between the two markets must be so extensive that entrants to one market (the "primary market") also would have to enter the other market (the "secondary market")[30] simultaneously. Second, the requirement of entry at the secondary level must make entry at the primary level significantly more difficult and less likely to occur. Finally, the structure and other characteristics of the primary market must be otherwise so conducive to noncompetitive performance that the increased difficulty of entry is likely to affect its performance. The following standards state the criteria by which the Department will determine whether these conditions are satisfied.

4.211 Need for Two-Level Entry

If there is sufficient unintegrated capacity[31] in the secondary market, new entrants to the primary market would not have to enter both markets simultaneously. The Department is unlikely to challenge a merger on this ground where post-merger sales (or purchases) by unintegrated firms in the secondary market would be sufficient to service two minimum-efficient-scale plants in the primary market. When the other conditions are satisfied, the Department is increasingly likely to challenge a merger as the unintegrated capacity declines below this level.

4.212 Increased Difficulty of Simultaneous Entry of Both Markets

The relevant question is whether the need for simultaneous entry to the secondary market gives rise to a substantial incremental difficulty as compared to entry into the primary market alone. If entry at the secondary level is easy in absolute terms, the requirement of simultaneous entry to that market is unlikely adversely to affect entry to the primary market. Whatever the difficulties of entry into the primary market may be, the Department is unlikely to challenge a merger on this ground if new entry into the secondary market can be accomplished under the conditions stated in Section 3.3.[32] When entry is not possible under those conditions, the Department is increasingly concerned about vertical mergers as the difficulty of entering the secondary market increases. The Department, however, will invoke this theory only where the need for secondary market entry significantly increases the costs (which may take the form of risks) of primary market entry.

More capital is necessary to enter two markets than to enter one. Standing alone, however, this additional capital requirement does not constitute a

---

[30] This competitive problem could result from either upstream or downstream integration, and could affect competition in either the upstream market or the downstream market. In the text, the term "primary market" refers to the market in which the competitive concerns are being considered, and the term "secondary market" refers to the adjacent market.

[31] Ownership integration does not necessarily mandate two-level entry by new entrants to the primary market. Such entry is most likely to be necessary where the primary and secondary markets are completely integrated by ownership and each firm in the primary market uses all of the capacity of its associated firm in the secondary market. In many cases of ownership integration, however, the functional fit between vertically integrated firms is not perfect, and an outside market exists for the sales (purchases) of the firms in the secondary market. If that market is sufficiently large and diverse, new entrants to the primary market may be able to participate without simultaneous entry to the secondary market. In considering the adequacy of this alternative, the Department will consider the likelihood of predatory price or supply "squeezes" by the integrated firms against their unintegrated rivals.

[32] Entry into the secondary market may be greatly facilitated in that an assured supplier (customer) is provided by the primary market entry.

barrier to entry to the primary market. If the necessary finds were available at a cost commensurate with the level of risk in the secondary market, there would be no adverse effect. In some cases, however, lenders may doubt that would-be entrants to the primary market have the necessary skills and knowledge to succeed in the secondary market and, therefore, in the primary market. In order to compensate for this risk of failure, lenders might charge a higher rate for the necessary capital. This problem becomes increasingly significant as a higher percentage of the capital assets in the secondary market are long-lived and specialized to that market and, therefore, difficult to recover in the event of failure. In evaluating the likelihood of increased barriers to entry resulting from increased cost of capital, therefore, the Department will consider both the degree of similarity in the essential skills in the primary and secondary markets and the economic life and degree of specialization of the capital assets in the secondary market.

Economies of sale in the secondary market may constitute an additional barrier to entry to the primary market in some situations requiring two-level entry. The problem could arise if the capacities of minimum-efficient-scale plants in the primary and secondary markets differ significantly. For example, if the capacity of a minimum-efficient-scale plant in the secondary market were significantly greater than the needs of a minimum-efficient-scale plant in the primary market, entrants would have to choose between inefficient operation at the secondary level (because of operating an efficient plant at an inefficient output or because of operating an inefficiently small plant) or a larger than necessary scale at the primary level. Either of these effects could cause a significant increase in the operating costs of the entering firm.[33]

4.213 Structure and Performance of the Primary Market

Barriers to entry are unlikely to affect performance if the structure of the primary market is otherwise not conducive to monopolization or collusion.[34] The Department is unlikely to challenge a merger on this ground unless overall concentration of the primary market is above 1800 HHI (a somewhat lower concentration will suffice if one or more of the factors discussed in Section 3.4 indicate that effective collusion is particularly likely). Above that threshold, the Department is increasingly likely to challenge a merger that meets the other criteria set forth above as the concentration increases.

4.22 Facilitating Collusion Through Vertical Mergers

4.221 Vertical Integration to the Retail Level

A high level of vertical integration by upstream firms into the associated retail market may facilitate collusion in the upstream market by making it easier to monitor price. Retail prices are generally more visible than prices in upstream markets, and vertical mergers may increase the level of vertical integration to the point at which the monitoring effect becomes significant. Adverse competitive consequences are unlikely unless the upstream market is generally conducive to collusion and a large percentage of the products produced there are sold through vertically integrated retail outlets.

---

[33] It is important to note, however, that this problem would not exist if a significant outside market exists at the secondary level. In that case, entrants could enter with the appropriately scaled plants at both levels, and sell or buy in the market as necessary.

[34] For example, a market with 100 firms of equal size would perform competitively despite a significant increase in entry barriers.

The Department is unlikely to challenge a merger on this ground unless 1) overall concentration of the upstream market is above 1800 HHI (a somewhat lower concentration will suffice if one or more of the factors discussed in Section 3.4 indicate that effective collusion is particularly likely), and 2) a large percentage of the upstream product would be sold through vertically-integrated retail outlets after the merger. Where the stated thresholds are met or exceeded, the Department's decision whether to challenge a merger on this ground will depend upon an individual evaluation of its likely competitive effect.

4.222 Elimination of a Disruptive Buyer

The elimination by vertical merger of a particularly disruptive buyer in a downstream market may facilitate collusion in the upstream market. If upstream firms view sales to a particular buyer as sufficiently important, they may deviate from the terms of a collusive agreement in an effort to secure that business, thereby disrupting the operation of the agreement. The merger of such a buyer with an upstream firm may eliminate that rivalry, making it easier for the upstream firms to collude effectively. Adverse competitive consequences are unlikely unless the upstream market is generally conducive to collusion and the disruptive firm is significantly more attractive to sellers than the other firms in its market.

The Department is unlikely to challenge a merger on this ground unless 1) overall concentration of the upstream market is 1800 HHI or above (a somewhat lower concentration will suffice if one or more of the factors discussed in Section 3.4 indicate that effective collusion is particularly likely), and 2) the allegedly disruptive firm differs substantially in volume of purchases or other relevant characteristics from the other firms in its market. Where the stated thresholds are met or exceeded, the Department's decision whether to challenge a merger on this ground will depend upon an individual evaluation of its likely competitive effect.

4.23 Evasion of Rate Regulation

Non-horizontal mergers may be used by monopoly public utilities subject to rate regulation as a tool for circumventing that regulation. The clearest example is the acquisition by a regulated utility of a supplier of its fixed or variable inputs. After the merger, the utility would be selling to itself and might be able arbitrarily to inflate the prices of internal transactions. Regulators may have great difficulty in policing these practices, particularly if there is no independent market for the product (or service) purchased from the affiliate.[35] As a result, inflated prices could be passed along to consumers as "legitimate" costs. In extreme cases, the regulated firm may effectively preempt the adjacent market, perhaps for the purpose of suppressing observable market transactions, and may distort resource allocation in that adjacent market as well as in the regulated market. In such cases, however, the Department recognizes that genuine economies of integration may be involved. The Department will consider challenging mergers that create substantial opportunities for such abuses.[36]

---

[35] A less severe, but nevertheless serious, problem can arise when a regulated utility acquires a firm that is not vertically related. The use of common facilities and managers may create an insoluble cost allocation problem and provide the opportunity to charge utility customers for non-utility costs, consequently distorting resources allocation in the adjacent as well as the regulated market.

[36] Where a regulatory agency has the responsibility for approving such mergers, the Department may express its concerns to that agency in its role as competition advocate.

4.24 Efficiencies

As in the case of horizontal mergers, the Department will consider expected efficiencies in determining whether to challenge a vertical merger. See Section 3.5 (Efficiencies). An extensive pattern of vertical integration may constitute evidence that substantial economies are afforded by vertical integration. Therefore, the Department will give relatively more weight to expected efficiencies in determining whether to challenge a vertical merger than in determining whether to challenge a horizontal merger.

* * *

17

ANTITRUST POLICY GUIDE TO MERGER REMEDIES

U.S. DEPARTMENT OF JUSTICE ANTITRUST DIVISION

October 2004

TABLE OF CONTENTS

I. Overview

The Antitrust Division is authorized to challenge acquisitions and mergers ("mergers") under Section 15 of the Clayton Act, 15 U.S.C. § 25, and Section 4 of the Sherman Act, 15 U.S.C. § 4. If the Division has concluded that a merger may substantially lessen competition, it can "fix" the problem in several ways. The Division may seek a full-stop injunction that would prevent the parties from consummating the transaction. The Division may choose, instead, to negotiate a settlement (a consent decree) or accept a "fix-it-first" remedy that allows the merger to proceed with modifications that restore or preserve the competition.[1]

The purpose of this Guide is to provide Antitrust Division attorneys and economists with a framework for fashioning and implementing appropriate relief short of a full-stop injunction in merger cases. The Guide focuses on the remedies available to the Division and is designed to ensure that those remedies are based on sound legal and economic principles and are closely related to the identified competitive harm. The Guide also sets forth policy issues that may arise in connection with different types of relief and offers Division attorneys and economists guidance on how to resolve them.

This Guide is a policy document, not a practice handbook. It is not a compendium of decree provisions, and it does not list or give "best practices" or the particular language or provisions that should be included in any given decree. Rather, it sets forth the policy considerations that should guide Division attorneys and economists when fashioning remedies for anticompetitive mergers. The Guide is intended to provide Division attorneys and economists with the tools they need—the pertinent economic and legal principles, appropriate analytical framework, and relevant legal limitations—to craft and implement the proper remedy for the case at hand.

Remedial provisions in Division decrees must be appropriate, effective, and principled. While there is no need to reinvent the wheel with each decree, neither is it appropriate to include a remedy in a decree merely because a similar provision was included in one or more previous decrees, particularly where there has been no clear articulation of the purpose behind the inclusion of that provision. There must be a significant nexus between the proposed transaction, the nature of the competitive harm, and the proposed remedial provisions. Focusing carefully on the specific facts of the case at hand will not only result in the selection of the appropriate remedies but will also permit the adoption of remedies specifically tailored to the competitive harm.

The Guide has five sections. The section immediately following this Overview describes guiding principles governing merger remedies. The third section discusses the policies for fashioning merger remedies, while the fourth addresses implementation of those remedies. Each of these sections sets forth the Antitrust Division's general policies for a variety of remedial issues, including the legal and economic support for those policies and the caveats to those policies.

---

[1] A consent decree is a binding agreement between the Division and defendants that is filed publicly in federal district court and, upon entry, becomes a binding court order. With a fix-it-first remedy, in contrast, the parties modify or "fix" the transaction before consummation to eliminate any competitive concern. There is no complaint or other court filing. Although a fix-it-first remedy technically preserves, rather than restores, competition, this Guide uses the terms restore and preserve interchangeably. *See infra* Section IV.A.

Finally, the last section of the Guide addresses steps the Division will take to ensure that, once a remedy is established, it is effectively complied with and enforced.

II. Guiding Principles

The following principles guide the development of remedies in all Antitrust Division merger cases:

- **The Antitrust Division Will Not Accept a Remedy Unless There Is a Sound Basis for Believing a Violation Will Occur.** Before recommending a specific remedy, there should be a sound basis for believing that the merger would violate Section 7 of the Clayton Act and that the resulting harm is sufficient to justify remedial action. The Division should not seek decrees or remedies that are not necessary to prevent anticompetitive effects, because that could unjustifiably restrict companies and raise costs to consumers. Consequently, even though a party may be willing to settle early in an investigation, the Division must have sufficient information to be satisfied that there is a sound basis for believing that a violation will otherwise occur before negotiating any settlement.

- **Remedies Must Be Based upon a Careful Application of Sound Legal and Economic Principles to the Particular Facts of the Case at Hand.** Carefully tailoring the remedy to the theory of the violation is the best way to ensure that the relief obtained cures the competitive harm.[2] Before recommending a proposed remedy to an anticompetitive merger, the staff should satisfy itself that there is a close, logical nexus between the recommended remedy and the alleged violation—that the remedy fits the violation and flows from the theory of competitive harm. Effective remedies preserve the efficiencies created by a merger, to the extent possible, without compromising the benefits that result from maintaining competitive markets.

  This assessment will necessarily be fact-intensive. It will normally require determining (a) what competitive harm the violation has caused or likely will cause and (b) how the proposed relief will remedy that particular competitive harm. Only after these determinations are made can the Division decide whether the proposed remedy will effectively redress the violation and, just as importantly, be no more intrusive on market structure and

---

[2] Ford Motor Co. v. United States, 405 U.S. 562, 575 (1972) (In a Section 7 action, relief "necessarily must 'fit the exigencies of the particular case.' "); Zenith Radio Corp. v. Hazeltine Research, Inc., 395 U.S. 100, 133 (1969); United States v. United States Gypsum Co., 340 U.S. 76, 89 (1950) ("In resolving doubts as to the desirability of including provisions designed to restore future freedom of trade, courts should give weight to . . . the circumstances under which the illegal acts occur."); United States v. Bausch & Lomb Optical Co., 321 U.S. 707, 726 (1944) ("The test is whether or not the required action reasonably tends to dissipate the restraints and prevent evasions."); Massachusetts v. Microsoft Corp., 373 F.3d 1199, 1228 (D.C. Cir. 2004) ("[T]he court carefully considered the 'causal connection' between Microsoft's anticompetitive conduct and its dominance of the market. . . ."); United States v. Microsoft Corp., 253 F.3d 34, 105–07 (D.C. Cir. 2001) (Relief "should be tailored to fit the wrong creating the occasion for the remedy."); Yamaha Motor Co. v. FTC, 657 F.2d 971, 984 (8th Cir. 1981) (Relief barring certain vertical restrictions "goes beyond any reasonable relationship to the violations found."); United States v. Microsoft Corp., 231 F. Supp. 2d 144, 154, 202 (D.D.C. 2002), *aff'd sub nom*, 373 F.3d 1199 (D.C. Cir. 2004).

conduct than necessary to cure the competitive harm. Basing remedies on the application of sound economic and legal analysis to the particular facts of each case avoids merely copying past relief proposals or adopting relief proposals divorced from guiding principles.

- **Restoring Competition Is the Key to an Antitrust Remedy.** Once the Division has determined that the merger is anticompetitive, the Division will insist on a remedy that resolves the competitive problem. Accepting remedies without analyzing whether they are sufficient to redress the violation involved is a disservice to consumers.

  Although the remedy should always be sufficient to redress the antitrust violation, the purpose of a remedy is not to enhance premerger competition but to restore it. The Division will insist upon relief sufficient to restore competitive conditions the merger would remove. Restoring competition is the "key to the whole question of an antitrust remedy,"[3] and restoring competition is the only appropriate goal with respect to crafting merger remedies. The Supreme Court has stressed repeatedly that the purpose of an antitrust remedy is to protect or restore competition.[4] Restoring competition requires replacing the competitive intensity lost as a result of the merger rather than focusing narrowly on returning to premerger HHI levels. Thus, for example, assessing the competitive strength of a firm purchasing divested assets requires more analysis than simply attributing to this purchaser past sales associated with those assets.

- **The Remedy Should Promote Competition, Not Competitors.** Because the goal is reestablishing competition—rather than determining outcomes or picking winners and losers—decree provisions should promote competition generally rather than protect or favor particular competitors.[5]

- **The Remedy Must Be Enforceable.** A remedy is not effective if it cannot be enforced.[6] Remedial provisions that are too vague to be enforced or that could be construed when enforced in such a manner as to fall short of their intended purpose can render useless the enforcement effort that went into investigating the transaction and obtaining the decree, leaving the competitive harm unchecked. The same is true of a decree that fails to bind a person or entity necessary to implementing the remedy. A defendant will scrupulously obey a decree only when the decree's meaning is clear, and when the defendant and its agents know that they face the prospect of fines or imprisonment if they disregard the decree.

---

[3] United States v. E.I. du Pont de Nemours & Co., 366 U.S. 316, 326 (1961).

[4] *Ford Motor Co.*, 405 U.S. at 573; *du Pont, id.*

[5] *E.g.*, Brooke Group Ltd. v. Brown & Williamson Tobacco Corp., 509 U.S. 209, 223 (1993); Spectrum Sports, Inc. v. McQuillan, 506 U.S. 447, 458–59 (1993); Atlantic Richfield Co. v. USA Petroleum Co., 495 U.S. 328, 338 (1990); Cargill, Inc. v. Monfort, Inc., 479 U.S. 104, 116–17 (1986); Brunswick Corp. v. Pueblo Bowl-O-Mat, Inc., 429 U.S. 477, 488 (1977); Brown Shoe Co. v. United States, 370 U.S. 294, 320 (1962); Massachusetts v. Microsoft Corp., 373 F.3d at 1211, 1230; United States v. Microsoft Corp., 253 F.3d at 58.

[6] *See, e.g.*, New York v. Microsoft Corp., 224 F. Supp. 2d 76, 137 (D.D.C. 2002), *aff'd sub nom.* Massachusetts v. Microsoft Corp., 373 F.3d 1199 (D.C. Cir. 2004) ("Plaintiffs' definition is vague and ambiguous, rendering compliance with the terms of Plaintiffs' remedy which are reliant on this definition to be largely unenforceable.").

Courts are certain to impose such sanctions only when (a) the decree provisions are clear and understandable and (b) the defendant's agents knew, or should have known, about the decree provisions.[7]

Consequently, decree provisions must be as clear and straightforward as possible, always focusing on how a judge not privy to the settlement negotiations is likely to construe those provisions at a later time.[8] Likewise, care must be taken to avoid potential loopholes and attempted circumvention of the decree. Attention must also be given to identifying those persons who must be bound by the decree to make the proposed relief effective and to ensuring that the judgment contains whatever provisions are necessary to put them on notice of their responsibilities.

- **The Antitrust Division Will Commit the Time and Effort Necessary to Ensure Full Compliance with the Remedy.** It is contrary to our law enforcement responsibilities to obtain a remedy and then not monitor and, if necessary, enforce it. Our work is not over until the remedies mandated in our consent decrees have been fully implemented, which means that decrees that place continuing obligations on defendants must be monitored. This requires, in the first instance, that decrees be drafted with sufficient reporting and access requirements to keep us apprised of how the decree is being implemented, and then a continuing commitment of Division resources to decree compliance and enforcement. Responsibility for enforcing all of the Division's outstanding judgments lies with its civil sections, to which the judgments are assigned according to the current allocation of industries or commodities among those sections, with assistance from a criminal section in criminal contempt cases.

III. Fashioning the Remedy

Merger remedies take two basic forms: one addresses the structure of the market, the other the conduct of the merged firm. Structural remedies generally will involve the sale of physical assets by the merging firms. In some instances, market structure can also be changed by requiring, for example, that the merged firm create new competitors through the sale or licensing of intellectual property ("IP") rights.[9] A conduct remedy usually entails injunctive provisions that would, in effect, manage or regulate the merged firm's postmerger business conduct. As discussed below, in some cases the remedy may require both structural and conduct relief.

---

[7] *E.g.*, United States v. Microsoft Corp., 147 F.3d 935, 940 (D.C. Cir. 1998); United States v. NYNEX Corp., 8 F.3d 52, 54 (D.C. Cir. 1993) ("There are three essential elements of criminal contempt under 18 U.S.C. § 401(3): (1) there must be a violation, (2) of a clear and reasonably specific order of the court, and (3) the violation must have been willful. United States v. Turner, 812 F.2d 1552, 1563 (11th Cir. 1987). The Government carries the burden of proof on each of these elements, and the evidence must be sufficient to establish guilt beyond a reasonable doubt."); United States v. Smith International, Inc., 2000-1 Trade Cas. ¶ 72,763 (D.D.C. 2000).

[8] *See* New York v. Microsoft Corp., 224 F. Supp. 2d at 100 ("Moreover, the case law counsels that the remedial decree should be 'as specific as possible, not only in the core of its relief, but in its outward limits, so that parties may know [ ] their duties and unintended contempts may not occur.' "); International Salt Co. v. United States, 332 U.S. 392, 400 (1947).

[9] U.S. v. 3D Systems Corp., 2002-2 Trade Cas. ¶ 73,738. (D.D.C. 2001).

A. Structural Remedies Are Preferred

The speed, certainty, cost, and efficacy of a remedy are important measures of its potential effectiveness. Structural remedies are preferred to conduct remedies in merger cases because they are relatively clean and certain, and generally avoid costly government entanglement in the market. A carefully crafted divestiture decree is "simple, relatively easy to administer, and sure" to preserve competition.[10] A conduct remedy, on the other hand, typically is more difficult to craft, more cumbersome and costly to administer, and easier than a structural remedy to circumvent.

Conduct remedies suffer from at least four potentially substantial costs that a structural remedy can in principle avoid. First, there are the direct costs associated with monitoring the merged firm's activities and ensuring adherence to the decree. Second, there are the indirect costs associated with efforts by the merged firm to evade the remedy's "spirit" while not violating its letter. As one example, a requirement that the merged firm not raise price may lead it profitably, and inefficiently, to reduce its costs by cutting back on quality—thereby effecting an anticompetitive increase in the "quality adjusted" price.

Third, a conduct remedy may restrain potentially procompetitive behavior. For instance, a requirement that the merged firm not discriminate against its rivals in the provision of a necessary input can raise difficult questions of whether cost-based differences justify differential treatment and thus are not truly discriminatory. Firms often sell to a wide range of customers, some of which have very intense demands for the product and would be willing to pay a high price based on that demand and others of which are not willing to pay nearly so much. When this is the case, and when price discrimination is feasible, permitting the firm to charge low prices to customers that have a low demand for the product and higher prices to customers that have a high demand for the product can increase not only the firm's profits, but total output and consumer welfare as a whole. Requiring the firm to charge a single price to all may, in such circumstances, result in a price that excludes the low demand group entirely.

Fourth, even where "effective," efforts to regulate a firm's future conduct may prevent it from responding efficiently to changing market conditions. For all of these reasons, structural merger remedies are strongly preferred to conduct remedies.[11]

B. A Divestiture Must Include All Assets Necessary for the Purchaser to Be an Effective, Long-Term Competitor

The assets consolidated in a merger may be tangible (factories capable of producing automobiles or raw materials used in the production of some other final good) or intangible (patents, copyrights, trademarks, or rights to facilities such as airport gates or landing slots). The goal of a divestiture is

---

[10] United States v. E.I. du Pont de Nemours & Co., 366 U.S. 316, 331 (1961); *see generally* California v. American Stores Co., 495 U.S. 271, 280–81 (1990) ("[I]n Government actions divestiture is the preferred remedy for an illegal merger or acquisition.").

[11] *See* discussion *infra* Section III.E.

to ensure that the purchaser[12] possesses both the means and the incentive to maintain the level of premerger competition in the market(s) of concern.[13]

This requires a clear identification of the assets a competitor needs to compete effectively in a timely fashion and over the long-term. Any divestiture should address whatever obstacles (for example, lack of a distribution system or necessary know-how) lead to the conclusion that a competitor, absent the divestiture, would not be able to discipline a merger-generated increase in market power.[14] That is, the divestiture assets must be substantial enough to enable the purchaser to maintain the premerger level of competition, and should be sufficiently comprehensive that the purchaser will use them in the relevant market and be unlikely to liquidate or redeploy them.[15]

If, for example, a constraint is the time or the incentive necessary for a potential entrant or small incumbent to construct production facilities, then sufficient production facilities should be part of the divestiture package. If the assets being combined through the merger are valuable brand names or other intangible rights, then the divestiture package should include a brand or a license that enables its purchaser to compete quickly and effectively. In markets where an installed base of customers is required in order to operate at an effective scale, the divested assets should either convey an installed base of customers to the purchaser or quickly enable the purchaser to obtain an installed customer base.

In any event, there are certain intangible assets that likely should be conveyed whenever tangible assets are divested. Many of these simply provide valuable information to the purchaser—for example, documents and computer records providing the purchaser with customer information or production information, research results, computer software, and market evaluations. Others pertain to patents, copyrights, trademarks, other IP rights, licenses, or access to key intangible inputs (for example, access to a particular range of broadcast spectrum) that are necessary to allow for the most productive use of any tangible assets being divested, or of any tangible assets already in the hands of the purchaser.

The package of assets to be divested must not only allow a purchaser quickly to replace the competition lost due to the merger, but also provide it

---

[12] The use of "purchaser" in this Guide refers to the third-party purchaser of the divested tangible or intangible assets from the merging firms.

[13] *See* Ford Motor Co. v. United States, 405 U.S. 562, 573 (1972) ("The relief in an antitrust case must be 'effective to redress the violations' and 'to restore competition.'. . . Complete divestiture is particularly appropriate where asset or stock acquisitions violate the antitrust laws.") (citation omitted).

[14] *See, e.g.*, White Consol. Indust. Inc. v. Whirlpool Corp., 612 F. Supp. 1009 (N.D. Ohio), *vacated on other grounds*, 619 F. Supp. 1022 (N.D. Ohio 1985), *aff'd*, 781 F.2d 1224 (6th Cir. 1986) (court analyzes sufficiency of a proposed divestiture package to restore effective competition).

[15] *See* Chemetron Corp. v. Crane Co., 1977-2 Trade Cas. ¶ 61,717 at 72,930 (N.D. Ill. 1977). In a merger between firm A and firm B, the Division generally would be indifferent as to which firm's assets are divested, despite possible qualitative differences between the firms' assets, so long as the divestiture restores competition to the premerger level. However, if the divestiture of one firm's assets would not restore competition, then the other firm's assets must be divested. For example, if firm A's productive assets can only operate efficiently in combination with other assets of the firm, while firm B's productive assets are free standing, the Division likely would require the divestiture of firm B's assets.

with the incentive to do so.[16] Unless the divested assets are sufficient for the purchaser to become an effective and efficient competitor, the purchaser may have a greater incentive to deploy them outside the relevant market.

A final issue to consider is whether and when it may be appropriate to permit flexibility in the specification of the divestiture assets. Although the appropriate identification of the divestiture assets is sometimes obvious, either due to the nature of the business or the homogeneity of potential purchasers, this is not always the case. The circumstances of potential bidders may vary in ways that affect the scope of the assets each would need to compete quickly and effectively. For example, one potential purchaser might require certain distribution assets and another may not. In other cases, the Division may be indifferent between two alternative sets of divestiture assets—for example, a manufacturing facility owned by merging firm A versus a similar facility owned by merging firm B, or even two differently configured sets of assets, either of which would enable a purchaser to maintain the premerger level of competition in the affected market(s). The Division recognizes the need for flexibility in defining the divestiture assets in such cases.

However, once the Division files a proposed consent decree, Division policy requires that the decree include a precise description of the package of assets that, when divested, will resolve the Division's competitive concerns by maintaining competition at premerger levels.[17] This will ordinarily require the identification of a single set of divestiture assets in the consent decree. In rare circumstances, the decree may include a description of more than one set of assets the divestiture of which would be acceptable to the Division, with the defendant permitted to sell any of the described asset packages during the initial divestiture period.[18] If, at any time after the decree is filed, the Division and the defendant agree that the sale of an asset package not described in the consent decree will resolve the competitive concerns raised by the proposed transaction, the consent decree must be modified to describe this new divestiture package and the reasons this new divestiture is appropriate must be set forth in the moving papers.[19]

C. Divestiture of an Existing Business Entity Is Preferred

As stated above, any divestiture must contain at least the minimal set of assets necessary to ensure the efficient current and future production and distribution of the relevant product and thereby replace the competition lost through the merger. The Division favors the divestiture of an existing business entity that has already demonstrated its ability to compete in the relevant market.[20] An existing business entity should possess not only all the physical assets, but also the personnel, customer lists, information systems, intangible assets, and management infrastructure necessary for the efficient production and distribution of the relevant product. Where an

---

[16] *See infra* Section IV.D. for a further discussion of the characteristics of an acceptable purchaser.

[17] Nothing, however, prohibits the merged firm from selling *additional* assets not specified in the decree.

[18] The decree may specify that a selling trustee have similar flexibility to sell the alternative sets of assets or may require the trustee to sell only one of the described sets of assets.

[19] However, a minor deletion of assets from the divestiture package may not require a decree modification.

[20] In some cases, an existing business entity may be a single plant that produces and sells the relevant product; in other cases, it may be an entire division.

existing business entity lacks certain of these characteristics, additional assets from the merging firms will need to be included in the divestiture package.

An existing business entity provides current and potential customers with a track record they can evaluate to assure themselves that the unit will continue to be a reliable provider of the relevant products. Importantly, an existing business entity's track record establishes a strong presumption that it can be a viable and effective competitor in the markets of concern going forward. It has, in a very real sense, been tested by the market.

Conversely, a set of assets that comprises only a portion of an existing business entity has not demonstrated the ability effectively to compete. Such a divestiture almost invariably raises greater concern about the viability or competitiveness of the purchaser, perhaps because it is missing some unanticipated yet valuable component.

The Division should scrutinize carefully the merging firm's proposal to sell less than an existing business entity because the merging firm has an obvious incentive to sell fewer assets than are required for the purchaser to compete effectively going forward. Further, at the right price, a purchaser may be willing to purchase these assets even if they are insufficient to produce competition at the premerger level. A purchaser's interests are not necessarily identical to those of the public, and so long as the divested assets produce something of value to the purchaser (possibly providing it with the ability to earn profits in some other market or enabling it to produce weak competition in the relevant market), it may be willing to buy them at a fire-sale price regardless of whether they cure the competitive concerns.

Caveats:

1. **Divestiture of Less than an Existing Business Entity May Be Considered if There Is No Existing Business Entity Smaller than Either of the Merging Firms and a Set of Acceptable Assets Can Be Assembled from Both of the Merging Firms**

    - There may be situations where there is no obvious existing business entity smaller than either of the merging firms. In limited circumstances, it may be possible to assemble an acceptable set of assets from both of the merging firms to create a viable divestiture. However, the Division must be persuaded that these assets will create a viable entity that will restore competition.

2. **Divestiture of Less than an Existing Business Entity Also May Be Considered When Certain of the Entity's Assets Are Already in the Possession of, or Readily Obtainable in a Competitive Market by, the Potential Purchaser**

    - The Division will approve the divestiture of less than an existing business entity if the evidence clearly demonstrates that certain of the entity's assets already are in the possession of, or readily obtainable in a competitive market by, the potential purchaser (e.g., general accounting or computer programming services). For example, if the likely purchaser already has its own distribution system, then insisting that a comparable distribution system be included in the divestiture package may create an unwanted and costly redundancy. In such a case, divesting only the assets required efficiently to design and build the relevant product may be appropriate.

3. Divestiture of More than an Existing Business Entity May Be Considered when It Is Necessary to Restore Competition

- Divesting an existing business entity, even if the divestiture includes all of the production and marketing assets responsible for producing and selling the relevant product, will not always enable the purchaser fully to replicate the competition eliminated by the merger. For example, in some industries, it is difficult to compete without offering a "full line" of products. In such cases, the Division may seek to include a full line of products in the divestiture package, even when our antitrust concern relates to only a subset of those products. Similarly, although the merger creates a competitive problem in a United States market, divestiture of a world-wide business may be necessary to restore competition. More generally, integrated firms can provide scale and scope economies that a purchaser may not be able to achieve after obtaining the divested assets. When available evidence suggests that this is likely to be the case (such as where only large integrated firms manage to remain viable in the marketplace), the entity that needs to be divested may actually be the firm itself, and blocking the entire transaction rather than accepting a divestiture may be the only effective solution.

D. The Merged Firm Must Divest Rights to Critical Intangible Assets

Where the critical asset is an intangible one—e.g., where firms with alternative patent rights for producing the same final product are merging—structural relief must provide one or more purchasers with rights to that asset.[21] Such rights can be provided either by sale to a different owner or through licensing.[22]

---

[21] A critical asset is one that is necessary for the purchaser to compete effectively in the market in question. When a patent covers the right to compete in multiple product or geographic markets, yet the merger adversely affects competition in only a subset of these markets, the Division will insist only on the sale or license of rights necessary to maintain competition in the affected markets. In some cases, this may require that the purchaser or licensee obtain the rights to produce and sell only the relevant product. In other circumstances, it may be necessary to give the purchaser or licensee the right to produce and sell other products (or use other processes), where doing so permits the realization of scale and scope economies necessary to compete effectively in the relevant market.

[22] United States v. National Lead Co., 332 U.S. 319, 348 (1947) (courts may order mandatory patent licensing as relief in antitrust cases where necessary to restore competition). When the divestiture involves licensing, the Division will generally insist on fully paid-up licenses rather than running royalties for two reasons. First, running royalty payments, even if they are less expensive to the licensee over the lifetime of the license, add a cost to the licensee's production and sale of incremental units, tending to increase the licensee's profit-maximizing price. The result will be less competition than the two merging firms had previously been providing. Second, running royalties require a continued relationship between the merged firm and the purchaser, which could soften competition between them. However, the Division may consider the use of running royalties if (a) no deal would otherwise be struck between the merged firm and the licensee (perhaps because the firms differ greatly in their estimates of future revenue streams under the license) and (b) blocking the deal entirely would likely sacrifice merger-specific efficiencies worth preserving.

When the remedy requires divestiture of intangible assets, often an issue arises as to whether the merged firm can retain rights to these assets, such as the right to operate under the divested patent itself. Because such intangible assets have the peculiar economic property that use of the asset by one party need not preclude unlimited use of that very same asset by others, there may be in this sense no cost to allowing the seller to retain the same rights as the purchaser.

Nonetheless, in the context of a merger, permitting the merged firm to retain access to the critical intangible assets may present a significant competitive risk. Because the purchaser of the intangible assets will not have the right to exclude all others (specifically, the merged firm), it may face a greater challenge in differentiating its product from rivals and therefore be a lesser competitive force in the market. Also, if the purchaser is required to share rights to an intangible asset (like a patent or a brand name), it may not engage in competitive conduct (including investments and marketing) that it might have engaged in otherwise. For example, the purchaser may face greater risks of misappropriation by its rival of future "add on" investments or marketing activities. Where the purchaser is unable effectively to differentiate its offering from that of the merged firm, this may weaken its ability and incentive to compete as aggressively as the two formerly independent firms had been competing premerger. Moreover, where multiple firms have rights to the same trademark or copyright, none may have the proper incentive to promote and maintain the quality and reputation of the brand. In these circumstances, the Division is likely to conclude that permitting the merged firm to retain rights to the critical intangible assets will prevent the purchaser from restoring effective competition and, accordingly, will require that the merged firm relinquish all rights to the intangible assets.[23]

However, there may be other circumstances when the merged firm needs to retain rights to the intangible assets to achieve demonstrable efficiencies—which are not otherwise obtainable through an efficient licensing agreement with the purchaser following divestiture—and a non-exclusive license is sufficient to restore competition and assure the purchaser's future viability and competitiveness. These conditions are more likely to be satisfied in, for example, the case of production process patents than with final product patents, copyrights, or trademarks. This is because the purchaser is almost certain to rely on the latter to distinguish its products from incumbent products. In contrast, patented production technology that is shared, in addition to having the beneficial effect of lowering both producers' marginal costs, is less likely significantly to affect competition since the production process generally does not affect the purchaser's ability to differentiate its product. Under these circumstances, the merged firm will likely be

---

Also, the Division will not generally require royalty free licenses since parties should ordinarily be compensated for the use or sale of their property, intangible as well as tangible. *See id.* at 349 ("[T]o reduce all royalties automatically to a total of zero, regardless of their nature and regardless of their number, appears, on its face, to be inequitable without special proof to support such a conclusion."); Massachusetts v. Microsoft Corp., 373 F.3d 1199, 1231 (D.C. Cir. 2004).

[23] For example, the Division required the exclusive licensing of brand names in United States v. Interstate Bakeries Corp., 1996-1 Trade Cas. ¶ 71,271 (N.D. Ill. 1995).

permitted to retain certain rights to the critical intangible assets and may only be required to provide the purchaser with a non-exclusive license.[24]

There also may be circumstances when licensing the intangible assets to multiple firms—or perhaps even to "all comers"—is necessary to replace the competition lost through the merger.[25] This might be the case, for example, if the number one and two firms merge and there is a significant gap between those firms and the competitive significance of smaller firms. Licensing to more than one of those smaller firms or new entrants may be required to replace the competition eliminated by the merger.

E. Conduct Relief Is Appropriate Only in Limited Circumstances

As discussed above, conduct remedies generally are not favored in merger cases because they tend to entangle the Division and the courts in the operation of a market on an ongoing basis and impose direct, frequently substantial, costs upon the government and public that structural remedies can avoid. However, there are limited circumstances when conduct remedies will be appropriate: (a) when conduct relief is needed to facilitate transition to or support a competitive structural solution, i.e., when the merged firm needs to modify its conduct for structural relief to be effective or (b) when a full-stop prohibition of the merger would sacrifice significant efficiencies and a structural remedy would also sacrifice such efficiencies or is infeasible. In either circumstance, the costs of the conduct relief must be acceptable in light of the expected benefits.

1. Conduct Relief as an Adjunct to a Structural Remedy

Limited conduct relief can be useful in certain circumstances to help perfect structural relief. One example of a potentially appropriate transitional conduct provision is a short-term supply agreement. While long-term supply agreements between the merged firm and third parties on terms imposed by the Division are generally undesirable,[26] short-term supply agreements on occasion can be useful when accompanying a structural remedy. For example, if the purchaser is unable to manufacture the product for a limited transitional period (perhaps as plants are reconfigured or product mixes are altered), a short-term supply agreement can help prevent the loss of a competitor from the market, even temporarily. In such a case, the potential problems arising from supply agreements are more limited, given their short duration, and may be outweighed by their ability to maintain another competitor during the interim.

---

[24] *See, e.g.*, United States v. 3D Systems Corp., 2002-2 Trade Cas. ¶ 73,738 (D.D.C. 2001).

[25] *See, e.g.*, United States v. Miller Industries, Inc., 2001-1 Trade Cas. ¶ 73,132 (D.D.C. 2000); United States v. Cookson Group plc, 1994-1 Trade Cas. ¶ 70,666 (D.D.C. 1993).

[26] Given the merged firm's incentive not to promote competition with itself, competitors reliant upon the merged firm for product or key inputs are likely to be disadvantaged in the long term. Contractual terms are difficult to define and specify with the requisite foresight and precision, and a firm compelled to help another compete against it is unlikely to exert much effort to ensure the products or inputs it supplies are of high quality, arrive as scheduled, match the order specifications, and satisfy other conditions that are necessary to restore competition. Moreover, close and persistent ties between two or more competitors (as created by such agreements) can serve to enhance the flow of information or align incentives that may facilitate collusion or cause the loss of a competitive advantage.

Similarly, temporary limits on the merged firm's ability to reacquire personnel assets as part of a divestiture may at times be appropriate to ensure that the purchaser will be a viable competitor. The divestiture of any portion of a business unit would normally involve the transfer of personnel from the merging firms to the purchaser of the assets. Incumbent employees often are essential to the productive operation of the divested assets, particularly in the period immediately following the divestiture (i.e., they may be integral to efficient operation of the other assets that are being divested). Current employees may have uncommon technical knowledge of particular manufacturing equipment or may be the authors of essential software. While knowledge is often transferrable or reproducible over time, the immediate loss of certain employees may substantially reduce the ability of the divested entity to compete effectively, at least at the outset. To protect against this impairment, the Division may prohibit the merged firm from re-hiring these employees for some limited period.[27]

Restricting the merged firm's right to compete in final output markets or against the purchaser of the divested assets, even as a transitional remedy, is strongly disfavored. Such restrictions directly limit competition in the short term, and any long-term benefits are inherently speculative. For this reason, the Division is unlikely to impose them as part of a merger remedy. When the purchaser appears incapable of surviving or competing effectively against the merged firm without such restrictions, the Division is likely to seek a full-stop injunction against the transaction.

Finally, in addition to temporary or transitional conduct remedies, there may be occasions when continuing conduct relief is needed to effectuate or bolster the structural remedy. For example, there can be instances under the Capper-Volstead Act, 7 U.S.C. § 291, and other statutes where antitrust exemptions could become applicable if the divested assets were owned by persons having certain characteristics. In those rare situations, a conduct provision providing that the merged firm and the purchaser of the divested assets cannot sell the divested assets to a person having those characteristics might be appropriate, if the efficiencies gained from allowing the merger to go forward are high.[28]

2. Stand-Alone Conduct Relief

While conduct remedies are used in limited circumstances as an adjunct to structural relief in merger cases, the use of conduct remedies standing alone to resolve a merger's competitive concerns is rare[29] and almost always in

---

[27] *See, e.g.*, United States v. AlliedSignal, Inc., 2000-2 Trade Cas. ¶ 73,023 (D.D.C. 2000); United States v. Aetna, Inc., 1999-2 Trade Cas. ¶ 72,730 (N.D.Tex. 1999). Of course, in a situation in which there are a limited number of key employees who are essential to any purchaser competing effectively in the market, the Division will scrutinize very carefully whether divestiture is an appropriate remedy. If the Division cannot be satisfied that the key personnel are likely to become and remain employees of the purchaser, a more appropriate action may be to block the entire transaction.

[28] An example of such a provision is found in the Final Judgment in United States v. Dairy Farmers of America, 2001-1 Trade Cas. ¶ 73,136 (E.D. Pa. 2000).

[29] For example, between October 1, 1993 and September 30, 2003, the Division filed about 113 merger cases. Less than ten had conduct relief without any structural remedy, and most of those cases involved the regulated telecommunications industry and the defense industry. See United States v. MCI Communications Corp, 1994-2 Trade Cas. ¶ 70,730 (D.D.C. 1994), *modified*, 1997-2 Trade Cas. ¶ 71,935 (D.D.C. 1997) (transparency provision); United States v. Sprint Corp., 1996-1 Trade Cas. ¶ 71,300 (D.D.C. 1996) (same); United States v. Tele-Communications, Inc., 1996-2 Trade Cas. ¶ 71,496 (D.D.C. 1994) (fair dealing provision); United States v. AT&T Corp., 59 Fed. Reg. 44158 (D.D.C. 1994) (same); United States v. Northrop Grumman Corp., 68 Fed. Reg. 1861 (D.D.C. 2003)

industries where there already is close government oversight. Stand-alone conduct relief is only appropriate when a full-stop prohibition of the merger would sacrifice significant efficiencies and a structural remedy would similarly eliminate such efficiencies or is simply infeasible.

Both horizontal and vertical mergers present the potential to create efficiencies.[30] Where merger-specific scale, scope, or other economies are significant but the merger is on balance anticompetitive, requiring a structural divestiture might remedy the competitive concerns only at the cost of unnecessarily sacrificing significant efficiencies. In such situations, a stand-alone conduct remedy may be appropriate. However, for the prospect of potentially attainable efficiencies to justify accepting a pure conduct remedy, the efficiencies in question need to be cognizable rather than merely asserted. Moreover, they must be unattainable (at reasonable cost) if there is a structural divestiture. Analogizing to the Merger Guidelines, the Division requires them to be "conduct-remedy specific."

Mergers may also present the situation where any possible structural remedy that would undo the competitive harm would result in the loss of pre-existing internal efficiencies, i.e., efficiencies already achieved by a merging firm, prior to the merger, that are not due to the merger. For example, in order to minimize costs a firm may use the same distribution system for the widgets and gadgets that it produces. A divestiture that requires breaking up the distribution system into a widget distribution system, entirely separate from the gadget distribution system, may eliminate efficiencies that had been created by their original consolidation. The Division would give consideration to a conduct remedy that retained these efficiencies and still remedied the anticompetitive concern arising from the proposed merger.

There also may be situations where a structural remedy is infeasible. Certain vertical mergers in particular may simply not be amenable to any type of structural relief, as is typically found in the case of an upstream firm with a single plant acquiring a downstream firm with a single plant. Where such a merger may substantially lessen competition yet would likely result in significant efficiencies, the Division's choice necessarily will come down to stopping the transaction or imposing a conduct remedy.

In deciding whether a conduct remedy is appropriate, the Division will also consider the costs of monitoring and enforcing the remedy. Monitoring and enforcing a conduct remedy may be easier in markets in which regulatory

---

(fair dealing and firewall provisions); and United States v. Lehman Bros. Holdings, Inc., 1998-2 Trade Cas. ¶ 72,269 (D.D.C. 1998) (firewall provision and prohibitions on certain joint bidding agreements). *See also* United States v. Morton Plant Health System, Inc., 1994-2 Trade Cas. ¶ 70,759 (M.D. Fla. 1994) (firewall provision and prohibitions on certain joint pricing).

[30] Horizontal and vertical mergers often produce different types of efficiencies. Examples of possible horizontal-merger-related efficiencies include achieving economies of scale or scope, and rationalization of sales forces, design teams, and distribution networks. Examples of vertical-merger-related efficiencies include elimination of the double-marginalization problem (i.e., the vertically integrated firm has an incentive to charge a lower price for the final good compared to the price that results from each of the merging firms setting prices independently), coordination of the design of intermediate and final products, and perhaps reduction or elimination of other types of transaction costs. See D. Carlton & J. Perloff, Modern Industrial Organization 377–417 (3rd ed. 2000) for an explanation of the various efficiencies that can arise from a vertical merger. For a discussion of the efficiencies that can arise from a horizontal merger, see Section 4 of the Horizontal Merger Guidelines.

oversight is already being employed and data on the merged firm's conduct would regularly be collected and audited in any event. Although those regulators will not generally have the same incentives and goals as the competition authorities, the greater transparency of market conduct that they permit can lower the cost to the Division and the courts of monitoring and enforcement.[31]

The most common forms of stand-alone conduct relief are firewall, fair dealing, and transparency provisions. As discussed below, however, their ongoing use, along with that of all other forms of stand-alone conduct relief, can present substantial policy and practical concerns.

a. Firewall Provisions

Firewalls are designed to prevent the dissemination of information within a firm. Suppose, for example, that an upstream monopolist proposes to merge with one of three downstream firms, all three of whom compete in the same relevant market. The Division may be concerned that the upstream firm will share information with its acquired downstream firm (and perhaps with the two other downstream firms) that will facilitate anticompetitive behavior.[32] A properly designed and enforced firewall could prevent that.

The problems with firewalls are those of every regulatory provision. The first concern is the considerable time and effort the Division and the courts have to expend in monitoring and enforcing such provisions. The second problem is devising a provision that will ensure that the pertinent information will not be disseminated in any event. The third is that a firewall may frequently destroy the very efficiency that the merger was designed to generate.

For these reasons, the use of firewalls in Division decrees is the exception and not the rule. They are infrequently used in horizontal mergers because, no matter how carefully crafted, the risks that the merging firms will act collaboratively in spite of the firewall are great. However, they have occasionally been used in some defense industry mergers, and in vertical and other non-horizontal mergers when both the loss of efficiencies from blocking the merger outright and the harm to competition from allowing the transaction to go unchallenged are high.

b. Fair Dealing Provisions

Fair dealing provisions include the concepts of equal access, equal efforts, and non-discrimination. However, as discussed previously, a non-discrimination requirement presents the difficult question of whether cost-based differences justify differential prices and thus are not truly discriminatory.[33]

---

[31] This will not, however, eliminate all mechanisms through which conduct-regulated firms can evade the conduct remedy. For instance, suppose the Division is considering a conduct remedy partly because a government agency accurately monitors the prices in the industry (but only the prices). One way to comply with the pricing provision (such as a non-discrimination provision) might be to keep prices the same, but decrease quality. However, if quality is not easily altered, or if there are other restraints on the merged firm's incentive to decrease quality, then the conduct remedy may be more acceptable.

[32] While coordination is perhaps the chief concern in such instances, such information sharing could also lead rivals concerned about misappropriation of their proprietary information to under-invest in product development and thus stifle innovation.

[33] *See supra* Section III.A. for a discussion of non-discrimination provisions.

Suppose, for example, an upstream monopolist proposes to merge with one of three downstream firms. The three downstream firms all compete in the same relevant market. A concern arising from this merger could be that the upstream firm will now have an incentive to favor the acquired downstream firm by offering less attractive terms to the acquired firm's two downstream competitors.

In such a case, consideration may be given to a fair dealing clause whereby the upstream firm must offer the same terms to all three downstream competitors. As with most forms of regulation, however, enforcing (and even drafting) this sort of requirement can be problematic. In the first instance, if the upstream and downstream firms have merged in such a manner that the sales price to the acquired downstream firm becomes a mere internal accounting factor, the upstream firm could set a high, non-discriminatory price to downstream firms that would nonetheless disadvantage the acquired downstream firm's competitors. A fair dealing provision might then be ineffective. Even where this is not the case, e.g., where regulation at one level dictates how transfer prices are measured or the vertical integration is only partial, difficulties remain with fair dealing provisions. In order to accept such a remedy, the Division must be convinced that it has protected against problems where the independent downstream firms get lesser quality product, slower delivery times, reduced service, or unequal access to the upstream firm's products.

Such provisions should not be undertaken without careful analysis. Fair dealing provisions have a great potential for harm as well as good, and the Division must always evaluate and weigh the benefits of using such a provision against the risks. When used at all in Division decrees, such provisions invariably require careful crafting so that the judgment accomplishes the critical goals of the antitrust remedy without damaging market performance.

c. Transparency Provisions

The Division on occasion has used so-called transparency provisions as the sole or principal form of relief in vertical merger cases. Such provisions usually require the merged firm to make certain information available to a regulatory authority that the firm would not otherwise be required to provide. For example, a telecommunications firm may be required to inform a regulatory authority of what prices the firm is charging customers for telephone equipment even though the regulatory agency may not have authority to regulate those prices. The theory is that the additional information will aid the regulatory authority in curtailing the telecommunications firm from engaging in regulatory evasion by, for example, charging telephone equipment clients with which it competes for telephone services higher prices than it charges its other telephone equipment customers.

Transparency provisions present the same problems that other regulatory provisions entail. First, they present the difficulty of devising a provision that will not be circumvented. Second, they require the Antitrust Division to educate the regulator on the significance of the additional information and ensure that the information is reviewed. Third, they require the Division and the courts to expend considerable resources in monitoring and enforcing the provision. For these reasons, transparency provisions are also used sparingly in Division decrees.

d. Other Types of Conduct Remedies

While firewall, fair dealing, and transparency provisions are the most common forms of stand-alone conduct relief (and even these provisions are quite rare), other conduct remedies are also possible. These include so-called competitive-rule joint ventures ("CRJV"),[34] non-compete clauses, long-term supply contracts, and restrictions on reacquisition of scarce personnel assets.[35]

IV. Implementing the Remedy

A. A Fix-It-First Remedy Is Acceptable if It Eliminates the Competitive Harm

A fix-it-first remedy is a structural remedy that the parties implement and the Division accepts before a merger is consummated.[36] A fix-it-first remedy eliminates the Division's antitrust concerns and therefore the need to file a case.[37]

The Division does not discourage acceptable fix-it-first remedies. If parties express an interest in pursuing a fix-it-first remedy that satisfies the conditions discussed below, the Division will consider the proposal. Indeed, in certain circumstances, a fix-it-first remedy may restore competition to the market more quickly and effectively than would a decree. This would be particularly important, for example, where a rapid divestiture would prevent asset dissipation or ensure the resolution of competitive concerns before an upcoming bid.

If an acceptable fix-it-first remedy can be implemented, the Division will exercise its Executive Branch prerogative to forego filing a case and conclude its investigation without imposing additional obligations on the parties. A fix-it-first remedy restores premerger competition, removes the need for litigation, allows the Division to use its resources more efficiently, and saves society from incurring real costs. Moreover, a fix-it-first remedy may provide more flexibility in fashioning the appropriate divestiture. Because different purchasers may require different sets of assets to be competitive, a fix-it-first remedy allows the assets to be tailored to a specific proposed purchaser. A consent decree, in contrast, must identify all of the assets necessary for effective competition by any potentially acceptable purchaser.

The Division will accept a fix-it-first remedy when it eliminates the competitive harm otherwise arising from the proposed merger. The same internal review is given to fix-it-first remedies as is given to consent

---

[34] A CRJV operates under a set of structural and behavioral rules designed to maintain the independence of multiple selling entities by ensuring that they will obtain the relevant product (or key input) at or near true marginal cost. Though theoretically appealing, the technical requirements for a CRJV to perform as advertised are many and subtle, and there are several potential pitfalls. Owners have a clear incentive to classify some fixed costs as variable costs, thereby increasing participants' marginal cost of production and reducing output. The Division might also need to insert firewalls to remove concerns about information sharing that would facilitate collusion and would have to exert resources to monitor the process. The Division has used a CRJV only once, in United States v. Alcan Aluminum, Inc., 605 F. Supp. 619 (W.D. Ky. 1985).

[35] *See supra* Section III.E.1.

[36] The parties may always *unilaterally* decide to restructure their transaction to eliminate any potential competitive harm. While this may obviate the need for the Division to further investigate the transaction, it is not considered a fix-it-first remedy for the purposes of this Guide since the Division did not "accept" the fix.

[37] A fix-it-first remedy usually involves the sale of a subsidiary or division, or specific assets of one or both of the merging parties, to a third party.

decrees. Before exercising its prerogative not to file a case, the Division must be satisfied that the fix-it-first remedy will protect the market from any adverse competitive effects attributable to the proposed transaction. A fix-it-first remedy will not eliminate the Division's concerns unless the Division is confident that the proposed fix will indeed preserve the premerger level of competition. In addition, Antitrust Division attorneys reviewing fix-it-first remedies should carefully screen the proposed divestiture for any relationships between the seller and the purchaser, since the parties have, in essence, self-selected the purchaser. An acceptable fix-it-first remedy should contain no less substantive relief than would be sought if a case were filed.[38] The Division, therefore, needs to conduct an investigation sufficient to determine both the nature and extent of the likely competitive harm and whether the proposed fix-it-first remedy will resolve it.[39]

Caveat: A Fix-It-First Remedy Is Unacceptable if the Remedy Must Be Monitored

- If the competitive harm requires remedial provisions that entail some continued obligations on the part of the merged firm (e.g., the use of firewalls or other conduct relief), a fix-it-first solution is unacceptable. In such situations, a consent decree is necessary to enforce and monitor any ongoing obligations. For example, a fix-it-first remedy would be unacceptable if the merged firm as part of the solution is required to provide the purchaser with a necessary input pursuant to a supply agreement. The Division would insist upon having recourse to a court's contempt power in such circumstances so as to ensure the merged firm's complete compliance with the agreement and the protection of competition.

B. A Hold Separate Provision Is a Necessary Component of Most Consent Decrees

Consent decrees requiring divestiture after the transaction closes should require defendants to take all steps necessary to ensure that the assets to be divested are maintained as separate, distinct, and saleable. A hold separate provision is designed to maintain the independence and viability of the divested assets as well as competition in the market during the pendency of the divestiture.

It is unrealistic, however, to think that a hold separate provision will entirely preserve competition. For example, managers operating entities kept apart by a hold separate provision are unlikely to engage in vigorous competition. Likewise, customers during the period before divestiture may be influenced in their purchasing decisions by the merger, even if the to-be-divested assets are being operated independently of the merged firm pursuant to a hold separate provision. Similarly, there may be some

---

[38] The parties should provide a written agreement regarding the fix-it-first remedy. The agreement should specify which assets will be sold, detail any conditions on those sales (*e.g.*, regulatory approval), provide that the Division be notified when the assets are sold, and state that the agreement constitutes the entire understanding with the Division concerning the divested assets. Unless the parties also enter into a timing agreement, a signed stipulation and consent decree (i.e., a "pocket decree") should be obtained that will be filed if the parties fail timely to comply with the written agreement.

[39] Although the parties may propose a fix-it-first remedy because they face substantial time pressures, the Division must allow itself adequate time to conduct the necessary investigation, including an evaluation of the proposed purchaser. *See* discussion *infra* Section IV.D.

dissipation of the soon-to-be-divested assets during the period before divestiture, notwithstanding the presence of a hold separate agreement—valuable employees may leave and critical investments may not be made. For these reasons, a hold separate agreement does not eliminate the need for a speedy divestiture.

Nevertheless, hold separate provisions are extremely important in Division merger enforcement. To ensure that there will be an independent, effective competitor after divestiture, the divestiture assets must remain independent and economically viable before divestiture.

C. The Divestiture Should Be Accomplished Quickly

The Division will require the parties to accomplish any divestiture quickly. A quick divestiture has two clear benefits. First, it restores premerger competition to the marketplace as soon as possible. Second, it mitigates the potential dissipation of asset value associated with a lengthy divestiture process. The Division recognizes that a comprehensive "shop" of the assets, the need for due diligence on the part of potential purchasers, and Division review of the purchaser take time. The Division will balance these considerations in developing an appropriate timetable for the divestiture process.

Depending on the size and complexity of the divestiture assets, the divesting firm normally will be given 60 to 90 days to locate a purchaser on its own.[40] The consent decree may also permit the Division to exercise discretion in granting short extensions when it appears that the divesting firm is making good faith efforts and an extension seems likely to result in a successful divestiture. On the other hand, the Division may insist upon more rapid divestiture in cases where critical assets appear likely to deteriorate quickly or there will be substantial competitive harm before the purchaser can operate the assets. In situations where an investment banker or other intermediary conducts the shop, the Division may require that the intermediary's compensation be based in part on speed of the sale.[41]

The Division will require regular reports on the divestiture process in order to ensure good faith efforts and to facilitate a quick review once a final settlement is proposed. Once a purchaser is proposed, the Division may require additional information to evaluate both the purchaser and the process by which the purchaser was chosen. The divesting firm and the proposed purchaser ordinarily will be required to respond to requests for such information within 30 days.

D. The Antitrust Division Must Approve Any Proposed Purchaser

The Division must approve any proposed purchaser.[42] Its approval will be conditioned on three fundamental tests. First, divestiture of the assets to

---

[40] The Tunney Act provides for a 60-day waiting period before the court can enter a proposed consent decree. 15 U.S.C. § 16(b). The Division will not oppose the sale of the divestiture assets to a purchaser acceptable to the Division before the judgment is entered if (a) the court is notified of the plan to complete the sale before the court enters the judgment and (b) there is no objection from the court. However, under no circumstance will such a sale preclude the Division from proceeding to trial, dismissing the case, or requesting additional or different relief if the court ultimately rejects the proposed decree. *See generally* United States v. BNS, Inc., 858 F.2d 456, 466 (9th Cir. 1988).

[41] *See infra* Section IV.I. for a discussion of the role of a trustee.

[42] As discussed above, the Division focuses on specifying in the decree the appropriate set of assets to be divested quickly rather than on the identification of an

the proposed purchaser must not itself cause competitive harm. For example, if the concern is that the merger will enhance an already dominant firm's ability unilaterally to exercise market power, divestiture to another large competitor in the market is not likely to be acceptable, although divestiture to a fringe incumbent might. On the other hand, if the concern is one of coordinated effects among a small set of postmerger competitors, divestiture to any firm in that set would itself raise competitive problems. In that situation, the Division would likely only approve divestiture to a firm outside that set.[43]

Second, the Division must be certain that the purchaser has the incentive to use the divestiture assets to compete in the relevant market. Even if the choice of a proposed purchaser does not raise competitive problems, the need for additional review arises because the seller has an obvious incentive not to sell to a purchaser that will compete effectively. A seller may wish to sacrifice a higher price for the assets today in return for selling to a rival that will not be especially competitive in the future. This is in contrast to a situation in which the firm selling the assets is itself exiting the market. The incentive of the latter firm is simply to identify and accept the highest offer.

Because the purpose of divestiture is to preserve competition in the relevant market, the Division will not approve a divestiture if the assets will be redeployed elsewhere.[44] Thus, there should be evidence of the purchaser's intention to compete in the relevant market. Such evidence might include business plans, prior efforts to enter the market, or status as a significant producer of a complementary product.[45] In addition, customers and suppliers of firms in the relevant market are often an important source of information concerning a proposed purchaser's intentions and ability to compete. Accordingly, their insights and views will be considered. However, in no case will they be given veto power over a proposed purchaser.

Third, the Division will perform a "fitness" test to ensure that the purchaser has sufficient acumen, experience, and financial capability to compete effectively in the market over the long term. Divestiture decrees state that it must be demonstrated to plaintiff's sole satisfaction that the purchaser has the "managerial, operational, technical and financial capability" to compete effectively with the divestiture assets.

In determining whether a proposed purchaser is "fit," the Division will evaluate the purchaser strictly on its own merits. The Division will not compare the relative fitness of multiple potential purchasers and direct a sale to that purchaser that it deems the fittest. The appropriate remedial goal is to ensure that the selected purchaser will be an effective, viable

---

acceptable buyer ("up front buyer") before entering into a consent decree. If the Division has done this correctly, then an acceptable buyer should be forthcoming. Moreover, the merging firms are always free to identify an acceptable buyer in a fix-it-first remedy.

[43] Indeed, if harmful coordination is feared because the merger is removing a uniquely-positioned maverick, the divestiture would likely have to be to a firm with maverick-like interests and incentives.

[44] *See supra* Section III.B.

[45] Complementary businesses often have a strong independent interest in maintaining competition in the relevant market, because higher prices in that market would impact them adversely as sellers of complementary goods or services. Further, if others in the relevant market are not also vertically integrated, creation of a vertically integrated rival may serve to disrupt postmerger coordinated conduct. *See* Horizontal Merger Guidelines ¶ 2.11.

competitor in the market, according to the requirements in the consent decree, not that it will necessarily be the best possible competitor.

If the divestiture assets have been widely shopped and the seller commits to selling to the highest paying, competitively acceptable bidder, then the review under the incentive/intention and fitness tests may be relatively simple.[46] Ideally, assets should be held by those who value them the most and, in general, the highest paying, competitively acceptable bidder will be the firm that can compete with the assets most effectively.[47] On the other hand, if (a) the seller has proposed a specific purchaser, (b) the shop has been narrowly focused, or (c) the Division has any other reason to believe that the proposed purchaser may not have the incentive, intention, or resources to compete effectively, then a more rigorous review may be warranted.

E. A Successful Divestiture Does Not Depend on the Price Paid for the Divestiture Assets

The Antitrust Division's interest in divestiture lies in the preservation of competition, not with whether the divesting firm or the proposed purchaser is getting the better of the deal. Therefore, the Division is not directly concerned with whether the price paid for the divestiture assets is "too low" or "too high." The divesting firm is being forced to dispose of assets within a limited time frame. Potential purchasers know this. If there are few potential purchasers to bid up the price, the divesting firm may fail to realize full competitive value. On the other hand, if there are many interested purchasers, the divesting firm may actually get a price above the appraised market value. In either event, the Division will not consider the price of the divestiture assets unless, as discussed below, it raises concerns about the effectiveness or viability of the purchaser.

Caveat: The Purchase Price Will Not Be Approved if It Clearly Indicates that the Purchaser Is Unable or Unwilling to Compete in the Relevant Market

- **"Too Low" a Price.** A purchase price that is "too low" may suggest that the purchaser does not intend to keep the assets in the market. In determining whether a price is "too low," the Division will look at the assets' liquidation value. Liquidation value is defined here as the highest value of the assets when redeployed to some use outside the relevant market. Liquidation value will be used as a constraint on minimum price only when (a) liquidation value can be reliably determined and (b) the constraint is needed as assurance that the proposed purchaser satisfies the fundamental test of intending to use the divestiture assets to compete in the relevant market. In many cases, however, liquidation value is difficult to determine reliably. Also, sale at a price below liquidation value does not

---

[46] The Division may identify specific firms that the seller should contact when the staff has learned of potential purchasers in the course of its original investigation. In addition, the Division may, under limited circumstances, require that an investment banker or other intermediary conduct the shop from the outset when the Division is concerned that the defendant will not complete the divestiture within a reasonable time. See *infra* Section IV.I. for a discussion of the role of a trustee.

[47] However, even when the divestiture assets have been widely shopped, it may sometimes be difficult reliably to rank competing offers. Ranking difficulties materialize when potential purchasers bid for different packages of assets or when offers are qualified by contingencies or otherwise depart from simple cash terms. In such cases, the Division may have to examine the competing offers more closely.

necessarily imply that the assets will be redeployed outside the relevant market. It may simply mean the purchaser is getting a bargain. Therefore, if the Division has other sufficient assurances that the proposed purchaser intends to compete in the relevant market, the Division will not require that the price exceed liquidation value.

- **"Too High" a Price.** In theory, a price that appears to be unusually high for the assets being sold could raise concerns for two reasons. First, it could indicate that the proposed purchaser is paying a premium for the acquisition of market power. However, this concern is adequately and more directly addressed in applying the fundamental test that the proposed purchaser must not itself raise competitive concerns. Second, a purchaser who pays too high a price might be handicapped by debt or lack of adequate working capital, increasing the chance of bankruptcy. Thus, a price that is unusually high may be taken into account when evaluating the financial ability of the purchaser to compete.

F. Restraints on the Resale of Divestiture Assets Will Ordinarily Not Be Permitted

Although the Division will insist that the purchaser have both the intention and ability to compete in the market for the foreseeable future, the Division will not insist that the assets, once successfully divested, continue to be employed in the relevant market indefinitely. Conditions change over time, and the divested assets may in the future be employed more productively elsewhere.

The market for corporate control is imperfect. In unusual cases, an unfit, poorly informed potential purchaser may overbid and win the divestiture assets. The Division is not able consistently to foresee and correct faulty market outcomes. Also, even when in retrospect the market for corporate control has made a mistake, the market itself tends to correct the mistake as long as the purchaser is free to resell the divestiture assets to the firm capable of operating them most efficiently. Therefore, the Division will not attempt to limit the purchaser's ability to resell the divestiture assets, nor will it permit the seller to do so.

Caveat: In Unusual Circumstances, the Purchaser's Ability To Sell the Divestiture Assets to a Particular Entity or Type of Entity Will Be Limited

- Where the Division is confident that during the life of the consent decree the resale of the divestiture assets to a particular entity or type of entity would be anticompetitive, it may seek to limit the purchaser's ability to sell those assets to such an entity.[48]
- There may also be circumstances when the merging firm will be permitted to limit a licensee's further licensing of the divested intangible assets. For example, suppose the remedy includes the right to use a particular brand name in the relevant market but not elsewhere. If the value of the brand name elsewhere is both significant and reasonably dependent on how the brand name is

[48] Division decrees also prohibit defendants from reacquiring the divested assets. *Cf. infra* Section V.A. This prohibition on reacquisition of assets is the key reason that the term of the decree in merger cases exceeds the completion of the divestiture. The typical term of Division merger decrees is 10 years.

used in the relevant market, the merging firm may have a legitimate interest in limiting the licensee's ability to re-license the brand name rights.

G. Seller Financing of Divestiture Assets Is Strongly Disfavored

Seller financing of the divestiture assets, whether in the form of debt or equity, raises a number of potential problems.[49] First, the seller may retain some partial control over the assets, which could weaken the purchaser's competitiveness. Second, the seller's incentive to compete with the purchaser may be impeded because of the seller's concern that vigorous competition may jeopardize the purchaser's ability to repay the financing. Similarly, the purchaser may be disinclined to compete vigorously out of concern that it may cause the seller to exercise various rights under the loan. Third, the seller may have some legal claim on the divestiture assets in the event the purchaser goes bankrupt. Fourth, the seller may use the ongoing relationship as a conduit for exchanging competitively sensitive information. Finally, the purchaser's inability to obtain financing from banks or other lending institutions raises questions about the purchaser's viability.

For these reasons, the Division is strongly disinclined ever to permit the seller to finance the sale of the divestiture assets. The Division will consider seller financing only when it is persuaded that none of the possible concerns discussed above exist. For example, in the relatively rare case where the information financial institutions need adequately to evaluate the purchaser's business prospects is either unavailable or costly to obtain relative to the amount of the financing, very limited seller financing may be considered.

H. Crown Jewel Provisions Are Strongly Disfavored

A crown jewel provision typically requires the addition of certain specified—and generally more valuable—assets to the initial divestiture package if the parties are unable to sell the initially agreed-upon divestiture assets to a viable purchaser within a certain period. The Division disfavors the use of crown jewel provisions because generally they represent acceptance of either less than effective relief at the outset or more than is necessary to remedy the competitive problem.

In some circumstances there may be a trade-off between requiring a somewhat smaller, less valuable package of divestiture assets and accepting greater risk that the remedy will prove inadequate, or demanding a more substantial divestiture in order to be highly confident that postmerger competition will be fully preserved. Because the Antitrust Division must be highly confident that the merger will not harm competition, its preference is to demand at the outset a remedy that provides this confidence—rather than one that may turn out later to require the addition of more assets, e.g., a crown jewel.

The staff's investigation should allow it to determine whether a particular package of assets proposed for divestiture will (a) solve the competitive problems with the proposed merger and (b) be sufficiently attractive to viable purchasers. Moreover, because restoring competition, rather than punishing the merging firm, is the goal of a merger remedy, the consent

---

[49] The Division may permit the purchaser to make staggered payments to the seller, such as disbursement out of an escrow account pending final due diligence. This is typically not considered seller financing.

decree should not require the divestiture of crown jewel assets that exceed the assets necessary to remedy the competitive problem.

Crown jewel provisions also provide an opportunity for purchaser manipulation. If there are only a few potential purchasers and they are aware of the crown jewel provision in the decree, they may intentionally delay negotiating for the agreed-upon divestiture assets so that they may later purchase the crown jewels at an attractive price.[50]

I. Selling Trustee Provisions Must Be Included in Consent Decrees

For divestiture to be an effective merger remedy, the Division must have the ability to seek appointment of a trustee to sell the assets if a defendant is unable to complete the ordered sale within the period prescribed by the decree.[51] A selling trustee provision provides a safeguard that ensures the decree is implemented in a timely and effective manner. In addition, to the extent that defendants desire to control to whom the decree assets are sold and the price at which they are sold, the potential for a selling trustee to assume that responsibility provides an incentive for defendants to divest the assets promptly. Thus, every decree in a Division merger case must include provisions for the appointment of a selling trustee.

In the vast majority of cases, the Division will allow the defendant a reasonable opportunity to divest the decree assets to an acceptable purchaser before it asks the court to appoint a trustee to complete the sale. The assumption is that the defendant, at least initially, is best positioned to have complete information about the operation and value of the assets to be divested and to communicate that information quickly to prospective buyers, thereby facilitating a speedy divestiture to an acceptable purchaser. However, as discussed in Section IV.D. supra, because a divestiture would introduce a viable new competitor into the market, the defendant also has economic incentives to delay or otherwise frustrate the ordered divestiture. Therefore, the Division will permit the defendant only a limited time to effect the ordered divestiture before seeking appointment of a trustee.

A defendant may fail to complete a divestiture to an acceptable purchaser for any number of reasons. The defendant's selling efforts may have been dilatory. It may have sought a more favorable price or other terms than potential purchasers were willing to pay. A decree-ordered divestiture may also languish for reasons unrelated to the defendant's diligence in seeking to divest the assets, e.g., an inability to obtain necessary approvals from a third party such as a government permitting agency, or the purchaser backed out of the deal at the last minute.

The divestiture decree should provide that whenever a divestiture has not been completed by the prescribed deadline for any reason, the Division may promptly nominate, and move the court to appoint, a trustee with responsibility for completing the divestiture to a purchaser acceptable to the Division as soon as possible. In addition, when the proposed remedy is

[50] As discussed in Section III.B. *supra,* the Division may permit the merging firms to offer two different asset packages for sale simultaneously in the rare circumstance where either package would remedy the competitive problem. Such a parallel shop does not present the same concerns raised by the use of crown jewel provisions.

[51] Indeed, even in cases in which a defendant has been ordered to divest the assets to a designated buyer, a trustee is necessary in the event that the ordered sale is not completed for some unforeseen reasons. *See* United States v. Cargill Inc., 1997-2 Trade Cas. ¶ 71,893 (W.D.N.Y. 1997).

contingent on the approval of a third party, and that approval will not be obtained prior to the entry of the decree, the decree should include a contingency provision setting forth alternative relief in the event that the required approval ultimately is not forthcoming.

Caveat:

1. **The Immediate Appointment of a Selling Trustee May Be Required in the Rare Instance when the Defendant Will Not Complete the Divestiture Within a Reasonable Time**

   - A decree that provides for the immediate appointment of a trustee to sell the divestiture assets is an unusual merger remedy, reserved for those situations in which the Division has reason to believe at the outset that a defendant will not complete an ordered divestiture within a reasonable time. For example, if the assets deteriorate quickly such that the seller has an incentive to delay divestiture, the Division may require the immediate appointment of a selling trustee. Also, when a defendant has taken an inordinately long time to complete an ordered divestiture in a previous case, the Division may conclude that the assets are likely to be promptly divested only if a selling trustee is immediately appointed to divest the assets in the current case.

2. **An Operating Trustee May Be Required in the Rare Instance when the Defendant Is Unlikely to Manage the Divestiture Assets During the Divestiture Period Without Impairing Their Value**

   - An operating trustee is responsible for day-to-day management of all or part of a business ordered to be divested pursuant to the terms of a decree. Installing a trustee to run a business before divestiture is an extraordinary remedy. It is highly unlikely that an operating trustee will have adequate knowledge and incentive in the short term to run the business effectively. Therefore, the Division will only require an operating trustee in the very rare instance in which the Division believes that the defendant is likely to mismanage the assets during the typical divestiture period and thereby impair the likelihood that the divestiture will restore effective competition. For example, this might occur if the nature of the assets to be divested is such that their competitive value could quickly deteriorate if inappropriately managed during the divestiture period. Appointment of an operating trustee might be warranted when intangible property such as computer software has been ordered divested, and under-investment in the development and improvement of the software in a rapidly changing business environment may irreparably impair the sale of the assets as a viable product to any acceptable purchaser.

3. **A Monitoring Trustee May Be Required in the Rare Instance when the Trustee's Expertise Is Critical to an Effective Divestiture**

- A monitoring trustee is responsible for reviewing a defendant's compliance with its decree obligations to sell the assets to an acceptable purchaser as a viable enterprise and to abide by injunctive provisions to hold separate certain assets from a defendant's other business operations. In a typical merger case, a monitoring trustee's efforts would simply duplicate, and could potentially conflict with, the Division's own decree enforcement efforts. For this reason, appointment of a monitoring trustee should be reserved for relatively rare situations where a monitoring trustee with technical expertise unavailable to the Division could perform a valuable role.

V. Consent Decree Compliance and Enforcement

Whether structured as a fix-it-first or a consent decree including structural or conduct provisions, the remedy agreed upon by the Antitrust Division and the parties must maintain competition at premerger levels. It is incumbent upon the Division, pursuant to its responsibility to the public interest, as well as to the court in the case of a consent decree, to ensure strict implementation of and compliance with the agreed-upon remedy.[52] To do so, Division attorneys must first ensure that the decree correctly binds the appropriate parties, provides sufficient notice of the decree to any persons against whom the decree may be enforced, and provides a means for Division attorneys to gather information necessary to monitor compliance. The Division will commit substantial resources to monitor parties' implementation of and compliance with the remedy and will not hesitate to bring actions to enforce consent decrees, typically through the use of civil or criminal contempt proceedings.[53]

A. The Consent Decree Must Bind the Entities Against Which Enforcement May Be Sought

For a decree to be effective, it must bind the parties needed to fulfill the consent decree objectives. Both parties to the transaction are generally named defendants even if only one will be making the required divestitures.[54] Furthermore, the decree should include language to bind the defendants' successors and assigns, so that a defendant cannot sell its interest in the assets to be divested before divestiture, thereby frustrating the sale of the divestiture package to the approved purchaser. If it is anticipated that a non-party to a decree could be instrumental to its enforcement, the decree should require that actual notice of the decree be

---

[52] The Antitrust Division will likewise commit all resources necessary to ensure that parties comply with a fix-it-first remedy. Because a fix-it-first divestiture will occur before or simultaneously with the closing of the main transaction, the attorney assigned to the matter will likely review the same materials with similar considerations—*e.g.*, viable purchaser and no limitation on ability to compete—as if the divestiture were taking place under a consent decree.

[53] Non-parties are not permitted to enforce Division decrees. The court in New York v. Microsoft Corp., 224 F. Supp. 2d 76, 181 (D.D.C. 2002), *aff'd sub nom.* Massachusetts v. Microsoft, 373 F.3d 1199 (D.C. Cir. 2004), likewise recently noted that "non-parties should not be allowed direct access to the enforcement mechanisms." *See also* Massachusetts v. Microsoft, 373 F.3d at 1243–1244.

[54] Naming both parties to the transaction as defendants increases the likelihood that (a) the assets to be divested are maintained as separate, distinct, and saleable until they are transferred to the purchaser, (b) the assets to be divested are actually divested, and (c) the Division can obtain appropriate relief in the event the court does not accept the decree or later orders revisions.

given to such a person.[55] The decree should also prohibit defendants from reacquiring or otherwise exerting control over the assets ordered to be divested.[56]

B. The Consent Decree Must Provide a Means to Investigate Compliance

Consent decrees must have provisions allowing the Division to monitor compliance. They may require defendants to submit written reports and permit the Division to inspect and copy all books and records, and to interview defendants' officers, directors, employees, and agents as necessary to investigate any possible violation of the decree. Although civil investigative demands may also be issued to investigate compliance,[57] access terms should nonetheless be included in the decree, both to monitor compliance and to examine possible decree modification or termination.

C. The Antitrust Division Will Ensure that Remedies Are Fully Implemented

Resources will be devoted before and after a decree is entered to ensure that the decree is fully implemented. Every decree is assigned to staff responsible for monitoring implementation and compliance. The specific steps necessary to ensure compliance with a decree will vary depending on its nature. For a divestiture decree, staff will closely monitor the sale, including reviewing (a) the sales process, (b) the financial and managerial viability of the purchaser, (c) any documents related to the sale, and (d) any relationships between the purchaser and defendants, to ensure that no such relationship will inhibit the purchaser's ability or incentive to compete vigorously.

Where a decree requires affirmative acts, such as the submission of periodic reports, Division staff will determine whether the required acts have occurred and evaluate the sufficiency of compliance. With respect to decrees that prohibit certain actions, staff may also need to conduct periodic inquiries to determine whether defendants are observing the prohibitions.[58]

D. The Antitrust Division Will Enforce Consent Decrees

If the Antitrust Division concludes that a consent decree has been violated, the Division will institute an enforcement action. There are two types of contempt proceedings, civil and criminal, and either or both may be used. Civil contempt has a remedial purpose—compelling compliance with the court's order or compensating the complainant for losses sustained.[59] Staff may consider seeking both injunctive relief and fines that accumulate on a daily basis until compliance is achieved.[60] Criminal contempt is not

---

[55] The parties' agents and employees, and others who are in active concert or participation with the parties, will be bound by the decree so long as they receive actual notice of the order. Fed. R. Civ. P. 65(d). If other non-parties are needed for effective enforcement, consideration should be given to joining them as parties, Fed. R. Civ. P. 19, 15 U.S.C. § 25, or otherwise obtaining their agreement to be bound by the decree.

[56] However, the decree may permit the merging firm in limited circumstances to retain rights to intangible assets. *See* discussion *supra* Section III.D.

[57] 15 U.S.C. §§ 1311(c), 1312(a).

[58] Use of special masters for Division decree enforcement is disfavored, Fed. R. Civ. P. 53(b); New York v. Microsoft Corp., 224 F. Supp. 2d at 179–82.

[59] *See* United Mine Workers v. Bagwell, 512 U.S. 821, 826–30 (1994); IBM v. United States, 493 F.2d 112, 115 (2d Cir. 1973).

[60] *See* United States v. United Mine Workers, 330 U.S. 258 (1947); United States v. Work Wear Corp., 602 F.2d 110 (6th Cir. 1979). Moreover, courts have recognized that,

remedial—its purpose is to punish the violator, to vindicate the authority of the court, and to deter others from engaging in similar conduct in the future.[61] Criminal contempt is established under 18 U.S.C. § 401(3) by proving beyond a reasonable doubt that there is a clear and definite order, applicable to the person charged, which was knowingly and willfully disobeyed. The penalty may be a fine or imprisonment, or both.

The Antitrust Division has instituted a number of contempt proceedings to enforce its judgments and will continue to do so where appropriate in the future.[62] In some situations, rather than seeking sanctions for contempt where the correct interpretation of a judgment is disputed, it may be appropriate simply to obtain a court order compelling compliance with the judgment.[63]

---

under appropriate circumstances, other equitable remedies may also be available (for example, compensation for harm or disgorgement of profits as a proxy for harm). In re General Motors Corp., 110 F.3d 1003, 1018 n.16 (4th Cir. 1997).

61 A criminal contempt proceeding may be instituted by indictment, see United States v. Snyder, 428 F.2d 520, 522 (9th Cir. 1970), or by petition following a grand jury investigation, see United States v. General Dynamics Corp., 196 F. Supp. 611 (E.D.N.Y. 1961).

62 *See, e.g., Work Wear Corp.*, 602 F.2d 110; United States v. Greyhound Corp., 508 F.2d 529 (7th Cir. 1974); United States v. Morton Plant Health System, Inc., No. CIV.A. 94-748-CIV-T-23E, 2000 WL 33223244 (M.D. Fla. July 14, 2000); United States v. Smith International, Inc., 2000-1 Trade Cas. ¶ 72,763 (D.D.C. 2000); United States v. North Suburban Multi-List, Inc., 1981-2 Trade Cas. ¶ 64,261 (W.D. Pa. 1981); United States v. FTD Corp., 1996-1 Trade Cas. ¶ 71,395 (E.D. Mich. 1995). *See also* United States v. Microsoft Corp., 147 F.3d 935, 940 (D.C. Cir. 1998); United States v. NYNEX Corp., 8 F.3d 52 (D.C. Cir. 1993).

63 *See, e.g.,* United States v. CBS Inc., 1981-2 Trade Cas. ¶ 64,227 (C.D. Cal. 1981).

PART 4

POLICY STATEMENTS AND AGREEMENTS

18

CORPORATE LENIENCY POLICY, U.S. DEPARTMENT OF JUSTICE

Issued August 10, 1993

The Division has a policy of according leniency to corporations reporting their illegal antitrust activity at an early stage, if they meet certain conditions. "Leniency" means not charging such a firm criminally for the activity being reported. (The policy also is known as the corporate amnesty or corporate immunity policy.)

A. Leniency Before an Investigation Has Begun

Leniency will be granted to a corporation reporting illegal activity before an investigation has begun, if the following six conditions are met:

1. At the time the corporation comes forward to report the illegal activity, the Division has not received information about the illegal activity being reported from any other source;
2. The corporation, upon its discovery of the illegal activity being reported, took prompt and effective action to terminate its part in the activity;
3. The corporation reports the wrongdoing with candor and completeness and provides full, continuing and complete cooperation to the Division throughout the investigation;
4. The confession of wrongdoing is truly a corporate act, as opposed to isolated confessions of individual executives or officials;
5. Where possible, the corporation makes restitution to injured parties; and
6. The corporation did not coerce another party to participate in the illegal activity and clearly was not the leader in, or originator of, the activity.

B. Alternative Requirements for Leniency

If a corporation comes forward to report illegal antitrust activity and does not meet all six of the conditions set out in Part A, above, the corporation, whether it comes forward before or after an investigation has begun, will be granted leniency if the following seven conditions are met:

1. The corporation is the first one to come forward and qualify for leniency with respect to the illegal activity being reported;
2. The Division, at the time the corporation comes in, does not yet have evidence against the company that is likely to result in a sustainable conviction;
3. The corporation, upon its discovery of the illegal activity being reported, took prompt and effective action to terminate its part in the activity;

4. The corporation reports the wrongdoing with candor and completeness and provides full, continuing and complete cooperation that advances the Division in its investigation;
5. The confession of wrongdoing is truly a corporate act, as opposed to isolated confessions of individual executives or officials;
6. Where possible, the corporation makes restitution to injured parties; and
7. The Division determines that granting leniency would not be unfair to others, considering the nature of the illegal activity, the confessing corporation's role in it, and when the corporation comes forward.

   In applying condition 7, the primary considerations will be how early the corporation comes forward and whether the corporation coerced another party to participate in the illegal activity or clearly was the leader in, or originator of, the activity. The burden of satisfying condition 7 will be low if the corporation comes forward before the Division has begun an investigation into the illegal activity. That burden will increase the closer the Division comes to having evidence that is likely to result in a sustainable conviction.

C. Leniency for Corporate Directors, Officers, and Employees

If a corporation qualifies for leniency under Part A, above, all directors, officers, and employees of the corporation who admit their involvement in the illegal antitrust activity as part of the corporate confession will receive leniency, in the form of not being charged criminally for the illegal activity, if they admit their wrongdoing with candor and completeness and continue to assist the Division throughout the investigation.

If a corporation does not qualify for leniency under Part A, above, the directors, officers, and employees who come forward with the corporation will be considered for immunity from criminal prosecution on the same basis as if they had approached the Division individually.

D. Leniency Procedure

If the staff that receives the request for leniency believes the corporation qualifies for and should be accorded leniency, it should forward a favorable recommendation to the Office of Operations, setting forth the reasons why leniency should be granted. Staff should not delay making such a recommendation until a fact memo recommending prosecution of others is prepared. The Director of Operations will review the request and forward it to the Assistant Attorney General for final decision. If the staff recommends against leniency, corporate counsel may wish to seek an appointment with the Director of Operations to make their views known. Counsel are not entitled to such a meeting as a matter of right, but the opportunity will generally be afforded.

19

LENIENCY POLICY FOR INDIVIDUALS, U.S. DEPARTMENT OF JUSTICE

Issued August 10, 1994

On August 10, 1993, the Division announced a new Corporate Leniency Policy under which a corporation can avoid criminal prosecution for antitrust violations by confessing its role in the illegal activities, fully cooperating with the Division, and meeting the other specified conditions. The Corporate Leniency Policy also sets out the conditions under which the directors, officers and employees who come forward with the company, confess, and cooperate will be considered for individual leniency. The Division today announces a new Leniency Policy for Individuals that is effective immediately and applies to all individuals who approach the Division on their own behalf, not as part of a corporate proffer or confession, to seek leniency for reporting illegal antitrust activity of which the Division has not previously been made aware. Under this Policy, "leniency" means not charging such an individual criminally for the activity being reported.

A. Requirements for Leniency for Individuals

Leniency will be granted to an individual reporting illegal antitrust activity before an investigation has begun, if the following three conditions are met:

1. At the time the individual comes forward to report the illegal activity, the Division has not received information about the illegal activity being reported from any other source;
2. The individual reports the wrongdoing with candor and completeness and provides full, continuing and complete cooperation to the Division throughout the investigation; and
3. The individual did not coerce another party to participate in the illegal activity and clearly was not the leader in, or originator of, the activity.

B. Applicability of the Policy

Any individual who does not qualify for leniency under Part A of this Policy will be considered for statutory or informal immunity from criminal prosecution. Such immunity decisions will be made by the Division on a case-by-case basis in the exercise of its prosecutorial discretion.

If a corporation attempts to qualify for leniency under the Corporate Leniency Policy, any directors, officers or employees who come forward and confess with the corporation will be considered for leniency solely under the provisions of the Corporate Leniency Policy.

C. Leniency Procedure

If the staff that receives the request for leniency believes the individual qualifies for and should be accorded leniency, it should forward a favorable recommendation to the Deputy Assistant Attorney General for Litigation, setting forth the reasons why leniency should be granted. The staff should not delay making such a recommendation until a fact memo recommending prosecution of others is prepared. The Deputy Assistant Attorney General for Litigation will review the request and forward it to the Assistant Attorney General for final decision. If the staff recommends against leniency, the individual and his or her counsel may wish to seek an appointment with the Deputy Assistant Attorney General for Litigation to make their views known. Individuals and their counsel are not entitled to such a meeting as a matter of right, but the opportunity will generally be afforded.

20

PROTOCOL FOR COORDINATION IN MERGER INVESTIGATIONS BETWEEN THE FEDERAL ENFORCEMENT AGENCIES AND STATE ATTORNEYS GENERAL

(1998)

Some mergers and acquisitions may become subject to simultaneous federal and state investigations by either the Antitrust Division of the U.S. Department of Justice ("Antitrust Division") or the Federal Trade Commission ("FTC"), and one or more State Attorneys General. To the extent lawful, practicable and desirable in the circumstances of a particular case, the Antitrust Division or the FTC and the State Attorneys General will cooperate in analyzing the merger. This protocol is intended to set forth a general framework for the conduct of joint investigations with the goals of maximizing cooperation between the federal and state enforcement agencies and minimizing the burden on the parties.

I. CONFIDENTIALITY

These joint investigations are generally nonpublic in nature and will routinely involve materials and information that are subject to statutes, rules, and policies governing when and how they may be disclosed. Participating agencies are required to protect confidential information and materials ("confidential information") from improper disclosure. Confidentiality obligations continue even if a receiving agency subsequently decides to pursue an enforcement avenue different from that chosen by one or more of the other agencies.

Agencies receiving confidential information from another agency ("the originating agency") will agree to take all appropriate steps to maintain its confidentiality, including:

1. timely notification to the originating agency of discovery requests or public access requests for that information;
2. a vigorous assertion of all privileges or exemptions from disclosure claimed by the originating agency;
3. intervention in legal proceedings, or provision of assistance to the originating agency in intervening in legal proceedings, if necessary, to assert such privileges or exemptions; and
4. complying with any conditions imposed by an agency that shares information it deems to be confidential.

Any agency that becomes aware that confidential information has been disclosed in contravention of this Protocol will promptly advise all other agencies conducting the joint investigation of the disclosure so that its significance and implications for further information-sharing can be assessed.

II. PROCEDURES INVOLVING THE MERGING PARTIES

The merging parties may be required to produce documents or other information to the Antitrust Division or FTC pursuant to the Hart-Scott-Rodino Antitrust Improvements Act of 1976 ("HSR Act"), Civil Investigative Demands, or other compulsory process, and to State Attorneys General pursuant to subpoena or other compulsory process. To minimize the burden on the merging parties and to expedite review of the transaction, the merging parties may wish to facilitate coordination between the enforcement agencies.

The Antitrust Division and the FTC will, with the consent of the merging parties, provide certain otherwise confidential information to State Attorneys General. The acquiring and acquired persons in the transaction must:

A. agree to provide the states, according to the National Association of Attorneys General Voluntary Premerger Disclosure Compact, or otherwise, all information submitted to the Antitrust Division or the FTC pursuant to the HSR Act, Civil Investigative Demands, or other compulsory process, or voluntarily; and

B. submit a letter to the Antitrust Division or the FTC that waives the confidentiality provisions under applicable statutes and regulations to allow communications between the Antitrust Division or FTC and State Attorneys General.[1]

Where these requirements have been satisfied, the Antitrust Division or FTC will provide to the state investigating the merger or, if there is a multistate working group, to the coordinating state:[2]

1. copies of requests for additional information issued pursuant to the HSR Act ("second requests");
2. copies of civil investigative demands issued pursuant to the Antitrust Civil Process Act and
3. copies of subpoenas and civil investigative demands issued by the FTC; and
4. the expiration dates of applicable waiting periods under the HSR Act.

III. <u>CONDUCT OF JOINT INVESTIGATION</u>

The following is intended to set forth suggested guidelines that may be followed to coordinate merger investigations by State Attorneys General and the FTC or Antitrust Division. All applicable investigatory, work product, or other privileges shall apply to any material exchanged.

---

[1] Examples of such a letter are annexed hereto as Exhibit 1.

[2] Pursuant to the NAAG Voluntary Pre-Merger Disclosure Compact, the merging parties may reduce their burden of complying with multiple state subpoenas by providing a set of all required materials to the designated "liaison state." The role of the liaison state is ministerial in nature. It differs from that of the "coordinating state," which is responsible for coordinating the investigation and any resulting litigation. The differences between the roles of the liaison and coordinating states are described more fully in the memorandum annexed hereto as Exhibit 2. Depending on the investigation, these roles may be performed by the same state or different states.

PROTOCOL FOR COORDINATION IN MERGER INVESTIGATIONS

A. STRATEGIC PLANNING

Coordination between federal and state enforcement agencies may be most effective at the earliest possible stage of a joint investigation. It should begin with an initial conference call among the FTC or Antitrust Division and State Attorneys General. To the extent lawful, practicable, and desirable in the circumstances of a particular case, subjects of the conference calls should include:

1. Identification of lawyers and other legal and economic team members working on the case, and assignment of areas of responsibility.
2. Identification of potential legal and economic theories of the case to be developed and assignment of research projects. It may be appropriate for state and federal enforcers to share memoranda, papers and/or briefs prepared in similar prior matters with appropriate redactions for confidential information, as well as those prepared during the current investigation to the extent permitted by the participating agencies.
3. Identification of categories of data, documents, and witness testimony needed to be obtained, and strategies for obtaining and sharing such information, including to the extent lawful, practicable, and desirable, the initiation of requests seeking the consent of past and future submitters to disclosure of such information. State Attorneys General should particularly be encouraged to take responsibility for obtaining data located within their respective geographic areas or maintained by state or local governmental agencies.
4. Identification of potential consulting economists or other experts.
5. Where multiple states are involved, understandings should be reached on how information can be most conveniently exchanged. For example, the coordinating state might assume responsibility for transmitting documents received from the FTC or Antitrust Division to other State Attorneys General.

B. DOCUMENT PRODUCTION

Coordinating both the request for, and review of, documentary materials can reduce the parties' burden and facilitate the agencies' investigation. To the extent lawful, practicable, and desirable, three steps should be taken in connection with issuing a second request or subpoenas, CID's, or voluntary requests for information from the merging parties or third parties:

1. Consideration of ideas from other investigating agencies on the content and scope of the request.
2. Providing correspondence to other investigating agencies memorializing agreements with parties to narrow or eliminate request specifications.
3. Division of responsibility among investigating agencies for document review and exchange of summaries and indices.

C. WITNESS EVIDENCE/EXPERTS

To the extent lawful, practicable, and desirable in a particular case, the State Attorneys General and the FTC or Antitrust Division should coordinate the joint development of testimonial evidence. The investigating agencies should try to integrate their efforts to the maximum extent possible. Specifically:

1. Identification and development of lists of potential interviewees/deponents should be undertaken in a coordinated manner. States should be encouraged to use their greater familiarity with local conditions/business to identify interviewees and schedule interviews.
2. Joint interviews and/or depositions of witnesses should be coordinated whenever lawful, practicable and desirable. An early understanding should be reached regarding the extent to which notes of interviews will be maintained and exchanged. Coordination of deposition summaries should also be discussed.
3. State Attorneys General and the FTC or the Antitrust Division should coordinate responsibility for the securing of declarations or affidavits.
4. State Attorneys General and the FTC or the Antitrust Division should discuss early during a joint investigation whether to employ experts jointly or separately. If the latter, a method should be provided for exchange of economic views/theories among the experts and with staff economists. The preparation of expert affidavits/testimony should be closely coordinated.

IV. SETTLEMENT DISCUSSIONS

To achieve the full benefits of cooperation it is imperative that federal and state antitrust enforcement agencies collaborate closely with respect to the settlement process. While each federal and state governmental entity is fully sovereign and independent, an optimal settlement is most likely to be achieved if negotiations with the merging parties are conducted, to the maximum extent possible, in a unified, coordinated manner.

It will normally be desirable for federal and state enforcement agencies to consult on settlement terms in advance of any meeting with the merging parties where settlement is likely to be discussed. Where possible, any such meeting should be attended by both federal and state representatives. Furthermore, each enforcement agency should keep the other enforcement agencies advised of communications regarding settlement with a merging party.

If any federal or state antitrust enforcement agency determines that circumstances require it to pursue a negotiation or settlement strategy different from that of the other investigating agencies, or decides to close its investigation, it should disclose that fact immediately.

V. STATEMENTS TO THE PRESS

It is important that understandings be reached between the enforcement agencies regarding the release of information to the news media. These agreements should cover the timing of and procedures for notifying the other enforcement agencies prior to the release of any information to the press.

EXHIBIT 1A

To: Assistant Director for Premerger Notification
Bureau of Competition
Federal Trade Commission
Washington, D.C. 20580

With respect to [the proposed acquisition of X Corp. by Y Corp.] the undersigned attorney or corporate officer, acting on behalf of [indicate entity], hereby waives confidentiality protections under the Hart-Scott-Rodino Act, 15 U.S.C. 18a(h), the Federal Trade Commission Act, 15 U.S.C. §§ 41 et seq., and the Federal Trade Commission's Rules of Practice, 16 C.F.R. §§ 4.9 et seq., insofar as these protections in any way limit confidential communications between the Federal Trade Commission and the Attorney(s) General of [insert pertinent State(s)].

Signed:____________________
Position: ____________________
Telephone: ____________________

EXHIBIT 1B

To: Director of Operations
Antitrust Division
Department of Justice
Tenth Street and Pennsylvania Avenue, N.W.
Washington, D.C. 20530

With respect to [the proposed acquisition of X Corp. by Y Corp.] the undersigned attorney or corporate officer, acting on behalf of [indicate entity], hereby waives confidentiality protections under the Hart-Scott-Rodino Act, 15 U.S.C. 18a(h), the Antitrust Civil Process Act, 15 U.S.C. §§ 1311 et seq., and any other applicable confidentiality provisions, for the purpose of allowing the United States Department of Justice and the Attorney(s) General of [insert pertinent State(s)] to share documents, information and analyses.

Signed:____________________
Position: ____________________
Telephone: ____________________

EXHIBIT 2

CORRESPONDENCE/MEMORANDUM
DEPARTMENT OF JUSTICE

Date: September 6, 1996

To: Antitrust Contacts

From: Kevin J. O'Connor
Assistant Attorney General

Subject: Memorandum of Clarification of Liaison and Coordinating States Under the NAAG Voluntary Pre-Merger Disclosure Compact

As our experience with the NAAG Voluntary Pre-Merger Disclosure Compact ("Compact") grows, additional questions concerning its application inevitably arise. The purpose of this memo is to clarify the distinction between the "liaison state" under the Compact and any multistate working groups or litigating groups which may be formed to deal with a matter that is the subject of a filing under the Compact.

LIAISON STATE

The function of the liaison state under the Compact is to receive the filing and to notify forthwith all signatories to the Compact of the filing and the identity of the merging parties. Upon request, the liaison state must permit signatories of the Compact to inspect the documents or obtain a photocopy of the filing from the liaison state. In short, the liaison state serves a ministerial function of receiving and distributing, upon request, copies of the confidential filings of the prospectively merging parties.[3]

COORDINATING STATE

In certain cases, two or more states may investigate or litigate regarding a particular transaction. This may occur whether or not the Compact has been invoked. As is the case with any Multistate Antitrust Task Force Working Group, the process of joint investigation and litigation operates largely by consensus. Although each enforcement agency retains its sovereignty, the synergies achievable from a joint investigation can only be realized if the states share a common interest in goals and process and organize effectively. Typically, the states most directly, and adversely, impacted by a proposed transaction, will take the lead in such investigations provided they have the resources to do so.

Chair Selection: Where a group of investigating states decides to work together, it will often be desirable to have a coordinating or "chair" state. The coordinating or "chair" state should be determined by the states actively involved in the investigation and litigation after consultation with the Chair of the Multistate Antitrust Task Force. The criteria for choosing a "coordinating state" should include, for example, whether the prospective chair state is (a) likely to be adversely affected by a proposed transaction,

---

[3] The Compact lists the order of preference for identifying the liaison state upon whom the merging parties may serve a copy of their filings. This order of preference includes: First, the principal place of business of the acquiring party to the merger; second, the attorney general of the state which is the principal place of business of the acquired party; third, the attorney general of the state of incorporation of the acquiring party; and, fourth, the attorney general of the state of incorporation of the acquired party. If no member of the Compact falls within the foregoing four preferences, the parties may make a filing upon the chair of the Multistate Antitrust Task Force or any other member of the Compact who is willing to act as liaison state for such transaction.

(b) is in a position to commit resources to the investigation, and (c) can coordinate effectively with the other states and the federal agencies that may be involved in reviewing the same transaction. Under these criteria, the state assuming the role of coordinating state is not necessarily the same state identified by the Compact as the state undertaking the largely ministerial duties set forth in the Compact.

Chair Function: The function of the coordinating state shall be to coordinate the investigative and enforcement activities of the working group states, to coordinate with any federal agency collaborating with the states, and to facilitate settlement discussions. Again, because this is largely a consensual process, the coordinating state should do all of the above in consultation with the other investigating states and federal agencies.

Settlement Negotiations: Because merger investigations often occur in a very short time frame, and because the issue of settlement is often raised during that time frame, it is imperative that the coordinating states and the investigating federal agency consult and collaborate early and often regarding terms and process of settlement. The interested enforcement agencies are more likely to achieve an optimal resolution by presenting the merging parties, to the maximum extent feasible, with a united front. If an individual enforcement agency, state or federal, determines that its interests require pursuing a negotiation or settlement strategy separate from the cooperating states and federal agencies, it is incumbent upon that agency to disclose its posture at the earliest possible opportunity and to implement its strategy in a way which minimizes any adverse impact upon the other states and enforcement agencies.

21

PROTOCOL TO EXPEDITE REVIEW PROCESS FOR TERMINATING OR MODIFYING OLDER ANTITRUST DECREES

ANTITRUST DIVISION, U.S. DEPARTMENT OF JUSTICE

April 13, 1999

ANTITRUST DIVISION ANNOUNCES NEW STREAMLINED PROCEDURE FOR PARTIES SEEKING TO MODIFY OR TERMINATE OLD SETTLEMENTS AND LITIGATED JUDGMENTS

Procedure Will Lower Costs and Expedite Review for Parties

WASHINGTON—The Department of Justice's Antitrust Division today announced a new streamlined procedure that will lower the costs and expedite the review process for parties seeking to modify or terminate old antitrust settlements and litigated judgments.

The new voluntary procedure, which is effective immediately, updates a 1999 protocol. The expedited process can be used by parties seeking to modify or terminate perpetual decrees—settlements and litigated judgments—entered prior to 1980.

In 1979, the department determined that entering into perpetual decrees was not in the public interest. Since that time, decrees have included "sunset" provisions that will automatically terminate them after a term of years, not to exceed 10 years. Most decrees entered into before 1980 do not contain this provision.

"The new streamlined procedure will expedite the review process for legacy decrees and will benefit both the defendants and the department by eliminating costly and time intensive investigations," said Bill Baer, Assistant Attorney General in charge of the Department of Justice's Antitrust Division. "The Antitrust Division will continue to look for ways to incorporate procedural efficiencies whenever possible as it is an important part of effective antitrust enforcement."

Pre-1980 perpetual decrees cannot be terminated or modified except by court order. Since 1980, there have been significant changes in markets and technology and substantial changes in antitrust law. Going forward, the department will advise courts that pre-1980 "legacy" decrees, except in limited circumstances, are presumptively no longer in the public interest. Those limited circumstances may include when there is a long-standing reliance by industry participants on the decree.

The updated procedure differs from the present procedure in two important ways. First, the party seeking termination or modification will no longer be subject to the extensive discovery that was required by the 1999 protocol. This should result in a substantial reduction in the cost of seeking decree termination. Second, when responding to a request to terminate or modify qualifying legacy decrees, the department will no longer conduct an in-depth investigation into the relevant markets due to the significant changes that have taken place. The updated procedure can be found in the Division Manual on the Antitrust Division's website.

Under the protocol, the requesting party will publish, at its own expense, notice of its intent to seek termination or modification and invite interested parties to provide the Antitrust Division with relevant information. The division will work with the requesting party to determine what form of cost-effective notice is appropriate. Because the process is expedited, the division believes that a pre-filing public comment period best serves the public interest by allowing interested parties to come forward early in the process so that their concerns may be considered and addressed prior to the filing of a motion to modify or terminate. The division will take into account issues that are brought to its attention and address them as appropriate. Other parts of the 1999 protocol will remain in effect.

DIVISION MANUAL

5. Judgment Modifications and Terminations

Perpetual final judgments, whether litigated judgments or consent decrees, were the norm from the early days of the Sherman Act until 1979, when the Division announced that future settlements would have "Sunset" provisions that would automatically terminate a decree on a date certain, usually after a period of 10 years. The 1979 change in policy was based on a judgment that perpetual decrees were not in the public interest. In 1994, the FTC made a similar judgment, and announced a policy of using sunset provisions. It also, through rulemaking, terminated all of its competition orders 20 years after entry of the order. The Division's final judgments, in contrast, constitute court orders and can only be modified or terminated by the relevant court.

In considering the modification or termination of final judgments, the Division distinguishes between decrees with sunset provisions and pre-1980, perpetual decrees ("legacy decrees"). Decrees with sunset provisions all have terms of no more than 10 years. They have been entered by courts after an APPA proceeding and "public interest" finding and presumptively remain in the public interest. Attorneys assigned to such decrees for enforcement purposes should, however, consider whether the decree has become, in whole or in part, anticompetitive or otherwise undesirable. If so, consideration should be given to opening an investigation into possible modification or termination of the decree, consistent with the Division's resource availability.

With some exceptions, there is no such presumption that legacy decrees remain in the public interest. The Division has said in briefs supporting the termination of legacy decrees that such decrees should presumptively be terminated except in limited circumstances, such as when there is a pattern of noncompliance with the decree or there is longstanding reliance by industry participants on the decree. *See, e.g.,* http://www.justice.gov/atr/cases/f273400/273471.pdf. Although the Division has supported terminating many legacy decrees, it routinely conducted a full investigation into possible changes in the market or law even when it believed that the decree should be presumptively terminated.

PROTOCOL TO EXPEDITE REVIEW PROCESS FOR TERMINATING OR MODIFYING OLDER ANTITRUST DECREES

In 1999, the Division announced a protocol to expedite the review process for legacy decrees because the length of the investigative process discouraged firms from seeking the termination of legacy decrees. The 1999 press release noted: "In the past, when the Division has agreed to support termination or modification, it has taken on average about two years between the party's initial request and the filing of the motion." Under the protocol, parties provided specific information up-front (essentially the information that the Division typically sought in its review) and published a notice of an intent to seek termination and solicit public comments. The 1999 protocol, however, did not significantly expedite decree termination reviews or reduce burdens on legacy defendants. Parties were subject to significant discovery and Division staff reviewed termination requests closely in order to explain to courts in detail why specific legacy decrees were no longer needed.

On March 28, 2014, the Division announced that it was updating its procedures for terminating or modifying qualifying legacy decrees to reduce the burden on defendants by no longer requiring them to submit detailed information and documents required by the 1999 protocol. Instead, the parties would certify that they are in compliance with the decree and have disclosed all known violations; they will notify other defendants bound by the decree; and will publish notification of their intent to seek termination or modification. Under the new procedure, absent information that leads the Division to decide that the requested decree termination or modification should not receive fast track review, the Division will support modification or termination of qualifying legacy decrees at the end of the public comment period on the basis that the decree presumptively is not in the public interest.

The 2014 update, therefore, creates two separate paths to decree modification and termination. The expedited path for qualifying legacy decrees is designed to be quick and to eliminate the burdens on the Division and the defendants of full investigation and discovery. The second path, for decrees with sunset provisions and when the Division believes that a legacy decree should not receive expedited review retains the traditional approach. Questions about whether the Division will likely use a fast track review for a specific judgment should be addressed to the appropriate section chief.

a. Obtaining Approval to Consent to Modification or Termination of Qualifying Legacy Decrees

i. Initiation of the Process

When a legacy judgment defendant asks the Division to terminate or modify its qualifying decree, the section or office should promptly request that the judgment defendant certify that they are in compliance with the decree and have disclosed all known decree violations; a commitment to notify other defendants bound by the decree that it is seeking termination or modification; and a commitment to pay the costs of Division-approved, appropriate public notices of the proposed judgment termination or modification. Ordinarily, publication should appear in the relevant trade press and The Wall Street Journal, but the Division will coordinate with the moving defendant to ensure cost-effective public notice. Staff should be clear that the publication costs for such notices are borne by the defendant and are not trivial. After receipt of a satisfactory response to the request, staff should submit a brief memorandum requesting preliminary investigation authority.

As soon as preliminary investigation authority is received and the Division has clearance from the FTC, the requesting defendant should inform other defendants bound by the decree and publish the Division-approved, appropriate notices. Ordinarily, the public comment period will be set for 30 days. In addition to the defendant's notice publication, the Division also voluntarily publishes on its Internet site a notice of the request to modify or terminate the judgment. The notice should summarize the Division's complaint and the Court's final judgment, provide links to the underlying relevant papers, and invite public comments.

ii. Recommendation, Review, and Applicable Standards

Under the expedited review process, absent information that leads the Division to decide that the requested termination or modification should not receive fast track review, staff should prepare a brief memorandum, concurred in by the General Counsel, setting forth its recommendation on whether to consent to terminate or modify the decree. The recommendation should be sent for review and processing to the Director of Civil Enforcement, who will obtain the concurrence of the DAAG for Operations, any Assigned DAAG, and the approval of the Assistant Attorney General. The memorandum should briefly describe the process followed to obtain public comments, describe any comments received from the public, evaluate whether the comments should remove the proposed modification or termination from fast-track approval, and evaluate whether a response to the comments should be filed with the court

iii. Necessary Papers

If staff's recommendation is to modify or terminate a decree, the recommendation memorandum should be accompanied by the following papers:

- A draft stipulation package, consisting of the Government's tentative consent to termination of the decree (prepared for the signatures of staff, the chief, the Director of Civil Enforcement, the General Counsel, the DAAG for Operations, any Assigned DAAG, the Assistant Attorney General, and the defendants) and an attached proposed order terminating or modifying the decree (designated as Exhibit A).

  (In some jurisdictions the stipulation and order may be combined in one pleading, depending upon the local rules.)

- A draft response to the decree defendant's memorandum of points and authorities that includes an explanation to the Court of the pre-filing public comment period.
- A draft Department press release.
- The public comments received by the Division and a draft response to such comments.

Samples of each of these documents are available from the FOIA/PA Unit and are available on ATRnet. Since these exemplars are subject to revision over time, particularly the Division's response, staff should consult with the General Counsel to ensure that they have current exemplars before preparing the necessary papers.

The defendant should likewise prepare its motion explaining to the Court why the decree should be terminated or modified. Further, where the Division is not aware of any violation of the decree, and the defendant asserts that it knows of no violations of the judgment, an officer of the defendant must attest to that effect. Before the Division's response is finalized, the moving defendant needs to provide its motion and supporting materials to the relevant section.

iv. Review, Filing, and Other Procedural Aspects

The final papers, approved by the General Counsel, including the stipulation already agreed to by the defendants, should be sent to the Director of Civil Enforcement to review and process the papers through the Assigned DAAG and the General Counsel, obtain authorization from the Assistant Attorney General, and then return them to staff.

Staff must coordinate the filing of the papers with the Office of Operations to ensure that the Office of Public Affairs has sufficient lead time to finalize a press release if it wishes to issue one. The actual filing process will vary depending on the jurisdiction, although normally it may be accomplished electronically.

The Division will recommend that a hearing not be held on the termination or modification motion of a qualifying legacy decree. Further, although the Division will not object if interested persons apply to appear as *amici curiae*, it will generally object vigorously if they attempt to intervene as parties.

b. Obtaining Approval to Consent to Modification or Termination of Decrees Containing Sunset provisions and Nonqualifying Legacy Decrees

i. Initiation of the Process

When a defendant to a judgment with sunset provisions or a nonqualifying legacy judgment asks the Division to terminate or modify its decree, the section or office should promptly request from each judgment defendant:

1. A detailed explanation as to (a) why the judgment should be vacated or modified, including information as to changes in circumstances or law that make the judgment inequitable or obsolete, and (b) the actual anticompetitive or other harmful effects of the judgment.
2. A statement of the changes, if any, in its method of operations or doing business that the defendant contemplates in the event that the judgment is vacated or modified.

3. A commitment to pay the costs of appropriate public notices in the trade press and The Wall Street Journal, or as may otherwise be required by the Division, in connection with the proposed termination or modification of the judgment. Staff should make clear to the defendant that the publication costs for such notices are borne by the defendant and are not trivial.

After receipt of a satisfactory response to the request, staff should submit a brief memorandum requesting preliminary investigation authority.

As soon as preliminary investigation authority is received and the Division has clearance from the FTC, an investigation, under the oversight of the General Counsel, should commence to determine whether termination or modification is in the public interest. At that time, the requesting defendant should inform other defendants bound by the decree and ensure the publication of the Division-approved, appropriate notices. In addition to the defendant's notice publication, the Division also voluntarily publishes on its Internet site a brief notice of the request to modify or terminate. The notice should summarize the Division's complaint and the Court's final judgment, provide links to the underlying relevant papers, and invite public comments.

ii. Recommendation, Review, and Applicable Standards

At the conclusion of the investigation, staff should prepare a memorandum, concurred in by the General Counsel, setting forth its recommendation on whether the Division should consent to terminate or modify the decree. The recommendation shall be sent for review and processing to the Director of Civil Enforcement, who will obtain the concurrence of the DAAG for Operations, any Assigned DAAG, and the approval of the Assistant Attorney General. For decrees with sunset provisions and for legacy decrees not eligible for fast track treatment, the Division will usually give its consent when changed circumstances in the industry render previously neutral provisions anticompetitive, such as when the decree unnecessarily prohibits a defendant from using efficient marketing techniques that (1) are available to other firms in the market and (2) would not today restrain competition. The Division is less likely to support termination of a decree if there are recent decree violations.

iii. Necessary Papers

If staff's recommendation is to modify or terminate a decree, its recommendation memorandum should be accompanied by the following papers:

- A draft stipulation package, consisting of the Government's tentative consent to termination or modification of the decree (prepared for the signatures of staff, the chief, the Director of Civil Enforcement, the General Counsel, the DAAG for Operations, the Assigned DAAG, the Assistant Attorney General, and the defendants) and the following attachments:

a. A form of notice to be printed in newspapers and periodicals (designated as Exhibit A).

b. A proposed order directing publication of the notice (designated as Exhibit B).

c. The proposed order terminating or modifying the decree (designated as Exhibit C).

(In some jurisdictions the stipulation and order may be combined in one pleading, depending upon the local rules.)

- A draft Division response to the decree defendant's memorandum of points and authorities.
- A draft Department press release.
- The public comments received by the Department during the investigation and a draft response to such comments.

Samples of each of these documents are available from the FOIA/PA Unit and are available on ATRnet. Since these exemplars are subject to revision over time, particularly the Division's response, staff should consult with the General Counsel to ensure that they have current exemplars before preparing the necessary papers.

The Division's response should also recommend whether the Court should rely on the prefiling notice and comment period in making its public interest determination that modification or termination are in the public interest or whether an additional notice and comment period may be beneficial to the Court's review. The Division is likely to recommend reliance on the prefiling notice and comment period when the modification or termination is not controversial and the Division has received no significant public comments or when the papers are filed shortly after the end of the original prefiling comment period.

The defendant should likewise prepare its motion explaining to the Court why the decree should be terminated or modified. Further, where the Division is not aware of any violation of the decree, and the defendant asserts that it knows of no violations of the judgment, an officer of the defendant must attest to that effect.

iv. Review, Filing, and Other Procedural Aspects

The final papers, approved by the General Counsel, including the stipulation already agreed to by the defendants, should be sent to the Director of Civil Enforcement to review and process the final papers through the Assigned DAAG and the General Counsel, obtain authorization from the Assistant Attorney General, and then return them to staff.

Staff must coordinate the filing of the papers with the Office of Operations to ensure that the Office of Public Affairs has sufficient lead time to finalize a press release if it wishes to issue one. The actual filing process will vary depending on the jurisdiction, although normally it may be accomplished electronically.

The Division will recommend that a hearing be held on the termination or modification motion, only when it appears that it would be useful to the Court's public interest determination. Further, although the Division will not object if interested persons apply to appear as *amici curiae*, it will generally object vigorously if they attempt to intervene as parties.

v. Notice, Publication Costs, and Multiple Defendants

If the Division recommends an additional comment period, or the Court otherwise orders an additional comment period, the notice requesting public comment should generally appear in two consecutive issues of (1) the national edition of The Wall Street Journal, and (2) the principal trade periodical serving the industry to which the decree relates, or as may otherwise be required by the Division. If the decree affects more than one industry, the notice should appear in the principal journal for each of the industries involved.

In addition to the defendant's notice publication, the Division may also voluntarily publish on its Internet site a brief notice of the motion to modify or terminate. The notice should summarize the Division's complaint and the Court's final judgment, provide links to the relevant underlying papers, and invite comments.

In cases that involve multiple defendants, it is Division policy to request the nonmoving defendants to provide the Division with affidavits similar to that prepared by the moving defendant (including the sworn statement of compliance with the decree), and if they do so, to insist that the notice published by the moving defendant recite the Division's consent to termination of the decree as to the other defendants.

22

STATEMENTS OF ANTITRUST ENFORCEMENT POLICY IN HEALTH CARE

DEPARTMENT OF JUSTICE AND FEDERAL TRADE COMMISSION

August 1996

DEPARTMENT OF JUSTICE AND FEDERAL TRADE COMMISSION STATEMENTS OF ANTITRUST ENFORCEMENT POLICY IN HEALTH CARE

TABLE OF CONTENTS

INTRODUCTION

In September 1993, the Department of Justice and the Federal Trade Commission (the "Agencies") issued six statements of their antitrust enforcement policies regarding mergers and various joint activities in the health care area. The six policy statements addressed:

1. hospital mergers;
2. hospital joint ventures involving high-technology or other expensive medical equipment;

3. physicians' provision of information to purchasers of health care services;
4. hospital participation in exchanges of price and cost information;
5. health care providers' joint purchasing arrangements; and
6. physician network joint ventures.

The Agencies also committed to issuing expedited Department of Justice business reviews and Federal Trade Commission advisory opinions in response to requests for antitrust guidance on specific proposed conduct involving the health care industry.

The 1993 policy statements and expedited specific Agency guidance were designed to advise the health care community in a time of tremendous change, and to address, as completely as possible, the problem of uncertainty concerning the Agencies' enforcement policy that some had said might deter mergers, joint ventures, or other activities that could lower health care costs. Sound antitrust enforcement, of course, continued to protect consumers against anticompetitive activities.

When the Agencies issued the 1993 health care antitrust enforcement policy statements, they recognized that additional guidance might be desirable in the areas covered by those statements as well as in other health care areas, and committed to issuing revised and additional policy statements as warranted. In light of the comments the Agencies received on the 1993 statements and the Agencies' own experience, the Agencies revised and expanded the health care antitrust enforcement policy statements in September 1994. The 1994 statements, which superseded the 1993 statements, added new statements addressing hospital joint ventures involving specialized clinical or other expensive health care services, providers' collective provision of fee-related information to purchasers of health care services, and analytical principles relating to a broad range of health care provider networks (termed "multiprovider networks"), and expanded the antitrust "safety zones" for several other statements.

Since issuance of the 1994 statements, health care markets have continued to evolve in response to consumer demand and competition in the marketplace. New arrangements and variations on existing arrangements involving joint activity by health care providers continue to emerge to meet consumers', purchasers', and payers' desire for more efficient delivery of high quality health care services. During this period, the Agencies have gained additional experience with arrangements involving joint provider activity. As a result of these developments, the Agencies have decided to amplify the enforcement policy statement on physician network joint ventures and the more general statement on multiprovider networks.

In these revised statements, the Agencies continue to analyze all types of health care provider networks under general antitrust principles. These principles are sufficiently flexible to take into account the particular characteristics of health care markets and the rapid changes that are occurring in those markets. The Agencies emphasize that it is not their intent to treat such networks either more strictly or more leniently than joint ventures in other industries, or to favor any particular procompetitive organization or structure of health care delivery over other forms that consumers may desire. Rather, their goal is to ensure a competitive marketplace in which consumers will have the benefit of high quality, cost-effective health care and a wide range of choices, including new provider-controlled networks that expand consumer choice and increase competition.

STATEMENTS OF ANTITRUST ENFORCEMENT POLICY IN HEALTH CARE

The revisions to the statements on physician network joint ventures and multiprovider networks are summarized below. In addition to these revisions, various changes have been made to the language of both statements to improve their clarity. No revisions have been made to any of the other statements.

Physician Network Joint Ventures

The revised statement on physician network joint ventures provides an expanded discussion of the antitrust principles that apply to such ventures. The revisions focus on the analysis of networks that fall outside the safety zones contained in the existing statement, particularly those networks that do not involve the sharing of substantial financial risk by their physician participants. The revised statement explains that where physicians' integration through the network is likely to produce significant efficiencies, any agreements on price reasonably necessary to accomplish the venture's procompetitive benefits will be analyzed under the rule of reason.

The revised statement adds three hypothetical examples to further illustrate the application of these principles: (1) a physician network joint venture that does not involve the sharing of substantial financial risk, but receives rule of reason treatment due to the extensive integration among its physician participants; (2) a network that involves both risk-sharing and non-risk-sharing activities, and receives rule of reason treatment; and (3) a network that involves little or no integration among its physician participants, and is per se illegal.

The safety zones for physician network joint ventures remain unchanged, but the revised statement identifies additional types of financial risk-sharing arrangements that can qualify a network for the safety zones. It also further emphasizes two points previously made in the 1994 statements. First, the enumeration in the statements of particular examples of substantial financial risk sharing does not foreclose consideration of other arrangements through which physicians may share substantial financial risk. Second, a physician network that falls outside the safety zones is not necessarily anticompetitive.

Multiprovider Networks

In 1994, the Agencies issued a new statement on multiprovider health care networks that described the general antitrust analysis of such networks. The revised statement on multiprovider networks emphasizes that it is intended to articulate general principles relating to a wide range of health care provider networks. Many of the revisions to this statement reflect changes made to the revised statement on physician network joint ventures. In addition, four hypothetical examples involving PHOs ("physician-hospital organizations"), including one involving "messenger model" arrangements, have been added.

Safety Zones and Hypothetical Examples

Most of the nine statements give health care providers guidance in the form of antitrust safety zones, which describe conduct that the Agencies will not challenge under the antitrust laws, absent extraordinary circumstances. The Agencies are aware that some parties have interpreted the safety zones as defining the limits of joint conduct that is permissible under the antitrust laws. This view is incorrect. The inclusion of certain conduct within the antitrust safety zones does not imply that conduct falling outside the safety zones is likely to be challenged by the Agencies. Antitrust analysis is inherently fact-intensive. The safety zones are designed to require consideration of only a few factors that are relatively easy to apply, and to provide the Agencies with a high degree of confidence that arrangements falling within them are unlikely to raise substantial competitive concerns. Thus, the safety zones encompass only a subset of provider arrangements that the Agencies are unlikely to challenge under the antitrust laws. The statements outline the analysis the Agencies will use to review conduct that falls outside the safety zones.

Likewise, the statements' hypothetical examples concluding that the Agencies would not challenge the particular arrangement do not mean that conduct varying from the examples is likely to be challenged by the Agencies. The hypothetical examples are designed to illustrate how the statements' general principles apply to specific situations. Interested parties should examine the business review letters issued by the Department of Justice and the advisory opinions issued by the Federal Trade Commission and its staff for additional guidance on the application and interpretation of these statements. Copies of those letters and opinions and summaries of the letters and opinions are available from the Agencies at the mailing and Internet addresses listed at the end of the statements.

The statements also set forth the Department of Justice's business review procedure and the Federal Trade Commission's advisory opinion procedure under which the health care community can obtain the Agencies' antitrust enforcement intentions regarding specific proposed conduct on an expedited basis. The statements continue the commitment of the Agencies to respond to requests for business reviews or advisory opinions from the health care community no later than 90 days after all necessary information is received regarding any matter addressed in the statements, except requests relating to hospital mergers outside the antitrust safety zone and multiprovider networks. The Agencies also will respond to business review or advisory opinion requests regarding multiprovider networks or other non-merger health care matters within 120 days after all necessary information is received. The Agencies intend to work closely with persons making requests to clarify what information is necessary and to provide guidance throughout the process. The Agencies continue this commitment to expedited review in an effort to reduce antitrust uncertainty for the health care industry in what the Agencies recognize is a time of fundamental change.

The Agencies recognize the importance of antitrust guidance in evolving health care contexts. Consequently, the Agencies continue their commitment to issue additional guidance as warranted.

---

1. STATEMENT OF DEPARTMENT OF JUSTICE AND FEDERAL TRADE COMMISSION ENFORCEMENT POLICY ON MERGERS AMONG HOSPITALS

Introduction

Most hospital mergers and acquisitions ("mergers") do not present competitive concerns. While careful analysis may be necessary to determine the likely competitive effect of a particular hospital merger, the competitive effect of many hospital mergers is relatively easy to assess. This statement sets forth an antitrust safety zone for certain mergers in light of the Agencies' extensive experience analyzing hospital mergers. Mergers that fall within the antitrust safety zone will not be challenged by the Agencies under the antitrust laws, absent extraordinary circumstances.[1] This policy statement also briefly describes the Agencies' antitrust analysis of hospital mergers that fall outside the antitrust safety zone.

A. *Antitrust Safety Zone*: Mergers of Hospitals That Will Not Be Challenged, Absent Extraordinary Circumstances, by the Agencies

The Agencies will not challenge any merger between two general acute-care hospitals where one of the hospitals (1) has an average of fewer than 100 licensed beds over the three most recent years, and (2) has an average daily inpatient census of fewer than 40 patients over the three most recent years, absent extraordinary circumstances. This antitrust safety zone will not apply if that hospital is less than 5 years old.

The Agencies recognize that in some cases a general acute care hospital with fewer than 100 licensed beds and an average daily inpatient census of fewer than 40 patients will be the only hospital in a relevant market. As such, the hospital does not compete in any significant way with other hospitals. Accordingly, mergers involving such hospitals are unlikely to reduce competition substantially.

The Agencies also recognize that many general acute care hospitals, especially rural hospitals, with fewer than 100 licensed beds and an average daily inpatient census of fewer than 40 patients are unlikely to achieve the efficiencies that larger hospitals enjoy. Some of those cost-saving efficiencies may be realized, however, through a merger with another hospital.

B. The Agencies' Analysis of Hospital Mergers That Fall Outside the Antitrust Safety Zone

Hospital mergers that fall outside the antitrust safety zone are not necessarily anticompetitive, and may be procompetitive. The Agencies' analysis of hospital mergers follows the five steps set forth in the Department of Justice/ Federal Trade Commission *1992 Horizontal Merger Guidelines.*

Applying the analytical framework of the Merger Guidelines to particular facts of specific hospital mergers, the Agencies often have concluded that an investigated hospital merger will not result in a substantial lessening of competition in situations where market concentration might otherwise raise an inference of anticompetitive effects. Such situations include transactions where the Agencies found that: (1) the merger would not increase the likelihood of the exercise of market power either because of the existence post-merger of strong competitors or because the merging hospitals were sufficiently differentiated; (2) the merger would allow the hospitals to realize significant cost savings that could not otherwise be realized; or (3) the merger would eliminate a hospital that likely would fail with its assets exiting the market.

Antitrust challenges to hospital mergers are relatively rare. Of the hundreds of hospital mergers in the United States since 1987, the Agencies have challenged only a handful, and in several cases sought relief only as to part of the transaction. Most reviews of hospital mergers conducted by the Agencies are concluded within one month.

---

[1] The Agencies are confident that conduct falling within the antitrust safety zones contained in these policy statements is very unlikely to raise competitive concerns. Accordingly, the Agencies anticipate that extraordinary circumstances warranting a challenge to such conduct will be rare.

* * *

If hospitals are considering mergers that appear to fall within the antitrust safety zone and believe they need additional certainty regarding the legality of their conduct under the antitrust laws, they can take advantage of the Department's business review procedure (28 C.F.R. 50.6 (1992)) or the Federal Trade Commission's advisory opinion procedure (16 C.F.R. 1.1–1.4 (1993)). The Agencies will respond to business review or advisory opinion requests on behalf of hospitals considering mergers that appear to fall within the antitrust safety zone within 90 days after all necessary information is submitted.

---

2. STATEMENT OF DEPARTMENT OF JUSTICE AND FEDERAL TRADE COMMISSION ENFORCEMENT POLICY ON HOSPITAL JOINT VENTURES INVOLVING HIGH-TECHNOLOGY OR OTHER EXPENSIVE HEALTH CARE EQUIPMENT

Introduction

Most hospital joint ventures to purchase or otherwise share the ownership cost of, operate, and market high-technology or other expensive health care equipment and related services do not create antitrust problems. In most cases, these collaborative activities create procompetitive efficiencies that benefit consumers. These efficiencies include the provision of services at a lower cost or the provision of services that would not have been provided absent the joint venture. Sound antitrust enforcement policy distinguishes those joint ventures that on balance benefit the public from those that may increase prices without providing a countervailing benefit, and seeks to prevent only those that are harmful to consumers. The Agencies have never challenged a joint venture among hospitals to purchase or otherwise share the ownership cost of, operate and market high-technology or other expensive health care equipment and related services.

This statement of enforcement policy sets forth an antitrust safety zone that describes hospital high-technology or other expensive health care equipment joint ventures that will not be challenged, absent extraordinary circumstances, by the Agencies under the antitrust laws. It then describes the Agencies' antitrust analysis of hospital high-technology or other expensive health care equipment joint ventures that fall outside the antitrust safety zone. Finally, this statement includes examples of its application to hospital high-technology or other expensive health care equipment joint ventures.

A. *Antitrust Safety Zone*: Hospital High-Technology Joint Ventures That Will Not Be Challenged, Absent Extraordinary Circumstances, by the Agencies

The Agencies will not challenge under the antitrust laws any joint venture among hospitals to purchase or otherwise share the ownership cost of, operate, and market the related services of, high-technology or other expensive health care equipment if the joint venture includes only the number of hospitals whose participation is needed to support the equipment, absent extraordinary circumstances.[2] This applies to joint

---

[2] A hospital or group of hospitals will be considered able to support high-technology or other expensive health care equipment for purposes of this antitrust safety zone if it could recover the costs of owning, operating, and marketing the equipment over its useful

ventures involving purchases of new equipment as well as to joint ventures involving existing equipment.[3] A joint venture that includes additional hospitals also will not be challenged if the additional hospitals could not support the equipment on their own or through the formation of a competing joint venture, absent extraordinary circumstances.

For example, if two hospitals are each unlikely to recover the cost of individually purchasing, operating, and marketing the services of a magnetic resonance imager (MRI) over its useful life, their joint venture with respect to the MRI would not be challenged by the Agencies. On the other hand, if the same two hospitals entered into a joint venture with a third hospital that independently could have purchased, operated, and marketed an MRI in a financially viable manner, the joint venture would not be in this antitrust safety zone. If, however, none of the three hospitals could have supported an MRI by itself, the Agencies would not challenge the joint venture.[4]

Information necessary to determine whether the costs of a piece of high-technology health care equipment could be recovered over its useful life is normally available to any hospital or group of hospitals considering such a purchase. This information may include the cost of the equipment, its expected useful life, the minimum number of procedures that must be done to meet a machine's financial breakeven point, the expected number of procedures the equipment will be used for given the population served by the joint venture and the expected price to be charged for the use of the equipment. Expected prices and costs should be confirmed by objective evidence, such as experiences in similar markets for similar technologies.

B. The Agencies' Analysis of Hospital High-Technology or Other Expensive Health Care Equipment Joint Ventures That Fall Outside the Antitrust Safety Zone

The Agencies recognize that joint ventures that fall outside the antitrust safety zone do not necessarily raise significant antitrust concerns. The Agencies will apply a rule of reason analysis in their antitrust review of such joint ventures.[5]

The objective of this analysis is to determine whether the joint venture may reduce competition substantially, and, if it might, whether it is likely to produce procompetitive efficiencies that outweigh its anticompetitive

---

life. If the joint venture is limited to ownership, only the ownership costs are relevant. If the joint venture is limited to owning and operating, only the owning and operating costs are relevant.

[3] Consequently, the safety zone would apply in a situation in which one hospital had already purchased the health care equipment, but was not recovering the costs of the equipment and sought a joint venture with one or more hospitals in order to recover the costs of the equipment.

[4] The antitrust safety zone described in this statement applies only to the joint venture and agreements reasonably necessary to the venture. The safety zone does not apply to or protect agreements made by participants in a joint venture that are related to a service not provided by the venture. For example, the antitrust safety zone that would apply to the MRI joint venture would not apply to protect an agreement among the hospitals with respect to charges for an overnight stay.

[5] This statement assumes that the joint venture arrangement is not one that uses the joint venture label but is likely merely to restrict competition and decrease output. For example, two hospitals that independently operate profitable MRI services could not avoid charges of price fixing by labeling as a joint venture their plan to obtain higher prices through joint marketing of their existing MRI services.

potential. This analysis is flexible and takes into account the nature and effect of the joint venture, the characteristics of the venture and of the hospital industry generally, and the reasons for, and purposes of, the venture. It also allows for consideration of efficiencies that will result from the venture. The steps involved in a rule of reason analysis are set forth below.[6]

Step one: Define the relevant market. The rule of reason analysis first identifies what is produced through the joint venture. The relevant product and geographic markets are then properly defined. This process seeks to identify any other provider that could offer what patients or physicians generally would consider a good substitute for that provided by the joint venture. Thus, if a joint venture were to purchase and jointly operate and market the related services of an MRI, the relevant market would include all other MRIs in the area that are reasonable alternatives for the same patients, but would not include providers with only traditional X-ray equipment.

Step two: Evaluate the competitive effects of the venture. This step begins with an analysis of the structure of the relevant market. If many providers would compete with the joint venture, competitive harm is unlikely and the analysis would continue with step four described below.

If the structural analysis of the relevant market showed that the joint venture would eliminate an existing or potentially viable competing provider and that there were few competing providers of that service, or that cooperation in the joint venture market may spill over into a market in which the parties to the joint venture are competitors, it then would be necessary to assess the extent of the potential anticompetitive effects of the joint venture. In addition to the number and size of competing providers, factors that could restrain the ability of the joint venture to raise prices either unilaterally or through collusive agreements with other providers would include: (1) characteristics of the market that make anticompetitive coordination unlikely; (2) the likelihood that other providers would enter the market; and (3) the effects of government regulation.

The extent to which the joint venture restricts competition among the hospitals participating in the venture is evaluated during this step. In some cases, a joint venture to purchase or otherwise share the cost of high-technology equipment may not substantially eliminate competition among the hospitals in providing the related service made possible by the equipment. For example, two hospitals might purchase a mobile MRI jointly, but operate and market MRI services separately. In such instances, the potential impact on competition of the joint venture would be substantially reduced.[7]

---

[6] Many joint ventures that could provide substantial efficiencies also may present little likelihood of competitive harm. Where it is clear initially that any joint venture presents little likelihood of competitive harm, the step-by-step analysis described in the text below will not be necessary. For example, when two hospitals propose to merge existing expensive health care equipment into a joint venture in a properly defined market in which many other hospitals or other health care facilities operate the same equipment, such that the market will be unconcentrated, then the combination is unlikely to be anticompetitive and further analysis ordinarily would not be required. See Department of Justice/Federal Trade Commission *1992 Horizontal Merger Guidelines*.

[7] If steps one and two reveal no competitive concerns with the joint venture, step three is unnecessary, and the analysis continues with step four described below.

Step three: Evaluate the impact of procompetitive efficiencies. This step requires an examination of the joint venture's potential to create procompetitive efficiencies, and the balancing of these efficiencies against any potential anticompetitive effects. The greater the venture's likely anticompetitive effects, the greater must be the venture's likely efficiencies. In certain circumstances, efficiencies can be substantial because of the need to spread the cost of expensive equipment over a large number of patients and the potential for improvements in quality to occur as providers gain experience and skill from performing a larger number of procedures.

Step four: Evaluate collateral agreements. This step examines whether the joint venture includes collateral agreements or conditions that unreasonably restrict competition and are unlikely to contribute significantly to the legitimate purposes of the joint venture. The Agencies will examine whether the collateral agreements are reasonably necessary to achieve the efficiencies sought by the joint venture. For example, if the participants in a joint venture formed to purchase a mobile lithotripter also agreed on the daily room rate to be charged lithotripsy patients who required overnight hospitalization, this collateral agreement as to room rates would not be necessary to achieve the benefits of the lithotripter joint venture. Although the joint venture itself would be legal, the collateral agreement on hospital room rates would not be legal and would be subject to challenge.

C. Examples of Hospital High-Technology Joint Ventures

The following are examples of hospital joint ventures that are unlikely to raise significant antitrust concerns. Each is intended to demonstrate an aspect of the analysis that would be used to evaluate the venture.

1. New Equipment That Can Be Offered Only by a Joint Venture

All the hospitals in a relevant market agree that they jointly will purchase, operate and market a helicopter to provide emergency transportation for patients. The community's need for the helicopter is not great enough to justify having more than one helicopter operating in the area and studies of similarly sized communities indicate that a second helicopter service could not be supported. This joint venture falls within the antitrust safety zone. It would make available a service that would not otherwise be available, and for which duplication would be inefficient.

2. Joint Venture to Purchase Expensive Equipment

All five hospitals in a relevant market agree to jointly purchase a mobile health care device that provides a service for which consumers have no reasonable alternatives. The hospitals will share equally in the cost of maintaining the equipment, and the equipment will travel from one hospital to another and be available one day each week at each hospital. The hospitals' agreement contains no provisions for joint marketing of, and protects against exchanges of competitively sensitive information regarding, the equipment.[8] There are also no limitations on the prices that each hospital will charge for use of the equipment, on the number of procedures that each hospital can perform, or on each hospital's ability to purchase the equipment on its own. Although any combination of two of the hospitals could afford to purchase the equipment and recover their costs within the equipment's useful life, patient volume from all five hospitals is required to maximize the efficient use of the equipment and lead to significant cost

---

[8] Examples of such information include prices and marketing plans.

savings. In addition, patient demand would be satisfied by provision of the equipment one day each week at each hospital. The joint venture would result in higher use of the equipment, thus lowering the cost per patient and potentially improving quality.

This joint venture does not fall within the antitrust safety zone because smaller groups of hospitals could afford to purchase and operate the equipment and recover their costs. Therefore, the joint venture would be analyzed under the rule of reason. The first step is to define the relevant market. In this example, the relevant market consists of the services provided by the equipment, and the five hospitals all potentially compete against each other for patients requiring this service.

The second step in the analysis is to determine the competitive effects of the joint venture. Because the joint venture is likely to reduce the number of these health care devices in the market, there is a potential restraint on competition. The restraint would not be substantial, however, for several reasons. First, the joint venture is limited to the purchase of the equipment and would not eliminate competition among the hospitals in the provision of the services. The hospitals will market the services independently, and will not exchange competitively sensitive information. In addition, the venture does not preclude a hospital from purchasing another unit should the demand for these services increase.

Because the joint venture raises some competitive concerns, however, it is necessary to examine the potential efficiencies associated with the venture. As noted above, by sharing the equipment among the five hospitals significant cost savings can be achieved. The joint venture would produce substantial efficiencies while providing access to high quality care. Thus, this joint venture would on balance benefit consumers since it would not lessen competition substantially, and it would allow the hospitals to serve the community's need in a more efficient manner. Finally, in this example the joint venture does not involve any collateral agreements that raise competitive concerns. On these facts, the joint venture would not be challenged by the Agencies.

3. Joint Venture of Existing Expensive Equipment Where One of the Hospitals in the Venture Already Owns the Equipment

Metropolis has three hospitals and a population of 300,000. Mercy and University Hospitals each own and operate their own magnetic resonance imaging device ("MRI"). General Hospital does not. Three independent physician clinics also own and operate MRIs. All of the existing MRIs have similar capabilities. The acquisition of an MRI is not subject to review under a certificate of need law in the state in which Metropolis is located.

Managed care plans have told General Hospital that, unless it can provide MRI services, it will be a less attractive contracting partner than the other two hospitals in town. The five existing MRIs are slightly underutilized—that is, the average cost per scan could be reduced if utilization of the machines increased. There is insufficient demand in Metropolis for six fully-utilized MRIs.

General has considered purchasing its own MRI so that it can compete on equal terms with Mercy and University Hospitals. However, it has decided based on its analysis of demand for MRI services and the cost of acquiring and operating the equipment that it would be better to share the equipment with another hospital. General proposes forming a joint venture in which it will purchase a 50 percent share in Mercy's MRI, and the two hospitals will work out an arrangement by which each hospital has equal access to the MRI. Each hospital in the joint venture will independently market and set prices for those MRI services, and the joint venture agreement protects against exchanges of competitively sensitive information among the hospitals. There is no restriction on the ability of each hospital to purchase its own equipment.

The proposed joint venture does not fall within the antitrust safety zone because General apparently could independently support the purchase and operation of its own MRI. Accordingly, the Agencies would analyze the joint venture under a rule of reason.

The first step of the rule of reason analysis is defining the relevant product and geographic markets. Assuming there are no good substitutes for MRI services, the relevant product market in this case is MRI services. Most patients currently receiving MRI services are unwilling to travel outside of Metropolis for those services, so the relevant geographic market is Metropolis. Mercy, University, and the three physician clinics are already offering MRI services in this market. Because General intends to offer MRI services within the next year, even if there is no joint venture, it is viewed as a market participant.

The second step is determining the competitive impact of the joint venture. Absent the joint venture, there would have been six independent MRIs in the market. This raises some competitive concerns with the joint venture. The fact that the joint venture will not entail joint price setting or marketing of MRI services to purchasers reduces the venture's potential anticompetitive effect. The competitive analysis would also consider the likelihood of additional entry in the market. If, for example, another physician clinic is likely to purchase an MRI in the event that the price of MRI services were to increase, any anticompetitive effect from the joint venture becomes less likely. Entry may be more likely in Metropolis than other areas because new entrants are not required to obtain certificates of need.

The third step of the analysis is assessing the likely efficiencies associated with the joint venture. The magnitude of any likely anticompetitive effects associated with the joint venture is important; the greater the venture's likely anticompetitive effects, the greater must be the venture's likely efficiencies. In this instance, the joint venture will avoid the costly duplication associated with General purchasing an MRI, and will allow Mercy to reduce the average cost of operating its MRI by increasing the number of procedures done. The competition between the Mercy/General venture and the other MRI providers in the market will provide some incentive for the joint venture to operate the MRI in as low-cost a manner as possible. Thus, there are efficiencies associated with the joint venture that could not be achieved in a less restrictive manner.

The final step of the analysis is determining whether the joint venture has any collateral agreements or conditions that reduce competition and are not reasonably necessary to achieve the efficiencies sought by the venture. For example, if the joint venture required managed care plans desiring MRI services to contract with both joint venture participants for those services, that condition would be viewed as anticompetitive and unnecessary to achieve the legitimate procompetitive goals of the joint venture. This example does not include any unnecessary collateral restraints.

On balance, when weighing the likelihood that the joint venture will significantly reduce competition for these services against its potential to result in efficiencies, the Agencies would view this joint venture favorably under a rule of reason analysis.

4. Joint Venture of Existing Equipment Where Both Hospitals in the Venture Already Own the Equipment

Valley Town has a population of 30,000 and is located in a valley surrounded by mountains. The closest urbanized area is over 75 miles away. There are two hospitals in Valley Town: Valley Medical Center and St. Mary's. Valley Medical Center offers a full range of primary and secondary services. St. Mary's offers primary and some secondary services. Although both hospitals have a CT scanner, Valley Medical Center's scanner is more sophisticated. Because of its greater sophistication, Valley Medical Center's scanner is more expensive to operate, and can conduct fewer scans in a day. A physician clinic in Valley Town operates a third CT scanner that is comparable to St. Mary's scanner and is not fully utilized.

Valley Medical Center has found that many of the scans that it conducts do not require the sophisticated features of its scanner. Because scans on its machine take so long, and so many patients require scans, Valley Medical Center also is experiencing significant scheduling problems. St. Mary's scanner, on the other hand, is underutilized, partially because many individuals go to Valley Medical Center because they need the more sophisticated scans that only Valley Medical Center's scanner can provide. Despite the underutilization of St. Mary's scanner, and the higher costs of Valley Medical Center's scanner, neither hospital has any intention of discontinuing its CT services.

Valley Medical Center and St. Mary's are proposing a joint venture that would own and operate both hospitals' CT scanners. The two hospitals will then independently market and set the prices they charge for those services, and the joint venture agreement protects against exchanges of competitively sensitive information between the hospitals. There is no restriction on the ability of each hospital to purchase its own equipment.

The proposed joint venture does not qualify under the Agencies' safety zone because the participating hospitals can independently support their own equipment. Accordingly, the Agencies would analyze the joint venture under a rule of reason. The first step of the analysis is to determine the relevant product and geographic markets. As long as other diagnostic services such as conventional X-rays or MRI scans are not viewed as a good substitute for CT scans, the relevant product market is CT scans. If patients currently receiving CT scans in Valley Town would be unlikely to switch to providers offering CT scans outside of Valley Town in the event that the price of CT scans in Valley Town increased by a small but significant amount, the relevant geographic market is Valley Town. There are three participants in this relevant market: Valley Medical Center, St. Mary's, and the physician clinic.

The second step of the analysis is determining the competitive effect of the joint venture. Because the joint venture does not entail joint pricing or marketing of CT services, the joint venture does not effectively reduce the number of market participants. This reduces the venture's potential anticompetitive effect. In fact, by increasing the scope of the CT services that each hospital can provide, the joint venture may increase competition between Valley Medical Center and St. Mary's since now both hospitals can provide sophisticated scans. Competitive concerns with this joint venture would be further ameliorated if other health care providers were likely to acquire CT scanners in response to a price increase following the formation of the joint venture.

The third step is assessing whether the efficiencies associated with the joint venture outweigh any anticompetitive effect associated with the joint venture. This joint venture will allow both hospitals to make either the sophisticated CT scanner or the less sophisticated, but less costly, CT scanner available to patients at those hospitals.

Thus, the joint venture should increase quality of care by allowing for better utilization and scheduling of the equipment, while also reducing the cost of providing that care, thereby benefitting the community. The joint venture may also increase quality of care by making more capacity available to Valley Medical Center; while Valley Medical Center faced capacity constraints prior to the joint venture, it can now take advantage of St. Mary's underutilized CT scanner. The joint venture will also improve access by allowing patients requiring routine scans to be moved from the sophisticated scanner at Valley Medical Center to St. Mary's scanner where the scans can be performed more quickly.

The last step of the analysis is to determine whether there are any collateral agreements or conditions associated with the joint venture that reduce competition and are not reasonably necessary to achieve the efficiencies sought by the joint venture. Assuming there are no such agreements or conditions, the Agencies would view this joint venture favorably under a rule of reason analysis.

As noted in the previous example, excluding price setting and marketing from the scope of the joint venture reduces the probability and magnitude of any anticompetitive effect of the joint venture, and thus reduces the likelihood that the Agencies will find the joint venture to be anticompetitive. If joint price setting and marketing were, however, a part of that joint venture, the Agencies would have to determine whether the cost savings and quality improvements associated with the joint venture offset the loss of competition between the two hospitals. Also, if neither of the hospitals in Valley Town had a CT scanner, and they proposed a similar joint venture for the purchase of two CT scanners, one sophisticated and one less sophisticated, the Agencies would be unlikely to view that joint venture as anticompetitive, even though each hospital could independently support the purchase of its own CT scanner. This conclusion would be based upon a rule of reason analysis that was virtually identical to the one described above.

* * *

Hospitals that are considering high-technology or other expensive equipment joint ventures and are unsure of the legality of their conduct under the antitrust laws can take advantage of the Department's expedited business review procedure for joint ventures and information exchanges announced on December 1, 1992 (58 Fed. Reg. 6132 (1993)) or the Federal Trade Commission's advisory opinion procedure contained at 16 C.F.R. 1.1–1.4 (1993). The Agencies will respond to a business review or advisory opinion request on behalf of hospitals that are considering a high-technology joint venture within 90 days after all necessary information is submitted. The Department's December 1, 1992 announcement contains specific guidance as to the information that should be submitted.

3. STATEMENT OF DEPARTMENT OF JUSTICE AND FEDERAL TRADE COMMISSION ENFORCEMENT POLICY ON HOSPITAL JOINT VENTURES INVOLVING SPECIALIZED CLINICAL OR OTHER EXPENSIVE HEALTH CARE SERVICES

Introduction

Most hospital joint ventures to provide specialized clinical or other expensive health care services do not create antitrust problems. The Agencies have never challenged an integrated joint venture among hospitals to provide a specialized clinical or other expensive health care service.

Many hospitals wish to enter into joint ventures to offer these services because the development of these services involves investments—such as the recruitment and training of specialized personnel—that a single hospital may not be able to support. In many cases, these collaborative activities could create procompetitive efficiencies that benefit consumers, including the provision of services at a lower cost or the provision of a service that would not have been provided absent the joint venture. Sound antitrust enforcement policy distinguishes those joint ventures that on balance benefit the public from those that may increase prices without providing a countervailing benefit, and seeks to prevent only those that are harmful to consumers.

This statement of enforcement policy sets forth the Agencies' antitrust analysis of joint ventures between hospitals to provide specialized clinical or other expensive health care services and includes an example of its application to such ventures. It does not include a safety zone for such ventures since the Agencies believe that they must acquire more expertise in evaluating the cost of, demand for, and potential benefits from such joint ventures before they can articulate a meaningful safety zone. The absence of a safety zone for such collaborative activities does not imply that they create any greater antitrust risk than other types of collaborative activities.

A. The Agencies' Analysis of Hospital Joint Ventures Involving Specialized Clinical or Other Expensive Health Care Services

The Agencies apply a rule of reason analysis in their antitrust review of hospital joint ventures involving specialized clinical or other expensive health care services.[9] The objective of this analysis is to determine whether the joint venture may reduce competition substantially, and if it might, whether it is likely to produce procompetitive efficiencies that outweigh its anticompetitive potential. This analysis is flexible and takes into account the nature and effect of the joint venture, the characteristics of the services involved and of the hospital industry generally, and the reasons for, and purposes of, the venture. It also allows for consideration of efficiencies that will result from the venture. The steps involved in a rule of reason analysis are set forth below.[10]

---

[9] This statement assumes that the joint venture is not likely merely to restrict competition and decrease output. For example, if two hospitals that both profitably provide open heart surgery and a burn unit simply agree without entering into an integrated joint venture that in the future each of the services will be offered exclusively at only one of the hospitals, the agreement would be viewed as an illegal market allocation.

[10] Many joint venturers that could provide substantial efficiencies also may present little likelihood of competitive harm. Where it is clear initially that any joint venture presents little likelihood of competitive harm, it will not be necessary to complete all steps

Step one: Define the relevant market. The rule of reason analysis first identifies the service that is produced through the joint venture. The relevant product and geographic markets that include the service are then properly defined. This process seeks to identify any other provider that could offer a service that patients or physicians generally would consider a good substitute for that provided by the joint venture. Thus, if a joint venture were to produce intensive care neonatology services, the relevant market would include only other neonatal intensive care nurseries that patients or physicians would view as reasonable alternatives.

Step two: Evaluate the competitive effects of the venture. This step begins with an analysis of the structure of the relevant market. If many providers compete with the joint venture, competitive harm is unlikely and the analysis would continue with step four described below.

If the structural analysis of the relevant market showed that the joint venture would eliminate an existing or potentially viable competing provider of a service and that there were few competing providers of that service, or that cooperation in the joint venture market might spill over into a market in which the parties to the joint venture are competitors, it then would be necessary to assess the extent of the potential anticompetitive effects of the joint venture. In addition to the number and size of competing providers, factors that could restrain the ability of the joint venture to act anticompetitively either unilaterally or through collusive agreements with other providers would include: (1) characteristics of the market that make anticompetitive coordination unlikely; (2) the likelihood that others would enter the market; and (3) the effects of government regulation.

The extent to which the joint venture restricts competition among the hospitals participating in the venture is evaluated during this step. In some cases, a joint venture to provide a specialized clinical or other expensive health care service may not substantially limit competition. For example, if the only two hospitals providing primary and secondary acute care inpatient services in a relevant geographic market for such services were to form a joint venture to provide a tertiary service, they would continue to compete on primary and secondary services. Because the geographic market for a tertiary service may in certain cases be larger than the geographic market for primary or secondary services, the hospitals may also face substantial competition for the joint-ventured tertiary service.[11]

Step three: Evaluate the impact of procompetitive efficiencies. This step requires an examination of the joint venture's potential to create procompetitive efficiencies, and the balancing of these efficiencies against any potential anticompetitive effects. The greater the venture's likely anticompetitive effects, the greater must be the venture's likely efficiencies. In certain circumstances, efficiencies can be substantial because of the need to spread the cost of the investment associated with the recruitment and training of personnel over a large number of patients and the potential for improvement in quality to occur as providers gain experience and skill from performing a larger number of procedures. In the case of certain specialized clinical services, such as open heart surgery, the joint venture may permit

---

in the analysis to conclude that the joint venture should not be challenged. *See* note 7, above.

[11] If steps one and two reveal no competitive concerns with the joint venture, step three is unnecessary, and the analysis continues with step four described below.

the program to generate sufficient patient volume to meet well-accepted minimum standards for assuring quality and patient safety.

Step four: Evaluate collateral agreements. This step examines whether the joint venture includes collateral agreements or conditions that unreasonably restrict competition and are unlikely to contribute significantly to the legitimate purposes of the joint venture. The Agencies will examine whether the collateral agreements are reasonably necessary to achieve the efficiencies sought by the venture. For example, if the participants in a joint venture to provide highly sophisticated oncology services were to agree on the prices to be charged for all radiology services regardless of whether the services are provided to patients undergoing oncology radiation therapy, this collateral agreement as to radiology services for non-oncology patients would be unnecessary to achieve the benefits of the sophisticated oncology joint venture. Although the joint venture itself would be legal, the collateral agreement would not be legal and would be subject to challenge.

B. Example—Hospital Joint Venture for New Specialized Clinical Service Not Involving Purchase of High-Technology or Other Expensive Health Care Equipment

Midvale has a population of about 75,000, and is geographically isolated in a rural part of its state. Midvale has two general acute care hospitals, Community Hospital and Religious Hospital, each of which performs a mix of basic primary, secondary, and some tertiary care services. The two hospitals have largely non-overlapping medical staffs. Neither hospital currently offers open-heart surgery services, nor has plans to do so on its own. Local residents, physicians, employers, and hospital managers all believe that Midvale has sufficient demand to support one local open-heart surgery unit.

The two hospitals in Midvale propose a joint venture whereby they will share the costs of recruiting a cardiac surgery team and establishing an open-heart surgery program, to be located at one of the hospitals. Patients will be referred to the program from both hospitals, who will share expenses and revenues of the program. The hospitals' agreement protects against exchanges of competitively sensitive information.

As stated above, the Agencies would analyze such a joint venture under a rule of reason. The first step of the rule of reason analysis is defining the relevant product and geographic markets. The relevant product market in this case is open-heart surgery services, because there are no reasonable alternatives for patients needing such surgery. The relevant geographic market may be limited to Midvale. Although patients now travel to distant hospitals for open-heart surgery, it is significantly more costly for patients to obtain surgery from them than from a provider located in Midvale. Physicians, patients, and purchasers believe that after the open heart surgery program is operational, most Midvale residents will choose to receive these services locally.

The second step is determining the competitive impact of the joint venture. Here, the joint venture does not eliminate any existing competition, because neither of the two hospitals previously was providing open-heart surgery. Nor does the joint venture eliminate any potential competition, because there is insufficient patient volume for more than one viable open-heart surgery program. Thus, only one such program could exist in Midvale, regardless of whether it was established unilaterally or through a joint venture.

Normally, the third step in the rule of reason analysis would be to assess the procompetitive effects of, and likely efficiencies associated with, the joint venture. In this instance, this step is unnecessary, since the analysis has concluded under step two that the joint venture will not result in any significant anticompetitive effects.

The final step of the analysis is to determine whether the joint venture has any collateral agreements or conditions that reduce competition and are not reasonably necessary to achieve the efficiencies sought by the venture. The joint venture does not appear to involve any such agreements or conditions; it does not eliminate or reduce competition between the two hospitals for any other services, or impose any conditions on use of the open-heart surgery program that would affect other competition.

Because the joint venture described above is unlikely significantly to reduce competition among hospitals for open-heart surgery services, and will in fact increase the services available to consumers, the Agencies would view this joint venture favorably under a rule of reason analysis.

* * *

Hospitals that are considering specialized clinical or other expensive health care services joint ventures and are unsure of the legality of their conduct under the antitrust laws can take advantage of the Department of Justice's expedited business review procedure announced on December 1, 1992 (58 Fed. Reg. 6132 (1993)) or the Federal Trade Commission's advisory opinion procedure contained at 16 C.F.R. 1.1–1.4 (1993). The Agencies will respond to a business review or advisory opinion request on behalf of hospitals that are considering jointly providing such services within 90 days after all necessary information is submitted. The Department's December 1, 1992 announcement contains specific guidance as to the information that should be submitted.

---

4. STATEMENT OF DEPARTMENT OF JUSTICE AND FEDERAL TRADE COMMISSION ENFORCEMENT POLICY ON PROVIDERS COLLECTIVE PROVISION OF NON-FEE-RELATED INFORMATION TO PURCHASERS OF HEALTH CARE SERVICES

Introduction

The collective provision of non-fee-related information by competing health care providers to a purchaser in an effort to influence the terms upon which the purchaser deals with the providers does not necessarily raise antitrust concerns. Generally, providers' collective provision of certain types of information to a purchaser is likely either to raise little risk of anticompetitive effects or to provide procompetitive benefits.

This statement sets forth an antitrust safety zone that describes providers' collective provision of non-fee-related information that will not be challenged by the Agencies under the antitrust laws, absent extraordinary circumstances.[12] It also describes conduct that is expressly excluded from the antitrust safety zone.

---

[12] This statement addresses only providers' collective activities. As a general proposition, providers acting individually may provide any information to any purchaser

STATEMENTS OF ANTITRUST ENFORCEMENT POLICY IN HEALTH CARE

A. *Antitrust Safety Zone:* Providers' Collective Provision of Non-Fee-Related Information That Will Not Be Challenged, Absent Extraordinary Circumstances, by the Agencies

Providers' collective provision of underlying medical data that may improve purchasers' resolution of issues relating to the mode, quality, or efficiency of treatment is unlikely to raise any significant antitrust concern and will not be challenged by the Agencies, absent extraordinary circumstances. Thus, the Agencies will not challenge, absent extraordinary circumstances, a medical society's collection of outcome data from its members about a particular procedure that they believe should be covered by a purchaser and the provision of such information to the purchaser. The Agencies also will not challenge, absent extraordinary circumstances, providers' development of suggested practice parameters—standards for patient management developed to assist providers in clinical decisionmaking—that also may provide useful information to patients, providers, and purchasers. Because providers' collective provision of such information poses little risk of restraining competition and may help in the development of protocols that increase quality and efficiency, the Agencies will not challenge such activity, absent extraordinary circumstances.

In the course of providing underlying medical data, providers may collectively engage in discussions with purchasers about the scientific merit of that data. However, the antitrust safety zone excludes any attempt by providers to coerce a purchaser's decisionmaking by implying or threatening a boycott of any plan that does not follow the providers' joint recommendation. Providers who collectively threaten to or actually refuse to deal with a purchaser because they object to the purchaser's administrative, clinical, or other terms governing the provision of services run a substantial antitrust risk. For example, providers' collective refusal to provide X-rays to a purchaser that seeks them before covering a particular treatment regimen would constitute an antitrust violation. Similarly, providers' collective attempt to force purchasers to adopt recommended practice parameters by threatening to or actually boycotting purchasers that refuse to accept their joint recommendation also would risk antitrust challenge.

* * *

Competing providers who are considering jointly providing non-fee-related information to a purchaser and are unsure of the legality of their conduct under the antitrust laws can take advantage of the Department of Justice's expedited business review procedure announced on December 1, 1992 (58 Fed. Reg. 6132 (1993)) or the Federal Trade Commission's advisory opinion procedure contained at 16 C.F.R. 1.1–1.4 (1993). The Agencies will respond to a business review or advisory opinion request on behalf of providers who are considering jointly providing such information within 90 days after all necessary information is submitted. The Department's December 1, 1992 announcement contains specific guidance as to the information that should be submitted.

---

without incurring liability under federal antitrust law. This statement also does not address the collective provision of information through an integrated joint venture or the exchange of information that necessarily occurs among providers involved in legitimate joint venture activities. Those activities generally do not raise antitrust concerns.

5. STATEMENT OF DEPARTMENT OF JUSTICE AND FEDERAL TRADE COMMISSION ENFORCEMENT POLICY ON PROVIDERS' COLLECTIVE PROVISION OF FEE-RELATED INFORMATION TO PURCHASERS OF HEALTH CARE SERVICES

Introduction

The collective provision by competing health care providers to purchasers of health care services of factual information concerning the fees charged currently or in the past for the providers' services, and other factual information concerning the amounts, levels, or methods of fees or reimbursement, does not necessarily raise antitrust concerns. With reasonable safeguards, providers' collective provision of this type of factual information to a purchaser of health care services may provide procompetitive benefits and raise little risk of anticompetitive effects.

This statement sets forth an antitrust safety zone that describes collective provision of fee-related information that will not be challenged by the Agencies under the antitrust laws, absent extraordinary circumstances.[13] It also describes types of conduct that are expressly excluded from the antitrust safety zone, some clearly unlawful, and others that may be lawful depending on the circumstances.

A. *Antitrust Safety Zone*: Providers, Collective Provision of Fee-Related Information That Will Not Be Challenged, Absent Extraordinary Circumstances, by the Agencies

Providers' collective provision to purchasers of health care services of factual information concerning the providers' current or historical fees or other aspects of reimbursement, such as discounts or alternative reimbursement methods accepted (including capitation arrangements, risk-withhold fee arrangements, or use of all-inclusive fees), is unlikely to raise significant antitrust concern and will not be challenged by the Agencies, absent extraordinary circumstances. Such factual information can help purchasers efficiently develop reimbursement terms to be offered to providers and may be useful to a purchaser when provided in response to a request from the purchaser or at the initiative of providers.

In assembling information to be collectively provided to purchasers, providers need to be aware of the potential antitrust consequences of information exchanges among competitors. The principles expressed in the Agencies' statement on provider participation in exchanges of price and cost information are applicable in this context. Accordingly, in order to qualify for this safety zone, the collection of information to be provided to purchasers must satisfy the following conditions:

(1) the collection is managed by a third party (*e.g.*, a purchaser, government agency, health care consultant, academic institution, or trade association);

(2) although current fee-related information may be provided to purchasers, any information that is shared among or is available to the

[13] This statement addresses only providers' collective activities. As a general proposition, providers acting individually may provide any information to any purchaser without incurring liability under federal antitrust law. This statement also does not address the collective provision of information through an integrated joint venture or the exchange of information that necessarily occurs among providers involved in legitimate joint venture activities. Those activities generally do not raise antitrust concerns.

competing providers furnishing the data must be more than three months old; and

(3) for any information that is available to the providers furnishing data, there are at least five providers reporting data upon which each disseminated statistic is based, no individual provider's data may represent more than 25 percent on a weighted basis of that statistic, and any information disseminated must be sufficiently aggregated such that it would not allow recipients to identify the prices charged by any individual provider.

The conditions that must be met for an information exchange among providers to fall within the antitrust safety zone are intended to ensure that an exchange of price or cost data is not used by competing providers for discussion or coordination of provider prices or costs. They represent a careful balancing of a provider's individual interest in obtaining information useful in adjusting the prices it charges or the wages it pays in response to changing market conditions against the risk that the exchange of such information may permit competing providers to communicate with each other regarding a mutually acceptable level of prices for health care services or compensation for employees.

B. The Agencies' Analysis of Providers' Collective Provision of Fee-Related Information That Falls Outside the Antitrust Safety Zone

The safety zone set forth in this policy statement does not apply to collective negotiations between unintegrated providers and purchasers in contemplation or in furtherance of any agreement among the providers on fees or other terms or aspects of reimbursement,[14] or to any agreement among unintegrated providers to deal with purchasers only on agreed terms. Providers also may not collectively threaten, implicitly or explicitly, to engage in a boycott or similar conduct, or actually undertake such a boycott or conduct, to coerce any purchaser to accept collectively-determined fees or other terms or aspects of reimbursement. These types of conduct likely would violate the antitrust laws and, in many instances, might be per se illegal.

Also excluded from the safety zone is providers' collective provision of information or views concerning prospective fee-related matters. In some circumstances, the collective provision of this type of fee-related information also may be helpful to a purchaser and, as long as independent decisions on whether to accept a purchaser's offer are truly preserved, may not raise antitrust concerns. However, in other circumstances, the collective provision of prospective fee-related information or views may evidence or facilitate an agreement on prices or other competitively significant terms by the competing providers. It also may exert a coercive effect on the purchaser by implying or threatening a collective refusal to deal on terms other than those proposed, or amount to an implied threat to boycott any plan that does not follow the providers' collective proposal.

The Agencies recognize the need carefully to distinguish possibly procompetitive collective provision of prospective fee-related information or views from anticompetitive situations that involve unlawful price agreements, boycott threats, refusals to deal except on collectively

---

[14] Whether communications between providers and purchasers will amount to negotiations depends on the nature and context of the communications, not solely the number of such communications.

determined terms, collective negotiations, or conduct that signals or facilitates collective price terms. Therefore, the collective provision of such prospective fee-related information or views will be assessed on a case-by-case basis. In their case-by-case analysis, the Agencies will look at all the facts and circumstances surrounding the provision of the information, including, but not limited to, the nature of the information provided, the nature and extent of the communications among the providers and between the providers and the purchaser, the rationale for providing the information, and the nature of the market in which the information is provided.

In addition, because the collective provision of prospective fee-related information and views can easily lead to or accompany unlawful collective negotiations, price agreements, or the other types of collective conduct noted above, providers need to be aware of the potential antitrust consequences of information exchanges among competitors in assembling information or views concerning prospective fee-related matters. Consequently, such protections as the use of a third party to manage the collection of information and views, and the adoption of mechanisms to assure that the information is not disseminated or used in a manner that facilitates unlawful agreements or coordinated conduct by the providers, likely would reduce antitrust concerns.

* * *

Competing providers who are considering collectively providing fee-related information to purchasers, and are unsure of the legality of their conduct under the antitrust laws, can take advantage of the Department of Justice's expedited business review procedure announced on December 1, 1992 (58 Fed. Reg. 6132 (1993)) or the Federal Trade Commission's advisory opinion procedure contained at 16 C.F.R. 1.1–1.4 (1993). The Agencies will respond to a business review or advisory opinion request on behalf of providers who are considering collectively providing fee-related information within 90 days after all necessary information is submitted. The Department's December 1, 1992 announcement contains specific guidance as to the information that should be submitted.

---

6. STATEMENT OF DEPARTMENT OF JUSTICE AND FEDERAL TRADE COMMISSION ENFORCEMENT POLICY ON PROVIDER PARTICIPATION IN EXCHANGES OF PRICE AND COST INFORMATION

Introduction

Participation by competing providers in surveys of prices for health care services, or surveys of salaries, wages or benefits of personnel, does not necessarily raise antitrust concerns. In fact, such surveys can have significant benefits for health care consumers. Providers can use information derived from price and compensation surveys to price their services more competitively and to offer compensation that attracts highly qualified personnel. Purchasers can use price survey information to make more informed decisions when buying health care services. Without appropriate safeguards, however, information exchanges among competing providers may facilitate collusion or otherwise reduce competition on prices or compensation, resulting in increased prices, or reduced quality and availability of health care services. A collusive restriction on the compensation paid to health care employees, for example, could adversely affect the availability of health care personnel.

This statement sets forth an antitrust safety zone that describes exchanges of price and cost information among providers that will not be challenged by the Agencies under the antitrust laws, absent extraordinary circumstances. It also briefly describes the Agencies' antitrust analysis of information exchanges that fall outside the antitrust safety zone.

A. *Antitrust Safety Zone:* Exchanges of Price and Cost Information Among Providers That Will Not Be Challenged, Absent Extraordinary Circumstances, by the Agencies

The Agencies will not challenge, absent extraordinary circumstances, provider participation in written surveys of (a) prices for health care services,[15] or (b) wages, salaries, or benefits of health care personnel, if the following conditions are satisfied:

(1) the survey is managed by a third-party (e.g., a purchaser, government agency, health care consultant, academic institution, or trade association);

(2) the information provided by survey participants is based on data more than 3 months old; and

(3) there are at least five providers reporting data upon which each disseminated statistic is based, no individual provider's data represents more than 25 percent on a weighted basis of that statistic, and any information disseminated is sufficiently aggregated such that it would not allow recipients to identify the prices charged or compensation paid by any particular provider.

The conditions that must be met for an information exchange among providers to fall within the antitrust safety zone are intended to ensure that an exchange of price or cost data is not used by competing providers for discussion or coordination of provider prices or costs. They represent a careful balancing of a provider's individual interest in obtaining information useful in adjusting the prices it charges or the wages it pays in response to changing market conditions against the risk that the exchange of such information may permit competing providers to communicate with each other regarding a mutually acceptable level of prices for health care services or compensation for employees.

B. The Agencies' Analysis of Provider Exchanges of Information That Fall Outside the Antitrust Safety Zone

Exchanges of price and cost information that fall outside the antitrust safety zone generally will be evaluated to determine whether the information exchange may have an anticompetitive effect that outweighs any procompetitive justification for the exchange. Depending on the circumstances, public, non-provider initiated surveys may not raise competitive concerns. Such surveys could allow purchasers to have useful information that they can use for procompetitive purposes.

Exchanges of future prices for provider services or future compensation of employees are very likely to be considered anticompetitive. If an exchange among competing providers of price or cost information results in an

[15] The "prices" at which providers offer their services to purchasers can take many forms, including billed charges for individual services, discounts off billed charges, or per diem, capitated, or diagnosis related group rates.

agreement among competitors as to the prices for health care services or the wages to be paid to health care employees, that agreement will be considered unlawful per se.

* * *

Competing providers that are considering participating in a survey of price or cost information and are unsure of the legality of their conduct under the antitrust laws can take advantage of the Department's expedited business review procedure announced on December 1, 1992 (58 Fed. Reg. 6132 (1993)) or the Federal Trade Commission's advisory opinion procedure contained at 16 C.F.R. 1.1–1.4 (1993). The Agencies will respond to a business review or advisory opinion request on behalf of providers who are considering participating in a survey of price or cost information within 90 days after all necessary information is submitted. The Department's December 1, 1992 announcement contains specific guidance as to the information that should be submitted.

---

7. STATEMENT OF DEPARTMENT OF JUSTICE AND FEDERAL TRADE COMMISSION ENFORCEMENT POLICY ON JOINT PURCHASING ARRANGEMENTS AMONG HEALTH CARE PROVIDERS

Introduction

Most joint purchasing arrangements among hospitals or other health care providers do not raise antitrust concerns. Such collaborative activities typically allow the participants to achieve efficiencies that will benefit consumers. Joint purchasing arrangements usually involve the purchase of a product or service used in providing the ultimate package of health care services or products sold by the participants. Examples include the purchase of laundry or food services by hospitals, the purchase of computer or data processing services by hospitals or other groups of providers, and the purchase of prescription drugs and other pharmaceutical products. Through such joint purchasing arrangements, the participants frequently can obtain volume discounts, reduce transaction costs, and have access to consulting advice that may not be available to each participant on its own.

Joint purchasing arrangements are unlikely to raise antitrust concerns unless (1) the arrangement accounts for so large a portion of the purchases of a product or service that it can effectively exercise market power[16] in the purchase of the product or service, or (2) the products or services being purchased jointly account for so large a proportion of the total cost of the services being sold by the participants that the joint purchasing arrangement may facilitate price fixing or otherwise reduce competition. If neither factor is present, the joint purchasing arrangement will not present competitive concerns.[17]

This statement sets forth an antitrust safety zone that describes joint purchasing arrangements among health care providers that will not be challenged, absent extraordinary circumstances, by the Agencies under the

---

[16] In the case of a purchaser, this is the power to drive the price of goods or services purchased below competitive levels.

[17] An agreement among purchasers that simply fixes the price that each purchaser will pay or offer to pay for a product or service is not a legitimate joint purchasing arrangement and is a per se antitrust violation. Legitimate joint purchasing arrangements provide some integration of purchasing functions to achieve efficiencies.

antitrust laws. It also describes factors that mitigate any competitive concerns with joint purchasing arrangements that fall outside the antitrust safety zone.[18]

A. *Antitrust Safety Zone:* Joint Purchasing Arrangements Among Health Care Providers That Will Not Be Challenged, Absent Extraordinary Circumstances, by the Agencies

The Agencies will not challenge, absent extraordinary circumstances, any joint purchasing arrangement among health care providers where two conditions are present: (1) the purchases account for less than 35 percent of the total sales of the purchased product or service in the relevant market; and (2) the cost of the products and services purchased jointly accounts for less than 20 percent of the total revenues from all products or services sold by each competing participant in the joint purchasing arrangement.

The first condition compares the purchases accounted for by a joint purchasing arrangement to the total purchases of the purchased product or service in the relevant market. Its purpose is to determine whether the joint purchasing arrangement might be able to drive down the price of the product or service being purchased below competitive levels. For example, a joint purchasing arrangement may account for all or most of the purchases of laundry services by hospitals in a particular market, but represent less than 35 percent of the purchases of all commercial laundry services in that market. Unless there are special costs that cannot be easily recovered associated with providing laundry services to hospitals, such a purchasing arrangement is not likely to force prices below competitive levels. The same principle applies to joint purchasing arrangements for food services, data processing, and many other products and services.

The second condition addresses any possibility that a joint purchasing arrangement might result in standardized costs, thus facilitating price fixing or otherwise having anticompetitive effects. This condition applies only where some or all of the participants are direct competitors. For example, if a nationwide purchasing cooperative limits its membership to one hospital in each geographic area, there is not likely to be any concern about reduction of competition among its members. Even where a purchasing arrangement's membership includes hospitals or other health care providers that compete with one another, the arrangement is not likely to facilitate collusion if the goods and services being purchased jointly account for a small fraction of the final price of the services provided by the participants. In the health care field, it may be difficult to determine the specific final service in which the jointly purchased products are used, as well as the price at which that final service is sold.[19] Therefore, the Agencies will examine whether the cost of the products or services being purchased jointly accounts, in the aggregate, for less than 20 percent of the total revenues from all health care services of each competing participant.

---

[18] This statement applies to purchasing arrangements through which the participants acquire products or services for their own use, not arrangements in which the participants are jointly investing in equipment or providing a service. Joint ventures involving investment in equipment and the provision of services are discussed in separate policy statements.

[19] This especially is true because some large purchasers negotiate prices with hospitals and other providers that encompass a group of services, while others pay separately for each service.

B. Factors Mitigating Competitive Concerns with Joint Purchasing Arrangements That Fall Outside the Antitrust Safety Zone

Joint purchasing arrangements among hospitals or other health care providers that fall outside the antitrust safety zone do not necessarily raise antitrust concerns. There are several safeguards that joint purchasing arrangements can adopt to mitigate concerns that might otherwise arise. First, antitrust concern is lessened if members are not required to use the arrangement for all their purchases of a particular product or service. Members can, however, be asked to commit to purchase a voluntarily specified amount through the arrangement so that a volume discount or other favorable contract can be negotiated. Second, where negotiations are conducted on behalf of the joint purchasing arrangement by an independent employee or agent who is not also an employee of a participant, antitrust risk is lowered. Third, the likelihood of anticompetitive communications is lessened where communications between the purchasing group and each individual participant are kept confidential, and not discussed with, or disseminated to, other participants.

These safeguards will reduce substantially, if not completely eliminate, use of the purchasing arrangement as a vehicle for discussing and coordinating the prices of health care services offered by the participants.[20] The adoption of these safeguards also will help demonstrate that the joint purchasing arrangement is intended to achieve economic efficiencies rather than to serve an anticompetitive purpose. Where there appear to be significant efficiencies from a joint purchasing arrangement, the Agencies will not challenge the arrangement absent substantial risk of anticompetitive effects.

The existence of a large number and variety of purchasing groups in the health care field suggests that entry barriers to forming new groups currently are not great. Thus, in most circumstances at present, it is not necessary to open a joint purchasing arrangement to all competitors in the market. However, if some competitors excluded from the arrangement are unable to compete effectively without access to the arrangement, and competition is thereby harmed, antitrust concerns will exist.

C. Example—Joint Purchasing Arrangement Involving Both Hospitals in Rural Community That the Agencies Would Not Challenge

Smalltown is the county seat of Rural County. There are two general acute care hospitals, County Hospital ("County") and Smalltown Medical Center ("SMC"), both located in Smalltown. The nearest other hospitals are located in Big City, about 100 miles from Smalltown.

County and SMC propose to join a joint venture being formed by several of the hospitals in Big City through which they will purchase various hospital supplies—such as bandages, antiseptics, surgical gowns, and masks. The joint venture will likely be the vehicle for the purchase of most such products by the Smalltown hospitals, but under the joint venture agreement, both retain the option to purchase supplies independently.

The joint venture will be an independent corporation, jointly owned by the participating hospitals. It will purchase the supplies needed by the

[20] Obviously, if the members of a legitimate purchasing group engage in price fixing or other collusive anticompetitive conduct as to services sold by the participants, whether through the arrangement or independently, they remain subject to antitrust challenge.

hospitals and then resell them to the hospitals at average variable cost plus a reasonable return on capital. The joint venture will periodically solicit from each participating hospital its expected needs for various hospital supplies, and negotiate the best terms possible for the combined purchases. It will also purchase supplies for its member hospitals on an ad hoc basis.

Competitive Analysis

The first issue is whether the proposed joint purchasing arrangement would fall within the safety zone set forth in this policy statement. In order to make this determination, the Agencies would first inquire whether the joint purchases would account for less than 35 percent of the total sales of the purchased products in the relevant markets for the sales of those products. Here, the relevant hospital supply markets are likely to be national or at least regional in scope. Thus, while County and SMC might well account for more than 35 percent of the total sales of many hospital supplies in Smalltown or Rural County, they and the other hospitals in Big City that will participate in the arrangement together would likely not account for significant percentages of sales in the actual relevant markets. Thus, the first criterion for inclusion in the safety zone is likely to be satisfied.

The Agencies would then inquire whether the supplies to be purchased jointly account for less than 20 percent of the total revenues from all products and services sold by each of the competing hospitals that participate in the arrangement. In this case, County and SMC are competing hospitals, but this second criterion for inclusion in the safety zone is also likely to be satisfied, and the Agencies would not challenge the joint purchasing arrangement.

* * *

Hospitals or other health care providers that are considering joint purchasing arrangements and are unsure of the legality of their conduct under the antitrust laws can take advantage of the Department of Justice's expedited business review procedure for joint ventures and information exchanges announced on December 1, 1992 (58 Fed. Reg. 6132 (1993)) or the Federal Trade Commission's advisory opinion procedure contained at 16 C.F.R. 1.1–1.4 (1993). The Agencies will respond to a business review or advisory opinion request on behalf of health care providers considering a joint purchasing arrangement within 90 days after all necessary information is submitted. The Department's December 1, 1992 announcement contains specific guidance as to the information that should be submitted.

---

8. STATEMENT OF DEPARTMENT OF JUSTICE AND FEDERAL TRADE COMMISSION ENFORCEMENT POLICY ON PHYSICIAN NETWORK JOINT VENTURES

Introduction

In recent years, health plans and other purchasers of health care services have developed a variety of managed care programs that seek to reduce the costs and assure the quality of health care services. Many physicians and physician groups have organized physician network joint ventures, such as individual practice associations ("IPAs"), preferred provider organizations

("PPOs"), and other arrangements to market their services to these plans.[21] Typically, such networks contract with the plans to provide physician services to plan subscribers at predetermined prices, and the physician participants in the networks agree to controls aimed at containing costs and assuring the appropriate and efficient provision of high quality physician services. By developing and implementing mechanisms that encourage physicians to collaborate in practicing efficiently as part of the network, many physician network joint ventures promise significant procompetitive benefits for consumers of health care services.

As used in this statement, a physician network joint venture is a physician-controlled venture in which the network's physician participants collectively agree on prices or price-related terms and jointly market their services.[22] Other types of health care network joint ventures are not directly addressed by this statement.[23]

This statement of enforcement policy describes the Agencies' antitrust analysis of physician network joint ventures, and presents several examples of its application to specific hypothetical physician network joint ventures. Before describing the general antitrust analysis, the statement sets forth antitrust safety zones that describe physician network joint ventures that are highly unlikely to raise substantial competitive concerns, and therefore will not be challenged by the Agencies under the antitrust laws, absent extraordinary circumstances.

The Agencies emphasize that merely because a physician network joint venture does not come within a safety zone in no way indicates that it is unlawful under the antitrust laws. On the contrary, such arrangements may be procompetitive and lawful, and many such arrangements have received favorable business review letters or advisory opinions from the Agencies.[24] The safety zones use a few factors that are relatively easy to

---

[21] An IPA or PPO typically provides medical services to the subscribers of health plans but does not act as their insurer. In addition, an IPA or PPO does not require complete integration of the medical practices of its physician participants. Such physicians typically continue to compete fully for patients who are enrolled in health plans not served by the IPA or PPO, or who have indemnity insurance or pay for the physician's services directly "out of pocket."

[22] Although this statement refers to IPAs and PPOs as examples of physician network joint ventures, the Agencies' competitive analysis focuses on the substance of such arrangements, not on their formal titles. This policy statement applies, therefore, to all entities that are substantively equivalent to the physician network joint ventures described in this statement.

[23] The physician network joint ventures discussed in this statement are one type of the multiprovider network joint ventures discussed below in the Agencies' Statement Of Enforcement Policy On Multiprovider Networks. That statement also covers other types of networks, such as networks that include both hospitals and physicians, and networks involving non-physician health professionals. In addition, that statement (*see infra* pp. 106–141), and Example 7 of this statement, address networks that do not include agreements among competitors on prices or price-related terms, through use of various "messenger model" arrangements. Many of the issues relating to physician network joint ventures are the same as those that arise and are addressed in connection with multiprovider networks generally, and the analysis often will be very similar for all such arrangements.

[24] For example, the Agencies have approved a number of non-exclusive physician or provider networks in which the percentage of participating physicians or providers in the market exceeded the 30% criterion of the safety zone. *See, e.g.,* Letter from Anne K. Bingaman, Assistant Attorney General, Department of Justice, to John F. Fischer (Oklahoma Physicians Network, Inc.) (Jan. 17, 1996) ("substantially more" than 30% of several specialties in a number of local markets, including more than 50% in one specialty); Letter from Anne K. Bingaman to Melissa J. Fields (Dermnet, Inc.) (Dec. 5,

apply, to define a category of ventures for which the Agencies presume no anticompetitive harm, without examining competitive conditions in the particular case. A determination about the lawfulness of physician network joint ventures that fall outside the safety zones must be made on a case-by-case basis according to general antitrust principles and the more specific analysis described in this statement.

A. *Antitrust Safety Zones*

This section describes those physician network joint ventures that will fall within the antitrust safety zones designated by the Agencies. The antitrust safety zones differ for "exclusive" and "non-exclusive" physician network joint ventures. In an "exclusive" venture, the network's physician participants are restricted in their ability to, or do not in practice, individually contract or affiliate with other network joint ventures or health plans. In a "non-exclusive" venture, on the other hand, the physician participants in fact do, or are available to, affiliate with other networks or contract individually with health plans. This section explains how the Agencies will determine whether a physician network joint venture is exclusive or non-exclusive. It also illustrates types of arrangements that can involve the sharing of substantial financial risk among a network's physician participants, which is necessary for a network to come within the safety zones.

1. Exclusive Physician Network Joint Ventures That the Agencies Will Not Challenge, Absent Extraordinary Circumstances

The Agencies will not challenge, absent extraordinary circumstances, an exclusive physician network joint venture whose physician participants share substantial financial risk and constitute 20 percent or less of the physicians[25] in each physician specialty with active hospital staff privileges who practice in the relevant geographic market.[26] In relevant markets with fewer than five physicians in a particular specialty, an exclusive physician network joint venture otherwise qualifying for the antitrust safety zone may include one physician from that specialty, on a non-exclusive basis, even though the inclusion of that physician results in the venture consisting of more than 20 percent of the physicians in that specialty.

2. Non-Exclusive Physician Network Joint Ventures That the Agencies Will Not Challenge, Absent Extraordinary Circumstances

The Agencies will not challenge, absent extraordinary circumstances, a non-exclusive physician network joint venture whose physician participants

---

1995) (44% of board-certified dermatologists); Letter from Anne K. Bingaman to Dee Hartzog (International Chiropractor's Association of California) (Oct. 27, 1994) (up to 50% of chiropractors); Letter from Mark Horoschak, Assistant Director, Federal Trade Commission, to Stephen P. Nash (Eastern Ohio Physicians Organization) (Sept. 28, 1995) (safety zone's 30% criterion exceeded for primary care physicians by a small amount, and for certain subspecialty fields "to a greater extent"); Letter from Mark Horoschak to John A. Cook (Oakland Physician Network) (Mar. 28, 1995) (multispecialty network with 44% of physicians in one specialty).

[25] For purposes of the antitrust safety zones, in calculating the number of physicians in a relevant market and the number of physician participants in a physician network joint venture, each physician ordinarily will be counted individually, whether the physician practices in a group or solo practice.

[26] Generally, relevant geographic markets for the delivery of physician services are local.

share substantial financial risk and constitute 30 percent or less of the physicians in each physician specialty with active hospital staff privileges who practice in the relevant geographic market. In relevant markets with fewer than four physicians in a particular specialty, a non-exclusive physician network joint venture otherwise qualifying for the antitrust safety zone may include one physician from that specialty, even though the inclusion of that physician results in the venture consisting of more than 30 percent of the physicians in that specialty.

3. Indicia of Non-Exclusivity

Because of the different market share thresholds for the safety zones for exclusive and non-exclusive physician network joint ventures, the Agencies caution physician participants in a non-exclusive physician network joint venture to be sure that the network is non-exclusive in fact and not just in name. The Agencies will determine whether a physician network joint venture is exclusive or non-exclusive by its physician participants' activities, and not simply by the terms of the contractual relationship. In making that determination, the Agencies will examine the following indicia of non-exclusivity, among others:

(1) that viable competing networks or managed care plans with adequate physician participation currently exist in the market;

(2) that physicians in the network actually individually participate in, or contract with, other networks or managed care plans, or there is other evidence of their willingness and incentive to do so;

(3) that physicians in the network earn substantial revenue from other networks or through individual contracts with managed care plans;

(4) the absence of any indications of significant de-participation from other networks or managed care plans in the market; and

(5) the absence of any indications of coordination among the physicians in the network regarding price or other competitively significant terms of participation in other networks or managed care plans.

Networks also may limit or condition physician participants' freedom to contract outside the network in ways that fall short of a commitment of full exclusivity. If those provisions significantly restrict the ability or willingness of a network's physicians to join other networks or contract individually with managed care plans, the network will be considered exclusive for purposes of the safety zones.

4. Sharing of Substantial Financial Risk by Physicians in a Physician Network Joint Venture

To qualify for either antitrust safety zone, the participants in a physician network joint venture must share substantial financial risk in providing all the services that are jointly priced through the network.[27]

[27] Physician network joint ventures that involve both risk-sharing and non-risk-sharing arrangements do not fall within the safety zones. For example, a network may have both risk-sharing and non-risk-sharing contracts. It also may have contracts that involve risk sharing, but not all the physicians in the network participate in risk sharing or not all of the services are paid for on a risk-sharing basis. The Agencies will consider each of the network's arrangements separately, as well as the activities of the venture as a whole, to determine whether the joint pricing with respect to the non-risk-sharing aspects of the venture is appropriately analyzed under the rule of reason. See *infra* Example 2. The mere presence of some risk-sharing arrangements, however, will not necessarily result in rule of reason analysis of the non-risk-sharing aspects of the venture.

The safety zones are limited to networks involving substantial financial risk sharing not because such risk sharing is a desired end in itself, but because it normally is a clear and reliable indicator that a physician network involves sufficient integration by its physician participants to achieve significant efficiencies.[28] Risk sharing provides incentives for the physicians to cooperate in controlling costs and improving quality by managing the provision of services by network physicians.

The following are examples of some types of arrangements through which participants in a physician network joint venture can share substantial financial risk:[29]

(1) agreement by the venture to provide services to a health plan at a "capitated" rate;[30]

(2) agreement by the venture to provide designated services or classes of services to a health plan for a predetermined percentage of premium or revenue from the plan;[31]

(3) use by the venture of significant financial incentives for its physician participants, as a group, to achieve specified cost-containment goals. Two methods by which the venture can accomplish this are:

(a) withholding from all physician participants in the network a substantial amount of the compensation due to them, with distribution of that amount to the physician participants based on group performance in meeting the cost-containment goals of the network as a whole; or

(b) establishing overall cost or utilization targets for the network as a whole, with the network's physician participants subject to subsequent substantial financial rewards or penalties based on group performance in meeting the targets; and

(4) agreement by the venture to provide a complex or extended course of treatment that requires the substantial coordination of care by physicians in different specialities offering a complementary mix of services, for a fixed, predetermined payment, where the costs of that course of treatment for any individual patient can vary greatly due to the individual patient's condition, the choice, complexity, or length of treatment, or other factors.[32]

---

[28] The existence of financial risk sharing does not depend on whether, under applicable state law, the network is considered an insurer.

[29] Physician participants in a single network need not all be involved in the same risk-sharing arrangement within the network to fall within the safety zones. For example, primary care physicians may be capitated and specialists subject to a withhold, or groups of physicians may be in separate risk pools.

[30] A "capitated" rate is a fixed, predetermined payment per covered life (the "capitation") from a health plan to the joint venture in exchange for the joint venture's (not merely an individual physician's) providing and guaranteeing provision of a defined set of covered services to covered individuals for a specified period, regardless of the amount of services actually provided.

[31] This is similar to a capitation arrangement, except that the amount of payment to the network can vary in response to changes in the health plan's premiums or revenues.

[32] Such arrangements are sometimes referred to as "global fees" or "all-inclusive case rates." Global fee or all-inclusive case rate arrangements that involve financial risk sharing as contemplated by this example will require that the joint venture (not merely an individual physician participant) assume the risk or benefit that the treatment provided through the network may either exceed, or cost less than, the predetermined payment.

The Agencies recognize that new types of risk-sharing arrangements may develop. The preceding examples do not foreclose consideration of other arrangements through which the participants in a physician network joint venture may share substantial financial risk in the provision of medical services through the network.[33] Organizers of physician networks who are uncertain whether their proposed arrangements constitute substantial financial risk sharing for purposes of this policy statement are encouraged to take advantage of the Agencies' expedited business review and advisory opinion procedures.

B. The Agencies' Analysis of Physician Network Joint Ventures That Fall Outside the Antitrust Safety Zones

Physician network joint ventures that fall outside the antitrust safety zones also may have the potential to create significant efficiencies, and do not necessarily raise substantial antitrust concerns. For example, physician network joint ventures in which the physician participants share substantial financial risk, but which involve a higher percentage of physicians in a relevant market than specified in the safety zones, may be lawful if they are not anticompetitive on balance.[34] Likewise, physician network joint ventures that do not involve the sharing of substantial financial risk also may be lawful if the physicians' integration through the joint venture creates significant efficiencies and the venture, on balance, is not anticompetitive.

The Agencies emphasize that it is not their intent to treat such networks either more strictly or more leniently than joint ventures in other industries, or to favor any particular procompetitive organization or structure of health care delivery over other forms that consumers may desire. Rather, their goal is to ensure a competitive marketplace in which consumers will have the benefit of high quality, cost-effective health care and a wide range of choices, including new provider-controlled networks that expand consumer choice and increase competition.

1. Determining When Agreements Among Physicians in a Physician Network Joint Venture Are Analyzed Under the Rule of Reason

Antitrust law treats naked agreements among competitors that fix prices or allocate markets as per se illegal. Where competitors economically integrate in a joint venture, however, such agreements, if reasonably necessary to accomplish the procompetitive benefits of the integration, are analyzed under the rule of reason.[35] In accord with general antitrust principles, physician network joint ventures will be analyzed under the rule of reason, and will not be viewed as per se illegal, if the physicians' integration through the network is likely to produce significant efficiencies that benefit

[33] The manner of dividing revenues among the network's physician participants generally does not raise antitrust issues so long as the competing physicians in a network (continued . . .) share substantial financial risk. For example, capitated networks may distribute income among their physician participants using fee-for-service payment with a partial withhold fund to cover the risk of having to provide more services than were originally anticipated.

[34] *See infra* Examples 5 and 6. Many such physician networks have received favorable business review or advisory opinion letters from the Agencies. The percentages used in the safety zones define areas in which the lack of anticompetitive effects ordinarily will be presumed.

[35] In a network limited to providers who are not actual or potential competitors, the providers generally can agree on the prices to be charged for their services without the kinds of economic integration discussed below.

consumers, and any price agreements (or other agreements that would otherwise be per se illegal) by the network physicians are reasonably necessary to realize those efficiencies.[36]

Where the participants in a physician network joint venture have agreed to share substantial financial risk as defined in Section A.4. of this policy statement, their risk-sharing arrangement generally establishes both an overall efficiency goal for the venture and the incentives for the physicians to meet that goal. The setting of price is integral to the venture's use of such an arrangement and therefore warrants evaluation under the rule of reason.

Physician network joint ventures that do not involve the sharing of substantial financial risk may also involve sufficient integration to demonstrate that the venture is likely to produce significant efficiencies. Such integration can be evidenced by the network implementing an active and ongoing program to evaluate and modify practice patterns by the network's physician participants and create a high degree of interdependence and cooperation among the physicians to control costs and ensure quality. This program may include: (1) establishing mechanisms to monitor and control utilization of health care services that are designed to control costs and assure quality of care; (2) selectively choosing network physicians who are likely to further these efficiency objectives; and (3) the significant investment of capital, both monetary and human, in the necessary infrastructure and capability to realize the claimed efficiencies.

The foregoing are not, however, the only types of arrangements that can evidence sufficient integration to warrant rule of reason analysis, and the Agencies will consider other arrangements that also may evidence such integration. However, in all cases, the Agencies' analysis will focus on substance, rather than form, in assessing a network's likelihood of producing significant efficiencies. To the extent that agreements on prices to be charged for the integrated provision of services are reasonably necessary to the venture's achievement of efficiencies, they will be evaluated under the rule of reason.

In contrast to integrated physician network joint ventures, such as these discussed above, there have been arrangements among physicians that have taken the form of networks, but which in purpose or effect were little more than efforts by their participants to prevent or impede competitive forces from operating in the market. These arrangements are not likely to produce significant procompetitive efficiencies. Such arrangements have been, and will continue to be, treated as unlawful conspiracies or cartels, whose price agreements are per se illegal.

Determining that an arrangement is merely a vehicle to fix prices or engage in naked anticompetitive conduct is a factual inquiry that must be done on a

[36] In some cases, the combination of the competing physicians in the network may enable them to offer what could be considered to be a new product producing substantial efficiencies, and therefore the venture will be analyzed under the rule of reason. *See Broadcast Music, Inc. v. Columbia Broadcasting System, Inc.*, 441 U.S. 1, 21–22 (1979) (competitors' integration and creation of a blanket license for use of copyrighted compositions results in efficiencies so great as to make the blanket license a "different product" from the mere combination of individual competitors and, therefore, joint pricing of the blanket license is subject to rule of reason analysis, rather than the per se rule against price fixing). The Agencies' analysis will focus on the efficiencies likely to be produced by the venture, and the relationship of any price agreements to the achievement of those efficiencies, rather than on whether the venture creates a product that can be labeled "new" or "different."

case-by-case basis to determine the arrangement's true nature and likely competitive effects. However, a variety of factors may tend to corroborate a network's anticompetitive nature, including: statements evidencing anticompetitive purpose; a recent history of anticompetitive behavior or collusion in the market, including efforts to obstruct or undermine the development of managed care; obvious anticompetitive structure of the network (*e.g.*, a network comprising a very high percentage of local area physicians, whose participation in the network is exclusive, without any plausible business or efficiency justification); the absence of any mechanisms with the potential for generating significant efficiencies or otherwise increasing competition through the network; the presence of anticompetitive collateral agreements; and the absence of mechanisms to prevent the network's operation from having anticompetitive spillover effects outside the network.

2. Applying the Rule of Reason

A rule of reason analysis determines whether the formation and operation of the joint venture may have a substantial anticompetitive effect and, if so, whether that potential effect is outweighed by any procompetitive efficiencies resulting from the joint venture. The rule of reason analysis takes into account characteristics of the particular physician network joint venture, and the competitive environment in which it operates, that bear on the venture's likely effect on competition.

A determination about the lawfulness of a network's activity under the rule of reason sometimes can be reached without an extensive inquiry under each step of the analysis. For example, a physician network joint venture that involves substantial clinical integration may include a relatively small percentage of the physicians in the relevant markets on a non-exclusive basis. In that case, the Agencies may be able to conclude expeditiously that the network is unlikely to be anticompetitive, based on the competitive environment in which it operates. In assessing the competitive environment, the Agencies would consider such market factors as the number, types, and size of managed care plans operating in the area, the extent of physician participation in those plans, and the economic importance of the managed care plans to area physicians. See infra Example 1. Alternatively, for example, if a restraint that facially appears to be of a kind that would always or almost always tend to reduce output or increase prices, but has not been considered per se unlawful, is not reasonably necessary to the creation of efficiencies, the Agencies will likely challenge the restraint without an elaborate analysis of market definition and market power.[37]

The steps ordinarily involved in a rule of reason analysis of physician network joint ventures are set forth below.

Step one: Define the relevant market. The Agencies evaluate the competitive effects of a physician network joint venture in each relevant market in which it operates or has substantial impact. In defining the relevant product and geographic markets, the Agencies look to what substitutes, as a practical matter, are reasonably available to consumers for the services in question.[38] The Agencies will first identify the relevant services that the physician network joint venture provides. Although all services provided by

---

[37] *See FTC v. Indiana Federation of Dentists*, 476 U.S. 447, 459–60 (1986).

[38] A more extensive discussion of how the Agencies define relevant markets is contained in the Agencies' *1992 Horizontal Merger Guidelines.*

each physician specialty might be a separate relevant service market, there may be instances in which significant overlap of services provided by different physician specialties, or in some circumstances, certain nonphysician health care providers, justifies including services from more than one physician specialty or category of providers in the same market. For each relevant service market, the relevant geographic market will include all physicians (or other providers) who are good substitutes for the physician participants in the joint venture.

Step two: Evaluate the competitive effects of the physician joint venture. The Agencies examine the structure and activities of the physician network joint venture and the nature of competition in the relevant market to determine whether the formation or operation of the venture is likely to have an anticompetitive effect. Two key areas of competitive concern are whether a physician network joint venture could raise the prices for physician services charged to health plans above competitive levels, or could prevent or impede the formation or operation of other networks or plans.

In assessing whether a particular network arrangement could raise prices or exclude competition, the Agencies will examine whether the network physicians collectively have the ability and incentive to engage in such conduct. The Agencies will consider not only the proportion of the physicians in any relevant market who are in the network, but also the incentives faced by physicians in the network, and whether different groups of physicians in a network may have significantly different incentives that would reduce the likelihood of anticompetitive conduct. The Department of Justice has entered into final judgments that permit a network to include a relatively large proportion of physicians in a relevant market where the percentage of physicians with an ownership interest in the network is strictly limited, and the network subcontracts with additional physicians under terms that create a sufficient divergence of economic interest between the subcontracting physicians and the owner physicians so that the owner physicians have an incentive to control the costs to the network of the subcontracting physicians.[39] Evaluating the incentives faced by network physicians requires an examination of the facts and circumstances of each particular case. The Agencies will assess whether different groups of physicians in the network actually have significantly divergent incentives that would override any shared interest, such as the incentive to profit from higher fees for their medical services. The Agencies will also consider whether the behavior of network physicians or other market evidence indicates that the differing incentives among groups of physicians will not prevent anticompetitive conduct.

If, in the relevant market, there are many other networks or many physicians who would be available to form competing networks or to contract directly with health plans, it is unlikely that the joint venture would raise significant competitive concerns. The Agencies will analyze the availability of suitable physicians to form competing networks, including the exclusive or non-exclusive nature of the physician network joint venture.

[39] *See, e.g.*, Competitive Impact Statements in *United States v. Health Choice of Northwest Missouri, Inc.*, Case No. 95-6171-CV-SJ-6 (W.D. Mo.; filed Sept. 13, 1995), 60 Fed. Reg. 51808, 51815 (Oct. 3, 1995); *United States and State of Connecticut v. HealthCare Partners, Inc.*, Case No. 395-CV-01946-RNC (D. Conn.; filed Sept. 13, 1995), 60 Fed. Reg. 52018, 52020 (Oct. 4, 1995).

The Agencies recognize that the competitive impact of exclusive arrangements or other limitations on the ability of a network's physician participants to contract outside the network can vary greatly. For example, in some circumstances exclusivity may help a network serve its subscribers and increase its physician participants' incentives to further the interests of the network. In other situations, however, the anticompetitive risks posed by such exclusivity may outweigh its procompetitive benefits. Accordingly, the Agencies will evaluate the actual or likely effects of particular limitations on contracting in the market situation in which they occur.

An additional area of possible anticompetitive concern involves the risk of "spillover" effects from the venture. For example, a joint venture may involve the exchange of competitively sensitive information among competing physicians and thereby become a vehicle for the network's physician participants to coordinate their activities outside the venture. Ventures that are structured to reduce the likelihood of such spillover are less likely to result in anticompetitive effects. For example, a network that uses an outside agent to collect and analyze fee data from physicians for use in developing the network's fee schedule, and avoids the sharing of such sensitive information among the network's physician participants, may reduce concerns that the information could be used by the network's physician participants to set prices for services they provide outside the network.

Step three: Evaluate the impact of procompetitive efficiencies.[40] This step requires an examination of the joint venture's likely procompetitive efficiencies, and the balancing of these efficiencies against any likely anticompetitive effects. The greater the venture's likely anticompetitive effects, the greater must be the venture's likely efficiencies. In assessing efficiency claims, the Agencies focus on net efficiencies that will be derived from the operation of the network and that result in lower prices or higher quality to consumers. The Agencies will not accept claims of efficiencies if the parties reasonably can achieve equivalent or comparable savings through significantly less anticompetitive means. In making this assessment, however, the Agencies will not search for a theoretically least restrictive alternative that is not practical given business realities.

Experience indicates that, in general, more significant efficiencies are likely to result from a physician network joint venture's substantial financial risk sharing or substantial clinical integration. However, the Agencies will consider a broad range of possible cost savings, including improved cost controls, case management and quality assurance, economies of scale, and reduced administrative or transaction costs.

In assessing the likelihood that efficiencies will be realized, the Agencies recognize that competition is one of the strongest motivations for firms to lower prices, reduce costs, and provide higher quality. Thus, the greater the competition facing the network, the more likely it is that the network will actually realize potential efficiencies that would benefit consumers.

Step four: Evaluation of collateral agreements. This step examines whether the physician network joint venture includes collateral agreements or conditions that unreasonably restrict competition and are unlikely to contribute significantly to the legitimate purposes of the physician network joint venture. The Agencies will examine whether the collateral agreements

---

[40] If steps one and two reveal no competitive concerns with the physician network joint venture, step three is unnecessary, and the analysis continues with step four, below.

are reasonably necessary to achieve the efficiencies sought by the joint venture. For example, if the physician participants in a physician network joint venture agree on the prices they will charge patients who are not covered by the health plans with which their network contracts, such an agreement plainly is not reasonably necessary to the success of the joint venture and is an antitrust violation.[41] Similarly, attempts by a physician network joint venture to exclude competitors or classes of competitors of the network's physician participants from the market could have anticompetitive effects, without advancing any legitimate, procompetitive goal of the network. This could happen, for example, if the network facilitated agreements among the physicians to refuse to deal with such competitors outside the network, or to pressure other market participants to refuse to deal with such competitors or deny them necessary access to key facilities.

C. Examples of Physician Network Joint Ventures

The following are examples of how the Agencies would apply the principles set forth in this statement to specific physician network joint ventures. The first three are new examples: 1) a network involving substantial clinical integration, that is unlikely to raise significant competitive concerns under the rule of reason; 2) a network involving both substantial financial risk-sharing and non-risk-sharing arrangements, which would be analyzed under the rule of reason; and 3) a network involving neither substantial financial risk-sharing nor substantial clinical integration, and whose price agreements likely would be challenged as per se unlawful. The last four examples involve networks that operate in a variety of market settings and with different levels of physician participants; three are networks that involve substantial financial risk-sharing and one is a network in which the physician participants do not jointly agree on, or negotiate, price.

1. Physician Network Joint Venture Involving Clinical Integration

Charlestown is a relatively isolated, medium-sized city. For the purposes of this example, the services provided by primary care physicians and those provided by the different physician specialties each constitute a relevant product market; and the relevant geographic market for each of them is Charlestown.

Several HMOs and other significant managed care plans operate in Charlestown. A substantial proportion of insured individuals are enrolled in these plans, and enrollment in managed care is expected to increase. Many physicians in each of the specialties participate in more than one of these plans. There is no significant overlap among the participants on the physician panels of many of these plans.

A group of Charlestown physicians establishes an IPA to assume greater responsibility for managing the cost and quality of care rendered to Charlestown residents who are members of health plans. They hope to reduce costs while maintaining or improving the quality of care, and thus to attract more managed care patients to their practices.

The IPA will implement systems to establish goals relating to quality and appropriate utilization of services by IPA participants, regularly evaluate both individual participants' and the network's aggregate performance with respect to those goals, and modify individual participants' actual practices,

[41] This analysis of collateral agreements also applies to physician network joint ventures that fall within the safety zones.

where necessary, based on those evaluations. The IPA will engage in case management, preauthorization of some services, and concurrent and retrospective review of inpatient stays. In addition, the IPA is developing practice standards and protocols to govern treatment and utilization of services, and it will actively review the care rendered by each doctor in light of these standards and protocols.

There is a significant investment of capital to purchase the information systems necessary to gather aggregate and individual data on the cost, quantity, and nature of services provided or ordered by the IPA physicians; to measure performance of the group and the individual doctors against cost and quality benchmarks; and to monitor patient satisfaction. The IPA will provide payers with detailed reports on the cost and quantity of services provided, and on the network's success in meeting its goals.

The IPA will hire a medical director and a support staff to perform the above functions and to coordinate patient care in specific cases. The doctors also have invested appreciable time in developing the practice standards and protocols, and will continue actively to monitor care provided through the IPA. Network participants who fail to adhere to the network's standards and protocols will be subject to remedial action, including the possibility of expulsion from the network.

The IPA physicians will be paid by health plans on a fee-for-service basis; the physicians will not share substantial financial risk for the cost of services rendered to covered individuals through the network. The IPA will retain an agent to develop a fee schedule, negotiate fees, and contract with payers on behalf of the venture. Information about what participating doctors charge non-network patients will not be disseminated to participants in the IPA, and the doctors will not agree on the prices they will charge patients not covered by IPA contracts.

The IPA is built around three geographically dispersed primary care group practices that together account for 25 percent of the primary care doctors in Charlestown. A number of specialists to whom the primary care doctors most often refer their patients also are invited to participate in the IPA. These specialists are selected based on their established referral relationships with the primary care doctors, the quality of care provided by the doctors, their willingness to cooperate with the goals of the IPA, and the need to provide convenient referral services to patients of the primary care doctors. Specialist services that are needed less frequently will be provided by doctors who are not IPA participants. Participating specialists constitute from 20 to 35 percent of the specialists in each relevant market, depending on the specialty. Physician participation in the IPA is non-exclusive. Many IPA participants already do and are expected to continue to participate in other managed care plans and earn substantial income from those plans.

Competitive Analysis

Although the IPA does not fall within the antitrust safety zone because the physicians do not share substantial financial risk, the Agencies would analyze the IPA under the rule of reason because it offers the potential for creating significant efficiencies and the price agreement is reasonably necessary to realize those efficiencies. Prior to contracting on behalf of competing doctors, the IPA will develop and invest in mechanisms to provide cost-effective quality care, including standards and protocols to govern treatment and utilization of services, information systems to measure and monitor individual physician and aggregate network performance, and procedures to modify physician behavior and assure adherence to network standards and protocols. The network is structured to achieve its efficiencies through a high degree of interdependence and cooperation among its physician participants. The price agreement, under these circumstances, is subordinate to and reasonably necessary to achieve these objectives.[42]

Furthermore, the Agencies would not challenge under the rule of reason the doctors' agreement to establish and operate the IPA. In conducting the rule of reason analysis, the Agencies would evaluate the likely competitive effects of the venture in each relevant market. In this case, the IPA does not appear likely to limit competition in any relevant market either by hampering the ability of health plans to contract individually with area physicians or with other physician network joint ventures, or by enabling the physicians to raise prices above competitive levels. The IPA does not appear to be overinclusive: many primary care physicians and specialists are available to other plans, and the doctors in the IPA have been selected to achieve the network's procompetitive potential. Many IPA participants also participate in other managed care plans and are expected to continue to do so in the future. Moreover, several significant managed care plans are not dependent on the IPA participants to offer their products to consumers. Finally, the venture is structured so that physician participants do not share competitively sensitive information, thus reducing the likelihood of anticompetitive spillover effects outside the network where the physicians still compete, and the venture avoids any anticompetitive collateral agreements.

Since the venture is not likely to be anticompetitive, there is no need for further detailed evaluation of the venture's potential for generating procompetitive efficiencies. For these reasons, the Agencies would not challenge the joint venture. However, they would reexamine this conclusion and do a more complete analysis of the procompetitive efficiencies if evidence of actual anticompetitive effects were to develop.

2. Physician Network Joint Venture Involving Risk-Sharing and Non-Risk-Sharing Contracts

An IPA has capitation contracts with three insurer-developed HMOs. Under its contracts with the HMOs, the IPA receives a set fee per member per month for all covered services required by enrollees in a particular health plan. Physician participants in the IPA are paid on a fee-for-service basis, pursuant to a fee schedule developed by the IPA. Physicians participate in the IPA on a non-exclusive basis. Many of the IPA's physicians participate in managed care plans outside the IPA, and earn substantial income from those plans.

The IPA uses a variety of mechanisms to assure appropriate use of services under its capitation contracts so that it can provide contract services within its capitation budgets. In part because the IPA has managed the provision of care effectively, enrollment in the HMOs has grown to the point where HMO patients are a significant share of the IPA doctors' patients.

---

42 Although the physicians in this example have not directly agreed with one another on the prices to be charged for services rendered through the network, the venture's use of an agent, subject to its control, to establish fees and to negotiate and execute contracts on behalf of the venture amounts to a price agreement among competitors. However, the use of such an agent should reduce the risk of the network's activities having anticompetitive spillover effects on competition among the physicians for non-network patients.

The three insurers that offer the HMOs also offer PPO options in response to the request of employers who want to give their employees greater choice of plans. Although the capitation contracts are a substantial majority of the IPA's business, it also contracts with the insurers to provide services to the PPO programs on a fee-for-service basis. The physicians are paid according to the same fee schedule used to pay them under the IPA's capitated contracts. The IPA uses the same panel of providers and the same utilization management mechanisms that are involved in the HMO contracts. The IPA has tracked utilization for HMO and PPO patients, which shows similar utilization patterns for both types of patients.

Competitive Analysis

Because the IPA negotiates and enters into both capitated and fee-for-service contracts on behalf on its physicians, the venture is not within a safety zone. However, the IPA's HMO contracts are analyzed under the rule of reason because they involve substantial financial risk-sharing. The PPO contracts also are analyzed under the rule of reason because there are significant efficiencies from the capitated arrangements that carry over to the fee-for-service business. The IPA's procedures for managing the provision of care under its capitation contracts and its related fee schedules produce significant efficiencies; and since those same procedures and fees are used for the PPO contracts and result in similar utilization patterns, they will likely result in significant efficiencies for the PPO arrangements as well.

3. Physician Network That Is Per Se Unlawful

A group of physicians in Clarksville forms an IPA to contract with managed care plans. There is some limited managed care presence in the area, and new plans have announced their interest in entering. The physicians agree that the only way they can effectively combat the power of the plans and protect themselves from low fees and intrusive utilization review is to organize and negotiate with the plans collectively through the IPA, rather than individually.

Membership in the IPA is open to any licensed physician in Clarksville. Members contribute $2,000 each to fund the legal fees associated with incorporating the IPA and its operating expenses, including the salary of an executive director who will negotiate contracts on behalf of the IPA. The IPA will enter only into fee-for-service contracts. The doctors will not share substantial financial risk under the contracts. The Contracting Committee, in consultation with the executive director, develops a fee schedule.

The IPA establishes a Quality Assurance and Utilization Review Committee. Upon recommendation of this committee, the members vote to have the IPA adopt two basic utilization review parameters: strict limits on documentation to be provided by physicians to the payers, and arbitration of disputes regarding plan utilization review decisions by a committee of the local medical society. The IPA refuses to contract with plans that do not accept these utilization review parameters. The IPA claims to have its own utilization review/quality assurance programs in development, but has taken very few steps to create such a program. It decides to rely instead on the hospital's established peer review mechanisms.

Although there is no formal exclusivity agreement, IPA physicians who are approached by managed care plans seeking contracts refer the plans to the IPA. Except for some contracts predating the formation of the IPA, the physicians do not contract individually with managed care plans on terms other than those set by the IPA.

Competitive Analysis

This IPA is merely a vehicle for collective decisions by its physicians on price and other significant terms of dealing. The physicians' purpose in forming the IPA is to increase their bargaining power with payers. The IPA makes no effort to selectively choose physicians who are likely to further the network's achievement of efficiencies, and the IPA involves no significant integration, financial or otherwise. IPA physicians' participation in the hospital's general peer review procedures does not evidence integration by those physicians that is likely to result in significant efficiencies in the provision of services through the IPA. The IPA does not manage the provision of care or offer any substantial potential for significant procompetitive efficiencies. The physicians are merely collectively agreeing on prices they will receive for services rendered under IPA contracts and not to accept certain aspects of utilization review that they do not like.

The physicians' contribution of capital to form the IPA does not make it a legitimate joint venture. In some circumstances, capital contributions by an IPA's participants can indicate that the participants have made a significant commitment to the creation of an efficiency-producing competitive entity in the market.[43] Capital contributions, however, can also be used to fund a cartel. The key inquiry is whether the contributed capital is being used to further the network's capability to achieve substantial efficiencies. In this case, the funds are being used primarily to support the joint negotiation, and not to achieve substantial procompetitive efficiencies. Thus, the physicians' agreement to bargain through the joint venture will be treated as per se illegal price fixing.

4. *Exclusive Physician Network Joint Venture with Financial Risk-Sharing and Comprising More Than Twenty Percent of Physicians with Active Admitting Privileges at a Hospital*

County Seat is a relatively isolated, medium-sized community of about 350,000 residents. The closest town is 50 miles away. County Seat has five general acute care hospitals that offer a mix of basic primary, secondary, and tertiary care services.

Five hundred physicians have medical practices based in County Seat, and all maintain active admitting privileges at one or more of County Seat's hospitals. No physician from outside County Seat has any type of admitting privileges at a County Seat hospital. The physicians represent 10 different specialties and are distributed evenly among the specialties, with 50 doctors practicing each specialty.

One hundred physicians (also distributed evenly among specialties) maintain active admitting privileges at County Seat Medical Center. County Seat's other 400 physicians maintain active admitting privileges at other County Seat hospitals.

Half of County Seat Medical Center's 100 active admitting physicians propose to form an IPA to market their services to purchasers of health care services. The physicians are divided evenly among the specialties. Under the proposed arrangement, the physicians in the network joint venture would agree to meaningful cost containment and quality goals, including

---

[43] *See supra* Example 1.

utilization review, quality assurance, and other measures designed to reduce the provision of unnecessary care to the plan's subscribers, and a substantial amount (in this example 20 percent) of the compensation due to the network's physician participants would be withheld and distributed only if these measures are successfully met. This physician network joint venture would be exclusive: Its physician participants would not be free to contract individually with health plans or to join other physician joint ventures.

A number of health plans that contract selectively with hospitals and physicians already operate in County Seat. These plans and local employers agree that other County Seat physicians, and the hospitals to which they admit, are good substitutes for the active admitting physicians and the inpatient services provided at County Seat Medical Center. Physicians with medical practices based outside County Seat, however, are not good substitutes for area physicians, because such physicians would find it inconvenient to practice at County Seat hospitals due to the distance between their practice locations and County Seat.

Competitive Analysis

A key issue is whether a physician network joint venture, such as this IPA, comprising 50 percent of the physicians in each specialty with active privileges at one of five comparable hospitals in County Seat would fall within the antitrust safety zone. The physicians within the joint venture represent less than 20 percent of all the physicians in each specialty in County Seat.

County Seat is the relevant geographic market for purposes of analyzing the competitive effects of this proposed physician joint venture. Within each specialty, physicians with admitting privileges at area hospitals are good substitutes for one another. However, physicians with practices based elsewhere are not considered good substitutes.

For purposes of analyzing the effects of the venture, all of the physicians in County Seat should be considered market participants. Purchasers of health care services consider all physicians within each specialty, and the hospitals at which they have admitting privileges, to be relatively interchangeable. Thus, in this example, any attempt by the joint venture's physician participants collectively to increase the price of physician services above competitive levels would likely lead third-party purchasers to recruit non-network physicians at County Seat Medical Center or other area hospitals.

Because physician network joint venture participants constitute less than 20 percent of each group of specialists in County Seat and agree to share substantial financial risk, this proposed joint venture would fall within the antitrust safety zone.

5. *Physician Network Joint Venture with Financial Risk-Sharing and a Large Percentage of Physicians in a Relatively Small Community*

Smalltown has a population of 25,000, a single hospital, and 50 physicians, most of whom are family practitioners. All of the physicians practice exclusively in Smalltown and have active admitting privileges at the Smalltown hospital. The closest urban area, Big City, is located some 35 miles away and has a population of 500,000. A little more than half of Smalltown's working adults commute to work in Big City. Some of the health plans used by employers in Big City are interested in extending their network of providers to Smalltown to provide coverage for subscribers who live in Smalltown, but commute to work in Big City (coverage is to include the families of commuting subscribers). However, the number of commuting Smalltown subscribers is a small fraction of the Big City employers' total workforce.

Responding to these employers' needs, a few health plans have asked physicians in Smalltown to organize a non-exclusive IPA large enough to provide a reasonable choice to subscribers who reside in Smalltown, but commute to work in Big City. Because of the relatively small number of potential enrollees in Smalltown, the plans prefer to contract with such a physician network joint venture, rather than engage in what may prove to be a time-consuming series of negotiations with individual Smalltown physicians to establish a panel of physician providers there.

A number of Smalltown physicians have agreed to form a physician network joint venture. The joint venture will contract with health plans to provide physician services to subscribers of the plans in exchange for a monthly capitation fee paid for each of the plans' subscribers. The physicians forming this joint venture would constitute about half of the total number of physicians in Smalltown. They would represent about 35 percent of the town's family practitioners, but higher percentages of the town's general surgeons (50 percent), pediatricians (50 percent), and obstetricians (67 percent). The health plans that serve Big City employers say that the IPA must have a large percentage of Smalltown physicians to provide adequate coverage for employees and their families in Smalltown and in a few scattered rural communities in the immediate area and to allow the doctors to provide coverage for each other.

In this example, other health plans already have entered Smalltown, and contracted with individual physicians. They have made substantial inroads with Smalltown employers, signing up a large number of enrollees. None of these plans has had any difficulty contracting with individual physicians, including many who would participate in the proposed joint venture.

Finally, the evidence indicates that Smalltown is the relevant geographic market for all physician services. Physicians in Big City are not good substitutes for a significant number of Smalltown residents.

Competitive Analysis

This proposed physician network joint venture would not fall within the antitrust safety zone because it would comprise over 30 percent of the physicians in a number of relevant specialties in the geographic market. However, the Agencies would not challenge the joint venture because a rule of reason analysis indicates that its formation would not likely hamper the ability of health plans to contract individually with area physicians or with other physician network joint ventures, or enable the physicians to raise prices above competitive levels. In addition, the joint venture's agreement to accept capitated fees creates incentives for its physicians to achieve cost savings.

That health plans have requested formation of this venture also is significant, for it suggests that the joint venture would offer additional efficiencies. In this instance, it appears to be a low-cost method for plans to enter an area without investing in costly negotiations to identify and contract with individual physicians.

Moreover, in small markets such as Smalltown, it may be necessary for purchasers of health care services to contract with a relatively large number of physicians to provide adequate coverage and choice for enrollees. For instance, if there were only three obstetricians in Smalltown, it would not be possible for a physician network joint venture offering obstetrical services to have less than 33 percent of the obstetricians in the relevant area. Furthermore, it may be impractical to have less than 67 percent in the plan, because two obstetricians may be needed in the venture to provide coverage for each other.

Although the joint venture has a relatively large percentage of some specialties, it appears unlikely to present competitive concerns under the rule of reason because of three factors: (1) the demonstrated ability of health plans to contract with physicians individually; (2) the possibility that other physician network joint ventures could be formed; and (3) the potential benefits from the coverage to be provided by this physician network joint venture. Therefore, the Agencies would not challenge the joint venture.

6. Physician Network Joint Venture with Financial Risk Sharing and a Large Percentage of Physicians in a Small, Rural County

Rural County has a population of 15,000, a small primary care hospital, and ten physicians, including seven general and family practitioners, an obstetrician, a pediatrician, and a general surgeon. All of the physicians are solo practitioners. The nearest urban area is about 60 miles away in Big City, which has a population of 300,000, and three major hospitals to which patients from Rural County are referred or transferred for higher levels of hospital care. However, Big City is too far away for most residents of Rural County routinely to use its physicians for services available in Rural County.

Insurance Company, which operates throughout the state, is attempting to offer managed care programs in all areas of the state, and has asked the local physicians in Rural County to form an IPA to provide services under the program to covered persons living in the County. No other managed care plan has attempted to enter the County previously.

Initially, two of the general practitioners and two of the specialists express interest in forming a network, but Insurance Company says that it intends to market its plan to the larger local employers, who need broader geographic and specialty coverage for their employees. Consequently, Insurance Company needs more of the local general practitioners and the one remaining specialist in the IPA to provide adequate geographic, specialty, and backup coverage to subscribers in Rural County. Eventually, four of the seven general practitioners and the one remaining specialist join the IPA and agree to provide services to Insurance Company's subscribers, under contracts providing for capitation. While the physicians' participation in the IPA is structured to be non-exclusive, no other managed care plan has yet entered the local market or approached any of the physicians about joining a different provider panel. In discussing the formation of the IPA with Insurance Company, a number of the physicians have made clear their intention to continue to practice outside the IPA and have indicated they would be interested in contracting individually with other managed care plans when those plans expand into Rural County.

Competitive Analysis

This proposed physician network joint venture would not fall within the antitrust safety zone because it would comprise over 30 percent of the general practitioners in the geographic market. Under the circumstances, a rule of reason analysis indicates that the Agencies would not challenge the formation of the joint venture, for the reasons discussed below.

For purposes of this analysis, Rural County is considered the relevant geographic market. Generally, the Agencies will closely examine joint ventures that comprise a large percentage of physicians in the relevant market. However, in this case, the establishment of the IPA and its inclusion of more than half of the general practitioners and all of the specialists in the network is the result of the payer's expressed need to have more of the local physicians in its network to sell its product in the market. Thus, the level of physician participation in the network does not appear to be overinclusive, but rather appears to be the minimum necessary to meet the employers' needs.

Although the IPA has more than half of the general practitioners and all of the specialists in it, under the particular circumstances this does not, by itself, raise sufficient concerns of possible foreclosure of entry by other managed care plans, or of the collective ability to raise prices above competitive levels, to warrant antitrust challenge to the joint venture by the Agencies. Because it is the first such joint venture in the county, there is no way absolutely to verify at the outset that the joint venture in fact will be non-exclusive. However, the physicians' participation in the IPA is formally non-exclusive, and they have expressed a willingness to consider joining other managed care programs if they begin operating in the area. Moreover, the three general practitioners who are not members of the IPA are available to contract with other managed care plans. The IPA also was established with participation by the local area physicians at the request of Insurance Company, indicating that this structure was not undertaken as a means for the physicians to increase prices or prevent entry of managed care plans.

Finally, the joint venture can benefit consumers in Rural County through the creation of efficiencies. The physicians have jointly put themselves at financial risk to control the use and cost of health care services through capitation. To make the capitation arrangement financially viable, the physicians will have to control the use and cost of health care services they provide under Insurance Company's program. Through the physicians' network joint venture, Rural County residents will be offered a beneficial product, while competition among the physicians outside the network will continue.

Given these facts, the Agencies would not challenge the joint venture. If, however, it later became apparent that the physicians' participation in the joint venture in fact was exclusive, and consequently other managed care plans that wanted to enter the market and contract with some or all of the physicians at competitive terms were unable to do so, the Agencies would re-examine the joint venture's legality. The joint venture also would raise antitrust concerns if it appeared that participation by most of the local physicians in the joint venture resulted in anticompetitive effects in markets outside the joint venture, such as uniformity of fees charged by the physicians in their solo medical practices.

7. Physician Network Joint Venture with No Price Agreement and Involving All of the Physicians in a Small, Rural County

Rural County has a population of 10,000, a small primary care hospital, and six physicians, consisting of a group practice of three family practitioners, a general practitioner, an obstetrician, and a general surgeon. The nearest urban area is about 75 miles away in Big City, which has a population of 200,000, and two major hospitals to which patients from Rural County are referred or transferred for higher levels of hospital care. Big City is too far away, however, for most residents of Rural County to use for services available in Rural County.

HealthCare, a managed care plan headquartered in another state, is thinking of marketing a plan to the larger employers in Rural County. However, it finds that the cost of contracting individually with providers, administering the system, and overseeing the quality of care in Rural County is too high on a per capita basis to allow it to convince employers to switch from indemnity plans to its plan. HealthCare believes its plan would be more successful if it offered higher quality and better access to care by opening a clinic in the northern part of the county where no physicians currently practice.

All of the local physicians approach HealthCare about contracting with their recently-formed, non-exclusive, IPA. The physicians are willing to agree through their IPA to provide services at the new clinic that HealthCare will establish in the northern part of the county and to implement the utilization review procedures that HealthCare has adopted in other parts of the state.

HealthCare wants to negotiate with the new IPA. It believes that the local physicians collectively can operate the new clinic more efficiently than it can from its distant headquarters, but HealthCare also believes that collectively negotiating with all of the physicians will result in it having to pay higher fees or capitation rates. Thus, it encourages the IPA to appoint an agent to negotiate the non-fee related aspects of the contracts and to facilitate fee negotiations with the group practice and the individual doctors. The group practice and the individual physicians each will sign and negotiate their own individual contracts regarding fees and will unilaterally determine whether to contract with HealthCare, but will agree through the IPA to provide physician, administrative, and utilization review services. The agent will facilitate these individual fee negotiations by discussing separately and confidentially with each physician the physician's fee demands and presenting the information to HealthCare. No fee information will be shared among the physicians.

Competitive Analysis

For purposes of this analysis, Rural County is considered the relevant geographic market. Generally, the Agencies are concerned with joint ventures that comprise all or a large percentage of the physicians in the relevant market. In this case, however, the joint venture appears on balance to be procompetitive. The potential for competitive harm from the venture is not great and is outweighed by the efficiencies likely to be generated by the arrangement.

The physicians are not jointly negotiating fees or engaging in other activities that would be viewed as per se antitrust violations. Therefore, the IPA would be evaluated under the rule of reason. Any possible competitive harm would be balanced against any likely efficiencies to be realized by the venture to see whether, on balance, the IPA is anticompetitive or procompetitive.

Because the IPA is non-exclusive, the potential for competitive harm from foreclosure of competition is reduced. Its physicians are free to contract with other managed care plans or individually with HealthCare if they desire. In addition, potential concerns over anticompetitive pricing are minimized because physicians will continue to negotiate prices individually. Although the physicians are jointly negotiating non-price terms of the contract, agreement on these terms appears to be necessary to the successful operation of the joint venture. The small risk of anticompetitive harm from this venture is outweighed by the substantial procompetitive benefits of improved quality of care and access to physician services that the venture will engender. The new clinic in the northern part of the county will make it easier for residents of that area to receive the care they need. Given these facts, the Agencies would not challenge the joint venture.

* * *

Physicians who are considering forming physician network joint ventures and are unsure of the legality of their conduct under the antitrust laws can take advantage of the Department of Justice's expedited business review procedure announced on December 1, 1992 (58 Fed. Reg. 6132 (1993)) or the Federal Trade Commission's advisory opinion procedure contained at 16 C.F.R. 1.1–1.4 (1993). The Agencies will respond to a business review or advisory opinion request on behalf of physicians who are considering forming a network joint venture within 90 days after all necessary information is submitted. The Department's December 1, 1992 announcement contains specific guidance about the information that should be submitted.

---

9. STATEMENT OF DEPARTMENT OF JUSTICE AND FEDERAL TRADE COMMISSION ENFORCEMENT POLICY ON MULTIPROVIDER NETWORKS

Introduction

The health care industry is changing rapidly as it looks for innovative ways to control costs and efficiently provide quality services. Health care providers are forming a wide range of new relationships and affiliations, including networks among otherwise competing providers, as well as networks of providers offering complementary or unrelated services.[44] These affiliations, referred to herein as multiprovider networks, can offer significant procompetitive benefits to consumers. They also can present antitrust questions, particularly if the network includes otherwise competing providers.

As used in this statement, multiprovider networks are ventures among providers that jointly market their health care services to health plans and other purchasers. Such ventures may contract to provide services to subscribers at jointly determined prices and agree to controls aimed at containing costs and assuring quality. Multiprovider networks vary greatly regarding the providers they include, the contractual relationships among those providers, and the efficiencies likely to be realized by the networks.

[44] The multiprovider networks covered by this statement include all types and combinations of health care providers, such as networks involving just a single type of provider (e.g., dentists or hospitals) or a single provider specialty (e.g., orthodontists), as well as networks involving more than one type of provider (e.g., physician-hospital organizations or networks involving both physician and non-physician professionals). Networks containing only physicians, which are addressed in detail in the preceding enforcement policy statement, are a particular category of multiprovider network. Many of the issues relating to multiprovider networks in general are the same as those that arise, and are addressed, in connection with physician network joint ventures, and the analysis often will be very similar for all such arrangements.

Competitive conditions in the markets in which such networks operate also may vary greatly.

In this statement, the Agencies describe the antitrust principles that they apply in evaluating multiprovider networks, address some issues commonly raised in connection with the formation and operation of such networks, and present examples of the application of antitrust principles to hypothetical multiprovider networks. Because multiprovider networks involve a large variety of structures and relationships among many different types of health care providers, and new arrangements are continually developing, the Agencies are unable to establish a meaningful safety zone for these entities.

A. Determining When Agreements Among Providers in a Multiprovider Network Are Analyzed Under the Rule of Reason

Antitrust law condemns as per se illegal naked agreements among competitors that fix prices or allocate markets. Where competitors economically integrate in a joint venture, however, such agreements, if reasonably necessary to accomplish the procompetitive benefits of the integration, are analyzed under the rule of reason.[45] In accord with general antitrust principles, multiprovider networks will be evaluated under the rule of reason, and will not be viewed as per se illegal, if the providers' integration through the network is likely to produce significant efficiencies that benefit consumers, and any price agreements (or other agreements that would otherwise be per se illegal) by the network providers are reasonably necessary to realize those efficiencies.[46]

In some multiprovider networks, significant efficiencies may be achieved through agreement by the competing providers to share substantial financial risk for the services provided through the network.[47] In such cases, the setting of price would be integral to the network's use of such an arrangement and, therefore, would warrant evaluation under the rule of reason.

The following are examples of some types of arrangements through which substantial financial risk can be shared among competitors in a multiprovider network:

---

[45] In a network limited to providers who are not actual or potential competitors, the providers generally can agree on the prices to be charged for their services without the kinds of economic integration discussed below.

[46] In some cases, the combination of the competing providers in the network may enable them to offer what could be considered to be a new product producing substantial efficiencies, and therefore the venture will be analyzed under the rule of reason. *See Broadcast Music, Inc. v. Columbia Broadcasting System, Inc.*, 441 U.S. 1 (1979) (competitors' integration and creation of a blanket license for use of copyrighted compositions result in efficiencies so great as to make the blanket license a "different product" from the mere combination of individual competitors and, therefore, joint pricing of the blanket license is subject to rule of reason analysis, rather than the per se rule against price fixing). The Agencies' analysis will focus on the efficiencies likely to be produced by the venture, and the relationship of any price agreements to the achievement of those efficiencies, rather than on whether the venture creates a product that can be labeled "new" or "different."

[47] The existence of financial risk sharing does not depend on whether, under applicable state law, the network is considered an insurer.

(1) agreement by the venture to provide services to a health plan at a "capitated" rate;[48]

(2) agreement by the venture to provide designated services or classes of services to a health plan for a predetermined percentage of premium or revenue from the plan;[49]

(3) use by the venture of significant financial incentives for its provider participants, as a group, to achieve specified cost-containment goals. Two methods by which the venture can accomplish this are:

(a) withholding from all provider participants a substantial amount of the compensation due to them, with distribution of that amount to the participants based on group performance in meeting the cost-containment goals of the network as a whole; or

(b) establishing overall cost or utilization targets for the network as a whole, with the provider participants subject to subsequent substantial financial rewards or penalties based on group performance in meeting the targets; and

(4) agreement by the venture to provide a complex or extended course of treatment that requires the substantial coordination of care by different types of providers offering a complementary mix of services, for a fixed, predetermined payment, where the costs of that course of treatment for any individual patient can vary greatly due to the individual patient's condition, the choice, complexity, or length of treatment, or other factors.[50]

The Agencies recognize that new types of risk-sharing arrangements may develop. The preceding examples do not foreclose consideration of other arrangements through which the participants in a multiprovider network joint venture may share substantial financial risk in the provision of health care services or products through the network.[51] Organizers of multiprovider networks who are uncertain whether their proposed arrangements constitute substantial financial risk sharing for purposes of this policy statement are encouraged to take advantage of the Agencies' expedited business review and advisory opinion procedures.

Multiprovider networks that do not involve the sharing of substantial financial risk may also involve sufficient integration to demonstrate that the venture is likely to produce significant efficiencies. For example, as

---

[48] A "capitated" rate is a fixed, predetermined payment per covered life (the "capitation") from a health plan to the joint venture in exchange for the joint venture's (not merely an individual provider's) furnishing and guaranteeing provision of a defined set of covered services to covered individuals for a specified period, regardless of the amount of services actually provided.

[49] This is similar to a capitation arrangement, except that the amount of payment to the network can vary in response to changes in the health plan's premiums or revenues.

[50] Such arrangements are sometimes referred to either as "global fees" or "all-inclusive case rates." Global fee or all-inclusive case rate arrangements that involve financial risk sharing as contemplated by this example will require that the joint venture (not merely an individual provider participant) assume the risk or benefit that the treatment provided through the network may either exceed, or cost less than, the predetermined payment.

[51] The manner of dividing revenues among the network's provider participants generally does not raise antitrust issues so long as the competing providers in a network share substantial financial risk. For example, capitated networks frequently distribute income among their participants using fee-for-service payment with a partial withhold fund to cover the risk of having to provide more services than were originally anticipated.

discussed in the Statement Of Enforcement Policy On Physician Network Joint Ventures, substantial clinical integration among competing physicians in a network who do not share substantial financial risk may produce efficiency benefits that justify joint pricing.[52] However, given the wide range of providers who may participate in multiprovider networks, the types of clinical integration and efficiencies available to physician network joint ventures may not be relevant to all multiprovider networks. Accordingly, the Agencies will consider the particular nature of the services provided by the network in assessing whether the network has the potential for producing efficiencies that warrant rule of reason treatment. In all cases, the Agencies' analysis will focus on substance, not form, in assessing a network's likelihood of producing significant efficiencies. To the extent that agreements on prices to be charged for the integrated provision of services promote the venture's achievement of efficiencies, they will be evaluated under the rule of reason.

A multiprovider network also might include an agreement among competitors on service allocation or specialization. The Agencies would examine the relationship between the agreement and efficiency-enhancing joint activity. If such an agreement is reasonably necessary for the network to realize significant procompetitive benefits, it similarly would be subject to rule of reason analysis.[53] For example, competing hospitals in an integrated multiprovider network might need to agree that only certain hospitals would provide certain services to network patients in order to achieve the benefits of the integration.[54] The hospitals, however, would not necessarily be permitted to agree on what services they would provide to non-network patients.[55]

B. Applying the Rule of Reason

A rule of reason analysis determines whether the formation and operation of the joint venture may have a substantial anticompetitive effect and, if so, whether that potential effect is outweighed by any procompetitive efficiencies resulting from the venture. The rule of reason analysis takes into account characteristics of the particular multiprovider network and the competitive environment in which it operates to determine the network's likely effect on competition.

---

[52] *See* Section B(1) of the Agencies' Statement Of Enforcement Policy On Physician Network Joint Ventures (pp. 71–74).

[53] A unilateral decision to eliminate a service or specialization, however, does not generally present antitrust issues. For example, a hospital or other provider unilaterally may decide to concentrate on its more profitable services and not offer other less profitable services, and seek to enter a network joint venture with competitors that still provides the latter services. If such a decision is made unilaterally, rather than pursuant to an express or implied agreement, the arrangement would not be considered a per se illegal market allocation.

[54] Hospitals, even if they do not belong to a multiprovider network, also could agree jointly to develop and operate new services that the participants could not profitably support individually or through a less inclusive joint venture, and to decide where the jointly operated services are to be located. Such joint ventures would be analyzed by the Agencies under the rule of reason. The Statement of Enforcement Policy On Hospital Joint Ventures Involving Specialized Clinical Or Other Expensive Health Care Services offers additional guidance on joint ventures among hospitals to provide such services.

[55] The Agencies' analysis would take into account that agreements among multiprovider network participants relating to the offering of services might be more likely than those relating to price to affect participants' competition outside the network, and to persist even if the network is disbanded.

A determination about the lawfulness of a multiprovider network's activity under the rule of reason sometimes can be reached without an extensive inquiry under each step of the analysis. For example, a multiprovider network that involves substantial integration may include a relatively small percentage of the providers in each relevant product market on a non-exclusive basis. In that case, the Agencies may be able to conclude expeditiously that the network is unlikely to be anticompetitive, based on the competitive environment in which it operates. In assessing the competitive environment, the Agencies would consider such market factors as the number, type, and size of managed care plans operating in the area, the extent of provider participation in those plans, and the economic importance of the managed care plans to area providers. Alternatively, for example, if a restraint that facially appears to be of a kind that would always or almost always tend to reduce output or increase prices, but has not been considered per se unlawful, is not reasonably necessary to the creation of efficiencies, the Agencies will likely challenge the restraint without an elaborate analysis of market definition and market power.[56]

The steps ordinarily involved in a rule of reason analysis of multiprovider networks are set forth below.

1. Market Definition

The Agencies will evaluate the competitive effects of multiprovider networks in each of the relevant markets in which they operate or have substantial impact. In defining the relevant product and geographic markets, the Agencies look to what substitutes, as a practical matter, are reasonably available to consumers for the services in question.[57]

A multiprovider network can affect markets for the provision of hospital, medical, and other health care services, and health insurance/financing markets. The possible product markets for analyzing the competitive effects of multiprovider networks likely would include both the market for such networks themselves, if there is a distinct market for such networks, and the markets for service components of the network that are, or could be, sold separately outside the network. For example, if two hospitals formed a multiprovider network with their medical and other health care professional staffs, the Agencies would consider potential competitive effects in each market affected by the network, including but not necessarily limited to the markets for inpatient hospital services, outpatient services, each physician and non-physician health care service provided by network members, and health insurance/financing markets whose participants may deal with the network and its various types of health care providers.

The relevant geographic market for each relevant product market affected by the multiprovider network will be determined through a fact-specific analysis that focuses on the location of reasonable alternatives. The relevant geographic markets may be broader for some product markets than for others.

2. Competitive Effects

In applying the rule of reason, the Agencies will examine both the potential "horizontal" and "vertical" effects of the arrangement. Agreements between or among competitors (e.g., competing hospitals or competing physicians)

---

56 *See FTC v. Indiana Federation of Dentists*, 476 U.S. 447, 459–60 (1986).

57 A more extensive discussion of how the Agencies define relevant markets is contained in the Agencies' *1992 Horizontal Merger Guidelines*.

are considered "horizontal" under the antitrust laws. Agreements between or among parties that are not competitors (such as a hospital and a physician in a physician-hospital organization ("PHO")), may be considered "vertical" in nature.

a. Horizontal Analysis

In evaluating the possible horizontal competitive effects of multiprovider networks, the Agencies will define the relevant markets (as discussed earlier) and evaluate the network's likely overall competitive effects considering all market conditions.

Determining market share and concentration in the relevant markets is often an important first step in analyzing a network's competitive effects. For example, in analyzing a PHO, the Agencies will consider the network's market share (and the market concentration) in such service components as inpatient hospital services (as measured by such indicia as number of institutions, number of hospital beds, patient census, and revenues), physician services (in individual physician specialty or other appropriate service markets)[58], and any other services provided by competing health care providers, institutional or noninstitutional, participating in the network.

If a particular multiprovider network had a substantial share of any of the relevant service markets, it could, depending on other factors, increase the price of such services above competitive levels. For example, a network that included most or all of the surgeons in a relevant geographic market could create market power in the market for surgical services and thereby permit the surgeons to increase prices.

If there is only one hospital in the market, a multiprovider network, by definition, cannot reduce any existing competition among hospitals. Such a network could, however, reduce competition among other providers, for example, among physicians in the network and, thereby, reduce the ability of payers to control the costs of both physician and hospital services.[59] It also could reduce competition between the hospital and non-hospital providers of certain services, such as outpatient surgery.

Although market share and concentration are useful starting points in analyzing the competitive effects of multiprovider networks, the Agencies' ultimate conclusion is based upon a more comprehensive analysis. This will include an analysis of collateral agreements and spillover effects.[60] In addition, in assessing the likely competitive effects of a multiprovider network, the Agencies are particularly interested in the ability and willingness of health plans and other purchasers of health care services to switch between different health care providers or networks in response to a price increase, and the factors that determine the ability and willingness of plans to make such changes. The Agencies will consider not only the proportion of the providers in any relevant market who are in the network,

---

[58] Although all services provided by each physician specialty or category of non-physician provider might be a separate relevant service market, there may be instances in which significant overlap of services provided by different physician specialties or categories of providers justifies including services from more than one physician specialty or provider category in the same market.

[59] By aligning itself with a large share of physicians in the market, a monopoly hospital may effectively be able to insulate itself from payer efforts to control utilization of its services and thus protect its monopoly profits.

[60] *See* Statement of Enforcement Policy on Physician Network Joint Ventures, pp.61–105.

but also the incentives faced by providers in the network, and whether different groups of providers in a network may have significantly different incentives that would reduce the likelihood of anticompetitive conduct.[61] If plans can contract at competitive terms with other networks or with individual providers, and can obtain a similar quality and range of services for their enrollees, the network is less likely to raise competitive concerns.

In examining a multiprovider network's overall competitive effect, the Agencies will examine whether the competing providers in the network have agreed among themselves to offer their services exclusively through the network or are otherwise operating, or are likely to operate, exclusively. Such exclusive arrangements are not necessarily anticompetitive.[62] Exclusive networks, however, mean that the providers in the network are not available to join other networks or contract individually with health plans, and thus, in some circumstances, exclusive networks can impede or preclude competition among networks and among individual providers. In determining whether an exclusive arrangement of this type raises antitrust concerns, the Agencies will examine the market share of the providers subject to the exclusivity arrangement; the terms of the exclusive arrangement, such as its duration and providers' ability and financial incentives or disincentives to withdraw from the arrangement; the number of providers that need to be included for the network and potentially competing networks to compete effectively; and the justification for the exclusivity arrangement.

Networks also may limit or condition provider participants' freedom to contract outside the network in ways that fall short of a commitment of full exclusivity. The Agencies recognize that the competitive impact of exclusive arrangements or other limitations on the ability of a network's provider participants to contract outside the network can vary greatly.

b. Vertical Analysis

In addition to the horizontal issues discussed above, multiprovider networks also can raise vertical issues. Generally, vertical concerns can arise if a network's power in one market in which it operates enables it to limit competition in another market.

Some multiprovider networks involve "vertical" exclusive arrangements that restrict the providers in one market from dealing with non-network providers that compete in a different market, or that restrict network provider participants' dealings with health plans or other purchasers. For example, a multiprovider network owned by a hospital and individually contracting with its participating physicians might limit the incentives or ability of those physicians to participate in other networks. Similarly, a hospital might use a multiprovider network to block or impede other hospitals from entering a market or from offering competing services.

In evaluating whether such exclusive arrangements raise antitrust concerns, the Agencies will examine the degree to which the arrangement may limit the ability of other networks or health plans to compete in the market. The factors the Agencies will consider include those set forth in the discussion of exclusive arrangements on pages 118–119, above.

---

[61] *See* discussion in Statement of Enforcement Policy on Physician Network Joint Ventures, pp. 61–105.

[62] For example, an exclusive arrangement may help ensure the multiprovider network's ability to serve its subscribers and increase its providers' incentives to further the interests of the network.

For example, if the multiprovider network has exclusive arrangements with only a small percentage of the physicians in a relevant market, and there are enough suitable alternative physicians in the market to allow other competing networks to form, the exclusive arrangement is unlikely to raise antitrust concerns. On the other hand, a network might contract exclusively with a large percentage of physicians in a relevant market, for example general surgeons. In that case, if purchasers or payers could not form a satisfactory competing network using the remaining general surgeons in the market, and could not induce new general surgeons to enter the market, those purchasers and payers would be forced to use this network, rather than put together a panel consisting of those providers of each needed service who offer the most attractive combination of price and quality. Thus, the exclusive arrangement would be likely to restrict competition unreasonably, both among general surgeons (the horizontal effect) and among health care providers in other service markets and payers (the vertical effects).

The Agencies recognize that exclusive arrangements, whether they are horizontal or vertical, may not be explicit, so that labeling a multiprovider network as "non-exclusive" will not be determinative. In some cases, providers will refuse to contract with other networks or purchasers, even though they have not entered into an agreement specifically forbidding them from doing so. For example, if a network includes a large percentage of physicians in a certain market, those physicians may perceive that they are likely to obtain more favorable terms from plans by dealing collectively through one network, rather than as individuals.

In determining whether a network is truly non-exclusive, the Agencies will consider a number of factors, including the following:

(1) that viable competing networks or managed care plans with adequate provider participation currently exist in the market;

(2) that providers in the network actually individually participate in, or contract with, other networks or managed care plans, or there is other evidence of their willingness and incentive to do so;

(3) that providers in the network earn substantial revenue from other networks or through individual contracts with managed care plans;

(4) the absence of any indications of substantial departicipation from other networks or managed care plans in the market; and

(5) the absence of any indications of coordination among the providers in the network regarding price or other competitively significant terms of participation in other networks or managed care plans.

c. Exclusion of Particular Providers

Most multiprovider networks will contract with some, but not all, providers in an area. Such selective contracting may be a method through which networks limit their provider panels in an effort to achieve quality and cost-containment goals, and thus enhance their ability to compete against other networks. One reason often advanced for selective contracting is to ensure that the network can direct a sufficient patient volume to its providers to justify price concessions or adherence to strict quality controls by the providers. It may also help the network create a favorable market reputation based on careful selection of high quality, cost-effective providers. In addition, selective contracting may be procompetitive by giving non-participant providers an incentive to form competing networks.

A rule of reason analysis usually is applied in judging the legality of a multiprovider network's exclusion of providers or classes of providers from the network, or its policies on referring enrollees to network providers. The focus of the analysis is not on whether a particular provider has been harmed by the exclusion or referral policies, but rather whether the conduct reduces competition among providers in the market and thereby harms consumers. Where other networks offering the same types of services exist or could be formed, there are not likely to be significant competitive concerns associated with the exclusion of particular providers by particular networks. Exclusion or referral policies may present competitive concerns, however, if providers or classes of providers are unable to compete effectively without access to the network, and competition is thereby harmed. In assessing such situations, the Agencies will consider whether there are procompetitive reasons for the exclusion or referral policies.

3. Efficiencies

Finally, the Agencies will balance any potential anticompetitive effects of the multiprovider network against the potential efficiencies associated with its formation and operation. The greater the network's likely anticompetitive effects, the greater must be the network's likely efficiencies. In assessing efficiency claims, the Agencies focus on net efficiencies that will be derived from the operation of the network and that result in lower prices or higher quality to consumers. The Agencies will not accept claims of efficiencies if the parties reasonably can achieve equivalent or comparable savings through significantly less anticompetitive means. In making this assessment, however, the Agencies will not search for a theoretically least restrictive alternative that is not practical given business realities.

Experience indicates that, in general, more significant efficiencies are likely to result from a multiprovider network joint venture's substantial financial risk-sharing or substantial clinical integration. However, the Agencies will consider a broad range of possible cost savings, including improved cost controls, case management and quality assurance, economies of scale, and reduced administrative or transaction costs.

In assessing the likelihood that efficiencies will be realized, the Agencies recognize that competition is one of the strongest motivations for firms to lower prices, reduce costs, and provide higher quality. Thus, the greater the competition facing the network, the more likely the network will actually realize potential efficiencies that would benefit consumers.

4. Information Used in the Analysis

In conducting a rule of reason analysis, the Agencies rely upon a wide variety of data and information, including the information supplied by the participants in the multiprovider network, purchasers, providers, consumers, and others familiar with the market in question. The Agencies may interview purchasers of health care services, including self-insured employers and other employers that offer health benefits, and health plans (such as HMOs and PPOs), competitors of the providers in the network, and any other parties who may have relevant information for analyzing the competitive effects of the network.

The Agencies do not simply count the number of parties who support or oppose the formation of the multiprovider network. Instead, the Agencies seek information concerning the competitive dynamics in the particular community where the network is forming. For example, in defining relevant markets, the Agencies are likely to give substantial weight to information provided by purchasers or payers who have attempted to switch between providers in the face of a price increase. Similarly, an employer or payer with locations in several communities may have had experience with a network comparable to the proposed network, and thus be able to provide the Agencies with useful information about the likely effect of the proposed network, including its potential competitive benefits.

In assessing the information provided by various parties, the Agencies take into account the parties' economic incentives and interests. In addition, the Agencies attach less significance to opinions that are based on incomplete, biased, or inaccurate information, or opinions of those who, for whatever reason, may be simply indifferent to the potential for anticompetitive harm.

C. Arrangements That Do Not Involve Horizontal Agreements on Prices or Price-Related Terms

Some networks that are not substantially integrated use a variety of "messenger model" arrangements to facilitate contracting between providers and payers and avoid price-fixing agreements among competing network providers. Arrangements that are designed simply to minimize the costs associated with the contracting process, and that do not result in a collective determination by the competing network providers on prices or price-related terms, are not per se illegal price fixing.[63]

Messenger models can be organized and operate in a variety of ways. For example, network providers may use an agent or third party to convey to purchasers information obtained individually from the providers about the prices or price-related terms that the providers are willing to accept.[64] In some cases, the agent may convey to the providers all contract offers made by purchasers, and each provider then makes an independent, unilateral decision to accept or reject the contract offers. In others, the agent may have received from individual providers some authority to accept contract offers on their behalf. The agent also may help providers understand the contracts offered, for example by providing objective or empirical information about the terms of an offer (such as a comparison of the offered terms to other contracts agreed to by network participants).

The key issue in any messenger model arrangement is whether the arrangement creates or facilitates an agreement among competitors on prices or price-related terms. Determining whether there is such an agreement is a question of fact in each case. The Agencies will examine whether the agent facilitates collective decision-making by network providers, rather than independent, unilateral, decisions.[65] In particular, the Agencies will examine whether the agent coordinates the providers' responses to a particular proposal, disseminates to network providers the views or intentions of other network providers as to the proposal, expresses an opinion on the terms offered, collectively negotiates for the providers, or decides whether or not to convey an offer based on the agent's judgment

---

[63] *See infra* Example 4.

[64] Guidance about the antitrust standards applicable to collection and exchange of fee information can be found in the Statement of Enforcement Policy On Providers' Collective Provision Of Fee-Related Information To Purchasers Of Health Care Services, and the Statement of Enforcement Policy On Provider Participation In Exchanges Of Price And Cost Information.

[65] Use of an intermediary or "independent" third party to convey collectively determined price offers to purchasers or to negotiate agreements with purchasers, or giving to individual providers an opportunity to "opt" into, or out of, such agreements does not negate the existence of an agreement.

about the attractiveness of the prices or price-related terms. If the agent engages in such activities, the arrangement may amount to a per se illegal price-fixing agreement.

D. Examples of Multiprovider Network Joint Ventures

The following are four examples of how the Agencies would apply the principles set forth in this statement to specific multiprovider network joint ventures, including: 1) a PHO involving substantial clinical integration, that does not raise significant competitive concerns under the rule of reason; 2) a PHO providing services on a per case basis, that would be analyzed under the rule of reason; 3) a PHO involving substantial financial risk sharing and including all the physicians in a small rural county, that does not raise competitive concerns under the rule of reason; and 4) a PHO that does not involve horizontal agreements on price.

1. PHO Involving Substantial Clinical Integration

Roxbury is a relatively isolated, medium-sized city. For the purposes of this example, the services provided by primary care physicians and those provided by the different physician specialists each constitute a relevant product market; and the relevant geographic market for each of them is Roxbury.

Several HMOs and other significant managed care plans operate in Roxbury. A substantial proportion of insured individuals are enrolled in these plans, and enrollment in managed care is expected to increase. Many physicians in each of the specialties and Roxbury's four hospitals participate in more than one of these plans. There is no significant overlap among the participants on the physician panels of many of these plans, nor among the active medical staffs of the hospitals, except in a few specialties. Most plans include only 2 or 3 of Roxbury's hospitals, and each hospital is a substitute for any other.

One of Roxbury's hospitals and the physicians on its active medical staff establish a PHO to assume greater responsibility for managing the cost and quality of care rendered to Roxbury residents who are members of health plans. They hope to reduce costs while maintaining or improving the quality of care, and thus to attract more managed care patients to the hospital and their practices.

The PHO will implement systems to establish goals relating to quality and appropriate utilization of services by PHO participants, regularly evaluate both the hospital's and each individual doctor's and the network's aggregate performance concerning those goals, and modify the hospital's and individual participants' actual practices, where necessary, based on those evaluations. The PHO will engage in case management, preadmission authorization of some services, and concurrent and retrospective review of inpatient stays. In addition, the PHO is developing practice standards and protocols to govern treatment and utilization of services, and it will actively review the care rendered by each doctor in light of these standards and protocols.

There is a significant investment of capital to purchase the information systems necessary to gather aggregate and individual data on the cost, quantity, and nature of services provided or ordered by the hospital and PHO physicians; to measure performance of the PHO, the hospital, and the individual doctors against cost and quality benchmarks; and to monitor patient satisfaction. The PHO will provide payers with detailed reports on the cost and quantity of services provided, and on the network's success in meeting its goals.

The PHO will hire a medical director and support staff to perform the above functions and to coordinate patient care in specific cases. The doctors and the hospital's administrative staff also have invested appreciable time in developing the practice standards and protocols, and will continue actively to monitor care provided through the PHO. PHO physicians who fail to adhere to the network's standards and protocols will be subject to remedial action, including the possibility of expulsion from the network.

Under PHO contracts, physicians will be paid by health plans on a fee-for-service basis; the hospital will be paid a set amount for each day a covered patient is in the hospital, and will be paid on a fee-for-service basis for other services. The physicians will not share substantial financial risk for the cost of services rendered to covered individuals through the network. The PHO will retain an agent to develop a fee schedule, negotiate fees, and contract with payers. Information about what participating doctors charge non-network patients will not be disseminated to participants of the PHO, and the doctors will not agree on the prices they will charge patients not covered by PHO contracts.

All members of the hospital's medical staff join the PHO, including its three geographically dispersed primary care group practices that together account for about 25 percent of the primary care doctors in Roxbury. These primary care doctors generally refer their patients to specialists on the hospital's active medical staff. The PHO includes all primary care doctors and specialists on the hospital's medical staff because of those established referral relationships with the primary care doctors, the admitting privileges all have at the hospital, the quality of care provided by the medical staff, their commitment to cooperate with the goals of the PHO, and the need to provide convenient referral services to patients of the primary care doctors. Participating specialists include from 20 to 35 percent of specialists in each relevant market, depending on the specialty. Hospital and physician participation in the PHO is non-exclusive. Many PHO participants, including the hospital, already do and are expected to continue to participate in other managed care plans and earn substantial income from those plans.

Competitive Analysis

The Agencies would analyze the PHO under the rule of reason because it offers the potential for creating significant efficiencies and the price agreement among the physicians is reasonably necessary to realize those efficiencies. Prior to contracting on behalf of competing physicians, the PHO will develop mechanisms to provide cost-effective, quality care, including standards and protocols to govern treatment and utilization of services, information systems to measure and monitor both the individual performance of the hospital and physicians and aggregate network performance, and procedures to modify hospital and physician behavior and assure adherence to network standards and protocols. The network is structured to achieve its efficiencies through a high degree of interdependence and cooperation among its participants. The price agreement for physician services, under these circumstances, is subordinate to and reasonably necessary to achieve these objectives.[66]

---

[66] Although the physicians have not directly agreed among themselves on the prices to be charged, their use of an agent subject to the control of the PHO to establish fees and

Furthermore, the Agencies would not challenge establishment and operation of the PHO under the rule of reason. In conducting the rule of reason analysis, the Agencies would evaluate the likely competitive effects of the venture in each relevant market. In this case, the PHO does not appear likely to limit competition in any relevant market either by hampering the ability of health plans to contract individually with area hospitals or physicians or with other network joint ventures, or by enabling the hospital or physicians to raise prices above competitive levels. The PHO does not appear to be overinclusive: many primary care physicians as well as specialists are available to other plans, and the doctors in the PHO have been included to achieve the network's procompetitive potential. Many PHO doctors also participate in other managed care plans and are expected to continue to do so in the future. Moreover, several significant managed care plans are not dependent on the PHO doctors to offer their products to consumers. Finally, the venture is structured so that physician participants do not share competitively sensitive information, thus reducing the likelihood of anticompetitive spillover effects outside the network where the physicians still compete, and the venture avoids any anticompetitive collateral agreements.

Since the venture is not likely to be anticompetitive, there is no need for further detailed evaluation of the venture's potential for generating procompetitive efficiencies. For these reasons, the Agencies would not challenge the joint venture. They would reexamine this conclusion, however, and do a more complete analysis of the procompetitive efficiencies if evidence of actual anticompetitive effects were to develop.

2. PHO That Provides Services on a Per Case Basis

Goodville is a large city with a number of hospitals. One of Goodville's hospitals, together with its oncologists and other relevant health care providers, establishes a joint venture to contract with health plans and other payers of health care services to provide bone marrow transplants and related cancer care for certain types of cancers based on an all inclusive per case payment. Under these contracts, the venture will receive a single payment for all hospital, physician, and ancillary services rendered to covered patients requiring bone marrow transplants. The venture will be responsible for paying for and coordinating the various forms of care provided. At first, it will pay its providers using a fee schedule with a withhold to cover unanticipated losses on the case rate. Based on its operational experience, the venture intends to explore other payment methodologies that may most effectively provide the venture's providers with financial incentives to allocate resources efficiently in their treatment of patients.

Competitive Analysis

The joint venture is a multiprovider network in which competitors share substantial financial risk, and the price agreement among members of the venture will be analyzed under the rule of reason. The per case payment arrangement involves the sharing of substantial financial risk because the venture will receive a single, predetermined payment for a course of treatment that requires the substantial coordination of care by different

---

to negotiate and execute contracts on behalf of the venture would amount to a price agreement among competitors. The use of such an agent, however, should reduce the risk of the PHO's activities having anticompetitive spillover effects on competition among provider participants for non-network patients.

types of providers and can vary significantly in cost and complexity from patient to patient. The venture will pay its provider participants in a way that gives them incentives to allocate resources efficiently, and that spreads among the participants the risk of loss and the possibility of gain on any particular case. The venture adds to the market another contracting option for health plans and other payers that is likely to result in cost savings because of its use of a per case payment method. Establishment of the case rate is an integral part of the risk sharing arrangement.

3. PHO with All the Physicians in a Small, Rural County

Frederick County has a population of 15,000, and a 50-bed hospital that offers primary and some secondary services. There are 12 physicians on the active medical staff of the hospital (six general and family practitioners, one internist, two pediatricians, one otolaryngologist, and two general surgeons) as well as a part-time pathologist, anesthesiologist, and radiologist. Outside of Frederick County, the nearest hospitals are in Big City, 25 miles away. Most Frederick County residents receive basic physician and hospital care in Frederick County, and are referred or transferred to the Big City physician specialists and hospitals for higher levels of care.

No managed care plans currently operate in Frederick County. Nor are there any large employers who selectively contract with Frederick County physicians. Increasingly, Frederick County residents who work for employers in Big City are covered under managed care contracts that direct Frederick County residents to hospitals and to numerous primary care and specialty physicians in Big City. Providers in Frederick County who are losing patients to hospitals and doctors in Big City want to contract with payers and employers so that they can retain these patients. However, the Frederick County hospital and doctors have been unsuccessful in their efforts to obtain contracts individually; too few potential enrollees are involved to justify payers' undertaking the expense and effort of individually contracting with Frederick County providers and administering a utilization review and quality assurance program for a provider network in Frederick County.

The hospital and all the physicians in Frederick County want to establish a PHO to contract with managed care plans and employers operating in Big City. Managed care plans have expressed interest in contracting with all Frederick County physicians under a single risk-sharing contract. The PHO also will offer its network to employers operating in Frederick County.

The PHO will market the services of the hospital on a per diem basis, and physician services on the basis of a fee schedule that is significantly discounted from the doctors' current charges. The PHO will be eligible for a bonus of up to 20 percent of the total payments made to it, depending on the PHO's success in meeting utilization targets agreed to with the payers. An employee of the hospital will develop a fee schedule, negotiate fees, and contract with payers on behalf of the PHO. Information about what participating doctors charge non-PHO patients will not be disseminated to the doctors, and they will not agree on the prices they will charge patients not covered by PHO contracts.

Physicians' participation in the PHO is structured to be non-exclusive. Because no other managed care plans operate in the area, PHO physicians do not now participate in other plans and have not been approached by other plans. The PHO physicians have made clear their intention to continue to practice outside the PHO and to be available to contract individually with any other managed care plans that expand into Frederick County.

Competitive Analysis

The agreement of the physicians on the prices they will charge through the PHO would be analyzed under the rule of reason, because they share substantial financial risk through the use of a pricing arrangement that provides significant financial incentives for the physicians, as a group, to achieve specified cost-containment goals. The venture thus has the potential for creating significant efficiencies, and the setting of price promotes the venture's use of the risk-sharing arrangement.

The Agencies would not challenge formation and operation of the PHO under the rule of reason. Under the rule of reason analysis, the Agencies would evaluate the likely competitive effects of the venture. The venture does not appear likely to limit competition in any relevant market. Managed care plans' current practice of directing patients from Frederick County to Big City suggests that the physicians in the PHO face significant competition from providers and managed care plans that operate in Big City. Moreover, the absence of managed care contracting in Frederick County, either now or in the foreseeable future, indicates that the network is not likely to reduce any actual or likely competition for patients who do not travel to Big City for care.

While the venture involves all of the doctors in Frederick County, this was necessary to respond to competition from Big City providers. It is not possible to verify at the outset that the venture will in fact be non-exclusive, but the physicians' participation in the venture is structured to be non-exclusive, and the doctors have expressed a willingness to consider joining other managed care plans if they begin operating in the area.

For these reasons, the Agencies would not challenge the joint venture. However, if it later became apparent that the physicians' participation in the PHO was exclusive in fact, and consequently managed care plans or employers that wanted to contract with some or all of the physicians at competitive terms were unable to do so, or that the PHO doctors entered into collateral agreements that restrained competition for services furnished outside the PHO, the Agencies likely would challenge the joint venture.

4. PHO That Does Not Involve Horizontal Agreements on Price

A hospital and doctors and other health care providers on its medical staff have established a PHO to market their services to payers, including employers with self-funded health benefits plans. The PHO contracts on a fee-for-service basis. The physicians and other health care providers who are participants in the PHO do not share substantial financial risk or otherwise integrate their services so as to provide significant efficiencies. The payers prefer to continue to use their existing third-party administrators for contract administration and utilization management, or to do it in-house.

There is no agreement among the PHO's participants to deal only through the PHO, and many of them participate in other networks and HMOs on a variety of terms. Some payers have chosen to contract with the hospital and some or all of the PHO physicians and other providers without going through the PHO, and a significant proportion of the PHO's participants contract with payers in this manner.

In an effort to avoid horizontal price agreements among competing participants in the PHO while facilitating the contracting process, the PHO considers using the following mechanisms:

A. An agent of the PHO, not otherwise affiliated with any PHO participant, will obtain from each participant a fee schedule or conversion factor that represents the minimum payment that participant will accept from a payer. The agent is authorized to contract on the participants' behalf with payers offering prices at this level or better. The agent does not negotiate pricing terms with the payer and does not share pricing information among competing participants. Price offers that do not meet the authorized fee are conveyed to the individual participant.

B. The same as option A, with the added feature that the agent is authorized, for a specified time, to bind the participant to any contract offers with prices equal, to or better than, those in a contract that the participant has already approved.

C. The same as option A, except that in order to assist payers in developing contract offers, the agent takes the fee authorizations of the various participants and develops a schedule that can be presented to a payer showing the percentages of participants in the network who have authorized contracts at various price levels.

D. The venture hires an agent to negotiate prices with payers on behalf of the PHO's participants. The agent does not disclose to the payer the prices the participants are willing to accept, as in option C, but attempts to obtain the best possible prices for all the participants. The resulting contract offer then is relayed to each participant for acceptance or rejection.

Competitive Analysis

In the circumstances described in options A through D, the Agencies would determine whether there was a horizontal agreement on price or any other competitively significant terms among PHO participants. The Agencies would determine whether such agreements were subject to the per se rule or the rule of reason, and evaluate them accordingly.

The existence of an agreement is a factual question. The PHO's use of options A through C does not establish the existence of a horizontal price agreement. Nor is there sharing of price information or other evidence of explicit or implicit agreements among network participants on price. The agent does not inform PHO participants about others' acceptance or rejection of contract offers; there is no agreement or understanding that PHO participants will only contract through the PHO; and participants deal outside the network on competitive terms.

The PHO's use of option D amounts to a per se unlawful price agreement. The participants' joint negotiation through a common agent confronts the payer with the combined bargaining power of the PHO participants, even though they ultimately have to agree individually to the contract negotiated on their behalf.

* * *

Persons who are considering forming multiprovider networks and are unsure of the legality of their conduct under the antitrust laws can take advantage of the Department of Justice's expedited business review procedure for joint ventures and information exchange programs announced on December 1, 1992 (58 Fed. Reg. 6132 (1993)) or the Federal Trade Commission's advisory opinion procedure contained at 16 C.F.R. 1.1–1.4

(1993). The Agencies will respond to a business review or advisory opinion request on behalf of parties considering the formation of a multiprovider network within 120 days after all necessary information is submitted. The Department's December 1, 1992 announcement contains guidance as to information that should be submitted.

Separate Statement of Commissioner Christine A. Varney on the Revised Health Care Guidelines

The Federal Trade Commission and the Department of Justice today issued revisions to Statements 8 and 9 of the Statements *of Antitrust Enforcement Policy in Health Care* ("health care guidelines"). I am writing separately for two basic reasons. First, I have been somewhat critical of the health care guidelines in the past, suggesting that they should reflect greater receptiveness to new and innovative forms of provider arrangements that do not necessarily involve financial risk sharing and suggesting factors that should be taken into account in reviewing provider arrangements that fall outside of the safety zones. I believe that the revised health care guidelines address these previous concerns. I commend the Agencies' staffs for the tremendous progress that is reflected in these guidelines. Second, the issuance of the guidelines is an iterative process, and I invite continued input from interested parties. The health care marketplace is undergoing rapid change, and it is primarily through an open dialogue with all involved in the health care industry that the Agencies can continue to provide appropriate and relevant antitrust guidance.

23

STATEMENT OF ANTITRUST ENFORCEMENT POLICY REGARDING ACCOUNTABLE CARE ORGANIZATIONS PARTICIPATING IN THE MEDICARE SHARED SAVINGS PROGRAM

AGENCIES: FTC, DOJ

ACTION: Final Policy Statement

SUMMARY: The FTC and DOJ (the "Agencies") are issuing the final *Statement of Antitrust Enforcement Policy Regarding Accountable Care Organizations Participating in the Medicare Shared Savings Program* (the "Policy Statement") in conjunction with the final rule issued today by the Centers for Medicare and Medicaid Services ("CMS") under Section 3022 of the Affordable Care Act (the Patient Protection and Affordable Care Act, Pub. L. 111-48, 124 Stat. 119 (2010), and the Health Care and Education Reconciliation Act of 2010, Pub. L. 111-52, 124 Stat. 1029 (2010)).

The final Policy Statement differs from the proposed Policy Statement issued earlier this year, 76 Fed. Reg. 21,894 (Apr. 19, 2011), in two significant respects. First, the entire final Policy Statement—with the exception of the voluntary expedited antitrust review— applies to all collaborations among otherwise independent providers and provider groups that are eligible and intend, or have been approved, to participate in the Medicare Shared Savings Program (the "Shared Savings Program"); its applicability is no longer limited to those collaborations formed after March 23, 2010, the date on which the Patient Protection and Affordable Care Act was enacted. Second, because the Shared Savings Program final rule will no longer require a mandatory antitrust review for certain collaborations as a condition of entry into the Shared Savings Program, the final Policy Statement no longer contains provisions relating to mandatory antitrust review.

However, as discussed in the final rule, the Agencies will continue to protect competition in markets served by accountable care organizations ("ACOs") that participate in the Shared Savings Program, aided by data and information from CMS that will assist the Agencies in monitoring the competitive effects of ACOs. Specifically, CMS will provide the Agencies with aggregate claims data regarding allowed charges and fee-for-service payments for all ACOs accepted into the Shared Savings Program and also with copies of all of the applications to the Shared Savings Program of ACOs formed after March 23, 2010. The Agencies will vigilantly monitor complaints about an ACO's formation or conduct and take whatever enforcement action may be appropriate. Additionally, upon request, the Agencies will provide an expedited 90 day review for newly formed ACOs that wish to obtain additional antitrust guidance.

ANTITRUST ENFORCEMENT POLICY REGARDING ORGANIZATIONS IN THE MEDICARE SHARED SAVINGS PROGRAM

SUPPLEMENTARY INFORMATION

Statement of Antitrust Enforcement Policy Regarding Accountable Care Organizations Participating in the Medicare Shared Savings Program

I. Introduction

The Patient Protection and Affordable Care Act and the Health Care and Education Reconciliation Act of 2010 (collectively, the "Affordable Care Act") seek to improve the quality and reduce the costs of health care services in the United States by, among other things, encouraging physicians, hospitals, and other health care providers to become accountable for a patient population through integrated health care delivery systems.[1] One delivery system reform is the Affordable Care Act's Medicare Shared Savings Program (the "Shared Savings Program"), which promotes the formation and operation of Accountable Care Organizations ("ACOs"[2]) to serve Medicare fee-for-service beneficiaries.[3] Under this provision, "groups of providers of services and suppliers meeting criteria specified by the [Department of Health and Human Services] Secretary may work together to manage and coordinate care for Medicare fee-for-service beneficiaries through an [ACO]."[4] An ACO may share in some portion of any savings it creates if the ACO meets certain quality performance standards established by the Secretary of Health and Human Services through the Centers for Medicare and Medicaid Services ("CMS"). The Affordable Care Act requires an ACO that wishes to participate in the Shared Savings Program to enter into an agreement with CMS for not less than three years.[5]

Recent commentary suggests that some health care providers are likely to create and participate in ACOs that serve both Medicare beneficiaries and commercially insured patients.[6] The Federal Trade Commission and the Antitrust Division of the Department of Justice (the "Agencies") recognize that ACOs may generate opportunities for health care providers to innovate in both the Medicare and commercial markets and achieve for many other consumers the benefits Congress intended for Medicare beneficiaries through the Shared Savings Program. Therefore, to maximize and foster opportunities for ACO innovation and better health for patients, the Agencies wish to clarify their antitrust enforcement policy regarding collaborations among independent providers that seek to become ACOs in the Shared Savings Program. The Agencies recognize that not all such ACOs are likely to benefit consumers, and under certain conditions ACOs could reduce competition and harm consumers through higher prices or lower quality of care. Thus, the antitrust analysis of ACO applicants to the Shared Savings Program seeks to protect both Medicare beneficiaries and

---

[1] Health Care and Education Reconciliation Act of 2010, Pub. L. No. 111-52, 124 Stat. 1029 (2010); Patient Protection and Affordable Care Act, Pub. L. No. 111-48, 124 Stat. 119 (2010).

[2] As used in this document, "ACO" refers to Accountable Care Organizations under the Medicare Shared Savings Program, which also may operate in commercial markets. Patient Protection and Affordable Care Act § 3022, 124 Stat. at 395–99.

[3] Id.

[4] Id. at 395.

[5] Id. at 396.

[6] Fed. Trade Comm'n & Dep't of Health and Human Serv., Workshop Regarding Accountable Care Organizations, and Implications Regarding Antitrust, Physician Self-Referral, Anti-Kickback, and Civil Monetary Penalty (CMP) Laws (Oct. 5, 2010).

commercially insured patients from potential anticompetitive harm while allowing ACOs the opportunity to achieve significant efficiencies.

To achieve these goals, the Agencies have developed this Statement of Antitrust Enforcement Policy Regarding Accountable Care Organizations Participating in the Medicare Shared Savings Program (the "Policy Statement"). The Policy Statement is intended to ensure that health care providers have the antitrust clarity and guidance needed to form procompetitive ACOs that participate in both the Medicare and commercial markets. The Policy Statement describes (1) the ACOs to which the Policy Statement will apply;[7] (2) when the Agencies will apply rule of reason treatment to those ACOs; (3) an antitrust safety zone; and (4) additional antitrust guidance for ACOs that are outside the safety zone, including a voluntary expedited antitrust review process for newly formed ACOs.[8]

II. Applicability of the Policy Statement

The Policy Statement applies to collaborations among otherwise independent providers and provider groups[9] that are eligible and intend, or have been approved, to participate in the Shared Savings Program. For ease of reference, the Policy Statement refers to such collaborations as ACOs, although they may not yet have been approved to participate as ACOs in the Shared Savings Program. The Policy Statement refers to the otherwise independent providers and provider groups that constitute the ACO as ACO participants.[10] The Policy Statement does not apply to mergers. Merger transactions, including transactions that meet the criteria set forth in Section 1.3 of the *Antitrust Guidelines for Collaborations Among Competitors*,[11] will be evaluated under the Agencies' *Horizontal Merger Guidelines*.[12] The Policy Statement also does not apply to single, fully integrated entities.

III. The Agencies Will Apply Rule of Reason Analysis to ACOs That Meet Certain Conditions

The antitrust laws treat naked price-fixing and market-allocation agreements among competitors as per se illegal. Joint price agreements among competing health care providers are evaluated under the rule of reason, however, if the providers are financially or clinically integrated and

---

7 The analytical principles underlying the Policy Statement also would apply to various ACO initiatives undertaken by the Innovation Center within CMS as long as those ACOs are substantially clinically or financially integrated.

8 The Policy Statement provides guidance to assist ACOs in determining whether they are likely to present competitive concerns. It does not reflect the full analysis that the Agencies may use in evaluating ACOs or any other transaction or course of conduct. "Newly formed ACOs" are defined *infra* at note 23.

9 A "collaboration" comprises an agreement or set of agreements, other than merger agreements, among otherwise independent entities jointly to engage in economic activity, and the resulting economic activity. U.S. DEP'T OF JUSTICE & FED. TRADE COMM'N, ANTITRUST GUIDELINES FOR COLLABORATIONS AMONG COMPETITORS § 1.1 (2000) [hereinafter COLLABORATION GUIDELINES], *available at* http://www.ftc.gov/os/2000/04/ftcdojguidelines.pdf.

10 An ACO participant can be an independent physician solo practice, a fully integrated physician group practice, an inpatient facility, or an outpatient facility. The Policy Statement's definition of ACO participant may differ from CMS's use of the term.

11 COLLABORATION GUIDELINES, *supra* note 9, § 1.3.

12 U.S. DEP'T OF JUSTICE & FED. TRADE COMM'N, HORIZONTAL MERGER GUIDELINES (rev. ed. 2010), *available at* http://www.justice.gov/atr/public/guidelines/hmg-2010.pdf.

the agreement is reasonably necessary to accomplish the procompetitive benefits of the integration.

A rule of reason analysis evaluates whether the collaboration is likely to have anticompetitive effects and, if so, whether the collaboration's potential procompetitive efficiencies are likely to outweigh those effects. The greater the likely anticompetitive effects, the greater the likely efficiencies must be for the collaboration to pass muster under the antitrust laws. The Agencies have articulated the standards for both financial and clinical integration in various policy statements, speeches, business reviews, and advisory opinions. For example, the Agencies' *Statements of Antitrust Enforcement Policy in Health Care* (the "Health Care Statements") explain that where participants in physician or multiprovider joint ventures have agreed to share substantial financial risk as defined in the Health Care Statements, their risk-sharing arrangement generally establishes both an overall efficiency goal for the venture and the incentives for the participants to meet that goal.[13] Accordingly, the setting of price is integral to the venture's use of such an arrangement and therefore warrants evaluation under the rule of reason.[14] The Health Care Statements provide examples of financial risk-sharing arrangements that can satisfy this standard, but also recognize that other acceptable financial risk-sharing arrangements might develop.[15]

The Health Care Statements further explain that provider joint ventures also may involve clinical integration sufficient to ensure that the venture is likely to produce significant efficiencies.[16] Clinical integration can be evidenced by the joint venture implementing an active and ongoing program to evaluate and modify practice patterns by the venture's providers and to create a high degree of interdependence and cooperation among the providers to control costs and ensure quality.[17] Federal Trade Commission staff advisory opinions discuss evidence that appears sufficient to demonstrate clinical integration in specific factual circumstances.[18]

The Affordable Care Act provides that CMS may approve ACOs that meet certain eligibility criteria, including (1) a formal legal structure that allows the ACO to receive and distribute payments for shared savings; (2) a leadership and management structure that includes clinical and administrative processes; (3) processes to promote evidence-based medicine and patient engagement; (4) reporting on quality and cost measures; and (5)

---

[13] U.S. DEP'T OF JUSTICE & FED. TRADE COMM'N, STATEMENTS OF ANTITRUST ENFORCEMENT POLICY INHEALTH CARE, Statements 8 and 9 (1996) [hereinafter HEALTH CARE STATEMENTS], *available at* http://www.ftc.gov/reports/hlth3s.pdf. [Eds. Updated link can be found at http://www.ftc.gov/sites/default/files/attachments/competition-policy-guidance/statements_of_antitrust_enforcement_policy_in_health_care_august_1996.pdf]

[14] *Id.*

[15] *Id.*

[16] *Id.*

[17] *See, e.g.*, Christine A. Varney, Assistant Attorney Gen., Antitrust Div., U.S. Dep't of Justice, Antitrust and Healthcare at 12 (May 24, 2010), *available at* http://www.justice.gov/atr/public/speeches/258898.pdf.

[18] *See* FED. TRADE COMM'N, ADVISORY OPINIONS (1982–2010), *available at* http://www.ftc.gov/bc/healthcare/industryguide/advisory.htm#2010.

coordinated care for beneficiaries.[19] CMS has further defined these eligibility criteria through regulations.[20]

By contrast, the Agencies have not previously listed specific criteria required to establish clinical integration, but instead have responded to detailed proposals from health care providers who have decided on specific ways to integrate their health care delivery systems to improve quality and lower costs.[21] The Agencies have chosen to avoid prescribing how clinical integration should take place. Nonetheless, the Agencies recognize that health care providers seeking to create ACOs in the context of the Shared Savings Program could benefit from additional antitrust guidance in evaluating whether an ACO that satisfies the CMS eligibility criteria could be subject to an antitrust investigation and potential challenge as engaging in per se illegal conduct.

The Agencies have determined that CMS's eligibility criteria are broadly consistent with the indicia of clinical integration that the Agencies previously set forth in the Health Care Statements and identified in the context of specific proposals for clinical integration from health care providers.[22] The Agencies also have determined that organizations meeting the eligibility requirements for the Shared Savings Program are reasonably likely to be bona fide arrangements intended to improve the quality, and reduce the costs, of providing medical and other health care services through their participants' joint efforts.

To assess whether an ACO has improved quality and reduced costs to Medicare, CMS will collect and evaluate cost, utilization, and quality metrics relating to each ACO's performance in the Shared Savings Program. The results of this monitoring will help the Agencies determine whether the CMS eligibility criteria have required a sufficient level of clinical integration to produce cost savings and quality improvements, and may help inform the Agencies' future analysis of ACOs and other provider organizations.

In light of CMS's eligibility criteria, and its monitoring of each ACO's results, the Agencies will treat joint negotiations with private payers as reasonably necessary to an ACO's primary purpose of improving health care delivery, and will afford rule of reason treatment to an ACO that meets CMS's eligibility requirements for, and participates in, the Shared Savings Program and uses the same governance and leadership structures and clinical and administrative processes it uses in the Shared Savings Program to serve patients in commercial markets. The Agencies further note that CMS's regulations allow an ACO to propose alternative ways to establish

---

[19] Patient Protection and Affordable Care Act, Pub. L. No. 111-48, § 3022, 124 Stat. 119, 395–99 (2010).

[20] Medicare Program; Medicare Shared Savings Program: Accountable Care Organizations, 42 C.F.R. pt. 425 (2011) [hereinafter CMS ACO Rule].

[21] *See generally* FTC Staff Advisory Opinions (2002–Present), *available at* www.ftc.gov/bc/healthcare/industryguide/opinionguidance.htm; *see also* U.S. DEP'T OF JUSTICE & FED. TRADE COMM'N, IMPROVING HEALTH CARE: ANOTHER DOSE OF COMPETITION ch. 2 at 34–41 (July 2004), *available at* http://www.ftc.gov/reports/healthcare/040723healthcarerpt.pdf.

[22] *Id. See also, e.g.*, TriState Health Partners, Inc. Advisory Opinion from FTC Staff (Apr. 13, 2009) (evaluating TriState Health Partners' proposal and stating that, if implemented as proposed, FTC staff would not recommend that the Commission challenge the proposed program), *available at* www.ftc.gov/os/closings/staff/090413tristateaoletter.pdf. [Eds. Updated link can be found at http://www.ftc.gov/sites/default/files/documents/advisory-opinions/tristate-health-partners-inc./090413tristateaoletter.pdf]

clinical management and oversight of the ACO, and the Agencies are willing to consider other proposals for clinical integration as well.

IV. The Agencies' Antitrust Analysis of ACOs That Meet CMS Eligibility Criteria

The following Sections provide additional antitrust guidance for ACOs that are eligible and intend, or have been approved, to participate in the Shared Savings Program, including those ACOs that also plan to operate in the commercial market. Section A sets forth a safety zone for certain ACOs that are highly unlikely to raise significant competitive concerns and, therefore, will not be challenged by the Agencies under the antitrust laws, absent extraordinary circumstances.

The Agencies emphasize that ACOs outside the safety zone may be procompetitive and legal. An ACO that does not impede the functioning of a competitive market will not raise competitive concerns. The creation of a safety zone reflects the view that ACOs that fall within the safety zone are highly unlikely to raise significant competitive concerns; it does not imply that ACOs outside the safety zone necessarily present competitive concerns.

Section B offers options for ACOs that seek additional antitrust guidance. It describes certain conduct all ACOs generally should avoid, other conduct that ACOs with high Primary Service Area ("PSA") shares or other possible indicia of market power may wish to avoid, and the process by which a newly formed ACO[23] may obtain a voluntary expedited antitrust review.

A. The Antitrust Safety Zone for ACOs in the Shared Savings Program

This Section sets forth an antitrust safety zone for ACOs that meet the CMS eligibility criteria for and intend, or have been approved, to participate in the Shared Savings Program and are highly unlikely to raise significant competitive concerns. The Agencies will not challenge ACOs that fall within the safety zone, absent extraordinary circumstances.[24]

To determine whether it falls within the safety zone, an ACO should evaluate the ACO's share of services in each ACO participant's PSA. Although a PSA does not necessarily constitute a relevant antitrust geographic market, it nonetheless serves as a useful screen for evaluating potential competitive effects.

The Policy Statement focuses on PSA shares for three major categories of services: physician specialties, major diagnostic categories ("MDCs") for inpatient facilities, and outpatient categories, as defined

[23] "Newly formed ACOs" are those ACOs that, as of March 23, 2010, the date on which the Patient Protection and Affordable Care Act was enacted, had not yet signed or jointly negotiated any contracts with private payers, and have not yet participated in the Shared Savings Program. Patient Protection and Affordable Care Act, Pub. L. No. 111-48, 124 Stat. 119 (2010). An ACO is not newly formed if it comprises only the same, or a subset of the same, providers that signed or jointly negotiated contracts with private payers on or before March 23, 2010.

[24] Extraordinary circumstances could include, for example, ACO participants engaging in collusion or improper exchanges of price information or other competitively sensitive information with respect to their sale of competing services outside the ACO. *See infra* IV(B)(1)(a).

by CMS, for outpatient facilities.[25] Although these services are useful in evaluating potential anticompetitive effects, they do not necessarily constitute relevant antitrust product markets. The Appendix to the Policy Statement describes how to calculate an ACO's shares of these services in the relevant PSAs, identifies data sources available for these calculations, and provides illustrative examples.[26]

For an ACO to fall within the safety zone, independent ACO participants that provide the same service (a "common service") must have a combined share of 30 percent or less of each common service in each participant's PSA, wherever two or more ACO participants provide that service to patients from that PSA.[27] As noted above, a service is defined as a primary specialty for physicians, an MDC for inpatient facilities, or an outpatient category for outpatient facilities. The PSA for each participant is defined as "the lowest number of postal zip codes from which the [ACO participant] draws at least 75 percent of its [patients],"[28] separately for all physician, inpatient, or outpatient services. Thus, for purposes of determining whether the ACO is eligible for the safety zone, each independent physician solo practice, each fully integrated physician group practice, each inpatient facility (even if part of a hospital system), and each outpatient facility will have its own PSA. In addition, each inpatient facility hospital will have separate PSAs for its (1) inpatient services, (2) outpatient services, and (3) physician services provided by its physician employees, if any.[29]

As described below, the availability of the PSA safety zone differs in some cases depending on whether an ACO participant is exclusive or non-exclusive to the ACO. To participate in an ACO on a non-exclusive basis, a participant must be allowed to contract with private payers through entities other than the ACO, including contracting individually or through other ACOs or analogous collaborations. The ACO must be non-exclusive in fact and not just in name. Exclusivity may be present explicitly or implicitly, formally or informally, through a written or de facto agreement as shown by conduct.[30]

> *Hospitals and Ambulatory Surgical Centers.* Any hospital or ambulatory surgery center ("ASC") participating in an ACO must be non-exclusive to the ACO to fall within the safety zone, regardless of its PSA share.

---

[25] The Policy Statement does not apply to other types of providers (e.g., clinical laboratories or nursing homes). Nonetheless, the Agencies recognize that those providers may participate in ACOs.

[26] The ACO may send questions regarding PSA share calculations to aco_psa_questions@ftc.gov.

[27] Thus, if two otherwise independent physician group practices form an ACO and each includes cardiologists and oncologists, each physician group practice would be an independent participant in the ACO, and cardiology and oncology would be common services. If, on the other hand, one physician group practice consists only of cardiologists and the other only of oncologists, then there would be no common services and the ACO would fall within the safety zone regardless of its share, subject to the dominant participant limitation described below.

[28] Medicare Program: Physicians' Referrals to Health Care Entities with Which They Have Financial Relationships (Phase II), 69 Fed. Reg. 16,094 (Mar. 26, 2004).

[29] *See* Appendix to the Policy Statement.

[30] The Health Care Statements further explain the indicia of non-exclusivity that the Agencies consider relevant to this evaluation. HEALTH CARE STATEMENTS, *supra* note 13, at 66–67.

Physicians. The safety zone for physicians (regardless of whether the physicians are hospital employees) does not differ based on whether the physicians are exclusive or non-exclusive to the ACO, unless they fall within the rural exception or dominant participant limitation described below.

1. Rural Exception

An ACO that exceeds the 30 percent PSA share may still fall within the safety zone if it qualifies for this rural exception. The rural exception allows such an ACO to include one physician or physician group practice[31] per specialty from each rural area[32] *on a non-exclusive basis* and still fall within the safety zone, provided the physician's or physician group practice's primary office is in a zip code that is classified as "isolated rural" or "other small rural."[33] Thus, an ACO may qualify for the safety zone as long as it includes only one physician or physician group practice per specialty for each county that contains at least one "isolated rural" or "other small rural" zip code, even if the inclusion of these physicians causes the ACO's share of any common service to exceed 30 percent in any ACO participant's PSA.

Likewise, an ACO may include Rural Hospitals[34] *on a non-exclusive basis* and qualify for the safety zone, even if the

---

[31] To qualify for the rural exception, the physician group practice must be treating patients as a fully integrated practice group as of the date of the Policy Statement. The practice group can add or eliminate physicians and still remain in the safety zone, as long as the number of full-time equivalent physicians in the practice group does not increase during the ACO's Shared Savings Program agreement period. For the purposes of the Policy Statement, Federally Qualified Health Centers and Rural Health Clinics, as defined by the Social Security Act, are considered physician group practices. 42 U.S.C. § 1396d (2006); 42 U.S.C. § 1395x(aa) (2006). A physician or physician group practice that qualifies for the rural exception may obtain "call coverage" from other physicians in the same rural area without losing its safety zone status as long as those physicians do not participate in the ACO.

[32] For the purposes of the Policy Statement, a "rural area" means any county containing at least one zip code that has been classified as "isolated rural," or "other small rural," according to the WWAMI Rural Health Research Center of the University of Washington's seven category classification. http://depts.washington.edu/uwruca/ruca-maps.php. These are zip codes that have a Rural Urban Commuting Area ("RUCA") code of 10.0, 10.2–10.6, 8.0, 8.2–8.4, or 9.0–9.2 as developed by the WWAMI Rural Health Research Center of the University of Washington and the U.S. Department of Agriculture's Economic Research Service. http://www.ers.usda.gov/briefing/Rurality/RuralUrbanCommutingAreas/. [Eds. Updated link can be found at http://depts.washington.edu/uwruca/] The RUCA code for any particular zip code can be found at http://depts.washington.edu/uwruca/ruca-download.php.

[33] A physician's or physician group practice's primary office is the office in which the majority of the physician's or physician group practice's patient visits take place. If no office serves a majority of a physician's patients, the majority of patient visits must take place in offices located in "isolated rural" or "other small rural" zip codes to qualify for the rural exception.

[34] For the purposes of the Policy Statement, a Rural Hospital is defined as a Sole Community Hospital, a Critical Access Hospital, or any other acute care hospital located in a rural area that has no more than 50 acute care inpatient beds and is located at least 35 miles from any other inpatient acute care hospital. A Sole Community Hospital is a hospital that is paid under the Medicare hospital inpatient prospective payment system and meets the criteria for Sole Community Hospital status as specified at 42 C.F.R. § 412.92. *See also* DEP'T OF HEALTH AND HUMAN SERVS., CTRS. FOR MEDICARE & MEDICAID SERVS., SOLE COMMUNITY HOSPITAL, RURAL HEALTH FACT SHEET SERIES (Oct. 2010), *available at* https:// www. cms.gov/MLNProducts/downloads/

inclusion of a Rural Hospital causes the ACO's share of any common service to exceed 30 percent in any ACO participant's PSA.

2. Dominant Participant Limitation

The dominant participant limitation applies to any ACO that includes a participant with a greater than 50 percent share in its PSA of any service that no other ACO participant provides to patients in that PSA. Under these conditions, the ACO participant must be *non-exclusive* to the ACO for the ACO to fall within the safety zone.[35] In addition, to fall within the safety zone, an ACO with a dominant participant cannot require a private payer to contract exclusively with the ACO or otherwise restrict a private payer's ability to contract or deal with other ACOs or provider networks.

* * *

The safety zone will remain in effect for the duration of an ACO's agreement with CMS, provided the ACO continues to meet the safety zone's requirements. An ACO will not lose its safety zone status solely because it attracts more patients.

B. ACOs Outside the Safety Zone

ACOs that fall outside the safety zone may be procompetitive and lawful. An ACO that does not impede the functioning of a competitive market will not raise competitive concerns.[36]

Nonetheless, there may be circumstances in which an ACO would raise competitive concerns. This section describes some types of conduct by an ACO that, under certain circumstances, may raise competitive concerns and outlines how an ACO may obtain further antitrust guidance from the Agencies.

1. Conduct to Avoid

a. Improper Sharing of Competitively Sensitive Information

Regardless of an ACO's PSA shares or other indicia of market power, significant competitive concerns can arise when an ACO's operations lead to price-fixing or other collusion among ACO participants in their sale of competing services outside the ACO. For example,

---

SoleCommHospfctsht508-09.pdf; Social Security Act, 42 U.S.C. § 1395ww(d)(5)(D)(iii) (2006). A Critical Access Hospital is a hospital that has been certified as a Medicare Critical Access Hospital, as described in 42 C.F.R. § 485 Subpart F. *See also* 42 U.S.C. § 1395i-4(c)(2).

[35] For example, a physician group participating in the ACO may comprise a specialty not found in any other ACO participant. In this case, the ACO may be eligible for the safety zone even if the physician group's share exceeds 50 percent, but only if the physician group participates in the ACO on a non-exclusive basis and the ACO does not restrict a private payer's ability to contract or deal with other ACOs or provider groups.

[36] The Agencies emphasize that PSA shares are useful as a screening device and that alternative data and information also may be useful in evaluating the likely competitive significance of a particular ACO. The Agencies recognize that an ACO may have reliable evidence other than PSA shares from which the ACO may reasonably conclude that the ACO is unlikely to raise competitive concerns.

improper exchanges of prices or other competitively sensitive information among competing participants could facilitate collusion and reduce competition in the provision of services outside the ACO, leading to increased prices or reduced quality or availability of health care services.[37] ACOs should refrain from, and implement appropriate firewalls or other safeguards against, conduct that may facilitate collusion among ACO participants in the sale of competing services outside the ACO.[38]

b. Conduct by ACOs with High PSA Shares or Other Possible Indicia of Market Power That May Raise Competitive Concerns

For ACOs with high PSA shares or other possible indicia of market power, the Agencies identify four types of conduct that may raise competitive concerns.[39] The Agencies recognize that some of the conduct described in (1) through (4) below may be competitively neutral or even procompetitive, depending on the circumstances, including whether the ACO has market power. For example, an ACO that requires its participants to contract exclusively through the ACO to increase the ACO's efficiency is generally less likely to raise competitive concerns the greater the number of competing ACOs or independent providers available to contract with private payers or to participate in competing ACOs or other analogous collaborations.

An ACO with high PSA shares or other possible indicia of market power may wish to avoid the conduct set forth in (1) through (4) below. Depending on the circumstances, the conduct identified below may prevent private payers from obtaining lower prices and better quality service for their enrollees:

1. Preventing or discouraging private payers from directing or incentivizing patients to choose certain providers, including providers that do not participate in the ACO, through "anti-steering," "anti-tiering," "guaranteed inclusion," "most-favored-nation," or similar contractual clauses or provisions
2. Tying sales (either explicitly or implicitly through pricing policies) of the ACO's services to the private

---

[37] Health Care Statements 4, 5, and 6 relate to the sharing of data and information among competing providers. The Health Care Statements set forth safety zones for providers' collective provision of fee- and non-fee-related information to health care purchasers and participation in exchanges of price and cost information. The Health Care Statements also provide further guidance on the distinctions between legitimate information sharing and information sharing that may facilitate collusion or otherwise raise competitive concerns. HEALTH CARE STATEMENTS, *supra* note 13, at 40–52.

[38] ACOs within the safety zone should also refrain from this conduct. *See supra* note 24.

[39] ACOs with high PSA shares or other possible indicia of market power also should consider the likely competitive effects of other types of conduct in which they engage.

payer's purchase of other services from providers outside the ACO (and vice versa), including providers affiliated with an ACO participant (e.g., an ACO should not require a purchaser to contract with *all* of the hospitals under common ownership with a hospital that participates in the ACO)

3. Contracting on an exclusive basis with ACO physicians, hospitals, ASCs, or other providers, thereby preventing or discouraging those providers from contracting with private payers outside the ACO, either individually or through other ACOs or analogous collaborations[40]

4. Restricting a private payer's ability to make available to its health plan enrollees cost, quality, efficiency, and performance information to aid enrollees in evaluating and selecting providers in the health plan, if that information is similar to the cost, quality, efficiency, and performance measures used in the Shared Savings Program

2. Availability of Expedited Voluntary Antitrust Review

Any newly formed ACO[41] that desires further antitrust guidance regarding its formation and planned operation can seek expedited 90 day review from the Agencies.[42] During expedited review, the reviewing Agency will examine whether the ACO will likely harm competition by increasing the ACO's ability or incentive profitably to raise prices above competitive levels or reduce output, quality, service, or innovation below what likely would prevail in the absence of the ACO.[43] To the extent possible in the 90 day review period, the Agency will consider factors in the rule of reason analysis as explained in the *Antitrust Guidelines for Collaborations Among Competitors* and the Health Care Statements.[44]

The ACO should submit its request for expedited review, along with a completed cover sheet (available on the Agencies' websites), to both Agencies before its entrance into the Shared Savings Program, and the Agencies will then promptly determine, and notify the applicant, which Agency will be the reviewing Agency.[45] As soon as the Agencies notify the applicant which

---

[40] Note that, although CMS requires the physician practice through which physicians bill for primary care services and to which Medicare beneficiaries are assigned to contract exclusively with one ACO for the purposes of beneficiary assignment, CMS does *not* require either those individual physicians or physician practices to contract exclusively through the same ACO for the purposes of providing services to private health plans' enrollees. CMS ACO Rule, *supra* note 20.

[41] *See supra* note 23.

[42] When the Federal Trade Commission is the reviewing Agency, Commission staff will perform the ACO review pursuant to the Commission's authorization of its staff in 16 C.F.R. § 1.1(b). When the Antitrust Division is the reviewing Agency, the Assistant Attorney General in charge of the Antitrust Division or the Assistant Attorney General's delegate will sign the review letter. 28 C.F.R § 50.6.

[43] *See* COLLABORATION GUIDELINES, *supra* note 9, § 1.2.

[44] *See id.* § 3.3; HEALTH CARE STATEMENTS, *supra* note 13, Statements 8 and 9.

[45] A request for an expedited review must be submitted in writing to either (1) the Office of the Assistant Attorney General, Antitrust Division, Department of Justice, Main Justice Building, Room 3109, 950 Pennsylvania Avenue, NW, Washington, DC 20530 (for

Agency will be the reviewing Agency, the applicant should provide all of the documents and information listed below to the reviewing Agency. The Agencies shall establish a Federal Trade Commission/Department of Justice ACO Working Group to collaborate and discuss issues arising out of the ACO reviews. This process will allow ACOs to rely on the expertise of both Agencies and ensure efficient, cooperative, and expeditious reviews.[46]

To start the 90-day review, the reviewing Agency must receive all of the following documents and information:[47]

1. The application and all supporting documents that the ACO plans to submit, or has submitted, to CMS, including a sample of each type of participation agreement and each type of document that reflects a financial arrangement between or among the ACO and its participants, as well as the ACO's bylaws and operating policies
2. Documents discussing
   a. the ACO's business strategies or plans to compete in the Medicare and commercial markets, including those relating to the ACO's likely impact on the prices, cost, or quality of any service provided by the ACO to Medicare beneficiaries, commercial health plans, or other payers; and
   b. the level and nature of competition among participants in the ACO, and the competitive significance of the ACO and ACO participants in the markets in which they provide services
3. Information sufficient to show the following:
   a. The common services that two or more ACO participants provide to patients from the same PSA, as described in the Appendix, and the identity of the ACO participants or providers providing those services
   b. The PSA of each ACO participant, and either PSA share calculations the ACO may have performed or other data that show the current competitive significance of the ACO or ACO participants, including any data that describe the geographic

---

non-U.S. Postal Service deliveries, use ZIP code 20004), and to the Federal Trade Commission, Bureau of Competition, Premerger Notification Office, Room 303, 600 Pennsylvania Avenue, NW, Washington, DC 20580 or (2) acorequest@usdoj.gov and acorequest@ftc.gov.

[46] For example, it has been standard practice for the Agencies to share with each other their proposed health care business review and staff advisory opinion letters before issuing them in final form to ensure application of consistent standards of antitrust review.

[47] The ACO must represent in writing that it has undertaken a good-faith search for the documents and information specified in the Policy Statement and, where applicable, provided all responsive material. Moreover, the Agencies may request additional documents and information where necessary to evaluate the ACO. A request for additional documents and information, however, will not extend the 90 day review period.

service area of each participant and the size of each participant relative to other providers serving patients from that area

c. Restrictions that prevent ACO participants from obtaining information regarding prices that other ACO participants charge private payers that do not contract through the ACO

d. The identity, including points of contact, of the five largest commercial health plans or other private payers, actual or projected, for the ACO's services

e. The identity of any other existing or proposed ACO known to operate, or known to plan to operate, in any market in which the ACO will provide services

Moreover, the ACO may submit any other documents and information that it believes may be helpful to the Agency in assessing the ACO's likely impact on competition. The documents and information may include anything that may establish a clearer picture of competitive realities in the market, including

1. evidence that the ACO is not likely to have market power in the relevant market;
2. any substantial procompetitive justification for why the ACO needs its proposed composition to provide high-quality, cost-effective care to Medicare beneficiaries and patients in the commercial market; and
3. if relevant, an explanation as to why the ACO engaging in any of the four types of conduct listed in Section IV.B of the Policy Statement would not be anticompetitive or might even be procompetitive.

Within 90 days of receiving all of the above documents and information,[48] the reviewing Agency will advise the ACO that the ACO's formation and operation, as described in the documents and information provided to the Agency,

1. does not likely raise competitive concerns or, if appropriate, does not likely raise competitive concerns conditioned on the ACO's written agreement to take specific steps to remedy concerns raised by the Agency;
2. potentially raises competitive concerns; or
3. likely raises competitive concerns.

As is current practice, both the request letter and the reviewing Agency's response will be made public consistent with applicable confidentiality provisions.[49] Also, consistent with

---

[48] Upon the applicant's request, the reviewing Agency may extend the review beyond 90 days, subject to the availability of resources or other discretionary considerations.

[49] The provisions regarding public access to review information, non-disclosure of competitively sensitive or business confidential information, and retention of review information set forth in 28 C.F.R. § 50.6 (2010) (U.S. Department of Justice business review letters) and 16 C.F.R. §§ 1.1–1.4 (2010) (FTC advisory opinions) will generally apply to the expedited review process. Requesters should follow applicable Agency procedures governing the designation of competitively sensitive business information and other information the requesters wish not to be made public in connection with a review

current practice, if it appears that an ACO's formation or conduct may be anticompetitive, the Agency may investigate the ACO and, if appropriate, take enforcement action at any time before or during the ACO's participation in the Shared Savings Program.

Appendix

This Appendix explains how to calculate the PSA shares of common services discussed in the Policy Statement.[50] There are three steps:

1. Identify each service provided by at least two independent ACO participants (i.e., each common service). A service is defined as follows:
   a. For physicians, a service is the physician's primary specialty, as designated on the physician's Medicare Enrollment Application. Each specialty is identified by its Medicare Specialty Code ("MSC"), as defined by CMS.[51]
   b. For inpatient facilities (e.g., hospitals), a service is an MDC.[52]
   c. For outpatient facilities (e.g., ASCs or hospitals), a service is an outpatient category, as defined by CMS.[53]
2. Identify the PSA(s) for each participant (e.g., physician group, inpatient facility, or outpatient facility) in the ACO that provides any common service. For each participant, the PSA is defined as the lowest number of postal zip codes from which the participant draws at least 75 percent of its patients.[54] Each independent physician solo practice, each fully integrated physician group practice, each inpatient facility (even if part of a hospital system), and each outpatient facility will have its own PSA. In addition, each inpatient facility will have a separate PSA for inpatient services, outpatient services, and physician services provided by its physician employees.
3. Separately for each common service, calculate the ACO's PSA share in the PSA of each participant that provides that service if at least two participants provide that service to patients from that PSA. If an entity owned by an ACO participant provides services in a PSA, those services should be included in the share calculation regardless of whether the affiliated organization participates in the ACO.

---

request. *See* 28 C.F.R. § 50.56 (U.S. Department of Justice procedures); 16 C.F.R. §§ 4.2, 4.9, and 4.10 (FTC procedures).

[50] Any ACO participant that wants to determine whether it meets the dominant participant limitation of the safety zone should calculate its PSA share in a similar manner.

[51] CMS will make publicly available the most current list of applicable specialties. Specialty Codes 01 (general practice), 08 (family practice), 11 (internal medicine), and 38 (geriatric medicine) are considered

"Primary Care" specialties, and are treated as a single service for the purposes of the Policy Statement.

[52] CMS will make publicly available the most current list of MDCs.

[53] CMS will make publicly available a list of applicable outpatient categories as well as data necessary to assign procedure codes to the appropriate category.

[54] This PSA calculation is based on the Stark II regulations. Medicare Program: Physicians' Referrals to Health Care Entities with Which They Have Financial Relationships (Phase II), 69 Fed. Reg. 16,094 (Mar. 26, 2004).

a. For physician services, the ACO should calculate its shares of Medicare fee-for-service allowed charges (i.e., the amount that a provider is entitled to receive for the service provided) during the most recent calendar year for which data are available. CMS will make public the data necessary to identify the full range of services and the aggregate fee-for-service allowed charges for each service, by zip code.

b. For inpatient services, the ACO should calculate its shares of inpatient discharges, using state-level all-payer hospital discharge data where available, for the most recent calendar year for which data are available. For ACOs located in a state where all-payer hospital discharge data are not available, the ACO should calculate its shares of Medicare fee-for-service payments during the most recent federal fiscal year for which data are available. CMS will make public the data necessary to identify the full range of services and the aggregate fee-for-service payments for each service, by zip code.

c. For outpatient services, the ACO should calculate its shares of Medicare fee-for-service payments for hospitals and fee-for-services allowed charges for ASCs during the most recent calendar year for which data are available, or the ACO can use state-level all-payer claims data, if available. CMS will make public the data necessary to identify the full range of services and the aggregate fee-for-service payments and allowed charges for each service, by zip code.

For those services that are rarely used by Medicare beneficiaries (e.g., pediatrics, obstetrics, gynecology, and neonatal care) and for which all-payer data are not available, the ACO may use other available data to determine the relevant shares. For example, for those services, data on the number of active physicians within the specialty and located within the PSA may be a reasonable alternative for the purposes of calculating shares of physician services.

Example of How to Calculate an ACO's PSA Shares

The following example illustrates how to calculate the ACO's relevant PSA shares. Assume that two independent physician practices, two independent hospitals, and an ASC propose to form an ACO. For purposes of this example, further assume that the hospitals do not directly employ physicians. If they do, then services provided by the hospitals' employed physicians would need to be taken into account in determining the PSA and calculating the ACO's shares for each common physician service where at least two participants provide that service to patients from the same PSA.

For the physician groups:

1. Identify the physician groups' common MSCs. In this example, Physician Group A ("PG A") has physicians with general surgery (MSC 02) and orthopedic surgery specialties (MSC 20). Physician Group B ("PG B") has physicians with orthopedic surgery (MSC 20) and cardiology (MSC 06) specialties. The only common service is orthopedic surgery, not general surgery or cardiology, because PG A does not have cardiologists and PG B does not have general surgeons.

2. Identify the zip codes that make up the PSA for each physician group. In this example, there will be two PSAs: one for PG A ("PSA A") and one for PG B ("PSA B").

3. Determine the ACO's share in each of the PSAs. In this example, both PG A's and PG B's orthopedic surgeons serve patients located in both PSAs. Thus, shares need to be calculated in PSA A and PSA B. The ACO's share of orthopedic surgery in PSA A would be the total Medicare allowed charges for claims billed by the ACO's orthopedic surgeons (which are PG A's and PG B's total allowed charges for claims billed by orthopedic surgeons for Medicare beneficiaries in PSA A's zip codes) divided by the total allowed charges for orthopedic surgery for all Medicare beneficiaries in PSA A. Likewise, the ACO's share of orthopedic surgery services in PSA B would be the total Medicare allowed charges for claims billed by the ACO's orthopedic surgeons (which are PG A's and PG B's total allowed charges for claims billed by orthopedic surgeons for Medicare beneficiaries in PSA B's zip codes) divided by the total allowed charges for orthopedic surgery for all Medicare beneficiaries in PSA B.

For the inpatient services:

1. Identify the hospitals' common MDCs. In this example, Hospital 1 and Hospital 2 each provide services in 10 MDCs, but only two are common services: cardiac care (i.e., services related to diseases and disorders of the circulatory system— MDC 05) and orthopedic care (i.e., services related to diseases and disorders of the musculoskeletal system and connective tissue—MDC 08).

2. Identify the zip codes that make up the PSA for inpatient services for each hospital. In this example, there will be two PSAs: Hospital 1's PSA and Hospital 2's PSA.

3. Determine the ACO's share in each of the PSAs. In this example, Hospital 1 and Hospital 2 both serve cardiac patients located in each hospital's PSA and both serve orthopedic patients in each hospital's PSA. Thus, shares need to be calculated in both PSAs, resulting in four shares. This hypothetical ACO is located in a state for which all-payer hospital discharge data are available, so the ACO's share of cardiac care in Hospital 1's PSA would be the ACO's total number of inpatient discharges for MDC 05 (which are Hospital 1's and Hospital 2's total inpatient discharges for cardiac care in Hospital l's PSA) divided by the total number of inpatient discharges for MDC 05 for all residents of this PSA. Use the analogous process to calculate the ACO's share of cardiac care in Hospital 2's PSA, the ACO's share of orthopedic care in Hospital 1's PSA, and the ACO's share of orthopedic care in Hospital 2's PSA.

For the outpatient services:

1. Identify the hospitals' and ASC's common outpatient categories. In this example, Hospital 1 does not provide outpatient services, while Hospital 2 and the ASC each provide services in 10 outpatient categories, but only two are common services: cardiovascular tests/procedures (outpatient category 2) and musculoskeletal procedures (outpatient category 5).

2. Identify the zip codes that make up the PSA for outpatient services for Hospital 2 and the ASC. In this example, there will be two PSAs: Hospital 2's PSA for outpatient services and the ASC's PSA.

3. Determine the ACO's share in each of the PSAs. In this example, Hospital 2 and the ASC both provide cardiovascular tests/procedures to patients located in each facility's PSA, and both provide musculoskeletal procedures to patients located in each facility's PSA. Thus, shares need to be calculated in both PSAs, resulting in four shares. The ACO's share of cardiovascular tests/procedures in Hospital 2's PSA would be the ACO's total Medicare fee-for-service payments/charges for outpatient category 2 (which are Hospital 2's total payments and the ASC's total allowed charges for outpatient cardiovascular tests/procedures for Medicare beneficiaries in Hospital 2's PSA) divided by the total payments/charges for outpatient category 2 for all Medicare beneficiaries in this PSA. Use the analogous process to calculate the ACO's share of cardiovascular tests/procedures in the ASC's PSA, the ACO's share of musculoskeletal procedures in Hospital 2's PSA, and the ACO's share of musculoskeletal procedures in the ASC's PSA.

Application to the Safety Zone: In this example, the ACO would calculate ten PSA shares. If *all* of the shares are 30 percent or below, and the hospitals and the ASC are non-exclusive to the ACO, then the ACO would fall within the safety zone. In other words, the 30 percent threshold must be met in *each* relevant PSA for each common service. If that condition is not met, then the ACO does not fall within the safety zone, unless it qualifies for the rural exception.

For the Antitrust Division of the Department of Justice.

Sharis A. Pozen

Acting Assistant Attorney General

For the Federal Trade Commission.

Donald S. Clark

Secretary

PART 5

PROCEDURAL STATUTES AND EXEMPTIONS

24

ANTITRUST CIVIL PROCESS ACT

§ 2. [15 U.S.C. § 1311]. Definitions

For the purposes of this Act [15 USCS §§ 1311 et seq.]—

(a) The term "antitrust law" includes:

(1) Each provision of law defined as one of the antitrust laws by section 1 of the Act entitled "An Act to supplement existing laws against unlawful restraints and monopolies, and for other purposes," approved October 15, 1914 (38 Stat. 730, as amended; 15 U. S. C. 12), commonly known as the Clayton Act; and

(2) Any statute hereafter [after Sept. 19, 1962] enacted by the Congress which prohibits, or makes available to the United States in any court of the United States any civil remedy with respect to any restraint upon or monopolization of interstate or foreign trade or commerce;

(b) The term "antitrust order" means any final order, decree, or judgment of any court of the United States, duly entered in any case or proceeding arising under any antitrust law;

(c) The term "antitrust investigation" means any inquiry conducted by any antitrust investigator for the purpose of ascertaining whether any person is or has been engaged in any antitrust violation or in any activities in preparation for a merger, acquisition, joint venture, or similar transaction, which, if consummated, may result in an antitrust violation;

(d) The term "antitrust violation" means any act or omission in violation of any antitrust law, any antitrust order or, with respect to the International Antitrust Enforcement Assistance Act of 1994, any of the foreign antitrust laws;

(e) The term "antitrust investigator" means any attorney or investigator employed by the Department of Justice who is charged with the duty of enforcing or carrying into effect any antitrust law;

(f) The term "person" means any natural person, partnership, corporation, association, or other legal entity, including any person acting under color or authority of State law;

(g) The term "documentary material" includes the original or any copy of any book, record, report, memorandum, paper, communication, tabulation, chart, or other document, and any product of discovery;

(h) The term "custodian" means the custodian or any deputy custodian designated under section 4(a) of this Act [15 USCS § 1313(a)]; and

(i) The term "product of discovery" includes without limitation the original or duplicate of any deposition, interrogatory, document, thing, result of the inspection of land or other property, examination, or admission obtained by any method of discovery in any judicial litigation or in any administrative litigation of an adversarial nature;

any digest, analysis, selection, compilation, or any derivation thereof; and any index or manner of access thereto; and

(j) The term "agent" includes any person retained by the Department of Justice in connection with the enforcement of the antitrust laws.

(k) The term "foreign antitrust laws" has the meaning given such term in section 12 of the International Antitrust Enforcement Assistance Act of 1994 [15 USCS § 6211].

(Sept. 19, 1962, P.L. 87-664, § 2, 76 Stat. 548; Sept. 30, 1976, P.L. 94-435, Title I, § 101, 90 Stat. 1383; Sept. 12, 1980, P.L. 96-349, §§ 2(a), 7(a)(1), 94 Stat. 1154, 1158. As amended Nov. 2, 1994, P.L. 103-438, § 3(e)(1)(A), 108 Stat. 4598.)

§ 3. [15 U.S.C. § 1312]. Civil investigative demand

(a) Issuance; service; production of material; testimony.

Whenever the Attorney General, or the Assistant Attorney General in charge of the Antitrust Division of the Department of Justice, has reason to believe that any person may be in possession, custody, or control of any documentary material, or may have any information, relevant to a civil antitrust investigation or, with respect to the International Antitrust Enforcement Assistance Act of 1994, an investigation authorized by section 3 of such Act [15 USCS § 6202], he may, prior to the institution of a civil or criminal proceeding by the United States thereon, issue in writing, and cause to be served upon such person, a civil investigative demand requiring such person to produce such documentary material for inspection and copying or reproduction, to answer in writing written interrogatories, to give oral testimony concerning documentary material or information, or to furnish any combination of such material, answers, or testimony. Whenever a civil investigative demand is an express demand for any product of discovery, the Attorney General or the Assistant Attorney General in charge of the Antitrust Division shall cause to be served, in any manner authorized by this section, a copy of such demand upon the person from whom the discovery was obtained and notify the person to whom such demand is issued of the date on which such copy was served.

(b) Contents; return date for demand for product of discovery.

Each such demand shall—

(1) state the nature of—

(A) the conduct constituting the alleged antitrust violation, or

(B) the activities in preparation for a merger, acquisition, joint venture, or similar transaction, which, if consummated, may result in an antitrust violation, which are under investigation and the provision of law applicable thereto;

(2) if it is a demand for production of documentary material—

(A) describe the class or classes of documentary material to be produced thereunder with such definiteness and certainty as to permit such material to be fairly identified;

(B) prescribe a return date or dates which will provide a reasonable period of time within which the material so demanded may be assembled and made available for inspection and copying or reproduction; and

(C) identify the custodian to whom such material shall be made available; or

(3) if it is a demand for answers to written interrogatories—

(A) propound with definiteness and certainty the written interrogatories to be answered;

(B) prescribe a date or dates at which time answers to written interrogatories shall be submitted; and

(C) identify the custodian to whom such answers shall be submitted; or

(4) if it is a demand for the giving of oral testimony—

(A) prescribe a date, time, and place at which oral testimony shall be commenced; and

(B) identify an antitrust investigator who shall conduct the examination and the custodian to whom the transcript of such examination shall be submitted.

Any such demand which is an express demand for any product of discovery shall not be returned or returnable until twenty days after a copy of such demand has been served upon the person from whom the discovery was obtained.

(c) Protected material or information; demand for product of discovery superseding disclosure restrictions except trial preparation materials.

(1) No such demand shall require the production of any documentary material, the submission of any answers to written interrogatories, or the giving of any oral testimony, if such material, answers, or testimony would be protected from disclosure under—

(A) the standards applicable to subpenas or subpenas duces tecum issued by a court of the United States in aid of a grand jury investigation, or

(B) the standards applicable to discovery requests under the Federal Rules of Civil Procedure, to the extent that the application of such standards to any such demand is appropriate and consistent with the provisions and purposes of this Act [15 USCS §§ 1311 et seq.].

(2) Any such demand which is an express demand for any product of discovery supersedes any inconsistent order, rule, or provision of law (other than this Act [15 USCS §§ 1311 et seq.]) preventing or restraining disclosure of such product of discovery to any person. Disclosure of any product of discovery pursuant to any such express demand does not constitute a waiver of any right or privilege, including without limitation any right or privilege which may be invoked to resist discovery of trial preparation materials, to which the person making such disclosure may be entitled.

(d) Service; jurisdiction.

(1) Any such demand may be served by any antitrust investigator, or by any United States marshal or deputy marshal, at any place

within the territorial jurisdiction of any court of the United States.

(2) any such demand or any petition filed under section 5 of this Act [15 USCS § 1314] may be served upon any person who is not to be found within the territorial jurisdiction of any court of the United States, in such manner as the Federal Rules of Civil Procedure prescribe for service in a foreign country. To the extent that the courts of the United States can assert jurisdiction over such person consistent with due process, the United States District Court for the District of Columbia shall have the same jurisdiction to take any action respecting compliance with this Act [15 USCS §§ 1311 et seq.] by such person that such court would have if such person were personally within the jurisdiction of such court.

(e) Service upon legal entities and natural persons.

(1) Service of any such demand or of any petition filed under section 5 of this Act [15 USCS § 1314] may be made upon a partnership, corporation, association, or other legal entity by—

(A) delivering a duly executed copy thereof to any partner, executive officer, managing agent, or general agent thereof, or to any agent thereof authorized by appointment or by law to receive service of process on behalf of such partnership, corporation, association, or entity;

(B) delivering a duly executed copy thereof to the principal office or place of business of the partnership, corporation, association, or entity to be served; or

(C) depositing such copy in the United States mails, by registered or certified mail, return receipt requested, duly addressed to such partnership, corporation, association, or entity at its principal office or place of business.

(2) Service of any such demand or of any petition filed under section 5 of this Act [15 USCS § 1314] may be made upon any natural person by—

(A) delivering a duly executed copy thereof to the person to be served; or

(B) depositing such copy in the United States mails, by registered or certified mail, return receipt requested, duly addressed to such person at his residence or principal office or place of business.

(f) Proof of service.

A verified return by the individual serving any such demand or petition setting forth the manner of such service shall be proof of such service. In the case of service by registered or certified mail, such return shall be accompanied by the return post office receipt of delivery of such demand.

(g) Sworn certificates.

The production of documentary material in response to a demand served pursuant to this section shall be made under a sworn certificate, in such form as the demand designates, by the person, if a natural person, to whom the demand is directed or, if not a natural person, by a person or persons having knowledge of the facts and circumstances relating to such production, to the effect that all of the documentary material required by the demand and in the possession, custody, or control of the person to whom the demand is directed has been produced and made available to the custodian.

(h) Interrogatories.

Each interrogatory in a demand served pursuant to this section shall be answered separately and fully in writing under oath, unless it is objected to, in which event the reasons for the objection shall be stated in lieu of an answer, and it shall be submitted under a sworn certificate, in such form as the demand designates, by the person, if a natural person, to whom the demand is directed or, if not a natural person, by a person or persons responsible for answering each interrogatory, to the effect that all information required by the demand and in the possession, custody, control, or knowledge of the person to whom the demand is directed has been submitted.

(i) Oral examinations.

(1) The examination of any person pursuant to a demand for oral testimony served under this section shall be taken before an officer authorized to administer oaths and affirmations by the laws of the United States or of the place where the examination is held. The officer before whom the testimony is to be taken shall put the witness on oath or affirmation and shall personally, or by someone acting under his direction and in his presence, record the testimony of the witness. The testimony shall be taken stenographically and transcribed. When the testimony is fully transcribed, the officer before whom the testimony is taken shall promptly transmit a copy of the transcript of the testimony to the custodian.

(2) The antitrust investigator or investigators conducting the examination shall exclude from the place where the examination is held all other persons except the person being examined, his counsel, the officer before whom the testimony is to be taken, and any stenographer taking such testimony. The provisions of the Act of March 3, 1913 (Ch. 114, 37 Stat. 731; 15 U.S.C. 30), shall not apply to such examinations.

(3) The oral testimony of any person taken pursuant to a demand served under this section shall be taken in the judicial district of the United States within which such person resides, is found, or transacts business, or in such other place as may be agreed upon by the antitrust investigator conducting the examination and such person.

(4) When the testimony is fully transcribed, the antitrust investigator or the officer shall afford the witness (who may be accompanied by counsel) a reasonable opportunity to examine the transcript; and the transcript shall be read to or by the witness, unless such examination and reading are waived by the witness. Any changes in form or substance which the witness desires to make shall be entered and identified upon the transcript by the officer or the antitrust investigator with a statement of the reasons given by the witness for making such changes. The transcript shall then be signed by the witness, unless the witness

in writing waives the signing, is ill, cannot be found, or refuses to sign. If the transcript is not signed by the witness within thirty days of his being afforded a reasonable opportunity to examine it, the officer or the antitrust investigator shall sign it and state on the record the fact of the waiver, illness, absence of the witness, or the refusal to sign, together with the reason, if any, given therefor.

(5) The officer shall certify on the transcript that the witness was duly sworn by him and that the transcript is a true record of the testimony given by the witness, and the officer or antitrust investigator shall promptly deliver it or send it by registered or certified mail to the custodian.

(6) Upon payment of reasonable charges therefor, the antitrust investigator shall furnish a copy of the transcript to the witness only, except that the Assistant Attorney General in charge of the Antitrust Division may for good cause limit such witness to inspection of the official transcript of his testimony.

(7) (A) Any person compelled to appear under a demand for oral testimony pursuant to this section may be accompanied, represented, and advised by counsel. Counsel may advise such person, in confidence, either upon the request of such person or upon counsel's own initiative, with respect to any question asked of such person. Such person or counsel may object on the record to any question, in whole or in part, and shall briefly state for the record the reason for the objection. An objection may properly be made, received, and entered upon the record when it is claimed that such person is entitled to refuse to answer the question on grounds of any constitutional or other legal right or privilege, including the privilege against self-incrimination. Such person shall not otherwise object to or refuse to answer any question, and shall not by himself or through counsel otherwise interrupt the oral examination. If such person refuses to answer any question, the antitrust investigator conducting the examination may petition the district court of the United States pursuant to section 5 of this Act [15 USCS § 1314] for an order compelling such person to answer such question.

(B) If such person refuses to answer any question on grounds of the privilege against self-incrimination, the testimony of such person may be compelled in accordance with the provisions of part V of title 18, United States Code [18 USCS §§ 6001 et seq.].

(8) Any person appearing for oral examination pursuant to a demand served under this section shall be entitled to the same fees and mileage which are paid to witnesses in the district courts of the United States.

(Sept. 19, 1962, P.L. 87-664, § 3, 76 Stat. 548; Sept. 30, 1976, P.L. 94-435, Title I, § 102, 90 Stat. 1384; Sept. 12, 1980, P.L. 96-349, § 2(b)(1)–(3), 94 Stat. 1154. As amended Nov. 2, 1994, P.L. 103-438, § 3(e)(1)(B), 108 Stat. 4598.)

§ 4. [15 U.S.C. § 1313]. Custodian of documents, answers and transcripts

(a) Designation.

The Assistant Attorney General in charge of the Antitrust Division of the Department of Justice shall designate an antitrust investigator to serve as custodian of documentary material, answers to interrogatories, and transcripts of oral testimony received under this Act [15 USCS §§ 1311 et seq.], and such additional antitrust investigators as he shall determine from time to time to be necessary to serve as deputies to such officer.

(b) Production of materials.

Any person, upon whom any demand under section 3 of this Act [15 USCS § 1312] for the production of documentary material has been duly served, shall make such material available for inspection and copying or reproduction to the custodian designated therein at the principal place of business of such person (or at such other place as such custodian and such person thereafter may agree and prescribe in writing or as the court may direct, pursuant to section 5(d) of this Act) on the return date specified in such demand (or on such later date as such custodian may prescribe in writing). Such person may upon written agreement between such person and the custodian substitute copies for originals of all or any part of such material.

(c) Responsibility for materials; disclosure

(1) The custodian to whom any documentary material, answers to interrogatories, or transcripts of oral testimony are delivered shall take physical possession thereof, and shall be responsible for the use made thereof and for the return of documentary material, pursuant to this Act [15 USCS §§ 1311 et seq.].

(2) The custodian may cause the preparation of such copies of such documentary material, answers to interrogatories, or transcripts of oral testimony as may be required for official use by any duly authorized official, employee, or agent of the Department of Justice under regulations which shall be promulgated by the Attorney General. Notwithstanding paragraph (3) of this subsection, such material, answers, and transcripts may be used by any such official, employee, or agent in connection with the taking of oral testimony pursuant to this Act [15 USCS §§ 1311 et seq.].

(3) Except as otherwise provided in this section, while in the possession of the custodian, no documentary material, answers to interrogatories, or transcripts of oral testimony, or copies thereof, so produced shall be available for examination, without the consent of the person who produced such material, answers, or transcripts, and, in the case of any product of discovery produced pursuant to an express demand for such material, of the person from whom the discovery was obtained, by any individual other than a duly authorized official, employee, or agent of the Department of Justice. Nothing in this section is intended to prevent disclosure to either body of the Congress or to any authorized committee or subcommittee thereof.

(4) While in the possession of the custodian and under such reasonable terms and conditions as the Attorney General shall prescribe, (A) documentary material and answers to interrogatories shall be available for examination by the person who produced such material or answers, or by any duly authorized representative of such person, and (B) transcripts of

oral testimony shall be available for examination by the person who produced such testimony, or his counsel.

(d) Use of investigative files

(1) Whenever any attorney of the Department of Justice has been designated to appear before any court, grand jury, or Federal administrative or regulatory agency in any case or proceeding, the custodian of any documentary material, answers to interrogatories, or transcripts of oral testimony may deliver to such attorney such material, answers, or transcripts for official use in connection with any such case, grand jury, or proceeding as such attorney determines to be required. Upon the completion of any such case, grand jury, or proceeding, such attorney shall return to the custodian any such material, answers, or transcripts so delivered which have not passed into the control of such court, grand jury, or agency through the introduction thereof into the record of such case or proceeding.

(2) The custodian of any documentary material, answers to interrogatories, or transcripts of oral testimony may deliver to the Federal Trade Commission, in response to a written request, copies of such material, answers, or transcripts for use in connection with an investigation or proceeding under the Commission's jurisdiction. Such material, answers, or transcripts may only be used by the Commission in such manner and subject to such conditions as apply to the Department of Justice under this Act [15 USCS §§ 1311 et seq.].

(e) Return of material to producer.

If any documentary material has been produced in the course of any antitrust investigation by any person pursuant to a demand under this Act [15 USCS §§ 1311 et seq.] and—

(1) any case or proceeding before any court or grand jury arising out of such investigation, or any proceeding before any Federal administrative or regulatory agency involving such material, has been completed, or

(2) no case or proceeding, in which such material may be used, has been commenced within a reasonable time after completion of the examination and analysis of all documentary material and other information assembled in the course of such investigation, the custodian shall, upon written request of the person who produced such material, return to such person any such material (other than copies thereof furnished to the custodian pursuant to subsection (b) of this section or made by the Department of Justice pursuant to subsection (c) of this section) which has not passed into the control of any court, grand jury, or agency through the introduction thereof into the record of such case or proceeding.

(f) Appointment of successor custodians.

In the event of the death, disability, or separation from service in the Department of Justice of the custodian of any documentary material, answers to interrogatories, or transcripts of oral testimony produced under any demand issued pursuant to this Act [15 USCS §§ 1311 et seq.], or the official relief of such custodian from responsibility for the custody and control of such material, answers, or transcripts, the Assistant Attorney

General in charge of the Antitrust Division shall promptly (1) designate another antitrust investigator to serve as custodian of such material, answers, or transcripts, and (2) transmit in writing to the person who produced such material, answers, or testimony notice as to the identity and address of the successor so designated. Any successor designated under this subsection shall have with regard to such material, answers, or transcripts all duties and responsibilities imposed by this Act [15 USCS §§ 1311 et seq.] upon his predecessor in office with regard thereto, except that he shall not be held responsible for any default or dereliction which occurred prior to his designation.

(Sept. 19, 1962, P.L. 87-664, § 4, 76 Stat. 549; Sept. 30, 1976, P.L. 94-435, Title I, § 103, 90 Stat. 1387; Sept. 12, 1980, P.L. 96-349, §§ 2(b)(4), 7(a)(2), 94 Stat. 1155, 1158.)

§ 5. [15 U.S.C. § 1314]. Judicial proceedings

(a) Petition for enforcement; venue.

Whenever any person fails to comply with any civil investigative demand duly served upon him under section 3 [15 USCS § 1312] or whenever satisfactory copying or reproduction of any such material cannot be done and such person refuses to surrender such material, the Attorney General, through such officers or attorneys as he may designate, may file, in the district court of the United States for any judicial district in which such person resides, is found, or transacts business, and serve upon such person a petition for an order of such court for the enforcement of this Act [15 USCS §§ 1311 et seq.].

(b) Petition for order modifying or setting aside demand; time for petition; suspension of time allowed for compliance with demand during pendency of petition; grounds for relief.

(1) Within twenty days after the service of any such demand upon any person, or at any time before the return date specified in the demand, whichever period is shorter, or within such period exceeding twenty days after service or in excess of such return date as may be prescribed in writing, subsequent to service, by any antitrust investigator named in the demand, such person may file and serve upon such antitrust investigator, and in the case of an express demand for any product of discovery upon the person from whom such discovery was obtained, a petition for an order modifying or setting aside such demand—

(A) in the district court of the United States for the judicial district within which such person resides, is found, or transacts business; or

(B) in the case of a petition addressed to an express demand for any product of discovery, only in the district court of the United States for the judicial district in which the proceeding in which such discovery was obtained is or was last pending.

(2) The time allowed for compliance with the demand in whole or in part as deemed proper and ordered by the court shall not run during the pendency of such petition in the court, except that such person shall comply with any portions of the demand not sought to be modified or set aside. Such petition shall specify each ground upon which the petitioner relies in seeking such relief and may be based upon any failure of such demand to comply with the

provisions of this Act [15 USCS §§ 1311 et seq.], or upon any constitutional or other legal right or privilege of such person.

(c) Petition for order modifying or setting aside demand for production of product of discovery; grounds for relief; stay of compliance with demand and of running of time allowed for compliance with demand.

Whenever any such demand is an express demand for any product of discovery, the person from whom such discovery was obtained may file, at any time prior to compliance with such express demand, in the district court of the United States for the judicial district in which the proceeding in which such discovery was obtained is or was last pending, and serve upon any antitrust investigator named in the demand and upon the recipient of the demand, a petition for an order of such court modifying or setting aside those portions of the demand requiring production of any such product of discovery. Such petition shall specify each ground upon which the petitioner relies in seeking such relief and may be based upon any failure of such portions of the demand to comply with the provisions of this Act [15 USCS §§ 1311 et seq.], or upon any constitutional or other legal right or privilege of the petitioner. During the pendency of such petition, the court may stay, as it deems proper, compliance with the demand and the running of the time allowed for compliance with the demand.

(d) Petition for order requiring performance by custodian of duties; venue.

At any time during which any custodian is in custody or control of any documentary material or answers to interrogatories delivered, or transcripts of oral testimony given by any person in compliance with any such demand, such person, and in the case of an express demand for any product of discovery, the person from whom such discovery was obtained, may file, in the district court of the United States for the judicial district within which the office of such custodian is situated, and serve upon such custodian a petition for an order of such court requiring the performance by such custodian of any duty imposed upon him by this Act [15 USCS §§ 1311 et seq.].

(e) Jurisdiction; appeal; contempts.

Whenever any petition is filed in any district court of the United States under this section, such court shall have jurisdiction to hear and determine the matter so presented, and to enter such order or orders as may be required to carry into effect the provisions of this Act [15 USCS §§ 1311 et seq.]. Any final order so entered shall be subject to appeal pursuant to section 1291 of title 28 of the United States Code. Any disobedience of any final order entered under this section by any court shall be punished as a contempt thereof.

(f) Applicability of USCS Federal Rules of Civil Procedure.

To the extent that such rules may have application and are not inconsistent with the provisions of this Act [15 USCS §§ 1311 et seq.], the Federal Rules of Civil Procedure shall apply to any petition under this Act [15 USCS §§ 1311 et seq.].

(g) Disclosure exemption.

Any documentary material, answers to written interrogatories, or transcripts of oral testimony provided pursuant to any demand issued under this Act [15 USCS §§ 1311 et seq.] shall be exempt from disclosure under section 552 of title 5, United States Code.

(Sept. 19, 1962, P.L. 87-664, § 5, 76 Stat. 551; Sept. 30, 1976, P.L. 94-435, Title I, § 104, 90 Stat. 1389; Sept. 12, 1980, P.L. 96-349, § 2(b)(5), 94 Stat. 1155.)

§ 6(a). [18 U.S.C. § 1505]. Obstruction of proceedings before departments, agencies, and committees

Whoever, with intent to avoid, evade, prevent, or obstruct compliance, in whole or in part, with any civil investigative demand duly and properly made under the Antitrust Civil Process Act [15 USCS §§ 1311 et seq.], willfully withholds, misrepresents, removes from any place, conceals, covers up, destroys, mutilates, alters, or by other means falsifies any documentary material, answers to written interrogatories, or oral testimony, which is the subject of such demand; or attempts to do so or solicits another to do so; or

Whoever corruptly, or by threats or force, or by any threatening letter or communication influences, obstructs, or impedes or endeavors to influence, obstruct, or impede the due and proper administration of the law under which any pending proceeding is being had before any department or agency of the United States, or the due and proper exercise of the power of inquiry under which any inquiry or investigation is being had by either House, or any committee of either House or any joint committee of the Congress—

Shall be fined under this title, imprisoned not more than 5 years or, if the offense involves international or domestic terrorism (as defined in section 2331), imprisoned not more than 8 years, or both.

(June 25, 1948, ch 645, § 1, 62 Stat. 770; Sept. 19, 1962, P.L. 87-664, § 6(a), 76 Stat. 551; Oct. 15, 1970, P.L. 91-452, Title IX, § 903, 84 Stat. 947; Sept. 30, 1976, P.L. 94-435, Title I, § 105, 90 Stat. 1389; Oct. 12, 1982, P.L. 97-291, § 4(d), 96 Stat. 1253. As amended Sept. 13, 1994, P.L. 103-322, Title XXXIII, § 330016(1)(K), 108 Stat. 2147; Dec. 17, 2004, P.L. 108-458, Title VI, Subtitle H, § 6703(a), 118 Stat. 3766.)

25

ANTITRUST CRIMINAL PENALTY ENFORCEMENT AND REFORM ACT OF 2004

§ 201. Short Title

This title may be cited as the "Antitrust Criminal Penalty Enhancement and Reform Act of 2004."

§ 211. Sunset

(a) In General.—Except as provided in subsection (b), the provisions of sections 211 through 214 of this subtitle shall cease to have effect 16 years after the date of enactment of this Act.

(b) Exceptions.—With respect to—

(1) a person who receives a marker on or before the date on which the provisions of section 211 through 214 of this subtitle shall cease to have effect that later results in the execution of an antitrust leniency agreement; or

(2) an applicant who has entered into an antitrust leniency agreement on or before the date on which the provisions of sections 211 through 214 of this subtitle shall cease to have effect,

the provisions of sections 211 through 214 of this subtitle shall continue in effect.

§ 212. Definitions

In this subtitle:

(1) Antitrust division.— The term "Antitrust Division" means the United States Department of Justice Antitrust Division.

(2) Antitrust leniency agreement.— The term "antitrust leniency agreement," or "agreement," means a leniency letter agreement, whether conditional or final, between a person and the Antitrust Division pursuant to the Corporate Leniency Policy of the Antitrust Division in effect on the date of execution of the agreement.

(3) Antitrust leniency applicant.— The term "antitrust leniency applicant," or "applicant," means, with respect to an antitrust leniency agreement, the person that has entered into the agreement.

(4) Claimant.— The term "claimant" means a person or class, that has brought, or on whose behalf has been brought, a civil action alleging a violation of section 1 or 3 of the Sherman Act or any similar State law, except that the term does not include a State or a subdivision of a State with respect to a civil action brought to recover damages sustained by the State or subdivision.

(5) Cooperating individual.— The term "cooperating individual" means, with respect to an antitrust leniency agreement, a current or former director, officer, or employee of the antitrust leniency applicant who is covered by the agreement.

(6) Marker.— The term "marker" means an assurance given by the Antitrust Division to a candidate for corporate leniency that no other company will be considered for leniency, for some finite period of time, while the candidate is given an opportunity to perfect its leniency application.

(7) Person.— The term "person" has the meaning given it in subsection (a) of the first section of the Clayton Act.

§ 213. Limitation on recovery

(a) In General.—Subject to subsection (d), in any civil action alleging a violation of section 1 or 3 of the Sherman Act, or alleging a violation of any similar State law, based on conduct covered by a currently effective antitrust leniency agreement, the amount of damages recovered by or on behalf of a claimant from an antitrust leniency applicant who satisfies the requirements of subsection (b), together with the amounts so recovered from cooperating individuals who satisfy such requirements, shall not exceed that portion of the actual damages sustained by such claimant which is attributable to the commerce done by the applicant in the goods or services affected by the violation.

(b) Requirements.—Subject to subsection (c), an antitrust leniency applicant or cooperating individual satisfies the requirements of this subsection with respect to a civil action described in subsection (a) if the court in which the civil action is brought determines, after considering any appropriate pleadings from the claimant, that the applicant or cooperating individual, as the case may be, has provided satisfactory cooperation to the claimant with respect to the civil action, which cooperation shall include—

(1) providing a full account to the claimant of all facts known to the applicant or cooperating individual, as the case may be, that are potentially relevant to the civil action;

(2) furnishing all documents or other items potentially relevant to the civil action that are in the possession, custody, or control of the applicant or cooperating individual, as the case may be, wherever they are located; and

(3) (A) in the case of a cooperating individual—

(i) making himself or herself available for such interviews, depositions, or testimony in connection with the civil action as the claimant may reasonably require; and

(ii) responding completely and truthfully, without making any attempt either falsely to protect or falsely to implicate any person or entity, and without intentionally withholding any potentially relevant information, to all questions asked by the claimant in interviews, depositions, trials, or any other court proceedings in connection with the civil action; or

(B) in the case of an antitrust leniency applicant, using its best efforts to secure and facilitate from cooperating individuals covered by the agreement the cooperation described in clauses (i) and (ii) and subparagraph (A).

(c) Timeliness.—The court shall consider, in making the determination concerning satisfactory cooperation described in subsection (b), the timeliness of the applicant's or cooperating individual's cooperation with the claimant.

(d) Cooperation After Expiration of Stay or Protective Order.—If the Antitrust Division does obtain a stay or protective order in a civil action based on conduct covered by an antitrust leniency agreement, once the stay or protective order, or a portion thereof, expires or is terminated, the antitrust leniency applicant and cooperating individuals shall provide without unreasonable delay any cooperation described in paragraphs (1) and (2) of subsection (b) that was prohibited by the expired or terminated stay or protective order, or the expired or terminated portion thereof, in order for the cooperation to be deemed satisfactory under such paragraphs.

(e) Continuation.—Nothing in this section shall be construed to modify, impair, or supersede the provisions of sections 4, 4A, and 4C of the Clayton Act relating to the recovery of costs of suit, including a reasonable attorney's fee, and interest on damages, to the extent that such recovery is authorized by such sections.

§ 214. Rights, authorities, and liabilities not affected

Nothing in this subtitle shall be construed to—

(1) affect the rights of the Antitrust Division to seek a stay or protective order in a civil action based on conduct covered by an antitrust leniency agreement to prevent the cooperation described in section 213(b) of this subtitle from impairing or impeding the investigation or prosecution by the Antitrust Division of conduct covered by the agreement;

(2) create any right to challenge any decision by the Antitrust Division with respect to an antitrust leniency agreement; or

(3) affect, in any way, the joint and several liability of any party to a civil action described in section 213(a) of this subtitle, other than that of the antitrust leniency applicant and cooperating individuals as provided in section 213(a) of this subtitle.

§ 215. Increased Penalties for Antitrust Violations

(a) Restraint of Trade Among the States.—Section 1 of the Sherman Act (15 U.S.C. 1) is amended by—

(1) striking "$ 10,000,000" and inserting "$ 100,000,000";

(2) striking "$ 350,000" and inserting "$ 1,000,000"; and

(3) striking "three" and inserting "10."

(b) Monopolizing Trade.—Section 2 of the Sherman Act (15 U.S.C. 2) is amended by—

(1) striking "$ 10,000,000" and inserting "$ 100,000,000";

(2) striking "$ 350,000" and inserting "$ 1,000,000"; and

(3) striking "three" and inserting "10."

(c) Other Restraints of Trade.—Section 3 of the Sherman Act (15 U.S.C. 3) is amended by—

(1) striking "$ 10,000,000" and inserting "$ 100,000,000";

(2) striking "$ 350,000" and inserting "$ 1,000,000"; and

(3) striking "three" and inserting "10."

(Pub.L. 108-237, Title II, §§ 211 to 215, June 22, 2004, 118 Stat. 665.)

26

EXPORT TRADING COMPANIES ACT OF 1982

§ 101. Short title

This title may be cited as the "Export Trading Company Act of 1982."

§ 102. [15 U.S.C. § 4001]. Congressional findings and declaration of purpose

(a) The Congress finds that—

(1) United States exports are responsible for creating and maintaining one out of every nine manufacturing jobs in the United States and for generating one out of every seven dollars of total United States goods produced;

(2) the rapidly growing service-related industries are vital to the well-being of the United States economy inasmuch as they create jobs for seven out of every ten Americans, provide 65 per centum of the Nation's gross national product, and offer the greatest potential for significantly increased industrial trade involving finished products;

(3) trade deficits contribute to the decline of the dollar on international currency markets and have an inflationary impact on the United States economy;

(4) tens of thousands of small- and medium-sized United States businesses produce exportable goods or services but do not engage in exporting;

(5) although the United States is the world's leading agricultural exporting nation, many farm products are not marketed as widely and effectively abroad as they could be through export trading companies;

(6) export trade services in the United States are fragmented into a multitude of separate functions, and companies attempting to offer export trade services lack financial leverage to reach a significant number of potential United States exporters;

(7) the United States needs well-developed export trade intermediaries which can achieve economies of scale and acquire expertise enabling them to export goods and services profitably, at low per unit cost to producers;

(8) the development of export trading companies in the United States has been hampered by business attitudes and by Government regulations;

(9) those activities of State and local governmental authorities which initiate, facilitate, or expand exports of goods and services can be an important source for expansion of total United States exports, as well as for experimentation in the development of

innovative export programs keyed to local, State, and regional economic needs;

(10) if United States trading companies are to be successful in promoting United States exports and in competing with foreign trading companies, they should be able to draw on the resources, expertise, and knowledge of the United States banking system, both in the United States and abroad; and

(11) the Department of Commerce is responsible for the development and promotion of United States exports, and especially for facilitating the export of finished products by United States manufacturers.

(b) It is the purpose of this Act to increase United States exports of products and services by encouraging more efficient provision of export trade services to United States producers and suppliers, in particular by establishing an office within the Department of Commerce to promote the formation of export trade associations and export trading companies, by permitting bank holding companies, bankers' banks, and Edge Act corporations and agreement corporations that are subsidiaries of bank holding companies to invest in export trading companies, by reducing restrictions on trade financing provided by financial institutions, and by modifying the application of the antitrust laws to certain export trade.

(Oct. 8, 1982, P.L. 97-290, Title I, § 102, 96 Stat. 1233.)

§ 103 [15 U.S.C. § 4002]. Definitions

(a) For purposes of this title [15 USCS §§ 4001 et seq.]—

(1) the term "export trade" means trade or commerce in goods or services produced in the United States which are exported, or in the course of being exported, from the United States to any other country;

(2) the term "services" includes, but is not limited to, accounting, amusement, architectural, automatic data processing, business, communications, construction franchising and licensing, consulting, engineering, financial, insurance, legal, management, repair, tourism, training, and transportation services;

(3) the term "export trade services" includes, but is not limited to, consulting, international market research, advertising, marketing, insurance, product research and design, legal assistance, transportation, including trade documentation and freight forwarding, communication and processing of foreign orders to and for exporters and foreign purchasers, warehousing, foreign exchange, financing, and taking title to goods, when provided in order to facilitate the export of goods or services produced in the United States;

(4) the term "export trading company" means a person, partnership, association, or similar organization, whether operated for profit or as a nonprofit organization, which does business under the laws of the United States or any State and which is organized and operated principally for purposes of—

(A) exporting goods or services produced in the United States; or

(B) facilitating the exportation of goods or services produced in the United States by unaffiliated persons by providing one or more export trade services;

(5) the term "State" means any of the several States of the United States, the District of Columbia, the Commonwealth of Puerto Rico, the Virgin Islands, American Samoa, Guam, the Commonwealth of the Northern Mariana Islands, and the Trust Territory of the Pacific Islands;

(6) the term "United States" means the several States of the United States, the District of Columbia, the Commonwealth of Puerto Rico, the Virgin Islands, American Samoa, Guam, the Commonwealth of the Northern Mariana Islands, and the Trust Territory of the Pacific Islands; and

(7) the term "antitrust laws" means the antitrust laws as defined in subsection (a) of the first section of the Clayton Act (15 U.S.C. 12(a)), section 5 of the Federal Trade Commission Act (15 U.S.C. 45) to the extent that section 5 [15 USCS § 45] applies to unfair methods of competition, and any State antitrust or unfair competition law.

(b) The Secretary of Commerce may by regulation further define any term defined in subsection (a), in order to carry out this title [15 USCS §§ 4001 et seq.].

(Oct. 8, 1982, P.L. 97-290, Title I, § 102, 96 Stat. 1233.)

§ 104 [15 U.S.C. § 4003]. Office of Export Trade in Department of Commerce; establishment

The Secretary of Commerce shall establish within the Department of Commerce an office to promote and encourage to the greatest extent feasible the formation of export trade associations and export trading companies. Such office shall provide information and advice to interested persons and shall provide a referral service to facilitate contact between producers of exportable goods and services and firms offering export trade services. The office shall establish a program to encourage and assist the operation of other export intermediaries, including existing and newly formed export management companies.

(Oct. 8, 1982, P.L. 97-290, Title I, § 104, 96 Stat. 1235; Aug. 23, 1988, P.L. 100-418, Title II, Subtitle C, § 2310, 102 Stat. 1346.)

§ 301 [15 U.S.C. § 4011]. Export trade promotion; duties of Secretary of Commerce

To promote and encourage export trade, the Secretary may issue certificates of review and advise and assist any person with respect to applying for certificates of review.

(Oct. 8, 1982, P.L. 97-290, Title III, § 301, 96 Stat. 1240.)

§ 302 [15 U.S.C. § 4012]. Application for issuance of certificate of review

(a) Written form; limitation to export trade; compliance with regulations.

To apply for a certificate of review, a person shall submit to the Secretary a written application which—

(1) specifies conduct limited to export trade, and

(2) is in a form and contains any information, including information pertaining to the overall market in which the applicant operates, required by rule or regulation promulgated under section 310 [15 USCS § 4020].

(b) Publication of notice of application; transmittal to Attorney General.

(1) Within ten days after an application submitted under subsection (a) is received by the Secretary, the Secretary shall publish in the Federal Register a notice that announces that an application for a certificate of review has been submitted, identifies each person submitting the application, and describes the conduct for which the application is submitted.

(2) Not later than seven days after an application submitted under subsection (a) is received by the Secretary, the Secretary shall transmit to the Attorney General—

(A) a copy of the application,

(B) any information submitted to the Secretary in connection with the application, and

(C) any other relevant information (as determined by the Secretary) in the possession of the Secretary, including information regarding the market share of the applicant in the line of commerce to which the conduct specified in the application relates.

(Oct. 8, 1982, P.L. 97-290, Title III, § 302, 96 Stat. 1240.)

§ 303 [15 U.S.C. § 4013]. Issuance of certificate

(a) Requirements

A certificate of review shall be issued to any applicant that establishes that its specified export trade, export trade activities, and methods of operation will—

(1) result in neither a substantial lessening of competition or restraint of trade within the United States nor a substantial restraint of the export trade of any competitor of the applicant,

(2) not unreasonably enhance, stabilize, or depress prices within the United States of the goods, wares, merchandise, or services of the class exported by the applicant,

(3) not constitute unfair methods of competition against competitors engaged in the export of goods, wares, merchandise, or services of the class exported by the applicant, and

(4) not include any act that may reasonably be expected to result in the sale for consumption or resale within the United States of the goods, wares, merchandise, or services exported by the applicant.

(b) Time for determination; specification in certificate.

Within ninety days after the Secretary receives an application for a certificate of review, the Secretary shall determine whether the applicant's export trade, export trade activities, and methods of operation meet the standards of subsection (a). If the Secretary, with the concurrence of the Attorney General, determines that such standards are met, the Secretary shall issue to the applicant a certificate of review. The certificate of review shall specify—

(1) the export trade, export trade activities, and methods of operation to which the certificate applies,

(2) the person to whom the certificate of review is issued, and

(3) any terms and conditions the Secretary or the Attorney General deems necessary to assure compliance with the standards of subsection (a).

(c) Expedited action.

If the applicant indicates a special need for prompt disposition, the Secretary and the Attorney General may expedite action on the application, except that no certificate of review may be issued within thirty days of publication of notice in the Federal Register under section 302(b)(1) [15 USCS § 4012(b)(1)].

(d) Notification of denial; request for reconsideration.

(1) If the Secretary denies in whole or in part an application for a certificate, he shall notify the applicant of his determination and the reasons for it.

(2) An applicant may, within thirty days of receipt of notification that the application has been denied in whole or in part, request the Secretary to reconsider the determination. The Secretary, with the concurrence of the Attorney General, shall notify the applicant of the determination upon reconsideration within thirty days of receipt of the request.

(e) Return of documents upon request after denial.

If the Secretary denies an application for the issuance of a certificate of review and thereafter receives from the applicant a request for the return of documents submitted by the applicant in connection with the application for the certificate, the Secretary and the Attorney General shall return to the applicant, not later than thirty days after receipt of the request, the documents and all copies of the documents available to the Secretary and the Attorney General, except to the extent that the information contained in a document has been made available to the public.

(f) Fraudulent procurement of certificate.

A certificate shall be void ab initio with respect to any export trade, export trade activities, or methods of operation for which a certificate was procured by fraud.

(Oct. 8, 1982, P.L. 97-290, Title III, § 303, 96 Stat. 1241.)

§ 304 [15 U.S.C. § 4014]. Reporting requirement; amendment of certificate; revocation

(a) Report of changes in matters specified; application to amend; treatment as application for issuance.

(1) Any applicant who receives a certificate of review—

(A) shall promptly report to the Secretary any change relevant to the matters specified in the certificate, and

(B) may submit to the Secretary an application to amend the certificate to reflect the effect of the change on the conduct specified in the certificate.

(2) An application for an amendment to a certificate of review shall be treated as an application for the issuance of a certificate. The effective date of an amendment shall be the date on which the application for the amendment is submitted to the Secretary.

(b) Request for compliance information; failure to provide; notice of noncompliance; revocation or modification; antitrust investigation; no civil investigative demand.

(1) If the Secretary or the Attorney General has reason to believe that the export trade, export trade activities, or methods of operation of a person holding a certificate of review no longer comply with the standards of section 303(a) [15 USCS § 4013(a)], the Secretary shall request such information from such person as the Secretary or the Attorney General deems necessary to resolve the matter of compliance. Failure to comply with such request shall be grounds for revocation of the certificate under paragraph (2).

(2) If the Secretary or the Attorney General determines that the export trade, export trade activities, or methods of operation of a person holding a certificate no longer comply with the standards of section 303(a) [15 USCS § 4013(a)], or that such person has failed to comply with a request made under paragraph (1), the Secretary shall give written notice of the determination to such person. The notice shall include a statement of the circumstances underlying, and the reasons in support of, the determination. In the 60-day period beginning 30 days after the notice is given, the Secretary shall revoke the certificate or modify it as the Secretary or the Attorney General deems necessary to cause the certificate to apply only to the export trade, export trade activities, or methods of operation which are in compliance with the standards of section 303(a) [15 USCS § 4013(a)].

(3) For purposes of carrying out this subsection, the Attorney General, and the Assistant Attorney General in charge of the antitrust division of the Department of Justice, may conduct investigations in the same manner as the Attorney General and the Assistant Attorney General conduct investigations under section 3 of the Antitrust Civil Process Act [15 USCS § 1312], except that no civil investigative demand may be issued to a person to whom a certificate of review is issued if such person is the target of such investigation.

(Oct. 8, 1982, P.L. 97-290, Title III, § 304, 96 Stat. 1242.)

§ 305 [15 U.S.C. § 4015]. Judicial review; admissibility

(a) District court review of grants or denials; erroneous determination.

If the Secretary grants or denies, in whole or in part, an application for a certificate of review or for an amendment to a certificate, or revokes or modifies a certificate pursuant to section 304(b) [15 USCS § 4014(b)], any person aggrieved by such determination may, within 30 days of the determination, bring an action in any appropriate district court of the

United States to set aside the determination on the ground that such determination is erroneous.

(b) Exclusive provision for review.

Except as provided in subsection (a), no action by the Secretary or the Attorney General pursuant to this title [15 USCS §§ 4011 et seq.] shall be subject to judicial review.

(c) Inadmissibility in antitrust proceedings

If the Secretary denies, in whole or in part, an application for a certificate of review or for an amendment to a certificate, or revokes or amends a certificate, neither the negative determination nor the statement of reasons therefor shall be admissible in evidence, in any administrative or judicial proceeding, in support of any claim under the antitrust laws.

(Oct. 8, 1982, P.L. 97-290, Title III, § 305, 96 Stat. 1243.)

§ 306 [15 U.S.C. § 4016]. Protection conferred by certificate of review

(a) Protection from civil or criminal antitrust actions.

Except as provided in subsection (b), no criminal or civil action may be brought under the antitrust laws against a person to whom a certificate of review is issued which is based on conduct which is specified in, and complies with the terms of, a certificate issued under section 303 [15 USCS § 4013] which certificate was in effect when the conduct occurred.

(b) Special restraint of trade civil action; time limitations; certificate governed conduct presumed in compliance; award of costs to successful defendant; suit by Attorney General.

(1) Any person who has been injured as a result of conduct engaged in under a certificate of review may bring a civil action for injunctive relief, actual damages, the loss of interest on actual damages, and the cost of suit (including a reasonable attorney's fee) for the failure to comply with the standards of section 303(a) [15 USCS § 4013(a)]. Any action commenced under this title [15 USCS §§ 4011 et seq.] shall proceed as if it were an action commenced under section 4 or section 16 of the Clayton Act [15 USCS § 15 or 26], except that the standards of section 303(a) of this title [15 USCS § 4013(a)] and the remedies provided in this paragraph shall be the exclusive standards and remedies applicable to such action.

(2) Any action brought under paragraph (1) shall be filed within two years of the date the plaintiff has notice of the failure to comply with the standards of section 303(a) [15 USCS § 4013(a)] but in any event within four years after the cause of action accrues.

(3) In any action brought under paragraph (1), there shall be a presumption that conduct which is specified in and complies with a certificate of review does comply with the standards of section 303(a) [15 USCS § 4013(a)].

(4) In any action brought under paragraph (1), if the court finds that the conduct does comply with the standards of section 303(a) [15 USCS § 4013(a)], the court shall award to the person against whom the claim is brought the cost of suit attributable to

defending against the claim (including a reasonable attorney's fee).

(5) The Attorney General may file suit pursuant to section 15 of the Clayton Act (15 U.S.C. 25) to enjoin conduct threatening clear and irreparable harm to the national interest.

(Oct. 8, 1982, P.L. 97-290, Title III, § 306, 96 Stat. 1243.)

§ 307 [15 U.S.C. § 4017]. Guidelines

(a) Issuance; content.

To promote greater certainty regarding the application of the antitrust laws to export trade, the Secretary, with the concurrence of the Attorney General, may issue guidelines—

(1) describing specific types of conduct with respect to which the Secretary, with the concurrence of the Attorney General, has made or would make, determinations under sections 303 and 304 [15 USCS §§ 4013 and 4014], and

(2) summarizing the factual and legal bases in support of the determinations.

(b) Administrative rulemaking requirements not applicable.

Section 553 of title 5, United States Code, shall not apply to the issuance of guidelines under subsection (a).

(Oct. 8, 1982, P.L. 97-290, Title III, § 307, 96 Stat. 1244.)

§ 308 [15 U.S.C. § 4018]. Annual reports

Every person to whom a certificate of review is issued shall submit to the Secretary an annual report, in such form and at such time as the Secretary may require, that updates where necessary the information required by section 302(a) [15 USCS § 4012(a)].

(Oct. 8, 1982, P.L. 97-290, Title III, § 308, 96 Stat. 1244.)

§ 309 [15 U.S.C. § 4019]. Disclosure of information

(a) Exemption.

Information submitted by any person in connection with the issuance, amendment, or revocation of a certificate of review shall be exempt from disclosure under section 552 of title 5, United States Code.

(b) Protection of potentially harmful confidential information; exceptions: Congress; judicial or administrative proceedings; consent; necessity for determination; Federal law; regulations.

(1) Except as provided in paragraph (2), no officer or employee of the United States shall disclose commercial or financial information submitted in connection with the issuance, amendment, or revocation of a certificate of review if the information is privileged or confidential and if disclosure of the information would cause harm to the person who submitted the information.

(2) Paragraph (1) shall not apply with respect to information disclosed—

(A) upon a request made by the Congress or any committee of the Congress,

(B) in a judicial or administrative proceeding, subject to appropriate protective orders,

(C) with the consent of the person who submitted the information,

(D) in the course of making a determination with respect to the issuance, amendment, or revocation of a certificate of review, if the Secretary deems disclosure of the information to be necessary in connection with making the determination,

(E) in accordance with any requirement imposed by a statute of the United States, or

(F) in accordance with any rule or regulation promulgated under section 310 [15 USCS § 4020] permitting the disclosure of the information to an agency of the United States or of a State on the condition that the agency will disclose the information only under the circumstances specified in subparagraphs (A) through (E).

(Oct. 8, 1982, P.L. 97-290, Title III, § 309, 96 Stat. 1244.)

§ 310 [15 U.S.C. § 4020]. Rules and regulations

The Secretary, with the concurrence of the Attorney General, shall promulgate such rules and regulations as are necessary to carry out the purposes of this Act.

(As added Oct. 8, 1982, P.L. 97-290, Title III, § 310, 96 Stat. 1245.)

§ 311 [15 U.S.C.§ 4021]. Definitions

As used in this title [15 USCS §§ 4011 et seq.]—

(1) the term "export trade" means trade or commerce in goods, wares, merchandise, or services exported, or in the course of being exported, from the United States or any territory thereof to any foreign nation,

(2) the term "service" means intangible economic output, including, but not limited to—

(A) business, repair, and amusement services,

(B) management, legal, engineering, architectural, and other professional services, and

(C) financial, insurance, transportation, informational and any other data-based services, and communication services,

(3) the term "export trade activities" means activities or agreements in the course of export trade,

(4) the term "methods of operation" means any method by which a person conducts or proposes to conduct export trade,

(5) the term "person" means an individual who is a resident of the United States; a partnership that is created under and exists pursuant to the laws of any State or of the United States; a State or local government entity; a corporation, whether organized as a profit or nonprofit corporation, that is created under and exists pursuant to the laws of any State or of the United States; or any

association or combination, by contract or other arrangement, between or among such persons,

(6) the term "antitrust laws" means the antitrust laws, as such term is defined in the first section of the Clayton Act (15 U.S.C. 12), and section 5 of the Federal Trade Commission Act (15 U.S.C 45) (to the extent that section 5 [15 USCS § 45] prohibits unfair methods of competition), and any State antitrust or unfair competition law,

(7) the term "Secretary" means the Secretary of Commerce or his designee, and

(8) the term "Attorney General" means the Attorney General of the United States or his designee.

(Oct. 8, 1982, P.L. 97-290, Title III, § 311, 96 Stat. 1245.)

27

FOREIGN SOVEREIGN IMMUNITIES ACT OF 1976

28 U.S.C. § 1602. Findings and declaration of purpose

The Congress finds that the determination by United States courts of the claims of foreign states to immunity from the jurisdiction of such courts would serve the interests of justice and would protect the rights of both foreign states and litigants in United States courts. Under international law, states are not immune from the jurisdiction of foreign courts insofar as their commercial activities are concerned, and their commercial property may be levied upon for the satisfaction of judgments rendered against them in connection with their commercial activities. Claims of foreign states to immunity should henceforth be decided by courts of the United States and of the States in conformity with the principles set forth in this chapter [28 USCS §§ 1602 et seq.].

(Added Oct. 21, 1976, P.L. 94-583, § 4(a), 90 Stat. 2892.)

28 U.S.C. § 1603. Definitions

For purposes of this chapter [28 USCS §§ 1602 et seq.]—

(a) A "foreign state," except as used in section 1608 of this title [28 USCS § 1608], includes a political subdivision of a foreign state or an agency or instrumentality of a foreign state as defined in subsection (b).

(b) An "agency or instrumentality of a foreign state" means any entity—

(1) which is a separate legal person, corporate or otherwise, and

(2) which is an organ of a foreign state or political subdivision thereof, or a majority of whose shares or other ownership interest is owned by a foreign state or political subdivision thereof, and

(3) which is neither a citizen of a State of the United States as defined in section 1332(c) and (e) of this title [28 USCS § 1332(c) and (e)] nor created under the laws of any third country.

(c) The "United States" includes all territory and waters, continental or insular, subject to the jurisdiction of the United States.

(d) A "commercial activity" means either a regular course of commercial conduct or a particular commercial transaction or act. The commercial character of an activity shall be determined by reference to the nature of the course of conduct or particular transaction or act, rather than by reference to its purpose.

(e) A "commercial activity carried on in the United States by a foreign state" means commercial activity carried on by such state and having substantial contact with the United States.

(Added Oct. 21, 1976, P.L. 94-583, § 4(a), 90 Stat. 2892. As amended Feb. 18, 2005, P.L. 109-2, § 4(b)(2), 119 Stat. 12.)

28 U.S.C. § 1604. Immunity of a foreign state from jurisdiction

Subject to existing international agreements to which the United States is a party at the time of enactment of this Act [enacted Oct. 21, 1976] a foreign state shall be immune from the jurisdiction of the courts of the United States and of the States except as provided in sections 1605–1607 of this chapter [28 USCS §§ 1605–1607].

(Added Oct. 21, 1976, P.L. 94-583, § 4(a), 90 Stat. 2892.)

28 U.S.C. § 1605. General exceptions to the jurisdictional immunity of a foreign state

(a) A foreign state shall not be immune from the jurisdiction of courts of the United States or of the States in any case—

(1) in which the foreign state has waived its immunity either explicitly or by implication, notwithstanding any withdrawal of the waiver which the foreign state may purport to effect except in accordance with the terms of the waiver;

(2) in which the action is based upon a commercial activity carried on in the United States by the foreign state; or upon an act performed in the United States in connection with a commercial activity of the foreign state elsewhere; or upon an act outside the territory of the United States in connection with a commercial activity of the foreign state elsewhere and that act causes a direct effect in the United States;

(3) in which rights in property taken in violation of international law are in issue and that property or any property exchanged for such property is present in the United States in connection with a commercial activity carried on in the United States by the foreign state; or that property or any property exchanged for such property is owned or operated by an agency or instrumentality of the foreign state and that agency or instrumentality is engaged in a commercial activity in the United States;

(4) in which rights in property in the United States acquired by succession or gift or rights in immovable property situated in the United States are in issue;

(5) not otherwise encompassed in paragraph (2) above, in which money damages are sought against a foreign state for personal injury or death, or damage to or loss of property, occurring in the United States and caused by the tortious act or omission of that foreign state or of any official or employee of that foreign state while acting within the scope of his office or employment; except this paragraph shall not apply to—

(A) any claim based upon the exercise or performance or the failure to exercise or perform a discretionary function regardless of whether the discretion be abused, or

(B) any claim arising out of malicious prosecution, abuse of process, libel, slander, misrepresentation, deceit, or interference with contract rights; or

(6) in which the action is brought, either to enforce an agreement made by the foreign state with or for the benefit of a private party to submit to arbitration all or any differences

which have arisen or which may arise between the parties with respect to a defined legal relationship, whether contractual or not, concerning a subject matter capable of settlement by arbitration under the laws of the United States, or to confirm an award made pursuant to such an agreement to arbitrate, if (A) the arbitration takes place or is intended to take place in the United States, (B) the agreement or award is or may be governed by a treaty or other international agreement in force for the United States calling for the recognition and enforcement of arbitral awards, (C) the underlying claim, save for the agreement to arbitrate, could have been brought in a United States court under this section or section 1607 [28 USCS § 1607], or (D) paragraph (1) of this subsection is otherwise applicable.

(7) Repealed. Pub.L. 110-181, Div. A, § 1083(b)(1)(A)(iii), Jan. 28, 2008, 122 Stat. 341[1]

(b) A foreign state shall not be immune from the jurisdiction of the courts of the United States in any case in which a suit in admiralty is brought to enforce a maritime lien against a vessel or cargo of the foreign state, which maritime lien is based upon a commercial activity of the foreign state: *Provided*, That—

(1) notice of the suit is given by delivery of a copy of the summons and of the complaint to the person, or his agent, having possession of the vessel or cargo against which the maritime lien is asserted; and if the vessel or cargo is arrested pursuant to process obtained on behalf of the party bringing the suit, the service of process of arrest shall be deemed to constitute valid delivery of such notice, but the party bringing the suit shall be liable for any damages sustained by the foreign state as a result of the arrest if the

---

[1] 28 U.S.C. § 1605(a)(7) formerly read:

(7) not otherwise covered by paragraph (2), in which money damages are sought against a foreign state for personal injury or death that was caused by an act of torture, extrajudicial killing, aircraft sabotage, hostage taking, or the provision of material support or resources (as defined in section 2339A of title 18) for such an act if such act or provision of material support is engaged in by an official, employee, or agent of such foreign state while acting within the scope of his or her office, employment, or agency, except that the court shall decline to hear a claim under this paragraph—

(A) if the foreign state was not designated as a state sponsor of terrorism under section 6(j) of the Export Administration Act of 1979 (50 U.S.C. App. 2405(j)) or section 620A of the Foreign Assistance Act of 1961 (22 U.S.C. 2371) at the time the act occurred, unless later so designated as a result of such act or the act is related to Case Number 1:00CV03110(EGS) in the United States District Court for the District of Columbia; and

(B) even if the foreign state is or was so designated, if—

(i) the act occurred in the foreign state against which the claim has been brought and the claimant has not afforded the foreign state a reasonable opportunity to arbitrate the claim in accordance with accepted international rules of arbitration; or

(ii) neither the claimant nor the victim was a national of the United States (as that term is defined in section 101(a)(22) of the Immigration and Nationality Act) when the act upon which the claim is based occurred

party bringing the suit had actual or constructive knowledge that the vessel or cargo of a foreign state was involved; and

(2) notice to the foreign state of the commencement of suit as provided in section 1608 of this title [28 USCS § 1608] is initiated within ten days either of the delivery of notice as provided in paragraph (1) of this subsection or, in the case of a party who was unaware that the vessel or cargo of a foreign state was involved, of the date such party determined the existence of the foreign state's interest.

(c) Whenever notice is delivered under subsection (b)(1), the suit to enforce a maritime lien shall thereafter proceed and shall be heard and determined according to the principles of law and rules of practice of suits in rem whenever it appears that, had the vessel been privately owned and possessed, a suit in rem might have been maintained. A decree against the foreign state may include costs of the suit and, if the decree is for a money judgment, interest as ordered by the court, except that the court may not award judgment against the foreign state in an amount greater than the value of the vessel or cargo upon which the maritime lien arose. Such value shall be determined as of the time notice is served under subsection (b)(1). Decrees shall be subject to appeal and revision as provided in other cases of admiralty and maritime jurisdiction. Nothing shall preclude the plaintiff in any proper case from seeking relief in personam in the same action brought to enforce a maritime lien as provided in this section.

(d) A foreign state shall not be immune from the jurisdiction of the courts of the United States in any action brought to foreclose a preferred mortgage, as defined in the section 31301 of title 46. Such action shall be brought, heard, and determined in accordance with the provisions of chapter 313 of title 46 and in accordance with the principles of law and rules of practice of suits in rem, whenever it appears that had the vessel been privately owned and possessed a suit in rem might have been maintained.

(e), (f) Repealed. Pub.L. 110-181, Div. A, Title X, § 1083(b)(1)(B), Jan. 28, 2008, 122 Stat. 341

(g) Limitation on discovery.

(1) In general.

(A) Subject to paragraph (2), if an action is filed that would otherwise be barred by section 1604 [28 USCS § 1604], but for section 1605A [28 USCS § 1605A], the court, upon request of the Attorney General, shall stay any request, demand, or order for discovery on the United States that the Attorney General certifies would significantly interfere with a criminal investigation or prosecution, or a national security operation, related to the incident that gave rise to the cause of action, until such time as the Attorney General advises the court that such request, demand, or order will no longer so interfere.

(B) A stay under this paragraph shall be in effect during the 12-month period beginning on the date on which the court issues the order to stay discovery. The court shall renew the order to stay discovery for additional 12-month periods upon motion by the United States if the Attorney General certifies that discovery would significantly interfere with a criminal investigation or prosecution, or a national security operation, related to the incident that gave rise to the cause of action.

(2) Sunset.

(A) Subject to subparagraph (B), no stay shall be granted or continued in effect under paragraph (1) after the date that is 10 years after the date on which the incident that gave rise to the cause of action occurred.

(B) After the period referred to in subparagraph (A), the court, upon request of the Attorney General, may stay any request, demand, or order for discovery on the United States that the court finds a substantial likelihood would—

(i) create a serious threat of death or serious bodily injury to any person;

(ii) adversely affect the ability of the United States to work in cooperation with foreign and international law enforcement agencies in investigating violations of United States law; or

(iii) obstruct the criminal case related to the incident that gave rise to the cause of action or undermine the potential for a conviction in such case.

(3) Evaluation of evidence.

The court's evaluation of any request for a stay under this subsection filed by the Attorney General shall be conducted ex parte and in camera.

(4) Bar on motions to dismiss.

A stay of discovery under this subsection shall constitute a bar to the granting of a motion to dismiss under rules 12(b)(6) and 56 of the Federal Rules of Civil Procedure.

(5) Construction.

Nothing in this subsection shall prevent the United States from seeking protective orders or asserting privileges ordinarily available to the United States.

(Added Pub.L. 94-583, § 4(a), Oct. 21, 1976, 90 Stat. 2892, and amended Pub.L. 100-640, § 1, Nov. 9, 1988, 102 Stat. 3333; Pub.L. 100-669, § 2, Nov. 16, 1988, 102 Stat. 3969; Pub.L. 101-650, Title III, § 325(b)(8), Dec. 1, 1990, 104 Stat. 5121; Pub.L. 104-132, Title II, § 221(a), Apr. 24, 1996, 110 Stat. 1241; Pub.L. 105-11, Apr. 25, 1997, 111 Stat. 22; Pub.L. 107-77, Title VI, § 626(c), Nov. 28, 2001, 115 Stat. 803; Pub.L. 107-117, Div. B, Ch. 2, § 208, Jan. 10, 2002, 115 Stat. 2299; Pub.L. 109-304, § 17(f)(2), Oct. 6, 2006, 120 Stat. 1708; Pub.L. 110-181, Title X, § 1083(b)(1), Jan. 28, 2008, 122 Stat. 341.)

28 U.S.C. § 1605A. Terrorism exception to the jurisdictional immunity of a foreign state

(a) In general.—

(1) No immunity.—A foreign state shall not be immune from the jurisdiction of courts of the United States or of the States in any case not otherwise covered by this chapter in which money damages are sought against a foreign state for personal injury or death that was caused by an act of torture, extrajudicial killing, aircraft sabotage, hostage taking, or the provision of material support or resources for such an act if such act or provision of material support or resources is engaged in by an official, employee, or agent of such foreign state while acting within the scope of his or her office, employment, or agency.

(2) Claim heard.—The court shall hear a claim under this section if—

(A)(i)(I) the foreign state was designated as a state sponsor of terrorism at the time the act described in paragraph (1) occurred, or was so designated as a result of such act, and, subject to subclause (II), either remains so designated when the claim is filed under this section or was so designated within the 6-month period before the claim is filed under this section; or

(II) in the case of an action that is refiled under this section by reason of section 1083(c)(2)(A) of the National Defense Authorization Act for Fiscal Year 2008 or is filed under this section by reason of section 1083(c)(3) of that Act, the foreign state was designated as a state sponsor of terrorism when the original action or the related action under section 1605(a)(7) (as in effect before the enactment of this section) or section 589 of the Foreign Operations, Export Financing, and Related Programs Appropriations Act, 1997 (as contained in section 101(c) of division A of Public Law 104-208) was filed;

(ii) the claimant or the victim was, at the time the act described in paragraph (1) occurred—

(I) a national of the United States;

(II) a member of the armed forces; or

(III) otherwise an employee of the Government of the United States, or of an individual performing a contract awarded by the United States Government, acting within the scope of the employee's employment; and

(iii) in a case in which the act occurred in the foreign state against which the claim has been brought, the claimant has afforded the foreign state a reasonable opportunity to arbitrate the claim in accordance with the accepted international rules of arbitration; or

(B) the act described in paragraph (1) is related to Case Number 1:00CV03110 (EGS) in the United States District Court for the District of Columbia.

(b) Limitations.—An action may be brought or maintained under this section if the action is commenced, or a related action was commenced under section 1605(a)(7) (before the date of the enactment of this section) or section 589 of the Foreign Operations, Export Financing, and Related Programs Appropriations Act, 1997 (as contained in section 101(c) of division A of Public Law 104-208) not later than the latter of—

(1) 10 years after April 24, 1996; or

(2) 10 years after the date on which the cause of action arose.

(c) Private right of action.—A foreign state that is or was a state sponsor of terrorism as described in subsection (a)(2)(A)(i), and any official, employee, or agent of that foreign state while acting within the scope of his or her office, employment, or agency, shall be liable to—

(1) a national of the United States,

(2) a member of the armed forces,

(3) an employee of the Government of the United States, or of an individual performing a contract awarded by the United States Government, acting within the scope of the employee's employment, or

(4) the legal representative of a person described in paragraph (1), (2), or (3),

for personal injury or death caused by acts described in subsection (a)(1) of that foreign state, or of an official, employee, or agent of that foreign state, for which the courts of the United States may maintain jurisdiction under this section for money damages. In any such action, damages may include economic damages, solatium, pain and suffering, and punitive damages. In any such action, a foreign state shall be vicariously liable for the acts of its officials, employees, or agents.

(d) Additional damages.—After an action has been brought under subsection (c), actions may also be brought for reasonably foreseeable property loss, whether insured or uninsured, third party liability, and loss claims under life and property insurance policies, by reason of the same acts on which the action under subsection (c) is based.

(e) Special masters.—

(1) In general.—The courts of the United States may appoint special masters to hear damage claims brought under this section.

(2) Transfer of funds.—The Attorney General shall transfer, from funds available for the program under section 1404C of the Victims of Crime Act of 1984 (42 U.S.C. 10603c), to the Administrator of the United States district court in which any case is pending which has been brought or maintained under this section such funds as may be required to cover the costs of special masters appointed under paragraph (1). Any

amount paid in compensation to any such special master shall constitute an item of court costs.

(f) Appeal.—In an action brought under this section, appeals from orders not conclusively ending the litigation may only be taken pursuant to section 1292(b) of this title.

(g) Property disposition.—

(1) In general.—In every action filed in a United States district court in which jurisdiction is alleged under this section, the filing of a notice of pending action pursuant to this section, to which is attached a copy of the complaint filed in the action, shall have the effect of establishing a lien of lis pendens upon any real property or tangible personal property that is—

(A) subject to attachment in aid of execution, or execution, under section 1610;

(B) located within that judicial district; and

(C) titled in the name of any defendant, or titled in the name of any entity controlled by any defendant if such notice contains a statement listing such controlled entity.

(2) Notice.—A notice of pending action pursuant to this section shall be filed by the clerk of the district court in the same manner as any pending action and shall be indexed by listing as defendants all named defendants and all entities listed as controlled by any defendant. (3) Enforceability.—Liens established by reason of this subsection shall be enforceable as provided in chapter 111 of this title.

(h) Definitions.—For purposes of this section—

(1) the term "aircraft sabotage" has the meaning given that term in Article 1 of the Convention for the Suppression of Unlawful Acts Against the Safety of Civil Aviation;

(2) the term "hostage taking" has the meaning given that term in Article 1 of the International Convention Against the Taking of Hostages;

(3) the term "material support or resources" has the meaning given that term in section 2339A of title 18;

(4) the term "armed forces" has the meaning given that term in section 101 of title 10;

(5) the term "national of the United States" has the meaning given that term in section 101(a)(22) of the Immigration and Nationality Act (8 U.S.C. 1101(a)(22));

(6) the term "state sponsor of terrorism" means a country the government of which the Secretary of State has determined, for purposes of section 6(j) of the Export Administration Act of 1979 (50 U.S.C. App. 2405(j)), section 620A of the Foreign Assistance Act of 1961 (22 U.S.C. 2371), section 40 of the Arms Export Control Act (22 U.S.C. 2780), or any other provision of law, is a government that has repeatedly provided support for acts of international terrorism; and

(7) the terms "torture" and "extrajudicial killing" have the meaning given those terms in section 3 of the Torture Victim Protection Act of 1991 (28 U.S.C. 1350 note).

(Added Pub.L. 110-181, Div. A, Title X, § 1083(a)(1), Jan. 28, 2008, 122 Stat. 338.)

28 U.S.C. § 1606. Extent of liability

As to any claim for relief with respect to which a foreign state is not entitled to immunity under section 1605 or 1607 of this chapter [28 USCS § 1605 or 1607], the foreign state shall be liable in the same manner and to the same extent as a private individual under like circumstances; but a foreign state except for an agency or instrumentality thereof shall not be liable for punitive damages; if, however, in any case wherein death was caused, the law of the place where the action or omission occurred provides, or has been construed to provide, for damages only punitive in nature, the foreign state shall be liable for actual or compensatory damages measured by the pecuniary injuries resulting from such death which were incurred by the persons for whose benefit the action was brought.

(Added Oct. 21, 1976, P.L. 94-583, § 4(a), 90 Stat. 2894; Oct. 21, 1998, P.L. 105-277, Div A, § 101(h) [Title I, § 117(b)], 112 Stat. 2681-491; Oct. 28, 2000, P.L. 106-386, Div C, § 2002(g)[(f)](2), 114 Stat. 1543; Nov. 26, 2002, P.L. 107-297, Title II, § 201(c)(3), 116 Stat. 2337.)

28 U.S.C. § 1607. Counterclaims

In any action brought by a foreign state, or in which a foreign state intervenes, in a court of the United States or of a State, the foreign state shall not be accorded immunity with respect to any counterclaim—

(a) for which a foreign state would not be entitled to immunity under section 1605 of this chapter [28 USCS § 1605] or 1605A [28 USCS § 1605A] had such claim been brought in a separate action against the foreign state; or

(b) arising out of the transaction or occurrence that is the subject matter of the claim of the foreign state; or

(c) to the extent that the counterclaim does not seek relief exceeding in amount or differing in kind from that sought by the foreign state.

(Added Pub.L. 94-583, § 4(a), Oct. 21, 1976, 90 Stat. 2894, and amended Pub.L. 110-181, Div. A, Title X, § 1083(b)(2), Jan. 28, 2008, 122 Stat. 341.)

28 U.S.C. § 1608. Service; time to answer; default

(a) Service in the courts of the United States and of the States shall be made upon a foreign state or political subdivision of a foreign state:

(1) by delivery of a copy of the summons and complaint in accordance with any special arrangement for service between the plaintiff and the foreign state or political subdivision; or

(2) if no special arrangement exists, by delivery of a copy of the summons and complaint in accordance with an applicable international convention on service of judicial documents; or

(3) if service cannot be made under paragraphs (1) or (2), by sending a copy of the summons and complaint and a notice of

suit, together with a translation of each into the official language of the foreign state, by any form of mail requiring a signed receipt, to be addressed and dispatched by the clerk of the court to the head of the ministry of foreign affairs of the foreign state concerned, or

(4) if service cannot be made within 30 days under paragraph (3), by sending two copies of the summons and complaint and a notice of suit, together with a translation of each into the official language of the foreign state, by any form of mail requiring a signed receipt, to be addressed and dispatched by the clerk of the court to the Secretary of State in Washington, District of Columbia, to the attention of the Director of Special Consular Services—and the Secretary shall transmit one copy of the papers through diplomatic channels to the foreign state and shall send to the clerk of the court a certified copy of the diplomatic note indicating when the papers were transmitted.

As used in this subsection, a "notice of suit" shall mean a notice addressed to a foreign state and in a form prescribed by the Secretary of State by regulation.

(b) Service in the courts of the United States and of the States shall be made upon an agency or instrumentality of a foreign state:

(1) by delivery of a copy of the summons and complaint in accordance with any special arrangement for service between the plaintiff and the agency or instrumentality; or

(2) if no special arrangement exists, by delivery of a copy of the summons and complaint either to an officer, a managing or general agent, or to any other agent authorized by appointment or by law to receive service of process in the United States; or in accordance with an applicable international convention on service of judicial documents; or

(3) if service cannot be made under paragraphs (1) or (2), and if reasonably calculated to give actual notice, by delivery of a copy of the summons and complaint, together with a translation of each into the official language of the foreign state—

(A) as directed by an authority of the foreign state or political subdivision in response to a letter rogatory or request or

(B) by any form of mail requiring a signed receipt, to be addressed and dispatched by the clerk of the court to the agency or instrumentality to be served, or

(C) as directed by order of the court consistent with the law of the place where service is to be made.

(c) Service shall be deemed to have been made—

(1) in the case of service under subsection (a)(4), as of the date of transmittal indicated in the certified copy of the diplomatic note; and

(2) in any other case under this section, as of the date of receipt indicated in the certification, signed and returned postal

receipt, or other proof of service applicable to the method of service employed.

(d) In any action brought in a court of the United States or of a State, a foreign state, a political subdivision thereof, or an agency or instrumentality of a foreign state shall serve an answer or other responsive pleading to the complaint within sixty days after service has been made under this section.

(e) No judgment by default shall be entered by a court of the United States or of a State against a foreign state, a political subdivision thereof, or an agency or instrumentality of a foreign state, unless the claimant establishes his claim or right to relief by evidence satisfactory to the court. A copy of any such default judgment shall be sent to the foreign state or political subdivision in the manner prescribed for service in this section.

(Added Oct. 21, 1976, P.L. 94-583, § 4(a), 90 Stat. 2894.)

28 U.S.C. § 1609. Immunity from attachment and execution of property of a foreign state

Subject to existing international agreements to which the United States is a party at the time of enactment of this Act [enacted Oct. 21, 1976] the property in the United States of a foreign state shall be immune from attachment arrest and execution except as provided in sections 1610 and 1611 of this chapter [28 USCS §§ 1610 and 1611].

(Added Oct. 21, 1976, P.L. 94-583, § 4(a), 90 Stat. 2895.)

28 U.S.C. § 1610. Exceptions to the immunity from attachment or execution

(a) The property in the United States of a foreign state, as defined in section 1603(a) of this chapter [28 USCS § 1603(a)], used for a commercial activity in the United States, shall not be immune from attachment in aid of execution, or from execution, upon a judgment entered by a court of the United States or of a State after the effective date of this Act, if—

(1) the foreign state has waived its immunity from attachment in aid of execution or from execution either explicitly or by implication, notwithstanding any withdrawal of the waiver the foreign state may purport to effect except in accordance with the terms of the waiver, or

(2) the property is or was used for the commercial activity upon which the claim is based, or

(3) the execution relates to a judgment establishing rights in property which has been taken in violation of international law or which has been exchanged for property taken in violation of international law, or

(4) the execution relates to a judgment establishing rights in property—

(A) which is acquired by succession or gift, or

(B) which is immovable and situated in the United States: *Provided*, That such property is not used for purposes of maintaining a diplomatic or consular mission or the residence of the Chief of such mission, or

(5) the property consists of any contractual obligation or any proceeds from such a contractual obligation to indemnify or hold harmless the foreign state or its employees under a policy of automobile or other liability or casualty insurance covering the claim which merged into the judgment, or

(6) the judgment is based on an order confirming an arbitral award rendered against the foreign state, provided that attachment in aid of execution, or execution, would not be inconsistent with any provision in the arbitral agreement, or

(7) the judgment relates to a claim for which the foreign state is not immune under section 1605A [28 USCS § 1605A], regardless of whether the property is or was involved with the act upon which the claim is based.

(b) In addition to subsection (a), any property in the United States of an agency or instrumentality of a foreign state engaged in commercial activity in the United States shall not be immune from attachment in aid of execution, or from execution, upon a judgment entered by a court of the United States or of a State after the effective date of this Act if—

(1) the agency or instrumentality has waived its immunity from attachment in aid of execution or from execution either explicitly or implicitly, notwithstanding any withdrawal of the waiver the agency or instrumentality may purport to effect except in accordance with the terms of the waiver, or

(2) the judgment relates to a claim for which the agency or instrumentality is not immune by virtue of section 1605(a)(2), (3), or (5), 1605(b), or 1605A of this chapter [28 USCS § 1605(a)(2), (3), or (5), 1605(b), or 1605A], regardless of whether the property is or was involved in the act upon which the claim is based.

(c) No attachment or execution referred to in subsections (a) and (b) of this section shall be permitted until the court has ordered such attachment and execution after having determined that a reasonable period of time has elapsed following the entry of judgment and the giving of any notice required under section 1608(e) of this chapter [28 USCS § 1608(e)].

(d) The property of a foreign state, as defined in section 1603(a) of this chapter [28 USCS § 1603(a)], used for a commercial activity in the United States, shall not be immune from attachment prior to the entry of judgment in any action brought in a court of the United States or of a State, or prior to the elapse of the period of time provided in subsection (c) of this section, if—

(1) the foreign state has explicitly waived its immunity from attachment prior to judgment, notwithstanding any withdrawal of the waiver the foreign state may purport to effect except in accordance with the terms of the waiver, and

(2) the purpose of the attachment is to secure satisfaction of a judgment that has been or may ultimately be entered against the foreign state, and not to obtain jurisdiction.

(e) The vessels of a foreign state shall not be immune from arrest in rem, interlocutory sale, and execution in actions brought to foreclose a preferred mortgage as provided in section 1605(d) [28 USCS § 1605(d)].

(f) (1) (A) Notwithstanding any other provision of law, including but not limited to section 208(f) of the Foreign Missions Act (22 U.S.C. 4308(f)), and except as provided in subparagraph (B), any property with respect to which financial transactions are prohibited or regulated pursuant to section 5(b) of the Trading with the Enemy Act (50 U.S.C. App. 5(b)), section 620(a) of the Foreign Assistance Act of 1961 (22 U.S.C. 2370(a)), sections 202 and 203 of the International Emergency Economic Powers Act (50 U.S.C. 1701–1702), or any other proclamation, order, regulation, or license issued pursuant thereto, shall be subject to execution or attachment in aid of execution of any judgment relating to a claim for which a foreign state (including any agency or instrumentality or such state) claiming such property is not immune under section 1605(a)(7) (as in effect before the enactment of 1605A) or section 1605A [28 USCS §§ 1605(a)(7), 1605A].

(B) Subparagraph (A) shall not apply if, at the time the property is expropriated or seized by the foreign state, the property has been held in title by a natural person or, if held in trust, has been held for the benefit of a natural person or persons.

(2) (A) At the request of any party in whose favor a judgment has been issued with respect to a claim for which the foreign state is not immune under section 1605(a)(7) (as in effect before the enactment of 1605A) or section 1605A [28 USCS § 1605(a)(7), 1605A], the Secretary of the Treasury and the Secretary of State should make every effort to fully, promptly, and effectively assist any judgment creditor or any court that has issued any such judgment in identifying, locating, and executing against the property of that foreign state or any agency or instrumentality of such state.

(B) In providing such assistance, the Secretaries—

(i) may provide such information to the court under seal; and

(ii) should make every effort to provide the information in a manner sufficient to allow the court to direct the United States Marshall's office to promptly and effectively execute against that property.

(3) Waiver.

The President may waive any provision of paragraph (1) in the interest of national security.

(g) Property in certain actions.—

(1) In general.—Subject to paragraph (3), the property of a foreign state against which a judgment is entered under section 1605A, and the property of an agency or instrumentality of such a state, including property that is a separate juridical entity or is an interest held directly or indirectly in a separate juridical entity, is subject to

attachment in aid of execution, and execution, upon that judgment as provided in this section, regardless of—

(A) the level of economic control over the property by the government of the foreign state;

(B) whether the profits of the property go to that government;

(C) the degree to which officials of that government manage the property or otherwise control its daily affairs;

(D) whether that government is the sole beneficiary in interest of the property; or

(E) whether establishing the property as a separate entity would entitle the foreign state to benefits in United States courts while avoiding its obligations.

(2) United States sovereign immunity inapplicable.—Any property of a foreign state, or agency or instrumentality of a foreign state, to which paragraph (1) applies shall not be immune from attachment in aid of execution, or execution, upon a judgment entered under section 1605A because the property is regulated by the United States Government by reason of action taken against that foreign state under the Trading With the Enemy Act or the International Emergency Economic Powers Act.

(3) Third-party joint property holders.—Nothing in this subsection shall be construed to supersede the authority of a court to prevent appropriately the impairment of an interest held by a person who is not liable in the action giving rise to a judgment in property subject to attachment in aid of execution, or execution, upon such judgment.

(Added Pub.L. 94-583, § 4(a), Oct. 21, 1976, 90 Stat. 2896, and amended Pub.L. 100-640, § 2, Nov. 9, 1988, 102 Stat. 3333; Pub.L. 100-669, § 3, Nov. 16, 1988, 102 Stat. 3969; Pub.L. 101-650, Title III, § 325(b)(9), Dec. 1, 1990, 104 Stat. 5121; Pub.L. 104-132, Title II, § 221(b), Apr. 24, 1996, 110 Stat. 1243; Pub.L. 105-277, Div. A, § 101(h) [Title I, § 117(a)], Oct. 21, 1998, 112 Stat. 2681-491; Pub.L. 106-386, Div. C, § 2002(g)(1), Oct. 28, 2000, 114 Stat. 1543; Pub.L. 107-297, Title II, § 201(c)(3), Nov. 26, 2002, 116 Stat. 2337; Pub.L. 110-181, Div. A, Title X, § 1083(b)(3), Jan. 28, 2008, 122 Stat. 341.)

28 U.S.C. § 1611. Certain types of property immune from execution

(a) Notwithstanding the provisions of section 1610 of this chapter [28 USCS § 1610], the property of those organizations designated by the President as being entitled to enjoy the privileges, exemptions, and immunities provided by the International Organizations Immunities Act shall not be subject to attachment or any other judicial process impeding the disbursement of funds to, or on the order of, a foreign state as the result of an action brought in the courts of the United States or of the States.

(b) Notwithstanding the provisions of section 1610 of this chapter [28 USCS § 1610], the property of a foreign state shall be immune from attachment and from execution, if—

(1) the property is that of a foreign central bank or monetary authority held for its own account, unless such bank or

authority, or its parent foreign government, has explicitly waived its immunity from attachment in aid of execution, or from execution, notwithstanding any withdrawal of the waiver which the bank, authority or government may purport to effect except in accordance with the terms of the waiver; or

(2) the property is, or is intended to be, used in connection with a military activity and

(A) is of a military character, or

(B) is under the control of a military authority or defense agency.

(c) Notwithstanding the provisions of section 1610 of this chapter [28 USCS § 1610], the property of a foreign state shall be immune from attachment and from execution in an action brought under section 302 of the Cuban Liberty and Democratic Solidarity (LIBERTAD) Act of 1996 [22 USCS § 6082] to the extent that the property is a facility or installation used by an accredited diplomatic mission for official purposes.

(Added Oct. 21, 1976, P.L. 94-583, § 4(a), 90 Stat. 2897; March 12, 1996, P.L. 104-114, Title III, § 302(e), 110 Stat. 818.)

28

HEALTH CARE QUALITY IMPROVEMENT ACT OF 1986

§ 402. [42 U.S.C. § 11101]. Findings

The Congress finds the following:

(1) The increasing occurrence of medical malpractice and the need to improve the quality of medical care have become nationwide problems that warrant greater efforts than those that can be undertaken by any individual State.

(2) There is a national need to restrict the ability of incompetent physicians to move from State to State without disclosure or discovery of the physician's previous damaging or incompetent performance.

(3) This nationwide problem can be remedied through effective professional peer review.

(4) The threat of private money damage liability under Federal laws, including treble damage liability under Federal antitrust law, unreasonably discourages physicians from participating in effective professional peer review.

(5) There is an overriding national need to provide incentive and protection for physicians engaging in effective professional peer review.

(Pub.L. 99-660, Title IV, § 402, Nov. 14, 1986, 100 Stat. 3784.)

§ 411. [42 U.S.C. § 11111]. Professional review

(a) In general.

(1) Limitation on damages for professional review actions.

If a professional review action (as defined in section 11151(9) of this title) of a professional review body meets all the standards specified in section 11112(a) of this title, except as provided in subsection (b) of this section—

(A) the professional review body,

(B) any person acting as a member or staff to the body,

(C) any person under a contract or other formal agreement with the body, and

(D) any person who participates with or assists the body with respect to the action,

shall not be liable in damages under any law of the United States or of any State (or political subdivision thereof) with respect to the action. The preceding sentence shall not apply to damages under any law of the United States or any State relating to the civil rights of any person or persons, including the Civil Rights Act of 1964, 42 U.S.C. 2000e, et seq. and the Civil Rights Acts, 42 U.S.C. 1981, et seq. Nothing in this paragraph shall prevent the United States or any Attorney General of a State from bringing an action, including an action under section 15c of Title 15, where such an action is otherwise authorized.

(2) Protection for those providing information to professional review bodies.

Notwithstanding any other provision of law, no person (whether as a witness or otherwise) providing information to a professional review body regarding the competence or professional conduct of a physician shall be held, by reason of having provided such information, to be liable in damages under any law of the United States or of any State (or political subdivision thereof) unless such information is false and the person providing it knew that such information was false.

(b) Exception

If the Secretary has reason to believe that a health care entity has failed to report information in accordance with section 11133(a) of this title, the Secretary shall conduct an investigation. If, after providing notice of noncompliance, an opportunity to correct the noncompliance, and an opportunity for a hearing, the Secretary determines that a health care entity has failed substantially to report information in accordance with section 11133(a) of this title, the Secretary shall publish the name of the entity in the Federal Register. The protections of subsection (a)(1) of this section shall not apply to an entity the name of which is published in the Federal Register under the previous sentence with respect to professional review actions of the entity commenced during the 3-year period beginning 30 days after the date of publication of the name.

(c) Treatment under State laws

(1) Professional review actions taken on or after October 14, 1989.

Except as provided in paragraph (2), subsection (a) of this section shall apply to State laws in a State only for professional review actions commenced on or after October 14, 1989.

(2) Exceptions

(A) State early opt-in

Subsection (a) of this section shall apply to State laws in a State for actions commenced before October 14, 1989, if the State by legislation elects such treatment.

(B) Effective date of election

An election under State law is not effective, for purposes of[1], for actions commenced before the effective date of the State law, which may not be earlier than the date of the enactment of that law.

(Pub.L. 99-660, Title IV, § 411, Nov. 14, 1986, 100 Stat. 3784; Pub.L. 100-177, Title IV, § 402(c), as added Pub.L. 101-239, Title VI, § 6103(e)(6)(A), Dec. 19, 1989, 103 Stat. 2208.)

---

1 So in original. Probably should be "for purposes of subparagraph (A),".

§ 412. [42 U.S.C. § 11112]. Standards for professional review actions

(a) In general

For purposes of the protection set forth in section 11111(a) of this title, a professional review action must be taken—

(1) in the reasonable belief that the action was in the furtherance of quality health care,

(2) after a reasonable effort to obtain the facts of the matter,

(3) after adequate notice and hearing procedures are afforded to the physician involved or after such other procedures as are fair to the physician under the circumstances, and

(4) in the reasonable belief that the action was warranted by the facts known after such reasonable effort to obtain facts and after meeting the requirement of paragraph (3).

A professional review action shall be presumed to have met the preceding standards necessary for the protection set out in section 11111(a) of this title unless the presumption is rebutted by a preponderance of the evidence.

(b) Adequate notice and hearing

A health care entity is deemed to have met the adequate notice and hearing requirement of subsection (a)(3) of this section with respect to a physician if the following conditions are met (or are waived voluntarily by the physician):

(1) Notice of proposed action

The physician has been given notice stating—

(A) (i) that a professional review action has been proposed to be taken against the physician,

(ii) reasons for the proposed action,

(B) (i) that the physician has the right to request a hearing on the proposed action,

(ii) any time limit (of not less than 30 days) within which to request such a hearing, and

(C) a summary of the rights in the hearing under paragraph (3).

(2) Notice of hearing

If a hearing is requested on a timely basis under paragraph (1)(B), the physician involved must be given notice stating—

(A) the place, time, and date, of the hearing, which date shall not be less than 30 days after the date of the notice, and

(B) a list of the witnesses (if any) expected to testify at the hearing on behalf of the professional review body.

(3) Conduct of hearing and notice

If a hearing is requested on a timely basis under paragraph (1)(B)—

(A) subject to subparagraph (B), the hearing shall be held (as determined by the health care entity)—

(i) before an arbitrator mutually acceptable to the physician and the health care entity,

(ii) before a hearing officer who is appointed by the entity and who is not in direct economic competition with the physician involved, or

(iii) before a panel of individuals who are appointed by the entity and are not in direct economic competition with the physician involved;

(B) the right to the hearing may be forfeited if the physician fails, without good cause, to appear;

(C) in the hearing the physician involved has the right—

(i) to representation by an attorney or other person of the physician's choice,

(ii) to have a record made of the proceedings, copies of which may be obtained by the physician upon payment of any reasonable charges associated with the preparation thereof,

(iii) to call, examine, and cross-examine witnesses,

(iv) to present evidence determined to be relevant by the hearing officer, regardless of its admissibility in a court of law, and

(v) to submit a written statement at the close of the hearing; and

(D) upon completion of the hearing, the physician involved has the right—

(i) to receive the written recommendation of the arbitrator, officer, or panel, including a statement of the basis for the recommendations, and

(ii) to receive a written decision of the health care entity, including a statement of the basis for the decision.

A professional review body's failure to meet the conditions described in this subsection shall not, in itself, constitute failure to meet the standards of subsection (a)(3) of this section.

(c) Adequate procedures in investigations or health emergencies

For purposes of section 11111(a) of this title, nothing in this section shall be construed as—

(1) requiring the procedures referred to in subsection (a)(3) of this section—

(A) where there is no adverse professional review action taken, or

(B) in the case of a suspension or restriction of clinical privileges, for a period of not longer than 14 days, during which an investigation is being conducted to determine the need for a professional review action; or

(2) precluding an immediate suspension or restriction of clinical privileges, subject to subsequent notice and hearing or other adequate procedures, where the failure to take such an action may result in an imminent danger to the health of any individual.

(Pub.L. 99-660, Title IV, § 412, Nov. 14, 1986, 100 Stat. 3785.)

§ 413. [42 U.S.C. § 11113]. Payment of reasonable attorneys' fees and costs in defense of suit

In any suit brought against a defendant, to the extent that a defendant has met the standards set forth under section 11112(a) of this title and the defendant substantially prevails, the court shall, at the conclusion of the action, award to a substantially prevailing party defending against any such claim the cost of the suit attributable to such claim, including a reasonable attorney's fee, if the claim, or the claimant's conduct during the litigation of the claim, was frivolous, unreasonable, without foundation, or in bad faith. For the purposes of this section, a defendant shall not be considered to have substantially prevailed when the plaintiff obtains an award for damages or permanent injunctive or declaratory relief.

(Pub.L. 99-660, Title IV, § 413, Nov. 14, 1986, 100 Stat. 3787.)

§ 414. [42 U.S.C. § 11114]. Guidelines of the Secretary

The Secretary may establish, after notice and opportunity for comment, such voluntary guidelines as may assist the professional review bodies in meeting the standards described in section 11112(a) of this title.

(Pub.L. 99-660, Title IV, § 414, Nov. 14, 1986, 100 Stat. 3787.)

§ 415. [42 U.S.C. § 11115]. Construction

(a) In general

Except as specifically provided in this subchapter, nothing in this subchapter shall be construed as changing the liabilities or immunities under law or as preempting or overriding any State law which provides incentives, immunities, or protection for those engaged in a professional review action that is in addition to or greater than that provided by this subchapter.

(b) Scope of clinical privileges

Nothing in this subchapter shall be construed as requiring health care entities to provide clinical privileges to any or all classes or types of physicians or other licensed health care practitioners.

(c) Treatment of nurses and other practitioners

Nothing in this subchapter shall be construed as affecting, or modifying any provision of Federal or State law, with respect to activities of professional review bodies regarding nurses, other licensed health care practitioners, or other health professionals who are not physicians.

(d) Treatment of patient malpractice claims

Nothing in this chapter shall be construed as affecting in any manner the rights and remedies afforded patients under any provision of Federal or State law to seek redress for any harm or injury suffered as a result of negligent treatment or care by any physician, health care practitioner, or health care entity, or as limiting any defenses or immunities available to any physician, health care practitioner, or health care entity.

(Pub.L. 99-660, Title IV, § 415, Nov. 14, 1986, 100 Stat. 3787; Pub.L. 100-177, Title IV, § 402(c), as added Pub.L. 101-239, Title VI, § 6103(e)(6)(A), Dec. 19, 1989, 103 Stat. 2208.)

§ 421. [42 U.S.C. § 11131]. Requiring reports on medical malpractice payments

(a) In general

Each entity (including an insurance company) which makes payment under a policy of insurance, self-insurance, or otherwise in settlement (or partial settlement) of, or in satisfaction of a judgment in, a medical malpractice action or claim shall report, in accordance with section 11134 of this title, information respecting the payment and circumstances thereof.

(b) Information to be reported

The information to be reported under subsection (a) of this section includes—

(1) the name of any physician or licensed health care practitioner for whose benefit the payment is made,

(2) the amount of the payment,

(3) the name (if known) of any hospital with which the physician or practitioner is affiliated or associated,

(4) a description of the acts or omissions and injuries or illnesses upon which the action or claim was based, and

(5) such other information as the Secretary determines is required for appropriate interpretation of information reported under this section.

(c) Sanctions for failure to report

Any entity that fails to report information on a payment required to be reported under this section shall be subject to a civil money penalty of not more than $10,000 for each such payment involved. Such penalty shall be imposed and collected in the same manner as civil money penalties under subsection (a) of section 1320a-7a of this title are imposed and collected under that section.

(d) Report on treatment of small payments

The Secretary shall study and report to Congress, not later than two years after November 14, 1986, on whether information respecting small payments should continue to be required to be reported under subsection (a) of this section and whether information respecting all claims made concerning a medical malpractice action should be required to be reported under such subsection.

(Pub.L. 99-660, Title IV, § 421, Nov. 14, 1986, 100 Stat. 3788.)

§ 422. [42 U.S.C. § 11132]. Reporting of sanctions taken by boards of medical examiners

(a) In general

(1) Actions subject to reporting

Each Board of Medical Examiners—

(A) which revokes or suspends (or otherwise restricts) a physician's license or censures, reprimands, or places on probation a physician, for reasons relating to the physician's professional competence or professional conduct, or

(B) to which a physician's license is surrendered,

shall report, in accordance with section 11134 of this title, the information described in paragraph (2).

(2) Information to be reported

The information to be reported under paragraph (1) is—

(A) the name of the physician involved,

(B) a description of the acts or omissions or other reasons (if known) for the revocation, suspension, or surrender of license, and

(C) such other information respecting the circumstances of the action or surrender as the Secretary deems appropriate.

(b) Failure to report

If, after notice of noncompliance and providing opportunity to correct noncompliance, the Secretary determines that a Board of Medical Examiners has failed to report information in accordance with subsection (a) of this section, the Secretary shall designate another qualified entity for the reporting of information under section 11133 of this title.

(Pub.L. 99-660, Title IV, § 422, Nov. 14, 1986, 100 Stat. 3789.)

§ 423. [42 U.S.C. § 11133]. Reporting of certain professional review actions taken by health care entities

(a) Reporting by health care entities

(1) On physicians

Each health care entity which—

(A) takes a professional review action that adversely affects the clinical privileges of a physician for a period longer than 30 days;

(B) accepts the surrender of clinical privileges of a physician—

(i) while the physician is under an investigation by the entity relating to possible incompetence or improper professional conduct, or

(ii) in return for not conducting such an investigation or proceeding; or

(C) in the case of such an entity which is a professional society, takes a professional review action which adversely affects the membership of a physician in the society, shall report to the Board of Medical Examiners, in accordance with section 11134(a) of this title, the information described in paragraph (3).

(2) Permissive reporting on other licensed health care practitioners

A health care entity may report to the Board of Medical Examiners, in accordance with section 11134(a) of this title, the information described in paragraph (3) in the case of a licensed health care practitioner who is not a physician, if the entity would be required to report such information under paragraph (1) with respect to the practitioner if the practitioner were a physician.

(3) Information to be reported

The information to be reported under this subsection is—

(A) the name of the physician or practitioner involved,

(B) a description of the acts or omissions or other reasons for the action or, if known, for the surrender, and

(C) such other information respecting the circumstances of the action or surrender as the Secretary deems appropriate.

(b) Reporting by Board of Medical Examiners

Each Board of Medical Examiners shall report, in accordance with section 11134 of this title, the information reported to it under subsection (a) of this section and known instances of a health care entity's failure to report information under subsection (a)(1) of this section.

(c) Sanctions

(1) Health care entities

A health care entity that fails substantially to meet the requirement of subsection (a)(1) of this section shall lose the protections of section 11111(a)(1) of this title if the Secretary publishes the name of the entity under section 11111(b) of this title.

(2) Board of Medical Examiners

If, after notice of noncompliance and providing an opportunity to correct noncompliance, the Secretary determines that a Board of Medical Examiners has failed to report information in accordance with subsection (b) of this section, the Secretary shall designate another qualified entity for the reporting of information under subsection (b) of this section.

(d) References to Board of Medical Examiners

Any reference in this subchapter to a Board of Medical Examiners includes, in the case of a Board in a State that fails to meet the reporting requirements of section 11132(a) of this title or subsection (b) of this section, a reference to such other qualified entity as the Secretary designates.

(Pub.L. 99-660, Title IV, § 423, Nov. 14, 1986, 100 Stat. 3789.)

§ 424. [42 U.S.C. § 11134]. Form of reporting

(a) Timing and form

The information required to be reported under sections 11131, 11132(a), and 11133 of this title shall be reported regularly (but not less often than monthly) and in such form and manner as the Secretary prescribes. Such information shall first be required to be reported on a date (not later than one year after November 14, 1986) specified by the Secretary.

(b) To whom reported

The information required to be reported under sections 11131, 11132(a), and 11133(b) of this title shall be reported to the Secretary, or, in the Secretary's discretion, to an appropriate private or public agency which has made suitable arrangements with the Secretary with respect to receipt, storage, protection of confidentiality, and dissemination of the information under this subchapter.

(c) Reporting to State licensing boards

(1) Malpractice payments

Information required to be reported under section 11131 of this title shall also be reported to the appropriate State licensing board (or boards) in the State in which the medical malpractice claim arose.

(2) Reporting to other licensing boards

Information required to be reported under section 11133(b) of this title shall also be reported to the appropriate State licensing board in the State in which the health care entity is located if it is not otherwise reported to such board under subsection (b) of this section.

(Pub.L. 99-660, Title IV, § 424, Nov. 14, 1986, 100 Stat. 3790.)

§ 425. [42 U.S.C. § 11135]. Duty of hospitals to obtain information

(a) In general

It is the duty of each hospital to request from the Secretary (or the agency designated under section 11134(b) of this title), on and after the date information is first required to be reported under section 11134(a) of this title—

(1) at the time a physician or licensed health care practitioner applies to be on the medical staff (courtesy or otherwise) of, or for clinical privileges at, the hospital, information reported under this subchapter concerning the physician or practitioner, and

(2) once every 2 years information reported under this subchapter concerning any physician or such practitioner who is on the medical staff (courtesy or otherwise) of, or has been granted clinical privileges at, the hospital.

A hospital may request such information at other times.

(b) Failure to obtain information

With respect to a medical malpractice action, a hospital which does not request information respecting a physician or practitioner as required under subsection (a) of this section is presumed to have knowledge of any information reported under this subchapter to the Secretary with respect to the physician or practitioner.

(c) Reliance on information provided

Each hospital may rely upon information provided to the hospital under this chapter and shall not be held liable for such reliance in the absence of the hospital's knowledge that the information provided was false.

(Pub.L. 99-660, Title IV, § 425, Nov. 14, 1986, 100 Stat. 3790.)

§ 426. [42 U.S.C. § 11136]. Disclosure and correction of information

With respect to the information reported to the Secretary (or the agency designated under section 11134(b) of this title) under this subchapter respecting a physician or other licensed health care practitioner, the Secretary shall, by regulation, provide for—

(1) disclosure of the information, upon request, to the physician or practitioner, and

(2) procedures in the case of disputed accuracy of the information.

(Pub.L. 99-660, Title IV, § 426, Nov. 14, 1986, 100 Stat. 3791.)

§ 427. [42 U.S.C. § 11137]. Miscellaneous provisions

(a) Providing licensing boards and other health care entities with access to information

The Secretary (or the agency designated under section 11134(b) of this title) shall, upon request, provide information reported under this subchapter with respect to a physician or other licensed health care practitioner to State licensing boards, to hospitals, and to other health care entities (including health maintenance organizations) that have entered (or may be entering) into an employment or affiliation relationship with the physician or practitioner or to which the physician or practitioner has applied for clinical privileges or appointment to the medical staff.

(b) Confidentiality of information

(1) In general

Information reported under this subchapter is considered confidential and shall not be disclosed (other than to the physician or practitioner involved) except with respect to professional review activity, as necessary to carry out subsections (b) and (c) of section 11135 of this title (as specified in regulations by the Secretary), or in accordance with regulations of the Secretary promulgated pursuant to subsection (a) of this section. Nothing in this subsection shall prevent the disclosure of such information by a party which is otherwise authorized, under applicable State law, to make such disclosure. Information reported under this subchapter that is in a form that does not permit the identification of any particular health care entity, physician, other health care practitioner, or patient shall not be considered confidential. The Secretary (or the agency designated under section 11134(b) of this title), on application by any person, shall prepare such information in such form and shall disclose such information in such form.

(2) Penalty for violations

Any person who violates paragraph (1) shall be subject to a civil money penalty of not more than $10,000 for each such violation involved. Such penalty shall be imposed and collected in the same manner as civil money penalties under subsection (a) of section 1320a-7a of this title are imposed and collected under that section.

(3) Use of information

Subject to paragraph (1), information provided under section 11135 of this title and subsection (a) of this section is intended to be used solely with respect to activities in the furtherance of the quality of health care.

(4) Fees

The Secretary may establish or approve reasonable fees for the disclosure of information under this section or section 11136 of this title. The amount of such a fee may not exceed the costs of processing the requests for disclosure and of providing such information. Such fees shall be available to the Secretary (or, in the Secretary's discretion, to the agency designated under section 11134(b) of this title) to cover such costs.

(c) Relief from liability for reporting

No person or entity (including the agency designated under section 11134(b) of this title) shall be held liable in any civil action with respect to any report made under this subchapter (including information provided under subsection (a) of this section[2] without knowledge of the falsity of the information contained in the report.

(d) Interpretation of information

In interpreting information reported under this subchapter, a payment in settlement of a medical malpractice action or claim shall not be construed as creating a presumption that medical malpractice has occurred.

(Pub.L. 99-660, Title IV, § 427, Nov. 14, 1986, 100 Stat. 3791; Pub.L. 100-177, Title IV, § 402(a), (b), Dec. 1, 1987, 101 Stat. 1007.)

§ 431. [42 U.S.C. § 11151]. Definitions

In this chapter:

(1) The term "adversely affecting" includes reducing, restricting, suspending, revoking, denying, or failing to renew clinical privileges or membership in a health care entity.

(2) The term "Board of Medical Examiners" includes a body comparable to such a Board (as determined by the State) with responsibility for the licensing of physicians and also includes a subdivision of such a Board or body.

(3) The term "clinical privileges" includes privileges, membership on the medical staff, and the other circumstances pertaining to the furnishing of medical care under which a physician or other licensed health care practitioner is permitted to furnish such care by a health care entity.

(4) (A) The term "health care entity" means—

(i) a hospital that is licensed to provide health care services by the State in which it is located,

---

[2] So in original. Probably should be followed by a closing parenthesis.

(ii) an entity (including a health maintenance organization or group medical practice) that provides health care services and that follows a formal peer review process for the purpose of furthering quality health care (as determined under regulations of the Secretary), and

(iii) subject to subparagraph (B), a professional society (or committee thereof) of physicians or other licensed health care practitioners that follows a formal peer review process for the purpose of furthering quality health care (as determined under regulations of the Secretary).

(B) The term "health care entity" does not include a professional society (or committee thereof) if, within the previous 5 years, the society has been found by the Federal Trade Commission or any court to have engaged in any anti-competitive practice which had the effect of restricting the practice of licensed health care practitioners.

(5) The term "hospital" means an entity described in paragraphs (1) and (7) of section 1395x(e) of this title.

(6) The terms "licensed health care practitioner" and "practitioner" mean, with respect to a State, an individual (other than a physician) who is licensed or otherwise authorized by the State to provide health care services.

(7) The term "medical malpractice action or claim" means a written claim or demand for payment based on a health care provider's furnishing (or failure to furnish) health care services, and includes the filing of a cause of action, based on the law of tort, brought in any court of any State or the United States seeking monetary damages.

(8) The term "physician" means a doctor of medicine or osteopathy or a doctor of dental surgery or medical dentistry legally authorized to practice medicine and surgery or dentistry by a State (or any individual who, without authority holds himself or herself out to be so authorized).

(9) The term "professional review action" means an action or recommendation of a professional review body which is taken or made in the conduct of professional review activity, which is based on the competence or professional conduct of an individual physician (which conduct affects or could affect adversely the health or welfare of a patient or patients), and which affects (or may affect) adversely the clinical privileges, or membership in a professional society, of the physician. Such term includes a formal decision of a professional review body not to take an action or make a recommendation described in the previous sentence and also includes professional review activities relating to a professional review action. In this chapter, an action is not considered to be based on the competence or professional conduct of a physician if the action is primarily based on—

(A) the physician's association, or lack of association, with a professional society or association,

(B) the physician's fees or the physician's advertising or engaging in other competitive acts intended to solicit or retain business,

(C) the physician's participation in prepaid group health plans, salaried employment, or any other manner of delivering health services whether on a fee-for-service or other basis,

(D) a physician's association with, supervision of, delegation of authority to, support for, training of, or participation in a private group practice with, a member or members of a particular class of health care practitioner or professional, or

(E) any other matter that does not relate to the competence or professional conduct of a physician.

(10) The term "professional review activity" means an activity of a health care entity with respect to an individual physician—

(A) to determine whether the physician may have clinical privileges with respect to, or membership in, the entity,

(B) to determine the scope or conditions of such privileges or membership, or

(C) to change or modify such privileges or membership.

(11) The term "professional review body" means a health care entity and the governing body or any committee of a health care entity which conducts professional review activity, and includes any committee of the medical staff of such an entity when assisting the governing body in a professional review activity.

(12) The term "Secretary" means the Secretary of Health and Human Services.

(13) The term "State" means the 50 States, the District of Columbia, Puerto Rico, the Virgin Islands, Guam, American Samoa, and the Northern Mariana Islands.

(14) The term "State licensing board" means, with respect to a physician or health care provider in a State, the agency of the State which is primarily responsible for the licensing of the physician or provider to furnish health care services.

(Pub.L. 99-660, Title IV, § 431, Nov. 14, 1986, 100 Stat. 3792.)

§ 432 [42 U.S.C. § 11152]. Reports and memoranda of understanding

(a) Annual reports to Congress

The Secretary shall report to Congress, annually during the three years after November 14, 1986, on the implementation of this chapter.

(b) Memoranda of understanding

The Secretary of Health and Human Services shall seek to enter into memoranda of understanding with the Secretary of Defense and the Administrator of Veterans' Affairs to apply the provisions of subchapter II of this chapter to hospitals and other facilities and health care providers under the jurisdiction of the Secretary or Administrator, respectively. The Secretary shall report to Congress, not later than two years after November 14, 1986, on any such memoranda and on the cooperation among such officials in establishing such memoranda.

(c) Memorandum of understanding with Drug Enforcement Administration

The Secretary of Health and Human Services shall seek to enter into a memorandum of understanding with the Administrator of Drug Enforcement relating to providing for the reporting by the Administrator to the Secretary of information respecting physicians and other practitioners whose registration to dispense controlled substances has been suspended or revoked under section 824 of Title 21. The Secretary shall report to Congress, not later than two years after November 14, 1986, on any such memorandum and on the cooperation between the Secretary and the Administrator in establishing such a memorandum.

(Pub.L. 99-660, Title IV, § 432, Nov. 14, 1986, 100 Stat. 3794.)

29

LOCAL GOVERNMENT ANTITRUST ACT OF 1984

§ 2. [15 U.S.C. § 34]. Definitions applicable to sections 34 to 36

For purposes of sections 34 to 36 of this title—

(1) the term "local government" means—

(A) a city, county, parish, town, township, village, or any other general function governmental unit established by State law, or

(B) a school district, sanitary district, or any other special function governmental unit established by State law in one or more States,

(2) the term "person" has the meaning given it in subsection (a) of the first section of the Clayton Act (15 U.S.C. 12(A)), but does not include any local government as defined in paragraph (1) of this section, and

(3) the term "State" has the meaning given it in section 4G(2) of the Clayton Act (15 U.S.C. 15g(2)).

(Pub.L. 98-544, § 2, Oct. 24, 1984, 98 Stat. 2750.)

§ 3. [15 U.S.C. § 35]. Recovery of damages, etc., for antitrust violations from any local government, or official or employee thereof acting in an official capacity

(a) Prohibition in general

No damages, interest on damages, costs, or attorney's fees may be recovered under section 4, 4A, or 4C of the Clayton Act (15 U.S.C. 15, 15a, or 15c) from any local government, or official or employee thereof acting in an official capacity.

(b) Preconditions for attachment of prohibition; prima facie evidence for nonapplication of prohibition

Subsection (a) of this section shall not apply to cases commenced before the effective date of this Act unless the defendant establishes and the court determines, in light of all the circumstances, including the stage of litigation and the availability of alternative relief under the Clayton Act, that it would be inequitable not to apply this subsection to a pending case. In consideration of this section, existence of a jury verdict, district court judgment, or any stage of litigation subsequent thereto, shall be deemed to be prima facie evidence that subsection (a) of this section shall not apply.

(Pub.L. 98-544, § 3, Oct. 24, 1984, 98 Stat. 2750.)

§ 4. [15 U.S.C. § 36]. Recovery of damages, etc., for antitrust violations on claim against person based on official action directed by local government, or official or employee thereof acting in an official capacity

(a) Prohibition in general

No damages, interest on damages, costs or attorney's fees may be recovered under section 4, 4A, or 4C of the Clayton Act (15 U.S.C. 15, 15a, or 15c) in any claim against a person based on any official action directed by a local government, or official or employee thereof acting in an official capacity.

(b) Nonapplication of prohibition for cases commenced before effective date of provisions

Subsection (a) of this section shall not apply with respect to cases commenced before the effective date of this Act.

(Pub.L. 98-544, § 4, Oct. 24, 1984, 98 Stat. 2750.)

30

MCCARRAN-FERGUSON ACT

§ 1. [15 U.S.C. § 1011]. Declaration of policy

Congress hereby declares that the continued regulation and taxation by the several States of the business of insurance is in the public interest, and that silence on the part of the Congress shall not be construed to impose any barrier to the regulation or taxation of such business by the several States.

(Mar. 9, 1945, c. 20, § 1, 59 Stat. 33.)

§ 2. [15 U.S.C. § 1012]. Regulation by State law; Federal law relating specifically to insurance; applicability of certain Federal laws after June 30, 1948

(a) State regulation

The business of insurance, and every person engaged therein, shall be subject to the laws of the several States which relate to the regulation or taxation of such business.

(b) Federal regulation

No Act of Congress shall be construed to invalidate, impair, or supersede any law enacted by any State for the purpose of regulating the business of insurance, or which imposes a fee or tax upon such business, unless such Act specifically relates to the business of insurance: *Provided*, That after June 30, 1948, the Act of July 2, 1890, as amended, known as the Sherman Act, and the Act of October 15, 1914, as amended, known as the Clayton Act, and the Act of September 26, 1914, known as the Federal Trade Commission Act, as amended [15 U.S.C.A. 41 et seq.], shall be applicable to the business of insurance to the extent that such business is not regulated by State law.

(Mar. 9, 1945, c. 20, § 2, 59 Stat. 34; July 25, 1947, c. 326, 61 Stat. 448.)

§ 3. [15 U.S.C. § 1013]. Suspension until June 30, 1948, of application of certain Federal laws; Sherman Act applicable to agreements to, or acts of, boycott, coercion, or intimidation

(a) Until June 30, 1948, the Act of July 2, 1890, as amended, known as the Sherman Act, and the Act of October 15, 1914, as amended, known as the Clayton Act, and the Act of September 26, 1914, known as the Federal Trade Commission Act [15 U.S.C.A. 41 et seq.], and the Act of June 19, 1936, known as the Robinson-Patman Anti-Discrimination Act, shall not apply to the business of insurance or to acts in the conduct thereof.

(b) Nothing contained in this chapter shall render the said Sherman Act inapplicable to any agreement to boycott, coerce, or intimidate, or act of boycott, coercion, or intimidation.

(Mar. 9, 1945, c. 20, § 3, 59 Stat. 34; July 25, 1947, c. 326, 61 Stat. 448.)

§ 4. [15 U.S.C. § 1014]. Effect on other laws

Nothing contained in this chapter shall be construed to affect in any manner the application to the business of insurance of the Act of July 5, 1935, as amended, known as the National Labor Relations Act [29 U.S.C.A.

151 et seq.], or the Act of June 25, 1938, as amended, known as the Fair Labor Standards Act of 1938 [29 U.S.C.A. 201 et seq.], or the Act of June 5, 1920, known as the Merchant Marine Act, 1920 [46 App. U.S.C.A. 861 et seq.].

(Mar. 9, 1945, c. 20, § 4, 59 Stat. 34.)

§ 5. [15 U.S.C. § 1015]. "State" Defined

As used in this chapter, the term "State" includes the several States, Alaska, Hawaii, Puerto Rico, Guam, and the District of Columbia.

(Mar. 9, 1945, c. 20, § 5, 59 Stat. 34; Aug. 1, 1956, c. 852, § 4, 70 Stat. 908.)

31

NATIONAL COOPERATIVE RESEARCH AND PRODUCTION ACT OF 1993 AS AMENDED BY THE STANDARDS DEVELOPMENT ORGANIZATION ADVANCEMENT ACT OF 2004

§ 2. [15 U.S.C. § 4301]. Definitions

(a) For purposes of this chapter:

(1) The term "antitrust laws" has the meaning given it in subsection (a) of section 12 of this title, except that such term includes section 45 of this title to the extent that such section 45 applies to unfair methods of competition.

(2) The term "Attorney General" means the Attorney General of the United States.

(3) The term "Commission" means the Federal Trade Commission.

(4) The term "person" has the meaning given it in subsection (a) of section 12 of this title.

(5) The term "State" has the meaning given it in section 15g(2) of this title.

(6) The term "joint venture" means any group of activities, including attempting to make, making, or performing a contract, by two or more persons for the purpose of—

(A) theoretical analysis, experimentation, or systematic study of phenomena or observable facts,

(B) the development or testing of basic engineering techniques,

(C) the extension of investigative findings or theory of a scientific or technical nature into practical application for experimental and demonstration purposes, including the experimental production and testing of models, prototypes, equipment, materials, and processes,

(D) the production of a product, process, or service,

(E) the testing in connection with the production of a product, process, or service by such venture,

(F) the collection, exchange, and analysis of research or production information, or

(G) any combination of the purposes specified in subparagraphs (A), (B), (C), (D), (E), and (F), and may include the establishment and operation of facilities for the conducting of such venture, the conducting of such venture on a protected and proprietary basis, and the prosecuting of applications for patents and the granting of licenses for the results of such venture, but does not include any activity specified in subsection (b) of this section.

(7) The term "standards development activity" means any action taken by a standards development organization for the purpose of developing, promulgating, revising, amending, reissuing, interpreting, or otherwise maintaining a voluntary consensus standard, or using such standard in conformity assessment activities, including actions relating to the intellectual property policies of the standards development organization.

(8) The term "standards development organization" means a domestic or international organization that plans, develops, establishes, or coordinates voluntary consensus standards using procedures that incorporate the attributes of openness, balance of interests, due process, an appeals process, and consensus in a manner consistent with the Office of Management and Budget Circular Number A-119, as revised February 10, 1998. The term "standards development organization" shall not, for purposes of this chapter, include the parties participating in the standards development organization.

(9) The term "technical standard" has the meaning given such term in section 12(d)(4) of the National Technology Transfer and Advancement Act of 1995.

(10) The term "voluntary consensus standard" has the meaning given such term in Office of Management and Budget Circular Number A-119, as revised February 10, 1998.

(b) The term "joint venture" excludes the following activities involving two or more persons:

(1) exchanging information among competitors relating to costs, sales, profitability, prices, marketing, or distribution of any product, process, or service if such information is not reasonably required to carry out the purpose of such venture,

(2) entering into any agreement or engaging in any other conduct restricting, requiring, or otherwise involving the marketing, distribution, or provision by any person who is a party to such venture of any product, process, or service, other than—

(A) the distribution among the parties to such venture, in accordance with such venture, of a product, process, or service produced by such venture,

(B) the marketing of proprietary information, such as patents and trade secrets, developed through such venture formed under a written agreement entered into before June 10, 1993, or

(C) the licensing, conveying, or transferring of intellectual property, such as patents and trade secrets, developed through such venture formed under a written agreement entered into on or after June 10, 1993,

(3) entering into any agreement or engaging in any other conduct—

(A) to restrict or require the sale, licensing, or sharing of inventions, developments, products, processes, or services not developed through, or produced by, such venture, or

(B) to restrict or require participation by any person who is a party to such venture in other research and development activities,

that is not reasonably required to prevent misappropriation of proprietary information contributed by any person who is a party to such venture or of the results of such venture,

(4) entering into any agreement or engaging in any other conduct allocating a market with a competitor,

(5) exchanging information among competitors relating to production (other than production by such venture) of a product, process, or service if such information is not reasonably required to carry out the purpose of such venture,

(6) entering into any agreement or engaging in any other conduct restricting, requiring, or otherwise involving the production (other than the production by such venture) of a product, process, or service,

(7) using existing facilities for the production of a product, process, or service by such venture unless such use involves the production of a new product or technology, and

(8) except as provided in paragraphs (2), (3), and (6), entering into any agreement or engaging in any other conduct to restrict or require participation by any person who is a party to such venture, in any unilateral or joint activity that is not reasonably required to carry out the purpose of such venture.

(c) The term "standards development activity" excludes the following activities:

(1) Exchanging information among competitors relating to cost, sales, profitability, prices, marketing, or distribution of any product, process, or service that is not reasonably required for the purpose of developing or promulgating a voluntary consensus standard, or using such standard in conformity assessment activities.

(2) Entering into any agreement or engaging in any other conduct that would allocate a market with a competitor.

(3) Entering into any agreement or conspiracy that would set or restrain prices of any good or service.

(Pub.L. 98-462, § 2, Oct. 11, 1984, 98 Stat. 1815; Pub.L. 103-42, § 3(b), (c), June 10, 1993, 107 Stat. 117, 118; Pub.L. 108-237, Title I, § 103, June 22, 2004, 118 Stat. 663.)

§ 3. [15 U.S.C. § 4302]. Rule of reason standard

In any action under the antitrust laws, or under any State law similar to the antitrust laws, the conduct of—

(1) any person in making or performing a contract to carry out a joint venture, or

(2) a standards development organization while engaged in a standards development activity,

shall not be deemed illegal per se; such conduct shall be judged on the basis of its reasonableness, taking into account all relevant factors affecting competition, including, but not limited to, effects on competition in properly defined, relevant research, development, product, process, and service markets. For the purpose of determining a properly defined, relevant market, worldwide capacity shall be considered to the extent that it may be appropriate in the circumstances.

(Pub.L. 98-462, § 3, Oct. 11, 1984, 98 Stat. 1816; Pub.L. 103-42, § 3(d), June 10, 1993, 107 Stat. 119; Pub.L. 108-237, Title I, § 104, June 22, 2004, 118 Stat. 663.)

§ 4. [15 U.S.C. § 4303]. Limitation on recovery

(a) Amount recoverable

Notwithstanding section 15 of this title and in lieu of the relief specified in such section, any person who is entitled to recovery on a claim under such section shall recover the actual damages sustained by such person, interest calculated at the rate specified in section 1961 of Title 28 on such actual damages as specified in subsection (d) of this section, and the cost of suit attributable to such claim, including a reasonable attorney's fee pursuant to section 4304 of this title if such claim—

(1) results from conduct that is within the scope of a notification that has been filed under section 4305(a) of this title for a joint venture, or for a standards development activity engaged in by a standards development organization against which such claim is made, and

(2) is filed after such notification becomes effective pursuant to section 4305(c) of this title.

(b) Recovery by States

Notwithstanding section 15c of this title, and in lieu of the relief specified in such section, any State that is entitled to monetary relief on a claim under such section shall recover the total damage sustained as described in subsection (a)(1) of such section, interest calculated at the rate specified in section 1961 of Title 28 on such total damage as specified in subsection (d) of this section, and the cost of suit attributable to such claim, including a reasonable attorney's fee pursuant to section 15c of this title if such claim—

(1) results from conduct that is within the scope of a notification that has been filed under section 4305(a) of this title for a joint venture, or for a standards development activity engaged in by a standards development organization against which such claim is made, and

(2) is filed after such notification becomes effective pursuant to section 4305(c) of this title.

(c) Conduct similar under State law

Notwithstanding any provision of any State law providing damages for conduct similar to that forbidden by the antitrust laws, any person who is entitled to recovery on a claim under such provision shall not recover in excess of the actual damages sustained by such person, interest calculated at the rate specified in section 1961 of Title 28 on such actual damages as specified in subsection (d) of this section, and the cost of suit attributable to such claim, including a reasonable attorney's fee pursuant to section 4304 of this title if such claim—

(1) results from conduct that is within the scope of a notification that has been filed under section 4305(a) of this title for a joint venture, or for a standards development activity engaged in by a standards development organization against which such claim is made, and

(2) is filed after notification has become effective pursuant to section 4305(c) of this title.

(d) Interest

Interest shall be awarded on the damages involved for the period beginning on the earliest date for which injury can be established and ending on the date of judgment, unless the court finds that the award of all or part of such interest is unjust in the circumstances.

(e) Subsections (a), (b), and (c) of this section shall not be construed to modify the liability under the antitrust laws of any person (other than a standards development organization) who—

(1) directly (or through an employee or agent) participates in a standards development activity with respect to which a violation of any of the antitrust laws is found,

(2) is not a fulltime employee of the standards development organization that engaged in such activity, and

(3) is, or is an employee or agent of a person who is, engaged in a line of commerce that is likely to benefit directly from the operation of the standards development activity with respect to which such violation is found.

(f) Applicability

This section shall be applicable only if the challenged conduct of a person defending against a claim is not in violation of any decree or order, entered or issued after October 11, 1984, in any case or proceeding under the antitrust laws or any State law similar to the antitrust laws challenging such conduct as part of a joint venture, or of a standards development activity engaged in by a standards development organization.

(Pub.L. 98-462, § 4, Oct. 11, 1984, 98 Stat. 1816; Pub.L. 103-42, § 3(e)(1), June 10, 1993, 107 Stat. 119; Pub.L. 108-237, Title I, § 105, June 22, 2004, 118 Stat. 663.)

§ 5. [15 U.S.C. § 4304]. Award of costs, including attorney's fees, to substantially prevailing party; offset

(a) Notwithstanding sections 15 and 26 of this title, in any claim under the antitrust laws, or any State law similar to the antitrust laws, based on the conducting of a joint venture, or of a standards development activity engaged in by a standards development organization, the court shall, at the conclusion of the action—

(1) award to a substantially prevailing claimant the cost of suit attributable to such claim, including a reasonable attorney's fee, or

(2) award to a substantially prevailing party defending against any such claim the cost of suit attributable to such claim, including a reasonable attorney's fee, if the claim, or the claimant's conduct during the litigation of the claim, was frivolous, unreasonable, without foundation, or in bad faith.

(b) The award made under subsection (a) of this section may be offset in whole or in part by an award in favor of any other party for any part of the cost of suit, including a reasonable attorney's fee, attributable to conduct during the litigation by any prevailing party that the court finds to be frivolous, unreasonable, without foundation, or in bad faith.

(c) Subsections (a) and (b) of this section shall not apply with respect to any person who—

(1) directly participates in a standards development activity with respect to which a violation of any of the antitrust laws is found,

(2) is not a fulltime employee of a standards development organization that engaged in such activity, and

(3) is, or is an employee or agent of a person who is, engaged in a line of commerce that is likely to benefit directly from the operation of the standards development activity with respect to which such violation is found.

(Pub.L. 98-462, § 5, Oct. 11, 1984, 98 Stat. 1817; Pub.L. 103-42, § 3(e)(2), June 10, 1993, 107 Stat. 119; Pub.L. 108-237, Title I, § 106, June 22, 2004, 118 Stat. 664.)

§ 6. [15 U.S.C. § 4305]. Disclosure of joint venture

(a) (1) Written notifications; filing

Any party to a joint venture, acting on such venture's behalf, may, not later than 90 days after entering into a written agreement to form such venture or not later than 90 days after October 11, 1984, whichever is later, file simultaneously with the Attorney General and the Commission a written notification disclosing—

(A) the identities of the parties to such venture,

(B) the nature and objectives of such venture, and

(C) if a purpose of such venture is the production of a product, process, or service, as referred to in section 4301(a)(6)(D) of this title, the identity and nationality of any person who is a party to such venture, or who controls any party to such venture whether separately or with one or more other persons acting as a group for the purpose of controlling such party.

Any party to such venture, acting on such venture's behalf, may file additional disclosure notifications pursuant to this section as are appropriate to extend the protections of section 4303 of this title. In order to maintain the protections of section 4303 of this title, such venture shall, not later than 90 days after a change in its membership, file simultaneously with the Attorney General and the Commission a written notification disclosing such change.

(2) A standards development organization may, not later than 90 days after commencing a standards development activity engaged in for the purpose of developing or promulgating a voluntary consensus standards or not later than 90 days after June 22, 2004, whichever is later, file simultaneously with the Attorney General and the Commission, a written notification disclosing—

(A) the name and principal place of business of the standards development organization, and

(B) documents showing the nature and scope of such activity.

Any standards development organization may file additional disclosure notifications pursuant to this section as are appropriate to extend the protections of section 4303 of this title to standards development activities that are not covered by the initial filing or that have changed significantly since the initial filing.

(b) Publication; Federal Register; notice

Except as provided in subsection (e) of this section, not later than 30 days after receiving a notification filed under subsection (a) of this section, the Attorney General or the Commission shall publish in the Federal Register a notice with respect to such venture that identifies the parties to such venture and that describes in general terms the area of planned activity of such venture, or a notice with respect to such standards development activity that identifies the standards development organization engaged in such activity and that describes such activity in general terms. Prior to its publication, the contents of such notice shall be made available to the parties to such venture or available to such organization, as the case may be.

(c) Effect of notice

If with respect to a notification filed under subsection (a) of this section, notice is published in the Federal Register, then such notification shall operate to convey the protections of section 4303 of this title as of the earlier of—

(1) the date of publication of notice under subsection (b) of this section, or

(2) if such notice is not so published within the time required by subsection (b) of this section, after the expiration of the 30-day period beginning on the date the Attorney General or the Commission receives the applicable information described in subsection (a) of this section.

(d) Exemption; disclosure; information

Except with respect to the information published pursuant to subsection (b) of this section—

(1) all information and documentary material submitted as part of a notification filed pursuant to this section, and

(2) all other information obtained by the Attorney General or the Commission in the course of any investigation, administrative proceeding, or case, with respect to a potential violation of the antitrust laws by the joint venture, or the standards development activity, with respect to which such notification was filed,

shall be exempt from disclosure under section 552 of Title 5, and shall not be made publicly available by any agency of the United States to which such section applies except in a judicial or administrative proceeding in which such information and material is subject to any protective order.

(e) Withdrawal of notification

Any person or standards development organization that files a notification pursuant to this section may withdraw such notification before notice of the joint venture involved is published under subsection (b) of this section. Any notification so withdrawn shall not be subject to subsection (b) of this section and shall not confer the protections of section 4303 of this title on any person or any standards development organization with respect to whom such notification was filed.

(f) Judicial review; inapplicable with respect to notifications

Any action taken or not taken by the Attorney General or the Commission with respect to notifications filed pursuant to this section shall not be subject to judicial review.

(g) Admissibility into evidence; disclosure of conduct; publication of notice; supporting or answering claims under antitrust laws

(1) Except as provided in paragraph (2), for the sole purpose of establishing that a person or standards development organization is entitled to the protections of section 4303 of this title, the fact of disclosure of conduct under subsection (a) of this section and the fact of publication of a notice under subsection (b) of this section shall be admissible into evidence in any judicial or administrative proceeding.

(2) No action by the Attorney General or the Commission taken pursuant to this section shall be admissible into evidence in any such proceeding for the purpose of supporting or answering any claim under the antitrust laws or under any State law similar to the antitrust laws.

(Pub.L. 98-462, § 6, Oct. 11, 1984, 98 Stat. 1818; Pub.L. 103-42, § 3(f), June 10, 1993, 107 Stat. 119; Pub.L. 108-237, Title I, § 107, June 22, 2004, 118 Stat. 664.)

§ 7. [15 U.S.C. § 4306]. Application of section 4303 protections to production of products, processes, and services

Notwithstanding sections 4303 and 4305 of this title, the protections of section 4303 of this title shall not apply with respect to a joint venture's production of a product, process, or service, as referred to in section 4301(a)(6)(D) of this title, unless—

(1) the principal facilities for such production are located in the United States or its territories, and

(2) each person who controls any party to such venture (including such party itself) is a United States person, or a foreign person from a country whose law accords antitrust treatment no less favorable to United States persons than to such country's domestic persons with respect to participation in joint ventures for production.

(Pub.L. 98-462, § 7, as added Pub.L. 103-42, § 3(g), June 10, 1993, 107 Stat. 119.)

32

NEWSPAPER PRESERVATION ACT OF 1970

§ 2. [15 U.S.C. § 1801]. Congressional declaration of policy

In the public interest of maintaining a newspaper press editorially and reportorially independent and competitive in all parts of the United States, it is hereby declared to be the public policy of the United States to preserve the publication of newspapers in any city, community, or metropolitan area where a joint operating arrangement has been heretofore entered into because of economic distress or is hereafter effected in accordance with the provisions of this chapter.

(Pub.L. 91-353, § 2, July 24, 1970, 84 Stat. 466.)

§ 3. [15 U.S.C. § 1802]. Definitions

As used in this chapter—

(1) The term "antitrust law" means the Federal Trade Commission Act [15 U.S.C.A. § 41 et seq.] and each statute defined by section 4 thereof [15 U.S.C.A. § 44] as "Antitrust Acts" and all amendments to such Act and such statutes and any other Acts in pari materia.

(2) The term "joint newspaper operating arrangement" means any contract, agreement, joint venture (whether or not incorporated), or other arrangement entered into by two or more newspaper owners for the publication of two or more newspaper publications, pursuant to which joint or common production facilities are established or operated and joint or unified action is taken or agreed to be taken with respect to any one or more of the following: printing; time, method, and field of publication; allocation of production facilities; distribution; advertising solicitation; circulation solicitation; business department; establishment of advertising rates; establishment of circulation rates and revenue distribution: *Provided*, That there is no merger, combination, or amalgamation of editorial or reportorial staffs, and that editorial policies be independently determined.

(3) The term "newspaper owner" means any person who owns or controls directly, or indirectly through separate or subsidiary corporations, one or more newspaper publications

(4) The term "newspaper publication" means a publication produced on newsprint paper which is published in one or more issues weekly (including as one publication any daily newspaper and any Sunday newspaper published by the same owner in the same city, community, or metropolitan area), and in which a substantial portion of the content is devoted to the dissemination of news and editorial opinion.

(5) The term "failing newspaper" means a newspaper publication which, regardless of its ownership or affiliations, is in probable danger of financial failure.

(6) The term "person" means any individual, and any partnership, corporation, association, or other legal entity existing under or authorized by the law of the United States, any State or possession of the United States, the District of Columbia, the Commonwealth of Puerto Rico, or any foreign country.

(Pub.L. 91-353, § 3, July 24, 1970, 84 Stat. 466.)

§ 4. [15 U.S.C. § 1803]. Antitrust exemptions

(a) Joint operating arrangements entered into prior to July 24, 1970

It shall not be unlawful under any antitrust law for any person to perform, enforce, renew, or amend any joint newspaper operating arrangement entered into prior to July 24, 1970, if at the time at which such arrangement was first entered into, regardless of ownership or affiliations, not more than one of the newspaper publications involved in the performance of such arrangement was likely to remain or become a financially sound publication: *Provided*, That the terms of a renewal or amendment to a joint operating arrangement must be filed with the Department of Justice and that the amendment does not add a newspaper publication or newspaper publications to such arrangement.

(b) Written consent for future joint operating arrangements

It shall be unlawful for any person to enter into, perform, or enforce a joint operating arrangement, not already in effect, except with the prior written consent of the Attorney General of the United States. Prior to granting such approval, the Attorney General shall determine that not more than one of the newspaper publications involved in the arrangement is a publication other than a failing newspaper, and that approval of such arrangement would effectuate the policy and purpose of this chapter.

(c) Predatory practices not exempt

Nothing contained in the chapter shall be construed to exempt from any antitrust law any predatory pricing, any predatory practice, or any other conduct in the otherwise lawful operations of a joint newspaper operating arrangement which would be unlawful under any antitrust law if engaged in by a single entity. Except as provided in this chapter, no joint newspaper operating arrangement or any party thereto shall be exempt from any antitrust law.

(Pub.L. 91-353, § 4, July 24, 1970, 84 Stat. 467.)

§ 5. [15 U.S.C. § 1804]. Reinstatement of joint operating arrangements previously adjudged unlawful under antitrust laws

(a) Notwithstanding any final judgment rendered in any action brought by the United States under which a joint operating arrangement has been held to be unlawful under any antitrust law, any party to such final judgment may reinstitute said joint newspaper operating arrangement to the extent permissible under section 1803(a) of this title.

(b) The provisions of section 1803 of this title shall apply to the determination of any civil or criminal action pending in any district court of the United State[1] on July 24, 1970, in which it is

---

[1] So in original. Probably should be "States".

alleged that any such joint operating agreement is unlawful under any antitrust law.

(Pub.L. 91-353, § 5, July 24, 1970, 84 Stat. 467.)

33

NORRIS LAGUARDIA ACT

§ 1. [29 U.S.C. § 101]. Issuance of restraining orders and injunctions; limitation; public policy

No court of the United States, as defined in this chapter, shall have jurisdiction to issue any restraining order or temporary or permanent injunction in a case involving or growing out of a labor dispute, except in a strict conformity with the provisions of this chapter; nor shall any such restraining order or temporary or permanent injunction be issued contrary to the public policy declared in this chapter.

(Mar. 23, 1932, c. 90, § 1, 47 Stat. 70.)

§ 2. [29 U.S.C. § 102]. Public policy in labor matters declared

In the interpretation of this chapter and in determining the jurisdiction and authority of the courts of the United States, as such jurisdiction and authority are defined and limited in this chapter, the public policy of the United States is declared as follows:

Whereas under prevailing economic conditions, developed with the aid of governmental authority for owners of property to organize in the corporate and other forms of ownership association, the individual unorganized worker is commonly helpless to exercise actual liberty of contract and to protect his freedom of labor, and thereby to obtain acceptable terms and conditions of employment, wherefore, though he should be free to decline to associate with his fellows, it is necessary that he have full freedom of association, self-organization, and designation of representatives of his own choosing, to negotiate the terms and conditions of his employment, and that he shall be free from the interference, restraint, or coercion of employers of labor, or their agents, in the designation of such representatives or in self-organization or in other concerted activities for the purpose of collective bargaining or other mutual aid or protection; therefore, the following definitions of and limitations upon the jurisdiction and authority of the courts of the United States are enacted.

(Mar. 23, 1932, c. 90, § 2, 47 Stat. 70.)

§ 3. [29 U.S.C. § 103]. Nonenforceability of undertakings in conflict with public policy; "yellow dog" contracts

Any undertaking or promise, such as is described in this section, or any other undertaking or promise in conflict with the public policy declared in section 102 of this title, is declared to be contrary to the public policy of the United States, shall not be enforceable in any court of the United States and shall not afford any basis for the granting of legal or equitable relief by any such court, including specifically the following:

Every undertaking or promise hereafter made, whether written or oral, express or implied, constituting or contained in any contract or agreement of hiring or employment between any individual, firm, company, association, or corporation, and any employee or prospective employee of the same, whereby

(a) Either party to such contract or agreement undertakes or promises not to join, become, or remain a member of any labor organization or of any employer organization; or

(b) Either party to such contract or agreement undertakes or promises that he will withdraw from an employment relation in the event that he joins, becomes, or remains a member of any labor organization or of any employer organization.

(Mar. 23, 1932, c. 90, § 3, 47 Stat. 70.)

§ 4. [29 U.S.C. § 104]. Enumeration of specific acts not subject to restraining orders or injunctions

No court of the United States shall have jurisdiction to issue any restraining order or temporary or permanent injunction in any case involving or growing out of any labor dispute to prohibit any person or persons participating or interested in such dispute (as these terms are herein defined) from doing, whether singly or in concert, any of the following acts:

(a) Ceasing or refusing to perform any work or to remain in any relation of employment;

(b) Becoming or remaining a member of any labor organization or of any employer organization, regardless of any such undertaking or promise as is described in section 103 of this title;

(c) Paying or giving to, or withholding from, any person participating or interested in such labor dispute, any strike or unemployment benefits or insurance, or other moneys or things of value;

(d) By all lawful means aiding any person participating or interested in any labor dispute who is being proceeded against in, or is prosecuting, any action or suit in any court of the United States or of any State;

(e) Giving publicity to the existence of, or the facts involved in, any labor dispute, whether by advertising, speaking, patrolling, or by any other method not involving fraud or violence;

(f) Assembling peaceably to act or to organize to act in promotion of their interests in a labor dispute;

(g) Advising or notifying any person of an intention to do any of the acts heretofore specified;

(h) Agreeing with other persons to do or not to do any of the acts heretofore specified; and

(i) Advising, urging, or otherwise causing or inducing without fraud or violence the acts heretofore specified, regardless of any such undertaking or promise as is described in section 103 of this title.

(Mar. 23, 1932, c. 90, § 4, 47 Stat. 70.)

§ 5. [29 U.S.C. § 105]. Doing in concert of certain acts as constituting unlawful combination or conspiracy subjecting person to injunctive remedies

No court of the United States shall have jurisdiction to issue a restraining order or temporary or permanent injunction upon the ground that any of the persons participating or interested in a labor dispute constitute or are engaged in an unlawful combination or conspiracy because of the doing in concert of the acts enumerated in section 104 of this title.

(Mar. 23, 1932, c. 90, § 5, 47 Stat. 71.)

§ 6. [29 U.S.C. § 106]. Responsibility of officers and members of associations or their organizations for unlawful acts of individual officers, members, and agents

No officer or member of any association or organization, and no association or organization participating or interested in a labor dispute, shall be held responsible or liable in any court of the United States for the unlawful acts of individual officers, members, or agents, except upon clear proof of actual participation in, or actual authorization of, such acts, or of ratification of such acts after actual knowledge thereof.

(Mar. 23, 1932, c. 90, § 6, 47 Stat. 71.)

§ 7. [29 U.S.C. § 107]. Issuance of injunctions in labor disputes; hearing; findings of court; notice to affected persons; temporary restraining order; undertakings

No court of the United States shall have jurisdiction to issue a temporary or permanent injunction in any case involving or growing out of a labor dispute, as defined in this chapter, except after hearing the testimony of witnesses in open court (with opportunity for cross-examination) in support of the allegations of a complaint made under oath, and testimony in opposition thereto, if offered, and except after findings of fact by the court, to the effect—

(a) That unlawful acts have been threatened and will be committed unless restrained or have been committed and will be continued unless restrained, but no injunction or temporary restraining order shall be issued on account of any threat or unlawful act excepting against the person or persons, association, or organization making the threat or committing the unlawful act or actually authorizing or ratifying the same after actual knowledge thereof;

(b) That substantial and irreparable injury to complainant's property will follow;

(c) That as to each item of relief granted greater injury will be inflicted upon complainant by the denial of relief than will be inflicted upon defendants by the granting of relief;

(d) That complainant has no adequate remedy at law; and

(e) That the public officers charged with the duty to protect complainant's property are unable or unwilling to furnish adequate protection.

Such hearing shall be held after due and personal notice thereof has been given, in such manner as the court shall direct, to all known persons against whom relief is sought, and also to the chief of those public officials of the county and city within which the unlawful acts have been threatened or committed charged with the duty to protect complainant's property: Provided, however, That if a complainant shall also allege that, unless a temporary restraining order shall be issued without notice, a substantial and irreparable injury to complainant's property will be unavoidable, such a temporary restraining order may be issued upon testimony under oath, sufficient, if sustained, to justify the court in issuing a temporary injunction upon a hearing after notice. Such a temporary restraining order shall be effective for no longer than five days and shall become void at the expiration of said five days. No temporary restraining order or temporary injunction shall be issued except on condition that complainant shall first file an undertaking with adequate security in an amount to be fixed by the court sufficient to recompense those enjoined for any loss, expense, or damage caused by the improvident or erroneous issuance of such order or injunction, including all reasonable costs (together with a reasonable attorney's fee) and expense of defense against the order or against the granting of any injunctive relief sought in the same proceeding and subsequently denied by the court.

The undertaking mentioned in this section shall be understood to signify an agreement entered into by the complainant and the surety upon which a decree may be rendered in the same suit or proceeding against said complainant and surety, upon a hearing to assess damages of which hearing complainant and surety shall have reasonable notice, the said complainant and surety submitting themselves to the jurisdiction of the court for that purpose. But nothing in this section contained shall deprive any party having a claim or cause of action under or upon such undertaking from electing to pursue his ordinary remedy by suit at law or in equity.

(Mar. 23, 1932, c. 90, § 7, 47 Stat. 71.)

§ 8. [29 U.S.C. § 108]. Noncompliance with obligations involved in labor disputes or failure to settle by negotiation or arbitration as preventing injunctive relief

No restraining order or injunctive relief shall be granted to any complainant who has failed to comply with any obligation imposed by law which is involved in the labor dispute in question, or who has failed to make every reasonable effort to settle such dispute either by negotiation or with the aid of any available governmental machinery of mediation or voluntary arbitration.

(Mar. 23, 1932, c. 90, § 8, 47 Stat. 72.)

§ 9. [29 U.S.C. § 109]. Granting of restraining order or injunction as dependent on previous findings of fact; limitation on prohibitions included in restraining orders and injunctions

No restraining order or temporary or permanent injunction shall be granted in a case involving or growing out of a labor dispute, except on the basis of findings of fact made and filed by the court in the record of the case prior to the issuance of such restraining order or injunction; and every restraining order or injunction granted in a case involving or growing out of a labor dispute shall include only a prohibition of such specific act or acts as may be expressly complained of in the bill of complaint or petition filed in such case and as shall be expressly included in said findings of fact made and filed by the court as provided in this chapter.

(Mar. 23, 1932, c. 90, § 9, 47 Stat. 72.)

§ 10. [29 U.S.C. § 110]. Review by court of appeals of issuance or denial of temporary injunctions; record

Whenever any court of the United States shall issue or deny any temporary injunction in a case involving or growing out of a labor dispute, the court shall, upon the request of any party to the proceedings and on his filing the usual bond for costs, forthwith certify as in ordinary cases the record of the case to the court of appeals for its review. Upon the filing of such record in the court of appeals, the appeal shall be heard and the temporary injunctive order affirmed, modified, or set aside expeditiously.

(Mar. 23, 1932, c. 90, § 10, 47 Stat. 72; June 25, 1948, c. 646, § 32(a), 62 Stat. 991; May 24, 1949, c. 139, § 127, 63 Stat. 107; Nov. 8, 1984, Pub.L. 98-620, Title IV, § 402(30), 98 Stat. 3359.)

§§ 11, 12 [29 U.S.C. §§ 111, 112]. Repealed. June 25, 1948, c. 645, § 21, 62 Stat. 862, eff. Sept. 1, 1948

§ 13. [29 U.S.C. § 113]. Definitions of terms and words used in chapter

When used in this chapter, and for the purposes of this chapter—

(a) A case shall be held to involve or to grow out of a labor dispute when the case involves persons who are engaged in the same industry, trade, craft, or occupation; or have direct or indirect interests therein; or who are employees of the same employer; or who are members of the same or an affiliated organization of employers or employees; whether such dispute is (1) between one or more employers or associations of employers and one or more employees or associations of employees; (2) between one or more employers or associations of employers and one or more employers or associations of employers; or (3) between one or more employees or associations of employees and one or more employees or associations of employees; or when the case involves any conflicting or competing interests in a "labor dispute" (as defined in this section) of "persons participating or interested" therein (as defined in this section).

(b) A person or association shall be held to be a person participating or interested in a labor dispute if relief is sought against him or it, and if he or it is engaged in the same industry, trade, craft, or occupation in which such dispute occurs, or has a direct or indirect interest therein, or is a member, officer, or agent of any association composed in whole or in part of employers or employees engaged in such industry, trade, craft, or occupation.

(c) The term "labor dispute" includes any controversy concerning terms or conditions of employment, or concerning the association or representation of persons in negotiating, fixing, maintaining, changing, or seeking to arrange terms or conditions of employment, regardless of whether or not the disputants stand in the proximate relation of employer and employee.

(d) The term "court of the United States" means any court of the United States whose jurisdiction has been or may be conferred or defined or limited by Act of Congress, including the courts of the District of Columbia.

(Mar. 23, 1932, c. 90, § 13, 47 Stat. 73.)

§ 14. [29 U.S.C. § 114]. Separability

If any provision of this chapter or the application thereof to any person or circumstance is held unconstitutional or otherwise invalid, the remaining provisions of this chapter and the application of such provisions to other persons or circumstances shall not be affected thereby.

(Mar. 23, 1932, c. 90, § 14, 47 Stat. 73.)

§ 15. [29 U.S.C. § 115]. Repeal of conflicting acts

All acts and parts of acts in conflict with the provisions of this chapter are repealed.

(Mar. 23, 1932, c. 90, § 15, 47 Stat. 73.)

34

PENSION FUNDING EQUITY ACT OF 2004

§207 [15 U.S.C. § 37b]. Confirmation of Antitrust Status of Graduate Medical Resident Matching Programs

(a) Findings and Purposes

(1) Findings

Congress makes the following findings:

(A) For over 50 years, most United States medical school seniors and the large majority of graduate medical education programs (popularly known as "residency programs") have chosen to use a matching program to match medical students with residency programs to which they have applied. These matching programs have been an integral part of an educational system that has produced the finest physicians and medical researchers in the world.

(B) Before such matching programs were instituted, medical students often felt pressure, at an unreasonably early stage of their medical education, to seek admission to, and accept offers from, residency programs. As a result, medical students often made binding commitments before they were in a position to make an informed decision about a medical specialty or a residency program and before residency programs could make an informed assessment of students' qualifications. This situation was inefficient, chaotic, and unfair and it often led to placements that did not serve the interests of either medical students or residency programs.

(C) The original matching program, now operated by the independent non-profit National Resident Matching Program and popularly known as "the Match," was developed and implemented more than 50 years ago in response to widespread student complaints about the prior process. This Program includes on its board of directors individuals nominated by medical student organizations as well as by major medical education and hospital associations.

(D) The Match uses a computerized mathematical algorithm, as students had recommended, to analyze the preferences of students and residency programs and match students with their highest preferences from among the available positions in residency programs that listed them. Students thus obtain a residency position in the most highly ranked program on their list that has ranked them sufficiently high among its preferences. Each year, about 85 percent of participating United States medical students secure a place in one of their top 3 residency program choices.

(E) Antitrust lawsuits challenging the matching process, regardless of their merit or lack thereof, have the potential to undermine this highly efficient, pro-competitive, and long-standing process. The costs of defending such litigation would divert the scarce resources of our country's teaching hospitals and medical schools from their crucial missions of patient care, physician training, and medical research. In addition, such costs may lead to abandonment of the matching process, which has effectively served the interests of medical students, teaching hospitals, and patients for over half a century.

(2) Purposes

It is the purpose of this section to—

(A) confirm that the antitrust laws do not prohibit sponsoring, conducting, or participating in a graduate medical education residency matching program, or agreeing to do so; and

(B) ensure that those who sponsor, conduct or participate in such matching programs are not subjected to the burden and expense of defending against litigation that challenges such matching programs under the antitrust laws.

(b) Application of antitrust laws to graduate medical education residency matching programs

(1) Definitions

In this subsection:

(A) Antitrust Laws

The term "antitrust laws"—

(i) has the meaning given such term in subsection (a) of section 12 of this title, except that such term includes section 45 of this title to the extent such section 45 of this title applies to unfair methods of competition; and

(ii) includes any State law similar to the laws referred to in clause (i).

(B) Graduate Medical Education Program

The term "graduate medical education program" means—

(i) a residency program for the medical education and training of individuals following graduation from medical school;

(ii) a program, known as a specialty or subspecialty fellowship program, that provides more advanced training; and

(iii) an institution or organization that operates, sponsors or participates in such a program.

(C) Graduate medical education residency matching program

The term "graduate medical education residency matching program" means a program (such as those conducted by the National Resident Matching Program) that, in connection with the admission of students to graduate medical education programs, uses an algorithm and matching rules to match students in accordance with the preferences of students and the preferences of graduate medical education programs.

(D) Student

The term "student" means any individual who seeks to be admitted to a graduate medical education program.

(2) Confirmation of antitrust status

It shall not be unlawful under the antitrust laws to sponsor, conduct, or participate in a graduate medical education residency matching program, or to agree to sponsor, conduct, or participate in such a program. Evidence of any of the conduct described in the preceding sentence shall not be admissible in Federal court to support any claim or action alleging a violation of the antitrust laws.

(3) Applicability

Nothing in this section shall be construed to exempt from the antitrust laws any agreement on the part of 2 or more graduate medical education programs to fix the amount of the stipend or other benefits received by students participating in such programs.

(c) Effective date

This section shall take effect on April 10, 2004, shall apply to conduct whether it occurs prior to, on, or after April 10, 2004, and shall apply to all judicial and administrative actions or other proceedings pending on April 10, 2004.

(Pub.L. 108-218, Title II, § 207, Apr. 10, 2004, 118 Stat. 611.)

35

REVENUE ACT OF 1916

§ 800 [15 U.S.C. § 71]. "Person" defined

When used in this subchapter the term "person" includes partnerships, corporations, and associations.

(Sept. 8, 1916, c. 463, Title VIII, § 800, 39 Stat. 798.)

§ 802 [15 U.S.C. § 73]. Agreements involving restrictions in favor of imported goods

If any article produced in a foreign country is imported into the United States under any agreement, understanding, or condition that the importer thereof or any other person in the United States shall not use, purchase, or deal in, or shall be restricted in his using, purchasing, or dealing in, the articles of any other person, there shall be levied, collected, and paid thereon, in addition to the duty otherwise imposed by law, a special duty equal to double the amount of such duty: Provided, That the above shall not be interpreted to prevent the establishing in this country on the part of a foreign producer of an exclusive agency for the sale in the United States of the products of said foreign producer or merchant, nor to prevent such exclusive agent from agreeing not to use, purchase, or deal in the article of any other person, but this proviso shall not be construed to exempt from the provisions of this section any article imported by such exclusive agent if such agent is required by the foreign producer or if it is agreed between such agent and such foreign producer that any agreement, understanding or condition set out in this section shall be imposed by such agent upon the sale or other disposition of such article to any person in the United States.

(Sept. 8, 1916, c. 463, Title VIII, § 802, 39 Stat. 799.)

§ 803 [15 U.S.C. § 74]. Rules and regulations

The Secretary of the Treasury shall make such rules and regulations as are necessary for the carrying out of the provisions of section 73 of this title.

(Sept. 8, 1916, c. 463, Title VIII, § 803, 39 Stat. 799.)

§ 804 [15 U.S.C. § 75]. Retaliation against country prohibiting importations

Whenever any country, dependency, or colony shall prohibit the importation of any article the product of the soil or industry of the United States and not injurious to health or morals, the President shall have power to prohibit, during the period such prohibition is in force, the importation into the United States of similar articles, or in case the United States does not import similar articles from that country, then other articles, the products of such country, dependency, or colony.

And the Secretary of the Treasury, with the approval of the President, shall make such rules and regulations as are necessary for the execution of the provisions of this section.

(Sept. 8, 1916, c. 463, Title VIII, § 804, 39 Stat. 799.)

36

SENTENCING REFORM ACT

[18 U.S.C. § 3571]. Sentence of fine

(a) In general.—A defendant who has been found guilty of an offense may be sentenced to pay a fine.

(b) Fines for individuals.—Except as provided in subsection (e) of this section, an individual who has been found guilty of an offense may be fined not more than the greatest of—

(1) the amount specified in the law setting forth the offense;

(2) the applicable amount under subsection (d) of this section;

(3) for a felony, not more than $250,000;

(4) for a misdemeanor resulting in death, not more than $250,000;

(5) for a Class A misdemeanor that does not result in death, not more than $100,000;

(6) for a Class B or C misdemeanor that does not result in death, not more than $5,000; or

(7) for an infraction, not more than $5,000.

(c) Fines for organizations.—Except as provided in subsection (e) of this section, an organization that has been found guilty of an offense may be fined not more than the greatest of—

(1) the amount specified in the law setting forth the offense;

(2) the applicable amount under subsection (d) of this section;

(3) for a felony, not more than $500,000;

(4) for a misdemeanor resulting in death, not more than $500,000;

(5) for a Class A misdemeanor that does not result in death, not more than $200,000;

(6) for a Class B or C misdemeanor that does not result in death, not more than $10,000; and

(7) for an infraction, not more than $10,000.

(d) Alternative fine based on gain or loss.—If any person derives pecuniary gain from the offense, or if the offense results in pecuniary loss to a person other than the defendant, the defendant may be fined not more than the greater of twice the gross gain or twice the gross loss, unless imposition of a fine under this subsection would unduly complicate or prolong the sentencing process.

(e) Special rule for lower fine specified in substantive provision.— If a law setting forth an offense specifies no fine or a fine that is lower than the fine otherwise applicable under this section and such law, by specific reference, exempts the offense from the applicability of the fine otherwise applicable under this section, the defendant may not be fined more than the amount specified in the law setting forth the offense.

(Added Pub.L. 98-473, Title II, § 212(a)(2), Oct. 12, 1984, 98 Stat. 1995, and amended Pub.L. 100-185, § 6, Dec. 11, 1987, 101 Stat. 1280.)

37

USA PATRIOT IMPROVEMENT AND REAUTHORIZATION ACT OF 2005

[18 U.S.C. § 2516]. Authorization for interception of wire, oral, or electronic communications

(1) The Attorney General, Deputy Attorney General, Associate Attorney General, or any Assistant Attorney General, any acting Assistant Attorney General, or any Deputy Assistant Attorney General or acting Deputy Assistant Attorney General in the Criminal Division or National Security Division specially designated by the Attorney General, may authorize an application to a Federal judge of competent jurisdiction for, and such judge may grant in conformity with section 2518 of this chapter [18 USCS § 2518] an order authorizing or approving the interception of wire or oral communications by the Federal Bureau of Investigation, or a Federal agency having responsibility for the investigation of the offense as to which the application is made, when such interception may provide or has provided evidence of—

***

(r) any criminal violation of section 1 (relating to illegal restraints of trade or commerce), 2 (relating to illegal monopolizing of trade or commerce), or 3 (relating to illegal restraints of trade or commerce in territories or the District of Columbia) of the Sherman Act (15 U.S.C. 1, 2, 3).

Added Pub.L. 90-351, Title III, § 802, June 19, 1968, 82 Stat. 216; amended Pub.L. 91-452, Title VIII, § 810, Title IX, § 902(a), Title XI, § 1103, Oct. 15, 1970, 84 Stat. 940, 947, 959; Pub.L. 91-644, Title IV, § 16, Jan. 2, 1971, 84 Stat. 1891; Pub.L. 95-598, Title III, § 314(h), Nov. 6, 1978, 92 Stat. 2677; Pub.L. 97-285, §§ 2(e), 4(e), Oct. 6, 1982, 96 Stat. 1220, 1221; Pub.L. 98-292, § 8, May 21, 1984, 98 Stat. 206; Pub.L. 98-473, Title II, § 1203(c), Oct. 12, 1984, 98 Stat. 2152; Pub.L. 99-508, Title I, §§ 101(c)(1)(A), 104, 105, Oct. 21, 1986, 100 Stat. 1851, 1855; Pub.L. 99-570, Title I, § 1365(c), Oct. 27, 1986, 100 Stat. 3207-35; Pub.L. 100-690, Title VI, § 6461, Title VII, §§ 7036, 7053(d), 7525, Nov. 18, 1988, 102 Stat. 4374, 4399, 4402, 4502; Pub.L. 101-298, § 3(b), May 22, 1990, 104 Stat. 203; Pub.L. 101-647, Title XXV, § 2531, Title XXXV, § 3568, Nov. 29, 1990, 104 Stat. 4879, 4928; Pub.L. 103-272, § 5(e)(11), July 5, 1994, 108 Stat. 1374; Pub.L. 103-322, Title XXXIII, §§ 330011(c)(1), (q)(1), (r), 330021(1), Sept. 13, 1994, 108 Stat. 2144, 2145, 2150; Pub.L. 103-414, Title II, § 208, Oct. 25, 1994, 108 Stat. 4292; Pub.L. 103-429, § 7(a)(4)(A), Oct. 31, 1994, 108 Stat. 4389; Pub.L. 104-132, Title IV, § 434, Apr. 24, 1996, 110 Stat. 1274; Pub.L. 104-208, Div. C, Title II, § 201, Sept. 30, 1996, 110 Stat. 3009-564; Pub.L. 104-287, § 6(a)(2), Oct. 11, 1996, 110 Stat. 3398; Pub.L. 104-294, Title I, § 102, Title VI, § 601(d), Oct. 11, 1996, 110 Stat. 3491, 3499; Pub.L. 105-318, § 6(b), Oct. 30, 1998, 112 Stat. 3011; Pub.L. 106-181, Title V, § 506(c)(2)(B), Apr. 5, 2000, 114 Stat. 139; Pub.L. 107-56, Title II, §§ 201, 202, Oct. 26, 2001, 115 Stat. 278; Pub.L. 107-197, Title III, § 301(a), June 25, 2002, 116 Stat. 728; Pub.L. 107-273, Div. B, Title IV, §§ 4002(c)(1), 4005(a)(1), Nov. 2, 2002, 116 Stat. 1808, 1812; Pub.L. 108-21, Title II, § 201, Apr. 30, 2003, 117 Stat. 659; Pub.L. 108-458, Title VI, § 6907, Dec. 17, 2004, 118 Stat. 3774; Pub.L. 109-162, Title XI, § 1171(b), Jan. 5, 2006, 119 Stat.

3123; Pub.L. 109-177, Title I, §§ 110(b)(3)(C), 113, Title V, § 506(a)(6), Mar. 9, 2006, 120 Stat. 208, 209, 248; Pub.L. 112-127, § 4, June 5, 2012, 126 Stat. 371; Pub.L. 112-186, § 5, Oct. 5, 2012, 126 Stat. 1429.)

38

WEBB-PROMERENE ACT OF 1918

§ 1 [15 U.S.C. § 61]. Export trade; definitions

The words "export trade" wherever used in this subchapter mean solely trade or commerce in goods, wares, or merchandise exported, or in the course of being exported from the United States or any Territory thereof to any foreign nation; but the words "export trade" shall not be deemed to include the production, manufacture, or selling for consumption or for resale, within the United States or any Territory thereof, of such goods, wares, or merchandise, or any act in the course of such production, manufacture, or selling for consumption or for resale.

The words "trade within the United States" wherever used in this subchapter mean trade or commerce among the several States or in any Territory of the United States, or in the District of Columbia, or between any such Territory and another, or between any such Territory or Territories and any State or States or the District of Columbia, or between the District of Columbia and any State or States.

The word "association" wherever used in this subchapter means any corporation or combination, by contract or otherwise, of two or more persons, partnerships, or corporations.

(Apr. 10, 1918, c. 50, § 1, 40 Stat. 516.)

§ 2 [15 U.S.C. § 62]. Export trade and antitrust legislation

Nothing contained in the Sherman Act [15 U.S.C.A. § 1 et seq.] shall be construed as declaring to be illegal an association entered into for the sole purpose of engaging in export trade and actually engaged solely in such export trade, or an agreement made or act done in the course of export trade by such association, provided such association, agreement, or act is not in restraint of trade within the United States, and is not in restraint of the export trade of any domestic competitor of such association: *Provided*, That such association does not, either in the United States or elsewhere, enter into any agreement, understanding, or conspiracy, or do any act which artificially or intentionally enhances or depresses prices within the United States of commodities of the class exported by such association, or which substantially lessens competition within the United States or otherwise restrains trade therein.

(Apr. 10, 1918, c. 50, § 2, 40 Stat. 517.)

§ 3 [15 U.S.C. § 63]. Acquisition of stock of export trade corporation

Nothing contained in section 18 of this title shall be construed to forbid the acquisition or ownership by any corporation of the whole or any part of the stock or other capital of any corporation organized solely for the purpose of engaging in export trade, and actually engaged solely in such export trade, unless the effect of such acquisition or ownership may be to restrain trade or substantially lessen competition within the United States.

(Apr. 10, 1918, c. 50, § 3, 40 Stat. 517.)

§ 4 [15 U.S.C. § 64]. Unfair methods of competition in export trade

The prohibition against "unfair methods of competition" and the remedies provided for enforcing said prohibition contained in the Federal Trade Commission Act [15 U.S.C.A. § 41 et seq.] shall be construed as extending to unfair methods of competition used in export trade against competitors engaged in export trade, even though the acts constituting such unfair methods are done without the territorial jurisdiction of the United States.

(Apr. 10, 1918, c. 50, § 4, 40 Stat. 517.)

§ 5 [15 U.S.C. § 65]. Information required from export trade corporation; powers of Federal Trade Commission

Every association which engages solely in export trade, within thirty days after its creation, shall file with the Federal Trade Commission a verified written statement setting forth the location of its offices or places of business and the names and addresses of all its officers and of all its stockholders or members, and if a corporation, a copy of its certificate or articles of incorporation and bylaws, and if unincorporated, a copy of its articles or contract of association, and on the 1st day of January of each year every association engaged solely in export trade shall make a like statement of the location of its offices or places of business and the names and addresses of all its officers and of all its stockholders or members and of all amendments to and changes in its articles or certificate of incorporation or in its articles or contract of association. It shall also furnish to the Commission such information as the Commission may require as to its organization, business, conduct, practices, management, and relation to other associations, corporations, partnerships, and individuals. Any association which shall fail so to do shall not have the benefit of the provisions of sections 62 and 63 of this title, and it shall also forfeit to the United States the sum of $100 for each and every day of the continuance of such failure, which forfeiture shall be payable into the Treasury of the United States, and shall be recoverable in a civil suit in the name of the United States brought in the district where the association has its principal office, or in any district in which it shall do business. It shall be the duty of the various United States attorneys, under the direction of the Attorney General of the United States, to prosecute for the recovery of the forfeiture. The costs and expenses of such prosecution shall be paid out of the appropriation for the expenses of the courts of the United States.

Whenever the Federal Trade Commission shall have reason to believe that an association or any agreement made or act done by such association is in restraint of trade within the United States or in restraint of the export trade of any domestic competitor of such association, or that an association either in the United States or elsewhere has entered into any agreement, understanding, or conspiracy, or done any act which artificially or intentionally enhances or depresses prices within the United States of commodities of the class exported by such association, or which substantially lessens competition within the United States or otherwise restrains trade therein, it shall summon such association, its officers, and agents to appear before it, and thereafter conduct an investigation into the alleged violations of law. Upon investigation, if it shall conclude that the law has been violated, it may make to such association recommendations for the readjustment of its business, in order that it may thereafter maintain its organization and management and conduct its business in accordance with law. If such association fails to comply with the recommendations of the Federal Trade Commission, said Commission shall refer its findings and recommendations to the Attorney General of the United States for such action thereon as he may deem proper.

For the purpose of enforcing these provisions the Federal Trade Commission shall have all the powers, so far as applicable, given it in the Federal Trade Commission Act [15 U.S.C.A. § 41 et seq.].

(Apr. 10, 1918, c. 50, § 5, 40 Stat. 517; June 25, 1948, c. 646, § 1, 62 Stat. 909.)

§ 6 [15 U.S.C. § 66]. Short title

This subchapter may be cited as the "Webb-Pomerene Act."

(Apr. 10, 1918, c. 50, § 6, as added Sept. 30, 1976, Pub.L. 94-435, Title III, § 305(c), 90 Stat. 1397.)

39

THE WILSON TARIFF ACT

§ 73 [15 U.S.C. § 8]. Trusts in restraint of import trade illegal; penalty

Every combination, conspiracy, trust, agreement, or contract is declared to be contrary to public policy, illegal, and void when the same is made by or between two or more persons or corporations, either of whom, as agent or principal, is engaged in importing any article from any foreign country into the United States, and when such combination, conspiracy, trust, agreement, or contract is intended to operate in restraint of lawful trade, or free competition in lawful trade or commerce, or to increase the market price in any part of the United States of any article or articles imported or intended to be imported into the United States, or of any manufacture into which such imported article enters or is intended to enter. Every person who shall be engaged in the importation of goods or any commodity from any foreign country in violation of this section, or who shall combine or conspire with another to violate the same, is guilty of a misdemeanor, and on conviction thereof in any court of the United States such person shall be fined in a sum not less than $100 and not exceeding $5,000, and shall be further punished by imprisonment, in the discretion of the court, for a term not less than three months nor exceeding twelve months.

(Aug. 27, 1894, c. 349, § 73, 28 Stat. 570; Feb. 12, 1913, c. 40, 37 Stat. 667.)

§ 74 [15 U.S.C. § 9]. Jurisdiction of courts; duty of United States attorneys; procedure

The several district courts of the United States are invested with jurisdiction to prevent and restrain violations of section 8 of this title; and it shall be the duty of the several United States attorneys, in their respective districts, under the direction of the Attorney General, to institute proceedings in equity to prevent and restrain such violations. Such proceedings may be by way of petitions setting forth the case and praying that such violations shall be enjoined or otherwise prohibited. When the parties complained of shall have been duly notified of such petition the court shall proceed, as soon as may be, to the hearing and determination of the case; and pending such petition and before final decree, the court may at any time make such temporary restraining order or prohibition as shall be deemed just in the premises.

(Aug. 27, 1894, c. 349, § 74, 28 Stat. 570; Mar. 3, 1911, c. 231, § 291, 36 Stat. 1167; June 25, 1948, c. 646, § 1, 62 Stat. 909.)

§ 75 [15 U.S.C. § 10]. Bringing in additional parties

Whenever it shall appear to the court before which any proceeding under section 9 of this title may be pending, that the ends of justice require that other parties should be brought before the court, the court may cause them to be summoned, whether they reside in the district in which the court is held or not; and subpoenas to that end may be served in any district by the marshal thereof.

(Aug. 27, 1894, c. 349, § 75, 28 Stat. 570.)

§ 76[15 U.S.C. § 11]. Forfeiture of property in transit

Any property owned under any contract or by any combination, or pursuant to any conspiracy, and being the subject thereof, mentioned in section 8 of this title, imported into and being within the United States or being in the course of transportation from one State to another, or to or from a Territory or the District of Columbia, shall be forfeited to the United States, and may be seized and condemned by like proceedings as those provided by law for the forfeiture, seizure, and condemnation of property imported into the United States contrary to law.

(Aug. 27, 1894, c. 349, § 76, 28 Stat. 570; Feb. 12, 1913, c. 40, 37 Stat. 667.)

PART 6

TREATIES AND INTERNATIONAL AGREEMENTS

40

TREATY ON THE FUNCTIONING OF THE EUROPEAN UNION

(1957)

Article 1

By this Treaty, the HIGH CONTRACTING PARTIES establish among themselves a EUROPEAN ECONOMIC COMMUNITY.

Article 2 (ex Article 2)

The Community shall have as its task, by establishing a common market and an economic and monetary union and by implementing common policies or activities referred to in Articles 3 and 4, to promote throughout the Community a harmonious, balanced and sustainable development of economic activities, a high level of employment and of social protection, equality between men and women, sustainable and non-inflationary growth, a high degree of competitiveness and convergence of economic performance, a high level of protection and improvement of the quality of the environment, the raising of the standard of living and quality of life, and economic and social cohesion and solidarity among Member States.

Article 3 (as amended)

1. For the purposes set out in Article 2, the activities of the Community shall include, as provided in this Treaty and in accordance with the timetable set out therein:

   (a) the prohibition, as between Member States, of customs duties and quantitative restrictions on the import and export of goods, and of all other measures having equivalent effect;

   (b) a common commercial policy;

   (c) an internal market characterized by the abolition, as between Member States, of obstacles to the free movement of goods, persons, services and capital;

   . . .

   (g) a system ensuring that competition in the internal market is not distorted;

   (h) the approximation of the laws of Member States to the extent required for the functioning of the common market;

   . . .

   (m) the strengthening of the competitiveness of Community industry;

   (n) the promotion of research and technological development;

   . . .

   (t) a contribution to the strengthening of consumer protection;

   (u) measures in the spheres of energy, civil protection and tourism.

2. In all the activities referred to in this Article, the Community shall aim to eliminate inequalities, and to promote equality, between men and women.

* * *

Article 101 (ex Article 81)*

1. The following shall be prohibited as incompatible with the common market: all agreements between undertakings, decisions by associations of undertakings and concerted practices which may affect trade between Member States and which have as their object or effect the prevention, restriction or distortion of competition within the common market, and in particular those which:

   (a) directly or indirectly fix purchase or selling prices or any other trading conditions;

   (b) limit or control production, markets, technical development, or investment;

   (c) share markets or sources of supply;

   (d) apply dissimilar conditions to equivalent transactions with other trading parties, thereby placing them at a competitive disadvantage;

   (e) make the conclusion of contracts subject to acceptance by the other parties of supplementary obligations which, by their nature or according to commercial usage, have no connection with the subject of such contracts.

2. Any agreements or decisions prohibited pursuant to this article shall be automatically void.

3. The provisions of paragraph 1 may, however, be declared inapplicable in the case of:

   —any agreement or category of agreements between undertakings;

   —any decision or category of decisions by associations of undertakings;

   —any concerted practice or category of concerted practices;

   which contributes to improving the production or distribution of goods or to promoting technical or economic progress, while allowing consumers a fair share of the resulting benefit, and which does not:

   (a) impose on the undertakings concerned restrictions which are not indispensable to the attainment of these objectives;

   (b) afford such undertakings the possibility of eliminating competition in respect of a substantial part of the products in question.

Article 102 (ex Article 82)**

Any abuse by one or more undertakings of a dominant position within the common market or in a substantial part of it shall be prohibited as incompatible with the common market in so far as it may affect trade between Member States.

---

* Amendments to other sections of the Treaty have caused Article 81 to be renumbered Article 101.

** Ibid.

Such abuse may, in particular, consist in:

(a) directly or indirectly imposing unfair purchase or selling prices or other unfair trading conditions;

(b) limiting production, markets or technical development to the prejudice of consumers;

(c) applying dissimilar conditions to equivalent transactions with other trading parties, thereby placing them at a competitive disadvantage;

(d) making the conclusion of contracts subject to acceptance by the other parties of supplementary obligations which, by their nature or according to commercial usage, have no connection with the subject of such contracts.

41

INTERNATIONAL ANTITRUST ENFORCEMENT ASSISTANCE ACT OF 1994

§ 2 [15 U.S.C. § 6201]. Disclosure to foreign antitrust authority of antitrust evidence.

In accordance with an antitrust mutual assistance agreement in effect under this chapter, subject to section 6207 of this title, and except as provided in section 6204 of this title, the Attorney General of the United States and the Federal Trade Commission may provide to a foreign antitrust authority with respect to which such agreement is in effect under this chapter, antitrust evidence to assist the foreign antitrust authority—

(1) in determining whether a person has violated or is about to violate any of the foreign antitrust laws administered or enforced by the foreign antitrust authority, or

(2) in enforcing any of such foreign antitrust laws.

(Pub.L. 103-438, § 2, Nov. 2, 1994, 108 Stat. 4597.)

§ 3 [15 U.S.C. § 6202]. Investigations to assist foreign antitrust authority in obtaining antitrust evidence

(a) Request for investigative assistance

A request by a foreign antitrust authority for investigative assistance under this section shall be made to the Attorney General, who may deny the request in whole or in part. No further action shall be taken under this section with respect to any part of a request that has been denied by the Attorney General.

(b) Authority to investigate

In accordance with an antitrust mutual assistance agreement in effect under this chapter, subject to section 6207 of this title, and except as provided in section 6204 of this title, the Attorney General and the Commission may, using their respective authority to investigate possible violations of the Federal antitrust laws, conduct investigations to obtain antitrust evidence relating to a possible violation of the foreign antitrust laws administered or enforced by the foreign antitrust authority with respect to which such agreement is in effect under this chapter, and may provide such antitrust evidence to the foreign antitrust authority, to assist the foreign antitrust authority—

(1) in determining whether a person has violated or is about to violate any of such foreign antitrust laws, or

(2) in enforcing any of such foreign antitrust laws.

(c) Special scope of authority

An investigation may be conducted under subsection (b) of this section, and antitrust evidence obtained through such investigation may be provided, without regard to whether the conduct investigated violates any of the Federal antitrust laws.

(d) Rights and privileges preserved

A person may not be compelled in connection with an investigation under this section to give testimony or a statement, or to produce a document or other thing, in violation of any legally applicable right or privilege.

(Pub.L. 103-438, § 3, Nov. 2, 1994, 108 Stat. 4597.)

§ 4 [15 U.S.C. § 6203]. Jurisdiction of district courts of United States

(a) Authority of district courts

On the application of the Attorney General made in accordance with an antitrust mutual assistance agreement in effect under this chapter, the United States district court for the district in which a person resides, is found, or transacts business may order such person to give testimony or a statement, or to produce a document or other thing, to the Attorney General to assist a foreign antitrust authority with respect to which such agreement is in effect under this chapter—

(1) in determining whether a person has violated or is about to violate any of the foreign antitrust laws administered or enforced by the foreign antitrust authority, or

(2) in enforcing any of such foreign antitrust laws.

(b) Contents of order

(1) Use of appointee to receive evidence

(A) An order issued under subsection (a) of this section may direct that testimony or a statement be given, or a document or other thing be produced, to a person who shall be recommended by the Attorney General and appointed by the court.

(B) A person appointed under subparagraph (A) shall have power to administer any necessary oath and to take such testimony or such statement.

(2) Practice and procedure

(A) An order issued under subsection (a) of this section may prescribe the practice and procedure for taking testimony and statements and for producing documents and other things.

(B) Such practice and procedure may be in whole or in part the practice and procedure of the foreign state, or the regional economic integration organization, represented by the foreign antitrust authority with respect to which the Attorney General requests such order.

(C) To the extent such order does not prescribe otherwise, any testimony and statements required to be taken shall be taken, and any documents and other things required to be produced shall be produced, in accordance with the Federal Rules of Civil Procedure.

(c) Rights and privileges preserved

A person may not be compelled under an order issued under subsection (a) of this section to give testimony or a statement, or to produce a document or other thing, in violation of any legally applicable right or privilege.

(d) Voluntary conduct

This section does not preclude a person in the United States from voluntarily giving testimony or a statement, or producing a document or other thing, in any manner acceptable to such person for use in an investigation by a foreign antitrust authority.

(Pub.L. 103-438, § 4, Nov. 2, 1994, 108 Stat. 4599.)

§ 5 [15 U.S.C. § 6204]. Limitations on authority

Sections 6201, 6202, and 6203 of this title shall not apply with respect to the following antitrust evidence:

(1) Antitrust evidence that is received by the Attorney General or the Commission under section 18a of this title. Nothing in this paragraph shall affect the ability of the Attorney General or the Commission to disclose to a foreign antitrust authority antitrust evidence that is obtained otherwise than under section 18a of this title.

(2) Antitrust evidence that is matter occurring before a grand jury and with respect to which disclosure is prevented by Federal law, except that for the purpose of applying Rule 6(e)(3)(C)(iv) of the Federal Rules of Criminal Procedure with respect to this section—

(A) a foreign antitrust authority with respect to which a particularized need for such antitrust evidence is shown shall be considered to be an appropriate official of any of the several States, and

(B) a foreign antitrust law administered or enforced by the foreign antitrust authority shall be considered to be a State criminal law.

(3) Antitrust evidence that is specifically authorized under criteria established by Executive Order 12356, or any successor to such order, to be kept secret in the interest of national defense or foreign policy, and—

(A) that is classified pursuant to such order or such successor, or

(B) with respect to which a determination of classification is pending under such order or such successor.

(4) Antitrust evidence that is classified under section 2162 of Title 42.

(Pub.L. 103-438, § 5, Nov. 2, 1994, 108 Stat. 4599.)

§ 6 [15 U.S.C. § 6205]. Exception to certain disclosure restrictions

Section 1313 of this title, and sections 46(f) and 57b-2 of this title, shall not apply to prevent the Attorney General or the Commission from providing to a foreign antitrust authority antitrust evidence in accordance with an antitrust mutual assistance agreement in effect under this chapter and in accordance with the other requirements of this chapter.

§ 7 [15 U.S.C. § 6206]. Publication requirements applicable to antitrust mutual assistance agreements

(a) Publication of proposed antitrust mutual assistance agreements

Not less than 45 days before an antitrust mutual assistance agreement is entered into, the Attorney General, with the concurrence of the Commission, shall publish in the Federal Register—

(1) the proposed text of such agreement and any modification to such proposed text, and

(2) a request for public comment with respect to such text or such modification, as the case may be.

(b) Publication of proposed amendments to antitrust mutual assistance agreements in effect

Not less than 45 days before an agreement is entered into that makes an amendment to an antitrust mutual assistance agreement, the Attorney General, with the concurrence of the Commission, shall publish in the Federal Register—

(1) the proposed text of such amendment, and

(2) a request for public comment with respect to such amendment.

(c) Publication of antitrust mutual assistance agreements, amendments, and terminations

Not later than 45 days after an antitrust mutual assistance agreement is entered into or terminated, or an agreement that makes an amendment to an antitrust mutual assistance agreement is entered into, the Attorney General, with the concurrence of the Commission, shall publish in the Federal Register—

(1) the text of the antitrust mutual assistance agreement or amendment, or the terms of the termination, as the case may be, and

(2) in the case of an agreement that makes an amendment to an antitrust mutual assistance agreement, a notice containing—

(A) citations to the locations in the Federal Register at which the text of the antitrust mutual assistance agreement that is so amended, and of any previous amendments to such agreement, are published, and

(B) a description of the manner in which a copy of the antitrust mutual assistance agreement, as so amended, may be obtained from the Attorney General and the Commission.

(d) Condition for validity

An antitrust mutual assistance agreement, or an agreement that makes an amendment to an antitrust mutual assistance agreement, with respect to which publication does not occur in accordance with subsections (a), (b), and (c) of this section shall not be considered to be in effect under this chapter.

(Pub.L. 103-438, § 7, Nov. 2, 1994, 108 Stat. 4600.)

§ 8 [15 U.S.C. § 6207]. Conditions on use of antitrust mutual assistance agreements

(a) Determinations.

Neither the Attorney General nor the Commission may conduct an investigation under section 6202 of this title, apply for an order under section 6203 of this title, or provide antitrust evidence to a foreign antitrust authority under an antitrust mutual assistance agreement, unless the Attorney General or the Commission, as the case may be, determines in the particular instance in which the investigation, application, or antitrust evidence is requested that—

(1) the foreign antitrust authority—

(A) will satisfy the assurances, terms, and conditions described in subparagraphs (A), (B), and (E) of section 6211(2) of this title, and

(B) is capable of complying with and will comply with the confidentiality requirements applicable under such agreement to the requested antitrust evidence,

(2) providing the requested antitrust evidence will not violate section 6204 of this title, and

(3) conducting such investigation, applying for such order, or providing the requested antitrust evidence, as the case may be, is consistent with the public interest of the United States, taking into consideration, among other factors, whether the foreign state or regional economic integration organization represented by the foreign antitrust authority holds any proprietary interest that could benefit or otherwise be affected by such investigation, by the granting of such order, or by the provision of such antitrust evidence.

(b) Limitation on disclosure of certain antitrust evidence

Neither the Attorney General nor the Commission may disclose in violation of an antitrust mutual assistance agreement any antitrust evidence received under such agreement, except that such agreement may not prevent the disclosure of such antitrust evidence to a defendant in an action or proceeding brought by the Attorney General or the Commission for a violation of any of the Federal laws if such disclosure would otherwise be required by Federal law.

(c) Required Disclosure of Notice Received.

If the Attorney General or the Commission receives a notice described in section 6211(2)(H) of this title, the Attorney General or the Commission, as the case may be, shall transmit such notice to the person that provided the evidence with respect to which such notice is received.

(Pub.L. 103-438, § 8, Nov. 2, 1994, 108 Stat. 4601.)

§ 9 [15 U.S.C. § 6208]. Limitations on judicial review

(a) Determinations

Determinations made under paragraphs (1) and (3) of section 6207(a) of this title shall not be subject to judicial review.

(b) Citations to and descriptions of confidentiality laws

Whether an antitrust mutual assistance agreement satisfies section 6211(2)(C) of this title shall not be subject to judicial review.

(c) Rules of construction

(1) Administrative procedure act

The requirements in section 6206 of this title with respect to publication and request for public comment shall not be construed to create any availability of judicial review under chapter 7 of Title 5.

(2) Laws referenced in section 6204 of this title.

Nothing in this section shall be construed to affect the availability of judicial review under laws referred to in section 6204 of this title.

(Pub.L. 103-438, § 9, Nov. 2, 1994, 108 Stat. 4602.)

§ 10 [15 U.S.C. § 6209]. Preservation of existing authority

(a) In general

The authority provided by this chapter is in addition to, and not in lieu of, any other authority vested in the Attorney General, the Commission, or any other officer of the United States.

(b) Attorney General and Commission

This chapter shall not be construed to modify or affect the allocation of responsibility between the Attorney General and the Commission for the enforcement of the Federal antitrust laws.

(Pub.L. 103-438, § 10, Nov. 2, 1994, 108 Stat. 4602.)

§ 11 [15 U.S.C. § 6210]. Report to Congress

In the 30-day period beginning 3 years after November 2, 1994, and with the concurrence of the Commission, the Attorney General shall submit, to the Speaker of the House of Representatives and the President pro tempore of the Senate, a report—

(1) describing how the operation of this chapter has affected the enforcement of the Federal antitrust laws,

(2) describing the extent to which foreign antitrust authorities have complied with the confidentiality requirements applicable under antitrust mutual assistance agreements in effect under this chapter,

(3) specifying separately the identities of the foreign states, regional economic integration organizations, and foreign antitrust authorities that have entered into such agreements and the identities of the foreign antitrust authorities with respect to which such foreign states and such organizations have entered into such agreements,

(4) specifying the identity of each foreign state, and each regional economic integration organization, that has in effect a law similar to this chapter,

(5) giving the approximate number of requests made by the Attorney General and the Commission under such agreements to foreign antitrust authorities for antitrust investigations and for antitrust evidence,

(6) giving the approximate number of requests made by foreign antitrust authorities under such agreements to the Attorney General and the Commission for investigations under section 6202 of this title, for orders under section 6203 of this title, and for antitrust evidence, and

(7) describing any significant problems or concerns of which the Attorney General is aware with respect to the operation of this chapter.

(Pub.L. 103-438, § 11, Nov. 2, 1994, 108 Stat. 4602.)

§ 12 [15 U.S.C. § 6211]. Definitions

For purposes of this chapter:

(1) The term "antitrust evidence" means information, testimony, statements, documents, or other things that are obtained in anticipation of, or during the course of, an investigation or proceeding under any of the Federal antitrust laws or any of the foreign antitrust laws.

(2) The term "antitrust mutual assistance agreement" means a written agreement, or written memorandum of understanding, that is entered into by the United States and a foreign state or regional economic integration organization (with respect to the foreign antitrust authorities of such foreign state or such organization, and such other governmental entities of such foreign state or such organization as the Attorney General and the Commission jointly determine may be necessary in order to provide the assistance described in subparagraph (A)), or jointly by the Attorney General and the Commission and a foreign antitrust authority, for the purpose of conducting investigations under section 6202 of this title, applying for orders under section 6203 of this title, or providing antitrust evidence, on a reciprocal basis and that includes the following:

(A) An assurance that the foreign antitrust authority will provide to the Attorney General and the Commission assistance that is comparable in scope to the assistance the Attorney General and the Commission provide under such agreement or such memorandum.

(B) An assurance that the foreign antitrust authority is subject to laws and procedures that are adequate to maintain securely the confidentiality of antitrust evidence that may be received under section 6201, 6202, or 6203 of this title and will give protection to antitrust evidence received under such section that is not less than the protection provided under the laws of the United States to such antitrust evidence.

(C) Citations to and brief descriptions of the laws of the United States, and the laws of the foreign state or regional economic integration organization represented by the foreign antitrust authority, that protect the confidentiality of antitrust evidence that may be provided under such agreement or such memorandum. Such citations and such descriptions shall include the enforcement mechanisms and penalties applicable under such laws and, with respect to a regional economic integration organization, the applicability of such laws, enforcement mechanisms, and penalties to the foreign states composing such organization.

(D) Citations to the Federal antitrust laws, and the foreign antitrust laws, with respect to which such agreement or such memorandum applies.

(E) Terms and conditions that specifically require using, disclosing, or permitting the use or disclosure of, antitrust evidence received under such agreement or such memorandum only—

(i) for the purpose of administering or enforcing the foreign antitrust laws involved, or

(ii) with respect to a specified disclosure or use requested by a foreign antitrust authority and essential to a significant law enforcement objective, in accordance with the prior written consent that the Attorney General or the Commission, as the case may be, gives after—

(I) determining that such antitrust evidence is not otherwise readily available with respect to such objective,

(II) making the determinations described in paragraphs (2) and (3) of section 6207(a) of this title, with respect to such disclosure or use, and

(III) making the determinations applicable to a foreign antitrust authority under section 6207(a)(1) of this title (other than the determination regarding the assurance described in subparagraph (A) of this paragraph), with respect to each additional governmental entity, if any, to be provided such antitrust evidence in the course of such disclosure or use, after having received adequate written assurances applicable to each such governmental entity.

(F) An assurance that antitrust evidence received under section 6201, 6202, or 6203 of this title from the Attorney General or the Commission, and all copies of such evidence, in the possession or control of the foreign antitrust authority will be returned to the Attorney General or the Commission, respectively, at the conclusion of the foreign investigation or proceeding with respect to which such evidence was so received.

(G) Terms and conditions that specifically provide that such agreement or such memorandum will be terminated if—

(i) the confidentiality required under such agreement or such memorandum is violated with respect to antitrust evidence, and

(ii) adequate action is not taken both to minimize any harm resulting from the violation and to ensure that the confidentiality required under such agreement or such memorandum is not violated again.

(H) Terms and conditions that specifically provide that if the confidentiality required under such agreement or such memorandum is violated with respect to antitrust evidence, notice of the violation will be given—

(i) by the foreign antitrust authority promptly to the Attorney General or the Commission with respect to antitrust evidence provided by the Attorney General or the Commission, respectively, and

(ii) by the Attorney General or the Commission to the person (if any) that provided such evidence to the Attorney General or the Commission.

(3) The term "Attorney General" means the Attorney General of the United States.

(4) The term "Commission" means the Federal Trade Commission.

(5) The term "Federal antitrust laws" has the meaning given the term "antitrust laws" in subsection (a) of section 12 of this title but also includes section 45 of this title to the extent that such section 45 applies to unfair methods of competition.

(6) The term "foreign antitrust authority" means a governmental entity of a foreign state or of a regional economic integration organization that is vested by such state or such organization with authority to enforce the foreign antitrust laws of such state or such organization.

(7) The term "foreign antitrust laws" means the laws of a foreign state, or of a regional economic integration organization, that are substantially similar to any of the Federal antitrust laws and that prohibit conduct similar to conduct prohibited under the Federal antitrust laws.

(8) The term "person" has the meaning given such term in subsection (a) of section 12 of this title.

(9) The term "regional economic integration organization" means an organization that is constituted by, and composed of, foreign states, and on which such foreign states have conferred sovereign authority to make decisions that are binding on such foreign states, and that are directly applicable to and binding on persons within such foreign states, including the decisions with respect to—

(A) administering or enforcing the foreign antitrust laws of such organization, and

(B) prohibiting and regulating disclosure of information that is obtained by such organization in the course of administering or enforcing such laws.

(Pub.L. 103-438, § 12, Nov. 2, 1994, 108 Stat. 4603.)

§ 13 [15 U.S.C. § 6212]. Authority to receive reimbursement

The Attorney General and the Commission are authorized to receive from a foreign antitrust authority, or from the foreign state or regional economic integration organization represented by such foreign antitrust authority, reimbursement for the costs incurred by the Attorney General or the

Commission, respectively, in conducting an investigation under section 6202 of this title requested by such foreign antitrust authority, applying for an order under section 6203 of this title to assist such foreign antitrust authority, or providing antitrust evidence to such foreign antitrust authority under an antitrust mutual assistance agreement in effect under this chapter with respect to such foreign antitrust authority.

(Pub.L. 103-438, § 13, Nov. 2, 1994, 108 Stat. 4605.)

42

AGREEMENT BETWEEN THE GOVERNMENT OF THE UNITED STATES OF AMERICA AND THE EUROPEAN COMMUNITIES ON THE APPLICATION OF POSITIVE COMITY PRINCIPLES IN THE ENFORCEMENT OF THEIR COMPETITION LAWS

(1998)

THE GOVERNMENT OF THE UNITED STATES OF AMERICA of the one part, and THE EUROPEAN COMMUNITY AND THE EUROPEAN COAL AND STEEL COMMUNITY of the other part (hereinafter "the European Communities"):

Having regard to the September 23, 1991 Agreement between the Government of the United States of America and the European Communities Regarding the Application of Their Competition Laws, and the exchange of interpretative letters dated May 31 and July 31, 1995 in relation to that Agreement (together hereinafter "the 1991 Agreement");

Recognizing that the 1991 Agreement has contributed to coordination, cooperation, and avoidance of conflicts in competition law enforcement;

Noting in particular Article V of the 1991 Agreement, commonly referred to as the "Positive Comity" Article, which calls for cooperation regarding anticompetitive activities occurring in the territory of one Party that adversely affect the interests of the other Party;

Believing that further elaboration of the principles of positive comity and of the implementation of those principles would enhance the 1991 Agreement's effectiveness in relation to such conduct; and

Noting that nothing in this Agreement or its implementation shall be construed as prejudicing either Party's position on issues of competition law jurisdiction in the international context,

HAVE AGREED AS FOLLOWS:

ARTICLE I

Scope and Purpose of this Agreement

1. This Agreement applies where a Party satisfies the other that there is reason to believe that the following circumstances are present:

(a) anticompetitive activities are occurring in whole or in substantial part in the territory of one of the Parties and are adversely affecting the interests of the other Party; and

(b) the activities in question are impermissible under the competition laws of the Party in the territory of which the activities are occurring.

2. The purposes of this Agreement are to:

(a) help ensure that trade and investment flows between the Parties and competition and consumer welfare within the territories of the Parties are not impeded by anticompetitive activities for which the competition laws of one or both Parties can provide a remedy, and

(b) establish cooperative procedures to achieve the most effective and efficient enforcement of competition law, whereby the competition authorities of each Party will normally avoid allocating enforcement resources to dealing with anticompetitive activities that occur principally in and are directed principally towards the other Party's territory, where the competition authorities of the other Party are able and prepared to examine and take effective sanctions under their law to deal with those activities.

ARTICLE II

Definitions

As used in this Agreement:

1. "Adverse effects" and "adversely affected" mean harm caused by anticompetitive activities to:

(a) the ability of firms in the territory of a Party to export to, invest in, or otherwise compete in the territory of the other Party, or

(b) competition in a Party's domestic or import markets.

2. "Requesting Party" means a Party that is adversely affected by anticompetitive activities occurring in whole or in substantial part in the territory of the other Party.

3. "Requested Party" means a Party in the territory of which such anticompetitive activities appear to be occurring.

4. "Competition law(s)" means

(a) for the European Communities, Articles 85, 86, and 89 of the Treaty establishing the European Community (EC), Articles 65 and 66(7) of the Treaty establishing the European Coal and Steel Community (ECSC), and their implementing instruments, to the exclusion of Council Regulation (EEC) No 4064/89 on the control of concentrations between undertakings, and

(b) for the United States of America, the Sherman Act (15 U.S.C. §§1–7), the Clayton Act (15 U.S.C. §§12–27, except as it relates to investigations pursuant to Title II of the Hart-Scott-Rodino Antitrust Improvements Act of 1976, 15 U.S.C. §18a), the Wilson Tariff Act (15 U.S.C. §§8–11), and the Federal Trade Commission Act (15 U.S.C. §§41–58, except as these sections relate to consumer protection functions),

as well as such other laws or regulations as the Parties shall jointly agree in writing to be a "competition law" for the purposes of this Agreement.

5. "Competition authorities" means:

(a) for the European Communities, the Commission of the European Communities, as to its responsibilities pursuant to the competition laws of the European Communities, and

(b) for the United States, the Antitrust Division of the United States Department of Justice and the Federal Trade Commission.

6. "Enforcement activities" means any application of competition law by way of investigation or proceeding conducted by the competition authorities of a Party.

7. "Anticompetitive activities" means any conduct or transaction that is impermissible under the competition laws of a Party.

ARTICLE III

Positive Comity

The competition authorities of a Requesting Party may request the competition authorities of a Requested Party to investigate and, if warranted, to remedy anticompetitive activities in accordance with the Requested Party's competition laws. Such a request may be made regardless of whether the activities also violate the Requesting Party's competition laws, and regardless of whether the competition authorities of the Requesting Party have commenced or contemplate taking enforcement activities under their own competition laws.

ARTICLE IV

Deferral or Suspension of Investigations in Reliance on Enforcement Activity by the Requested Party

1. The competition authorities of the Parties may agree that the competition authorities of the Requesting Party will defer or suspend pending or contemplated enforcement activities during the pendency of enforcement activities of the Requested Party.

2. The competition authorities of a Requesting Party will normally defer or suspend their own enforcement activities in favor of enforcement activities by the competition authorities of the Requested Party when the following conditions are satisfied:

   (a) The anticompetitive activities at issue:

      (i) do not have a direct, substantial and reasonably foreseeable impact on consumers in the Requesting Party's territory, or

      (ii) where the anticompetitive activities do have such an impact on the Requesting Party's consumers, they occur principally in and are directed principally towards the other Party's territory;

   (b) The adverse effects on the interests of the Requesting Party can be and are likely to be fully and adequately investigated and, as appropriate, eliminated or adequately remedied pursuant to the laws, procedures, and available remedies of the Requested Party. The Parties recognize that it may be appropriate to pursue separate enforcement activities where anticompetitive activities affecting both territories justify the imposition of penalties within both jurisdictions; and

   (c) The competition authorities of the Requested Party agree that in conducting their own enforcement activities, they will:

(i) devote adequate resources to investigate the anticompetitive activities and, where appropriate, promptly pursue adequate enforcement activities;

(ii) use their best efforts to pursue all reasonably available sources of information, including such sources of information as may be suggested by the competition authorities of the Requesting Party;

(iii) inform the competition authorities of the Requesting Party, on request or at reasonable intervals, of the status of their enforcement activities and intentions, and where appropriate provide to the competition authorities of the Requesting Party relevant confidential information if consent has been obtained from the source concerned. The use and disclosure of such information shall be governed by Article V;

(iv) promptly notify the competition authorities of the Requesting Party of any change in their intentions with respect to investigation or enforcement;

(v) use their best efforts to complete their investigation and to obtain a remedy or initiate proceedings within six months, or such other time as agreed to by the competition authorities of the Parties, of the deferral or suspension of enforcement activities by the competition authorities of the Requesting Party;

(vi) fully inform the competition authorities of the Requesting Party of the results of their investigation, and take into account the views of the competition authorities of the Requesting Party, prior to any settlement, initiation of proceedings, adoption of remedies, or termination of the investigation; and

(vii) comply with any reasonable request that may be made by the competition authorities of the Requesting Party.

When the above conditions are satisfied, a Requesting Party which chooses not to defer or suspend its enforcement activities shall inform the competition authorities of the Requested Party of its reasons.

3. The competition authorities of the Requesting Party may defer or suspend their own enforcement activities if fewer than all of the conditions set out in paragraph 2 are satisfied.

4. Nothing in this Agreement precludes the competition authorities of a Requesting Party that choose to defer or suspend independent enforcement activities from later initiating or reinstituting such activities. In such circumstances, the competition authorities of the Requesting Party will promptly inform the competition authorities of the Requested Party of their intentions and reasons. If the competition authorities of the Requested Party continue with their own investigation, the competition authorities of the two Parties shall, where appropriate, coordinate their respective investigations under the criteria and procedures of Article IV of the 1991 Agreement.